Innovation and the Transformation of Consumer Law

Dan Wei · James P. Nehf ·
Claudia Lima Marques
Editors

Innovation and the Transformation of Consumer Law

National and International Perspectives

SSAP

Springer

Editors
Dan Wei
University of Macau
Macao, Macao

James P. Nehf
Indiana University
Indianapolis, IN, USA

Claudia Lima Marques
Federal University of Rio Grande do Sul
Porto Alegre, Brazil

Funded: University of Macau

ISBN 978-981-15-8947-8 ISBN 978-981-15-8948-5 (eBook)
https://doi.org/10.1007/978-981-15-8948-5

Jointly published with Social Sciences Academic Press
The print edition is not for sale in China (Mainland). Customers from China (Mainland) please order the print book from: Social Sciences Academic Press.

This Springer imprint is published by the registered company Springer Nature Singapore Pte Ltd.
The registered company address is: 152 Beach Road, #21-01/04 Gateway East, Singapore 189721, Singapore

Preface

The 17th conference of the International Association of Consumer law was held at the Indiana University Robert H. McKinney School of Law in June 2019. The conference was organized around the theme of *Innovation and the Transformation of Consumer Law*, the title of this book. The goal of the conference was to provide a forum where leading international scholars, practitioners, representatives of consumer organizations, public authorities, and business could gather together to present and discuss issues relevant to consumer protection in many sectors and from various perspectives. Nearly 100 scholars from 27 countries attended. Presenters focused on technologies that create new challenges for consumer policy (e.g., the "internet of things"), creative developments that can assist consumers in protecting their economic interests (e.g., online consumer reviews), innovative approaches to solving traditional and continuing consumer concerns, and challenges presented by emerging ways of creating and delivering consumer products and services. Within the general theme, some presenters reflected on past successes (and failures) of consumer law and policy in a particular area of commerce, opportunities for moving consumer law in a different direction, or the potential threats to consumer welfare (particularly the impact of changes on the political landscape in some parts of the world). Papers focusing on consumer law in individual countries were also welcome, as well as papers with an international focus.

The International Association of Consumer Law was founded over 25 years ago to foster learning and debate on consumer issues and law. It is an association primarily for academics; one that engages with the wider community and has a long tradition of inviting those from that wider community to participate in its conferences. IACL conferences are held once every 2 years in different parts of the world and have hosted judges, regulators, legal practitioners, bureaucrats, bankers, business groups, and consumer organizations. The goal of the IACL is to develop research networks and stimulate research and joint research projects in the area of consumer law and policy and consumer relations, covering all regions of the world. Co-operation between government institutions, universities, consumer organizations, and individual experts is supported in order to develop research and teaching of consumer law.

This book includes not only selected papers of IACL conference in 2019 but also some outputs of the research project "Macau as a World Tourism Destination and Protection of Tourist and Visitor as a Consumer", by Dan Wei (PI) and Claudia Lima Marques (Co-PI) of the University of Macau.

The book is structured as follows. Part I focuses on consumer protection in a digital economy. Part II examines innovations in access to justice. Part III gathers analyses on the transformation of consumer laws.

The publication of the book has benefited from the research funding provided by the University of Macau. We also express our sincere thanks to the board members of IACL and to all who have contributed to the book in one way or the other.

Macao, Macao — Dan Wei
Indianapolis, USA — James P. Nehf
Porto Alegre, Brazil — Claudia Lima Marques
February 2020

Contents

Part I
Consumers in a Digital Economy

Principles and Programs to Protect Consumers from the Deleterious Effects of Technological Innovation

Mark E. Budnitz

1 Introduction

Technology has transformed the environment in which most consumers select products, promise to buy them, pay for them, and use them. Consumer law in the United States has failed to adjust to this new marketplace. Outdated legal approaches, concepts and terminology result in consumer law becoming less able to meet the needs of businesses for certainty and consumers for basic protection. After describing major issues that arise in the cyberspace environment this paper proposes principles and programs to aid in the development of new consumer laws that can bring greater certainty and safeguard consumer welfare.

2 Technological Innovation and the Changing Consumer Marketplace

2.1 Selecting Consumer Products

Consumers used to find products through advertisements in various media such as radio, television, newspapers, and visits to stores. Today, many rely on search engines and apps. While making important information such as comparative pricing and consumer reviews easily available, this also has resulted in new avenues for deceptive practices. For example, competitors complain that Google manipulates its search engine to favor products it sells. Company employees, posing as consumers, post

17th IACL Conference, June 2019

M. E. Budnitz (✉)
Georgia State University College of Law, Atlanta, GA, USA
e-mail: mbudnitz@gsu.edu

D. Wei et al. (eds.), *Innovation and the Transformation of Consumer Law*,
https://doi.org/10.1007/978-981-15-8948-5_1

complaints about their competitors' goods and services on consumer reviews. Courts have not yet explored the issue of whether apps should be treated differently from other methods of accessing a company's goods and services.

Many laws require disclosures,[1] but those disclosures as well as other information consumers are exposed to result in information overload. In addition, disclosure laws have not been modernized to account for shopping online, so they do not include provisions directing businesses on how to comply when making disclosures on the small screen of a smartphone.[2] Furthermore, consumers need laws that provide substantive protection and effective ways to enforce those laws, not merely disclosures.

Shopping online is a boon for the disabled and those living in rural areas, but it enables companies to collect and store personal information, then sell it to others.

Consumers purchasing goods and services online enter into contracts that obligate them to pay for their purchase and comply with other terms and conditions. The law has failed to develop specific rules to govern the formation of online contracts.

Most contracts are formed online by clicking, touching, tapping and talking. Consumers click on a mouse while shopping from their desktops or laptops. Or they touch or tap on the screens of tablets and smartphones. In addition, increasingly consumers contract by talking to virtual personal assistants such as Alexa and Siri.

Most websites use "clickwrap" contracts in which consumers click on a button labelled "I agree" or "Accept". Websites are specially designed to optimize the chances that consumers will agree to purchase goods and services, even if they did not intend to do so.[3] Often companies include a pop-up box that contains the firm's terms and conditions and a hyperlink to its privacy policy. They are usually voluminous and filled with legalese.[4] There is no ability for consumers to bargain; these are take-it-or-leave-it contracts.[5] Therefore, consumers correctly believe taking the time to read and try to understand the terms and conditions is "irrational and infeasible."[6]

Courts have largely upheld this form of contracting, as long as certain requirements are met.[7] If the requirements are not met, protecting consumers from invalid contracts

---

[1] The Truth in lending Act requires disclosure of credit terms, an error resolution procedure, limited liability for unauthorized charges, and a private right of action. 15 U.S.C. §§ 1604–106, 1631–1632, 1637–1638, 1640, 1643. The Electronic Fund Transfers Act requires disclosure of terms, an error resolution procedure, limited liability for unauthorized transfers, and a private right of action. 15 U.S.C. §§ 1693c, 1693f, 1693 h, 1693 m.

[2] *See* e.g., Georgia's Motor Vehicle Sales Finance Act that requires a notice to be "clear and conspicuous" and in at least 6 point type. O.C.G.A. § 10–1-32. The FTC has provided businesses some guidance about how to make proper online representations..com Disclosures, How to Make Effective Disclosures in Digital Advertising, *available at* www.ftc.gov.

[3] Yoreee Koh & Jessica Kuronen, *How Tech Giants Get You To Click This (and Not That),* Wall St. J., June 1–2, 219, at B3. Legislation has been introduced in the U.S. Senate to ban certain website design methods. *Id.*

[4] Hulu Terms of Use, Sept. 13, 2018, *available at* https://secure.hulu.com/terms.

[5] *See* generally Reporter's Introduction, Restatement of the Law Consumer Contracts, Tentative Draft 1 (April 18, 2019).

[6] *Id.*

[7] *Id.* at 44–46.

depends on enforcing these rules. Enforcement is dependent on consumers being able to obtain legal representation to fight the matter in court. Usually the amount in controversy in a consumer case does not justify the expense of hiring a lawyer.

Issues involving the formation of contracts is not the only issue that may arise in clickwrap agreements. For example, some businesses use deceptive practices to trick consumers into unintentionally purchasing goods and services, subjecting them to unfavorable terms and conditions.[8] The FTC Act and state laws prohibit unfair and deceptive practices, but public enforcement depends on the resources and priorities of public agencies and litigation by consumers. Federal resources depend on the willingness of Congress and the President to devote funds and agencies to give high priority to consumer protection. These vary considerably depending on which political party's candidate occupies the White House.[9] Even if a consumer can afford to retain a lawyer, state laws impose many obstacles to consumers' ability to obtain relief,[10] and the prevalence of arbitration clauses precludes access to the courts.[11]

Some companies employ "browsewrap" agreements in which consumers are not required to click on any button or indicate in any explicit manner that they agree to terms and conditions. Companies contend that just by visiting the site consumers have agreed as long as the pages the consumer visits include a link to the terms and conditions. Courts impose stricter requirements on browsewrap contracts, but do not prohibit them altogether.[12] There are an insufficient number of cases, however, for companies and consumers to have a clear idea of what is allowed. This is especially true because companies provide access to browsewrap contracts in so many different ways.

Complicating the legal landscape even further, at least one court categorized an agreement as a "hybrid" contract that included elements of both a clickwrap and a browsewrap agreement.[13] Another court identified four types of online agreements.[14]

---

[8]FTC v. Direct Benefits, 2013 WL 3,771,322 (M.D. Fla. 2013).

[9]Budnitz [1]; *CFPB Law Enforcement Plummets Under Trump Administration,* March 11, 2019, *available at* https://consumerfed.org/press_release/16137.

[10]Carolyn L. Carter & Jonathan Sheldon, Unfair and Deceptive Acts and Practices, §§ 2.2, 2.3, 12.5.2.1 (National Consumer Law Center 9th ed. 2016) (UDAP statutes exempt certain transactions, exempt many types of sellers, restriction and ban class actions).

[11]Paul Bland [2], Alderman [3].

[12]Courts require the "mutual manifestation of assent, whether by written or spoken word or by conduct." Nguyen v. Barnes & Noble Inc., 763 F.3d 1171, 1175 (9th Cir. 2014), quoting Specht v. Netscape Commc'ns Corp., 306 F.3d 17, 29 (2d Cir. 2002). To satisfy that requirement sellers must provide evidence the consumer had actual or constructive knowledge of the agreement's terms and conditions. Van Tassell v. United Mktg. Grp, LLC, 795 F.Supp. 2d 770, 790 (N.D. Ill. 2011). To prove constructive knowledge, sellers must show they put the consumer on inquiry notice. Nguyen, 793 F.3d at 1177. Courts determine whether inquiry notice was sufficient by reviewing the website's design and content. Nicosia v. Amazon.com Inc., 834 F.3d 220, 233 (2d Cir. 2016). Courts have failed to meet requirements in the following cases. Nguyen, 763 F.3d at 1175, 1177; Van Tassell v. United Mktg. Grp, LLC, 795 F.Supp. 2d at 792; Specht v. Netscape Commc'ns Corp., 306 F.3d at 35.

[13]Nicosia v. Amazon.com Inc., 834 F.3d 236.

[14]Berkson v. Gogo LLC, 97 F.Supp. 3d 359, 395–402 (E.D.N.Y. 2015).

At present, the courts have not provided guidance on how the law will treat contracting by touching or tapping on mobile device screens and talking to virtual personal assistants such as Siri and Alexa. Consequently, it is unclear whether they will treat touching and tapping as the same as clicking on a mouse. Ordering goods by talking presents circumstances that are distinctly different from traditional contracting. Perhaps the law on oral contracts is applicable or analogous, although that law presumes talking to a human and often there is an underlying written or digital agreement.

In addition to formation of contract issues, the digital divide is an important consideration because it determines which consumers are able to engage in on-line shopping. There are two facets to the digital divide. There are consumers who cannot afford the computer hardware and software necessary to engage in e-commerce. In addition, there are both businesses and consumers who live in rural communities that lack the infrastructure for high-speed broadband connections to the internet. The latter is considered below in the discussion of paying for goods and services.

Consumers who cannot afford to engage in e-commerce miss out on financial incentives and other types of opportunities. These include special offers, discounts and promotions. They miss the convenience of shopping on-line and consumer reviews. Online shopping is especially advantageous for those who are disabled or those who live in neighborhoods without convenient public transportation.

2.2 *Paying for Goods and Services*

Consumers increasingly pay for their purchases using digital wallets, new payment systems, unregulated financial institutions, and cryptocurrency. Natural disasters and human error have made access to online systems inaccessible for extended periods of time. Substantial gaps in the law leave consumers without protection. Examples include Apple Pay, Person-to-person (P2P) platforms such as Venmo and Zelle, PayPal, fintech companies and bitcoin.

Facebook's latest venture illustrates how companies are combining several of these features. According to recent reports, consumers can use cryptocurrency "to send to each other and use to make purchases both on Facebook and across the internet."[15] Consumers may receive payments in cryptocurrency when they view ads. The project "threatens to upend the traditional lucrative plumbing of e-commerce and would likely be the most mainstream application yet of cryptocurrency."[16] Major drawbacks of cryptocurrency include its volatility, lack of backing by the government and failure to qualify as legal tender. Facebook is seeking to overcome the volatility of cryptocurrency and absence of government imprimatur by seeking investments of about $1 billion (presumably in traditional sources of funds) from financial institutions. Merchants would benefit by not having to pay the swipe and card

[15] Andriotis et al. [4], at A1.

[16] *Id.*

processing fees that are imposed on them when they accept payment by credit or debit cards. "If it succeeds, the project threatens the card networks' dominance over global payments."[17]

Natural disasters play havoc with systems that depend on power. Online shopping and paying for goods and services are disrupted for long periods of time when tornadoes and hurricanes devastate large areas. Even if banks and stores are still standing, they cannot process transactions. Climate change contributes to more severe storms.[18]

Even brief power outages cause problems for consumers. These difficulties are particularly acute for lower income people living paycheck to paycheck.[19] They may not be able to receive their wages because they likely receive them as electronic direct deposits. They probably cannot obtain wages in the form of cash if ATMs are not working and branches do not have power. Lacking access to their funds, they cannot pay the rent, make monthly car payments, buy food, etc. They may not be able to pay for needed repairs to their homes caused by the storm. They will not be able to ascertain the balance in their checking account on-line or by calling the bank. Consequently, they may incur overdraft fees or their bank may refuse to honor the checks they write. Attempts to pay online or via mobile devices will not be successful. Preauthorized payments will not be made, resulting in late fees.

A recent example of a brief outage occurred February 7 and 8, 2019. Because of the outage Wells Fargo's website, mobile app and ATMs did not work.[20] Consumers' debit and credit cards were affected as well as the systems used by the bank's tellers. The most disturbing feature of the outage was that apparently it was not caused by any natural event such as a hurricane or tornado. According to the bank, there was "'a power shutdown at one of our facilities, initiated after smoke was detected following routine maintenance.'"[21] There were conflicting reports of what caused the smoke, and why backup systems and servers were not immediately activated. Another question is why smoke in one facility brought Wells' entire online operation off-line.

United States law is inadequate. The Electronic Fund Transfers Act (EFTA) provides that "If a system malfunction prevents the effectuation of an electronic fund transfer…the consumer's obligation to [another] person shall be suspended until the malfunction is corrected and the electronic transfer may be completed…."[22] The suspension ends, however, if that other person, such as a landlord or lender, makes a written request demanding payment by some other means. If the consumer's bank

---

[17] *Id.*

[18] National Climate Assessment (2014), *available at* https://nca2014.globalchange.gov/report.

[19] The Federal Reserve found that if faced with an unexpected expense of $400, only half of persons surveyed said they could pay the expense in cash or its equivalent. *Report on the Economic Well-Being of United States Households in 2018 – May 2019, available at* www.federalreserve.gov/publications.

[20] Neal [5].

[21] *Id.*

[22] 15 U.S.C. § 1693j.

is closed or unable to process transactions due to a power outage and the ATMs are not operating, the consumer will not be able to pay the rent, make the car payment or pay other bills.

In a situation such as the Wells Fargo outage, it is not clear if the bank is liable under the EFTA. The Act provides that a financial institution is liable for its "failure to make an electronic fund transfer, in accordance with or in a timely manner when properly instructed by the consumer…"[23] The Act, however, also says the financial institution is not liable if its action or failure to act was due to "an act of God or other circumstance beyond its control, that it exercised reasonable care to prevent such an occurrence, and that it exercised such diligence as the circumstances required…."[24] Furthermore, if the bank's failure to make the transfers the consumer ordered "was not intentional and …resulted from a bona fide error, notwithstanding the maintenance of procedures reasonably adapted to avoid any such error, the financial institution shall be liable [only] for actual damages proved."[25] If the consumer can somehow overcome the inevitable mandatory pre-dispute arbitration clause and get to court, the bank can easily use these escape hatches in the EFTA to raise defenses that would make a consumer's litigation too expensive to justify in most instances.

The EFTA governs only electronic transfers. It will not help consumers who do not have a bank account or do not have sufficient funds in their accounts to transfer because the power outage prevented their wages or other funds from being transferred through direct deposit. The Act provides no help to consumers who can pay for needed goods and services only with a credit card if the card networks are down due to the outage.

Lawmakers have not considered whether or how the law should be modernized to deal with new ways to pay for goods and services. Examples of these new methods include the services offered by fintech firms and person-to-person payments using mobile devices such as Zelle and Venmo. Problems have already occurred, demonstrating the need for legislators to look into these. For example, fraudsters have used Zelle to hack into consumers' bank accounts and transfer funds to an account controlled by the fraudster.[26] The FTC sued PayPal's Venmo not only for misrepresenting its security program, but also having inadequate security procedures and no written security policy at all for some length of time.[27] The FTC sued fintech Avant,

---

[23] 15 U.S.C. § 1693 h(a)(1). For check transactions, *see* UCC § 4–109.

[24] 15 U.S.C. § 1693 h(b). *See also* federal law that requires banks to make the funds a consumer deposits available in a timely manner but includes exceptions for emergency situations such as computer or other technical problems and severe weather conditions. Expedited Funds Availability Act, 12 U.S.C. §§ 4001 – 4010; Reg. CC,12 C.F.R., pt.229. Saunders et al. [6], at 140.

[25] 15 U.S.C. § 1693 h(c).

[26] Sullivan [7].

[27] *PayPal Settles FTC Charges that Venmo Failed to Disclose Information to Consumers About the Ability to Transfer Funds and Privacy Settings; Violated Gramm-Leach-Bliley Act*, Feb. 27, 2018, *available at* www.ftc.gov.

an online lender, for unauthorized transfers from consumer accounts, unauthorized charges to credit and debit cards and other unfair and deceptive practices.[28]

Cryptocurrencies are increasingly popular, but the industry has been plagued with problems and scandals. For example, $136 million in cryptocurrency was inaccessible because the founder and only employee died without telling anyone the password. Without the password, the funds could not be reached.[29] In 2017, a cryptocurrency exchange admitted that during a software upgrade it inadvertently transferred $14 million to a digital wallet it was unable to access.[30] The value of cryptocurrencies is very volatile. It often is used to launder money.

The lack of broadband access in rural areas has important consequences for consumers' paying for goods and services.[31] They miss the advantages of fast and automatic deposit of wages and other funds they need to make payments, and the convenience of preauthorized and other electronic payments out of their bank accounts. Low income consumers are disadvantaged in additional ways.[32] For those living paycheck to paycheck, the ability to make almost immediate transfers just before a credit card or other payment is due makes transactions less expensive compared to mailing a check that may or may not reach the company in time to prevent the imposition of finance charges and other fees.

Consumers are not the only ones in rural areas who are hurt by the lack of access to broadband. Lack of broadband infrastructure also hurts rural businesses. They cannot take advantage of the efficiencies offered by electronic technology. They are unable to use the online environment to reach potential customers in communities who may have to travel great distances to come to them, potential customers those companies could contact easily through the internet. Furthermore, they suffer from poor service and an inability to process credit card charges.[33]

2.3 *Privacy and Security*

Security breaches and privacy invasions are a common occurrence. Hundreds of millions of American consumers have been subject to them. Major corporations have fallen victim including Equifax,Target, Home Depot, JP Morgan and Anthem.[34]

---

[28]The FTC announced on April 15, 2019 that the case was settled. The FTC includes within the term fintech mobile payments and virtual currencies as well as online lenders. *Available at* www.ftc.gov

[29]Paul Vigna, *Crypto Mystery: One Lost Password, Missing Millions and a Death in India*, Wall St. J., Feb. 7, 2019, at B1.

[30]Vigna and Shifflett [8], at B6.

[31]*See generally* Smith [9].

[32]*See generally* Mersa Baradaran, How the Other Half Banks (2015).

[33]Quinn [10], at A9.

[34]Bloomberg News [11], 2019 WLNR 14,722,412.

Within a few days of one another in June 2019, there were breaches affecting millions of Quest Diagnostics and LabCorp.[35]

Despite the prevalence of security breaches and privacy invasions, the United States has no comprehensive laws to protect consumers. Although the FTC has brought several actions, its authority to safeguard consumer privacy and police companies' security measures has been challenged because there is nothing in federal law specifically granting them that authority.[36]

2.4 *Consumers Lack Effective Remedies*

Consumers are more dependent than ever on the goods and services they purchase online, yet they have few practical remedies. There are serious gaps in the law. Examples include the almost total lack of laws protecting privacy and security. Current law has not been modernized to deal with the many new products and services available and the new ways to shop and pay online. Many consumer protection statutes are ineffective. For example, many bar class actions. Courts often construe and interpret consumer protection laws narrowly to reduce their scope. Agreements containing mandatory pre-dispute arbitration clauses make access to the courts impossible. Contracts banning consumer class actions in court and arbitration make legal representation for consumers financially infeasible. Arbitration renders the laws on the books useless because arbitrators can ignore the law.

3 Solutions: Principles and Programs to Protect Consumers

The above discussion demonstrates that technology has brought substantial benefits to consumers. But it also has caused serious harm and the substantial risk of continuing harm. The law in the United States has not been modernized to protect consumers under these changed circumstances. What is needed is the enactment of new laws to govern new ways of purchasing goods and services and modernization of present laws. Moreover, in addition to specific law reform, consumers and businesses need to develop principles to guide future laws and best practices. Finally, policymakers need to identify those goals that can be met only through creative cooperative public–private partnerships, and assist the partnerships to accomplish those goals.

The term "laws" as used here is meant to be understood in its broadest sense. Whether the laws are state or federal, and whether they are in the form of statutes, regulations or case law is beyond the scope of this paper.

---

[35] Siegel [12], at A11.

[36] Whall [13].

3.1 *Principles*[37]

Laws should be revised to take into account online disclosures.

Laws should be revised to deal with unfair and deceptive online practices.

The law on contract formation should take into account contracting by conduct online including clicking, touching and tapping as well as by talking to virtual assistants.

Laws involving consumer e-commerce should be technology-neutral.

Regulators should fill in the gaps in laws governing digital wallets, cryptocurrency, new types of financial institutions, and novel methods to process payments.

The federal government should establish minimum security standards and privacy safeguards.

Consumers must have adequate judicial remedies; mandatory pre-dispute arbitration and class action bans should be prohibited.

3.2 *New and Modernized Laws to Implement the Principles*

Any proposal for new and modernized laws typically alarms both businesses and consumers, each fearing changes in the laws will work to their detriment. Many of the law reform that is needed, however, is not anti-business or anti-consumer. Businesses need clarity and certainty. Because most of our consumer law was written assuming face-to-face interaction and paper documents, it is not clear how current law applies.

For example, laws require "clear and conspicuous" notices and disclosures in at least a specified size type. Companies need to know how to comply with those statutes when the consumer receives communications electronically on a small computer screen. They need guidance on whether a notice is properly placed if the consumer must scroll down the web page to reach the notice. If not updated to take the changes brought by technology into account, the law will continue to lack certainty. That situation harms both businesses and consumers.

One of businesses' major concerns is that regulation will stifle innovation. For that reason, laws should be technology neutral. Furthermore, laws must not be so specific that companies are unable to try different ways to advertise, sell and get paid for goods and services. But companies' desire to experiment must be balanced against consumers' reasonable expectations, disclosure of vital information and protection from abuse. Laws requiring "commercial reasonableness" and those prohibiting unfair and deceptive acts and practices illustrate laws that impose general standards that do not unduly restrict honest firms.

But when there is clear evidence of widespread and/or serious abuse, lawmakers should prohibit specific conduct. Those laws protect consumers and help honest companies by hopefully deterring scammers & fraudsters.

---

[37]The list of principles is intended to be suggestive rather than exhaustive.

An example of this type of law is the Restore Online Shoppers Confidence Act (ROSCA).[38] ROSCA deals with deceptive practices that are made possible because of the opaque nature of internet transactions. The consumer never interacts with an actual person, so it is easy for merchants to arrange lucrative arrangements with third parties to the detriment of consumers who are unaware of the involvement of the third parties.

ROSCA applies to third party sellers where those third party sellers obtain the consumer's credit information, including credit and debit card numbers from the merchant with which the consumer thinks she is dealing. The third party charges the consumer for goods or services the third party is selling. The consumer never intended to purchase anything from the third party. Furthermore, she reasonably believed she had not bought anything from the third party because she never gave any payment information to it. ROSCA imposes notices, prohibitions and restrictions on this practice. The Federal trade Commission is granted enforcement authority.

Although a step in the right direction, the statute is very limited in scope and provides no private right of action. New laws are needed that apply to specific acts and practices that merchants engage in, not just the conduct of third parties. In addition, without a consumer private right of action and prohibition or restriction of arbitration clauses, vigorous and widespread enforcement is not assured, given the limited resources and other priorities of the FTC.

A bill recently filed in the United States Senate does apply to the conduct of merchants with whom consumers deal with directly. The bill also illustrates how a statute can be designed to deal with a specific problem. The Deceptive Experiences To Online Users Reduction Act (DETOUR Act) would prohibit (1) designing and manipulating a user interface to impair user decision-making for the purpose of obtaining user consent or user data; (2) subdividing consumers of online services into groups for purposes of behavioral or psychological experiments or studies, except with informed consent; and (3) designing or manipulating a user interface on a website or online service directed to children under 13 with the purpose or substantial effect of "cultivating compulsive usage."[39]

Many laws require disclosure of important information to consumers. These laws, however, were drafted before electronic disclosures were possible and consequently do not take into account that increasingly consumers view the disclosures on the small screens of mobile devices. Businesses need to know how to comply with these laws in a very different communication environment.

The formation of contracts is a fundamental element of contract law. But contract case law and statutes have failed to answer the most basic issues. For example, the Restatement of Contracts (Second) employs the concept of "mutual assent to a writing."[40] Furthermore, [W]here the other party has reason to believe that the party

[38] 15 U.S.C §§ 8401–8405.

[39] S. 108, filed April 9, 2019.

[40] Restatement of the Law of Contracts (Second), § 211(1).

manifesting assent would not do so if he knew that the writing contained a particular term, the term is not part of the agreement."[41]

In stark contrast, the current proposed Restatement of the Law of Consumer Contracts, which purports to reflect current case law, pays lip service to consumers manifesting assent.[42] The Comment, however, severely dilutes the concept. The explanation in the Comment demonstrates that online contracts were a major focus of the Reporters. For example, the Comment states: "Most often, assent to the transaction is manifested by signing an agreement, paying, or clicking "Purchase Now" or "I Agree" after the consumer has been put on reasonable notice that such actions would result in the formation of a legal obligation."[43] In other words, notice followed by clicking constitutes manifest assent.

The proposed restatement also follows a much-reviled case and its progeny that permits online sellers and sellers in stores to provide consumers with major contract terms, not when the consumer orders the goods, but rather when the goods are delivered. The restatement permits this despite contrary case law and academic commentary pointing out the leading case misunderstood and misapplied applicable law in the Uniform Commercial Code.[44] The proposed consumer restatement omits the provision in the Restatement of Contracts protecting the party who assents when the other party had reason to believe there would not have been assent if the assenting party knew the writing included a particular term.

At the American Law Institute's Annual meeting in May 2019, the ALI members approved the definitions section of the proposed Consumer Contracts restatement but were not even able to finish discussion of the section on formation of contracts before the allotted time expired. Completion of discussion on that section and the remaining seven sections was left for another day.

The recent experience of the ALI members illustrates the difficulty of attempting to summarize the case law on consumer contracts, especially since the cases include transactions where the parties are face-to-face and paper-based as well as others where the consumer is online, interacting with electronic software. Consumers and businesses need laws that clarify the rules. It might be best if those rules were developed case-by-case as courts apply contract rules to the specific circumstances before them. Because of the pervasiveness of arbitration clauses, however, it is unlikely

---

[41] *Id.* § 211(3).

[42] Restatement of the Law, Consumer Contracts, Tentative Draft, April 18, 2019, § 2(a), at 18.

[43] *Id.* § 2, Comment 3, at 20.

[44] *Id.* Reporters' Notes at 49. The Reporters rely on a commercial case, not a case involving consumers. ProCD v. Zeidenberg, 86 F.3d 1447 (7th Cir. 1996). Contra Klocek v. Gateway, 104 F.Supp. 2d 1332 (D. Kan 2000). The Reporters' method of collecting and analyzing cases has been criticized. Levitin [14]. For academic criticism of ProCD, *see e.g.,* White [15] ("hard cases making bad law (ProCD and Hill)"); Bern [16]. Bern claims Judge Easterbrook "deftly discarded clear statutory language and foundational common law principles and created in their place, virtually out of whole cloth, a new doctrine of contract formation" *Id.* at 649, and that despite his citing the Restatement (Second) of Contracts to support his position, that restatement offers no support. *Id.* at 654.

for that development to occur in a timely manner. That leaves only the legislative alternative.

There are many new ways for consumers to store and transfer their funds. Consumers need the same legal protection as they have when using debit and credit cards. Regulators should fill in the gaps in laws governing digital wallets, cryptocurrency, new types of financial institutions, and novel methods to process payments.[45]

Data breaches have become commonplace, putting consumers at great risk of injury from resulting identity theft and unauthorized transfers of their funds. Legislation should establish minimum security standards and privacy safeguards.

Consumers must have adequate judicial remedies. They need laws that provide a private right of action, actual and statutory damages, and reimbursement for court costs and attorney fees. These are already included in many consumer protection statutes and should be in all of them.[46] Consumers also need legislation to prohibit mandatory pre-dispute arbitration. There is no regulation of companies that provide arbitration services. One major organization specializing in consumer arbitration abruptly stopped offering this service after being sued by the Minnesota Attorney General, demonstrating there is clearly a need for regulation.[47] The Consumer Financial Protection Bureau refused to ban consumer arbitration altogether, but imposed restrictions. Congress repealed the regulation.[48] Contractual class action bans also should be prohibited.

3.3 Public–private Joint Ventures

Some of the problems that have resulted from technology's impact on the consumer marketplace ecommerce can be ameliorated more quickly, cheaper and hopefully more efficiently by a partnership between the public and private sector.

A prime example is the need to bridge the digital divide. Most of the activity to bridge the digital divide has been the effort to build infrastructure in rural areas that will enable high-speed broadband that consumers and businesses can use to their great advantage. Bringing broadband access will result in significant benefits, not only for ecommerce transactions, but in other important ways. "Without a proper broadband connection, these communities can't start or run a modern business, access telemedicine, take an online class, digitally transform their farm or research a school project online."[49]

---

[45] *See generally* Levitin [17].

[46] E.g., 15 U.S.C. § 1693 h (Electronic Fund Transfers Act); 15 U.S.C. § 1640 (Truth in Lending Act).

[47] Merzer [18]

[48] H. J. Res. 111, Pub. L. No. 115–74. 115th Congress.

[49] Smith [9].

A consortium of technology companies, Internet Service Providers and component and device manufacturers are working on this effort. That group has partnered with farm organizations such as the National 4-H Council and National Future Farmers of America to involve the people who live in the affected communities. Two federal government agencies, the Federal Communications Commission (FCC) and the Department of Agriculture have provided $22 billion in subsidies and grants to telecommunication carriers who are building this infrastructure.[50] Federal government agencies such as the FCC also will play a vital regulatory role. They will have to balance industry's wish for rules that promote broadband development against the need to ensure consumers are treated fairly. One way to accomplish that is to fully involve all the stakeholders, including consumers, in the planning and execution of this endeavor.

Sprint and T-Mobile have requested a unique type of public–private cooperation. They promise to close the digital divide in rural areas in return for government approval of their proposed merger. Their strategy may work. In May 2019, the chairman of the FCC recommended that the FCC approve the merger, in part, because of the agency's commitment to build rural broadband.[51] The merger also must be approved by the Department of Justice.

In addition to the need to bridge the digital divide in rural communities, there is a pressing need to bridge the divide in low-income urban neighborhoods. An example of public sector efforts is a 2016 rule issued by the Department of Housing and Urban Development (HUD) requiring the installation of broadband infrastructure in all new construction or substantially rehabilitated rental housing funded or supported by HUD.[52] Public–private initiatives are sorely needed for these long-neglected places.

Another area needing public–private initiatives is cybersecurity and privacy for consumer ecomerce. The United States has no general law providing cyberspace security protection. In addition, unlike the European Union, the United States has no general comprehensive privacy legislation.[53] Members of Congress have supported the need for federal legislation but have not been able to reach consensus on the details.[54] Democrats favor granting wide authority to the FTC and preserving state privacy law. Republicans fear the FTC might stifle innovation and prefer that any

---

[50] *Id.*

[51] Lee [19], at B1. The FCC chairman said closing the digital divide was a top agency priority. *See It's time to close The Digital* Divide, full page advertisement, Wall St. J., June 1–2, 2019, at A5.

[52] Miller and Walker [20].

[53] The European Union's Data Protection Regulations became effective May 25, 2018. From the effective date until January 2019 there were almost 60,000 breaches of the GDPR. Smith [21]. California has the most comprehensive state legislation in the U.S. California Consumer Privacy Act of 2018. That law, however, has a partial carve-out for financial institutions. David M. Stauss, Kristen Poetzel & Malia K. Rogers, *GLBA and the California Privacy Act: Analyzing SB 1121's Change to the Financial Institution Carve-Out Provision*, Ballard Spahr Cyber Adviser Blog, *available at* www.cyberadviserblog.com

[54] Tracy [22], *at A2.*

federal law pre-empt state law.[55] Some have urged establishment of a cabinet-level department of cybersecurity.[56] The debate over privacy involves fundamental issues such as the question of who, if anyone, owns data about consumers' identity and behavior.[57]

A private–public partnership might be able to break the logjam. All stakeholders, including consumers and the many types of businesses affected, should be involved. Those businesses include telecoms, ISPs, social media, insurance companies, financial institutions and retailers.[58]

4 Conclusion

Improving the consumer online marketplace will not be easy. Enacting new laws and modernizing current laws require compromise among opposing parties. The two major American political parties agree on little and are influenced by lobbyists, interest groups and political contributions. There is fierce competition among industry groups. Lines between different types of industries become blurred as companies in one type of industry enters the marketplace of another type.[59]

Even if a government agency has the authority and will to fill in the gaps in the law through regulations, those regulations can be reversed by succeeding hostile administrations or rendered ineffective due to the refusal of the future administration to enforce the law.

Programs to ameliorate problems that cannot be solved solely by legal means, such as the digital divide, require substantial resources and cooperation between the public and private sectors.

Complicating and confounding any effort to tackle the serious problems in the consumer ecommerce environment is the reality of ever-changing technological advances that impact the consumer marketplace in often profound and unpredictable ways.

Nevertheless, businesses need certainty and consumers need legal protection. Without certainty, companies are not able to devise rational business plans because they cannot calculate risk. If consumers cannot be confident that the law will provide basic protection, they may be less willing to spend their money in the ecommerce marketplace.

---

[55]The Consumer Financial Protection Bureau offered businesses a "sandbox" program that allowed them to test innovative financial products and services. Companies did not take up the offer because the CFPB retained its supervisory and enforcement role. In April 2019 the Office of the Comptroller of the Currency proposed its own sandbox program to national banks and federal thrifts. Under the OCC's Innovation Pilot Program, banks could apply individually or with a non-bank fintech partner. As proposed, the OCC would not provide regulatory relief. Hill [23].

[56]Schlein [24], at R4. For an argument opposing such a department, *see* Spaulding [25], at R4.

[57]Determan [26]; Schwartz [27].

[58]*See* Nishi [28], at R8.

[59]*See* text accompanying notes 15–17, *supra*.

References

1. Mark E. Budnitz, *The FTC's Consumer Protection Program During the Miller Years: Lessons for Administrative Agency Structure and Operation*, 46 Cath. L. Rev. 371 (1987)
2. F. Paul Bland *et al.*, Consumer Arbitration Agreements (National Consumer Law Center, 7th ed. 2015)
3. Richard A. Alderman, *Pre-Dispute Mandatory Arbitration in Consumer Contracts: A Call for Reform, 38 Hous. L. Rev 1237 (2001)*
4. AnnaMaria Andriotis, Lis Hoffman, Peter Rudegeair & Jeff Horwitz, *Facebook Plans for Crypto Payments*, Wall St. J., May 3, 2019
5. Ryan W. Neal, *Wells Fargo outage has security professionals puzzled*, www.investmentnews.com. Feb. 8, 2019
6. Lauren K. Saunders *et al.*, Consumer Banking and Payments Law (National Consumer Law Center 2018)
7. Bob Sullivan, *Here's how hackers are using Zelle to raid bank accounts; and why victim was out $1,800 until I wrote to the bank*, April 25, 2019, *available at* https://bobsullivan.net.
8. Paul Vigna & Shane Shifflett, *Crypto Customers Hunt for Missing Cash*, Wall St. J., Feb. 20, 2019
9. Brad Smith, *The rural broadband divide: An urgent national problem that we can solve, Dec. 3, 2018, available at* https://blogs.microsoft.com
10. Christopher Quinn, *Bankrupt firm still will serve Georgia,* Atlanta J.-Constitution, Feb. 28, 2019
11. Bloomberg News, *Chinese Citizen indicted in Anthem hack of records of 80M*, May 10, 2019
12. Rachel Siegel, *LabCorp discloses data breach*, Atlanta J-Constitution, June 6, 2019
13. Julia Whall, *Policing Cyberspace: The Uncertain Future of Data Privacy and Security Enforcement in the Wake of LabMD*, 60 B.C. L. Rev. E-Supp. 11, 149 (2019)
14. Adam Levitin, *et al.*, The Faulty Foundation of the Draft Restatement of Consumer Contracts, 36 Yale J. on Regulation 447 (2019)
15. 15. James J. White, *Default Rules in Sales and the Myth of Contracting Out*, 48 Loy. L. Rev. 53, 80 (2002)
16. Roger C. Bern, *"Terms Later" Contracting: Bad Economics, Bad Morals, and a Bad Idea for a Uniform Law, Judge Easterbrook Not Withstanding*, 12 J. L. & Pol'y 641 (2004)
17. Adam J. Levitin, *Pandora's Digital Box: The Promise and Perils Of Digital Wallets*, 166 U. Penn. L. Rev. 305 (2018)
18. Martin Merzer, *Leading arbitration firm quits the business after lawsuit*, July 20, 2009, *available at* www.creditcards.com
19. Edmund Lee, *T-Mobile-Sprint Union Gets Key Win*, Wall St. J., May 21, 2019
20. Stephen R. Miller & Lisa L. Walker, *The Fair Housing Act Turns 50 Years Old – Part 1: A Legal Retrospective From the Public & Affordable Housing World*, 47 Real Estate Rev. J. 2 (2018)
21. Adam Smith, *Over 10,000 GDPR Breaches in UK, Says Law Firm,* UK PC Magazine, *available at* https://uk.pcmag.com
22. Ryan Tracy, *Lawmakers Differ on Privacy-Breach Fix, Wall St. J., May 9, 2019*
23. Jon Hill, *Does The OCC's Sandbox Substitute Have A Fatal Flaw?* Law 360, June 6, 2019, *available at* www.law360.com
24. Ted Schlein, *To Be Safe, the U.S. Needs to Be a Lot More Organized,* Wall St. J., June 5, 2019
25. Suzanne Spaulding, *A New Department Would Do More Harm Than Good*, Wall St. J., June 5, 2019
26. Lothar Determan, *No One Owns Data,* 70 Hast. L. J. 1 (2018)
27. Paul M. Schwartz, *Property, Privacy, and Personal Data,* 117 Harv. L. Rev. 2055 (2004)
28. Dennis Nishi, *Explaining Cyberinsurance*, Wall St. J., June 5, 2019

Consumer Protection and Sharing Economy. Preliminary Ideas from the Argentine View

Sergio Sebastián Barocelli

1 Introduction

Legal protection of consumers tries to respond to the consequences suffered by the effects of the so-called "society of consumers" [1–4], also describes in Economics as "market failures" [5–7].

Consumer Law recognizes the structural vulnerability of consumers in the market in their relations with suppliers of goods and services, establishing a series of norms, principles and institutions of protection in their favor.

With different traditions and intensities, legal protection of consumers is present today all over the world -even in Argentina—thanks to the visibility of the problems and demands of consumers in public sphere by the "Consumer Movement" [8].

This structural vulnerability has been especially accentuated by the impact of information and communications technologies (ICT) in business. The vulnerability of the consumers in mass consumption, which is depersonalized and globalized, is compounded by the unnaturally of the technological event, the control of the electronic media by the supplier and a greater propensity to risks related to security and self-determination in terms of personal data, means of payments, breach of trust, fraud, and trademark fraud, among others.

In the present paper we will try to delineate some reflections regarding the legal protection of consumers in the digital environment, in particular, regarding the so-called "sharing economy".

S. S. Barocelli (✉)
Universidad de Buenos Aires, Buenos Aires, Argentina
e-mail: sbarocelli@derecho.uba.ar

Universidad del Salvador, Buenos Aires, Argentina

D. Wei et al. (eds.), *Innovation and the Transformation of Consumer Law*,
https://doi.org/10.1007/978-981-15-8948-5_2

2 E-commerce and the Phenomenon of "Sharing Economy"

E-commerce began in 1993, when the government of the United States ceases to administer the network governmentally and the prohibition that existed until then for the commercial use of the Internet is lifted. From that same year, the public domain of the network allowed the exponential multiplication of its users, year after year, reaching according to statistical studies 46% of the world population for the year 2016 [9].

According to the latest Annual E-Commerce Study 2018 of the Argentine Chamber of Electronic Commerce in Argentina, 90% of connected Argentine adults have already purchased online, representing 18.3 million people, while 92% of total Sales was made through credit cards.

E-commerce presents, in front of its traditional physical version, an accumulation of intrinsic characteristics that make it very attractive for the consuming public. E-commerce transcends geographic and temporal barriers, has a very broad scope, allows standardization and exploitation of economies of scale. E-commerce allows a greater communicational richness, interactivity with the consumer and a correlative reduction of the information costs and increase of the informative quality available. It allows a greater personalization and adaptation of the goods and services marketed, introduces novel models of social interaction, and generates an experience on occasions of higher quality for the consumer, by using data processing technologies that allow narrowing the commercial profiling of the consumer and the optimization of your satisfaction.

Nonetheless, E-commerce also has its disadvantages. Naturally, a large part of the consuming public has well-founded fears and uncertainty in the conduct of their transactions by this means, which is linked to the inherent risks of their use. When using technologies, the use made of them must be safe, so that the consumer is required to know fully what are the normal conditions for their use, to master their use, to be informed how to do it correctly, and which the risks that your safety can suffer are and what preventive mechanisms you should take. On the other hand, consumers may have the perception that their confidence is compromised.

In this context, a significant phenomenon is that of the so-called "sharing economy" or "collaborative consumption".

The term "collaborative consumption" was coined by Marcus Felson and Joe L. Spaeth in their paper "Community Structure and Collaborative Consumption: A routine activity approach" published in 1978 in the American Behavioral Scientist. However, this expression began to become popular thanks 2010 Botsman and Rogers' book "What's mine is yours: The rise of collaborative consumption".

The "sharing economy" is defined as a movement that encompasses new economic practices that have in common some degree of participation or collective organization in the provision of goods and services. On 2 June 2016, the European Commission published a Communication containing "A European Agenda for the Collaborative Economy" in which it defined the sharing economy as "business models where activities are facilitated by collaborative platforms that create an open marketplace for the temporary usage of goods or services often provided by private individuals" (European Commission 2016).

This definition places emphasis on those practices and business models based on horizontal networks and the participation of a community, built on distributed energy and trust within communities instead of centralized institutions. It highlights the collective and community aspect, as well as the need for trust and participation to develop the activity, and extends the scope of the sharing economy beyond information and communication technologies (ICT), including exchanges and collaboration in the local environment. The philosophy of sharing economy emphasizes the creation of communities that, in a framework of trust, allow access to underutilized goods by sharing them.

It highlights the collective and community aspect, as well as the need for trust and participation to develop the activity, and extends the scope of the collaborative economy.

We can mention the experiences of "community fairs" or "barter clubs". However, the collaborative economy is essentially linked to peer-to-peer (P2P) and business-to-peer (B2P) technology for its operation, in the supply based on access to the unproductive good as opposed to its acquisition; combination that can sometimes be based on a relationship between equals (P2P) or in the provision by a company to access by users of goods on demand when it is more convenient (B2P), differentiating between companies that they try to monetize services around communities of users and those technological companies that connect some users with others and charge a fee for it.

In Argentina, the phenomenon of collaborative economy has had a special impact in several sectors:

(a) In the transport sector, with *Uber* and *Cafiby;*
(b) In online food ordering, delivery and errands, with applications such as *Pedidos Ya, Glovo*, and *Rappi;*
(c) In the tourism sector, with *Airbnb.*

3 Rules Implicated to This Phenomenon

The consumer is thus linked, with two subjects:

(a) with a supplier, which may be professional or occasional, who provides the good or service; and
(b) with a professional supplier, who is the organizing subject of the app or platform where the operations are carried out and which It has powers to include and exclude members, supervise operations, establish activity rules (for example, qualifications) and receive fee (direct profit) or manage spaces for advertising or preferential publication (indirect profit).

There are several direct or indirect rules that regulate this activity.

(a) The United Nations Guidelines for the Protection of Consumers of 1985, reformed in 1999 and 2015, are an internationally recognized set of basic objectives, prepared especially for Governments of developing countries and newly independent countries will use them for structuring and strengthening consumer protection policies and laws. While these directives have no binding force for States, we can argue that they constitute a major support in the international custom in the matter and are part of the so-called *soft law*.
The Guidelines, in terms of electronic consumer protection, establish:

   (I) Consumers who resort to electronic commerce should have a degree of protection that is not lower than that granted in other forms of commerce (Paragraph 5º, j, and 63). This is considered to be the most important rule, since it allows us to maintain that just as in the face-to-face trade, consumers deserve the protection of law and public authorities in terms of the structural vulnerability of which they suffer from the ravages of the "society of consumers", so they are empowered with a series of rights, recognized by Argentinian constitution and regulated by various regulations issued by national authorities and local authorities and all those involved in the marketing chain, constituting the vertical of the consumption relationship in terms of the various related contracts developed from the role of provider are bound to fulfill those rights and must respond concurrently in front of the consumer, also that same rule must be applied in the field of electronic commerce.
   (II) Consumer confidence in electronic commerce must be promoted (Paragraph 63). The protection of trust is one of the central axes of the protection of electronic consumers, of which we will refer in the following section.
   (III) It must be ensured that consumers are informed and aware of their rights and obligations in the digital market (Paragraph 64). The right to information is of vital importance, due to the special vulnerability of consumers in electronic contracting and should be combined with other rules that regulates compulsory disclosure and establish that information must be adequate, true, certain, clear, detailed, free, understandable, transparent and timely.
   (IV) It is suggested that States adopt the criteria of the Guidelines for the Protection of Consumers in the Context of Electronic Commerce of the Organization for Economic Cooperation and Development (OECD). These Guidelines state that: consumers who participate in electronic commerce must be granted transparent and effective protection that is not inferior to the level of protection granted in other forms of commerce; the interests of consumers should be respected and act in accordance with fair practices in the exercise of their business, advertising and marketing activities; companies should not perform no statement, incur any omission, or engage in any practice that proves false, deceitful, fraudulent or disloyal; companies engaged in the sale, promotion or marketing of goods or services should not carry out commercial practices that could cause

irrational risks to the detriment of consumers; provided that companies publish information about themselves or about the goods or services that they offer, they should present it clearly, visibly, accurately and easily accessible and should comply with any statement they make regarding their policies and practices related to their transactions with consumers; companies should not take advantage of the special characteristics of electronic commerce to hide their true identity or location, or to evade compliance with the rules of protection to consumer or the mechanisms for applying said standards; companies should not use terms disloyal contractual advertising and marketing should be clearly identifiable as such; the advertising and marketing should identify the company in whose name they are made, when it is not met this requirement is considered deceptive; companies should have the ability to check any express or implicit affirmation, during the entire time it is made, and maintain this capacity during a reasonable time, once said statement is concluded; companies should develop and implement effective and easy-to-use procedures that allow consumers to express their decision to receive or refuse unsolicited commercial messages through electronic mail and respect the decision of the consumers not to receive commercial messages; entrepreneurs should take special care with the advertising or marketing aimed at children, the elderly, the seriously ill, and other groups that they probably do not have the capacity to fully understand the information presented to them; questions about the information of the company, about the goods or services offered, about the terms, conditions and costs associated with the operation, especially when applicable and appropriate depending on the Transaction Type; means of error detection and preservation of a complete and accurate record of the transaction; entrepreneurs should provide consumers with safe and easy payment mechanisms use and information about the level of security provided by such mechanisms and delimit the responsibility for unauthorized or fraudulent use of payment systems and refund mechanisms on credit cards (chargebacks); consumers should be provided with easy access to alternative mechanisms for a fair and timely process of compensation and resolution of disputes without costs or burdensome charges and that companies and consumer representatives should establish continuous, impartial internal mechanisms, effective and transparent to meet and respond to complaints and difficulties of consumers, in a way that fair and timely and without undue costs or charges for consumers.

(b) Resolution 21/04 of the Common Market Group of Mercosur on electronic commerce through Internet. This rule establishes, in general terms, the protection of the right-duty of information, the means technicians to identify and correct data entry errors before making the transaction and the rule of the "double click" in terms of consent.

(c) Argentine Consumer Protection Act also has specific rules regarding the contracts, without prejudice to the general rules that are applicable to consumer relations, including those relating to liability for damages. They are:

   (I) Parallelism of rescission forms, with respect to contracts concluded by electronic media (Paragraph 10 ter);
   (II) Written instrumentation, informing the right of withdrawal (Paragraph 34);
   (III) 10 days´ right of withdrawal (Paragraph 34). It is true that there are no specific rules on liability. But it is not true that there are no rules applicable. They are applicable, as we said previously the general rules in security obligation (Paragraphs 5 and 6 LDC), regarding non-compliance (Paragraph 10 bis LDC) and solidarity liability in case of risk or vice of the thing or service (Paragraph 40 LDC). The ruling betrays the need for specific rules that depart from these criteria; In our view, they are not necessary.

(d) Argentine Civil and Commercial Code also established:

   (I) Instrumentation in writing, with understandable and self-sufficient clauses and clear, complete and easily readable and prohibition of forwarding (Paragraph 985);
   (II) Obligation of the consumer data provider, in addition to the minimum content of the contract and the power to revoke, all the necessary data to correctly use the chosen medium, to understand risks derived from its use, and to be absolutely clear who assumes those risks (Paragraph 1107);
   (III) Regulation of the place of performance and unfairness of the jurisdiction clause (Paragraph 1109);
   (IV) Right of withdrawal (Paragraph 1110–1116).

We also believe that the theory of "contractual connection" contributes to sustain these arguments (1073–1075 Argentine Civil Code). That is, by virtue of the proven connection, the interpretation and intercontractual effects, thus finding a limit the classical rule of the relative effect of the contracts. The operations in sharing economy apps, whether they are intermediated or not, represent a triad of related contracts:

(a) the contract between the user-provider and the user-consumer (consumer contract),
(b) the contract between the user-provider and sharing economy apps (contracts of adhesion), and
(c) the contract between the user-consumer and sharing economy apps (consumer contract).

Also, as in the case, it may be complemented by other related contracts regarding the payment system. In this scheme, sharing economy apps it occupies the role of organizer of the contractual system, so its actions directly affect the supra-contractual cause and all contracts linked to it. This allows simplify the question of how risks should be distributed in a contractual system that mixes a scheme of institutional trust with another of distributed trust. Using the doctrine on contracts related to the principles of consumer law, in the doubt of who should bear the risks of the injury of trust, these should fall on the party that occupies both roles of provider and organizer of the system of related contracts.

Sharing economy apps have the role of provider, in our view, for several reasons: organizer of the platform and the payment system, by its brand in the good and as an apparent provider under of the guardianship of trust. Its activity is not limited to the storage and transmission of data but as organizer of the system, determining rules, payment methods and scoring systems. They uses a mixed system of institutional trust (brand) and trust distributed (scoring system) as a business model.

Scoring systems are an algorithm that informs—based on data downloaded by different users of the platform—the reliability of a particular user. It is based on that reliability that a consumer contracts with a supplier that does not know or has seen his face. Now, move users the risk of reliability represented on the platform is an abusive practice, since whoever makes the representation is not the users themselves, but the algorithm, from which you cannot get finished information. Furthermore, it is this algorithm that gives the platform institutional reliability, which is why it is part of business model of the platform, and, being an asset that depends on its guardian, is the platform who must take responsibility for the representations of reliability of the algorithm. It fits remember also that the apparent supplier assumption assumes the provider's perception that a certain product is backed by a brand, even if that is not real. In these cases, the owner of the brand must respond for the injury in the confidence generated in the consumer and assume the risk generated [10].

It is also important to highlight the forecasts made by the Preliminary Draft of a new Consumer Protection Act. In addition to collecting the aforementioned rules of the guidelines, it is established that in accordance with the rules of connected contracts, the exemption from liability of the electronic operator will only be possible when:

1. Has not played an active role in the legal-economic operation, limited to provide only a transaction forum, reporting it clearly, prominently and easily understandable;
2. It has not generated a particular confidence in the consumer.

4 Preliminary Conclusions

E-consumers deserve a level of protection that is not less than that afforded in other forms of commerce. In addition, the hypervulnerability of consumers in the digital environment obliges States to adopt specific protection policies.

The phenomenon of the collaborative economy and electronic commerce in general has produced important impacts on our economic and social realities.

This forces legal operators to review the classical postulates in light of these new challenges. However, the north of this road should not be forgotten: consumers should be protected in their dignity and in their rights.

In that sense we believe that:

(a) Consumers should receive adequate information that promotes their trust in the electronic community;
(b) Health and safety of consumers should be protected, especially in relation to their personal data and payment methods;
(c) Unfair practices must be controlled;
(d) Unfair clauses should be ineffective, especially those relating to use of personal data, exclusion clauses, extension of jurisdiction, etc.;
(e) Organizers of collaborative economy networks are strictly liable for damages suffered by consumers in context of consumption.

References

1. Bauman, Z. (2000) Trabajo, consumismo y nuevos pobres. Gedisa, Madrid.
2. Bauman, Z. (2007) Vida de consumo, Fondo de Cultura Económica, Buenos Aires.
3. Bocock, R. (1995) El Consumo. Talasa, Madrid.
4. Carrasco Rosa, A (2007) La sociedad de consumo: origen y características. https://www.eumed.net/ce/2.007a/acr.htm [28–01–2.018];
5. Reich, N. (1985) Mercado y derecho. Ariel, Barcelona.
6. Bourgoignie, T. (1994), Elementos para una teoría del Derecho del Consumidor. Departamento de Comercio, Consumo y Turismo del País Vasco, San Sebastián.
7. Ramsay, I. (1989) Consumer Protection: Text and Materials (Law in Context) , Weidenfeld and Nicolson, Londron.
8. Sánchez Legrán, F. et al (2008) FACUA y el movimiento de consumidores. Ediciones FACUA-Consumidores en Acción, Sevilla.
9. Faliero, J. Barocelli, S. (2017) La protección del consumidor en el comercio electrónico. Un caso de responsabilidad de los intermediarios comerciales en Internet. LA LEY 04/04/2017, 04/04/2017, 5 - LA LEY2017-B, 275.
10. Estevarena, E. Barocelli, S. (2018) La protección de los consumidores en plataformas de comercio electrónico. LA LEY 30/05/2018, 30/05/2018, 6.
11. Annual E-Commerce Study 2018 of the Argentine Chamber of Electronic Commerce in Argentina https://cace-static.s3-us-west-2.amazonaws.com/uploads/estudios/estudio-anual-comercio-electronico-argentina-2018-resumen.pdf [20–03–2.019].
12. Botsman, R. (2017) "Who can you trust? How Technology Brought Us Together and Why It Might Drive Us Apart", Hachette Book Group, New York.
13. Diaz-Foncea, M. et al (2018) Economía social y economía colaborativa: encaje y potencialidades. Revista Economía Industrial, https://www.minetad.gob.es/Publicaciones/Publicacionesperiodicas/EconomiaIndustrial/RevistaEconomiaIndustrial/402/D%C3%8DAZ%20FONCEA,%20MARCUELLO%20Y%20MONREAL.pdf [18–01–2.018].
14. Felson, Marcus and Joe L. Spaeth (1978), "Community Structure and Collaborative Consumption: A routine activity approach," American Behavioral Scientist, 21 (March–April), 614–24.
15. Rusconi, D., (2007) La confianza del consumidor como factor de atribución de responsabilidad del proveedor aparente. SJA 03/10/2007.

Freedom of Contract and New Economic Models

A New Approach of European and French Consumers Law for Internet of Things

Malo Depincé

What would be new issues in Europe for consumers Law? Economic models of many companies have probably evolved and there's no doubt that the foundations upon which legal frame for these practices is established might not be as relevant as it used to be forty years ago (date of adoption of the first explicitly protective consumers' Act in France[1]). New technologies now allow professionals to enforce a new relation to consumers. Coming into consumers' home thanks to new connected objects and a network setting together several systems, it might bring new services, new values and also new risks. If, for instance, fidelity could previously be considered as a tool or invitation to renew contracts with immediate execution, it might be relevant today to wonder if the practice would not have evolved towards a new economic model favoring a constant contractual link or presented so. For such a purpose, professionals multiply the mechanisms to strengthen the contractual relationship. Technology, and the knowledge of consumer's behavior that such a technology proposes, then offer new relations that Law should consider. Interfaces might evolve or be totally different, and one of the main consequences of such an evolution might be to reconsider the importance of contract as the model of economic relationship. If algorithms were to be considered as the new way of ordering, which place would remain to human consent?[2] Main question for such an issue would be to determinate if Internet of Things by creating a permanent link with providers can also assure professionals (or others, I shall mention it later) access a large scope of information about lifestyles or consumer preferences. Then, what economists have described as captive ecosystems,

[1]**Loi n° 72-1137 du 22 décembre 1972** relative à la protection des consommateurs en matière de démarchage et de vente à domicile (consumers protection for canvassing and home sales). This is the very first act which first purpose is to protect consumers and not specifically professionals.

[2]*Algorithmic consumers*, Gal and Niva [1].

M. Depincé (✉)
Maître de Conférences HDR à La Faculté de Droit et de Science Politique de Montpellier, 34060 Montpellier, France
e-mail: malo.depince@umontpellier.fr

D. Wei et al. (eds.), *Innovation and the Transformation of Consumer Law*,
https://doi.org/10.1007/978-981-15-8948-5_3

where consumer remains bound by a provider thanks to this object that remains in his daily life, can be set up. In such systems, data is highly valued. As a driver of this new economy, the valorized data can make it possible to constitute dominant positions by offering the professional who collects and treats it a priority over its competitors. This is an issue of competition Law, obviously important for consumers. These systems can also bind consumer and they potentially call into question his freedom of contract. Of course, consumer law can also apply to it. Yet the issue of the most relevant way of protecting consumers and competitors remain. National laws present different solutions: some are global such as in United States for instance which prohibit misleading consumers and deal with bankruptcy. Such solutions can obviously apply but require a large work of interpretation, which is not always done, and don't allow consumers to have easy knowledge of their rights. With such a sentence as "it is forbidden to mislead a consumer", it is quite difficult for this consumer to understand that some professional practices are forbidden or might be so. Still requiring Loyalty, other countries also set up very specific and technical prescriptions. So is it in France for example, and later in European Law. Unfair terms, for instance, might be considered as a violation of this requirement of Loyalty, as well as a violation of specific unfair terms Law. In France justice decisions condemning a professional practice of unfair terms were very rare before the unfair terms Law was adopted in 1978.[3] We then might consider that if specific settlements are not necessary, they certainly are very useful. The disadvantages of specific and technical settlements however are to be considered. Their scope is much narrow and as they suggest very specific solutions to very specific issues, they let neglected other issues. They also may let professional think that any practice that would not be specifically prohibited could be admitted.[4] This is the main issue of specific Law: it only offers specific solutions, whereas issues remain wilder. What we are discussing here is about differences between common consumers Law and specific consumers Law. European countries have, for the past thirty years, considerably developed specific consumers Law, while maintaining of course common Law without huge evolution. The purpose of our paper shall consider the required evolutions of competition and consumers Law to protect effectively consumers without hindering growth. What would be the most efficient, the most relevant for assuring a fair competition? This fair competition isn't so easy to define, it must allow to fight misleading practices to consumers as well as to establish clear rules between professionals that should improve competition. Consumers Law then should assure a wide offer to consumers that would be clearly representative.

---

[3] *Loi* n° 78-23 du 10 janvier *1978* sur la protection et l'information des consommateurs.

[4] We here would like to recall the words of Portalis, one of authors of the French civil Code: « *Ce qui n'est pas contraire aux lois, est licite. Mais ce qui leur est conforme, n'est pas toujours honnête; car les lois s'occupent plus du bien politique de la société que de la perfection morale de l'homme* » , discours préliminaire sur le premier projet de Code civil, 1801.

We intend to analyze the way the Internet of things might influence consumers' situation within a short period of time. This evolution therefore may require to reconsider consumers' protection through the description of a new relation to consumers (I) and proposal of new protections (II).

I. The new relation between professionals and consumers

It is now obvious that we are close to note new practices from professionals based upon their habilities to know much more about each one's behaviour. This technology (A) which offers new Data, shall allow new practicies (B).

A. New technologies for new data

There are, at least in Europe, two movements that explain an evolution of practices. First of all sales are probably no longer interesting for major companies. Better than selling which is a one shot operation, they prefer to rent, in order to enjoy longer relationship. Secondly, Internet Of Things also allow new services. I often repeat that untill nowadays we've been pretty well isolated at home. This might no longer be so.

Closing the door of home meant leaving each one outdoor (today this is still mostly the case). The walls protect us all, so that today's sweet home still is quite a protected place isolated from everyone's look. With new connected objects in our houses, this might change by tomorrow. Walls may fall. Of course placing, for instance, a connected speaker in a living room is a choice of the occupant (yet we might discuss the fact that each consumer doesn't always know the capacities of this objet). Such a decision also offers a possibility for professionals to present new services to consumers, and of course let them know much more about consumers behaviour and needs. We may also wonder placing a connected objet is a choice, it would still be so if professionals only offered connected objects (would someone refuse to have a refrigerator if all these objects were connected?). However it is quite difficult today to evaluate evolution of such offers (we can estimate the technology to come, it is more difficult to evaluate how they'll be used).

In order to have a better idea of what might be, we decided in Montpellier to set up an experimentation in vivo. This experiment can be introduced within a few words.[5] The HUT project focuses on a connected apartment, our ambition is to place all the sensors available today on the market as well as those that could be put in the short, medium or long term on the market, or to design completely new. To do so, we organised a team of 14 disciplines, and we are financed by european and french public founds.

It is important, first of all, to remind the reader of what is technically possible today (even if the possibilities mentioned below are not yet offered for sale): an occupant enters his home. The opening of the door triggers a sensor (which makes it possible to determine when he comes in and comes out) and which justifies the setting in function of a whole series of actuators (ex: light, music or heating, etc.)

[5]For more information, www.hut-occitanie.eu.

which gives the time of its arrival (to a computer system in isolation or more likely connected to others). The occupant walks on the floor, the system can determine if he is alone or accompanied, if he is dragging a cart or (eventually) carries a bag. He goes by the fridge to take a beer or a multivitamin juice (we know what individual consumes and what's left, who in the apartment consumed what). He then opens the cupboard to take chips or dried fruits (same analysis) and lies on the couch to watch a program on television (a documentary or a movie?). He then goes to the bathroom etc. What are the potentially collected information? We may know (the inventory below does not claim to be exhaustive) his sociability rate, his schedules, his habits and the state of his urinary system to detect any difficulties. This is a neutral analysis (which we consider as a potentially dangerous idea) of the technique, but it is also often presented as inevitable because technically possible. And we are then guided, driven, even directed by the technique. This inevitability of technological progress can be frightening and all the more so if the information circulates freely beyond any control by the subject of this tracing.

Such a flat doesn't exist yet and this not what we built. Fortunatly, Setting up such an appartement with so many sensors wasn't so easy and mostly for a lawyer in charge of coordinating the project.[6] In the case of a connected apartment or simply the use of connected objects, the data collected will be personal data. The main interest of these objects relies in the individualization of advice and decisions made from the information collected, elements that can always be attached to the home of the individual or its digital or nominative identity. The legal regime that will be applicable to them will therefore be that of the IT law and freedoms but also the european Regulation on the protection of natural persons with regard to the processing of personal data and on the free movement of such data.[7]

The need to obtain the consent of the user of the connected object results in particular from Article 7 of the Data Protection Act, which states that the processing must have received the consent of the person whose data are collected. This principle has been completed by the european Regulation, which is applicable from May 2018. Articles 6 and 7 reproduce the articles of the Data Protection Act and deepen them. The continuity is only apparent because the requirements of the RGPD are stricter. Article 4 lays down a definition of consent which must henceforth be interpreted as a clear positive act. This means that the person whose data is collected must formally express their agreement separately from their general consent to the contract that binds them. Article 6 further specifies that this consent must be given for one or more purposes. If consent is not provided for all purposes of the treatment, it will not be considered valid. This implies that the user whose data is collected must have been informed of these different purposes and how they will be processed. He must know what will be the personal data he has accepted treatment. This of course complicates our own experimentation in HUT since it means that we have to inform the occupant of all processed data and all the observed purposes. In case of change, or addition, this occupant must be informed and accept it. Is this general reglement duly applied?

[6]The author of this note.

[7]2016, April 27th, JOUE L.119/1.

Each observer would say not yet and we must confess that requires important reforms of professional contemporary practices.

B. What would be new practices?

Common language rightly invoked exclusively and until a recent period a "fidelity" of the clientele, an elegant formula that calls for a constancy of faith. The system consisted in offering advantages to the customer who registered with the operator (essentially on a customer file) in return for his payments. The practice does not seem dangerous, it leaves the client free to pursue, renew or interrupt the economic relationship. But beside this known mechanism grow much more restrictive systems thanks to new technologies described below. The question then arises of whether a legislative evolution, comparable to the evolution of the practices in question, would be relevant, as we already discussed. We would like here to recall the very evolution of French consumers' Code, the content of which has grown considerably over the years, to the detriment no doubt, of the general prohibitions it contains. Yet by privileging the technical or sectoral provisions, the eye of the practitioner is more and more focused on the predetermined models, sometimes making him hesitate to apply the general principles (this is probably even more obvious for consumer). A legislative intervention or an evolution of the jurisprudential answer can then be relevant here, as for example the reform of the framework of the contracts containing a clause of tacit renewal was set up after many abuses.[8]

It must then be possible to consider the protection of consumer outside its walls and excluding only the provisions of Consumer Code and Consumer Law as it may have been circumscribed by the legislator. Competition law is also a tool for consumer protection (as far as consumer law, through its regulatory function, is a tool for protecting the market). The immediate objective of competition law is certainly the free play of competition in the interests of the operators, but this objective must work for the benefit of all and also achieve the protection of consumers. In concrete terms, this means that competition law will only protect consumer if his interests are thwarted by a market anomaly, but it is an important protection. Competition Law must guarantee the plurality of the offer and its transparency, thereby it can also guarantee consumer's freedom of choice. The law of personal data, with the new general regulation on the protection of personal data that is applicable today, because it intends to promote the portability of data, also guarantees just like the competition law, the plurality of the offer. By doing so again, it facilitates the change of contractor by consumer and thus again his freedom of choice. There again it is an usefull tool for the consumers' freedom: what would his right to deal with a new professional if, in case of interpretating data, this data remained the only property of the previous professional contractor?

---

[8]LOI n° 2005-67 du 28 janvier 2005 tendant à conforter la confiance et la protection du consommateur.

It is therefore more likely to be a question of consumer protection against captive ecosystems[9] by consumer Law and by the two most commonly used techniques: information or, more intrusively, the revision of contracts. We here consider consumers Law as any economic right, it must necessarily evolve with society to adapt to new aspirations of individuals and the practices of professionals who also evolve as technology advances.

II. The new way of protecting

What would be new protection? There are, in our opinion three issues to consider: first, the need for more freedom, within or without the contract consideration and the requirement of a relevant information of consumers. Second, the place of contract in Consumer Law and a new consideration of consumers rights. Nowadays all french consumers' Code is based upon the model of sale contract.

A. More freedom

The exclusivity sometimes exists thanks to the appropriation of data by the professional. These data can be raw or processed. In this second hypothesis, the data collected from consumer, once analyzed, make it possible to create new data which have been the subject of the professional's expertise. If this information can be of value to consumer, it strongly encourages him in fact for an accessory service to contract only with this professional or to use (and acquire) only compatible hardware. Of course, under the computer law and freedoms of 1978 several times modified, consumer retains a right of access to his data, but only the raw data that is to say those that have been transmitted to the professional or automatically captured by him, but more difficult in fact to the analysis which has been made and which remains the only one which for him, has a value. If we take the example of activity tracer bracelets, the raw data correspond to those captured by this bracelet and which resume the activity of the wearer by associating them with a time scale. The processed data correspond to the analysis that is made and their representation (am I in good physical condition? What may I do to improve it?). If consumer can only access these raw data and leave only with them, he faces two difficulties in implementing his choice to prefer a competing offer: he often loses the analysis of these data and does not receive them when he does so. request that in a form that does not ensure an immediate and effective transmission thereof to a second operator. Here arises the difficulty of interoperability of the data. If ever consumer desires to contract with another professional offering similar services, he has to request the transfer of data to a new system. If the transferred data are in a raw format (which would need to be entered again in the system? of the new operator) and if furthermore the second operator offers no other mode of data recovery than the capture by his own system, the consumer remains bounded. Here the question of the protection of personal data has been legally considered from the point of view of the protection of privacy (which is obviously an important objective), but not always from the point of view of maintaining a full competition between

[9] Malo Depincé, *Du consommateur fidèle au consommateur captif*, Revue Lamy de droit des affaires, juillet/août 2019, p. 54 et s.

operators. The question of interoperability was initially addressed in a situation that did not raise exclusivity problems a priori in France (on the protection measures of digital media prohibiting reading on certain devices). It is now much wider. It is interesting here to recall Article L. 111-1 of Consumer Code, which has essentially taken over the Court of Cassation's solution by imposing an information obligation on: « *Where appropriate, information safeguards, the functionalities of the digital content and, where appropriate, its interoperability, the existence and implementation of guarantees and other contractual conditions* » . However, this is exclusively a matter of obligation of information which obviously does not promote interoperability but on the contrary valid any "closed" system on the condition that consumer had been previously informed. Article L. 111-1 then validates, what we regret, the partitioning of the data market. Article 20 of the european Regulation which confers a right to the portability of data has to be recalled: « *Data subjects have the right to receive the personal data concerning them which they have provided to a person in charge of the data. processing, in a structured, commonly used and machine-readable format, and have the right to transmit such data to another controller without the controller responsible for the processing of the personal data being obstructed* [...] » , but the portability is probably not complete if this right is in fact only the raw data so that the data produced by the professional from these first data would not have to be transmitted to consumer who would make it asks and if, in addition, technical restrictions could justify a refusal of this portability. The regulation nevertheless brings a major breakthrough for portability, which should favor the switch from one data operator to another or the sharing of this data between several devices.

B. A new model of contracts and new rights for consumers

The purpose of this part of the article is to discuss the way new model of contract may change the consumers' situation and require new rights: in our opinion a larger right to deny or withdraw.

It is today very easy, in a formal consideration, to sign and consent to a contract, but in practice it is often more complicated to resign. Here we have, sometimes in France and Europe an inequality in forms. Parties to the contract are free, except some specific exceptions (such as for canvassing in France), to determine the way consent must be expressed. So that some professional, who write the frame of the contract, usually suggest a form of signature that would make the consent to the contract easier. This is on of the reasons why some of them no longer make sign sheets of paper but suggest an electronic signature on an electronic device: consumer in such a form, doesn't realize the length of the contract and reads even less its content. Yet it is, to the opposite more complicated for consumer to resign it. Some professional who encouraged electronic signature to validate the contract, require to resign, a more formal and a more restrictive form, such as a letter with a proof of sending. In some others cases, we may even wonder if there is a possible consent. This consent to contract may today be guided, or even Substituted by algorithms: « *Will it still make sense, for example, to speak about consumer's choice when preferences are defined, predicted and shaped by algorithms*?".[10] Therefore the model of contract for market regulation and consumers Law, upon which most of French consumers Law is based could no longer be relevant. This Law protect consumer as a party to a contact. If there is no contract, consumers Law could not be relevant. If there is no more contract (because there would be no more consent of the individual), how to find a new way of regulation? Option may then be introduced: whether the requirement of a contract and so of consent prevails, so that algorithms should now be strictly limited in their introduction. Whether contract is only considered as relevant for framework ones (to be regulated then upon a new model). Whether, for the very last solution, regulation should no longer be based upon contract but facts and unilateral acts. This issue is raised today because of an amazing development of algorithm science (the capacity of professionals to predict a rational behavior) and because of the huge increase of available data about consumers. The more is known, the best is the prediction and the less consent would be appropriate. With this final proposal for a new European frame of consumers Law, no matter then the consideration of contract if free consent can not be admitted. What matters is that consumer may access general conditions of contract (which shall not change) or requirement of the professional, whatever they might be. This is the prohibition of certain terms, or the obligation to insert terms in contracts and conditions that shall only protect. Here are many issues raised by new technologies for consumers Law, requiring a new debate of the best consumers' protection and market regulation.

Reference

1. Michal S. Gal &Niva Elkin-Koren, Harvard Journal of Law & Technology, Volume 30, Number 2 Spring 2017.

[10]*Algorithmic consumers*, Gal and Niva [1].

Consumer Protection in e-Commerce and Online Services

Ashfaq M. Naikwadi

1 Introduction

Consumer Protection has become a great concern to all world countries. It has gained importance to Political, Social, Corporate, Cultural and overall Human developments. In India the Consumer is Called as "King". It is an obligation on the states to provide a fair and transparent market to its population at the same time to protect its rights and interests as consumer. On the guidelines of the UN several states have framed legislations and regulations with the intent of protecting the consumer through judicial and/or quasi-judicial provisions. When it comes to e-commerce trade or online services, the issue of executing a judicial order always remains hanging.

This paper analysis the disputes arising out of e-commerce and online services and puts forth possible redressal mechanisms. For this, Consumer protection in different countries was studied with the help of internet. It is found that no country could firmly make provisions for cross border or e-commerce transactions of consumers to protect their interests and rights.

2 Issues of e-Commerce and Online Services

With the Internet, followed unending innovations and applications in the digital world. Supplemented by the smartphone, the internet became easy access to the grass-root population with rapid developments in the information technology. The whole world has come into the hands of an individual.

A. M. Naikwadi (✉)
District Consumer Disputes Redressal Forum, Satara, Maharashtra, India
e-mail: ash02@dr.com

D. Wei et al. (eds.), *Innovation and the Transformation of Consumer Law*,
https://doi.org/10.1007/978-981-15-8948-5_4

Digitalization has brought in vast applications in the field of Online shopping, Banking, Tourism, Travel, Cross border Trade, Government schemes, Documentation, Education and things to come in the daily life. Most of the complaints in the digital world arise from online shopping and financial transactions like banking. The issues in online shopping are—non delivery of product, delayed delivery, defective product, unoriginal product, after sales services, return of defective product, product and services not complying with the requirements and other. The issues in Financial services like banking are related to internet banking, debit cards, credit cards, fraudulent transactions, private information sharing, ATM services and other.

Many nations have Consumer Affairs Department or the Fair Trading Department in their Ministry. Also there are Consumer Complaints Redressing Agencies. In India there is a three tier Quasi Judicial system for consumer complaints redressal. One at the District level, second at the State level and the third at the National level. Consumer complaints are flowing to these forums. Recently there is a rise in consumer complaints pertaining to online shopping and services. It is found that in most of the complaints the necessary parties are missed and mostly only the platform provider is made as the opposite party. The seller is often is not identified with true and proper address. Same thing in case of the manufacturer of the product. So the process of litigation goes on becoming lengthy.

In online banking services issues pertaining to debit cards and credit cards are at a rise. Monetary transactions only with a PIN have become more risky and number of frauds are occurring day by day. Private data of a consumer is shared and personal codes are acquired using this personal information. Frauders are not identified and do not have a fixed location. Transactions are made within a short span of time from over many distant locations. Financial institutes take defence of private data being shared by consumers themselves. The consumer doesn't know the exact mechanism of consumer complaint redressal and to whom he should approach. In the developing countries majority of the population is still computer illiterate but still use the online facilities as the service providers give them access via smartcards and digital accounts without ascertaining whether they are oriented with the use of computers with internet or not. It is suggested that each bank should have a consumer complaint redressing cell at each branch along with the customer service centre.

The issue of Cross border e-commerce needs to be addressed by a integrated process by the nations of the world. Monetary judgments in consumer complaints can be made executable by making provisions through a International Regulatory Authority. Time has come when existence of such a body is necessary and steps be taken towards it by the Groups of Nations and brought for consideration at the United Nations. This Authority can function under the directions of the International Court of Justice.

3 Conclusion

The present Consumer Complaint Redressal in any nation stands to be in-adequate in the case of e-commerce and online services. As there is complexity of processes and issues of cross border jurisdiction and adjudication, it remains to be addressed in conglomeration of international laws, guidelines on international trade and commerce, consideration of consumer protection at bilateral international agreements and laws on information technology. The solution is far but very much possible with the consideration, co-operation and cognizance of consumer protection by all the nations for a better world of trust between the businesses and the consumers.

Consumers Users, by Definition, Include Us All—The Problems and Consequences of a New Approach to Consumer Protection in the Digital Era

Monika Jagielska

"Consumers, by definition, include us all." This sentence, contained in the Special Message of American President J.F. Kennedy on March 15, 1962 is often cited to emphasize the importance of consumer rights. The message itself is considered a decisive point in the development of consumer law.

It is worth looking at these words today from a slightly different perspective, in terms of the ideas they expressed at the time when they were said, and their relevance today. Market transformations indicate that contemporary customers are ceasing to be consumers of goods and are becoming their users. Consequently, consumer protection measures based on the traditional design of a sales contract are ceasing to be sufficient to ensure an equivalent position of the parties on the market, they need to be rethought and, as a result, most likely should undergo significant change.

Nowadays we are facing tremendous changes in consumer law, notwithstanding whether we deal with American, European or international one, which is slowly but surely ceasing to be consumer law and becoming user law. We are now at a turning point, which we as lawyers cannot miss. Otherwise the law will be out of touch with reality, social expectations and needs. The process is one of many various transformations that consumer law is facing today. For the time being, it may even seem not to be the most important one, but from a wider perspective it may become a milestone in the evolution of at least European private law. The law that, for 2000 years, has been based on the concept that sales law lies at the heart of the system and constitutes a starting point for the legislator.

The publication was prepared in frame of the NCN Project 2015/17/B/HS/01416 "Protection of a weaker party to the contract".

Special Message to the Congress on Protecting the Consumer Interest. March 15, 1962; available at https://www.jfklibrary.org/asset-viewer/archives/JFKPOF/037/JFKPOF-037-028.

M. Jagielska (✉)
University of Silesia in Katowice, Katowice, Poland
e-mail: monika.jagielska@us.edu.pl

D. Wei et al. (eds.), *Innovation and the Transformation of Consumer Law*,
https://doi.org/10.1007/978-981-15-8948-5_5

The dictionary definition defines the verb "to consume" as "to do away with completely; to spend wastefully."[1] This definition shows the essence of consuming—to use up, to destroy. The consumer is a person that consumes the purchased products, is the final link in the chain of the economic process that goes from the production of the goods up to the person who has to use the product (service) without treating it as a good suitable for further trade."

This approach fully corresponded to the market and the situation of consumers in the second half of thetwentieth century. In the industrial economy the chain was simple, and roles were clearly defined. It was for the business to produce and for the final buyers to consume. Each actor in the process would be responsible to either creating value or consuming value. In the industrial era value chain, the consumer would 'eat' value, being the final link and end of the chain of value.[2] Mass production, sales of finished products, the acquisition of goods for final consumption characterized the economic turnover of those times.

The traditional sales contract at least in European legal system was the most important contract, the basic structure for the legal regulations. Until the end of the twentieth century, the law protected the consumer as the final purchaser of goods. The legal means of consumer protection were adapted to the existing market challenges. Therefore, the consumer law of that time focused on ensuring the safety and the quality of goods on the market. Again, as President J. F. Kennedy pointed out "All of us deserve the right to be protected against unsafe or worthless drugs and other products". Concepts such as strict product liability, warranty and guarantees aimed at consumers, the control of unfair contract terms, and finally the consumer right to withdraw from a contract were supposed to be instruments for restoring market balance in trade involving consumers.

The situation has changed significantly in the last few years, along with the development of new technologies[3] and digital revolution.[4] On the one hand, the role of digital content on the market has significantly increased, while on the other the sharing economy, which is implemented mainly via online platforms, is gaining importance.

Modern consumers (known as 3.0 consumers), especially the younger generation, do not show a far-reaching need to own goods.[5] Research shows that the so-called millennial generation, so called "the generation of renters" rarely buy houses and

---

[1] https://www.merriam-webster.com/dictionary/consume.

[2] https://www.brandingstrategyinsider.com/2017/01/unveiling-marketings-new-definition-of-consumers.html#.XWuTgy3US00.

[3] Social and Economic Transformation in the Digital Era, G. Doukidis, N. Mylonopoulos, N. Pouloudi (eds), Idea Group Publishing 2004.

[4] Digital Revolution. Challenges for Contract Law in Practice, R. Schulze, D. Staudenmayer (eds), Nomos 2016.

[5] See more I, Scott; E. Brown, "Redefining and Regulating the New Sharing Economy," University of Pennsylvania Journal of Business Law 2017, vol. 19, no. 3.

even more rarely — cars.[6] They focus more on the possibility to have an access[7] to the goods for a period of time corresponding to their needs. "I rent just about everything in my life: what I wear, what I watch, what I listen to, how I eat."[8] Among the most famous are the services offered by Uber[9] or Airbnb,[10] but also home exchanges, inviting tourists to a free room in a private apartment, taking passengers to places in a car, sharing parking lots, city bike systems, renting clothing or renting unused areas of land for gardening enthusiasts.

The development of digital technologies has also radically changed the number and quality of contracts concluded through internet platforms.[11]

The shift from ownership to the temporary use of things is also evident in traditional forms of distribution for goods normally purchased "forever". An example of this is the Ikea initiative, which plans to partially replace the sale of furniture with rental schemes.[12] In 2019, IKEA announced[13] that the company is testing a system in which customers will be able to use furniture (initially for the office, but in the future also for the kitchen), and then return it to the store. At the beginning this will be in four European countries: Poland, the Netherlands, Switzerland and Sweden, and only office furniture (chairs, tables, desks and so on), but starting from 2021 this strategy should cover other stock, primarily kitchen furniture. After using the good for some time, the consumer would be entitled to give it back, in which case IKEA will refresh the furniture and rent it back to other clients.

Renting jeans is another example. As part of the service proposed by Mudjenas, customers receive pants for which they pay a monthly fee and later, after at least a year, they can exchange them for a new pair. As the company declares "After a year of leasing a pair of you have the option to keep wearing them, switching them for a new model—only paying the monthly fee of €7,50, or sending them back for reuse or recycling. Once recovered, we sell the used clothing as vintage items, or, depending on the status of the jeans, recycle the fabrics into new products."[14]

Consumer interest in the temporary use or access to goods is even more pronounced in relation to digital content. The popularity of services such as Spotify[15] (in relation to music), Netflix[16] (in relation to films) or e-books and audiobooks

---

[6]https://brightside.me/inspiration-psychology/why-young-people-dont-buy-cars-and-apartments-anymore-238710/.

[7]https://www.digitalnewsreport.org/survey/2019/how-younger-generations-consume-news-differently/.

[8]https://money.cnn.com/2015/05/13/pf/millennial-rent-economy-clothes-jewelry/index.html.

[9]https://www.statista.com/topics/4826/uber-technologies/.

[10]https://ipropertymanagement.com/airbnb-statistics/.

[11]https://influencermarketinghub.com/influencer-marketing-2019-benchmark-report/.

[12]https://www.ft.com/content/da461f24-261c-11e9-8ce6-5db4543da632.

[13]https://www.ikea.com/us/en/about_ikea/newsitem/040319-IKEA-will-test-furniture-leasing-2020.

[14]https://mudjeans.eu/lease-a-jeans/.

[15]https://www.theverge.com/2019/4/29/18522297/spotify-100-million-users-apple-music-podcasting-free-users-advertising-voice-speakers.

[16]https://edition.cnn.com/2019/01/17/media/netflix-earnings-q4/index.html.

services[17] (as Kindle Unlimited), in which users gain temporary access to digital content in exchange for paying a subscription fee, or for free, shows the growing importance of transactions in which the essence of the benefit is the possibility to use goods, and not their permanent possession.

The above examples indicate a trend on the market consisting in moving away from traditionally understood consumption and ownership towards the temporary use of goods. The customer ceases to be a consumer (in the sense indicated at the beginning of these considerations) and becomes a user, who needs an access. This applies not only to goods traditionally offered for rent (such as apartments and cars), but also those that have so far been purchased for final consumption or sale (clothing and furniture, as well as books or films in digital form), which have become the subject of the longer term contracts of use.

It should be assumed that this tendency will deepen. On the one hand, the younger generations, as opposed to their parents, are not "burdened" (43% of consumers agree that "owning today feels like a burden")[18] by the need to own things, resulting from life experience of a lack or shortage of goods. On the other hand, they see the burdens and responsibilities associated with the permanent possession of goods. The sharing economy also goes along with the growing public awareness of the need for action to protect the natural environment, in which the indicated projects fit very well.

In this situation, it becomes necessary to reorient consumer law focused on protecting the final purchaser of consumer goods into a system that protects the user, usually long-term, of the various types of goods. Over the past 50 years, and not only in the European Union,[19] appropriate legal mechanisms have been developed to protect traditional consumers.[20] These means of protection may require improvement, but not wholesale change. For the time being, it is necessary to focus on ensuring adequate protection for a new category of entities—users of goods. To paraphrase JFK's sentence cited at the beginning, currently "Users include—or will include—all of us," whereas consumer law is not fully adapted to such a situation.

The rationale behind creating an appropriate system of user protection is the same as for consumers.[21] They are the weaker party to the contract, deprived of full

---

[17]https://www.forbes.com/sites/ellenduffer/2018/07/27/amazon-e-book-sales-grow-in-2017-and-2018/.

[18]Consumer Intelligence Series: The Sharing Economy, Pricewaterhousecoopers 2015, https://www.pwc.fr/fr/assets/files/pdf/2015/05/pwc_etude_sharing_economy.pdf.

[19]Since 1985 EU has developed a wide range of consumer protection instruments, mainly via consumer law directives, more S.Weatherill, EU Consumer Law and Policy, 2014; G. Howells, Ch. Twigg-Flesner, T. Wilhelmsson, Rethinking EU Consumer Law, 2019; H. Micklitz, N. Reich, EU Consumer Law, 2014; EC Consumer Law Compendium. The Consumer Acquis and its transposition in the Member States, H.Schulte-Noelke, Ch.Twigg-Flesner, M. Ebers (eds) Munich 2008; Cases, Materials and Text on Consumer Law, H. W > Micklitz, J. Stuyck, E. Terryn (eds), Oxford 2010.

[20]I. Ramsay, Consumer Law and Policy, 1974; G. Howells, S. Weatherill, Consumer Protection Law, London 2017; G. Howells, I. Ramsay, T. Wilhelmsson, Handbook of Research on International Consumer Law Elgar 2010.

[21]See footnote 17 and reference 14.

information about concluded contracts, and at the same time not equipped with full protection measures corresponding to those created to protect traditional consumers.

This applies especially to protection in the case of non-conformity and defective goods. *De lege lata* it is not possible to use the non-conformity and warranty concepts for contracts concluded by users. Apart from general regulations on liability for non-performance, there are no system solutions that would give the user protection similar to what the buyer receives.

It is a truism for a lawyer to say that the fact that the user is not the owner of the thing has far-reaching legal effects. However, this is not so obvious to the average user. In a situation where more and more goods, which until now were most often the object of ownership, are becoming the object of use, (the lack of) the possibility of disposing of them becomes a problem. "It does not appear that consumers have a clear understanding whether they own or license the products and services they purchase online due in part to the length and opacity of most EULAs, the labelling of the "buy" button, and the lack of clear and conspicuous information regarding ownership status on websites".[22]

In the virtual world, the idea of being a user is even more evident. Very often we only want access—to music, films and books. In this case, the same questions appear—how can we protect the users of digital content in the case of non-conformity and throughout the whole lifespan of the contract. The situation becomes more complicated when we "buy" the digital goods. In many jurisdictions one can only own things, which is understood as tangible goods. So those who "buy" are not, in fact, actually buying, they are merely the owners, they are users. In such a situation, users are not usually entitled to sell, gift or dispose of in the event of death. Users cannot rely on remedies that apply in the case of ownership—such as vindication claims. In the case of a cloud services provider's bankruptcy, they can only rely on contractual remedies.

In situations where the sales contract is replaced by a contract for the use of goods, usually concluded for an extended period of time, the mechanisms of controlling the content of the contract begin to play a very important role. Contracts for the sale of consumer goods are usually concluded without complying with any formal requirements, based solely on a consensus as to the parties' main benefits, whereas contracts for the use of goods are usually formal and, above all, are concluded on the basis of the standard contract terms. In permanent relations, the provisions relating to the possibility of unilaterally shaping the content of a contract and the mutual obligations of the parties, including liability, as well as the termination of the legal relationship, are of particular importance.

An analysis of the contractual patterns used in this type of contract indicates that they contain provisions that may be considered unfair. European law provides protection against such clauses in relation to all types of contracts concluded with

[22]U.S. Department of Commerce's Internet Policy Task Force WHITE PAPER ON REMIXES, FIRST SALE, AND STATUTORY DAMAGES 2016 https://www.uspto.gov/sites/default/files/documents/copyrightwhitepaper.pdf.

consumers,[23] though it may be worth considering which abusive clauses are characteristic for temporary use contracts, violate the contractual balance and then introduce such clauses to the catalog of unfair contract terms. From a similar perspective, it would also be necessary to analyze the information obligations posed on the business, as well as the unfair market practices.

Another important issue is the regulation of the complex issue of online platforms. It is somewhat outside the scope of this study, as it does not directly relate to the consumer transformation process and its legal consequences, but it is nevertheless closely related to it. In the literature, the new legal regulations[24] or draft regulations,[25] attention is drawn to numerous legal problems that internet platforms bring with them. First of all, it is about clarifying the legal status of the platform actors, in particular determining whether and when they are professionals or consumers, with all the resulting consequences; secondly, what the nature of the links are connecting the three parties participating in the platform system, and thirdly, the problem of liability. The issue of the reliability of information and opinions/comments is also at stake.

The latter issue also gains significant importance in the context of the need to build consumer confidence in the market, which has been pointed out over the past few decades. Platform mechanisms indicate that the user is looking for confidence, not so much in legal instruments but elsewhere—in the reputation of the platform and the opinions of other users. For this mechanism to function properly, however, legal instruments are needed. Moreover, if the correct functioning of evaluation systems could be guaranteed, they could become a very useful instrument of consumer/user protection in the future, and at least partly fulfill an informative function.

In recent years, the process of transforming a traditional consumer into a user is becoming more and more important. This, of course, does not mean that traditional consumers will disappear from the market. There are people who are not and will not be interested in obtaining only temporary access to goods and who would prefer to stay with traditional sales. Secondly, there are goods that will always have the nature of purely consumer goods, the use of which consists in their consumption. In these areas, traditional consumer law will continue to play an essential role and, as

---

[23]Council Directive 93/13/EEC of 5 April 1993 on unfair terms in consumer contracts. OJ L 95, 21.4.1993, p. 29–34.

[24]For example in France LOI n° 2016–1321 du 7 octobre 2016 pour une République numérique, https://www.legifrance.gouv.fr/affichTexte.do;jsessionid=DC8EDE50354DC7C7EAC3D02ACAC70E33.tplgfr23s_2?cidTexte=JORFTEXT000033202746&categorieLien=id.

[25]In Italy Proposta di legge No. 3564: Disciplina delle piattaforme digitali per la condivisione di beni e servizi e disposizioni per la promozione dell'economia della condivisione; on the EU level Model Rules on Online Intermediary Platforms https://www.elsi.uni-osnabrueck.de/projekte/model_rules_on_online_intermediary_platforms.html Christoph Busch; Gerhard Dannemann; Hans Schulte-Nölke; Aneta Wiewiórowska-Domagalska; Fryderyk Zoll, Discussion Draft of a Directive on Online Intermediary Platforms, in: 5 Journal of European Consumer and Market Law (EuCML) (2016); Christoph Busch; Gerhard Dannemann; Hans Schulte-Nölke; Aneta Wiewiórowska-Domagalska; Fryderyk Zoll (eds) Discussion Draft of a Directive on Online Intermediary Platforms: Commentary, Jagiellonian University Press 2019.

already indicated above, will require improvements but not significant changes. The issue of ensuring adequate protection for users should be approached differently.

The situation is still simpler compared to the times when consumer law was being created in the second half of the twentieth century. The idea of protecting the weaker party and its justification is generally approved, appropriate protective measures have been developed and traders have grown accustomed to the idea of providing adequate protection to both parties to the transaction. Moreover, in many areas, such as unfair contract terms and unfair market practices, perhaps it would be possible to provide users with adequate protection under existing regulations. However, we should think about developing a protection system for users that is similar to the system of consumer protection, so that not only a lawyer specializing in consumer law, but also an ordinary user will be able to effectively enforce his rights. This is important, because the move from consumerism towards the idea of sharing should be fully supported. It is a beneficial process for society and the environment.

References

1. Y. van Rooy, Consumer Law: The First Fifty Years, 1 J. Eur. Consumer & Mkt. L. 209 (2012).
2. K. Gutman, Development of Consumer Law in the US: Comparison with the EU Experience, 1 J. Eur. Consumer & Mkt. L. 212 (2012).
3. R. Zimmermann, "Roman Law and European Culture," New Zealand Law Review 2007, no. 2.
4. J. A. Jolowicz, "The Protection of the Consumer and Purchaser of Goods under English Law," Modern Law Review 1969, vol. 32, no. 1.
5. W. Prosser, The Assault Upon the Citadel (Strict Liability to the Consumer), Yale Law Journal 1960, vol. 69, s. 1099–1134; T. Cowan, Some Policy Basis of Products Liability, Stanford Law Review 1965, vol. 17; S. Simitis, Grundfragen der Produzentenhaftung, Tübingen 1965; F.Kessler, Product Liability, Yale Law Journal, 1967, Vol. 76; M. Shapo, Product Liability, Cases and Materials, Mineola 1980; J. Wade, On the Nature of Strict Tort Liability for Products, Missisipi Law]ournal 1973, vol. 44; D. Montgomery, W. Owen, Reflections on the Theory and Administration of Strict Tort Liability for Defective Products, Santa Clara Law Review 1976, vol. 27; V. Palmer, A General Theory of the Inner Structure of Strict Liability: Common Law, Civil Law and Comparative Law, JPTL 1989, vol. 12; J. Fleming, Mass Torts, AJCL 1994, vol. 42.
6. F. Kessler, The Protection of the Consumer under the Modern Sales Law, Yale Law Journal 1964, Vol. 74; "Disclaimer of Warranty in **Consumer Sales**," Harv. L. R. 1963, vol.77); A.Mueller, Contract of Frustration, Yale Law Journal 1969 , Vol. 78; E.Murphy, Another Assault upon the Citadel: Limiting the Use of Negotiable Notes and Waiver-of-Defense Clauses in Consumer Sales. Consumer Protection Symposium, Ohio State Law Journal 1968, Vol. 29.
7. E. Hondious, Unfair Contracts terms: New Control System, American Journal of Comparative Law 1978, Vol. 26; Gluck G, Standard Form Contracts: The Contract Theory Reconsidered, International and Comparative Law Quarterly,1979 Vol. 28.
8. O. Ben-Shahar; E.A. Posner, The right to withdraw in contract law. Journal of Legal Studies 2011, vol. 40.
9. J.B. Meisel, "Entry into the Market for Online Distribution of Digital Content: Economic and Legal Ramifications," SCRIPTed: A Journal of Law, Technology and Society 2008, vol. 5, no. 1.
10. D. Selloni, New Forms of Economies: Sharing Economy, Collaborative Consumption, Peer-to-Peer Economy, Springer 2017.

11. K. Stanoevska-Slabeva, V. Lenz-Kesekamp, V. Suter, Platforms and the Sharing Economy: An Analysis. https://www.bi.edu/globalassets/forskning/h2020/ps2share_platform-analysis-paper_final.pdf.
12. P. Houdek, A Perspective on Consumers 3.0: They Are Not Better Decision-Makers than Previous Generations, "Frontiers in Psychology" 2016, https://www.ncbi.nlm.nih.gov/pmc/articles/PMC4891336/.
13. More B. Cohen, P. Munoz, Sharing Cities and Sustainable Consumption and Production: Towards an Integrated Framework, Journal of Cleaner Production 2016, 134 https://core.ac.uk/download/pdf/30273386.pdf; B. Morgan; D. Kuch, "Radical Transactionalism: Legal Consciousness, Diverse Economies, and the Sharing Economy," Journal of Law and Society 2015, vol. 42, no. 4.
14. B. Morgan; D. Kuch, "Radical Transactionalism: Legal Consciousness, Diverse Economies, and the Sharing Economy," Journal of Law and Society 2015, vol. 42, no. 4.
15. J. Beck, The Decline of the Driver's License, The Atlantic 22 January 2016, https://www.theatlantic.com/technology/archive/2016/01/the-decline-of-the-drivers-license/425169/ https://www.umich.edu/~umtriswt/PDF/UMTRI-2016-4_Abstract_English.pdf.
16. V. Mak, E. Lujinovic: Towards a Circular Economy in EU Consumer Markets – Legal Possibilities and Legal Challenges and the Dutch Example, EuCML 2019, nr 4; B. Morgan; D. Kuch, "Radical Transactionalism: Legal Consciousness, Diverse Economies, and the Sharing Economy," Journal of Law and Society 2015, vol. 42, no. 4.
19. More S. Kreiczer-Levy, "Consumption Property in the Sharing Economy," Pepperdine Law Review 2015, vol 43, no. 1.
20. Aaron Perzanowski; Chris Jay Hoofnagle, What We Buy When We Buy Now, 165 U. Pa. L. Rev. (2017).
21. More Sjef van Erp, Ownership of Data: The Numerus Clausus of Legal Objects, 6 Brigham-Kanner Prop. Rts. Conf. J. 2017.
22. More Benjamin Hayward, What's in a Name: Software, Digital Products, and the Sale of Goods, 38 Sydney L. Rev. 2016, s. 447.
23. J. Luzak: Digital age: time to say goodbye to traditional concepts, EuCML 2018, vol.17.
24. E.Terryn: The sharing economy in Belgium – a case for regulation?, EuCML 2016, 45.
25. Ch. Busch, H. Schulte-Nölke, A. Wiewiórowska-Domagalska, F. Zoll, The Rise of the Platform Economy: A New Challenge for EU Consumer Law? EuCML 2016, nr 3; K.Nemeth, J.Morais Carvalho: Current Challenges for Consumer Law, EuCML 2019.
26. T. McSweeny, "FTC 2.0: Keeping Pace with Online Platforms," Berkeley Technology Law Journal 32, no. 3 (2017); A. Wiewiórowska-Domagalska, Online Platforms: How to Adapt Regulatory Framework to the Digital Age?, European Parliament Briefing, PE 607.323, 2017, available at https://www.europarl.europa.eu/RegData/etudes/BRIE/2017/607323/IPOL_BRI(2017)607323_EN.pdf.
27. M. Narciso, The Regulation of Online Reviews in European Consumer Law, European Review of Private Law 2019, vol.27, nr 3.

Digital Platformers' Responsibilities to Platform Users; 'Consumer Protection' in B2C and C2C e-Commerce

Shizuko Tanaka

1 Introduction

As internet use is expanded, variable internet businesses are appearing. The purpose of this study is to clarify whether digital platforms, which provide online shopping and auction services, have a responsibility to provide a proper platform service which fully protects its users. The business model of such digital platforms is more different and rapidly evolving than ever. Hence, we find that there is insufficient legislation to protect users, and hence we need a new worldwide framework of rules to maintain platformer's responsibilities to one another.

Such a framework has been often discussed in the context of antitrust legislation. However, the coverage of antitrust law is normally in direct reference to a certain market(s) and specific businesses engaged in said market(s). Consumer protection does not, therefore, adequately, cover it. Of course, there are some laws and regulations which cover consumer-buyer's rights regarding the sale of goods and services on the internet. However, they cover simply B2C transactions. Is there no problem to refer the resolution to antitrust law? Must we always ignore C2C transactions?

Online shopping malls and internet auction platforms are places that offer services such as facilitating the conclusion of the contract of sales, their closing as well as supporting the payments and deliveries of related products. Such places are business models belonging to platform operators which make use of platform users. Thus, the platform operators do not act as an intermediator in the classical business (and legal) sense. Furthermore, C2C transactions using digital platforms (e.g., Internet flea markets) take place very frequently. C2C transactions are not protected to the same level as those of B2C transactions. Hence, consumers in this area are at a disadvantage.

S. Tanaka (✉)
Faculty of Law, Momoyamagakuin University, 1-1 Manabino, Izumi-city, Osaka 594-1198, Japan
e-mail: shizut@andrew.ac.jp

D. Wei et al. (eds.), *Innovation and the Transformation of Consumer Law*,
https://doi.org/10.1007/978-981-15-8948-5_6

In order to trade in Internet malls and via Internet auctions, the systems provided by platform operators must be used. There is less trust for the counterpart in such contract of sales than in face-to-face transactions given that there is a possibility that the product will not be delivered, and even if delivered, it may not conform to the agreement and/or description. Of course, the primary responsibility coming from a contract of sales lies with the seller. However, when the seller does not bear the responsibility, the user is not obliged to simply accept the disadvantages caused to them by a system that the platform operator. However, these operators have built these platforms and have exclusive control of them. Therefore, platform operators should be obliged to provide systems that enable secure transactions based on the terms of use.

In this paper, I shall do the following: firstly, I highlight the characteristics of digital platforms by making use of economic analysis; secondly, I discuss the terms of use on digital platforms, especially online shopping malls, internet auctions and internet flea markets; and, finally I'Il compare buyer's/consumer's remedies briefly under the laws and platforms' policies.

Digital platform operators are evolving on a daily basis, so there are various business types and forms of transaction but as yet, no established definitions. In this paper, the word "digitalplatformer" refers to operators/providers of a digital platform or an online platform.[1] A digital platform is hereinafter referred to as digital platform or "platform."

2 Features of Digital Platform

In two-sided and multi-sided markets, there is an indirect network effect of "an increase in the number of users of a platform which increases the benefits for other users".[2] A digital platformer who uses the indirect network effect is an entity that provides an essential foundation for social economics by designing, operating and managing the very place where many consumers and businesses participate in transactions. Its peculiarity lies in the fact that such a place has intrinsic operability and technical intransparency.

It also happens that there are cases when platform services are even provided free of charge. "In some marketplaces, free services without any monetary compensation, such as SNS are provided to consumers, while other marketplaces often receive monetary compensations." Also, even when such services are "free," as various

[1] Digital platformer Study Group on trading environment improvement, the Intermediate Discussion Paper on *the Trading Environment Improvement Over the Digital Platformer* (December 12, 2018) 1 original note 1. https://www.meti.go.jp/press/2018/12/20181212002/20181212002-1.pdf.

[2] Hiroyuki Odagiri has argued "Network effect" means that "the more users who use the same product, brand, standard, technology, etc., the greater the benefits, etc. that individual users gain from that product," *Competitive Policy in the Innovation Era: Law and Economy of Research, Patents, and Platforms* (Yuhikaku, 2016) 228. See also, Shinnosuke Fukuoka and Hidetoshi Matsumura, *Data Law and Contract* (Shojihomu, First Edition, 2019) 32.

other services are provided to consumers on SNS and in online shopping malls, it is said that "non-price competition for quality among competitors takes place".[3]

3 Terms and Conditions

In the case of online shopping malls, internet auctions and internet flea markets, platformers provide platform services such as management systems for shopping malls, auctions and flea markets.

In an online shopping mall, a seller who sets up a shop on the platform is a business owner, and other business owners or consumers who are buyers purchase goods which that seller has displayed in the shopping mall. A contract of sales for items in question is a contract between the business which has set up the shop and a purchaser.

In Internet flea markets, many sellers and buyers who sell goods on the platform are consumers, and the contract of sales will be concluded between a consumer-seller and a consumer-buyer.

In Internet auctions, the seller who "lists" an item on the platform and the buyer, a successful bidder who purchases it, may be other businesses or consumers and the contract of sales will be between such a seller who is the lister, and the buyer who is the successful bidder.

Platformers define the terms of use for their platforms. In order to sell or buy goods, shop owners (sellers) and bidders (buyers) enter a platform usage agreement which is the base of a contract of sales with the platformer. The platforms' terms of use are the "terms and conditions" which are the contents of the platform usage agreement set forth for that purpose by the platformer. In order to trade using a platform, one must use the system provided by the platformer.

Many of the terms of usage for platforms provide a disclaimer stating the platformer is not liable even if a transaction between users causes damage to one of the parties. Therefore, even if one party to a platform-based contract of sales suffers damage, in principle, the platformer is not to be held liable. Also, there may be cases in which return of goods, exchanges or compensations in case of non-delivery of goods is permitted by laws or terms and conditions. However, this aspect is not uniform (Fig. 1).

[3]Japan Fair Trade Commission, Competition Policy Research Center, "*Committee on Data and Competition Policy Report* (2017) pp. 28–29. https://www.jftc.go.jp/cprc/conference/index_files/170606data01.pdf.

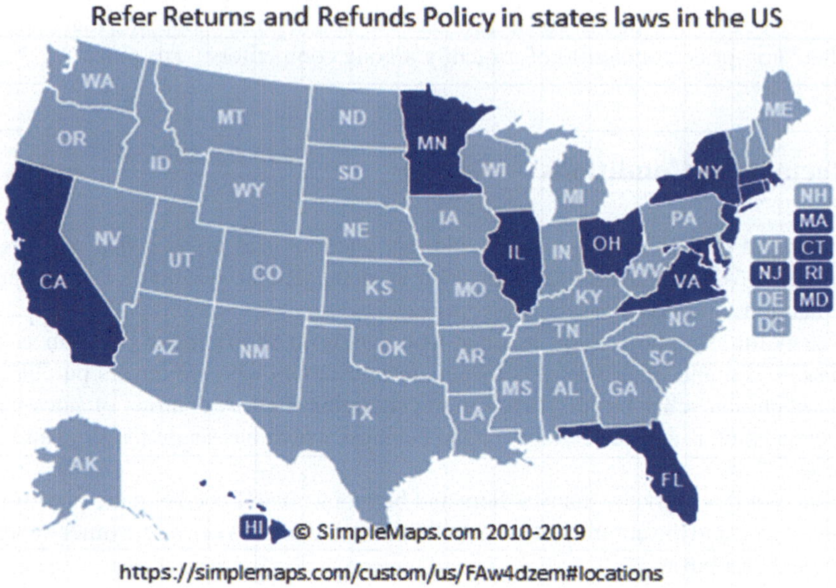

Fig. 1 Legistation in the U.S.

4 Variable Policy and Law

In the U.S., there are no federal laws affecting returns and refunds. Some states in the U.S. lay returns and refund terms down prior to purchasing. For example, according Civil Code Sect. 1723 of the California penal code, a retail seller should display a returns and refunds policy which does not include full refund, not allowing equal exchanges, or any combination thereof.

In the EU, if consumers have purchased faulty goods or which have a lack of conformity to the description, a trader must repair, replace, reduce the price or refund the item(s). Also, if the consumer in question bought a product or a service online, or outside of a shop, the consumer has the right to cancel and return it within 14 days, for any reason and without a justification. These are stated as Directives, so every EU country should integrate these requirements into their own national laws (Fig. 2).

In Japan, a consumer may withdraw the offer for a sales contract or cancel the sales contract via Mail Order Sales in 8 days. However, that does not apply if there are unique conditions that the seller has previously indicated in its advertisement e.g., "Consumer can cancel the contract and return the goods only if the goods is defective product."

In the case of an Internet auction service, the first instance decision in a case in which the platformer's responsibility before a successful bidder who paid for a product, but was deceived by the seller and the product did not arrive, has been discussed as follows.

Distance Sale (via mail order sale)

- Withdraw the offer
- Cancel the contract

Under the Specified Commercial Transactions Act

Buyer's Remedies	There are reasons for return to the buyer	There is no reason for return for both	The seller has a reason for return
Damages	X	X	✓
Cancel	X	✓	✓
Replacement or exchange	X	✓	✓
Price reduction	X	✓	✓

Revised Japanese Civil Law comes into force on 1st April 2020.

Fig. 2 Legistation in Japan

"Because the Usage Agreement is based on the system usage for this service, under the principle of good faith covered in the Usage Agreement the defendant has an obligation to provide this service by constructing a system without defects for its users who include the plaintiffs."[4]

In addition, global platformer like Amazon has slightly different return policy in each countries or areas, because of different legal background.

5 Conclusion

On 11th April 2018, the European Commission adopted a proposal for a directive on "better enforcement and modernization of EU consumer protection rules".[5] The proposal, which would amend four consumer protection Directives, focuses on various consumer issues, including penalties for infringements, transparency on online marketplaces, protection for consumers of 'free' digital services, the right of withdrawal and dual quality of products.

---

[4]3/20/2008 Nagoya District Court Decision. https://www.courts.go.jp/app/files/hanrei_jp/445/036445_hanrei.pdf.

[5]COM/2018/0185 final-2018/090 (COD).

Transparency on online marketplaces would be required to clearly inform consumers about how the offers are ranked in a search engine, and paid placements would have to be indicated. The scope of the Consumer Rights Directive would be extended to cover free digital services.[6] However, there is still keeping of sellers' and buyers' contracts without explanation of how to rank the offers.

Also, Regulation (EU) 2019/1150 of the European Parliament and of the Council of 20 June 2019 on promoting fairness and transparency for business users of online intermediation services came into force on the twentieth day following that of its publication in the Official Journal of the European Union, 11st July 2019. And it will apply from 12nd July 2020. These proposed rules are intended to regulate businesses that provide platforms to businesses that provide goods and services to consumers within the EU, and does not regulate the responsibility of platformers before consumers. Also, it does not apply to regulations on providers who provide platforms for C2C transactions.

In the first instance, it came from the times when platformers designed systems that ignored consumer protection. Furthermore, as a result of platformers changing the terms and conditions so that the sellers had to bear the costs of returns from the buyers, it became necessary to have the limitations according to the competition law for such cases as abuse of a dominant bargaining position, etc.

It has been decided that it is necessary to introduce new regulations with regards to digital platforms in the field of competition law. Can the relationships between platformers and platform users be governed by conventional interpretations of laws in the field of trade law?

Trading via the Internet easily crosses borders. In particular, in order to protect consumers from large platforms, it is necessary not only to develop laws in each individual country, but for all countries to coordinate their legislation.

---

[6]Nikolina Šajn, "Modernization of EU consumer protection rules; A new deal for consumers," EPRS PE 623.547 2, https://www.europarl.europa.eu/RegData/etudes/BRIE/2018/623547/EPRS_BRI(2018)623547_EN.pdf.

Towards Tourists Protection in the Digital Age

Ezequiel N. Mendieta

1 Introduction

Ever since the emergence of consumer protection in the second half of the twentieth century, there has been an expansion of important amendments to legislation worldwide. Nowadays, consumer law as a discipline also faces new scenarios inherent to the twenty-first century, and tries to provide answers to the challenges that these scenarios pose.

In this context, it is worth highlighting the exponential growth of e-commerce in the last twenty years, in a year-to-year basis. This phenomenon allows consumers to acquire goods and services worldwide, and thus create cross-border consumption relationships. Supply-wise, these agreements offer consumers wider opportunities for good and services, which go beyond the formal borders of a country. Notwithstanding that, the advancement of e-commerce also poses risks for consumers, which go from data theft (e.g. payment means data theft) to possible hindrances to dispute resolution access due to the lack of appropriate instruments for filing claims.

In parallel, tourism has also grown considerably in the last thirty years. According to the World Tourism Organization (hereinafter "UNWTO",) the aggregate international arrivals worldwide increased by 7% in 2017; the highest growth registered since the 2009 crisis.[1] In this industry, several agreements and consumption relationships are entered into by tourist consumers.

Between the two aforementioned phenomena, an intersection may be set. E-commerce and tourist consumption relationships have become intertwined, as tourist consumers habits have changed as a result of the digital revolution. Nowadays,

[1] World Tourism Organization (2018), *UNWTO Tourism Highlights*, 2018 Edition, UNWTO, Madrid.

E. N. Mendieta (✉)
University of Buenos Aires, Buenos Aires, Argentina

Castilla-La Mancha University, Ciudad Real, Spain

D. Wei et al. (eds.), *Innovation and the Transformation of Consumer Law*,
https://doi.org/10.1007/978-981-15-8948-5_7

consumers may enter into agreements through several platforms or purchase plane tickets in an airline's website or through agents online. Furthermore, consumers may also access to accommodations through collaborative economy services.

Said intersection exposes electronic tourist consumers to many disadvantages, as consumers bear not only with their structural vulnerability but also with the vulnerabilities inherent to tourism and online agreements; issues which shall be later expanded on.

Therefore, the starting point set herein are the results of the research project The Issue of Hyper-vulnerable Consumers in Argentine Consumer Law, directed by Sergio S.Barocelli, which took place between 2016 and 2018 in the Gioja Research Institute at the School of Law of the University of Buenos Aires. Therein are defined the concepts of hyper-vulnerable consumers,[2] including tourist consumers[3] and electronic consumers.[4]

On this issue, it has been held that hyper-vulnerable consumers are those consumers "…which, to their structural vulnerability as a consumer, a further vulnerability is added, generally linked to age; psycho-physical condition; gender; socioeconomic or cultural background; as well as any other permanent or temporary condition".[5]

In this sense, regarding tourist consumers, it was held that hyper-vulnerability stems from the difficulties that may be faced while staying in a place different to ones home, with different customs and language, added to the short time for claiming upon a breach of contract or any other harm that may be held.[6]

Likewise, when addressing to electronic consumers as hyper-vulnerable, special consideration is taken to the fact that consumers are immersed in a completely unknown medium, which cannot be managed or fully understood; poses further challenges for consumers; and accentuates the technical asymmetry between consumer and provider.[7]

---

[2]Barocelli, Sergio S., "Hacia la construcción de la categoría de consumidores hipervulnerables" in Barocelli, Sergio S. (Director), *Consumidores Hipervulnerables*, Ed. El Derecho, Ciudad Autónoma de Buenos Aires, 2018, p. 9, ff. It is worth highlighting that this work is the publication of the results of the research project "The Issue of Hyper-Vulnerable Consumer in Argentine Consumer Law," directed by Sergio S. Barocelli, which took place between 2016 and 2018 in the Gioja Research Institute at the School of Law of the University of Buenos Aires.

[3]Orduna, Javier and Santana, Carolina, "El turista: Un consumidor hipervulnerable" in Barocelli, Sergio S. (Director), *Consumidores Hipervulnerables*, Ed. El Derecho, Ciudad Autónoma de Buenos Aires, 2018, p. 187, ff.

[4]Beltramo, Andrés Nicolás and Faliero, Johana Caterina, "El consumidor electrónico como consumidor hipervulnerable" en Barocelli, Sergio S. (Director), *Consumidores Hipervulnerables*, op. cit., p. 205, ff.

[5]Barocelli, Sergio S., "Hacia la construcción de la categoría…" op. cit., p. 16.

[6]Orduna, Javier and Santana, Carolina, "El turista: Un consumidor…", op. cit., pp. 187–188.

[7]Beltramo, Andrés Nicolás and Faliero, Johana Caterina, "El consumidor electrónico…", op. cit., p. 212.

Consequently, an electronic tourist consumer[8] may be defined as any consumer in a consumption relationship that has been entered into through e-commerce and has a service in the tourism industry as a bargain for consideration or subject matter. These consumers face specific challenges which require a specific protection frame. Therefore, the various rules of said protection frame are further explained, and possible solutions to the challenges faced by these consumers are devised.

2 Electronic Tourist Consumer Protection in International and Compared Law

In the last fifteen years, international law has attempted to provide answers to the issues inherent to touristic services and e-commerce. On their own, the European Union has also provided for protective rules for such cases.

Therefore, the different rules and declarations made by international law and the European Union on different protection mechanisms for electronic tourist consumers shall be briefly recounted.

(A) UN Guidelines for Consumer Protection

It is inevitable to start mentioning the rules set forth by the UN Guidelines for Consumer Protection, as adopted by the General Assembly in Resolution 39/248 of 16 April 1985 and revised in Resolution 70/186 of 22 December 2015.

The first part of the Guidelines contains provisions which point out that the protection of consumers and hyper-vulnerable consumers is a legitimate necessity (Guideline 5(b)[9]). On this account, protection for electronic consumers under the Guidelines shall not be lesser than that afforded in other forms of commerce (Guideline 5(j).[10])

Then, in Guideline 44(g),[11] the Member States were advised to include in their consumer information and education program, the issues related to e-commerce, underlining the importance of that phenomena in the daily life of consumers.

In the same order of ideas, the Guidelines provide for specific rules for e-commerce, comprised by Guidelines 63 to 65. In Guideline 63, focus was placed

---

[8]Throughout this paper, references to "electronic tourist consumers" shall identify the subject of protection, thus intertwining the previously defined concepts of tourist consumer and electronic consumer.

[9]"5. The legitimate needs which the guidelines are intended to meet are the following … (b) The protection of vulnerable and disadvantaged consumers…".

[10]"5. The legitimate needs which the guidelines are intended to meet are the following … (j) A level of protection for consumers using electronic commerce that is not less than that afforded in other forms of commerce…".

[11]"44. Consumer education and information programmes should cover such important aspects of consumer protection as the following … (g) Electronic commerce…".

in the importance of the efforts of Member States to foster consumers trust in e-commerce, by setting forth some mechanisms that may be implemented to that end.[12] This shows the great concern existing on the security of electronic transactions and the trust that these media should create so that consumers agree to purchase goods and services online. Trust is a key component for e-commerce, and its progress depends on it.

In this context, during the second period of sessions of the Intergovernmental Group of Experts on Consumer Protection Law and Policy operating within the framework of Trade and Development Board of the United Nations Conference on Trade and Development (hereinafter "IGE"), it has been recognized that e-commerce weakens the relationship between providers and consumers by increasing the vulnerability of the latter. In that light, e-commerce becomes a place for unfair practices. Therefore, it was concluded that the main challenge for e-commerce development was fostering consumers trust in the digital market.[13]

Guideline 64[14] commends Member States to take into account the specificities of e-commerce in their consumer protection policies, and to guarantee that consumers be informed of their rights and duties in the digital market. In this point, the idea of providing information to consumers is reinforced mainly on the specific characteristics of e-commerce.

Guideline 65[15] advices Member States to consider all guidelines and recommendations on e-commerce as revised, especially those provided for by the Organization for Economic Co-operation and Development (hereinafter, "OECD".)

As regards tourism, Guideline 78[16] provides that Member States shall implement protective policies to deal with the supply and commercialization of goods and services related to the industry, highlighting issues related to travel, accommodations

[12]"63. Member States should work towards enhancing consumer confidence in electronic commerce by the continued development of transparent and effective consumer protection policies, ensuring a level of protection that is not less than that afforded in other forms of commerce".

[13]UNCTAD, "Consumer protection in electronic commerce" (note by the secretariat TD/B/C.I.CPLP/7), para 16.

[14]"64. Member States should, where appropriate, review existing consumer protection policies to accommodate the special features of electronic commerce and ensure that consumers and businesses are informed and aware of their rights and obligations in the digital marketplace".

[15]"65. Member States may wish to consider the relevant international guidelines and standards on electronic commerce and the revisions thereof, and, where appropriate, adapt those guidelines and standards to their economic, social and environmental circumstances so that they can adhere to them, as well as collaborate with other Member States in their implementation across borders. In so doing, Member States may wish to study the Guidelines for Consumer Protection in the Context of Electronic Commerce of the Organization for Economic Cooperation and Development".

[16]"78. Tourism. Member States should ensure that their consumer protection policies are adequate to address the marketing and provision of goods and services related to tourism, including, but not limited to, travel, traveller accommodation and timeshares. Member States should, in particular, address the cross-border challenges raised by such activity, including enforcement cooperation and information-sharing with other Member States, and should also cooperate with the relevant stakeholders in the tourism-travel sector".

and timeshare systems. This provision underlines the main aspects related to tourism, and also coincides with the biggest issues a tourist consumer usually faces.

On this regard, the lack of liable persons within the consumers jurisdiction makes it harder to protect tourist consumers who purchase services online, given the growth of agreements entered into through the Internet and the resulting decrease of activity of tourism agencies.[17]

Consequently, the Guidelines provide for the three aspects herein analyzed, as they provide guides for hyper-vulnerable consumer protection, e-commerce and tourism. Upon the convergence of these three elements, it is possible to devise a specific protection for electronic tourist consumer, as the above mentioned Guidelines complement with each other and accentuate protection for these cases. In this sense, the IGEs work shall be paramount to set forth the minimum protection standards for this group of consumers, given its role as an international forum wide enough to debate this kind of policies.

(B) OECD Recommendation on Consumer Protection in E-commerce

In 2016, the OECD revised the recommendations adopted in 1999 on consumer protection in e-commerce.[18] The recommendations together with the Toolkit for protecting digital consumers especially devised for G20 Member State bodies which formulate consumer protection policies set forth various principles that may help States on their e-commerce protection policymaking.

The recommendations are divided in three parts. Part one establishes the general principles on consumer protection in e-commerce. Part two proposes possible ways of implementing said principles. Part three sets the principles for State cooperation worldwide.

The OECD has provided for the following general principles on e-commerce, which include but are not limited to:

(a) Transparent and Effective Protection.
(b) Fair Business, Advertising and Marketing Practices.
(c) Online Disclosure.
(d) Confirmation Process.
(e) Payment.
(f) Dispute Resolution and Redress.
(g) Privacy and Security.
(h) Education, Awareness and Digital Competence.

Most of the recommendations are applicable to electronic tourist consumers. Among these stand out those which indicate the minimum information that goods and services providers must disclose to consumers, such as, identification of the provider; prompt, easy, and effective communication with consumers; appropriate

[17]UNCTAD, *Manual on Consumer Protection*, 2017, p. 56.

[18]OECD (2016) *Consumer Protection in E-commerce: OECD Recommendation.*

and effective dispute resolution mechanisms; service of process for local and cross-border disputes; and the providers place of business.[19] Interpretations point out that the recommendation seeks to trump providers nondisclosure of information with intent to avoid facing possible liabilities. Moreover, this recommendation should foster consumers trust by pinpointing the providers location with certainty.[20]

These measures are useful for electronic tourist consumers, who have little time to formulate claims and, sometimes, find it hard to obtain proper answers in due time upon the inconveniences that may arise in a consumption relationship.

Finally, the recommendations mirror the State Members concern in finding a uniform regulation on e-commerce, given the massive amount of cross-border transactions.

(C) Reports of the International Law Association Committee on International Protection of Consumers

On November 2008, the Committee on International Protection of Consumers was created within the International Law Association (hereinafter "ILA".) The Committee's main goal is to study consumer protection at an international level, especially protection on e-commerce, tourism and accidents. Therefore, the Committees Reports are paramount for the issues studied herein.

From the beginning, the Committee acknowledged in its Reports that setting protective rules dealing with the difficulties inherent to e-commerce was needed to strengthen consumers trust. Moreover, trust would be enhanced by eradicating any difference between local and cross-border consumers.[21]

From there on, the Committee focused its efforts on tourist consumers and cross-border dispute resolution. The Reports acknowledge the features enhancing consumer vulnerability in international trade. Special regard was taken on tourists, who are generally exposed to aggressive marketing practices or ignore foreign laws and customs, among other issues. For instance, substitute performance is acknowledged as a rare relief for breach of contract, such as loss of excursions, while damages are the most usual relief.[22]

---

[19]"28. Businesses engaged in e-commerce with consumers should make readily available information about themselves that is sufficient to allow, at a minimum: (i) identification of the business; (ii) prompt, easy and effective consumer communication with the business; (iii) appropriate and effective resolution of any disputes that may arise; (iv) service of legal process in domestic and crossborder disputes; and (v) location of the business".

[20]Serra Cambaceres, Antonino, "Generando confianza en los consumidores. Comentario a la recomendación del Consejo de la OCDE relativa a directrices para la protección en el contexto del comercio electrónico", JA 2004-I-1224.

[21]First Interim Report of ILA Committee on International Protection of Consumers, The Hague Conference (2010), point II.4).3.

[22]Final Report of ILA Committee on International Protection of Consumers, Sofia Conference (2012), point II.5.E.This Conference adopted the Sofia Principles, consisting of five points in common for consumer protection.

The Committee has also identified the main issues suffered by tourists, such as the quality of the service; nonperformance, especially failure to register a booking; or vulnerability upon a providers insolvency or bankruptcy.[23]

By 2016, the Committee had ten years worth of study of compared law and recommended to continue efforts on assuring international cooperation on consumer protection, especially on tourists.[24] Moreover, the Committee recommended that legislation should acknowledge the consumers structural weakness as a principle for both local and cross-border transactions.[25]

Consequently, it is possible to appreciate the Committees active work on recounting tourism and cross-border transaction regulations worldwide while determining their protective scope.

(D) European Union

In the last fifteen years, the European Union (hereinafter "EU") has issued several rules for electronic tourist consumers. In fact, there are several guidelines and reports related to the protection of tourist consumers and electronic consumers.

To start with, it is worth mentioning the European Parliament Research Service recount on how deep an impact the digital revolution has made on touristic services. It has been seen that upon tourism platforms and intermediaries, consumers have changed their habits and started entering into agreements online, therefore abandoning the habit of hiring such services through a tourism agency.[26]

As a consequence: the following changes have been noticed[27]:

(a) Trips are planned by the consumer on its own account.
(b) Increased usage of mobile applications.
(c) Exchange of personal experiences in several platforms or travel blogs.
(d) Use of automated translation applications.
(e) Online check-in of flights.
(f) Automated answers for questions and services or attractions offers.
(g) Virtual guides for museum and attractions tours available for smartphones.

From a legal standpoint, mention must be made on Articles 6(d) and 195 of the Treaty on the Functioning of the European Union (hereinafter, TFEU,) where the EU's competence in complementing the Member States efforts for fostering and developing tourism were set forth.

---

[23]Interim Report of ILA Committee on International Protection of Consumers, Washington Conference (2014), point III.3.2.

[24]Final Report of ILA Committee on International Protection of Consumers, Johannesburg Conference (2016), recommendation 3.

[25]Final Report of ILA Committee on International Protection of Consumers, Johannesburg Conference (2016), recommendation 1.

[26]European Parliament Research Service, "Digital tourism in the European Union", by Maria Niestadt, PE 628.236, September 2018.

[27]European Parliament Research Service, "Digital tourism in the European…", op. cit., p. 3.

In exercise of said competence, the EU has issued regulations related to the protection of electronic tourist consumers, such as Regulation 2018/302 on addressing unjustified geo-blocking, Regulation 2017/1953 on the promotion of internet connectivity in local communities or Directive 2015/2302 on package travel and linked travel arrangements, among others.

All of these aims, in one way or another, to set minimum protection standards for electronic tourist consumers, foster their trust in e-commerce, and thus promote the development of the tourism industry.

3 Common Issues of Electronic Tourist Consumers

(A) Sharing Economies

One of the main changes brought by the boom of e-commerce is sharing economies. This phenomenon has drastically changed the way in which various services are consumed. The tourism industry was one of the most permeable to these changes. In fact, platforms[28] such as Airbnb or Couchsurfing managed to get consumers to hire touristic services on their own, instead of hiring travel agents for those effects.[29]

In such platforms, one of the most common difficulties faced by electronic consumers is identifying services providers. This matter should be interpreted within the scope of OECD recommendations regarding disclosure of data that may allow to identify providers online.[30] Thus, this new type of agreements raises the question of whether and how much liability should the platforms face.

As a response, the EU is working on a proposal for regulation on promoting equity and transparency of businesses utilizing online intermediation services. This proposal seeks to regulate platforms' activity, and the relationship with the businesses using the platform. As far as this work is concerned, the proposal sets the understanding that sharing economies are some of the online intermediation services intended to be subject to regulation.

In this order of ideas, it is important to highlight that the rules recounted in Chapter II herein apply to sharing economies. In fact, despite their role as intermediaries, a consumption relationship may be set between the platform and the consumer.

In touristic services, there are platforms through which persons offer accommodations, and tourist consumers may hire them for their stay. These platforms not only charge their users for the intermediation, but also demand that accommodations suppliers comply with their policies, including posting and tourist consumer management, among others. These actions trespass the limits of a mere intermediation, and allow the platform to exercise a huge amount of power to mold the consumption relationships to be entered into through their intermediation. That is to say, that these

[28]UNCTAD, *Manual on Consumer Protection*, 2017, p. 90.

[29]European Parliament Research Service, "Digital tourism in the European...", op. cit., p. 4.

[30]UNCTAD, "Consumer protection in electronic...", op.cit., para 10.

platforms may direct advertisement, set guest approval policies, exclude defaulting users, among any other rights they may hold for themselves.

Finally, it is convenient to stress that these platforms should accommodate to the UN Guidelines on Consumer Protection and the OECD Recommendation on Consumer Protection in E-commerce, which are uniform guidelines accepted worldwide as proper consumer protection instruments.

(B) Geo-Blocking

Sometimes, goods and services providers exercise practices that either hinder or limit the access to goods and services to consumers wishing to enter into cross-border agreements. Among this practices is geo-blocking, by which a provider blocks or limits certain consumers from accessing to their goods and services based on their location or nationality.

As a response, the EU has recently issued Regulation (EU) 2018/302 on addressing unjustified geo-blocking and other forms of discrimination. The Regulation defines geo-blocking as a practice where a provider blocks or limits access to their online interfaces to consumers from other States wishing to enter into cross-border agreements, including the implementation of differentiated terms and conditions for the access to their products and services.[31] This regulation aims to avoid discrimination in cross-border transactions based on nationality, place of residence or physical location of customers.[32]

Think, for instance, of consumers planning their holidays. They generally arrange a schedule including sites, attractions or shows that they want to visit or see. Then, on their premises, they start gathering data on prices with views on booking them beforehand. These are all situations in which a provider may establish a differentiated set of terms and conditions for cross-border consumers. The Regulation provides for all these scenarios, especially with respect to the sale of tickets for the transport of passengers.[33]

[31] "In order to realise the full potential of the internal market, as an area without internal frontiers in which the free movement of, inter alia, goods and services is ensured, it is not sufficient to abolish, between Member States, State barriers alone. Such abolition can be undermined by private parties putting in place obstacles inconsistent with internal market freedoms. That occurs where traders operating in one Member State block or limit access to their online interfaces, such as websites and apps, by customers from other Member States wishing to engage in cross-border transactions (a practice known as 'geo-blocking'). It also occurs when certain traders apply different general conditions of access to their goods and services with respect to such customers from other Member States, both online and offline" ¨[Regulation (EU) 2018/302, para. (1)].

[32] See Whereas clause (6).

[33] See Whereas clause (9).

For all of these scenarios, Article 3[34] of the Regulation forbids any unjustified blocks to the access of a provider's online interface. It is also forbidden to redirect consumers to a different interface to the one the consumer wishes to interact with. Some touristic services, like platforms, may fall within the scope of said prohibition due to Article 4.1(c),[35] which forbids differentiation of terms and services to consumers who wish to receive services from a provider, other than electronically supplied services, in a physical location within the territory where the provider operates.

To sum up, the Regulation seeks to avoid unjustified discrimination based only on a consumer's nationality or place of residence. This measure underpins consumers' trust, boosts the benefits inherent to e-commerce, and thus expands the possibilities of consumers to enjoy cross-border experiences.

Hence, those providers who exercise said discriminatory practices shall be held liable for the harm caused by unlawful refusals to enter into an agreement. Within the scope of the Regulation and beyond, these practices constitute a breach to the principle of equality, and clash with all provisions mentioned in the previous chapter regarding prohibitions on differentiation of practices among local and cross-border consumers.

(C) Dispute Resolution and Redress

As mentioned in Chapter II, both the UN Guidelines and the OECD Recommendations identify the lack of effective dispute resolution systems as a key difficulty for electronic consumers, a condition that becomes even harsher when the consumer is also a tourist.

---

[34]"Article 3. Access to online interfaces. 1. A trader shall not, through the use of technological measures or otherwise, block or limit a customer's access to the trader's online interface for reasons related to the customer's nationality, place of residence or place of establishment. 2. A trader shall not, for reasons related to a customer's nationality, place of residence or place of establishment, redirect that customer to a version of the trader's online interface that is different from the online interface to which the customer initially sought access, by virtue of its layout, use of language or other characteristics that make it specific to customers with a particular nationality, place of residence or place of establishment, unless the customer has explicitly consented to such redirection. In the event of redirection with the customer's explicit consent, the version of the trader's online interface to which the customer initially sought access shall remain easily accessible to that customer. 3. The prohibitions set out in paragraphs 1 and 2 shall not apply where the blocking or limitation of access, or the redirection is necessary in order to ensure compliance with a legal requirement laid down in Union law, or in the laws of a Member State in accordance with Union law, to which the trader's activities are subject. In such instances, the trader shall provide a clear and specific explanation to customers regarding the reasons why the blocking or limitation of access, or the redirection is necessary in order to ensure such compliance. That explanation shall be given in the language of the online interface that the customer initially sought to access".

[35]"Article 4. Access to goods or services. 1. A trader shall not apply different general conditions of access to goods or services, for reasons related to a customer's nationality, place of residence or place of establishment, where the customer seeks to (…) (c) receive services from a trader, other than electronically supplied services, in a physical location within the territory of a Member State where the trader operates".

In this sense, it is worth remembering UN Guideline 37,[36] which encourages Member States to develop fair, effective, transparent and impartial mechanisms to address consumer complaints through administrative, judicial and alternative dispute resolution, including cross-border cases. Upon a claim from a hyper-vulnerable consumer, the Guidelines provide for a dispute resolution that attends to the specific needs of said consumer, including electronic touristic consumers. Consequently, Member States should provide the means necessary for this group of consumers to adequately channel any claim, while having special regard to the vulnerability these consumers bear.

The ILA Committee studied the difficulties bore by tourist consumers, and concluded that they suffered grave hindrances to access to justice, including[37]:

(a) An information gap.
(b) Inability to use mediation/conciliation beyond the stay period in the visited country.
(c) An inability to initiate court proceedings beyond the stay in the visited country.
(d) An impossibility to continue court proceeding beyond the stay in the visited country.
(e) The unavailability of a small claims procedure tailored for cross-border cases.
(f) The absence of governmentally funded authorities in charge of helping tourist to access justice.
(g) The absence of appropriate liaison mechanism between authorities of the visited country and the country of the tourist.

This issue is being debated by various international law fora. For instance, the Hague Conference on Private Law published the Draft Convention on Co-operation and Access to Justice for International Tourist. This proposal focuses on tourist consumers and seeks to unify criteria for filing claims upon breach of contract by the provider or any other harm the consumer may endure.

In the whereas clauses, the Draft Convention gives detailed explanations on the vulnerabilities bore by the consumer tourist and the need for effective dispute resolution mechanisms that allow tourists to access to justice. Therefore, the Draft Convention seeks to make it possible to file claims in the place of stay in a prompt manner and, ideally, in the consumer's native language. The Draft also pushes for the disclosure of information on the channels and procedures available for filing claims (See

---

[36]"37. Member States should encourage the development of fair, effective, transparent and impartial mechanisms to address consumer complaints through administrative, judicial and alternative dispute resolution, including for cross-border cases. Member States should establish or maintain legal and/or administrative measures to enable consumers or, as appropriate, relevant organizations to obtain redress through formal or informal procedures that are expeditious, fair, transparent, inexpensive and accessible. Such procedures should take particular account of the needs of vulnerable and disadvantaged consumers. Member States should provide consumers with access to remedies that do not impose a cost, delay or undue burden on the economic value at stake and at the same time do not impose excessive or undue burdens on society and businesses".

[37]Interim Report of ILA Committee on International Protection of Consumers, Sydney Conference (2018), The Hague Conference Report on the Tourism Project (Contributed by Claudia Lima Marques and Dan Wei).

article 1°.) In article 4°, the Draft proposes a standardized form for filing claims, whereas articles 7° and 8° set forth a principle of no discrimination in the access to dispute resolution (judicially and alternatively) between locals and foreign tourists.

This ambitious project could effectively unify criteria globally on applicable jurisdiction to electronic tourist consumers who, as herein explained, mainly enter into cross-border contracts. The project could foster international cooperation as provided for by UN Guideline 78.

In this point, international cooperation seems an almost inevitable path to adequately protect electronic tourist consumers. As the disputes are mainly cross-border in nature, a healthy consumer protection policy would entail States facilitating means for filing claims in the consumer's jurisdiction, regardless from the place of performance or execution of the agreement. Therefore, for an adequate access to justice, it would be extremely beneficial to have a convention unifying jurisdictional rules for all tourist consumers without regard to their place of origin.

4 Conclusion

The twenty-first century poses crucial challenges for consumers. The technological revolution has caused an impact in every aspect of daily life, including consumption. The growth of e-commerce gives new opportunities by offering a wider range of products of services independently from the place where consumers reside.

This growth also pushed forward the size of the tourism industry. The possibility of advertising new accommodations online, the access to information on different localities, and the possibility to share travel experiences in blogs boost the possibilities of travelling around the globe.

In this context, beyond the opportunities that stem from the expansion of e-commerce, new challenges arise, which add up to those faced by tourist consumers. The coming of sharing economies and practices such as geo-blocking are some of the consequences of the technological revolution. More than often, the electronic tourist consumer is defenseless against these challenges, and does not know how to react or where to look for help. There is where the States should appear, providing for adequate mechanisms so that consumers may file their claims or clear their doubts. The alienation experienced while visiting other lands, the cultural differences, the exchange rates, all these are situations which deepen the vulnerability bore by a tourist consumer. These vulnerabilities are further increased when adding e-commerce to the equation.

As previously explained, there are various rules (mainly pertaining to soft law) on the different issues involving tourism and e-commerce, which declare the main concerns of the States worldwide. The international community is starting to attend to the features of cross-border consumer, while attempting to encourage States to adopt measures tending to provide an adequate protection. International fora such as UNCTAD's IGE Consumer and the ILA Committee give important guidelines for consumer protection policymaking.

On this order of ideas, international cooperation is paramount to the protection of electronic tourist consumers. The particular circumstances of this group requires the adoption of measures tending to facilitate the formulation of claims without any barriers, giving special regard to the vulnerabilities bore by a tourist. Therefore, the creation of UN's IGE Consumer to review the application of the UN Guidelines or the Draft Convention for access to justice for international tourists are valuable initiatives that should be supported. States should use these as a foundation for electronic tourist consumer protection policymaking. All in all, in a globalized world, only the cooperation among States may create an effective protection network for consumers worldwide.

Goods with Embedded Software: Consumer Protection 2.0 in Times of Digital Content?

Jasper Vereecken and Jarich Werbrouck

1 Introduction

Software has acquired a central role in the lives of almost anyone taking part in modern society. People buy watches measuring their blood pressure and heart pulsation, cars slowing down automatically when getting to close to the car in front and computers with pre-installed software. However, digital content is not only dispersed via tangible media. People also acquire digital content and digital services apart from a tangible medium (mostly online). Streaming music and downloading movies are just two of the many examples.

But what if it goes wrong? What if the digital content (or services) does not work properly? Until recently, litigants had to rely on legal concepts and systems designed by the European legislator, without the latter having had special (or any) attention for the specificities of digital content or software. As a consequence, application problems are often around the corner. Section I of this contribution will bring up these problems. Since a couple of years, however, the European legislator seems to be catching up with reality in the sense that multiple initiatives have been taken to (try to) develop systems that take into appropriate account the particularities of

---

This Article is based on an earlier contribution, written for the Symposium of the Consumer Law Institute held in Ghent (Belgium) on the 24th of May 2019.

PhD Researcher University of Antwerp and Ghent University (Joint PhD); LL.M., Ghent University Law School, 2018.

PhD Researcher Ghent University; LL.M., Ghent University Law School, 2017.

J. Vereecken (✉)
LL.M, University of Antwerp and Ghent University (Joint PhD), Ghent University Law School, Antwerp, Ghent, Belgium
e-mail: Jasper.Vereecken@uantwerpen.be

J. Werbrouck
LL.M, Ghent University, Ghent University Law School, Ghent, Belgium
e-mail: Jarich.Werbrouck@UGent.be

D. Wei et al. (eds.), *Innovation and the Transformation of Consumer Law*,
https://doi.org/10.1007/978-981-15-8948-5_8

digital content. Section II will examine to what extent these new systems will entail ameliorations in comparison to the current ones, and to what extent the European legislator missed an opportunity. The focus will be more specifically on goods with embedded software. Section III will throw a glance at the present and the future, in order to conclude whether or not the envisaged adaptations will add much to a high(er) degree of consumer protection *ex* Article 38 of the Charter of Fundamental Rights of the European Union. Finally, section IV will examine the enforcement of these substantive law provisions. After all, one of the most large-scale infringements on consumer law in the EU until today concerned embedded software, the Dieselgate scandal. Hence, the possibilities of the previous Consumer Sales Directive and new Goods Directive for effective enforcement of such an infringement will be examined. Emphasis will be placed on possible defects and the repercussions thereof for effective enforcement. The analysis will then look whether legislative solutions within an EU law perspective exist outside said former and current legal framework for the protection of consumer interests.

This contribution will focus specifically on the special consumeristic legislation the European legislator has supplied. It should be borne in mind, however, that the general provisions of the law of obligations still apply as well. The latter remain beyond the scope of the current contribution.

2 Lack of Conformity of Digital Content—De Lege Lata

When we look at the situation as it stands at present, a distinction has to be made depending on the way in which the consumer acquires the digital content or the good in which it is incorporated. Should they acquire the digital content or the good by means of an off-premises contract or by means of a distance contract, the consumer will be entitled to rely on specific provisions foreseen in Directive 2011/83/EU (hereinafter: 'Consumer Rights Directive', 'CRD') (A.).[1] Furthermore—and in the hypothesis that there is a tangible medium—he will also be able to fall back on the specific provisions concerning consumer sales as foreseen in Directive 1999/44/EC (hereinafter: 'Consumer Sales Directive', 'CSD') (B.).[2] In case there is no off-premises or distance contract (i.e. the classical store visit; on-premises contracts), only the rules concerning consumer sales will apply, in as far as there is a tangible medium.

[1] Directive (EU) No 2011/83 of the European Parliament and of the Council of 25 October 2011 on consumer rights, amending Council Directive 93/13/EEC and Directive 1999/44/EC of the European Parliament and of the Council and repealing Council Directive 85/577/EEC and Directive 97/7/EC of the European Parliament and of the Council, Official Journal of the European Union 304/64–88 (2011). This directive entailed maximum harmonisation, meaning that the Member States could not foresee in any protection within the harmonised area, other than that foreseen by the directive.

[2] Directive (EC) 1999/44 of the European Parliament and of the Council of 25 May 1999 on certain aspects of the sale of consumer goods and associated guarantees, Official Journal of the European Union 171/12–16 (1999).

A. *Specific provisions for off-premises contracts or distance contracts*

1. *Scope of application*

Both the specific rules concerning off-premises contracts and these concerning distance contracts are applicable to sales contracts, service contracts, contracts for the supply of digital content which is not supplied on a tangible medium ('contracts for online digital content') and contracts for the supply of water, gas or electricity, where they are not put up for sale in a limited volume of set quantity, or of district heating.[3] In this context, the first and third type of contracts are especially relevant.

Digital content is defined as 'data which are produced and supplied in digital form' (Article 2 (11) CRD).[4] Digital content can be distributed both in a materialised (e.g. DVD or CD) and a non-materialised (e.g. downloading or streaming) way. The borderline between these two coincides with the one between sales contracts on the one hand, respectively contracts for online digital content on the other hand. The division between these two types of contracts is translated into diverging applicable provisions. Materialised digital content (digital content distributed on a tangible medium) has to be considered as a 'good' for the application of the specific provisions concerning off-premises contracts and distance contracts.[5] Consequently, the contract has to be considered as a sales contract.[6] It should be noted that goods with embedded software will always be considered as 'goods' in this context and that, consequently, the contract concerning its supply to consumers will always be deemed a sales contract, irrespective of the exact 'relationship' between the tangible medium and the digital content.[7] In the event where the digital content is distributed in a non-materialised way, the contract will be a *sui generis* one ('a contract for online digital

---

[3] DG JUST Guidance Document concerning Directive 2011/83/EU of the European Parliament and of the Council of 25 October 2011 on consumer rights, amending Council Directive 93/13/EEC and Directive 1999/44/EC of the European Parliament and of the Council and repealing Council Directive 85/577/EEC and Directive 97/7/EC of the European Parliament and of the Council, June 2014, 5.

[4] *See* Reinhard Steennot, *Art. I.8, 33°-35° WER* in Reinhard Steennot, Jules Stuyck, Hendrik Vanhees & Eddy Wymeersch, Handels- en economisch recht. Commentaar met overzicht van rechtspraak en rechtsleer [Commercial and economic law. Commentary with overview of case law and doctrine] 53 (Wolters Kluwer 2016). It may concern computer programs, applications, games, music, videos or texts. See recital 19 CDR. As Reinhard Steennot rightly suggests, the use of the word 'and' indicates cumulativity. Consequently, it does not suffice that the date are produced *or* supplied in digital form.

[5] Recital 19 CDR. 'Goods' are defined as 'tangible movable items' (Article 2 (3) CRD).

[6] 'Sales contracts' are described as 'any contract under which the trader transfers or undertakes to transfer the ownership of goods to the consumer and the consumer pays or undertakes to pay the price thereof, including any contract having as its object both goods and services' (Article 2 (5) CRD).

[7] As will be shown further, this relationship will play in an important role in the future in determining the applicable legislative framework.

content'),[8] for which diverging rules may exist in comparison to the ones applicable to digital content on a tangible medium.

Generally, in the event that a contract concerns digital content the trader has to inform the consumer about the functionality, including applicable technical protection measures, and the relevant interoperability of digital of digital content with hardware and software that the trader is aware of or that he can reasonably be expected to have been aware of (Article 6.1 (r) and (s) CRD). Moreover, in case of digital content which is not supplied on a tangible medium, the consumer bears no cost for the supply, in full or in part where (i) the consumer has not given his prior express consent to the beginning of the performance before the end of the fourteen day period during which he can exercise his right of withdrawal, (ii) the consumer has not acknowledged that he loses his right of withdrawal when giving his consent *or* (iii) the trader has failed to provide the consumer with written confirmation of the pre-contractual information which had to be supplied initially where appropriate along with the prior express consent and the acknowledgment of the consumer that he loses his right of withdrawal (Article 14.4 (b) CRD).[9] Finally, the Directive also foresees in specific provisions for digital content supplied on a tangible medium: the consumer will not be able to exercise his right of withdrawal in the event of the supply of sealed audio or video recordings or sealed computer software which were unsealed after delivery (Article 16 (i) CRD).

2. *Right of withdrawal: principle and consequences*

In as far as the contract between the consumer and the trader falls under the scope of the specific provisions concerning off-premises contracts or distance contracts, the consumer has in principle the right to withdraw from the contract during the first fourteen calendar days upon delivery of the goods. In the event of a contract concerning the sale of digital content which is not supplied on a tangible medium, however, the period starts to run from the day of the conclusion of the contract (Article 9 CRD). The consumer does not have to give any reason for the exercise of his right of withdrawal. Consequently it is also possible for the consumer to send back perfectly working digital content, next to digital content with a lack of conformity.[10] The only thing the consumer has to do to exercise this right is sending a notification to the trader informing him of his decision to withdraw from the contract before the expiry of the withdrawal period. The burden of proof of informing the trader in time is on the consumer (Article 11 CRD).

---

[8] Some national legislators, among which the Belgian one, have perceived these contracts for online digital content as service contracts. See *Travaux Préparatoires* [Preparatory documents] 2012–2013, doc. 53, 3018/001, 16.

[9] The use of the word 'or' clearly shows that these conditions are alternative. As soon as one of these three criteria is not fulfilled, the consumer shall bear no cost.

[10] In this aspect the CRD diverges from the CSD, where the consumer has to prove a lack of conformity.

The exercise of the right of withdrawal terminates the obligations of the parties to perform or conclude the contract (Article 12 CRD).[11] The trader has to reimburse all payments received from the consumer, including costs of delivery, without undue delay and in any event not later than fourteen days from the day on which he is informed of the decision to withdraw. This reimbursement has to be carried out using the same means of payment as the consumer used for the initial transaction, unless the consumer expressly agreed otherwise. However, the trader is entitled to withhold the reimbursement until he has received the goods back or until the consumer has supplied evidence of having sent back the goods, depending on whichever is earliest, unless he offered to collect the goods himself (Article 13 CRD). On the side of the consumer, the obligation emerges to send back the goods or hand them over to the trader or person authorised by the trader to receive the goods, without undue delay and in any event not later than fourteen days from the day on which he has informed the trader of the withdrawal, unless the trader has offered to collect the goods himself. Only the direct costs of returning the goods are to be borne by the consumer, unless the trader failed to inform the consumer that the latter has to bear them. In the latter event, the consumer does not bear these costs. Furthermore, the consumer is in principle only liable for any diminished value of the goods resulting from their handling other than what is necessary to establish the nature, characteristics and functioning of the goods (Article 14 CRD).

Diverging rules apply, however, in the event that the trader omitted to correctly supply the information concerning the right of withdrawal (Article 10 CRD). In that case, the withdrawal period expires twelve months from the end of the initial withdrawal period. Should, however, the trader provide the consumer with the correct information concerning the right of withdrawal within this extended period, the withdrawal period expires fourteen days after the day upon which the consumer receives that information. Another consequence of the omission to correctly supply the information concerning the right of withdrawal, the consumer is in any event not liable for any diminished value of the goods, even not if this diminished value is the result of their handling other than what is necessary to establish their nature, characteristics and functioning (Article 14.2 CRD). In case there is no right of withdrawal for the consumer, the omission to inform the consumer thereof is not sanctioned.

3. *Right of withdrawal: exceptions*

The Directive prescribes some binding exceptions in relation to the aforementioned principle, where the consumer has no right of withdrawal (Article 16 CRD). Given the maximum harmonisation aimed at by the Directive, it is no longer possible for national legislators to give extra protection to consumers within the harmonised area (e.g. by not implementing certain exceptions, or by restricting their conditions of applicability). Neither is it possible to add new exceptions to the limitative list

---

[11] The latter hypothesis applies in case the consumer made the proposition for the contract.

foreseen in the Directive.[12] This does not take away the possibility to adopt additional exceptions in contracts concluded between traders and consumers.

In the context of digital content, two exceptions deserve specific mention. First of all, there is no right of withdrawal for contacts for the supply of sealed audio or video recordings or sealed computer software which were unsealed after delivery (Article 16 (i) CRD). On the contrary, the consumer retains his right of withdrawal if the seal has not been broken or if there was no seal applied.[13] Evidently, 'tangible seals' first spring to mind (e.g. the strip incorporated in the packaging of a CD or DVD). However, there is in our opinion no reason to assume that this exception should be limited to this kind of seals. At present, audio or video files are also distributed via non-tangible media (downloading, streaming,...) where the consumer has to enter a digital key to break a digital seal, in order to get access to the actual content (e.g. the code on the back of gift cards for the App Store). Consequently, this exception is relevant both for digital content supplied on a tangible medium, as well as for digital content not supplied on a tangible medium.

The second relevant exception confines itself to digital content which is not supplied on a tangible medium. In case the performance started within the withdrawal period of fourteen days with the consumer's prior express consent and his acknowledgment that he loses his right of withdrawal, the consumer effectively loses his right of withdrawal (Article 16 (m) CRD). The consumer does maintain a right of withdrawal if one of these conditions is not fulfilled, since he then falls under the general scope of Article 9 CRD. In the latter event, the trader should have supplied information concerning this right of withdrawal *ex* Article 6.1 (h) CRD. Subsequently, in case the trader did not supply this information the period expires twelve months from the end of the initial withdrawal period (Article 10 CRD).[14] Moreover, the consumer's prior express consent and his acknowledgment that he loses his right of withdrawal have to be provided to him on a durable medium within a within a reasonable time after the conclusion of the distance contract, and at the latest at the time of the delivery

[12]Reinhard Steennot, Gert Straetmans, Evelyne Terryn, Bert Keirsbilck & Bert Wyseur, *Overzicht van rechtspraak. Consumentenbescherming (2008–2014)—Marktpraktijken (2011–2014)* [Overview of case law. Consumer protection (2008–2014)—Commercial practices (2011–2014)], 52 TPR 1311, 1651 (2015).

[13]Note that in the context of the exceptions to the right of withdrawal, no specific rules concerning the burden of proof apply. Consequently, according to *actori incumbit probation* the claimant has to prove his allegations. In our opinion, however, account should be taken of the fact that sometimes this might lead to the requirement of proving a negative fact (e.g. the absence of a seal). In these types of cases, reversal of the burden of proof might be justified.

[14]*See* Reinhard Steennot, *Art. VI.48 WER* in R. Steennot, J. Stuyck, H. Vanhees & E. Wymeersch, *supra* note 4 at 178. More concrete this means that if not all conditions are met for the exception to apply, and if the trader did not inform the consumer properly concerning the right of withdrawal which exists in the latter case, the period is prolonged to twelve months and fourteen days. This situation has to be clearly distinguished from the general rule that the lack of information concerning the absence of a right of withdrawal *ex* Article 16 CRD does not lead to the coming into existence of a right of withdrawal or the prolongation of such right. Only the pre-contractual liability of the trader will in this case be at stake. Whereas most exceptions enacted in Article 16 CRD do not require for their application that the consumer is informed about their existence, Article 16 (m) does require this.

of the goods or before the performance of the service begins (Article 8.7 CRD). As far as it concerns off-premises contracts, the trader has to supply the consumer with a copy of the signed contract or the confirmation of the contracts on paper or, if the consumer agrees, on another durable medium, including—where applicable—the confirmation of the consumer's prior express consent and acknowledgment that his right of withdrawal ceases to exist (Article 7.2 CRD). In case of supply, in full or in part, of digital content which is not supplied on a tangible medium, the consumer bears no cost when he has not given his prior express consent for the beginning of the performance before the end of the initial withdrawal period. The same holds true if he has not acknowledged that he loses his right of withdrawal when giving this consent or if the trader failed to provide the aforementioned confirmation (Article 14.4, (b) CRD).[15] Evidently, the consumer has to send back the (non-materialised) digital content.[16]

4. *Application problems of the current legislative framework*

Now some guidance has been given concerning the current legislative framework for off-premises and distance contracts, some deficiencies can be uncovered.

First of all, a period of fourteen days from the day of delivery is in some cases (very) short to establish the nature, characteristics and (potentially defective) functioning of goods. Should, for example, digital content be bought as a gift, the risk exists that by the time the recipient of the gift receives (and thus gets the chance to assess) it, the period for withdrawal has already expired.[17] Moreover, it is possible (maybe even normal) for certain digital content that it takes a while before the consumer operates/can operate all functionalities. The consumer often 'discovers' the possibilities. Should it turn out after a period (e.g. three weeks) that a certain application does not function, it would already be too late for the consumer to withdraw from the contract. Subsequently, it is clear that the right of withdrawal cannot intercept the non-existence of a guarantee. This should not surprise, however, since the right of withdrawal is not meant for these types of situations. Nevertheless, as we will see further on, the Consumer Sales Directive does not apply in an important share of the situations where digital content is involved (more precisely, the supply of digital

[15]It should be noted that, if the former two conditions are met cumulatively (i.e. the consumer consented expressly with the beginning of the performance before the initial period expires and the consumer acknowledged the loss of the right of withdrawal) the third condition becomes irrelevant. After all, in this hypothesis there *is* no right of withdrawal *ex* Article 16 (m).

[16]The question arises as how this has to be done, since it concerns the supply of digital content which is not supplied on a tangible medium. The content may already have been saved somewhere by the consumer. Should the content function via or under the form of an online platform or access thereto, the trader could evidently cut of the access of the consumer to this platform.

[17]If, for example, Edward orders a smartphone via Amazon to give to Elsie as a Christmas present, which is delivered on 10th December, the last day on which the right of withdrawal might be exercised with success would be 24th December.

content which is not supplied on a tangible medium). In this hypothesis, the right of withdrawal might be the only remaining straw to clutch at.[18]

On the other side of the spectrum a withdrawal period of fourteen days may in certain instances be too long, more specifically against the background of illegal copying and spreading of digital content followed by the exercise of the right of withdrawal. However, it should be noted that in addition to the digital possibilities to make illegal copying and spreading impossible, the Directive provides two exceptions on the right of withdrawal that can be relied on by the trader.

Finally, the question arises of what must happen if digital content is being updated. Depending on the circumstances, the update might be considered as a new off-premises or distance contract, or as the fulfilment by the trader of an obligation flowing from the initial contract. Consequently, it can be questioned whether or not a new withdrawal period starts to run as from the day of the update. The provisions seem at first sight flexible enough to be employed in the context of software updates, though specific provisions might have been in place in order to avoid legal uncertainty.

B. *Specific provisions for consumer sales contracts*

1. *Scope of application*

The specific provisions on consumer sales apply to contracts of sale of (nearly)[19] all tangible movable items (i.e. consumer goods) by a seller to a consumer, as well as to contracts for the supply of such items to be manufactured or produced (Article 1 CSD).

Contrary to the Consumer Rights Directive, the Consumer Sales Directive does not contain specific provisions concerning digital content.[20] Once again, however, we can rely on the *summa divisio* between digital content supplied on a tangible medium on the one side, and digital content not supplied on a tangible medium on the other side. Since the latter is by definition not distributed on a tangible medium, and is thus not incorporated in a tangible movable item (e.g. CD, DVD, computer,...), this entire category of digital content—to which belong among other things streamed and downloaded data—falls out of the scope of application of the provisions on consumer sales.[21] Digital content supplied on a tangible medium, to which category goods with

---

[18] Apart from the general law of obligations, that is. As indicated above, however, the latter falls out of the scope of the current contribution.

[19] Goods sold by way of execution or otherwise by authority of law, water and gas where they are not put up for sale in a limited volume or set quantity and electricity fall out of the scope of application.

[20] It should be noted, however, that given the minimum harmonisation aimed at by the Consumer Sales Directive, Member States were/are allowed to incorporate specific provisions in the context of digital content, similar to the ones adopted by the European legislator. Whereas some Member States have done so (e.g. the Netherlands), others did not (e.g. Belgium).

[21] Caroline Cauffman & Alain Verbeke, *Een jaar wet consumentenkoop* [One year Consumer Sales Act] in Bernard Tilleman & Alain Verbeke, Themis 32 – Bijzondere overeenkomsten [Themis 32 – Specific Contracts] 25, 29 (die Keure 2005); Bernard Tilleman, *Consumentenkoop* [Consumer sales] in Bernard Tilleman, Overeenkomsten. Deel 2. Bijzondere overeenkomsten. A. Verkoop. Deel 2. Gevolgen van de koop 577 [Contracts. Part 2. Specific Contracts. A. Sales. Part 2. Consequences

embedded software belong per definition, does fall under the scope of application of the Directive, irrespective of the relationship between the digital content itself on the one hand and the tangible movable item which serves as medium on the other hand.

2. *Lack of conformity of consumer goods*

Sellers have to deliver goods in conformity with the contract of sale. This is the case if the goods (i) comply with the description given by the seller and possess the qualities of the goods that the seller holds out to the consumer as a sample or model, (ii) are fit for any particular purpose for which the consumer requires them and which he made known to the seller at the time of conclusion of the contract and which the seller has accepted, (iii) are fit for the purposes for which goods of the same type are normally used and (iv) show the quality and performance which are normal in goods of the same type and which the consumer can reasonably expect, given the nature of the goods and taking into account any public statements on the specific characteristics of the goods made about them by the seller, the producer or his representative, particularly in advertising or on labelling (Article 2.1 in conjunction with 2.2 CSD).,[22, 23] Moreover, a lack of conformity for which the seller is liable will also occur if there is an incorrect installation of the consumer goods if the installation forms part of the contract of sale of the goods and the goods were installed by the seller or under his responsibility. Also if the consumer good is intended to be installed by the consumer, is installed by the consumer and the incorrect installation is due to a shortcoming in the installation instructions, there is deemed to be a lack of conformity for which the seller is liable (Article 2.5 CSD). If for instance a smartphone is advertised with a memory capacity of 128 gigabyte, it can be reasonably expected that the consumer can call, text, surf,… with it. As soon as one of these applications lacks or does not work, there is a lack of conformity. Should afterwards the memory capacity turn out to be only 32 gigabyte, the smartphone will equally be deemed to be not conform with the contract.

---

of a sales contract], 581, (Kluwer 2012); Jules Stuyck, *Bijzondere overeenkomsten en economisch recht* [Specific contracts and economic law] in X., XXXIVste Postuniversitaire Cyclus Willy Delva – Bijzondere overeenkomsten [XXXIVth postgraduate cycle Willy Delva – Specific contracts] (2007–2008) 8, (Wolters Kluwer 2008); Reinhard Steennot, *Art. 1649bis BW* in Eric Dirix & Aloïs Van Oevelen, Bijzondere overeenkomsten. Artikelsgewijze commentaar met overzicht van rechtspraak en rechtsleer [Specific contracts. Commentary with overview of case law and doctrine] 19, 28, (Wolters Kluwer 2015). As indicated, given the minimum harmonisation aimed at by the Directive, Member States could foresee in a similar system for digital content supplied not on a tangible medium. This has happened for instance in the Netherlands.

[22]Concerning the expectations of the consumer and the information based on which he could base them, it should be kept in mind that the Consumer Rights Directive prescribes a whole range of informational duties. In the context of digital content, it is especially relevant that the seller has to supply information concerning the functionality of digital content, including applicable technical protection measures, and the relevant interoperability of digital content with hardware and software that the trader is aware of or can reasonably be expected to have been aware of.

[23]The seller is not bound by public statements, however, if he shows (i) that he was not and could not reasonably have been aware of the statement in question, (ii) that by the time of conclusion of the contract the statement had been corrected or (iii) that the decision to buy the consumer goods could not have been influenced by the statement (Article 2.4 CSD).

Finally, the Directive foresees in two situations where a de facto lack of conformity is presumed not to exist *de jure*. More precisely, there is no lack of conformity which entails the seller's liability if, at the time the contract was concluded, the consumer was aware or could not reasonably be unaware of the lack of conformity. If, for instance, the consumer buys a second hand car of which the seller made clear during the selling process that the software in the encapsulated GPS is dated, the consumer will not be able to make the argument that there is a lack of conformity. In addition, the seller liability will not be endangered if the lack of conformity has its origin in materials supplied by the consumer (Article 2.3 CSD).

3. *Seller's liability*

The seller is liable to the consumer for any lack of conformity which exists at the time of delivery of the goods and which becomes apparent within two years as from the delivery of the goods (Article 3.1 in conjunction with 5.1 CSD). In case of second hand goods, the Directive foresees in the possibility for Member States to provide that seller and consumer may agree a shorter time period for the liability of the seller, without it being less than one year (Article 7.1 CSD).[24] The Directive does not lay down a binding period of time within which the consumer has to communicate the lack of conformity to the seller. However, it leaves the possibility to do the Member States to provide that the consumer must inform the seller within a period of at least two months from the date on which he detected the lack of conformity (Article 5.2 CSD). The burden of proof of informing the seller is on the consumer, whereas (eventually) the burden of proof that the consumer did not do this within the agreed time period is on the seller.[25] Though it may appear difficult to prove on which moment a lack of conformity came into existence and became apparent, the nature of goods with digital content often entails the possibility for the seller to track the exact moment on which the good was used.[26] The Directive does not provide for a binding limitation period, though it leaves the possibility to do so for the Member States. This limitation period cannot expire, however, before the end of the initial two years period within which the seller is liable (Article 5.1 CSD).

In order to facilitate the application of the rules on consumer sales, the European legislator has introduced the presumption *juris tantum* that a lack of conformity which becomes apparent within six months of delivery of the goods existed at the time of delivery, unless if this presumption is incompatible with the nature of the goods or the nature of the lack of conformity (Article 5.3 CSD).[27] If for example someone drops his smart phone five months after delivery, due to which the screen

[24]This has happened a.o. in Belgium.

[25]Reinhard Steennot, *Art. 1649quater BW* in Eric Dirix & Aloïs Van Oevelen, *supra* note 22 at 66.

[26]If, for example, a smart-tv does not work anymore on February 28th and the contract of sale provides a contractual time limit of two months within which the consumer has to report the lack of conformity, the consumer who informs the seller on May 10th will eat humble pie.

[27]Given the minimum harmonisation aimed at by the Directive, nothing prevented the Member States to extend the period during which this presumption is applicable. In France, for instance, the period has been extended to two years. Consequently, during the entire period of guarantee, the

is completely cracked and no longer useful, the nature of the lack of conformity will be incompatible with the presumption of anteriority.

4. *Hierarchy of remedies*

The Consumer Sales Directive provides for a hierarchy of remedies on which the consumer can rely in case of liability of the seller. Only in the event where the primary remedies are not (longer) fit to indemnify the consumer, he can demand application of the secondary remedies. Next to these specific remedies, it is also possible to claim damages from the seller.

First of all, the consumer is entitled to require the seller to repair the goods or to replace them, in both instances free of charge (the primary remedies) (Article 3.3 CSD).[28] This repair or replacement has to be completed within a reasonable period of time and without any significant inconvenience to the consumer. In light of the latter requirement, the seller may have to supply the consumer with a replacement good (e.g. mobile phone, car,…). The consumer is not entirely free in his choice between repair or replacement, however, in the sense that the remedy chosen may not be impossible or disproportionate in comparison with the alternative remedy. A remedy is deemed to be disproportionate in as far as it imposes costs on the seller which are unreasonable in comparison with the alternative remedy, taking into account the value the goods would have if there was no lack of conformity, the significance of the lack of conformity and whether or not the alternative remedy could be completed *in concreto* without significant inconvenience to the consumer. Should for instance a CD turn out to not work properly, repair will most likely be deemed disproportionate in relation to replacement. The costs of repair of the CD and the inconveniences caused to the consumer will namely be far higher than these of replacement. Should, on the other hand, the problem occur with a self-driving car of which certain sensors do not work properly, it is most likely that repair will (evidently depending on the circumstances) be favoured above replacement.

If the consumer is entitled to neither repair nor replacement, he may require an appropriate reduction of the price or have the contract rescinded (the secondary remedies) (Article 5.5). The same holds true if the seller has not completed the chosen primary remedy within a reasonable time, or if he has not completed it without significant inconvenience to the consumer. The dissolution of the contract will not be possible, however, if the lack of conformity is of minor importance, which is for

consumer enjoys the benefits of the presumption. Other Member States (e.g. Belgium) took over the period of six months.

[28] The European Court of Justice has interpreted the 'free of charge'-requirement very broad. For example, the seller cannot claim any usage fees for the normal use the consumer could have before the lack of conformity came into existence (Case 404/06, Quelle AG v. Bundesverband der Verbraucherzentralen und Verbraucherverbände, CURIA (April 17, 2008). Also, the consumer does not have to pay any costs of removal and new installation, if the consumer acted in good faith (i.e. before the lack of conformity was discovered) when installing the goods. However, according to the Court of Justice, nothing opposes to a national scheme allowing the consumer only to have a proportional part of the costs of replacement reimbursed (Joined Cases 65/09 and 87/09, Gebr. Weber GmbH v. Jürgen Wittmer and Ingrid Putz v. Medianess Electronics GmbH (June 16, 2011).

the judge to decide. Consequently, also within the secondary remedies the consumer does not have complete freedom of choice.

5. *Application problems of the current legislative framework*

Regardless of the fact that the rules on consumer sales are a welcome addition to the armoury of the consumer in pursuance of a high degree of consumer protection, once again application problems are not farfetched.

Evidently, the fact that digital content not supplied on a tangible medium completely falls outside of the scope of the Directive is a problem. This is especially true against the background of online distribution of digital content (streaming, downloading, etc.) gaining more and more importance. The consequences of this lack of applicability do not only concern digital content which was initially not supplied on a tangible medium (and thus ab initio fell outside of the scope of the rules on consumer sales), but also concern digital content which was initially supplied on a tangible medium (such as the digital content incorporated in goods with embedded software) which is later updated. Should this update be distributed online, which is very often the case, the question arises what the faith is of the goods with digital content incorporated therein. If as a consequence of the update the good is no longer in conformity with the contract, this lack of conformity was not present at the moment of delivery of the (initially materialised) digital content. Consequently, the seller's liability for the initially supplied good would not be endangered. If the consumer would argue that the lack of conformity is a consequence of the update, the seller could easily oppose that this update was distributed online and that as a consequence the 'new' digital content that was obtained via this update falls outside the material scope of application of the Consumer Sales Directive.

Another problem relates to the disparity between the period of two years during which the seller is basically liable on the one hand, and the presumption of anteriority which only covers six months from the day of delivery on the other hand.[29] In our opinion, the fact that after the expiry of six months from the day of delivery the consumer would have to prove that the lack of conformity was already present at the moment of delivery, de facto often comes down to a limitation of the liability of the seller to six months, given the heavy burden of proof resting on the consumer's shoulders. This observation is even more true in the context of digital content, which is very often complex to such an extent that the consumer would need technical expertise investigations to establish the exact moment on which the lack of conformity came into existence. Given the price tag of such investigations, there are convincing reasons to fear that the consumer will decide not to try to prove that the lack of conformity was already present at the moment of supply. The outcome of a costs/benefits-analysis between the expected costs of expert investigations on the one hand and the value of the goods on the other hand, taking into account the chances of success of proceedings, will from the viewpoint of the consumer be most likely negative. Moreover, a

[29]It should be borne in mind, however, that the Member States can/could extend the presumption period, given the minimum harmonisation aimed at by the Directive.

six-month period may be short in light of the nature of the good. As indicated above, consumers often 'discover' the goods; they do not always use all functionalities of a good from the start. If the consumer for example tries to play a CD on his computer after seven months and notices that this application does not work due to defective software, he will in principle not find redress in the Consumer Sales Directive.[30]

Finally, the presumption of anteriority also conflicts with the idea of software being updated. If digital content which is supplied on a tangible medium (*inter alia* goods with embedded software) is updated within the first six months from delivery and is no longer in conformity due to this update, the consumer will be able to rely on the presumption of anteriority. The seller would then have to prove that the lack of conformity was not present at the moment of supply, which he will most likely be only able to do by proving that the lack of conformity is due to the update.

3 A Two-Track System for Digital Content—(Goods with) Embedded Software

A. *Introduction—level of harmonisation*

The potential of online business, both purely domestic and cross-border, and the central position digital products have taken in our lives did not escape the attention of the Juncker-Commission. Even before he was actually installed, (future) Commission President Jean-Claude Juncker revealed his intentions to invest strongly in the creation of the 'Digital Single Market' (DSM). The realisation of the Digital Single Market would, according to him, generate an additional economic growth of 250 billion euros within the term of office of the current Commission. One of the points of focus was the adoption of new consumer protection legislation. Too often, sellers and consumers would relinquish doing business with one another because of the uncertainty surrounding the legal framework applicable to their relationships. This is all the more problematic if it concerns cross-border business. Given the minimum harmonisation provided for by the Consumer Sales Directive, which plays a central role in this whole story, both the seller and the consumer encounter legal uncertainty on the exact content of the applicable legislation. Moreover, if we assessed more specifically the context of digital content, it became clear that the existing provisions are often not adequate to react to the specific needs of consumer. Consequently, adaptations/additions to the existing legal framework were necessary.

On December 9th 2015, two proposals for Directives were presented: a proposal for a Directive on certain aspects concerning contracts for the supply of digital

[30]Note that others causes of action, such as liability for latent defects, may still prove to be useful. As indicated above, though, these remedies under general law of obligations are outside the scope of the current contribution.

content on one side,[31] and a proposal for a Directive on certain aspects concerning contracts for the online and other distance sales of goods on the other side.[32] These would complement each other with regard to digital content. The former would apply to any digital content, including any durable medium incorporating digital content where the durable medium was used exclusively as carrier of digital content (Article 3.3), whilst the latter would apply to goods where digital content is imbedded in such a way that its functions are subordinate to the main functionalities of the goods, and it operates as an integral part of the goods (Article 3.1).[33] The relationship between durable medium on one side and digital content on the other would thus decide which one of the Directives would be applicable.

The proposals have not been free of criticism, however.[34] As a consequence, on October 31st, 2017, the Commission launched an amended proposal for a directive on certain aspects concerning contracts for the sales of goods.[35] This amended proposal foresaw in the applicability of the new rules to all contracts of sale concluded between a seller and a consumer. Nothing changed with regard to the (non) applicability to digital content or digital services. No amended proposal was brought forth for the proposed Digital Content Directive, though a wide range of changes were proposed in a joint report from the Committee on the Internal Market and Consumer Protection and the Committee on Legal Affairs.[36] These included, *inter alia*, the application of the Digital Content Directive to embedded digital content or embedded digital services, but only in as far as the digital content or services were pre-installed (Article 2.1 (1b) in conjunction with 3.3 of the amended proposal). Given the fact that the Proposed Goods Directive would still apply to everything concerning goods with embedded digital content or embedded digital services irrespective of pre-installation or not, the scopes of applications of the two amended proposals would consequently overlap.

Apparently aware of the fact that the 'split approach' as proposed by the parliamentary committees would only enhance legal uncertainty, the Council indicated in a policy note of May 24th 2018 that it intended to maintain the original idea to bring

---

[31] *Proposal for a Directive of the European Parliament and of the Council of December 9 2015 on certain aspects concerning contracts for the supply of digital content*, COM (2015) 287 final (Dec. 9, 2015).

[32] *Proposal for a Directive of the European Parliament and of the Council of December 9 2015 on certain aspects concerning contracts for the online and other distance sales of goods*, COM (2015) 288 final, (Dec. 9, 2015).

[33] *Id.*, Recital 13.

[34] See for an elaborate overview the contributions of Sanne Jansen & Sophie Stijns and Simon Geiregat & Reinhard Steennot in Ignace Claeys & Evelyne Terryn, Digital Content & Distance Sales – New Developments at EU Level (Intersentia 2017).

[35] *Amended proposal for a Directive of the European Parliament and of the Council of October 31*th*2017 on certain aspects concerning contracts for the sales of goods, amending Regulation (EC) No 2006/2004 of the European Parliament and of the Council and Directive 2009/22/EC of the European Parliament and of the Council and repealing Directive 1999/44/EC of the European Parliament and of the Council*, COM (2017) 637 final (Oct. 31, 2017).

[36] Report of November 27th 2017 on the proposal for a directive of the European Parliament and of the Council on certain aspects concerning contracts for the supply of digital content (A8-0375/2017).

goods with embedded digital content completely under the scope of application of the Goods Directive.[37] It held that in case where on one good with embedded software two different sets of rules could apply, depending on whether the liability would flow from the hardware or from the digital content. Fierce and long lasting discussions would then be unavoidable concerning the question what exactly caused the defect. If both components are subject to the same system, these discussions would be unnecessary. On the other hand, the Council acknowledged that in the context of the Goods Directive attention had to be paid to the role of digital services. If these have the same function as embedded digital content, and/or are equally closely linked to the functioning of the good, these services should be covered by the goods rules in the same way as embedded digital content.[38] Consequently, the substance of the proposal was modified one last time on December 3rd 2018, in the hope of establishing a balanced compromise between the positions expressed by the different delegations from the Member States.[39] Finally, both directives were adopted on May 20th 2019 and published on May 22th 2019. The implementation in the national legislation of the Member States has to take place by July 1st 2021 (Article 24). The final versions hold on to the original two-track system, depending on whether or not the durable medium's only function was to carry the digital content.[40]

Both the Digital Content Directive and the Goods Directive aim at maximum harmonisation (Article 4 DCD, Article 4 GD). By doing so, the European legislator wants to do away with the negative consequences of the minimum harmonisation aimed at by the CSD, and the diverging national approaches.[41] Both proposals are very similar to each other, although on some points diverging rules have been enacted due to the broader scope of application of the Goods Directive in comparison to the Digital Content Directive. For the remaining of this contribution, we will focus on the Goods Directive, more specifically in the context of goods with embedded digital content/digital services.

B. *Digital content and digital services—goods with embedded software*

The Goods Directive uses the same concept of 'digital content' as the Digital Content Directive, based on the Consumer Sales Directive. Digital content means data which are produced and supplied in digital form (Article 2 (6) GD). Digital content entails

---

[37] Policy note of May 24th 2018, 9261/18, 4–5.

[38] Policy note of May 24th 2018, 9261/18, 5.

[39] *Supra* note 37.

[40] Directive (EU) 2019/771 of the European Parliament and of the Council of 20 May 2019 on certain aspects concerning contracts for the sale of goods, amending Regulation (EU) 2017/2394 and Directive 2009/22/EC, and repealing Directive 1999/44/EC (consultable via https://eur-lex.europa.eu/legal-content/en/TXT/?uri=CELEX:32019L0771) (hereinafter: 'Goods Directive') and Directive (EU) 2019/790 of the European Parliament and of the Council of 17 April 2019 on copyright and related rights in the Digital Single Market and amending Directives 96/9/EC and 2001/29/EC (consultable via https://eur-lex.europa.eu/legal-content/EN/TXT/?uri=CELEX%3A32019L0790) (hereinafter: 'Digital Content Directive').

[41] Recital 6 GD.

for example software programs, games, video and audio records, etc. New for the Goods Directive, is the introduction of 'digital services'. These are described in a very similar way as is the case for the Digital Content Directive. A digital service is (i) a service that allows the consumer to create, process, store or access data in digital form, or (ii) a service that allows the sharing of or any interaction with data in digital form uploaded or created by the consumer or other users of that service (Article 2 (7) GD). Examples include social media platforms (Facebook, Twitter, etc.), cloud services, etc.

Though the term 'embedded software' has already been used multiple times before, we did not yet describe exactly what it is, nor what exactly goods with embedded software are. The reason is that these concepts were up until now legally irrelevant. No legal consequences were attached to whether or not something was (a good with) embedded software. In the near future, however, this will change. More specifically for goods with digital content, a division will be made between 'goods with digital elements' on the one hand, and digital content of which the durable medium has no other function than medium of the digital content, on the other hand. The Goods Directive gives no definition of 'goods with embedded software'. 'Goods with digital elements', however, are defined as all tangible movable items that incorporate or are inter-connected with digital content or a digital service in such a way that the absence of that digital content or digital service would prevent the goods from performing their functions (Article 2 (5) GD).[42] Both digital content which was already installed at the moment of conclusion of the contract and digital content of which the installation is foreseen in the contract fall under the scope of application. Digital services inter-connected with a good may include services that allow the creation, processing or storage of data in digital form, or access thereto, such as the continuous supply of traffic data in a GPS-system.[43]

As mentioned above, goods with digital content/digital services cannot be seen as goods with digital elements in the sense of the Goods Directive if the good solely functions as medium of the digital content or digital service (Article 3.3 Goods Directive). Examples include CD's or USB flash drives on which a software program is supplied. In case of a defect which only concerns the tangible medium (e.g. the CD is scratched and as a consequence the software—with which nothing is wrong—cannot be installed), we are of the opinion that the consumer will have to fall back on the Goods Directive. Surely the CD which functions solely as medium for the digital content is not a good with digital elements, though the CD on its own is still a tangible movable item, and therefore a good in the sense of the Goods Directive (Article 2 (5) (a) GD).

---

[42] Recital 14 GD, which states that "[d]igital content that is incorporated in or inter-connected with a good can be any data which is produced and supplied in digital form, such as operating systems, applications and *any other software*", makes us presume that 'goods with embedded software' and 'goods with digital element' are synonyms.

[43] Recital 14 GD.

C. *Lack of conformity of goods with digital elements*

1. *Conformity of goods: general*

According to Article 5 GD, the seller has to deliver goods to the consumer that, depending on the circumstances, meet subjective and objective conformity requirements. The distinction between these two types of conformity requirements is also applied in the Digital Content Directive. Following the criticism made in the context of the Digital Content Directive, which initially held that the objective criteria would only come into play if the subjective criteria were not stipulated in a clear and comprehensive manner (*see* Article 6 of the original proposal of the DCD), the Goods Directive foresees the ab initio mutual application of both the subjective and objective conformity requirements. Moreover, the seller has to make sure under certain circumstances that the installation is properly conducted and that the rights of third-parties do not limit or prevent the use of the goods.

2. *Subjective conformity requirements*

The subjective conformity requirements are the ones parties agreed on at the moment of conclusion of the contract, as a consequence of which the seller is bound (*pacta sunt servanda*). More precisely the goods have to be (i) of the description, type, quantity and quality, and possess the functionality, compatibility, interoperability and other features, as required by the contract, (ii) fit for any particular purpose for which the consumer requires them an which he made known to the seller at the latest at the time of conclusion of the contract, and in respect of which the seller has given acceptance, (iii) delivered with al accessories and instruction, including on installation, as stipulated by the sales contract and (iv) supplied with updates as the contract stipulates (Article 6 GD). In pursuance of the Digital Content Directive, the European legislator clarified that the pre-contractual information forms an integral part of the contract for the application of the Goods Directive as well, as a consequence of which they have to be taken into account in order to determine whether or not the good is in conformity.[44]

3. *Objective conformity requirements*

Next to the conformity requirements as stipulated in the contract, the Goods Directive provides objective requirements which have to be fulfilled (Article 7 GD). The goods have to be (i) fit for the purposes for which goods of the same type would normally be used, taking into account, where applicable, technical standards or applicable sector-specific codes of conduct and (ii) of the quantity and possess the qualities and other features, including in relation to durability, functionality, compatibility and security normal for goods of the same type an which the consumer may reasonably expect, given the nature of the goods and taking into account any public statements made by or on behalf of the seller or other persons in previous links of the chain

---

[44]Recital 26 DCD.

of transactions, including the producer, particularly in advertising or on labelling. Where applicable, the goods have to be (iii) of the quality and correspond to the description of a sample or model that the seller made available to the consumer before the conclusion of the contract and (iv) delivered along with such accessories, including packaging, installation instructions or other instructions, as the consumer may reasonably expect.

In pursuance of the Consumer Sales Directive, the Goods Directive states that the seller is not bound by public statements if he proves that (i) he was not, and could not reasonably have been aware of the public statement in question, (ii) by the time of conclusion of the contract, the public statement had been corrected in the same way as, or in a way comparable to how, it had been made or (iii) the decision to buy the goods could not have been influenced by the abovementioned public statement (Article 7.2 GD). Moreover, there is no lack of conformity if at the time of the conclusion of the contract, the consumer was specifically informed that a particular characteristic of the goods was deviating from the objective requirements for conformity and he expressly and separately accepted that deviation when concluding the sales contract (Article 7.5 GD). The exception which existed under the Consumer Sales Directive according to which there would be no lack of conformity if the latter had its origin in materials supplied by the consumer, is not maintained in the new Goods Directive.

Entirely new is the developed framework concerning the objective conformity requirements of goods with digital elements.[45] Next to the abovementioned objective conformity requirements, the Goods Directive entails the seller's duty to ensure that the consumer is informed of and supplied with updates, including security updates, that are necessary to keep the goods in conformity. For contracts including a single act of supply of the digital content or digital service, this duty applies for the period that the consumer may reasonably expect, given the type and purpose of the goods and the digital elements and taking into account the circumstances and nature of the contract. In case of contracts that include a continuous supply of the digital content or digital service, the duty applies for a period of two years starting from the moment the goods with digital elements were delivered. Should the period during which the digital content or digital service has to be supplied be longer than two years (according to the contract), the duty for the seller to notify and supply updates applies for the entire period during which he has to supply the digital content or digital service (Article 7.3 GD). In the event where the consumer fails to install the updates, supplied by the seller, within a reasonable time, the seller cannot be held liable for any lack of conformity resulting solely from the lack of the relevant update, in as far as (i) the seller informed the consumer about the availability of the update and the consequences of failure of the consumer to install it and (ii) the failure of the consumer to install or the incorrect installation by the consumer was not due to

[45]This framework was still absent in the modified proposal of the Goods Directive. The latter only provided that the seller had to make sure that "in the case of goods with digital elements [these are] updated, including [...] security updates, as necessary to maintain conformity" (*see* Article 5.1 (b2) of this modified proposal).

shortcomings in the installation instructions provided to the consumer (Article 7.4 GD).

4. *Considerations concerning the conformity requirements*

It is obvious from the explicit references to updates that the European legislator is very well aware of the deficiencies of the Consumer Sales Directive in the context of updates/updated goods. More precisely, the Goods Directive now entails the duty for the seller to update goods with digital elements in as far as this is necessary to keep the goods in conformity, even after the moment of delivery. If not, these goods are not conform, as a consequence of which the seller may be held liable.

Some remarks can be made concerning this new legal framework, however. First of all, a tautology may be found in the description of the objective conformity criteria. Goods with digital elements have to be updated, including safety updates, *in order to keep them conform.* Consequently, the 'global concept' is filled in under reference to the idea of conformity itself. Evidently, the conformity that has to be maintained by means of updates has to be filled in by means of the other subjective and objective conformity requirements.

Next, it is apparent from the wording of the Goods Directive that the duty to notify and supply updates rests on the seller's shoulders (Article 7.3 GD). Should the good be no longer in conformity due to this update, though, only the seller is held liable by the Goods Directive. It follows from the recitals, however, that the updates can be provided by the seller or by a third party.[46] The Directive foresees in a right of redress for the seller, which is determined by the national law of the Member States (Article 18 GD). Though it does not directly concern the consumer, the question arises as to what extent this right of redress will turn out to be useful in practice in the context of goods with digital elements. If for example the local electro store sells a smartphone (e.g. iPhone) on which software is pre-installed, and due to a software-update supplied by Apple the device is no longer conform, the consumer would have the possibility to file liability claims based on the Goods Directive against the local seller. Subsequently, the latter theoretically has the right to claim redress from Apple. However, given the unequal playing field on which the local seller and Apple operate, it may be questioned whether this attempt would be fruitful. This could in turn trigger the local seller to stop distributing certain goods/certain brands, in order to avoid such tenuous situations.[47] The consumer might thus indirectly experience negative consequences, although it should be noted that commercial considerations will probably convince the seller to continue distributing a certain good/brand. Another point is that the right of redress is limited to redress against persons in previous links of the chain

[46]Recital 30 GD.

[47]Moreover, it exemplifies the necessity to consider the desirability of European harmonisation of provisions that impose rights on certain undertakings which are similar to the ones consumers derive from consumer protection law initiatives. It should be noted, however, that attempts to this end have already been taken. In Belgium, for example, there is a proposition pending in Parliament concerning unfair contract terms and unfair commercial practices between undertakings (Legislative proposal of 22nd February 2019, nr. 54–3595/001).

of transactions.[48] It cannot be excluded, however, that the third party supplying the updates is not a 'previous link' of the chain of transactions. If a sales contract provides that the digital content or digital service will be provided by a trading partner of the seller after delivery of the physical component, it is in our opinion still unclear whether or not this third party can be considered a 'previous link'. Consequently, application problems are not farfetched.

Another aspect concerns the period of time during which the seller has to notify and supply updates. As indicated above, the Goods Directive provides in the context of sales contract which foresee in a single act of supply that the seller has this duty 'during the period that the consumer may reasonably expect'. This wording is much vaguer than the one for contracts foreseeing in a continuous supply of digital content or digital service, where the duty exists for at least two years (and potentially longer, in case of contracts foreseeing in a continuous supply for a period of more than two years). However, given the fact that updates are necessary to keep the good in conformity and are taken into account when determining conformity itself, it would logically be most suitable to align the period of notification and supply of updates in the context of contracts entailing one single act of supply with the period during which the seller can be held liable for a lack of conformity (i.e. two years).

Finally, there seem to be (unjustified) inconsistencies between the Goods Directive and the Digital Content Directive. Whereas the latter refers to qualities and performance features such as accessibility, continuity and security of digital content or digital service for the conformity assessment (Article 8.1 (b) DCD), a similar reference is lacking in the Goods Directive. Whereas security is still mentioned (Article 7.1 (d) GD), every reference to accessibility and continuity is absent. Although these aspects can without any doubt be brought under the umbrella of 'other features' (Article 7.1 (d) GD), it would have been preferable to explicitly refer to them in the relevant legal provisions. This would a priori have excluded every *a contrario* reasoning in that regard.

5. *Incorrect installation and third-party rights*

In pursuance to the Consumer Sales Directive, the Goods Directive holds provisions for goods needing to be installed. In as far as the lack of conformity results from an incorrect installation, the seller is liable if the installation (i) forms part of the contract of sale and was carried out by the seller or under the latter's responsibility or (ii) was intended to be carried out by the consumer, was done by the consumer or under his supervision[49] and the incorrect installation was due to shortcomings in the installation instructions provided by the seller or, in case of goods with digital elements, by the supplier of the digital content or digital service (Article 8 GD). One can for example think of the delivery of a kitchen robot, on which the software still has to be installed by means of a CD which is supplied along with the device itself. This contract would fall under the scope of application of the Goods Directive (Article 3.3

[48] Recital 63 GD.

[49] This does not follow from the wording of Article 8, though is apparent from recital 34.

GD). Should, as a consequence of a shortcoming in the installation instructions, the digital content be wrongfully installed due to which the kitchen robot is no longer conform (e.g. it explodes), there will be a lack of conformity. However, if one looks at the two separate elements – the physical component and the digital content – one might conclude that *in se* nothing was wrong with both of them.

Lastly, a lack of conformity might also arise from third-party rights. If a restriction resulting from a violation of any right of a third party, in particular intellectual property rights, prevents or limits the use of the goods in accordance with the above-mentioned subjective and objective conformity requirements, the consumer has to be entitled to the remedies provided for by the Directive (Article 9 GD). This is only different in as far as national law of the Member State provides for the nullity or rescission of the sales contract in such circumstances.

D. *Liability of the seller—remedies*

1. *Liability*

The seller is liable to the consumer for any lack of conformity which exists at the time when the goods were delivered (Article 10.1 GD). This is also the case for goods with digital elements, without prejudice to the particular rules concerning updates.

Different rules apply in relation to goods with digital elements when the agreement stipulates a continues supply of the digital content or digital service over a period of time.[50] The seller shall then also be liable for any lack of conformity of the digital content or digital service that occurs or becomes apparent within two years from the time of delivery of the goods containing digital elements, unless the contract provides for a continuous supply of more than two years. In the latter situation, the seller is liable for any lack of conformity which occurs or becomes apparent within the period of time during which the digital content or digital service is to be supplied under the sales contract (Article 10.2 GD). The new directive ensures that the seller cannot be obligated to deliver digital content or digital services during a period of time in which he can no longer be held liable for desisting from such delivery. Member States may maintain or introduce longer time limits than those referred to (Article 10.3 GD). It remains doubtful, however, whether they will effectively use this opportunity, considering most Member States merely literally copied the time limits of the Consumer Sales Directive.[51]

It is again obvious that particular attention was given to goods with digital elements. The content of the discussed provisions remains suboptimal, in the sense that it seems unclear what can be precisely understood under the phrasing ‘delivery of goods with digital elements’. One could mistakenly suspect that the delivery of the physical component suffices. However, the time when physical delivery was the end of it is behind us and from the recitals it seems goods with digital elements

[50] Agreements concerning goods with digital elements which provide for a one-time delivery are subject to the general rule (i.e. liability of the seller during the first two years after delivery).

[51] *Communication on the implementation of Directive 1999/44/EC*, at 8, COM (2007) 210 final (Apr. 24, 2007).

are considered 'delivered' when both the physical and digital component are delivered. In a situation of continuous supply, the good with digital elements is considered delivered when delivery has begun, i.e. the moment of the first delivery.[52] In a situation where goods with digital elements have to be installed by the seller or under his responsibility, they are considered delivered when the installation has been completed.[53]

No different than the Consumer Sales Directive, the new Goods Directive provides for a time limit of seller liability of two years during which the lack of conformity *becomes apparent* since the delivery (Article 10.1 GD). In other words, the lack of conformity must manifest itself (and thus not arise![54]) within two years after delivery. When the consumer can prove the lack of conformity already existed at the time of the delivery but only appeared after those two years, he will not be able to invoke the rules of the Goods Directive.[55] In case of second-hand goods the existing arrangement has also been copied: the consumer and the seller can agree on shorter time limits, provided that such shorter periods shall not be less than one year (Article 10.6 GD).

In relation to goods with digital elements, the seller is liable for every lack of conformity of the digital content or the digital service which would become apparent during the above mentioned time limits, depending on whether the delivery occurred once or was continuous (Article 10.1 GD). Thus, when an update is carried out after the first two years upon delivery which causes the good to lack conformity, the consumer is let down, since this would constitute a lack of conformity which (per definition) manifested itself two years after the delivery of the good.[56] This can turn out to be especially problematic in relation to goods that the consumer seldom uses.

It is of importance to emphasize that the new legal framework concerning continuous supply of digital content or elements overlooks reality. It holds true that many goods, and also many goods with digital elements, remain unchanged after delivery of this good. This was also the angle of the Consumer Sales Directive. Where appropriate, the time limit of liability comes down to a 'critical time limit' during which a lack of conformity has time to manifest itself. When this lack of conformity manifests itself shortly after the delivery, then it is presumed to have been already present at this moment of delivery.[57] If it occurred later but still within two years, then the consumer could still prove the good was delivered lacking conformity with the contract of sale. Yet, when the lack of conformity manifested itself after the time limit of liability, then the consumer can no longer invoke the favourable regime. This declining regime of protection can be considered obvious to some extent since the probability of a lack

---

[52]Recital 39 GD.

[53]Recital 40 GD.

[54]The lack of conformity has to be present at the moment of delivery.

[55]As indicated above, non-consumer law ways of action are still possible but remain outside the scope of the current contribution however.

[56]Note that the period can be longer for contracts of sale providing for a continuous supply for a period longer than two years (*supra*).

[57]*See supra* with regard to the presumption of anteriority.

of conformity which was present at the time of delivery diminishes as time flows. This way of thinking is based upon the assumption that the seller has completed all his legal obligations (i.e. concerning delivery in conformity) at that moment. With goods with digital elements where the agreement provides for continuous supply, it's a different ballgame. As mentioned earlier, the lack of conformity can manifest itself after the goods were delivered (i.e. both the physical component as well as the (first) delivery of the digital content or service). This means the critical time limit has already commenced when the lack of conformity still has to arise. Delivery of digital content or digital services based upon the agreement are literally still possible up until minutes before the expiration of the time limit of liability and these can still give rise to a lack of conformity. By no means is it excluded that something goes wrong in the sense that (fraudulent?) sellers or third parties (i.e. producers) by delivering digital content or services, cause the good to lack conformity just moments before the passing of the time limit. The consumer will then have to react immediately, be it that this theory assumes that the consumer can actually also identify the lack of conformity within the short remainder of the critical time limit. If digital content were to be installed just fifteen minutes before the passing of the time limit and only the next day results in a lack of conformity of the good, then the consumer will be left out in the cold,[58] even though there is a lack of conformity which manifests itself within a short period after the good became non-conformant.

An example can shed light upon the previous. A consumer buys a smart TV on January 1st 2020. The agreement dictates that during five years the most recent version of the software will be continuously delivered. The consumer receives the good with the software (i.e. digital content) already installed and thus the good with digital elements can be considered delivered on that very same day. All goes well in the coming years but on December 31st 2024, 11:30 PM, the latest version of digital content is delivered, causing the good to be no longer in conformity with the contract of sale (e.g. the device can no longer boot). The consumer enjoys New Year's Eve with his friends and spends all of New Year's Day with his family. Exhausted on January 2nd, he wants to turn on the device but notices this doesn't work. Since the good was considered delivered on January 1st 2020 and as such the critical time limit of five years[59] expired on January 1st 2025, the consumer will no longer be able to invoke the favourable rules for a lack of conformity if this manifests itself on January 2nd 2025. When this case is regarded from the perspective of the lack of conformity, this only manifested itself less than two days after it was created. This seems unfair for a consumer who can now no longer invoke the favourable rules of the new directive.

In our opinion the legislative defect flows from the absolute and sole starting point of the 'critical time limit'. In relation to goods with digital elements of which the agreement provides for a continuous supply of digital content or digital services,

[58] Apart from the means of action under general law.

[59] The liability period is extended to five years, given the fact that Article 10 GD provides that in each case where the contract stipulates the continuous supply for a period of more than two years, the consumer can rely on the remedies provided for in the Goods Directive during that same period.

'the delivery' is indeed defined as the moment when both the physical component is delivered as well as the digital component is delivered *for the first time*. Hence, a better option would have been the establishment of an additional and variable starting point for a, possibly shorter, critical period from each new delivery of digital content or digital services (i.e. a critical period with variable starting point).

The above mentioned presumption of anteriority has been extended until one year (instead of six months). Any lack of conformity which becomes apparent within one year of the time when the goods were delivered shall be presumed to have existed at the time when the goods were delivered, unless proved otherwise or unless this presumption is incompatible with the nature of the goods or with the nature of the lack of conformity (Article 11.1 GD). The directive however also gives the opportunity to Member States to maintain or introduce a period of two years instead of one year (Article 11.2 GD). Even though a strict interpretation of the text of this second provision leads to the conclusion that Member States can't introduce or maintain other periods than either one or two years, the adage *qui peut le plus, peut le moins* ("he who can do more, can do less") contends that Member States can introduce or maintain periods in between one and two years.

In relation to goods with digital elements, both those where the agreement provides for a continuous supply and those where it does not, the Proposition of the Goods Directive was more generous. More specifically it immediately constituted a presumption of anteriority (and thus a reversed burden of proof) during the whole period in which the seller could be held liable (Article 8*ter*, 2). This stood in contrast to goods without digital elements, where the 'default rule' stated that there is a presumption of anteriority only during half of the period of liability (i.e. the current rule: one year). It can be considered appropriate from the perspective of consumer protection in relation to goods with digital elements if the period of a reversed burden of proof and the period of liability coincided.

The Goods Directive in its final version, however, stipulates that for contracts prescribing a *single act of supply* of digital content or services, only a one year period of reversed burden of proof will apply (Article 11.1 GD). Member States may however extend this period to two years. This adaptation is regrettable. First of all, the system as enacted in the proposition (i.e. reversed burden of proof during two years upon delivery) would have met the abovementioned criticism in relation to goods with digital elements. The disparity between the period of presumed anteriority and the period of liability *in fact* leads to only a guarantee for the consumer when the burden of proof is reversed. Even though the directive expressly provides for a possibility for Member States to equalise both periods, the past has shown that not all Member States are inclined to do so. After, all the minimal harmonisation nature of the previous Consumer Sales Directive did not prevent Member States to synchronise the period of a reversed burden of proof and the period of liability. If we look at the implementation of the previous directive in the Member States, it is apparent that not all Member States used this opportunity.[60] Consequently, it is hard to imagine that they would all suddenly do the opposite.

In relation to contracts prescribing a *continuous supply*, the final version of the Directive has it that the reversed burden of proof applies for a period of two years upon delivery (delivery of the physical and (first) delivery of the digital component), unless the contract foresees in a longer period during of continuous supply. In the latter event, the burden of proof is reversed during the same amount of time as the one during which digital content or services have to be supplied continuously. Consequently, it is argued that with regard to contracts prescribing a continuous supply, the Goods Directive is more consumer friendly and 'reality-proof' than it is in relation to contracts holding a single act of supply.

In accordance with Article 12, they can provide that the consumer must notify the seller "within a period of at least 2 months of the date on which the consumer detected such lack of conformity". Again, the phrasing leaves much to be desired. Based on the words of the provision it seems that the period may be shorter than two months. The provision would then have no additional value since nothing[61] hinders Member States to maintain or introduce shorter periods, in which case they could again envisage a longer period based upon the adage *qui peut le plus, peut le moins*. Additionally, the recitals show that the phrasing is wrong. It reads that Member States should be allowed to establish the obligation for the consumer to inform the seller "within a period *not shorter than* two months" from the date on which the consumer detected such lack of conformity.[62] Given the use of "not shorter than", nothing prevents the establishment of a longer period. The new directive thus seamlessly follows the previous one.[63]

2. *Remedies*

In accordance with the Consumer Sales Directive, the new Goods Directive provides for four remedies. It concerns repair or replacement free of charge, a proportionate reduction in the price or termination of contract (Article 13.1 Goods Directive). It should be made clear that the first two of these remedies are aiming at restoring the lack of conformity with the contract of sale and thus strive for a redress in kind, whilst the last two remedies rather entail redress by equivalence. Similar to the previous directive, the consumer can also attempt to receive damages.[64]

---

[60] Belgium, for example, did not extend the period of the presumption of anteriority. France on the other hand did.

[61] The literal wording of Article 12 GD provides that Member States *may* maintain or introduce such a period. Nothing obligates them to do so.

[62] Recital 46 GD.

[63] *See* in that regard the case *Froukje Faber* (*supra*), where the CJEU ruled that the notification to be given relates only to the existence of the lack of conformity and that it is not subject to rules of evidence which would make it impossible or excessively difficult for the consumer to exercise his rights.

[64] Recitals 18 and 61 GD.

Apart from the remedies, the hierarchy has also been maintained, be it that the Goods Directive elaborates more closely on the criteria which must or may be fulfilled before one or the other remedy can or cannot be requested. When the goods do not seems in conformity, then the consumer can firstly choose between repairor replacement, both which are free of charge. In principle, the consumer has freedom of choice between both remedies, unless the remedy chosen would be impossible or, compared to the other remedy, would impose costs on the seller that would be disproportionate[65] (Article 13.2 Goods Directive). In addition, the directive expressly provides for the right for the seller to refuse to bring the goods into conformity if repair or replacement are impossible or would impose costs on the seller that would be disproportionate (Article 13.3 Goods Directive). When both repair or replacement cannot be completed, is not in accordance with the legal conditions or when the seller has refused to bring the goods into conformity, then the consumer has a right to a proportionate reduction of the price or to terminate the agreement (Article 13.4 Goods Directive). This right to the secondary remedies also applies when the lack of conformity persists despite the seller having attempted to bring the goods into conformity,[66] when the lack of conformity is of such a serious nature as to justify an immediate price reduction or termination of the sales contract, or when the seller has declared, or it is clear from the circumstances, that the seller will not bring the goods into conformity within a reasonable time, or without significant inconvenience for the consumer. In principle the consumer then has freedom of choice between a proportionate reduction of the price or the termination of the agreement, except when the lack of conformity is only of minor importance (Article 13.5. Goods Directive). Termination of contract is in the latter case not permitted. These abstract concepts (minor importance, reasonable time, significant inconvenience) grant a wide margin of discretion to the judge. Nevertheless, this was also the case in the Consumer Sales Directive and therefore inspiration can be drawn from the case law which was then developed.

New is the legal base for the so-called '*exceptio non adimpleti contractus*'.[67] The consumer then has the right to withhold payment of any outstanding part of the price or a part thereof until the seller has fulfilled the seller's obligations under the directive (Article 13.6 Goods Directive). Finally, the new directive stipulates that Member States may regulate whether and to what extent a contribution of the consumer to the lack of conformity affects the consumer's right to remedies.

---

[65] The latter requires that all circumstances are taken into account, including (a) the value the goods would have if there were no lack of conformity, (b) the significance of the lack of conformity and (c) whether the alternative remedy could be provided without significant inconvenience to the consumer. For instance, it might be disproportionate to request the replacement of the good because of a minor scratch (*see* Recital 48 GD).

[66] In our opinion, this could mean both a lack of conformity which manifests itself again shortly afterwards or which continuous to manifest itself.

[67] In the circumstance of a reciprocal contract (e.g. an agreement of sales), this remedy of defence allows one party to suspend his or her contractual obligations when and after the other party defaults on his or her respectively.

The content of the provisions containing the remedies shows clearly that the new directive more or less copy-pasted its predecessor. Consequently, case law regarding the latter can be transposed insofar this is useful. For example, case law concerning the possibility for the consumer to, when he has asked for termination but this was refused because the lack of conformity was only of minor importance, then modify the original claim where no reduction of price was demanded to that effect.[68]

As previously mentioned, the first option for the consumer is to restore the lack of conformity with the contract of sale, notably by repairing or replacing the good (Article 14 Goods Directive). Enabling consumers to re require repair should, according to the recitals, encourage sustainable consumtion and could contribute to greater durability of products.[69] From the perspective of durability this consequently leads to a preference of repair over replacement.

Repair or replacement shall be carried out free of charge. This means, inter alia, that the consumer should not have to pay for the normal use in the period which precedes the replacement and that the seller should take back the replaceable goods at his expense. Additionally, this has to be carried out within a reasonable period of time from the moment the seller has been informed by the consumer of the lack of conformity and without any significant inconvenience to the consumer, taking into account the nature of the goods and the purpose for which the consumer required the goods. In turn, the consumer has to make the goods available to the seller so that the latter has the opportunity to carry out repair or replacement. Insofar it concerns goods that have to be installed, the obligation to repair or replace also entails the obligation of the removal of the non-conforming goods, or to bear the costs thereof.

When due to one of the above mentioned reasons redress in kind is out of the question, the consumer can still chose between the proportionate reduction of price, on the one hand, or termination of contract, on the other.

Concerning the reduction of price, the new directive states that this shall be in proportion to the decrease in value of the goods which were received by the consumer compared with the value that the goods would have had if they were in conformity (Article 15 Goods Directive). Once again this concerns a transposition of that which already existed under the Consumer Sales Directive.

The '*ultimum remedium*' of the new directive is however, again in accordance with the Consumer Sales Directive, the termination of contract. The consumer shall exercise this right by means of a statement to the seller expressing the decision to terminate the sales contract (Article 16.1 Goods Directive). Since no particular rules of evidence are specified, the consumer must by himself evaluate whether he possesses sufficient evidence. The main consequences of the termination are by contrast specified in the new directive: the seller has to reimburse to the consumer the price paid for the goods upon receipt of the goods or of evidence provided by the consumer of having sent back the goods whilst the consumer has to return to the seller, at the seller's expense, the goods (Article 16.3 Goods Directive). In respect

[68]Case 32/12, Soledad Duarte Hueros v. Autociba SA, Automóviles Citroën España SA, 2013 CURIA (Nov. 8 2013).

[69]Recital 48 GD.

to other consequences, the choice remains with the Member States, for example concerning the consequences of decrease of value, destruction or loss of the good.[70]

A novelty in the directive is the possibility of a 'partial termination'. Where the lack of conformity relates to only some of the goods delivered under the sales contract and there is a ground for termination of the sales contract pursuant to Article 13, the consumer may terminate the sales contract only in relation to those goods, and in relation to any other goods which the consumer has acquired together with the non-conforming goods if the consumer cannot reasonably be expected to accept to keep only the conforming goods (Article 16.2 Goods Directive). The purchase of a laptop can serve as an example. When the laptop appears to lack conformity but the charger does not, then the consumer cannot be expected to keep this charger.

The Goods Directive copied the Consumer Sales Directive to a great extent. Even though this is understandable since the former will replace the latter (and thus will apply to 'normal' goods), the lack of particular attention to goods with digital elements is remarkable. Where the new directive pays much attention to the specificities of goods with digital elements in respect to seller liability, not one word is mentioned in the domain of remedies. In view of remedies being the big stick of the directive, this can be regarded as a scourge.

The drafters of the new Goods Directive could have found useful inspiration in the Digital Content Directive. Without further elaboration on the latter, we want to point out, for example, the possibility for the consumer to oblige the trader to make available any content other than personal data, which was provided or created by the consumer when using the digital content or digital service supplied by the trader (Article 16.4 in conjunction with 16.5 Digital Content Directive). In respect of cloud services, this could mean that the movement of data of a cloud to a new location when this is no longer available in consequence of termination of contract. Such a possibility would also have been welcome in the new Goods Directive. When as a consequence of the termination the agreement is immediately ended, the risk exists that the consumer no longer has access to certain content (e.g. photos and documents) that he saved in a cloud service (e.g. iCloud) and is only accessible through certain goods (e.g. Apple products). Also the extensive arrangements in the Digital Content Directive on how a trader should act after termination (Articles 16 until 18) and in regard to the modification of digital content or services (Article 19), could to some extent have been adopted in the Goods Directive since digital content or digital services that are embedded in goods do not differ in essence from digital content or digital goods which is traded separately (i.e. not embedded).

[70]Recital 60 GD. Article 16.3 GD refers to the modalities for return and reimbursement.

4 Enforcement of Infringements Concerning Goods with Embedded Software

A. *The dieselgate scandal: facts of a large-scale infringement concerning embedded software*

This fourth part addresses the enforcement of infringements on the subject of goods with embedded software. To do so, the assessment will refer to the so-called 'Dieselgate scandal' to identify certain challenges for enforcement which flow thereof. It was discovered in September 2015[71] that about 11 million diesel fuelled cars of the Volkswagen AG group, 8 million of which had been retailed in the European Union, were equipped with fraudulent embedded software. Fraudulent because the programming was purposely meant to bypass diesel emission standards by activating certain emission control systems only during laboratory testing (i.e. 'defeat devices'). After emissions certification, the operating mode deactivated to improve acceleration and fuel consumption. These models were then sold under the pretext of being "eco-friendly" whilst they were not. The first sales of vehicles equipped with this embedded software dated back to approximately 2009. In other words, the scandal concerning this embedded software was Union wide (even global), wide spread and only detected after a long period of time due to its technical nature. Notwithstanding possible violations in the fields of environmental law, competition law, criminal law or whichever, the analysis only adopts a EU consumer law perspective. Several interests of consumers were harmed such as, inter alia, consumers who wanted to purchase "eco-friendly" cars were misled,[72] the resale value of their cars diminished after the discovery,[73] their cars were subjected to software updates which increased fuel consumption and degraded their horsepower[74] or they would no longer be able to enter low-emission zones in some urban areas.[75]

---

[71] *See* Meetu Kaul, *Notice of Violation*, U.S. Envtl. Prot. Agency (Sept. 18, 2015), https://www.epa.gov/sites/production/files/2015-10/documents/vw-nov-caa-09-18-15.pdf [https://perma.cc/G8WY-PWLT]. The United States Environmental Protection Agency (EPA) initially discovered the fraud.

[72] *Supra* note 77.

[73] Sandra Passinhas, *"Dieselgate" and Consumer Law: Repercussions of the Volkswagen scandal in Portugal*, 6 EuCML 42, 43 (2017). *See also* Charles Miller, *Volkswagen and Audi 'Clean Diesel' Owners See Decline in Vehicle Value Following VW Emissions Recall Scandal*, HG.ORG Legal Resources, https://www.hg.org/legal-articles/volkswagen-and-audi-clean-diesel-owners-see-decline-in-vehicle-value-following-vw-emissions-recall-scandal-36898 [https://perma.cc/RK6J-NHAU] (last visited March 25, 2019).

[74] Krachler & Rzehorska, *supra* note 76, at 36. *See also* Miles Brignall, *Thousands of drivers suffer loss of power following VW emissions 'fix'*, The Guardian (Jul. 12, 2017), https://www.theguardian.com/money/2017/jul/12/drivers-loss-of-power-vw-emissions-fix-class-action [https://perma.cc/24GW-9M58] (last visited March 20, 2019).

[75] *See* Peter Teffer, *Dieselgate casts doubt over low emission zones*, EUobserver (Nov 18, 2016, 1:25 PM), https://euobserver.com/regions/135941 [https://perma.cc/2AVN-CKFQ](last visited Apr. 1, 2019). Consumers' cars equipped with the Dieselgate software were categorised into a more polluting category (i.e. from EURO 5 to EURO 6) and could therefore then be banned from certain urban areas with low emission standards.

To protect these consumer interests, an effective enforcement response is required. This contribution does not aim to engage in an extensive debate on the general meaning[76] of *effective* enforcement. In simple terms it can be referred to as the implementation of law in practice[77] and thus as similar to compliance. Since a sound legal basis is a necessary condition[78] for effectiveness, the assessment examines the previous (CSD) and new directive (GD) concerning goods with embedded software and whether these can (i) restore the losses suffered of all the injured consumers involved ('compensation', or 'redress') and (ii) prevent similar infringements from happening in the future by discouraging (potential) perpetrators from committing these ('deterrence'). These two objectives of enforcement can traditionally[79] be regarded as instrumental for achieving compliance[80] and thus effective enforcement.

B. *Enforcement issues in the consumer sales directive and the goods directive*

1. *Repercussions on enforcement of the substantive law provisions*

Applying the previous Consumer Sales Directive shows that the Dieselgate scandal was a clear-cut situation of a lack of conformity of the delivered good with the contract of sale and hence an infringement on this requirement. The emission standards of the Dieselgate vehicles were of worse quality and performance than presented by the producer. Moreover, since the emission limits (i.e. EURO 5) were incorporated in the agreement between Volkswagen AG dealers (sellers) and consumers, one could say these were explicitly agreed upon. Based on Article 2.2 (d) of the previous directive, the good did not show the quality and performance that the consumer can reasonably expect, given the nature of the good and taking into account any public

---

[76]*See* Fabrizio Cafaggi & Paola Iamiceli, *The Principles of Effectiveness, Proportionality and Dissuasiveness in the Enforcement of EU Consumer Law: The Impact of a Triad on the Choice of Civil Remedies and Administrative Sanctions*, 25 ERPL 575, 577 and 581 (2017). *Effectiveness as a legal principle* in EU consumer law also exists but has to be distinguished from its general meaning. The latter can be applied as a benchmark for the enforcement of any substantive law provision in any legal jurisdiction.

[77]*See* Geneviève Saummier & Hans-W. Micklitz et al., Enforcement and Effectiveness of Consumer Law 5 (Springer International Publishing 2018). A definition of 'effectiveness' in the field of consumer law enforcement falls outside the scope and purpose of this contribution since, as Micklitz and Saummier rightly state, "effectiveness is one of the most complicated issues to 'measure'".

[78]*Id.*

[79]*See, e.g.,* Klaus Viitanen, *Enforcement of consumers' collective interests by regulatory agencies in the Nordic countries*, in Willem Van Boom & Marco Loos, Collective Enforcement of Consumer Law: Securing Compliance in Europe through Private Group Action and Public Authority Intervention 83, 83–103 (Europa Law Publishing 2007). Compliance through soft law methods is another viable option which will not be discussed in this contribution.

[80]*See* Louis Visscher, *Rechtseconomische beschouwingen over rechtshandhaving* [Considerations on enforcement from a law and economics perspective], at 5 (2009), https://hdl.handle.net/1765/31467 [https://perma.cc/C7XV-ECNY]. The successful exercise of compensatory private claims could *in theory* also deter traders from committing infringements and thus have a preventive effect. Compensation is of course, in our opinion, also of importance to restore the imbalance between perpetrator and victim after an infringement and thus reach implementation of law in practice.

statements on the specific characteristics of the goods made about them by the seller, the producer or his representative, particularly in advertising or on labelling. Under the new Goods Directive, lack of conformity still seems at hand since the good didn't have e.g. the description or quality (i.e. emissions performance) as the contract of sales specifies (subjective requirement, *see* Article 6 (a)) nor possesses the qualities and other features the consumer may reasonably expect (objective requirement, *see* Article 7.1 (d)).

The time limit of two years in the previous directive turned out to be a significant issue in the aftermath of the scandal. At the time of discovery of the infringement (September 2015), most of the models equipped with the fraudulent software were already well past said time limit and thus fell outside the scope of application of the Consumer Sales Directive.[81] After all, the bulk of the infringements in the EU occurred between 2010 and 2014.[82] The default period of two years has unfortunately been maintained by the new directive[83] (Article 10.1 GD) and some critical observations have already been made previously. Applied to Dieselgate, the two year liability period is first of all far too short since the delivery of some models dates back to even six years (2009) before the discovery of the infringement (2015). Secondly, the success of a consumer invoking one of the four civil law remedies in a court of law mostly depends upon the presumption period. Without this presumption, the consumer has to prove that the fraudulent software was installed at the time of the delivery of the good which constitutes a very heavy burden of proof due to the technical nature of the embedded software. This minimum period of the presumption is now extended from six months up until one year (Article 11.1 GD) and would still be too short in most cases. Granted, once the competent government authorities concluded that these defeat devices were indeed installed at the delivery and the goods therefore lacked conformity, this issue of proof would no longer have been relevant in private proceedings. These are, however, favourable circumstances specific to the Dieselgate case and will not always arise.

The fraud by Volkswagen AG was detected by the United States supervisor on environmental law[84] and only after a period of six years due to its technical aspects. The nature of goods with embedded software thus causes detection of infringements to be difficult when it is particularly related to this software. If these infringements are or were detected, it is likely this will or would only take place after some time. Moreover, it is improbable that the individual consumer has the expertise to detect infringements on such a technical level and then also prove them in court. In this respect, literature has already addressed some of these issues as pervasive barriers for individual private enforcement of consumer law. Consumers will often not exercise their rights in courts because they are unaware that an infringement is at hand or because the time-consuming and costly nature of litigation discourages them.

---

[81] Passinhas, *supra* note 80, at 43 (2017).

[82] Transport & Environment, *supra* note 78, at 3.

[83] As seen before, this default time limit can be extended when a continuous supply of more than two years is at hand.

[84] *Supra* note 7474.

Furthermore, the rational consumer will not act if the costs outweigh the benefits, for instance, when harm is very small and the investment to enforce the law is costly.[85]

This is no different with embedded software. If consumers invoked the remedies of the new Goods Directive, they would most likely only receive a repair of said software (e.g. an update). This was notably exemplified inDieselgate[86] where in some cases the lack of conformity was successfully remedied in this way.[87] Replacement as a remedy can only be invoked if this would not impose disproportionate costs on the seller. Consumers receiving, for instance, a new car instead of a software update can be considered as such. Only a full reimbursement of the price after termination of contract could therefore be an adequate financial incentive for an individual consumer to bring an action before court, albeit unlikely in both the previous Consumer Sales Directive and the Goods Directive. This is namely a secondary remedy which can only be invoked if repair or replacement have failed or are unfit. Moreover, it is required that the lack of conformity is not of minor importance to have the contract rescinded[88] or terminated.[89] In some cases it could be reasonable for the seller to argue that the (hidden) fraudulent software is of such minor importance.[90] The other secondary remedy, a proportionate price reduction, seems more probable but the potential benefit is then much smaller. Hence, the potential benefits of litigation when embedded software is involved are also small (e.g. receiving an update) compared with the cost thereof (basic costs of the trial with an additional cost of an expertise inquiry), even when the good in itself was initially of high value and purchased at a high price (e.g. a car).

These existing barriers now seem strengthened in very technical situations[91] such as goods with embedded software and this will probably become more of an issue due to the ever-growing presence of software components in consumer goods in the rapidly advancing digital age. Goods with embedded software are therefore hallmarked with an '*expertise barrier*' which hinders consumers from detecting infringements in time, or even at all, and also effectively enforcing their rights in court. Furthermore, if the technical nature of goods with embedded software causes infringements to be detected only after a long period of time, it will also be more

---

[85] *See* Michael Faure & Franziska Weber, *The Diversity of the EU Approach to Law Enforcement - Towards A Coherent Model Inspired by a Law and Economics Approach*, 18 German Law Journal 823, 838 (2017). This is commonly referred to as 'rational apathy'.

[86] *See* also Thomas Riehm & Lukas Lindner, *"Dieselgate" and Consumer Law: Repercussions of the Volkswagen scandal in Germany*, 6 EuCML 39, 39 (2017).

[87] *See* Dybus & Lemmen, *supra* note 89, at 91. Some Volkswagen models showed negative influences on the car's performance after the update, whilst others actually showed positive influences.

[88] Article 3.6 CSD.

[89] Article 13.5 GD.

[90] *See* Riehm & Lindner, *supra* note 96, at 40. We have to emphasize, however, that some consumers might consider the ecological aspect of a car of major importance, whilst others might not.

[91] *See* Monika Namyslowska, *"Dieselgate" and Consumer Law: Repercussions of the Volkswagen scandal in Poland*, 6 EuCML 87, at 90 (2017), who rightly states the Volkswagen case is complicated due to nuanced circumstances and a complex technical background.

likely to harm a larger number of consumers. Hence, it seems plausible that infringements concerning embedded software could, as time passes, become widespread as well.

Like its predecessor, the Goods Directive targets liability for these infringements concerning embedded software at the seller. The producer of the fraudulent software (or update) escapes legal action by the consumer and the (retail) seller is supposed to implement a redress action according to Article 18 GD (which remained nearly identical to Article 4 of the Consumer Sales Directive). If the lack of conformity resulted "from an act or omission, including omitting to provide updates to goods with digital elements in accordance with Article 7.3 by a person in previous links of the chain of transactions, the seller shall be entitled to pursue remedies against the person or persons liable in the chain of transactions. The persons against whom the seller may pursue remedies and the relevant actions and conditions of exercise, shall be determined by national law". The provision only obligates Member States to establish this right of redress, whilst the shaping of this right and the procedures leading thereunto were left to the Member States.[92]

The retail seller (e.g. a small salesman of a brand of Volkswagen AG cars) is in this manner placed in the difficult legal position where he has to bring an action before court against the (multinational) producer (e.g. Volkswagen AG). It seems unlikely that this cascade system of liability procedures is fit to provide the necessary deterrence towards the actual potential perpetrators. To ensure compliance, deterrence requires that *the perpetrators* are discouraged, i.e. producers, from committing future infringements. Hence, the prevention of similar future infringements cannot be achieved when only the seller is liable to the consumer in the directive.

Granted, neither liability nor the four civil law remedies mean to impose a deterrent sanction towards the infringing perpetrator, but most of all strive to compensate consumers for the lack of conformity.[93] Even so, the achievement of this compensatory objective in a court of law can only be met if the above mentioned enforcement barriers (time limit and burden of proof) are not of issue. Even if, for example, the time limit was extended, the discovery of the infringement could take some years due to its technical nature and it could be that the retail seller is no longer in business by then. A successful retail seller (e.g. of numerous Volkswagen AG models) could, moreover, go out of business when several consumers effectively exercise their remedies at the same time (e.g. through a collective redress procedure[94]). These concerns show the achievement of full compensation for *all* consumers seems doubtful when only sellers can be held liable. Direct and additional liability of the producer could support the achievement of actual compensation for affected consumers.

---

[92] Recital 63 GD.

[93] *See* Recital 10 CSD and Recitals 10 and 46 GD. Repair or replacement can be regarded as remedies which restore the lack of conformity, whilst price reduction or termination of contract offer redress by equivalence.

[94] *See* Krachler & Rzehorska, *supra* note 76, at 39. Volkswagen dealers (i.e. sellers) have been targeted by collective procedures in Austria.

A last concern lies in the use of updates. Volkswagen AG carried out updates to correct the fraudulent software, which did not always go without problems. The repair of the original lack of conformity, i.e. emission standards, resulted in a new lack of conformity with the contract of sale in some cases, i.e. higher fuel consumption and a loss of horsepower.[95] The Consumer Sales Directive did not provide any protection, but neither will the new Goods Directive since liability for updates again falls on the seller. It was also made clear previously that (even) when an update occurs (just) within the time limit of continuous supply, it offers no protection if this update shows issues. This new lack of conformity is clearly not caused by the original seller but by the producer, whilst it is again only the former who could be liable and has to commence redress actions against the latter. The above-mentioned issues are again at hand.

2. *Enforcement provisions: scope and meaning*

The previous section shows that even the new Goods Directive would still not provide the necessary legal basis for effective enforcement if Dieselgate had happened today. The gaps in substantive law for the protection of consumer interests that existed then, remain. Regardless of these identified gaps, that is to say in the hypothesis that these would not exist, could an enforcement provision in the new Goods Directive contribute to effective enforcement?

The establishment and shaping of remedies, sanctions and procedures traditionally falls under the so-called 'enforcement autonomy' of Member States. The Consumer Sales Directive and the Goods Directive poses an exception thereon due to remedies with a compensatory objective towards sellers already being present in both directives. Apart from that, the Consumer Sales Directive did not mention enforcement, whilst Article 19 GD now additionally states: "Member States shall ensure that*adequate and effective* means exist to ensure compliance with this Directive". The phrase "means to ensure compliance" could include both deterrent sanctions and the procedures due to its broad formulation, but not additional compensatory measures against sellers[96] since Article 4 GD prescribes maximum harmonisation. Moreover, these means have to be both adequate and effective. This condition can be interpreted through the principle of effectiveness as it is understood in consumer law enforcement.[97] *Effectiveness* has been defined as a principle enabling an *adequate* remedial response to a violation in terms of both (i) the aptness of a remedy or sanction to in fact perform the function for which it is designed (preventive, penal, compensatory, restitutionary, etc.) and (ii) the absence of obstacles (mostly procedural) that in fact prevent the attainment of said objectives. Based on this definition

[95] Brignall, *supra* note 81. *See also* Krachler & Rzehorska, *supra* note 76, at 37. Conformity with the contract is not established and the buyer could then, in theory, request price reduction or rescission of contract.

[96] *See* Recital 63 GD. Member States retained the freedom to establish remedies by consumers against producers.

[97] *See* Cafaggi & Iamiceli, *supra* note 83, at 577 and 581. A further elaboration on the complex conceptual meaning of these principles falls outside the scope of this contribution.

and recent case law of the Court of Justice of the European Union regarding this same phrase,[98] the seemingly separate condition of adequacy is already entailed in the phrase ‘effective means’.

Article 19 furthermore says these means shall include provisions whereby which one or more of three kinds of bodies, as determined by national law, may take action under national law before the courts or before the competent administrative bodies to ensure that the national provisions transposing the new directive are applied. These bodies can be (i) public bodies or their representatives, (ii) consumer organisations having a legitimate interest in protecting consumers or (iii) professional organisations having a legitimate interest in acting. This provision only obligates Member States to establish or appoint one of these three bodies and apt procedural provisions as to ensure the application of the directive, or in other words, the ensurance of compliance. This leaves room for professional organisations (e.g. of sellers) of which the provision only requires a legitimate interest in acting and not necessarily the interest of protecting consumers. The provision allows for an organisation of traders to be appointed in fulfilling this enforcement task by, for instance, bringing an injunction procedure for unfair competition. This could then also protect consumer interests.

Be it as it may, the vague and broad formulation of Article 19 leaves ample room to the discretion of Member States and therefore hardly, if even at all, affects enforcement autonomy.[99] As regards the Dieselgate scandal, the enforcement responses differed strongly in the EU due to this autonomy and the introduction of Article 19 in the Goods Directive does not seem capable of changing this. In some Member States, collective enforcement mechanisms are possible which could constitute an effective response to compensate consumers like in the Dieselgate scandal. Fully functioning collective redress mechanisms are, however, only available in a limited number of Member States[100] and even then the application of such a procedure in light of Dieselgate only benefitted a limited number of consumers in comparison to the total number of affected consumers.[101] In other Member States, the public watchdog

---

[98]Case 109/17, Bankia SA v. Juan Carlos Mari Merino and Others, CURIA (Sept. 19, 2018), points 35 and 43. In a case on the same phrase “adequate and effective means” from Article 11 of the Unfair Commercial Practices Directive, the CJEU seemingly did not consider *adequate* to be a separate condition for enforcement.

[99]*See* Case 388/13, Nemzeti Fogyasztóvédelmi Hatóság v. UPC Magyarország kft, CURIA (Apr. 16, 2015), point 57. Enforcement autonomy stands firm even when directives obligate Member States to follow these principles.

[100]*European Collective Redress - What is the EU waiting for?*, Bureau européenne des Unions des Consommateurs, at 6 (Jun. 31, 2017), https://www.beuc.eu/publications/beuc-x-2017-086_ama_european_collective_redress.pdf [https://perma.cc/AM3R-ULE3]. *See also, The EU’s Response to the “dieselgate” scandal*, European Court of Auditors, at 70–72 (February 2019) https://www.eca.europa.eu/lists/ecadocuments/brp_vehicle_emissions/brp_vehicle_emissions_en.pdf [https://perma.cc/63FJ-Q59J].

[101]*See* Namyslowska, *supra* note 101, at 90. The involvement of Polish consumers in collective redress against Volkswagen is still relatively small compared to approx. 140.000 defective Volkswagen cars. A positive outcome of the proceedings will only satisfy the private interests of a limited number of Polish consumers. The proceedings were, moreover, based on the Unfair Commercial Practices Directive, not the Consumer Sales Directive.

(or, 'public supervisor/authority') on consumer law responded (e.g. Italy[102] and the Netherlands[103]). Critical voices have rightly contended the applied sanctions were too low and therefore did not cause sufficient deterrence.[104] The maximum cap of the fine was insignificant (e.g. 450.000 Euros in the Netherlands[105]) in comparison with the financial means of the perpetrator (Volkswagen AG group) and the magnitude of the infringement (i.e. approx. 8 million cars lacking conformity). The legal consequences (i.e. remedies and sanctions) should correspond with the nature of the infringement so compensation and deterrence can be fully achieved.

Dieselgate showed this fragmentation of enforcement is detrimental for the full achievement of the objectives of compensation and deterrence, but also equal consumer protection[106] across the EU. Integration of the national markets within the Single Market of the European Union is ever-increasing.[107] If goods with embedded software from the same producer are increasingly being retailed all across the European Union due to outlet markets of producers transcending national markets or due to its further circulation as second-hand goods, it is not unlikely Unionwide infringements like Dieselgate[108] will happen more often. Hence, infringements concerning embedded software will not only be discovered after a long period of time and will therefore be widespread, they could also turn out to be Unionwide.

3. *Towards effective enforcement of infringements concerning embedded software*

Enforcement of Dieselgate-like infringements remains ineffective due to a defected legal basis and fragmented enforcement. An infringement like Dieselgate requires

---

102 *The Italian Competition Authority fines the Volkswagen Group for tampering with their vehicles' emissions control systems*, Autorità Garante della Concorrenza e del Mercato (Aug. 8, 2016) https://en.agcm.it/en/media/detail?id=0899f747-5c9e-4642-b866-c4ac22cc60e0 [https://perma.cc/X9MD-YLLQ].

103 *Besluit van de Autoriteit Consument en Markt tot het opleggen van een boete aan Volkswagen AG* [Decision of the Authority for Consumers & Markets to impose a fine on Volkswagen AG], Autoriteit Consument & Markt (Oct. 18, 2017), https://www.acm.nl/sites/default/files/documents/2017-12/besluit-acm-beboet-volkswagen-ag-voor-oneerlijke-handelspraktijken-2017-12-01.pdf [https://perma.cc/MY2P-K535].

104 Evelyne Terryn & Pauline Verbiest, *De herziene CPC verordening als oplossing voor grensoverschrijdend consumentenleed?* [The revised CPC Regulation as a solution for cross-border consumer detriment], 118 DCCR 5, 27 (2018).

105 *Supra* note 114.

106 *Collective Redress in the Member States of the European Union*, Parl. Eur. Doc. (PE 608.829) 58 (Oct. 2018).

107 *Intra-EU trade in goods - recent trends. Evolution of intra-EU trade in goods: 2002–2018*, Eurostat (Sept. 2018), https://ec.europa.eu/eurostat/statistics-explained/index.php/Intra-EU_trade_in_goods_-_recent_trends#Evolution_of_intra-EU_trade_in_goods:_2002-2018 [https://perma.cc/FWF2-DSG6] (last visited Apr. 3, 2019). The intra-EU trade in goods has nearly doubled since 2002 and keeps on rising. *See also Collective redress in the Member States of the European Union*, *supra* note 117. The increasing integration requires integrated enforcement since consumers in some Member States could not get redress in the aftermath of Dieselgate.

108 *See* Transport & Environment, *supra* note 78, at 23–24. Other car companies are also suspected of installing defeat devices.

enforcement that can overcome the 'expertise barrier', is aimed at the producer and is also in correspondence with the total number of affected consumers within the European Union. This corresponding response needs to go beyond a mere compensation and should also impose a punishment by means of sanctions[109] to discourage future potential offenders. Fragmentation of procedures should be avoided as they lead to unequal protection between consumers in different Member States. A single or coordinated procedural response is therefore required. The previous part showed these needs cannot be answered within the scope of the new Goods Directive. Could the answers to these needs for the effective enforcement of large-scale embedded software infringements like Dieselgate then be found outside of these directives? Indeed, both current and proposed EU legislation outside of the previously discussed directives could still provide the right solutions.

First of all, the expertise barrier could be overcome by the investigative powers and possibilities of a public enforcement body.[110] Even so, it is still questionable if even such a public watchdog on consumer protection laws always has the means to detect infringements of such a technical nature as in the domain of goods with embedded software, especially when it concerns a small Member State with lesser financial means. Currently, a public watchdog from another Member State can be called upon under the provisions of the Consumer Protection and Cooperation Regulation (CPC Regulation).[111] The watchdogs can then ideally aid each other within this CPC network in acquiring the necessary technical knowledge for detection and investigation. Nonetheless, it has been made clear that the effectiveness thereof depends heavily on the extent of the investigative powers of the addressed public watchdog and the procedures within the applicant[112] and requested[113] Member States.[114] When the requested information (finally) reached the applicant authority, limitation periods for taking action in the Member State of the applicant authority had already been reached.[115] Information sharing between public watchdogs has thus far not been

---

[109] *See Common principles for injunctive and compensatory collective redress mechanisms in the Member States concerning violations of rights granted under Union law*, at 17, COM (2018) 40 final (Jan. 25, 2018). Punitive damages are generally alien to the majority of the Member States' legal context. The European Commission is of the opinion these should be formally prohibited to avoid abusive proceedings.

[110] Visscher, *supra* note 88, at 6.

[111] Regulation 2006/2004 of the European Parliament and of the Council of 27 October 2004 on cooperation between national authorities responsible for the enforcement of consumer protection laws (the Regulation on consumer protection cooperation), 2004 O.J. (L 364) 1 (2004) [hereinafter CPC Regulation].

[112] 'Applicant authority' means the competent authority that makes a request for mutual assistance (*see* Article 3 (f) CPC Regulation).

[113] 'Requested authority' means the competent authority that receives a request for mutual assistance (*see* Article 3 (g) CPC Regulation).

[114] Mark Peacock et al., *(External) evaluation of the Consumer Protection Cooperation Regulation,* Consumer Policy Evaluation Consortium, at 60 (Dec. 17, 2012) https://ec.europa.eu/smart-regulation/evaluation/search/download.do;jsessionid=dQhE06qeWnqRejHtqjmPxi3pyN5vJXqyWzuIjtBfeRZcFVCukzZp!2131975131?documentId=6320865 [https://perma.cc/2WWV-UAY4].

[115] *Id.*

effective and the expertise barrier in relation to goods with embedded software could not be bridged despite the CPC network.

The revised CPC Regulation (CPC2 Regulation)[116] has been approved in 2017 and will enter into force in 2020 according to its Article 42. This seems to provide new possibilities that answer the discussed enforcement needs. In sum, the information sharing system has been strengthened. Article 9 provides for far-reaching minimum investigative powers and, according to Article 4, limitation periods will have to be shared between the competent authorities. Furthermore, Article 11 requires that requests for information have to be answered without delay and in any event within 30 days. Other bodies which serve the interests of consumers can also be involved which leads to the establishment of a broad information network. Article 27 states 'designated bodies' with the necessary expertise, such as European Consumer Centres,[117] consumer organisations and associations and where appropriate, trader associations,[118] will have the power to issue an alert to the competent authorities. These procedural innovations are encouraging for fulfilling the need to uncover and share[119] technical information, which is of importance for detecting and investigating infringements concerning embedded software, in a speedy[120] manner.

Apart from flaws in information sharing, the CPC Regulation also showed malfunctioning coordination procedures.[121] These have therefore also been strengthened in the revised CPC2 Regulation. Strongly developed coordinated operations between public enforcement authorities and under supervision of the European Commission will be possible. The coordination is most strongly developed when a 'widespread infringement with a Union dimension' is at hand, which basically means the infringement on consumer law has spread to at least two-thirds of the Member States, accounting together for at least two-thirds of the population of the EU. The Dieselgate case can be qualified as such.[122] Even within the revised CPC2 Regulation some defects[123] can still be identified. According to Article 17,

[116] Regulation 2017/2394 of the European Parliament and of the Council of 12 December 2017 on cooperation between national authorities responsible for the enforcement of consumer protection laws and repealing Regulation (EC) No 2006/2004, 2017 O.J. (L 345) 1 [hereinafter CPC2 Regulation].

[117] *Role of the ECC-Net*, European Commission, https://ec.europa.eu/info/live-work-travel-eu/consumers/resolve-your-consumer-complaint/european-consumer-centres-network_en (last visited Apr. 1, 2019). This is the so-called ECC Network.

[118] In theory, trader associations of sellers could alert (embedded) software infringements to the authorities of the CPC2 network. This gives them the possibility to escape redress actions by consumers by shifting the focus to producers.

[119] Albeit the information sharing procedures are only possible in a cross-border situation. Only when a competent authority suspects the same infringement has occurred or is occurring in another Member State can it request (technical) information. If it only occurs within Member State borders, then the competent authority would in principle have to fend for itself.

[120] *A Digital Single Market for Europe*, at 5, COM (2015) 192 final (May 6, 2015). Rapid information sharing was one of the identified needs in the Digital Single Market Policy.

[121] Mark Peacock et al., *supra* note 125, at 94.

[122] *See* Terryn & Verbiest, *supra* note 115, at 25.

[123] *Id.* at 24–28.

the coordinated action procedure can only be initiated if the competent authorities of all involved Member States unanimously agree thereto. A veto right by one of these for whichever reason could thus easily undermine effective enforcement. If the coordinated action can then still commence, the European Commission will be the coordinator and more inquiries and inspections will follow. The results thereof can be adopted in a common position of the involved competent authorities if appropriate and negotiations with the perpetrator can then be initiated. According to Article 20, on the basis of the common position the competent authorities may invite the trader responsible to propose commitments to cease the infringement. The trader may also propose commitments on his own initiative which cease the infringement or offer remedial commitments to consumers.

TheCPC2 Regulation seemingly offers a collective redress mechanism for consumers all over the European Union in a single procedural action, but an important defect remains: the commitments cannot be forced upon the perpetrator. The enforcement measures thereto (i.e. sanctions) still remain within the jurisdiction of the Member States.[124] Deterrence is not achieved due to sanctions and procedures varying in each Member State.[125] These would necessarily remain fragmented. One of the substantive consumer law directives or regulations in itself could prescribe harmonised sanctions (Article 21 CPC2 Regulation) which could then ensure deterrence (and hence compensation) if this sanction takes into account the total magnitude of the infringement across the EU.

In April 2018 the European Commission released its 'New Deal for Consumers'.[126] Strong emphasis was placed upon effective enforcement of consumer protection rules. The European Commission proposed a 'Modernization Directive' [127]to amend several existing directives containing the EU substantive consumer law provisions, such as the Unfair Commercial Practices Directive[128] (UCPD). These amendments include, among other things, a harmonisation of criteria for penalties striving towards a correspondence between the nature of the infringement (e.g. gravity, duration, number of consumers harmed, intent, etc.) and the fine.[129] Where the penalty to be imposed is a fine, the infringing trader's annual turnover and net

[124]*See* Cafaggi & Iamiceli, *supra* note 83, at 575. The consumer law directives only require these sanctions are effective, proportionate and dissuasive.

[125]Terryn & Verbiest, *supra* note 115, at 27.

[126]*A New Deal for Consumers*, COM (2018) 183 final (Apr. 11, 2018).

[127]*Proposal for a directive of the European Parliament and of the Council amending Council Directive 93/13/EEC of 5 April 1993, Directive 98/6/EC of the European Parliament and of the Council, Directive 2005/29/EC of the European Parliament and of the Council and Directive 2011/83/EU of the European Parliament and of the Council as regards better enforcement and modernisation of EU consumer protection rules*, COM (2018) 185 final (Apr. 11, 2018) [hereinafter Proposal Modernization Directive].

[128]Directive 2005/29/EC of the European Parliament and of the Council of 11 May 2005 concerning unfair business-to-consumer commercial practices in the internal market and amending Council Directive 84/450/EEC, Directives 97/7/EC, 98/27/EC and 2002/65/EC of the European Parliament and of the Council and Regulation (EC) No 2006/2004 of the European Parliament and of the Council ('Unfair Commercial Practices Directive'), 2005 O.J. (L 149), 22 [hereinafter UCPD].

[129]Article 11 (5) Proposal Modernization Directive.

profits as well as any fines imposed for the same or other infringements in other Member States shall also be taken into account in the determination of its amount. If the infringement is a widespread infringement with a Union dimension (i.e. Dieselgate) in the sense of the CPC2 Regulation, Member States have to ensure the possibility of such fines exist. These can mount up to 4% of the trader's annual turnover in the Member State or Member States concerned. It goes without saying this would constitute a seriously deterrent sanction[130] due to its correspondence with the magnitude of the infringement. It could then be used to force perpetrators to propose or accept and then comply with commitments.

In the same vein, a revision of the Injunctions Directive has also been proposed.[131] This directive introduces compensatory collective redress actions (i.e. 'class actions'), where a qualified entity (notably independent public bodies or consumer organisations) can represent a group of consumers who suffered losses from the same infringement. Interestingly, this procedural mechanism could aid in overcoming the expertise barrier since traders can be forced to disclose evidence in a confidential manner in a court of law or before an administrative authority.[132] Moreover, cross-border representative actions would be possible: qualified entities from other Member States could bring a collective redress action before courts in other Member States and strive for redress of foreign consumers. Single collective actions representing consumers from different Member States in front of a single forum would also be a possibility.[133]

In other words, the CPC2 Regulation in conjunction with these proposals could in fact enable the establishment of legal responses which meet needs to effectively enforce Dieselgate-like infringements. When an infringing trader would, for instance, refuse collective redress through commitments and even after being forced thereto through deterrent sanctions, collective redress could still be pursued in a court of law by the same public authority.

A sound legal basis upon which any enforcement procedure must be based remains a necessary requirement for effective enforcement. The new Goods Directive still seemed inadequate to address the needs for effectively enforcing infringements concerning embedded software like Dieselgate. Literature has often referred to the provisions of the UCPD[134] as a solution.[135] Knowingly promoting cars as "eco-friendly" whilst they are not could be regarded as misleading and could have caused the average consumer to have taken a transactional decision that he would not have

---

[130] *A New Deal for Consumers, supra* note 137, at 8.

[131] *Proposal for a directive of the European Parliament and of the Council on representative actions for the protection of the collective interests of consumers, and repealing Directive 2009/22/EC*, COM (2018) 184 final (Apr. 4, 2018) [hereinafter Proposal Injunctions Directive].

[132] Recital 37 and Article 13 Proposal Injunctions Directive.

[133] Recital 41 and Article 16 Proposal Injunctions Directive.

[134] *Supra* note 139.

[135] *See, e.g.*, Frauke Henning-Bodewig, *Corporate Social Responsibility, the VW Scandal and the UCP Directive*, 5 EuCML 153, 153 (2016).

taken otherwise.[136] This was, however, another favourable circumstance specific to this case. Volkswagen AG could as well have refrained from committing false advertising and still have equipped the concerned vehicles with fraudulent software with the goal to bypass emission standards. In other words, the qualification as a misleading commercial practice will not always offer a way out.

The practice could then still be qualified as an 'unfair' commercial practice. Under Article 5UCPD, the trader should act in line with the requirements of professional diligence. The violation of the first condition seems fulfilled in Dieselgate since Volkswagen AG clearly, by unduly informing consumers, did not demonstrate due care.[137] Additionally, it is also required the act materially distorted or was likely to distort the economic behaviour with regard to the product of the average consumer whom it reached or to whom it was addressed, or of the average member of the group when a commercial practice is directed to a particular group of consumers. Article 2 (e) UCPD further defines "to materially distort the economic behaviour of consumers" as using a commercial practice to appreciably impair the consumer's ability to make an informed decision, thereby causing the consumer *to take a transactional decision that he would not have taken otherwise.* Even though the Italian public supervisor on consumer protection (Autorità Garante della Concorrenza del Marcato) referred to the breach of these provisions in the Dieselgate case due to false information concerning the emissions in certificates of conformity,[138] serious doubts about the fulfilment of the conditions of this provision in this case have been made in literature. Whether a *material* distortion could have been at hand and whether this could have influenced the *average* consumer, can and has rightfully been called into question.

Summarily, the reliance on the broad norms of theUCPD does not seem convincing for effectively protecting consumers who are confronted with goods that lack conformity with the contract of sale, especially since this is the main objective of the new Goods Directive.[139] This begs the question whether the new Goods Directive should have implemented harmonised regimes of (either) liability, remedies or sanctions aimed at the producer.

5 Conclusion: Consumer Protection 2.0… Or Rather 1.1?

It was made clear throughout the article that the previous legal context was hardly appropriate in light of the ever-growing digitalisation of society. Where the Consumer Rights Directive and the national implementations thereof, to some extent, take

---

[136] Article 6.1 UCPD. *See also* Terryn & Verbiest, *supra* note 115, at 25.

[137] Case 310/15, Vincent Deroo-Blanquart v. Sony Europe Limited, 2015 CURIA (Sept. 7, 2016), point 37.

[138] *Supra* note 113.

[139] Article 1 GD.

into account the specificities of technological developments, the Consumer Sales Directive turned out to be outdated.

Even though nothing prevented Member States to adopt analogous legislative arrangements in the context of digital content and digital services (whether or not materialised), this did not happen everywhere. The consequence thereof is that immaterial digital content and services completely fell outside its scope of application. Updates also give rise to problems since lacks of conformity may be created which were not present at the moment of delivery.

These observations did not escape the attention of the Juncker Commission. To establish the development of the Digital Single Market, and thus fully take advantage of the potential of online trade and technological products, initiatives were taken for new legislative initiatives. On the one hand a new directive was adopted replacing the legal framework of the Consumer Sales Directive by a new but very comparable legal framework that, next to 'traditional' goods, also pays attention to the specificities of goods with digital elements.

Even though this attention for digital elements was without a doubt a step in the right direction, the initiatives are not yet on point. Strangely, the first part of the new directive extensively elaborates on goods with digital elements (i.e. liability and time periods), whilst the remedies remained utterly silent on that. In our opinion at least some legal arrangements of the remedies from the Digital Content Directive could have been transposed to the Goods Directive. The time limits as they are now also lack a sense of reality since the consumer loses out when the seller or third parties keep on delivering digital content or services shortly before the expiration of the period of liability which, however, brings about a new lack of conformity. An additional critical period with a variable starting point (i.e. after the last delivery of the digital content or service) would have been a welcome addition.

Additionally, these conclusions are regrettable in light of the notorious Dieselgate scandal. The previous Consumer Sales Directive was clearly inadequate to enforce this infringement. The new Goods Directive turned out to be incapable to mitigate this. Both fail to address the needs of effectively enforcing a situation where 8 million goods were delivered lacking conformity with the contract of sale caused by embedded software. Despite the new CPC2 Regulation and legislative proposals in the 'New Deal for Consumers', the main problem lies in the soundness of the legal basis which is a prerequisite for effective enforcement. Falling back on the Unfair Commercial Practices Directive did not seem convincing. In our opinion, liability of producers of the embedded software and harmonised legal consequences (i.e. remedies and sanctions) could therefore have at least been considered in the new Goods Directive, especially if Dieselgate was an omen for things to come in an increasingly integrating 'Digital Single Market'.

Whether we have now landed concerning the field of goods with digital elements in a scenario of consumer protection 2.0 or a scenario of consumer protection 1.1, should in our opinion be answered in between. One could refer to the current situation as consumer protection 1.9: even though certain steps have been taken into the right direction, not every imperfection has been eliminated and not every need has been addressed. Nevertheless, we can look hopeful to the future where we evolve towards a conclusive system that takes into account the needs of the digital age. *The future is now.*

References

1. Reinhard Steennot, Gert Straetmans, Evelyne Terryn, Bert Keirsbilck & Bert Wyseur, *Overzicht van rechtspraak. Consumentenbescherming (2008–2014) – Marktpraktijken (2011–2014)* [Overview of case law. Consumer protection (2008–2014) – Commercial practices (2011–2014)], 52 TPR 1311, 1651 (2015).
2. Jean-Claude Juncker, *A new start for Europe: My agenda for Jobs, Growth, Fairness and Democratic Change*, opening speech in the European Parliament plenary session in Strasbourg, July 15th, 2014.
3. Simon Geiregat & Reinhard Steennot, *Proposal for a Directive on Digital Content – Scope of Application and Liability for a Lack of Conformity*, in Ignace Claeys & Evelyne Terryn, *supra* note 36 at 121.
4. Christian Krachler & Martin Rzehorska, *"Dieselgate" and Consumer Law: Repercussions of the Volkswagen scandal in Austria*, 6 EuCML 2017 36, 36 (2017).
5. Marco Frigessi di Rattalma et al., The Dieselgate. A legal perspective, at ix (Springer International Publishing 2017)
6. Sara Landini, Environmental Law, in The Dieselgate. A legal perspective 159, 164 (2017)
7. Britt Blackwelder et al., *The Volkswagen Scandal. Case study*, University of Richmond: Robins School of Business, at 1 (January 2016), https://scholarship.richmond.edu/cgi/viewcontent.cgi?article=1016&context=robins-case-network [https://perma.cc/EU9T-NPFR] (last visited Apr. 3, 2019). *See also* Transport & Environment, *Dieselgate. Who? What? How?*, at 7, Transport & Environment (September 2016), https://www.transportenvironment.org/sites/te/files/publications/2016_09_Dieselgate_report_who_what_how_FINAL_0.pdf [https://perma.cc/QG4X-XGH5] (last visited Apr. 3, 2019).
8. Fabrizio Cafaggi & Hans-W. Micklitz et al., New frontiers of consumer protection: the interplay between private and public enforcement 2 (Intersentia 2009).
9. Charles Dybus & Jeroen Lemmen, "*Dieselgate and Consumer Law: Repercussions of the Volkswagen scandal in the Netherlands*, 6 EuCML 91, at 91 (2017). *See also* Krachler & Rzehorska, *supra* note 76, at 36. The permitted exhaust emission limits were listed in the standard sales contracts of Volkswagen dealers and can therefore be considered as explicitly agreed upon by the parties.
10. Kati Cseres, *Enforcement of collective consumer interests: a competition law perspective*, in Willem Van Boom & Marco Loos, Collective Enforcement of Consumer Law: Securing Compliance in Europe through Private Group Action and Public Authority Intervention 123, 129 (Europa Law Publishing 2007).
11. Olha Cherednychenko, *Public and Private Enforcement of European Private Law: Perspectives and Challenges*, 23 ERPL 481, 482 (2015).
12. Philipp Fabbio, "*Dieselgate" and Consumer Law: Repercussions of the Volkswagen scandal in Italy*, 6 EuCML 94, 95 (2017).

The Challenges of Smart Insurance Contracts to Consumers: Based on the Chinese Law

M. A. Kailiang

1 Introduction

Consumer rights have always been the focus of researching in consumer rights protection laws around the world. In fact, regardless of the civil law system or the Anglo-American legal system, the types of consumer rights have their similarities.[1] The difference is the specific protection methods of rights. Especially in today's fast-changing technology, a large amount of consumption has been heavily dependent on the network economy. Even the traditional business model has to adjust in terms of propaganda and payment methods to adapt to the major changes in social life. Correspondingly, the legal system for consumer rights protection should also be adjusted in a timely manner to solve the consumer protection problems brought about by technological development. After China's Consumer Rights Protection Act was revised in 2013, the main part of its revision was to increase the protection of consumer rights in online transactions.[2] In fact, this revision has indeed brought certain rights to the rights of Chinese online consumer groups. According to the statistics of China's famous judicial case website, since 2014, the number of consumer rights protection cases related to online consumption in China has reached more than 300,[3] and it has basically shown a trend of increasing year by year. However, with the development of society, the iteration of technology update and the emergence of a new Internet

[1] See Li [8], 193–195.

[2] See Hu and Zhou [5], 135–143.

[3] See Lawyee [18].

Kailiang MA is a law PhD student in the University of Paris-Sud/University of Paris-Saclay and he is sponsored by China Scholarship Council. He focusses on the research of company law, corporate governance, financial law, consumer law and family law.

M. A. Kailiang (✉)
University of Paris-Sud/University of Paris-Saclay, Orsay, France
e-mail: kailiang.ma@hotmail.com

D. Wei et al. (eds.), *Innovation and the Transformation of Consumer Law*,
https://doi.org/10.1007/978-981-15-8948-5_9

transaction model, it is a problem we have to think about that how to deal with the risks brought about by the new trading model.

To a certain extent, in the Internet society, the law cannot be arbitrarily revised at any time, which determines that the law regulating social relations will always be lagging behind. This does not mean that the risks brought about by the new trading model cannot be relied upon. In fact, the traditional legal system can adjust most of the social risks, but we need to think about how to achieve maximum judicial justice and social justice. Since the development of blockchain technology, smart contracts have been the core of related transactions. Although blockchain technology is still in the development stage, insurance companies in many countries, including China, have taken the lead in researching and using blockchain technology to reduce transactions cost to protect the interests of consumers. China is currently in a high-speed development stage in the research of blockchain technology and has a certain representativeness. We must also acknowledge that there are still certain risks in the application of smart contracts to the insurance market. Therefore, this paper will focus on the challenges and solutions for the protection of smart insurance contracts in the context of Chinese law.

2 Smart Contracts and Consumer Rights Protection

The main basis of consumers interacting with other market participants is the consumer contract, because a contract means that the production of a series of rights and obligations. And in the market, many situations that the consumer rights are violated are reflected in the contract and the interpretation of the contract, so no matter any time, we should pay close attention that how to safeguard the interests of the consumers more fairly when they want to conclude commercial contracts.

The development of technology has changed every aspect of social life, and also improved the way of contract conclusion in the protection of consumer rights. The generation and development of smart contracts can be said to be a double-edged sword for the protection of consumer rights. It is necessary for us to conduct in-depth analysis on this.

2.1 Understanding of Smart Contracts

The concept of a smart contract was first proposed by Nick Szabo, a famous American computer scientist and jurist in the 1990s, which can be regarded as the research of intersection between law and computer science in the early days.[4] However, due to the immature computer technology at that time and the lack of reliable execution environment for the application of smart contract, smart contracts were not

[4]See Savelyev [14], 116–134.

applied in the actual industry. But, since the birth of bitcoin, people have realized the underlying technology of bitcoin, namely blockchain technology, which can provide a more favorable execution environment for the development of smart contracts.[5] And, Ethereum, which is very popular now, first discovered the convergence point of blockchain and smart contracts.

A smart contract program is not just a computer program that can execute automatically. It is a system participant in its own right, and it can respond to the information it receives. At the same time, it can receive and store value as well as send out information and value. Generally speaking, smart contracts are contracts that can be automatically executed on computer systems under certain conditions.

However, as far as the current situation is concerned, the important reason that it has not been widely used, is still the issue of trust. Often in the real world, a contract is a paper that only takes effect after it has been signed. But in the computer world, where contracts are recorded in code, digitized contracts face the moral hazard of being tampered with, or the technical risk of being hacked.[6] If the service is provided by a large financial institution such as a bank, then consumers may trust it, but if the same service is applied to e-commerce or personal websites, once the risk occurs, the difficulty of consumer proof will be greatly increased. Therefore, it becomes a problem that how to design smart contract program effectively and we must consider seriously.

2.2 The Relationship Between Smart Contracts and Consumer Rights Protection

2.2.1 Ways to Protect Consumer Rights

In the traditional concept, the basic principle of contract law is contract autonomy. The counterparty can not only conclude and perform contracts based on the will of both parties, but also modify and violate contracts according to their own will, and even have the right to decide to refuse to perform. For smart contracts, due to the nature of their automatic execution, once the will of the parties is recorded in the code, the contract will automatically start running by default, unless the parties add procedures to modify or stop execution in the smart contract. Otherwise there will be no changes to the contract. In this case, the fair-trading rights of consumers can be better protected, because one of the biggest problems facing consumers when defending their rights is the burden of proof, and the openness of smart contracts and transparency narrows the information gap between consumers and sellers and producers.[7] When consumers feel that their rights have been violated, they can choose

[5] See Iansiti and Lakhani [6], 1–11.

[6] See Mostert and Wang [9], 15–42.

[7] See Witherspoon [16].

their traditional ways to protect their legitimate rights and interests, and they can also solve the disputes through technical means.

2.2.2 Challenges to Consumer Rights Protection in the Technological Age

In China, the legal system of consumer rights protection is regarded as special laws and regulations to protect vulnerable subjects, which is reflected in the design of legal provisions. Lawmakers believe that for goods and services, sellers and producers have much more information than consumers, so in the market economy, if the government does not take the initiative to intervene, consumers' rights are easily infringed. Therefore, in the legal system of consumer rights protection in China, consumers, as the weak subject, are given preferential protection.

However, smart contracts pursue an egalitarian philosophy and do not distinguish between the identity of the counterparty. At the same time, based on the pseudonym mechanism, in the process of running smart contracts, it is impossible to distinguish the identity of the parties.[8] In this context, this technical operation of smart contracts cannot better reflect the humanistic concept of protecting the weak. It can be said that this poses a serious challenge to the consumer rights protection law under the current legal background.

Moreover, in the current society, smart contracts are still in the stage of emerging development, and consumers have little experience with the automatic consequences of signing smart contracts. For example, in the scenario where loans are needed to purchase goods, it is difficult for consumers to pay for new payment systems. The guaranteed loan recovery risk is accurately estimated. Smart contracts put consumers into pre-set risks, and they themselves have difficulty recognizing the automatic consequences of violations. Even if consumers are aware of this, they may not fully understand the impact of lack of familiarity with this model.

3 New Attempts Made by Chinese Insurance Companies to Protect Consumers' Rights Under the Background of Technological Development

In the early days of blockchain and smart contracts, China has created a large number of entities that use smart contract technology to develop new business models. Especially in the insurance field, a number of Chinese insurance companies have started to develop smart contract products to assist them in signing contracts with customers. However, from the current situation, the actual implementation of blockchain technology in the insurance industry is still relatively small. The main problem is

[8]See Ryan [12], 14–21.

that insurance information is still limited by supervision, chain performance and authenticity.

3.1 The Concept of "Consumer" Under the Chinese Legal System

In China, customers who purchase insurance products can be called "consumers" in the Chinese consumer rights protection law system.[9] It has different understandings and arguments in China's theoretical and practical circles. According to the latest revised China Consumer Law, consumers are the mainstay of purchasing goods or services for the needs of life.[10] Then, when we consider the relationship between the insurance company's smart contract and consumer rights protection, we should first clarify the specific circumstances under which the entity that deals with the insurance company can be called a consumer.[11] And at the same time, it is necessary to clarify the basic characteristics of these subjects to know the problems arising from the commercial practices of Chinese insurance companies.

The main body of insurance products purchased by insurance companies is regarded as financial consumers in many countries and regions, such as the United Kingdom, Japan and Taiwan, but there are differences in the United States, which was mandated under the Dodd-frank Wall Street Reform and Consumer Protection Act.[12] There are corresponding regulations and explanations in the Protection Act. For the protection of the rights of financial consumers, many countries have also developed a special financial consumer bill, but the current China has not set up a special bill targeting the weak subjects in consumer behavior, and mainland China only has China Consumer Law to regulate the market subjects. But in fact, the subjects who buy insurance products from insurance companies can be bound by China Consumer Law, which is a controversial issue in China.

The "controversy point" is whether the original intention of purchasing insurance products is for the needs of life. China Consumer Law does not explicitly reject or deny this. And China also has another basis for the ruling, it clearly states that according to the regulations issued in 2016, financial consumers are natural persons who purchase and use financial products and services provided by financial institutions.[13] It should be noted that the field of financial consumption covers both financial products and financial services. The so-called financial institutions include the securities, insurance and banks, but they are not limited to those, as long as they provide

[9]Namely Law of the People's Republic of China on the Protection of Consumer Rights and Interests (hereinafter referred to as China Consumer Law).

[10]See Article 2 of China Consumer Law.

[11]See Thomas [15], 294–318.

[12]See Section 2 of Dodd-frank Wall Street Reform and Consumer Protection Act.

[13]See Article 2 of Notice of the People's Bank of China on Issuing the Implementation Measures of the People's Bank of China for Protecting Financial Consumers' Rights and Interests.

financial services to consumers.[14] And other financial institutions approved by the People's Bank of China are also included in the scope. The financial services here should be interpreted in a broad sense, including financial institutions selling financial products such as funds to consumers, as well as financial institutions providing financial services such as deposits, loans and insurance.[15]

In fact, the extension of the concept of consumers is not certain. In some specific situations, the subject of certain behaviors may be regarded as consumers, but also as other subjects. Then, for the identification of the consumer subject, law should be combined with social development. They can be private rights, but they also have the attributes of social rights. So, in many civil law countries, the consumer rights protection law system is classified as the composition of economic law.[16] In part, these reflect the complexity of consumer attributes. Consumers are the product of the changes in the legal personality era. The strength of legal subjects is increasingly differentiated with the development of the economy.[17] The specific personality of consumers as natural persons appears in the consumer society should be based on the development of technology in the traditional private rights system.

3.2 Attempts by Chinese Insurance Companies to Protect Consumer Rights

3.2.1 ZhongAn Online P&C Insurance Co. Ltd

ZhongAn Online P&C Insurance Co. Ltd (hereinafter referred to as ZhongAn) is China's first blockchain insurance company, and all business processes are online processing. In 2018, the company put forward the concept of universal certification of insurance and planned to gradually realize universal certification of its own and even the industry's insurance products under the premise of effective supervision.[18]At the same time, ZhongAn also launched the block chain foundation platform for chain cloud, to provide more than 10 areas of block chain solutions.[19]

In the second direction, ZhongAn launched the professional ecological cloud service platform: Security Chain Cloud based on artificial intelligence, block chain and cryptography. This platform is an independent research and development tool and ZhongAn Chain is the basic infrastructure and has developed nearly 10 vertical

[14]See Notice of the People's Bank of China on Issuing the Implementation Measures of the People's Bank of China for Protecting Financial Consumers' Rights and Interests.

[15]See Xu and Wei [17], 90–93.

[16]In China, consumer law is one part of economic law systems.

[17]See Joshua [7], 35–43.

[18]See Xu and Wei [17], 90–93.

[19]Block chain application: ZhongAn Online push insurance product certification. (2019). Retrieved from https://www.coinonpro.com/news/toutiao/41054.html.

applications such as electronic contract signing, digital identity, distributed encrypted storage, storage certificate, and traceability.[20]

3.2.2 Sunshine Insurance Group

Sunshine Insurance Group (hereinafter referred to as Sunshine Insurance) is a famous insurance company in China, which performs well in financial technology and introduces the basic application of its block chain: "Sunshine bay" integral plan and "Feichanghui" aviation accident insurance.[21]In March 2016, Sunshine Insurance launched the "Sunshine Shell" credits based on the block chain as the underlying technology architecture.[22]Users can transfer the credits to their friends in the form of "sending red envelopes" based on the ordinary credit function and exchange the credits with other companies' blockchain credits. At the end of July 2016, Sunshine Insurance and the professional company in the blockchain field: the Bubi blockchain cooperation launched the "blockchain + aviation accident insurance card list"—"Fei Chang Hui" aviation accident insurance card, which is China's first attempt to circulate mainstream financial assets on the blockchain.[23] It is also one of the main products of smart contracts in the insurance market in the Chinese market. In addition, Sunshine Insurance uses the certification and security features of the blockchain to perform secondary authentication. When the user logs in, the mobile phone can be swiped to achieve blockchain authentication.

4 Benefits Brought by Smart Contracts to the Protection of Consumer Rights in Insurance Companies Under the Chinese Legal System

China's current insurance companies' attempts to research smart contracts are essentially the exploration of blockchain technology in the insurance field. Therefore, when discussing the advantages of smart contracts, we cannot avoid the exploration of blockchain technology. Both in China and the rest of the world, blockchain and smart contracts have had an important impact on the rights of consumers.

---

[20]Distributed identity-the cornerstone of the future trust ecosystem. (2019). Retrieved from https://www.chainnews.com/articles/249423010519.htm.

[21]See Su [13].

[22]Creating the blockchain digital insurance development ecosystem. (2018). Retrieved from http://chsh.sinoins.com/2018-02/27/content_255520.htm.

[23]Blockchain application analysis report of domestic insurance industry. (2017). Retrieved from https://www.8btc.com/article/132541.

4.1 Smart Contracts and Consumer Trading Security Rights

The certainty of smart contracts and the invariance of blockchains ensure the safety of funds and information. The invariance of the blockchain is to maintain a complete and distributed continuous database using the new encryption authentication technology and the network-wide consensus mechanism.[24] The book system and the "time stamp mechanism" have high security traceability and are able to query every insurance transaction record which can ensure the security of funds and information, and avoid deliberate tampering.[25] This will greatly change the content ecology of existing insurance, make high-quality content more valuable and better disseminated, especially hope to reconstruct a new and sophisticated insurance credit system.

In addition, the use of smart contract methods for insurance transactions can ensure that the transaction automatically completes the corresponding obligations to ensure the security of the transaction, thereby reducing the credit risk of the transaction object. At the same time, it can help customers solve some complex trading obstacles while protecting customer privacy.

4.2 Smart Contracts and Fair-Trade Right

Smart contracts can solve many insurance problems, especially in the actual trading process. Fair trade often has a lot of uncertainty, and smart contract technology provides a new solution. According to China Consumer Law, fair trade means that consumers have the right to obtain fair trade conditions such as quality assurance, reasonable price, and correct measurement when purchasing goods or receiving services, and have the right to refuse the mandatory transaction of the operator.[26]

First, smart contracts are truly new tools for organizing complex systems that combine with the insurance industry, which can address the authenticity of information and the efficiency of delivery. The basic technical means of smart contracts has a unique and traceable source of information recognized by the participants. Therefore, in the value chain links such as insurance, underwriting, claims, and customer service,[27] it can solve the problem caused by information asymmetry. Specifically, it can help to prevent the fraud insurance, the insured customer information loss stolen. Technically, the preservation and inquiry of insurance records can also be achieved through traditional technology, but the major problem in traditional technology is that it cannot prevent tampering. The tampering with the data alone leads to mutual distrust between the organizations, mutual distrust between users and institutions,

---

[24] Peer-to-peer network. (2019). Retrieved from https://www.binance.vision/zh/blockchain/peer-to-peer-networks-explained.

[25] See Giancaspro [2], 825–835.

[26] See Article 10 of China Consumer Law.

[27] See Herian [4].

and ultimately the incompatibility of information.[28] This is why insurance companies spend huge sums of money each year to prevent insurance fraud, which is why annual insurance companies lose huge amounts of money because of insurance fraud. The emergence of smart contract technology has reduced the possibility of insurance fraud. The insurance contract is written to the distributed ledger through the smart contract. The so-called distributed ledger is the basic application of blockchain technology in building smart contracts. In this process, any institution participating in the alliance chain holds the same fully consistent ledger, and any institution that falsifies the ledger will be discovered or treated as invalid by the blockchain platform.[29] In addition, a large part of the distributed ledger is usually configurable, depending on the design of the blockchain platform architecture, which is the consensus mechanism chosen by the designer. If it is designed for higher transaction security, it can be designed as a full institutional consensus. Therefore, blockchain technology reduces the possibility of fraud.

Second, smart contract technology can further protect consumers' fair-trading rights by promoting regulatory technology. The irrevocable and non-repudiation retention characteristics of the smart contract approach will promote the regulation. Once the insurance company transfers the daily operational process to the blockchain and opens a billing node to the regulatory body, the regulator can easily observe all the insurance company's business trends in real time, including all transactions, smart contracts, capital flows and investment composition. It can track any transaction in real time and monitor risks in time without waiting for the event. It also facilitates automated compliance processing for participants to increase transparency, avoid fraud, and achieve more effective regulation.

4.3 Smart Contracts and the Claim of Consumers' Damages

In the process of purchasing any goods or services, consumers may encounter dissatisfaction with the purchases. In this regard, China Consumer Law gives relatively clear regulations to fully protect consumers' damages repayment.[30]

First, the decentralization of smart contracts increases the transparency of insurance claims. The application of smart contracts will enable insurers to implement automatic claims, improve claims efficiency, increase the transparency of claims, and reduce the need for centralized operations.[31] Moreover, since the smart contracts on the blockchain are all defined by code and then automatically enforced, the process is relatively transparent. So, the claim method is relatively simple, and the loss result is relatively more accurate, which avoids the subjective decision bias and errors caused by manual operation.

---

[28]See Oscar [10].

[29]See Oscar [11], 885–902.

[30]See Chapter VII Legal Liability of China Consumer Law.

[31]See Cuccuru [1], 179–195.

Secondly, due to the decentralized trust mechanism of the smart contract participants, real-time insurance transaction settlement and liquidation can be realized, and the insurance disintermediation mechanism can be realized, thereby greatly reducing the time for settlement or liquidation.[32] Moreover, in the insurance transaction process, many repeated verification and operation processes can be simplified or eliminated, thereby greatly improving operational efficiency.

4.4 Smart Contracts and the Innovation of Insurance Products as Well as Services

First of all, it is now the era of mobile Internet, and in the future, the Internet of Things[33] era will certainly become possible. "Internet of Everything" is an unstoppable trend. In this process, the Internet still plays a fundamental role, which also means the Internet will greatly benefit ordinary consumers in the future. Applying smart contracts to the field of Internet insurance will bring about tremendous changes in payments, clearing, transactions, and confirmation of rights in the Internet insurance field, and will help traditional insurance to transform to Internet insurance in terms of credit and security. It can make insurance and deep integration of Internet technologies, which will be helpful to promote scientific and reasonable, safe and efficient Internet insurance business model, so that Internet insurance will benefit social consumers on a larger scale and deeper level.

Secondly, data sharing can be achieved through smart contracts, which will enable consumers to more accurately assess their own risks and thus match more suitable insurance products, greatly enriching consumers' freedom of choice in insurance products. By big data, the consumer can share data on personal insurance, auto insurance, pension payments, and credit insurance. If blockchain technology is introduced into health records and electronic cases, hospitals, pharmacies, pensions, medical examinations, Internet medical care and insurance can share and use these data independently, creating huge possibilities for personal insurance, especially health insurance.

Finally, smart contracts will reduce the operating costs of insurance companies, which will encourage Chinese insurance companies to develop products that are more beneficial to consumers in the market competition. In order to prevent single points of failure and systemic risks, the insurance industry needs to conduct layer-by-layer audits to control risks, which also results in high internal costs. Blockchain technology can greatly reduce the cost of the entire insurance system by preventing tampering and a highly transparent approach.[34] Moreover, the insurance companies have very rich consumer data, and can directly add blockchain modules in the mobile backend, which can greatly reduce operating costs. Moreover, insurance products

---

[32]See Cuccuru [1], 179–195.

[33]See Internet of things. (2019). Retrieved from https://en.wikipedia.org/wiki/Internet_of_things.

[34]See Cuccuru [1], 179–195.

are mostly community products. Many mature products and certain users can be better combined with blockchain, making it easier to spread in the later promotion. Blockchain technology can also help create more cost-effective microinsurance products that can flexibly adjust insurance product coverage and pricing to meet needs of individual, customized, differentiated and fragmented product.

5 Challenges Posed by the Smart Contract to the Protection of Consumer Rights Under the Chinese Legal System

5.1 Accurate Expression of Contract Terms

In the insurance transaction process, the program code is not able to accurately express the semantics of the contract terms at present, and the terms of the smart contract are difficult to accurately express the meaning of the parties.[35] In real life, limited by the ambiguity of semantic expression and the volatility of objective conditions, there are often cases where the law does not stipulate or the parties have not agreed, and the legal provisions or contract terms need to be explained, and such interpretations often involve complex interest trade-offs. And value judgments should rely on credible third parties to decide from them; but smart contracts rely entirely on computer language-written procedures to verify and enforce between parties. In the current context, sometimes consumers do not understand smart contracts, which can easily lead to infringement of the consumer's right to know and fair trade.

Smart contract technology is still in the initial stage of exploration. Opportunities and risks coexist, and there are still many major problems.[36] There is still a gap between the theory and commercial operation. Although smart contract technology may subvert trade, capital markets, lending, cross-border payments and other industries, there is still a certain gap from the real commercial operation. Besides, the threshold of technical application should be reduced. It is necessary to reduce the application threshold of blockchain technology by introducing technologies and designs such as open chain access protocols, cornerstone programs, and distributed subscription gateways, so that insurance organizations can directly deploy and apply them. It is necessary to explore the feasibility of medium and high frequency trading. At present, the application of smart contracts in the insurance industry is still in the low-frequency commercial transaction stage in Chinese insurance companies, which means that we still need to continue to explore the feasibility of developing high-frequency commercial transactions in technology. Then in the era of rapid development of blockchain technology, the protection of consumer rights cannot rely solely on smart contracts. In fact, the protection of consumer rights should be systematic,

[35]See Raskin [19], 305–340.

[36]Smart contracts face an immediate challenge, code or legal dispute. (2016). Retrieved from http://www.sohu.com/a/120453524_556089.

and it requires the coordinated development of multiple technologies. Specifically, blockchain technology has yet to cooperate with other related technologies such as the big data, biometrics, artificial intelligence in order to form insurance technology capabilities and highlight financial technology attributes, and ultimately to build an "ecology" for insurance companies to protect consumer rights.[37] Furthermore, personal information data protection still needs improvement. In the trading parties of the smart contract, each participant can get a complete data backup, all transaction data is open and transparent, which is a significant advantage. But at the same time, this is also a big problem because users themselves want their account privacy and transaction information to be protected. At this point, conflicts between different interests are formed. After these conflicts are properly resolved, smart contract technology can really improve the quality of consumer rights protection. Insurance companies still need to face new regulatory issues and legal risks. With the application and development of blockchain technology, the existing legal framework may not provide a comprehensive consumer rights protection system, which means that new regulatory issues and legal risks may arise.[38] While the existing legal and regulatory frameworks are not fully applicable to smart contracts, it is a problem that how to enforce them in the international network of blockchains and smart contracts.

5.2 The Trouble with Computer Codes

In according with Article 15 and Article 16[39] of China's Insurance Law, contract cancellation and termination system are simply unable to be applied. Moreover, this has a great conflict with the "right of contrite" stipulated in Article 25[40] of China Consumer Law and will also affect the realization of consumers' right of claim. In smart contract execution process, all need to obey their set in advance good code. If a party want to have other options and codes do not provide alternatives, then codes are not intelligent.

---

[37]See Witherspoon [16].

[38]See Witherspoon [16].

[39]Article 15 of China's Insurance Law stipulates that after an insurance contract is formed, the insurance applicant may, but the insurer may not, rescind the contract, except as otherwise provided for by this Law or as otherwise agreed upon in the insurance contract. And Article 16 stipulates that where the insurance applicant fails to perform the obligation of telling the truth as prescribed in the preceding paragraph intentionally or for gross negligence, affecting the insurer's decision on whether to underwrite the insurance or raise the insurance premium, the insurer shall have the right to rescind the insurance contract.

[40]Article 25 of China Consumer Law stipulates that where business operators sell commodities on the Internet, on television, over telephone, or by mail order, among others, consumers shall have the right to return the commodities within seven days of receipt of them without cause, except the following commodities: (1) Custom-made commodities. (2) Fresh, live, or perishable commodities. (3) Audio-visual recordings, computer software, and other digital commodities downloaded online or unpacked by consumers. (4) Newspapers or periodicals delivered.

From another perspective, this also leads to the intensification of the conflict between efficiency and equity. The basic unit of smart contract is data, but in the process of automatic execution of contract, the screening of effective data should not only ensure the improvement of execution efficiency, but also ensure the fair screening process of data for both parties, which is determined by the advantages of smart contract and the nature of contract.[41] However, due to the complexity of the data itself, the existing data processing technology cannot fully achieve this. Secondly, China's civil code is being formulated, and there are some obstacles to the application of smart contract. According to the revised content, the parties may agree on the interests of a third party, but the premise must be favorable to the third party.[42] This raises questions about the automatic execution of smart contracts, because the process involves comparison of benefits and value judgment, which is inherently uncertain. Obviously, the code cannot fully explain values. In addition, China Contract Law provides for unpredictable situations in the execution of contracts,[43] while smart contracts themselves lack consideration in this aspect.

5.3 Difficulties in the Application of Laws by Multinational Corporations

China is pushing ahead with the Belt and Road Initiative, [44]which has led to Chinese companies interacting with foreign companies very frequently. At present, the two insurance companies mentioned above have certain ability to conduct exchanges with foreign companies. Therefore, there are a large number of transnational contracts in actual operation. However, the legal system of China is quite different from that of common law countries, so the procedural setting of transnational smart contract will present a more complicated situation. For the governance of Chinese insurance companies, the premise of integrating smart contract into Chinese legal system is to clarify its normative basis, evaluation standard and feasible business model. However, the application of smart contract in China is only limited to a specific simple scenario, and its future development still faces great challenges.

[41] See Savelyev [14], 116–134.

[42] For example, according to Article 35 of General Provisions of the Civil Law of the People's Republic of China, a guardian shall perform the duty of guardianship under the principle of most benefiting the ward. The guardian shall not dispose of the ward's property unless for safeguarding the ward's interests.

[43] Article 94 of China Contract Law stipulates that the parties to a contract may terminate the contract under any of the following circumstances: (1) it is rendered impossible to achieve the purpose of contract due to an event of force majeure.

[44] See Li [8], 193–197.

6 China's Response to the Challenges Brought by Smart Insurance Contracts to the Protection of Chinese Consumer Rights

6.1 Responsibilities of Consumer Organizations

In the future, consumer associations should set up special committees or departments to solve the contradictions caused by technologies such as financial technology, but they need to be composed of people with professional knowledge. From the perspective of state intervention, we must have a matching assessment mechanism for professional issues. This is mainly due to the existence of unfair terms or format clauses. Although smart contracts can effectively solve the fraud between consumers and sellers or producers, they can also make consumers' information about products or services more transparent to a certain extent. However, in essence, there is no way to completely guarantee transactions. The information of both parties is equal, so when a transaction situation similar to the overlord clause occurs, the interests of consumers will be easily lost. At this time, the society should have an effective rescue mechanism.

Consumer rights protection organizations have a long history of development, and their development in China has experienced a transition from civil organizations to state departments. However, regardless of its nature, in the context of the times, we all need specific professionals to achieve its role.

6.2 Attributes of Smart Contracts and the Reorganization of Relevant Legal Systems

Now, because a smart contract is still in the initial stage of development, the current application situation is still relatively limited, and the problems that may arise are still in the exploration stage. After China has collected enough information on legislative issues in the future, defining the nature will be very necessary.

Since China is a statute country, it is only a reference to the jurisprudence. It is not like the common law countries which are mainly based on precedents. Then, if there is a conflict in the application of the legal provisions, it will lead directly to similar cases but different judgments, which is not a good thing for the authority of the law. Therefore, from the perspective of the long-term development of China's blockchain technology, the law should give a clear definition at an appropriate time, which can promote the unification of relevant theories and social practices.[45]

[45]See Mostert and Wang [9], 15–42.

6.3 *Bilateral or Multilateral Agreements on Blockchain and Smart Contracts*

China can establish a series of bilateral or multilateral agreements on blockchain and smart contracts in the future to actively promote the establishment of an international science and technology legal system. As a matter of fact, blockchain and smart contract are still in the preliminary application stage, and their scenarios have great limitations. In international commercial business, countries and regions have not yet established some effective regulatory frameworks and legal systems, so they can only negotiate and communicate on the basis of existing laws. However, in the long run, the international commercial business of insurance companies still has great development potential, which requires their business teams to fully study the laws and regulations of various countries to achieve business compliance. On the other hand, it is also an opportunity for China's legal development. As China is now rich in research and practice in relevant fields, it should seek the possibility of establishing corresponding international rules in the future, which also has great potential for the business development of Chinese insurance companies and the protection of consumer rights.

7 Conclusion

China's consumer rights protection legal system is rapidly adapting to the needs of social development and is constantly being improved. In the wave of blockchain and smart contract development, Chinese insurance companies take the lead in conducting various forms of exploration, which is of great significance to China's long-term development of commercial technology in the future. Before the emergence of smart contracts, the relationship between insurance companies and consumers are tricky. The main problem is that insurance companies use information advantages to infringe on the legitimate interests of consumers. Smart contracts make using of technology to expand the transparency of the transaction process, save transaction costs, and greatly increase the possibility of consumer rights protection on the existing basis. However, it must be acknowledged that the development of smart contract technology still requires more business scenarios. Now the development of insurance companies still has great limitations. In the context of Chinese law, the commercial application of smart contract is faced with conflicts between legal provisions and interpretation. And its role in eliminating information disadvantage is still limited, which leads to more challenges in domestic and international communication. China should continuously update its laws and regulations in accordance with the development of insurance business in the future, so as to improve the consumer rights protection framework in other countries in the era of smart contracts. Smart contracts are both challenges and opportunities for countries around the world.

References

1. Cuccuru, P. (2017). *Beyond Bitcoin: An Early Overview on Smart Contracts*. International Journal of Law and Information Technology. 25: 179–195.
2. Giancaspro, M. (2017). Is a 'Smart Contract' Really a Smart Idea? Insights from a Legal Perspective. *Computer Law & Security Review*. 6: 825–835.
3. Gabriel, J. (2018). *Smart Contracts and the Role of Law*. Retrieved from https://ssrn.com/abstract=3099885.
4. Herian, R. (2018). *Legal Recognition of Blockchain Registries and Smart Contracts*. Retrieved from https://www.eublockchainforum.eu/sites/default/files/research-paper/legal_recognition_of_blockchain_registries_and_smart_contracts_final_draft_report_appendix.pdf?width=1024&height=800&iframe=true.
5. Hu, G.Z., & Zhou, Q. (2014). On Consumer Protection in China's Internet Finance Innovation. *Law Review*,6,135–143.
6. Iansiti, M., & Lakhani, K.R. (2017). The Truth About Blockchain. *Harvard Business Review*. 1–11.
7. *Joshua A, F.* (2014). Smart Contracts, Bitcoin Bots, and Consumer Protection. *Washington and Lee Law Review Online*,2, 35–43.
8. Li, G.Q. (2014). On the Interpretation of Consumer's Civil Subject Positioning in the Context of Civil Law on Consumer Rights Protection. *Chinese Journal of Law*. 6, 193–197.
9. Mostert, F. & Wang, J. (2018). The Application and Challenges of Blockchain in Intellectual Property Driven Businesses in China. *Tsinghua China Law Review*. 11:15–42.
10. Oscar, B. (2019). The Pursuit of Usefulness: On the Value of Smart Contracts for Consumers and Merchants. Retrieved from https://ssrn.com/abstract=3350128.
11. Oscar, B. (2018). Smart Contracts as the (New) Power of the Powerless? The Stakes for Consumers. *European Review of Private Law*. 6: 885–902.
12. Ryan, P. (2017). Smart Contract Relations in e-Commerce: Legal Implications of Exchanges Conducted on the Blockchain. *Technology Innovation Management Review*.7:14–21.
13. Su, W.L. (2017). *The Block Chain Brings in Brand New Opportunities*. Retrieved from https://www.soa.org/globalassets/assets/files/e-business/pd/events/2017/soa-china-symposium/2017-china-symposium-session-4-block.pdf.
14. Savelyev, A. (2017). Contract law 2.0: 'Smart' Contracts as the Beginning of the End of Classic Contract Law, *Information & Communications Technology Law*, 26:2, 116–134.
15. Thomas,K. (2018). Analysing the Notion of 'Consumer' in China's Consumer Protection Law. *The Chinese Journal of Comparative Law*,6, 294–318.
16. Witherspoon, Z. (2017). Advancing Consumer Adoption of Blockchain Applications. Retrieved from file:///Users/bruce/Downloads/SSRN-id2966321%20(2).pdf.
17. Xu, Z.Y., & Wei, T. (2013). On the Right of Withdrawal of Consumers from the Perspective of Civil Code. *Journal of Henan Normal University*, 2, 90–93.
18. Lawyee. (2019). Retrieved from http://www.lawyee.org/.
19. Raskin, M. (2017). The Law and Legality of Smart Contracts. The Georgetown Law Technology Review. 1:305–340.

Consumer Law Facing the Advent of the Child E-Consumer

Maxime Peron

1 Introduction

The current society is characterized by a mass-consumption, targeting all subjects of law, including a particularly vulnerable public: children.[1] Several scenes from everyday life can testify to the encounter between children and the consumer market, like the many advertisements aimed at them, the pocket money they can benefit from, products and services specially created for them, or the various celebrations in their honor as Christmas and birthday. It can also be considered that the various gifts offered to him contribute to the child's legal involvement by joining his patrimony. Moreover, although indirect, it could be the minor's first confrontation with the reality of the consumerist world in which he or she has just been born.

Should we legally legitimize this early confrontation of the child by this world pressing him to consume when he is recognized as particularly vulnerable and in need of an adequate legal protection ?[2]

The existence of an adequate protection for children is expressed in Human rights, since the child has become a subject of fundamental rights through the United Nations International Convention of children's rights, but also in the French and Brazilian legal systems, particularly through the civil law with the incapacity, which may have been influenced by international texts.

[1] In France and Brazil, the minor is the person up to the age of 18. This statement may also use the terms children and adolescents as provided for in the Statute of the child and the Brazilian teenager to refer to the minor.

[2] « The child, by reason of his physical and mental immaturity, needs special safeguards and care, including appropriate legal protection », Preamble of the Declaration of the Rights of the Child, 1959.

M. Peron (✉)
Univ. Brest, Brest, France
e-mail: maximeperon@yahoo.fr

LAB-LEX, University of São Paulo, São Paulo, EA 7480, Brazil

D. Wei et al. (eds.), *Innovation and the Transformation of Consumer Law*,
https://doi.org/10.1007/978-981-15-8948-5_10

The importance of consumption in the children's world raises doubts about the adequacy between traditional protective rules and the consumerist world's danger. Two questions are worth asking. The first question is to know if, in consumer matters, they are protected by the law. The analysis of positive law allows to plan two protection approaches: the first one, the civilist, meaning that the incapacity is enough for its protection; the second one is consumerist, where considered as consumers, the children would be protected by the consumer law. The second question is to know if the advent of new technologies doesn't disturb this protection link and doesn't weaken children's connection with any consumption's forms. The answer of both questions is indicator of the innovation and transformation of the consumer law.

Indeed, the particular vulnerability of children also consumers encourage to think about the consumer law, taking into account the aim of an adapted protection for children and teenagers. Nowadays, the consumer law gives only low protection to children. Therefore, this protection deserves to be extended to answer current and future issues of the child as consumer, involving a consumer law's evolution.

Furthermore, the new technologies' emergence participates to the innovation and transformation of consumer law by creating new risks for consumers, especially for children, who are particularly exposed to new way of communication, to e-trade and to limits porosity between the real and the virtual. Legal mechanisms of the consumer law have to adapt themselves to those new risks.

To give answer to these both questions, legal protection tools in the French and the Brazilian laws will be used to plan to improve the protection of the children as consumers. To achieve this improvement, compare the two laws' systems (II) can help to recognize children as particularly vulnerable consumers, which vulnerability would increase in terms of e-commerce (III). Improving the child's protection requires a law's transformation, and especially a consumer law's transformation, when there is a dematerialized consumer relation. These innovation and transformation of the consumer law are, in some aspects, beginning because specific protective rules already exist (IV).

2 The Comparative France-Brazil Approach as Reflection

If it seems difficult to define the comparative law, it is sure it is a legal science which allow to learn, to improve to understand his domestic law, to try to improve it, to meet new legal mechanisms, to think about it own law's understanding and about its aim in our society. To reach this goal, a "bridge" has to be built to compare. The simple compilation of information must be excluded because it is necessary to create original reflections by "entering" into foreign law. Consequently, one of the keys to comparative law is the knowledge of a foreign law, not only about the law but also of the culture, the philosophy and sociology of the country. The legal understanding's stage leads to the discovery of new legal mechanisms which can be confronted. Any comparative law research exposes to difficulties but also to advantages. However, rather than talking about the difficulties, it is better to see comparative law as a challenge. Thus, a comparative reflection oscillates between challenges (A) and advantages (B).

(A) **The challenge of the comparatist approach**

The challenge of the comparatist approach is revealed, for example, in the choice and with the meaning of words. In law, the choice of words has always been important because words can set the law in motion. Above all, word can give a meaning to the law.

In comparative law, words' choice characterizes an even more important step for the comparatist who during his translation, has to take precautions to ensure that the law's spirit is preserved. If research may require a translation, retaining the original text would be the most judicious option, allowing us to ask about the legitimacy of translating a foreign law. Indeed, the original version preserves the meaning and the spirit of law on the condition that we can understand this sense and this spirit.

It should also be remembered that the choice of words can show the importance which is given by the legislator to a point of law. The mere observation of the drafting of certain laws allows to speculate on some conclusions about the meaning given to the law, as it is possible to do when we are comparing the French and Brazilian laws.

For example, on one hand when French law deals with consumption law, on the other hand Brazilian law deals with consumer law. By choosing these words, we are allowed to think that the Brazilian law is based on (the person of) the consumer whereas French law seems to be based on the consumer relationship, or even more specifically on the consumption contract. This idea is confirmed by reading the codes in this area, because France has opted for a consumption code, and Brazil has opted for a code of defence and consumer protection. The words' choice seems to confirm the center of gravity of the French and Brazilian laws. While French law puts consumption relations at the forefront, Brazilian law is part of a consumer protection perspective. The choice of the terms "defence" and "protection" in the appellation reinforces this idea. Of course, this choice does not mean that French law does not protect the consumer or that the Brazilian law does not frame the consumption relationship,[3] but this words' choice helps to orient the analysis of these two laws.

If the choice of terms can be justified by the aim that the legislature intended to give to the laws, it can also be justified by a particular local context. In France, civil law regularly referres to children and teenager, but many studies evoke the existence of a minor law. At the international scale, the idea of childhood is met with the International Convention on the rights of the child by using the term « children ». However, in Brazil, the terms child and adolescent are used. This choice is justified by a particular historical context. The notion of « minor » was present in Brazilian laws for many years, particularly through the minors' code. However, this concept was part of the movement of the doctrine of irregular situation which had established a discriminatory distinction between minors based on several parameters including origins and social conditions. The current drafting of the Federal Constitution of 1988

---

[3]G. Paisant, id. at 6.

and the creation of a Statute for children and adolescents in 1990 have put an end to this doctrine of irregular situation. Henceforth, the doctrine of integral protection was inscribed in the Brazilian legal landscape by dismissing the term "minor" and emphasizing the terms "child" and "adolescent".

Concerning French law, the term "minor" does not have this discriminatory connotation, so his employment does not generate any difficulty. Nevertheless, the use of the term does not escape criticism because the "minor" opposed to the term "major", he describes a situation of inferiority. In addition, the term "child" appears neutral. Why does French law favor the term minor? Once again, this choice can be justified by the meaning of the word "child", which in French law describes the relationship of filiation: a person can be a child without being a minor.

Through this example, the importance of the historical and social context is demonstrated to understand a foreign law, and that this context influences the meaning of the words chosen in each law. As a result, and as the example of the formulations "child", "adolescent" and "minor" demonstrates it, it would be wrong to attempt to impose a term without taking into account the particular context of each State.

In order to meet the challenge of comparative law, the comparatist must be concerned with the words, and more particularly he has to understand them by looking at a world with a different legal language. Once this challenge is raised, the benefits of having a comparatist approach will emerge.

(B) **The advantages of the comparatist approach**

To be meaningful, comparative law must have advantages for the comparatist. The confrontation of the legal rules of each order can raise questions about the internal legal order and allow to propose, based on more or less antagonistic legal mechanisms, an improvement of the law. The advantages of a comparative law study are revealed here.

During the confrontation phase, it is necessary to analyze law's sources. As regards the protection of consumer minor, French law proposes protection under legal provisions whereas in Brazilian law, if the rules on disability arise from the civil law, protection is imposed by the Federal Constitution of 1988 which gives a fundamental character both to the rights of children and adolescents and to the consumer's rights. The fundamental nature of the protection's source demonstrates the importance given to these rights in the Brazilian legal order, while allowing them to be better legally protected.

The rule's place in the hierarchy of norms has a considerable impact on the people covered by these rights. The strength of these rights has helped to improve the protection of these subjects over the last twenty years in Brazil by influencing public policies. If there is no guarantee of the effectiveness of these rights, the sources' study shows a significant contrast to the approach given by each State to the protection of vulnerable subjects.

The current effectiveness of the protective rights of minors and consumers in France is based on the legal provisions in force but could be strengthened by a "fondamentalisation" of rights in the assumptions of a reduction in the effectiveness of the protection of vulnerable persons combined with an increase of the dangers faced by these fragile subjects. However, a trap could appear: the growth of fundamental rights could lead to a reduction in the importance of these rights and the effectiveness of protection.

The interplay of differences is not exclusive to the law's sources since it extends into their content, which may raise questions. In this sense, in Brazil, the Status of children and adolescents categorizes the minority in two phases: up to 12 years, the person is a "child", from 12 to 18 years of age, the person is a "teenager". This choice asks as well about a French inspiration for this minority distinction to improve its rights, as about the relevance of separating the minority in two stages.

We are allowed to ask about the reality of the inability of children and adolescents, especially since the French and Brazilian laws are opposed to each other on this issue.

On the one hand, in Brazil, the minor is considered an absolute incapable until the age of 16 years, forbidding the minor from contracting, and leaving his parents the burden of consuming for him; and as a relative incapable between 16 and 18 years old. On the other hand, in France, up to 18 years, the minor is an absolute incapable person, except for the current acts. These approaches have an interest for the comparatist who can think about the best protective regime, analyzing these two mechanisms to propose a new one inspired by the best elements of each.

The choice of splitting the incapacity in two stages have an interest to the protection's adaptation according to the minor's age to lead progressively to adulthood. If an age limit's choice can increase legal certainty by decreasing the judge's role, it remains questionable by arbitrarily defining an age that prevents adaptation to maturity and discernment, which varying according to each teenager. Also, the age of 16 is questionable because this choice dates from the Civil Code of 1916 and may no longer be adapted to the reality of the present time. The consumerist reality of the world and the dematerialization of today's relations dictate to question the choice of the age of 16 years and to reflect on a lowering of this age. The comparatist approach can provide tools to improve the mechanism of disability in positive law and the protection of minors.

The reflections stemming from comparative law can, more concretely, allow to reflect on an evolution of the law when the minor is confronted with the consumption. To take into account the aggravated vulnerability of the minor now becoming e-consumer, this law's evolution seems necessary. Above all, comparative law can raise question about this evolution but also about tomorrow's law.

3 The Recognition of the Minor as E-Consumer

The minor is protected because of its vulnerability. Because he's a little man, because he is not autonomous but fragile, the law has come to ensure its protection through the incapacity. This incapacity is in particular contractual preventing him, in principle, from acquiring goods and services. These few elements suggest that they cannot be consumers. Neither the consumer code nor the consumer protection and defence code seem to allow minors to do consumption's acts. However, many businesses offer to sell consumption's products for children and adolescents, such as toys, without forgetting the many services corresponding only to a juvenile public. Minors are therefore targeted by the consumption offer, and the many advertisements inciting children and adolescents to consume show the existence of a professionals' real attraction for a consumption of this age group. This consumerist world accentuates their vulnerability by presenting a real danger to minors and these fears are multiplied by the increasing use of new technologies by minors. These factors require to recognize the minor as a consumer and to study the ambivalence of this consumption (A) to consider the recognition of consumerist protection recognizing its aggravated e-consumption vulnerability (B).

(A) **Recognition of the ambivalence of the minor's consumption**

The minor's consumption is ambivalent, because it can be indirect or direct.

The minor can guide the purchases of his parents and his family, who do not hesitate to cover him with toys and other gifts from his birth and all his childhood. This form of consumption can be described as indirect and places the minor as a prescriber. In that position, he would only be a user of the property acquired by others, following a request from him or a desire of his parents to gratify him. On the one hand, such consumption seems to escape the definition of the consumer proposed by French law since it is the consumer who "acted" and that this term implies action by the person. On the other hand, in Brazilian law, such action is not necessary, since it is also the consumer of the "consignee" of the consumption's act. French law could be inspired by the Brazilian definition of the consumer to broaden the scope of the consumption code to any person addressed by an act of consumption, which would make sense when carrying out a risk.

It is also possible to ask what can induce the minor to guide the consumption of his elders, and the answer lies in the constant willingness of professionals to aim at a childish audience, in particular by using excessive publicity by all possible channels. These channels, due to the development of new technologies, are not only reduced to press or television, but extend to all digital sources: Internet, computer, smartphone, game platform.

To cope with this power of consumption on the consumer, the consumer law proposes a regulation of the consumption's offer and more specifically of the advertisements. Classically regulated by the consumer law, protection is found specifically strengthened because it can reach minors' health. This is the case for advertisements related to alcoholic and tobacco products, which are prohibited in order to discourage young people to consume these products. Also, it should be noted that domestic laws also prohibit the sale of these products to minors. However, the practice shows a fairly large consumption of these products among the adolescent public, demonstrating deficiencies in the protection system. Who's the wrongdoing? Perhaps it is the parents, brothers and sisters, the merchant? Perhaps it is also the consumer law which have to adapt his minor's protection in its indirect consumption.

If he can be indirect consumer, the minor can also be a direct consumer despite the absolute or relative incapacity that can weigh on him. To demonstrate this, it is sufficient to observe the erosion of its incapacity and the existence of its legal activity.

Concerning Brazilian law, the incapable relative minor has the possibility of performing acts, in particular of consumption. In the case of the absolute incapable minor, it seems possible to consider that he could do certain civil acts, particularly common.

Concerning French law, if the non-emancipated minor does not have the capacity to exercise, by exception, he has the possibility to carry out the common acts permitted by law or use according to articles 388–1-1 and 1148 of the civil code, failing which they are fulfilled by the representation. It remains to be known what the common acts may be, especially since the law is rather vague on this point. If, from a legal point of view, it seems possible to consider the acquisition of toys as being common acts, it is in practice the uses that allow to retain if the purchase is allowed. Although the jurisprudence is evolutionary and relatively poor, it is possible to establish criterias to consider an act as a current: the financial risk, the discernment of the minor, his age, the modest nature of the act or his dangerousness.

Also, this interpretation of the acts that he can do have to take into account the evolution of the manners and the increase of the products proposed. The minor is not only consumers of certain foods or products such as toys, but he is also a consumer of new technologies: computers, digital tablets, smartphones, connected objects, video games. This form of consumption is now substantial, can be carried out through the parents, but also without their intervention by being and presenting a form of significant autonomy. This is the case for the use of the Internet and social networks where children and especially adolescents expose themselves. Massive users of the Internet and social networks,[4] in any place, with computers, tablets, smartphones, smartwatch, minors are now caught in the Web. To cope with these risks, the law must adapt, and in particular the consumer law to protect minors facing new technologies.

(B) **Recognition of a heightened vulnerability in e-consumption**

The adaptation of consumer law to respond to the worsening of the minor's vulnerability to e-consumption requires recognition of this particular vulnerability. Is this recognition possible?

It may be considered that consumer law indiscriminately protects all consumers, and that taking into account the particular abilities of each consumer would bring about endless litigation and would reduce the efficiency of consumer law.[5] However, this principle may receive some mitigations.

In French law, attenuations are found with the offence of weakness' abuse which provides additional protection to consumers in a state of particular weakness or ignorance; where a commercial practice - for example an advertisement- refers to

---

[4]See: Génération numérique, Les 11–18 ans et les réseaux sociaux, consultable en ligne: https://asso-generationnumerique.fr/.

[5]J. Calais-Auloy and H. Temple, id. at. 14.

a category of particularly vulnerable consumers, its disloyalty must be assessed in terms of the average discernment capacity of the category referred toe; the advertising of certain products and services is framed specifically to protect minors, especially if it is an Internet advertisement.[6]

These exceptions may seem inadequate to specifically protect the minor in terms of consumption, especially since the philosophy of French consumer law remains the indistinguishable protection of all consumers, and that the consumption of minors is growing. Of course, the civil law, with the inability of the minor, can fill some gaps in consumer law and the development of the sources dialogue can overcome certain shortcomings by applying the law most favorable to the minor concerned by the consumption. However, new uses of consumption, such as new technologies, justify the evolution of protective rules by making them suitable for these new issues.

To improve the minor's protection in terms of consumption, it is possible to rely on the Brazilian law. By imposing respect for the consumer's dignity in its Constitution, Brazil has laid fundamental foundations for this subject's protection, which are found in the recognition of its vulnerability in the consumer protection and defence code. The consumer's vulnerability provided for in article 4. ° I of the code, poses an absolute presumption of vulnerability when he is a consumer.[7]

The Brazilian law above all clearly recognized the minor as a consumer, what is important in the application of consumerist protection to protect his person. Also, as minor and the consumer are considered vulnerables, the question of recognizing this particular vulnerability must be raised. If French law seems to reject this assumption, the Brazilian law has very clearly recognized in its jurisprudence the particular consumer's vulnerability by describing him as a hypervulnerable subject based on article 37 § 2° of the code.[8]

It would therefore be possible to rely on this objective social situation of worsening the vulnerability of the consumer due to personal circumstances known to the professional, such as the age,[9] that is hypervulnability to allow better protection of the minor consumer. In fact, relying on its constitutional basis, the legislature and the judge will have the objective to make every effort to ensure that protection.

The reflection raised by the qualification ofhypervulnerable asks the future of consumerist protection and more generally of private law, recognizing consumers with increased fragility, questioning the unity of the consumer's definition, and by

[6]CA Paris, 23 mai 2012, n° 11/15,591: the Paris Court of appeal retained "the intrusive nature of an advertisement" when downloading a social network because it could affect "a whole network of knowledge", including minors.

On the other hand, the judge of the proceedings considered that the advertisement was allowed on an online communication service, "it cannot be banned on networks such as Facebook, since the company officially restricts its target to persons aged over 21 years: TGI Paris, réf., 6 janv. 2012, n° 11/59,895.

[7]A. M. Nishiyama, R. Densa, *A proteção dos hipervulneráveis no Código de Defesa do Consumidor*, RDC 77/18.

[8]REsp 586.316 MG, j.17.04.2007, rel. Min. Herman Benjamin.

[9]REsp 980.860/SP, j. 23.04.2009, rel. Min. Nancy Andrighi, DJe 02.06.2009.

inviting a better articulation of the protective mechanisms.[10] Also, is it permit to ask whether the e-consumer could be considered like hypervulnerable. But what about the consumer minor? Would he have a triple vulnerability? Such recognition could harm the coherence of the law but would be rational for the protection of more fragile consumers.

If the idea of the recognition ofhypervulnerable consumer in French law is actually rejected, judges tend to extend the scope of consumerist rules to new horizons to allow for better protection of minors in the area of consumerism. This extension is particularly found for the minor user of a social network which has been considered as a consumer by the jurisprudence.[11] This could be an open door to taking into account the particular vulnerability of the minor now e-consumer. By this solution, it is already a specific protection of the e-consumer minor that seems envisaged.

4 The Specific Protection of the e-consumer Minor

As a continuation of the recognition of a specific status, the question arises as to the establishment of a specific protection of the e-consumer minor. There is no doubt that the dematerialized relations reduce the lighting and the freedom of consumers, justifying the reinforcement of the e-commerce's protection.[12] The protection must be fund as well as at the time of the offer and at the time of acceptance of the electronic commerce contract to anticipate any risk to the minor. More specifically, concerning a minor, it is the acceptance of the offer that must be limited to not commit its patrimony or that of its relatives. To protect him, online payment transactions must be secured (A). Moreover, if it seems difficult to prohibit him from communicating on social networks, it is essential to protect him against the capture of personal data that it can communicate when using the Internet or any online platform (B).

(A) **Protection by securing online payment**

The consumer electronic contract contributes to the weakening of consumer protection, which requires protection of the consent of the cyber-consumer.

A double acceptance is imposed by article 1127–2 of the French civil code, the addressee of the offer having the possibility to verify the details of his order and its total price, to correct any errors, before confirming the order again to validate the transaction. This double approval of the consumer, the so-called "double-click"

---

[10] See: C. L. Marques, B. Miragem, id. at. 8.

[11] TGI Paris, 7 août 2018, UFC Que choisir/Twitter; CJUE, 25 janv. 2018, aff. C-434/15, M. Schrems c/Sté Facebook Ireland Ltd.

[12] J. Passa, *Commerce électronique et protection du consommateur,* D. 2002. 555; J. Huet, *Libres propos sur la protection des consommateurs dans le commerce électronique*, in Mélanges *Calais-Auloy*, 507 (Dalloz, 2004); V. Fauchoux, P. Deprez, et J.-M. Bruguière, Le droit de l'Internet : lois, contrats et usages (2nd ed. LexisNexis 2013).

procedure, allows the consumer to check his order and then reiterate it at the time of payment to confirm it.

This payment is often concluded by the communication of the credit card numbers, such as the facial number, the expiry date and the cryptogram. If this formality of double-clicking is a condition of contract's validity and protects the consumer in the commitment of his consent and against any error of manipulation,[13] it becomes ineffective in the case of fraudulent use of the means of payment.

Payment card frauds are simple to realize since it is sufficient for the fraudsters to know the information on the credit card: facial number, expiration date, and cryptogram. This simplicity leads to the relatively common nature of these frauds.[14]

Different methods of capturing this information exist, which may be of family origin or criminal origin.[15] Family frauds correspond to the misappropriation of the payment's means by by the children of the holder.[16] Those, having no online payment way, find in their parents the solution to an e-commerce operation. Therefore, ineffective and insufficient to prevent fraudulent use of the payment card, the double-click procedure must be reinforced.

It could be imposed the additional requirement of a new mouse click, which would reinforce the rules concerning the electronic signature. Already used by some e-commerce sites, through the device « 3D secure », the so-called triple-click procedure adds an additional step to the double-click process. It consists of verifying, by the Bank, that the cardholder who makes the payment on the Internet is well the holder of the payment card. After communicating the information about its payment method, the cyber-consumer must enter a personal code to validate the order. This additional step allows only the holder of the payment method to contract, avoiding the risk of fraudulent use of the credit card.

Different degrees of authentications can be envisaged: it will be simple when communicating a pre-established password; it will be strong when the personal code is sent by SMS on the landline or mobile number of the consumer or by mail, provided that the number or/and the email address are known and reliable with the bank; it will be very strong when the personal code is transmitted on the secure email of the consumer's online bank account. The solution of the pre-established password must be discarded because it does not guarantee the security of the operation because the minor can know the password.

If the additional step of the third click may seem too demanding by imposing an additional constraint on the cyber-consumer, mainly a waste of time, but also the cyber-trader, and the banker, in terms of the cost of setting up, the triple-click method ensures the use of the payment card by its holder and reduces fraudulent uses of the means of payment by a minor.

---

[13]J.-M. Bruguière, *La protection du cyber-consommateur dans la loi pour la confiance dans l'économie numérique*, RLDI 2005–1/7.

[14]In 2015, the rate of credit card fraud on the Internet is 0.229%, for an amount 145,3 million euros: Annual report of the payment card security Observatory, fraud statistics for 2015, searchable online.

[15]E. Netter, *Réflexions sur la preuve et l'imputabilité des contrats électroniques*, RLDI 2013–1/89.

[16]Id.

(B) Protection against the capture of personal data

The new technologies' development is not without risk for the minor and especially for the preservation of his private life. In particular, it can be achieved when he is a consumer of social networks and when he is a consumer of connected toys.

When using a social network, the minor is tempted to unveil images or videos of them on the Internet, to let go to issue statements that they would never dare, or more difficult, to carry in real life. This constant exposure of his person on the Internet is not without consequence, since this can harm the e-reputation or third parties so the minor and his representative may wish to forget a part of his digital life. The legally accepted solution is the right to digital oblivion, which was instilled by the jurisprudence of the Court of Justice of the European Union in 2014,[17] by dedicating a right to dereference.

The right to be forgotten has been legally embodied in French law, since Parliament has devoted the possibility of deleting elements of the minor's past in article 63 of the law of 7 October 2016 for a digital Republic. The omission was consolidated by the entry into application of the European regulation of 27 April 2016, which provides for the possibility of deleting personal data.

Also, the minor or his parents are allowed to erase any personal content broadcast during the minority on the Internet by those responsible for processing such as social networks or search engines. Heard widely,[18] the protection afforded by the right to be forgotten may participate in the protection of the privacy of the minor Internet user.

It is also interesting to observe the formulation used in these texts, which refer to the information and service society offer, in order to conclude that the minor is, on the Internet, the recipient of this offer, and that when he joins a social network, he has subscribed to a consumer contract.

In conjunction with the use of the Internet, the use of objects and toys connected by minors imposes adequate protection. Indeed, they are carrying new dangers by being able to violate the child's privacy by listening to them through microphones and filming them with cameras located inside the toy.[19] After collecting many personal data, they could exchange them through an Internet connection, which would imply a risk for his user.[20] This spy toy has led European law to consider a protective scheme suitable for the minor consumer of these objects. In this sense, the general data protection regulation imposes on connected objects new obligations regarding the security of personal data, such as securing the doll by password, encrypting the processed data and a configuration that reduces the intrusion into the privacy of

---

[17]CJUE, 13 mai 2014, case C-131/12, Google Spain and Google vs Agencia Espanola de Proteccion de Datos (AEPD) and others : Comm. com. électr., 01/05/2015, n° 5, p. 15, note J.-M. Bruguière ; JCP 2014, n° 26, p. 1300, note L. Marino ; LPA, 11 sept. 2014, n° 182, p. 9, note G. de Malafosse.

[18]M. Péron, *Libre propos sur le droit à l'oubli numérique*, RDLF 2017, chron. 15.

[19]P. Sirinelli, S. Prévost, « Noël 3.0 », *Dalloz IP/IT* 2018. 653.

[20]N. Weinbaum, *Les données personnelles confrontées aux objets connectés*, *Comm. Com. Electr.* 2014, n°12, étude 22.

children and their entourage.[21] This regulation can address the fears raised by any toy connected to the risk of harm to the child's privacy but does not evacuate those related to prolonged exposure of the child to the electromagnetic waves generated by the object, and must also be considered by Brazilian law.

These few examples demonstrate the increased risk of e-commerce for the minor. A punctual protection is currently provided by the law, without being sufficient. In order to improve the protection of the e-consumer minor, a modernization of the consumer law could be the solution, in particular by excluding the solution of the ad hoc protective rules in favor of a specific regime of the minor consumer, which would integrate the problem of the e-consumer minor. This appropriate protection should be discussed. Necessary or utopic, thinking about the e-consumer miner probably means to remain connected to the future of consumer law.

References

1. C. Lavallée, La protection internationale des droits de l'enfant : entre idéalisme et pragmatisme, (Bruylant, 2015).
2. J. Commaille, *Les politiques publiques à destination de l'enfant*, *In* E. Paillet, J. J. Sueur, (Coord.). Le droit et les droits de l'enfant, 11–17, (L'Harmattan, 2017).
3. T. M. Macena de Lima et M. de Fátima Freire de Sá, *A criança e o adolescente no Mundo consumerista*, in M. De F. Freire de Sá, R. H. Porto Noguiera et B. Schettini (org.), Novos Direitos Privados, 111, (Arraes, 2016).
4. G. Paisant, Défense et illustration du droit de la consommation (LexisNexis, 2015).
5. L. Grynbaum, C. Le Goffic, L. Morlet-Haïdara, Droit des activités numériques (Précis Dalloz, 2014).
6. C. L. Marques, B. Miragem, O novo direito privado e a proteaçao dos vulneraveis (2nd ed. Revista dos Tribunais 2014).
7. C. L. Marques, L. R. Bessa, A. H. V. Benjamin, Manual de direito do consumidor (8th ed., Revista dos Tribunais, 2018).
8. A.-C. Papachristos, La réception des droits étrangers comme phénomène de sociologie juridique (LGDJ, 1975).
9. L. Leveneur, *Le choix des mots en droit des personnes et de la famille*, in N. Molfessis (ed.), Les mots de la loi, 11 (Economica, 1999).
10. E. Örücü, The Enigma of Comparative Law – variations on a theme for the twenty-first century (Leiden, M. Nijhoff publ., 2004).
11. V. G. Curran, *Comparive Law and Language*, in R. Zimmerman and M. Reimann (eds), 676 (The Oxford Handbook of Comparative Law, Oxford University Press, 2006).
12. J. Calais-Auloy, H. Temple, Droit de la consommation (9th ed. Précis Dalloz, 2015); R. Nunes, Curso de Direito do Consumidor, (11th ed. Saraiva, 2017).
13. J.-L. Raynaud, *A propos du code de la consommation*, Gaz. pal. 27 janv. 1994, 181.
14. L. De Medeiros Garcia, Codigo de Defesa do Consumidor comentado artigo por artigo, (13th ed. Editora JusPODIVM 2017).
15. A. C. Fonseca, Direitos da criança e do adolescente (Atlas, 2011).
16. M. Machado, A proteção constitucional de crianças e adolescentes e os direitos humanos (Manole, 2003).

[21] Regulation (EU) No. 2016/679 of the European Parliament and of the Council of 27 April 2016 on the protection of individuals with regard to the processing of personal data and on the free movement of such data and repealing Directive 95/46/EC.

17. R. J. Elias, Comentários ao Estatuto da Criança e do Adolescente, (4th ed. Saraiva, 2010).
18. M. Ancel, *Comment aborder le droit comparé*, in Mélanges Rodière, 3 (Dalloz, 1981).
19. K. Zweigert, H. Kotz, An introduction to comparative law, (3rd ed. Clarendon press, 1983).
20. B. L. COELHO, O Bloco de constitucionalidade e a proteção à criança. *Revista de Informação Legislativa*, Senado Federal, 123, 1994.
21. F. M. Milanezi, *Direitos humanos das crianças e dos adolescentes e as políticas públicas no brasil, de Fernando Henrique a Lula.* thesis, Univ. de Salamanca, 2015.
22. I. W. Sarlet, Dignidade (da pessoa) Humana e Direitos Fundamentais na Constituição Federal de 1988 (10th ed. Livraria do Advogado, 2015).
23. M. Fromont, M.-A. Frison-Roche, T. Morais da Costa, G. Cerqueira, B. Graeff, T. Martini Vilariño, Direito francês e Direito brasileiro : perspectivas nacionais e comparadas (Saraiva, 2017).
24. R. David, Le droit comparé : droits d'hier, droits de demain (Economica, 1982).
25. G. Wiederkehr, *Le contractant vulnérable*, in Mélanges C. Philippe, 349 (L'Harmattan, 2017).
26. J. Hauser, *Des petites hommes ou des petits d'hommes*, in J. Rubellin-Devichi, F. Rainer, *L'enfant et les conventions internationales*, (PUL, 1996).
27. P. Bonfils et A. Gouttenoire, Droit des mineurs (2nd ed. Précis Dalloz, 2015).
28. M.-C. Meyzeaud Garaud, *De la minorité à la majorité*, thesis, Univ. Limoges, 1998.
29. G. Raymond, Droit de l'enfance et de l'adolescence (5th ed. LexisNexis, 2006).
30. G. Raymond, *L'enfants cibles, Contrats, conc. consom.*, n° 8–9, p. 3 (2003).
31. M. N. Browne, N. Kubasek, J. Rex, R. Horton, *Commercializing children: law and regulations affecting advertisements directed at children in France, Spain and Sweden*, Indiana Int'l & Comp. Law Review, vol. 28, n°2, 2018.
32. K. R. D. Beroncello, *Os efeitos da publicidade na "vulnerabilidade agravada": como proteger as crianças consumidoras?*, Revista de Direito do Consumidor, , vol. 90, p. 70, nov.-dez. 2013.
33. L. A. Lopez de Magalhaes Dias, Publicidade e Direito, (3rd ed. Saraiva, 2018).
34. R. Nerson, *L'activité juridique du mineur non émancipé*, RTD civ. 1971, p. 613.
35. J.-P. Gridel, *L'âge et la capacité civile*, D. 1998 chron. 93, n° 16.
36. P. Lardellier et D. Moatti, Les ados pris dans la Toile : des cyberaddictions aux techno-dépendances (le Manuscrit, 2014).
37. N. de Lucca, Direito do Consumidor, (2nd ed. Quartier Latin 2008).
38. B. Miragem, *Proteção da criança e do adolescente consumidores*, Revista de Direito do Consumidor, vol. 95, set-out. 2014, p. 459.
39. B. Miragem, Curso de Direito do Consumidor (7th ed. RT 2017).
40. Silvia Fernandes Chaves, A vulnerabilidade e a hipossuficiência do consumidor nas contrataçoes eletrônicas (Editora Manole, 2015).
41. Patricia Peck Garrido Pinheiro, *Contratos digitais ou eletrônicos: apenas um meio ou uma nova modalidade contratual?*, Revista dos Tribunais, april 2016, vol. 966.
42. P.-Y. Gautier and X. Linant de Bellefonds, *De l'écrit électronique et des signatures qui s'y attachent*, JCP 2000, I, n ° 236.
43. C. Gavalda and J. Stoufflet, Instruments de paiement et de crédit : effets de commerce, chèque, carte de paiement, transfert de fonds (6th ed. Litec, 2006).
44. P. Leclercq and L. Khalil, *La confiance est-elle enfin possible dans les moyens de paiement en ligne?*, Comm. Comm. Electr., n° 12, étude 40, déc. 2004.
45. E. A. Caprioli, *Manquement à l'obligation d'information lors du déploiement du système "3D secure"*, Comm. com. électr., n° 1, janv. 2016, comm. 9, about : CA Aix-en-Provence, 8e ch. C, 19 févr. 2015, n° 12/16514.
46. F.-X. Roux-Demare, *L'appréhension pénale de la diffusion de son intimité sur Internet*, RPDP 2015, n° 1, p. 41.
47. V.-L. Benabou and J. Rochfeld, *Les moteurs de recherche, maîtres ou esclaves du droit à l'oubli numérique ?*, *D.* 2014. 1476.
48. A.-L. Villedieu, B. Benezeth, *La poupée trop connectée, une Toy's Story qui dérape*, *LPA* 13 juill. 2018, n° 137, p. 5 : Cnil, déc. n° MED-2017–073, 20 nov. 2017.

49. T. Piette-Coudol, Les objets connectés – Sécurité juridique et technique (LexisNexis, 2015).
50. P. Martinez Almeida and V. Oliveira da Silveira, *O direito ao esquecimento e a privacidade*, in Newton de Lucca, A. Simão Filho and C. R. Pereira de Lima, Direito & Internet III, T. I. 619 (Quartier Latin 2015).

Juridical Validity of (The) Artificial Intelligence in the Theory of Preventive Consumer Law in Digital Advertising

Camilo Alfonso Escobar Mora

1 About Juridical Validity of Artificial Intelligence in the Theory

Artificial intelligence is not a human being. It is a product. Is a product created and/or used (depending on the case) by the human being. So: the juridical liability (in general: the law—law) proceeds (applies) respect to the person (the physical—natural—or moral—juridical—person involved, according to the case) for which (the) artificial intelligence is working—functioning—(operating) on her/his/ist (if is a company) behalf (on behalf of) because its juridical effects (the juridical effects that causes artificial intelligence tailored to the case) are under the diligence of that person (under the juridical diligence that proceeds—applies—to the juridical profile that the person has in the case. Tailored to the case).

Therefore: the person who creates and/or uses artificial intelligence must be diligent. In the theory (the theory of preventive consumer law in digital advertising) the company must be diligent in foresee and make the valid advertising. So: it must be diligent in act in a valid form to make valid advertising and/or has to hire—in general: has to contract—its valid advertising (when there's a third party that makes the advertising in its representation and/or make valid advertising).

The relevant topic is that the diligence that applies to the company is the mercantile diligent. This means: the company has con act as a professional person in its market. So: it (the company) has to be diligent in defining the necessity of creation and/or

Camilo Alfonso Escobar Mora—Lawyer. Master in Law and Information Technology. Master in Telecommunications Law. LL.M. in Commercial Law. Ph.D. in Law. Postdoc in Law Candidate. Creator of *The Theory of Preventive Consumer Law in Digital Advertising*. Founder of JURÍDIA: Research Center for Preventive Consumer Law in Digital Advertising—Worldwide (www.juridi a.co).

C. A. Escobar Mora (✉)
Bogota, Colombia
e-mail: gerencia@juridia.co

D. Wei et al. (eds.), *Innovation and the Transformation of Consumer Law*,
https://doi.org/10.1007/978-981-15-8948-5_11

using (including: working—functioning. Operating—) of (the) artificial intelligence to make (the) valid advertising.

If its diligence defines that artificial intelligence is necessary to make it (to make valid digital business advertising) it (the company) has to act in a valid form when creates and/or uses (depending on the case) artificial intelligence (including: has to make and/or ensure, depending on the case, that artificial intelligence makes valid digital advertising). Because: artificial intelligence must be valid. And: that validity depends on the company's diligence (depends on that the company acts diligently). So: artificial intelligence must have the quality required for making valid advertising.

Simon shows the environment:

> This book does not attempt to list every possible cause of system failures. Too many factors are at play: type of system, industry, size of organization, budget, timeline, dates, and so on. Rather, this book delves into the "usual suspects," to borrow a phrase from one of my favorite films. To the extent that each implementation is different—if not unique—the causes of system failures can and do vary in each project. For example, consider data issues: one organization may have pristine data in its legacy system, whereas a second may have wildly divergent data. Still, a third may have minor data issues.[1]

That's why the company has to foresee and make valid (digital) advertising. Because: digital systems can fail. And: company has to be diligent avoiding the failures that are foreseeable (including: must be diligent hiring—in general: contracting—valid third parties that can create and/or use valid artificial intelligence (in its representation, when that situation applies in the case) and making artificial intelligence functioning in a valid form that makes valid advertising. That's why the company has to foresee and make (and/or contract, according to the case) valid (digital) advertising. Because: digital systems can fail. And: the company has to be diligent avoiding the failures that are foreseeable (including: must be diligent hiring—in general: contracting—valid third parties that can create and/or use valid artificial intelligence, when that situation applies in the case) and making artificial intelligence works—functions—(operates) in a valid form that makes valid advertising.

So: the company has to be diligent in making and/or ensuring (depending on the case) that artificial intelligence is valid. Artificial intelligence is valid when each of its parts is valid and its whole is valid. Properly: artificial intelligence is valid when its being is valid. Its being is valid when its creation, functioning and effect is—each one—(are—all—) valid.

Naughton said:

> So it is with us now. We're living through a radical transformation of our communications environment. Since we don't have the benefit of hindsight, we don't really know where it's taking us. And one thing we've learned from the history of communications technology is that people tend to overestimate the short-term effects of new technologies—and to underestimate their long-term implications.[2]

That's why the theory established that juridical validity depends on (the) diligence. On acting with diligence. On acting diligently. Because: only through diligence

---

[1]Simon [1, Chap. 1, p. 5].

[2]Naughton [2, Chap. 1, p. 1].

people can foresee and make validity in the subjects and/or objects (according to the case) that depends on that diligence to be valid. Properly: the diligent act make that the subject and/or object related to that act be valid. And: if that subject and/or object is valid the effect of it (of the subject and/or the object, depending on the case) is valid. Making the valid subject and/or subject.

That's why the company has to foresee the variables of each case in which artificial intelligence is involved. And: has to make and/or ensure (depending on the case) that those variables are (juridically) valid.

An example of the variables of artificial intelligence that are related with the law (law) is the personal data protection (and the right to privacy). Nugent express:

> Data assurance and privacy are governed by a variety of laws across the globe with certain data bodies being more protective of data and privacy rights that others. Prior to the technology advances we see presently, privacy and data security were easier to maintain as compromise in times past required proximity and physical access. Today, with modern communication systems, which link us all together in a basic virtual "One to All" electronic network (the Internet), the traditional protections afforded by "Borders and Trust" permit parties at long distances to now have virtual proximity and access to our most private data, often with little chance of notice, discovery, or punishment. And this condition is exacerbated via wireless communications where one may literally just take a copy of someone's data from the ether, and remain totally undetected, Today we are basically becoming "digital beings" with vast amounts of personal information collected, aggregated, and presented for sale by firms such as Accurint and ChoicePoint in the United States, among numerous others.[3]

So: the company has to create and apply a preventive law solution to make the valid artificial intelligence (according to the case) and/or to ensure that hires—in general: contracts—a third's party valid artificial intelligence. Marr says:

> Don't start with the data. If you do you will find yourself lost in and impossible rabbit warren of options. Start with strategy, get really clear about what you need to know and why and link that back to your strategic and tactical objectives. Just by starting with strategy and not data you will immediately focus in on your really important data requirements and what's needed instead of being overwhelmed by what's possible.[4]

That's why: in the theory the valid case (the valid case of the consumption relationship formed on the basis of a business digital advertising) is different than the valid system. The valid system is a part of the valid case. But: the valid case is when all its variables—digital and/or analog. Human and/or non-human—(properly: is when all the variables of each case fact, all the variables of all the facts and all the variables of the advertising as a whole) are valid.

Bertuglia and Vaio theorize:

> Systems are objects with varying degrees of complexity, although they are always acknowledged as containing different elements that interact with one other. Various kinds of relations may also exist between the system and the external environment, but these are either of a different nature or of a lesser intensity with respect to those that are encountered inside what we identify as 'system' and that contribute to its definition.[5]

---

[3] Withman and Mattord [3, p. 10].

[4] Marr [4, p. 231].

[5] Bertuglia and Vaio [5, Part 1.1, p. 3].

So: the company must be diligent in foresee the form to make the valid system and, in general, the form to make the valid case (including: the valid form to make the valid advertising). That's why: each party of the consumption relationship has to act validly. Has to have the moral (including: the ethics) that makes the juridical validity.

Vallor explains:

> My aim in this book has been to shine a light on this all too real disease: a widening cultural gap between the scope of our global technosocial power and the depth of our technomoral wisdom. Throughout the book, culminating with this chapter, I have suggested the only plausible first step toward a cure: to convene new institutions, communities, and cultural alliances in the service of global technomoral cultivation. This will require intense, cooperative, and sustained human efforts, many of them on a worldwide scale. Yet such efforts are not with-out precedent in a species well acquainted with fighting massive, protracted world wars for far less happy gains. A long-overdue commitment to the cultivation of technomoral habits and virtues may be the human family's only real chance for not merely continuing to live, but live well in this century and those to come. If we act now, while there is still time and hope, we may at last discover what kind of human, or posthuman, future is worth wishing for.[6]

So: there must be (there must exist) a moral conscience focused in juridical validity.

Aristotle explains:

> Now some things owe their necessity to something other than themselves; others do not, but are themselves the source of necessity in other things. Therefore, the necessary in the primary and strict sense is the simple; for this does not admit of more states than one, so that it cannot even be in one state and also in another; for if it did, it would already be in more than one. If, then, there are any things that are eternal and unmovable, nothing compulsory or against their nature attaches to them.[7]

So: the necessity of artificial intelligence is to be valid. Only in that form artificial intelligence can be created and/or used validly. Properly: only (the) valid artificial intelligence is valid for the law. And: (the) artificial intelligence is valid (is only valid—only is valid—) when in its being (if in its being) exist the juridical validity elements of existence. That is to say: if in its being exist the elements of the law (law)—those elements are: the elements of the philosophy of law, the elements of the theory of law and the elements of the norms of the Rule of Law involved in the case that are harmonious with that philosophy and theory—according to the form in which those elements proceeds (applies) in the being (tailored to the case).

[6] Vallor [6, Chap. 10, p. 249].

[7] Bosley and Tweedale [7, Chap. I.1 (Aristotle), p. 6].

2 About Juridical Effectiveness and Security of Artificial Intelligence in the Theory

When artificial intelligence has validity (juridical validity) has juridical effectiveness and security. Juridical effectiveness means (in the theory of preventive consumer law in digital advertising) that the rights (that apply in the case—tailored to the case—) are enjoyed and the duties (that apply in the case—tailored to the case—) are fulfilled. Properly: means that each party involved in the case (that is to say: means that each party of the juridical relationship that is defined as the case—and that is defined tailored to the case—) enjoy her/his/its rights and fulfills her/his/its duties tailored to the case.

So: artificial intelligence is a product. It is not the person who enjoys the rights and/or fulfills the duties. Therefore: the party of the relationship (and inside the party: the person liable for that matter) is the one that has to ensure the enjoyment of the other party right, has to enjoy the rights that has as a party (tailored to the case), has to fulfill the duties that has as a party (tailored to the case) and has the right to expect (and require) that the other party of the relationship fulfill the duties that has as a party (tailored to the case).

Maier clarifies:

> Knowledge management systems neither contain knowledge, nor do they manage it. This fact provoked substantial and partially justified critic from proponents of the human-oriented KM fraction. Despite its pragmatic foundation as an integrated set of information and communication technologies supporting knowledge management and the many unresolved questions, the term KMS seems to provide a powerful metaphor that is able to draw the attention of researchers from multiple disciplines an practitioners with diverse backgrounds alike.[8]

That's why: the human being is the one that has the rights and/or duties (tailored to the case). So: each human being has to be diligent in creating and/or using artificial intelligence. Because: is the form in which that human being and the other human beings involved in the case can enjoy the rights and fulfill the duties (tailored to the case).

Williams illustrates:

> It is not a trivial question, Socrates said: what we are talking about is how one should live. Or so Plato reports him, in one of the first books written about this subject. Plato thought that philosophy could answer the question. Like Socrates, he hoped that one could direct one's life, if necessary redirect it, through an understanding that was distinctively philosophical—that is to say, general and abstract, rationally reflective, and concerned with what can be known through different kinds of inquiry.[9]

So: human being has to be diligent in having a life (in living) making juridical effectiveness. And: if each human being make juridical effectiveness make (as a consequence of the juridical effectiveness) juridical security. In the theory (the theory of preventive consumer law in digital advertising) juridical security means that the

[8] Maier [8, Chap. 18, p. 621].

[9] Williams [9, Chap. 1, p. 1].

case (that is to say: the juridical relationship defined as the case) is enforceable because in its being there's (there exist) juridical effectiveness (as a consequence of its juridical validity—as a consequence of the existence of the juridical validity elements of existence in the being. In its being).

Mifsud affirms:

> The advantages of the customised regulation of self-regulation cannot be achieved however without the constant support of states and state legislation. As this study shows, there is a continuing relevance of national legal orders. States are especially indispensable in providing a general framework of legislation and legal mechanism that ground self-regulation. It is also important that states continue acting as 'watchdog' on the regulatory actions of the groups. Oversight by states is indispensable for the fair running of the customised rules. States should continue to assist in the development and maintenance of the self-regulation rules, including by continuing financial assistance.
>
> Ultimately, states need to consider self-regulation as an intertwining and complementary source of regulation. It is neither its competitor nor its subordinate. Thinking in this way, which corresponds to the reality of current self-regulation on the Internet, sales can consider moulding state legislation and policies to complement self-regulation. This is not a situation of 'losing' or abandoning power to groups. It is instead a way to honour the states' responsibility to citizens to provide adequate regulation and remedies and to protect the public interest.[10]

That grounds that (valid) self-regulation make the valid case. Because: make that the (juridical) relationship (properly: makes that the being of the relationship) coincides with the law (with its juridical must be). So: preventive law is the valid self-regulation. Because: is the form to make that being coincides with its juridical must be (including: is the form to make that advertising coincides with its juridical must be tailored to the case). And: when the being coincides with the law the being makes juridical effectiveness and security. Making quality of life (the quality of life that is established in the philosophy of law, the theory of law and the Rule of Law involved in the case, if it is harmonious with that philosophy and theory—because: the law, that is to say: law, only is the being that is harmonious with the philosophy and theory of law. Because: that philosophy and theory is the juridical must be of the being called: law. The law—).

An example of the valid self-regulation is the one that can be made through artificial intelligence in the consumption relationship formed on the basis of a business (company) digital advertising (when the diligence in charge of a party defines—tailored to the case—that artificial intelligence is necessary to make a part or the whole of valid advertising).

Liang defines:

> Enterprises can quickly and effectively find complex customer data from large quantities of data by data mining to help understand and interact with them by suitable marketing tactics, increase the value to the customer, and improve their competitive advantages of enterprises supposed that data mining technology could help business in customer relationship management as listed in the following:

---

[10] Mifsud [10, Chap. 8.7, p. 213].

1. Improve business efficiency in the least budget.
2. Utilize database marketing to maintain customer relationship.
3. Increase customer loyalty and customer value contribution, decrease loss rate.
4. Learn customer need to develop strategy.
5. Evaluate the effectiveness of advertising and promotion.
6. Control competitive advantages and improve brand orientation.
7. Respond to the expectation of customer and strengthen service quality.[11]

This clarifies that the party can be diligent in making (juridical) validity using the elements (subjects and/or objects, depending on the case) that are defined as necessary through the diligence to make the valid act. So: artificial intelligence is an element (product—good and/or service, according to the case—) that when is necessary make validity if is created and/or used diligently. And: if all the parties involved in a relationship act diligent make the valid case (because: if all the acts are valid the case is valid). Therefore: when artificial intelligence is necessary to make validity is diligent to create and/or use it.

Weiner proposes:

> The ideal computing machine must then have all its data inserted at the beginning, and must be as free as possible from human interference to the very end. This means that not only must the numerical data be inserted at the beginning, but also all the rules for combining them, in the form of instructions covering every situation which may arise in the course of the computation. Thus the computing machine must be a logical machine as well as an arithmetic machine, and must combine contingencies in accordance with a systematic algorithm. While these are many algorithms which might be used for combining contingencies, the simplest of these is known as the algebra of logic par excellence, or the Boolean algebra. This algorithm, like the binary arithmetic, is based on the dichotomy, the choice between yes and no, the choice between being in a class and outside it. The reasons for its superiority to other systems are binary arithmetic over other arithmetics.[12]

So (according to the state of the art that exist in the case) artificial intelligence can make the validity of the theory (the validity concept created in the theory of preventive consumer law in digital advertising). Because: can make that the being coincides with its juridical must be. For example: can foresee and make valid advertising (tailored to the case—the valid advertising is not the one that is tailored to the consumer. Is the one that is tailored to the case. Properly: is the one that is tailored to the form in which the law proceeds, that is to say: applies, in the case. According to the case, in the case and tailored to the case—).

Of course: the company must be diligent in ensuring that the artificial intelligence works validly and makes validity. And: has to be (must be) diligent in having other elements (subjects and/or objects) that can act and/or work—according to the case—(properly: that can serve to make—juridical—validity) if artificial intelligence presents or causes any invalidity. Because: the juridical must be of the company is to act professionally foreseeing and making valid acts and making the valid case

[11]Pedrycz and Chen [11, p. 351].

[12]Wiener [12, Chap. V, pp. 139–140].

(respect to the acts that depends on its diligence. Therefore: the consumer has to act diligent to make validity in the acts that depends on her/his diligence. That is the form to make the valid case in the theory. Because: is the form to make that all the acts involved in the case are valid).

Pariser gives the following premise:

> The days when the filter bubble disappears when we step away from our computers, in other words, are numbered.[13]

So: each party of the juridical (extracontractual and/or contractual, depending on the case) relationship must be diligent to make the valid case. Technology is just a means. Diligence (the diligence) of (the) human being (properly: the diligence that proceeds—applies—to each human being according to her/his juridical profile tailored to the case) is the form to make the valid case.

3 Conclusion

In the theory of preventive consumer law in digital advertising artificial intelligence is valid (juridical validly) when is created validly and works (function) validly (including: when is used validly and/or when it causes valid effects due to its valid working). So: the company must be diligent in foresee and make valid creation and working (functioning) of artificial intelligence (and/or in ensuring that third's parties artificial intelligence that is involved in the consumption relationship with its consumers for making a part or the whole of its business digital advertising is created and used validly).

And: when artificial intelligence is valid (the valid artificial intelligence) creates juridical effectiveness and security. So: when there's a valid artificial intelligence the applying rights are enjoyed and the applying duties are fulfilled. And: that makes that the case is enforceable (that makes it binding) because coincides with its juridical must be (that is to say: because the case—the being—coincides with the law—with the form in that the law proceeds, that is to say: applies, tailored to the case).

Acknowledgements To the people that read, listen, view, feedback, apply and/or spread my theory.

References

1. P. Simon (2011). Why new systems fail: an insider's guide to successful IT projects (revised Ed.). Course Technology, a part of Cengage Learning, Boston, MA, United States of America.
2. [2] J. Naughton (2014). From Gutenberg to Zuckerberg: disruptive innovation in the age of the internet (1st. Ed.). Quercus, New York, NY, United States of America.

[13]Pariser [13, Chap. 7, p. 192].

3. M.E. Withman & H.J. Mattord (2011). Readings and cases in information security: law and ethics (1st. Ed.). Course Technology, Cengage Learning, Boston, MA, United States of America, Case 3A (J.H. Nugent. Article: data privacy).
4. [4] B. Marr (2015). Big data: using smart big data, analytics and metrics to make better decisions and improve performance (1st. Ed.). John Wiley & Sons Ltd., Chichester, West Sussex, United Kingdom.
5. [5] C.S. Bertuglia & F. Vaio (2005). Momlinearity, chaos & complexity: the dynamics of natural and social systems (1st. Ed.). Oxford University Press, Cambridge, MA, United States of America.
6. [6] S. Vallor (2016). Technology and the virtues: a philosophical guide to a future worth wanting (1st. Ed.). Oxford University Press, New York, NY, United States of America.
7. [7] R.N. Bosley & M.M. Tweedale (Eds.) (2006). Basic issues in medieval philosophy: selected readings presenting the interactive discourses among the major figures (2nd. Ed.). Broadview Press, Peterborough, ON, Canada.
8. [8] R. Maier (2010). Knowledge management systems: information and communication technologies for knowledge management (3rd. Ed.). Springer, Berlin, Germany.
9. [9] B. Williams (1985). Ethics and the limits of philosophy (1st. Ed.). Harvard University Press, Cambridge, MA, United States of America.
10. J.P. Mifsud (2008). Self-Regulation in Cyberspace, information technology & law series, volume 19 (1st. Ed.). T.M.C Asser Press, The Hague, The Netherlands.
11. W. Pedrycz & S-M. Chen (Eds.) (2015). Information granularity, big data, and computational intelligence, studies in big data, volume 8 (1st. Ed.). Springer International Publishing Switzerland, New York, NY, United States of America, Part 3, (Y.H. Liang. Article: customer relationship management and big data mining).
12. N. Wiener (1949). Cybernetics or control and communication in the animal and the machine (7th. printing.). John Wiley & Sons, Inc., The Technology Press, New York, NY, United States of America.
13. [13] E. Pariser (2011). The filter bubble: how the new personalized web is changing what we read and how we think (1st. Ed.). Penguin Group, New York, NY, United States of America.

Part II
Innovations in Access to Justice

A Possible Future Convention on Cooperation and Access to Justice for International Tourists at the Hague Conference: Note on the Final Report and First Expert Group Meeting

Dan Wei and Claudia Lima Marques

1 Introduction

The focus of this paper is to debate thepossible future 'Convention on Cooperation and Access to Justice for International Tourists' at the Hague Conference suggested by the Brazilian government.[1,2] It is the first time that a Latin American country (Brazil) suggests a subject for the work of the Hague Conference on Private International Law: the protection of international tourists as consumers. It is also the first

[1]Full Professor of the University of Macau, Vice-Dean of the Law School-UM, Macau SAR, China. General-Rapporteur of the Committee of International Protection of Consumers of the International Law Association (London) and also Director of International Association of Consumer Law–IACL, Brussels. Bachelor of Law (Peking University), Master and Ph.D. Degree in Law (University of Coimbra, Portugal). Vice-President of International Academy of Comparative Law. General Director of Macao Association for Brazilian Studies. Member of Council of Economic Development of Macao Special Administrative Region. E-mail: danwei@um.edu.mo.

[2]Dean (12.2020–12.2024) and Full Professor of Private International Law at the Federal University of Rio Grande do Sul-UFRGS in Porto Alegre, Brazil. Chair of the Committee of International Protection of Consumers of the International Law Association (London). Director of International Association of Consumer Law–IACL and the Center for European and Germany Studies, CDEA-DAAD, Porto Alegre. *Doctor iuris utriusque* (Ruprecht-Karls Universität Heidelberg), *Legum Magister* (Eberhard-Karls Universität Tübingen), Diploma in European Integration (Universität des Saarlandes), SDJ (UFRGS). Former President of *Asociación Americana de Derecho Internacional Privado* (ASADIP, Asunción) and of BRASILCON (Brazilian Institut for Consumer Law and Policy, Brasilia). E-mail: cmarques.ufrgs@gmail.com.

The authors thank Dr. Pablo Baquero and Ph.D. Candidate Laís Bergstein for their suggestions and contributions to the text.

D. Wei (✉)
University of Macau, Macau, China
e-mail: danwei@um.edu.mo

C. L. Marques
Federal University of Rio Grande Do Sul, UFRGS, Porto Alegre, Brazil
e-mail: cmarques.ufrgs@gmail.com

D. Wei et al. (eds.), *Innovation and the Transformation of Consumer Law*,
https://doi.org/10.1007/978-981-15-8948-5_12

time that Brazil, China and other BRICS countries act together at this important global forum, the Hague Conference of Private International Law (HCCH). With the help of the Macau University and as experts[3] from the Committee on International Protection of Consumers established by the International Law Association (ILA, London) in 2008,[4] we have followed the negotiations of the text and the growing interest on the protection of tourists as consumers.[5]

On December 17th 2018, the Consultant's Final Report concerning this Draft Convention on Cooperation was sent to the HCCH Members States, as Annex III to Preliminary Document (Prel. Doc) No. 3, prepared for the Meeting of the Council on General Affairs and Policy, held from March 5th to the 7th of 2019. The aim of this article is to analyse this Report 'on the desirability and feasibility of further work on' the subject on tourist protection and the prospects of the so called 'Tourism Project' at the Hague Conference, especially in light of the text of the 'Aide Memoire of the Chair of the representative Experts' Group on the Cooperation and Access to Justice for International Tourists' (annex I of the Prel. Doc. No. 3) and the 'Conclusions and Recommendations of the representative Experts' Group on the Co-operation and Access to Justice for International Tourists' (Annex II of the Prel. Doc. No. 3).

Brazil is the author of the proposal to draft a Convention on this subject ("Proposal concerning a Draft Convention on Co-operation and Access to Justice for International Tourists") which has been strongly supported by other Latin-American countries and emergent economies in general. Nevertheless, this proposal has been disputed by countries with high consolidated consumer societies, e.g. the USA and Canada. At the first Experts Group Meeting, held in August 2018, there was no consensus regarding the future instrument to be negotiated, whether it should be a convention or a soft law instrument. The Final Report suggests a Convention and a complementary soft law instrument.

Many reasons can be found for such fragmented opinions worldwide. On one side, although international tourism moves more than 1.4 billion people each year,[6] individual tourist's complaints are almost inexistent. After all, the current cooperation network does not help the individual, as it helps only when a cross-border fraud scheme is identified, when one or more national agencies take the lead. On the other hand, tourists only remain a small amount of time in each country, and they rarely know how to find help in the language of the local consumer agencies. Besides, they have little (or no) access to justice, and no cross-border small

[3]See Marques [1].

[4]See Marques and Delaloye [2].

[5]A good example is the Guideline nr. 78 UN Consumer Protection Guideline (revised in 2015), that ensure the importance to address subjects like provide of goods and services related to tourism, specially, travel services, accommodation, marketing and timeshares, in cross-border cases stating in case of tourism that the *States should, in particular, address the cross-border challenges raised by such activity, including enforcement cooperation and information sharing with other Member States.*

[6]UNWTO World Tourism Barometer–January 2019, International tourism arrivals in 2018: 1,4 millions (growth of 7 % in relation to 2017) in: https://www.e-unwto.org/doi/abs/10.18111/wtobarometereng.2019.17.1.1.

claims court or arbitrations exist, with the exception of those made available for consumers domiciled in Europe. In light of this, the organization of a new 'information' and a 'cooperation network' for tourists and theirs small claims could be costly. Politically, as Jürgen Basedow states, national politicians normally think of the voters/tax payers/consumers and their protection via-*à-vis* both domestic and foreign professionals, but they are less concerned with foreign consumers via-a-vis national professionals/providers, and their practices against foreign tourists/consumers.[7]

In 2012, ASADIP (American Association of Private International Law) observe that in the XXI Century, the flow of international tourists has changed[8]: there are more and more tourists from developing countries, which are eager to contract directly with the professionals/providers, instead of using travel agencies. Besides, the number of tourists heading to countries with emergent economies are increasing. The UNWTO projects that in 2030 more than 1 billion people (more than 55 % of the international tourism) will have not developed countries as their destination.

The so-called 2012 ASADIP "Declaration of *Rio de Janeiro*" proposed the accomplishment of studies on the cooperation and protection of tourists as consumers considering all of their vulnerabilities as foreign people, i.e., the short time that they dispose at the visited country and the circumstances of being away from their culture, language and home country, the need for special information, the proper place to complain and to get access to justice, the availability of alternative means of dispute resolution and small claim courts, the access to easy administrative and legal aid without discrimination, and the usual need to pay a *caution judicatium solvi*.

These studies and changes on international tourism drove the Brazilian suggestion of a possible future Convention on Cooperation and Access to Justice for International Tourists at the Hague Conference (now at the second version).[9] As coming from China and Brazil, we will divide the article in two parts. On the first part, we will analyze the growth of mass international tourism and its impacts on emergent economies, and also the main substantial findings of the study of the Consultant, Emmanuel Guinchard, about the difficulties that the average tourist faces in his/her path to access justice. Thus, on the second part, we will study the prospects of the so-called 'Tourism Project' at the Hague Conference, especially after the Experts' Group on the Cooperation and Access to Justice for International Tourists' meeting held in 2018, and the new possibilities to change the proposed Draft of the Convention on Cooperation and Access to Justice for International Tourists, for it to be a more

---

[7]Basedow [3].

[8]https://asadip.files.wordpress.com/2012/04/carta-de-rio-de-janeiro8asadip230312en-espac3b1ol-y-portviii.pdf. In 2012, among the activities of the American Association on Private International Law (ASADIP) and considering the development of tourism services and the increasing of visitors and tourists in the world, 108 experts from more than 14 countries have officially manifested their support to the creation of a document with the objective to protect tourists and visitors internationally.

[9]As President of ASADIP, I have the honor to serve as author of the Brazilian proposal to draft a Convention on the protection of tourists as consumers ("Proposal concerning a Draft Convention on Co-operation and Access to Justice for International Tourists") at the Hague Conference of Private International Law, see Marques [4], ASADIP: Porto Alegre (2014) 823–848. See also Marques [5].

accepted international legal instrument. The future of this proposal is open, but we see merits on the evolution of the protection of international tourists worldwide.

2 Growth of Mass International Tourism and the Difficulties the Average Tourist Face in His Access to Justice

The UN World Tourism Organization (Madrid) defines tourist as the visitor or traveler, who stays longer than 24 h (an overnight stay) but less than one year in one country or place visited.[10] According to UNWTO, international tourist arrivals have increased from 25 million in 1950 to 1.4 billion in 2018.[11]

Destinations in international tourism have been varying: arrivals in developing countries' destinations increased from 30 % in 1980 to 45 % in 2014, and are expected to reach 57 % by 2030, what is equivalent to more than 1 billion international tourist arrivals in emergent economies.[12] The fact that 45 % of the tourist's destinations are in emergent economies today,[13] creating a new mass of cross-borders tourists/consumers, "*which not always are well equipped to inform, to assist and help the tourists to have access to justice, ADR and other channels to solve their problems quick and inexpensively*"[14] has called the attention of the Brazilian government.

[10]"2.9. A visitor is a traveler taking a trip to a main destination outside his/her usual environment, for less than a year, for any main purpose (business, leisure or other personal purpose) other than to be employed by a resident entity in the country or place visited. These trips taken by visitors qualify as tourism trips. Tourism refers to the activity of visitors… 2.13. A visitor (domestic, inbound or outbound) is classified as a tourist (or overnight visitor), if his/her trip includes an overnight stay, or as a same-day visitor (or excursionist) otherwise." https://unstats.un.org/unsd/statcom/doc08/BG-TourismStats.pdf.

[11]See UNWTO Tourism Highlights 2018 Edition. Avaliable in: https://www2.unwto.org/publication/unwto-tourism-highlights-2018. And for 2019, see.

UNWTO World Tourism Barometer–January 2019, Available in: https://www.e-unwto.org/doi/abs/10.18111/wtobarometereng.2019.17.1.1

[12]See UNWTO World Tourism Barometer–v. 16. January 2018. Available in: https://cf.cdn.unwto.org/sites/all/files/pdf/unwto_barom18_01_january_excerpt_hr.pdf.

[13]The data are: International tourism arrivals in 2017: 1,322 million (growth of 7 % in relation to 2016); Advanced economies arrivals in 2017: 724 million (54.8 %); Emerging economies arrivals in 2017: 597 million (45.2 %). Source: 2017 UNWTO Tourism Highlights. Available in: https://www.e-unwto.org/doi/pdf/10.18111/9789284419029.

[14]Letter from the Foro Iberoamericano de las Agencias Gubernamentales de Protección al Consumidor (FIAGC) to the Hague Conference´s Secretary-General, from 3. September 2018. The original is: "Vivimos en un tiempo de creciente diversificación de destinos y países generadores del turismo internacional, así como la auto-reserva de servicios turísticos. Hoy el 45 % de los destinos turísticos son economías emergentes (puntos destacados de la OMT 2017), que no siempre están bien equipados para informar, ayudar y ayudar a los turistas a tener acceso a Justicia, ADR y otros canales para resolver sus problemas demanera rápida y económica. Sabemos que su institución está estudiando canales para ayudar a llenar este vacío de instrumentos internacionales o esquemas cooperativos para ayudar a los consumidores que enfrentan problemas en el extranjero en los

2.1 The Changes on International Tourism and the Rapid Development of Tourism Industry in China, Brazil and Other Emergent Economies

In recent years, tourism has developed rapidly in emerging market countries, which greatly improved their economic development. In India, from 2012 to 2016, the number of inbound tourists increased from 6.5 million to 14.6 million, and annual inbound tourism revenue increased from 18.3 billion to 23.1 billion U.S. dollars. The number of outbound tourists increased from 14.92 million to 21.87 million, and annual expenditure on outbound travel increased from 14.1 billion to 19.2 billion U.S. dollars.[15] In Russia, from 2012 to 2016, the number of inbound tourists maintained at around 30 million per year, and the annual inbound tourism revenue was up to 20.2 billion U.S. dollars in 2013. The number of outbound tourists maintained at about 45.9 million per year, and the annual expenditure on outbound travel was up to 60 billion U.S. dollars in 2013.[16] In Brazil, from 2012 to 2016, the number of inbound tourists increased from 5.69 million to 6.57 million, and annual inbound tourism revenue remained at about 6.6 billion U.S. dollars. In 2014, it reached 7.4 billion U.S. dollars. The number of outbound tourists remained at around 8.5 million per year. In 2014, it reached 9.62 million. The annual expenditure on outbound travel was more than 17 billion U.S. dollars, and in 2014, it reached 30 billion U.S. dollars.[17]

China is the biggest potential market for outbound tourism, and it is also a major tourist destination. China's tourism industry started from the inbound tourism in the early 1980s. Under the overall planning of the national strategies, China actively explored overseas markets and the inbound tourism industry has constantly grown. Except for some special years, in the first two decades, the number of inbound tourists and foreign exchange income grew continuously. During that period, China received a total of 576 million overseas tourists with an average annual growth rate of 19.47 %. The total foreign exchange income was 782 billion U.S. dollars with an average annual growth rate of 20.55 %. In 2001–2010 decade, approximately 1.155 billion overseas tourists visited China, with an average annual growth rate of 4.6 %. The foreign exchange income was 312.82 billion U.S. dollars with an average annual growth rate of 11.1 %. The number of outbound tourists during the same period was

países visitados. En la actualidad, 1.300 millones depersonas que realizan turismo transfronterizo y la proyección de la OMT es que en 2030 habrá 1,8 millones: la mayoría de los destinos turísticos internacionales serán economías emergentes (57 %). Este turista debería tener sus derechos respetados en todo el mundo.".

[15] Compendium of Tourism Statistics, Data 2012–2016 (2018 Edition), World Tourism Organization, at 57.

[16] Compendium of Tourism Statistics, Data 2012–2016 (2018 Edition), World Tourism Organization, at 328.

[17] Compendium of Tourism Statistics, Data 2012–2016 (2018 Edition), World Tourism Organization, at 180.

335 million, and the number of inbound tourists exceeded the number of outbound tourists by 820 million.[18]

From 2012 to 2016, the number of inbound tourists increased from 132 to 142 million, and annual inbound tourism revenue remained at around 50 billion U.S. dollars. The number of outbound tourists increased from 83 to 135 million, and annual expenditure on outbound travel increased from 83.2 billion to 135.1 billion U.S. dollars.[19] It is worth noting that in 2016, the number of inbound tourists reached 28.15 million with the growth rate of 8.3 %, which was a record high since the financial crisis.[20]

The Number of Inbound and Outbound Tourists in China from 2006 to 2016 (Unit: 10,000).[21]

At the same time, in 2017, the outbound travel destinations for Chinese citizens have expanded to 151 countries and regions.[22] And Chinese citizens can travel to 65 countries without visas. Besides United Arab Emirates, China also signed a visa-free agreement with Bosnia and Herzegovina, and the approval procedure is in progress. Thus, there will be 12 countries that will have achieved full visa reciprocity with China. In addition, 40 countries and regions unilaterally granted Chinese citizens with ordinary passports the treatment of visa upon arrival; 16 countries and regions unilaterally allowed Chinese citizens with ordinary passports to travel without visas; China also reached 70 simplified visa agreements or arrangements with 41 countries. Among them, Indonesia both implements visa-free and landing visa policies.[23]

It is to mention that China has signed many bilateral Agreements or Memorandums of Understanding on cooperation in matters related to the protection of tourists, for

---

[18]Dai Bin, It is the Time to go on Expanding the International Tourism Surplus, Ministry of Culture and Tourism of the People's Republic of China. 戴斌,继续扩大国际旅游顺差正当时,中华人民共和国文化和旅游部,参见 HYPERLINK "sps:urlprefix::http" https://www.cnta.gov.cn/xxfb/jdxwnew2/201708/t20170801_833763.shtml,2018年4月11日最后访问.

[19]Compendium of Tourism Statistics, Data 2012–2016 (2018 Edition), World Tourism Organization, at 86.

[20]Dai Bin, It is the Time to go on Expanding the International Tourism Surplus, Ministry of Culture and Tourism of the People's Republic of China. 戴斌,继续扩大国际旅游顺差正当时,中华人民共和国文化和旅游部,参见 HYPERLINK "sps:urlprefix::http" https://www.cnta.gov.cn/xxfb/jdxwnew2/201708/t20170801_833763.shtml,2018年4月11日最后访问.

[21]Dai Bin, It is the Time to go on Expanding the International Tourism Surplus, Ministry of Culture and Tourism of the People's Republic of China. 戴斌,继续扩大国际旅游顺差正当时,中华人民共和国文化和旅游部,参见 HYPERLINK "sps:urlprefix::http" https://www.cnta.gov.cn/xxfb/jdxwnew2/201708/t20170801_833763.shtml,2018年4月11日最后访问.

[22]Annual Expenditure on Outbound Travel Reached 109.8 billion U.S. dollars, Chinese People Tends to be Rational Consumers, Ministry of Culture and Tourism of the People's Republic of China.去年出境游花费1098亿美元 国人消费趋于理性,中华人民共和国文化和旅游部,参见 HYPERLINK "sps:urlprefix::http" https://www.cnta.gov.cn/xxfb/hydt/201701/t20170117_812570.shtml,2018年4月11日最后访问.

[23]'Motherland is Always Beside us'- A Summary of Consular Protection of China in 2017, Xin Hua Net. "祖国一直在我们身旁"——2017年中国领事保护工作综述,新华网,参见 HYPERLINK "sps:urlprefix::http" https://www.xinhuanet.com/overseas/2018-01/10/c_1122240751.htm,2018年4月11日最后访问.

example with the EU and Brazil.[24] In these bilateral instruments the information where to get help and the language is one of the main concerns.

As we stated,[25] China is the second fastest growing Travel & Tourism Economy in the world and has the potential to become one of the world's great tourism economies—in terms of inbound, domestic and outbound travel. China has become the largest spender in international tourism globally since 2012. At the same time, its Special Administrative Region of Macau (Macau SAR) ranks at 9th place among the world's fastest growing Travel & Tourism economies. The transformation of Macau from a sleepy Portuguese colony to a mega world class tourism entertainment destination is staggering in its vision and scope.

There are no data available about the consumer problems the Chinese tourists face in foreign countries. With the rapid development of tourism in emerging market countries, tourism crisis events occur more and more frequently. In order to deal with tourism crisis properly, tourism crisis management becomes increasingly important. Due to limited time and energy in travel, tourists are often unable to look for help when their interests are infringed, or they give up remedies for various other reasons. At the same time, overseas security risks are ever more diversified. There are both traditional security threats and non-traditional ones. Coupled with lack of relevant concepts and awareness, overseas Chinese companies and citizens have a more complex living environment, and the security situation is becoming severer. The number of overseas consular protection cases has increased, and its development shows a trend from traditional to non-traditional, from accidental and single, to frequent and massive.[26]

From 2007 to 2018, together with Chinese embassies, consulates and relevant departments, the Chinese Ministry of Foreign Affairs accepted and disposed of nearly 160,000 cases of various types of consular protection, with an average of 40,000 cases per year, involving millions of Chinese citizens. In 2017, together with Chinese embassies, consulates and relevant departments, the Chinese Ministry of Foreign Affairs handled about 70,000 cases of consular protection and assistance properly, including the emergency assistance of helping Chinese citizens evacuate or return to China due to hurricane in Dominica, floods in Nepal, and volcanic eruptions in Bali, Indonesia, and other cases. Among them, the case involving the largest number of people and having biggest social impact is the one of emergency assistance of helping Chinese citizens return to China from Bali, Indonesia.[27]

Besides, the Department of Consular Affairs of the Ministry of Foreign Affairs has opened the '12,308′ hotline to set up an all-weather, zero-time difference and barrier-free channel between overseas travellers and their motherland. The main duties of the hotline are, as follow: (1) provide emergency guidance and consultation for people

[24] See mentioning 146 Bilateral Agremments and MoUs, Wei [6].

[25] Wei [7].

[26] Yang [8]. 杨洋,中国领事保护中存在的问题及对策, 国际政治研究,2013年,第17-29页.

[27] 'Motherland is Always Beside us'- A Summary of Consular Protection of China in 2017, Xin Hua Net. "祖国一直在我们身旁"——2017年中国领事保护工作综述,参见 HYPERLINK "sps:urlprefix::http" https://www.xinhuanet.com/overseas/2018-01/10/c_1122240751.htm,2018年4月11日最后访问.

who need help, and coordinate the foreign embassies and consulates to follow-up when necessary; (2) introduce the process of case handling and provide advice in accordance with the needs of people; (3) provide consulting services for public regarding emergency events; (4) provide consulting services for Chinese citizens with general knowledge of consular issues.[28] Currently, the '12,308′ hotline has become an important tool of the Ministry of Foreign Affairs to serve the people. Since it was opened three years ago, more than 370,000 calls have been received, of which more than 120,000 are hand-carried. Through the '12,308′ hotline, a lot of Chinese people who encountered difficulties overseas were able to get help in time.[29]

In addition to the US$ 1.340 billion in tourism receipts earned in the destinations (the travel item of the Balance of Payments), international tourism generated another US$ 240 billion from international passenger transport services rendered to non-residents. The total exports from international tourism reached US$ 1.6 trillion in 2017, or an average of US$ 4 billion a day. That means that, as a worldwide export category, tourism ranks in third after chemicals and fuels, and ahead of automotive products. In many developing countries, tourism is the top export category.[30]

The increase of mass tourism in and within emerging economies is an important change on the international tourism in our times. Between 2016 and 2017, China continued to lead global outbound travel, following ten years of double-digit growth in spending and after rising to the top of the rank in 2012. Expenditure of Chinese travellers grew by 12 % in 2016, reaching US$ 261 billion. The number of outbound travellers rose by 6 %, reaching 135 million in 2016. Also in 2016, the Republic of Korea spent 5 % more (US$ 27 billion) and moved up further to 7th place, after having entered the Top 10 list in 2015. The number of outbound travellers increased in Korea by 16 %,reaching 22 million.[31]

In 2017, Thailand received 35,381 million tourists–almost the same as the UK in 2015 (35.814 million). In 2017, Mexico received 39.3 million tourists–more than Germany in the same year (37.452 million). In 2017, there were 63 million arrivals in Africa, there were 58 million tourists in the Middle East, and there were 323 million in Asia and the Pacific region.[32]

---

[28]Disclose the '12,308′ Hotline Overseas: the Really Zero Time Difference, People's Daily. 独家揭秘12308海外热线:实打实的全天候零时差,人民网,参见 HYPERLINK "sps:urlprefix::http" https://chinese.people.com.cn/n/2015/0420/c42309-26872091.html,2018年4月12日最后访问.

[29]Disclose the '12,308′ Hotline Overseas: the Really Zero Time Difference, People's Daily. 独家揭秘12308海外热线:实打实的全天候零时差,人民网,参见 HYPERLINK "sps:urlprefix::http" https://chinese.people.com.cn/n/2015/0420/c42309-26872091.html,2018年4月12日最后访问.

[30]See UNWTO Tourism Highlights 2018 Edition. Avaliable in: https://www2.unwto.org/publication/unwto-tourism-highlights-2018.

[31]See 2017 UNWTO Tourism Highlights. Available in: https://www.eunwto.org/doi/pdf/10.18111/9789284419029.

[32]See UNWTO Tourism Highlights 2018 Edition. Avaliable in:: https://www2.unwto.org/publication/unwto-tourism-highlights-2018.

Destination	1995	2010	2016	2017 (%)	2030 (%)
Advanced economies	342 million	515 mi	686 mi	726 mi.-55	43
Emerging economies	189 million	437 mi	554 mi	597 mi.-45	57

Source UNWTO 2018 Highlights

As I have already stated,[33] consumer law scholars[34] also alert of the challenges presented by the international mass tourism to the law. These challenges do not derive only from technological progress (electronic booking, maps and information on *in locus* tourism services for foreigners, and remote reservation) and from the complexities and diversity range of the current tourism contracts (package tours, time-sharing, adventure tourism, young educational tourism, tourism for conferences, professional, language and religious training, etc.), but they are also connected to the changes of the tourist's profile (next to mass tourism to all social classes, a new elite tourism industry is blooming) and of the tourism industry itself.

Besides, Brazilian empirical data shows that with the impact of the development of new technologies on distance contracts, many tourists no longer use travel agencies,[35] opting for other public and private intermediaries instead, or even hire the services themselves, directly in the country of destination, as the current data suggests (e.g., today 65.4 % of the foreign tourists visiting Brazil have no travel agency at their home state).[36] We can affirm that these challenges are no longer answered by only with changes in national law and being responded by supranational laws of economic integration processes, like those from the EU[37] and MERCOSUR.[38]

So following the MERCOSUR experience regarding tourists-consumers[39] protection focused on the attention to conflict resolution regarding tourist among the country members, the Brazilian government drafted a proposal of an International Convention in order to protect international tourists as consumers presented at the Hague Conference of Private International Law: The Project concerning a possible future Convention on Co-operation and Access to Justice for International Tourists (so called 'Tourism Project'[40]).

This draft Convention proposes an *ex ante* intervention of consumer agencies to inform and help international tourists, and was consolidated by the Proposal of the Brazilian government. The second draft of the Proposal was presented in 2015 with

[33]Marques [9].

[34]Tonner [10].

[35]Atheniense [11].

[36]A research from the Brazilian government in preparation for the 2014 World Cup says that "most tourists visiting Brazil in 2010 did not use travel agencies (65.4 %)." https://www.turismo.gov.br/export/sites/default/turismo/o_ministerio/publicacoes/downloads_publicacoes/Documento_Referencial_Turismo_no_Brasil_2011-2014.pdf.

[37]See Tonner [12].

[38]See Pfeiffer [13].

[39]See Soares [14].

[40]https://www.hcch.net/en/projects/legislative-projects/protection-of-tourists (accessed 22.07.2018).

10 Articles.[41] A study of the Consultant Emmanuel Guinchard 'on the desirability and feasibility of further work on the Proposal on a Draft Convention on Co-operation and Access to Justice for International Tourists' has interesting findings about the impact of such changes in the protection of international tourists.

2.2 *The Main Substantial Findings of the Final Report About the Difficulties the Average Tourist Face in His Access to Justice*

The ILA's Committee on International Protection of Consumers describes the evolution of the proposal as followed: *"The Brazilian Proposal was submitted to the Council on General Affairs and Policy (Council) in 2013, together with an explanatory memorandum detailing the rationale for such an instrument. In 2013, with the support of member states such as Portugal and China (and most of South American countries) the theme was included in the Conference Agenda. The importance of such inclusion lies on the fact that for the first time in The Hague Conference on Private International Law (HCCH) a theme, proposed by a developing country, was considered to be officially discussed and, therefore included, in the Conference Agenda. In 2015, the Council decided that the Permanent Bureau (PB) should conduct a study on the desirability and feasibility of further work in the area of co-operation in respect of protection of tourists and visitors abroad, in view of compatibility of the topic with the mandate of the HCCH as well as the work conducted in other for a, such as the World Tourism Organization (UNWTO). Hague Conference expertise in building global networks organized by Central Authorities enhances the accessibility to foreign tourists to the legal assistance and also standard formularies in various languages to help the complains- The Central Authorities are a very good tools to organize networks and to assure mutual assistance, urgent measures and legal information, also to develop formulary in various languages and also to beware and register the complains and the data about it, for purposes of evidence in future complains at the State of origin of the tourist, so it is an instrument that is needed to protect foreign tourists. The report delivered by the expert consultant, Professor Emmanuel Guinchard after a deep research, made with the help of States Members and Non-Members of the Hague Conference concludes that "that work on the Tourism Project is desirable; is feasible; and that the work of the HCCH and UNWTO neither overlaps nor is it incompatible. To the contrary, the Final Report concludes that the work by the two organizations in this area would be complementary", member states have manifested the need of an extension of time for the analysis of such report…".*[42]

In 2018, the Council ordered the Permanent Bureau to prepare the establishment of an Experts' Group. This Experts' Group met from August 28th to August 31st, of 2018. Experts from sixteen jurisdictions, together with the Consultant and members

[41] https://assets.hcch.net/docs/74b12153-45a4-45fa-a86e-814fa5bf9d2a.pdf.

[42] Source: https://unctad.org/meetings/en/Contribution/cicplp3rd_c_brasilcon-ila_sd_en1.pdf.

of the Permanent Bureau, 'considered a wide range of issues pertinent to the Tourism Project'.

For the purpose of the Consultant´s Study, the UNWTO definition of tourists has been adopted with the important caveat that, unless otherwise stated, a tourist is a natural person who does not have his place of habitual residence in the State visited and it was suggest an amendment to the definition set out in the current Brazilian proposal (nr. 15, p. XII). The study analyzes the MERCOSUR and the ECC-Net experience, and also the Chinese experience.[43] The study has 117 pages, with 7 Parts (Part 1. Introduction; Part 2. Concepts, Statistics and Literature; Part 3. The particular vulnerability of the tourist; Part 4. Identifying difficulties faced by tourists; Part 5. Possible ways forward; Part 6. Compatibility of the Tourism Project with the mandate of the HCCH; Part 7 Compatibility of the Tourism Project with the work conducted in other *fora*).

To be able to identify the difficulties faced by tourists, the study analyzes the evidence gathered through questionnaires (a. In relation to Legal Standing/Sources of Law regarding Access to Justice; b. In relation to Information c. In relation to Mediation, Conciliation and Arbitration; d. In relation to Court Proceedings; e. In relation to Assistance; f. In relation to Assessment and Future) and through an especial 'questionnaire on Access to Justice in Latin American and Caribbean Countries' (analyzing a. Legal aid for extrajudicial proceedings; b. Legal aid in court proceedings; c. *Cautio judicatum solvi* and a survey among the Embassies of the Latin American countries accredited in Argentina on the difficulties encountered by tourists). There are also analysis of other specific points, such as the very interesting EU ODR Regulation and the European Small Claims Procedure.

The main findings of the study are that the Convention to protect international consumers is desirable and feasible. Particularly, the report of the consultant states:

"The report starts with the growth of tourism as a major trade sector in the last decades and the fact that tourism is expected to continue to grow, with international tourist arrivals reaching 1.8 billion by 2030. Tourism related expenditure follows the same trend. It is submitted that, almost inevitably, the probability of a larger number (in absolute terms) of dissatisfied tourists with the goods bought or the services provided will also increase, reinforcing the pressure on States to guarantee effective access to justice. The HCCH appears to be on the frontline of this development because all, or nearly all, key players in international tourism, whether in terms of arrivals/receipts or departures/expenditures, are either Member States or connected non-Member States. The profile of the new tourist contributes to the need for the Tourism Project on access to justice for tourists since many now travel without using

[43]Quoted is Dan "Wei, in the 2014 Discussion Interim Report of the Committee on the International Protection of Consumers, International Law Association, Washington Conference (2014), p 9, https://www.ila-hq.org/index.php/committees. Recently, "The Consumer Council [of Macao SAR of China] and Zhuhai City Association for Consumers' Rights and Interests Protection […] decided to launch the cross-border arbitration service between Macao and Zhuhai on March 15th 2018" (Interim Report 2017 2018 of the Committee on the International Protection of Consumers, International Law Association, Sydney Conference 2018, https://www.ila-hq.org/images/ILA/DraftReports/DraftReport_Consumers.pdf, p. 9)." Note 338 of the Study.

the services of a travel agent or tour operator and therefore do not benefit from the sometimes associated safety net. In most circumstances, the tourist coming from abroad finds himself in a position of added vulnerability in comparison to the local consumer for reasons which include the short length of stay in the visited country and the ignorance of the local language, culture, laws and customs, and social geography. There is a growing institutional recognition of the need and specificity of tourist protection in civil matters.

Evidence collected up to 1 December 2018 demonstrates that the average tourist may face several difficulties in his access to justice. These may include:

- *An information gap: Tourists often seem unaware of their rights and legal remedies. There is a lack of express and systematic dissemination of relevant information and assistance. Even pro-active tourists may find it difficult to identify information. This information gap may lead to a denial of justice in practice.*
- *An inability to use mediation/conciliation beyond the stay in the visited country: Mediation/conciliation is generally regarded as the most appropriate/proportionate method to resolve small claims (arguably a major proportion of tourists' claims). This method seems often available in theory, however may be unavailable in practice for two main reasons. First, physical presence is required by law, and the use of distance communication tools to substitute physical presence is impossible, leading to an unavailability, or discontinuance, of mediation/conciliation, especially where the stay in the visited country is of insufficient length, or where a return, while available, would not be reasonable. Secondly, even where distance communication tools are available, other limitations such as language barriers may hamper appropriate resolution of the claim.*

A persistence of obstacles to access to justice in cross-border matters, in particular the cautio judicatum solvi

- *An inability to initiate court proceedings beyond the stay in the visited country: Court proceedings may not be available in cases where physical presence is required. Requiring physical presence has a disproportionate impact on tourists, and especially short-stay tourists. Difficulties are compounded notably by the information gap and language barriers.*
- *An impossibility to continue court proceedings beyond the stay in the visited country: Even if a tourist can initiate proceedings during the stay in the visited country, the potential length of judicial proceedings may prove prohibitive to gain appropriate access to justice. The issue is compounded in situation where proceedings are discontinued in the absence of physical presence at the hearing, and exacerbated where proceedings last longer than a stay permitted by visa conditions, in which case delay can be used strategically.*
- *The unavailability of a small claims procedure tailored for cross-border cases: Tailored small claims procedures appear particularly desirable in tourism related disputes, which are typically akin to typical consumer claims, in that they are of small value and of little complexity.*

- *The absence of a governmentally funded authorities in charge of helping tourists to access justice: Most States do not have dedicated governmental agencies or bodies charged with assisting tourists to access justice, although some consumer agencies take on a comparable role. However, even where such bodies exist, they are often ill-equipped to assist appropriately, especially in light of time pressures and language barriers.*
- *The absence of appropriate liaison mechanisms between authorities of the visited country and the country of the tourist: Where tourists seek to complain to a (consumer) body after their return, then these bodies regularly have practical difficulties in liaising with the trader, whether in relation to the facts, or even to commence mediation/conciliation. Moreover, the complex enforcement of any settlement reached would prove a significant deterrent.*

The suggested Hague Convention on Cooperation and Access to Justice for International Tourists aims to address these difficulties by setting up an international cooperation mechanism between Central Authorities together with provisions on access to justice (in particular cautio judicatum solvi and legal aid). One of the key underlying ideas seems to be that the intervention of an Authority from the State of the trader should often be enough to convince him of the need to seriously take into account the complaint of the tourist from abroad, whilst at the same time offering him the possibility to understand this complaint in his own language. The tourist is for his part likely to know the contact details of his own relevant authority with whom he will be able to correspond in his own language. Any mediation attempt is made through the Authorities. The cooperation mechanism would also be of use in the event that the mediation attempt fails. This report is of the opinion that the mechanism set up by the suggested Hague Convention is fundamentally viable and has demonstrated its usefulness within the Mercosur and the EU (ECC-Net). The Tourism Project would build on these successes, albeit at global level. It may be added that a desire for more international cooperation on tourism matters has also been expressed at times by the ones most familiar with the practical issues faced by tourists/consumers. For example, in 2014, some members of the ECC-Net considered the issue of assistance for non-EU tourists and suggested a draft protocol to handle such requests from such tourists after liaising with their North American counterpart. This report however suggests some amendments and additions to the current suggested Hague Convention on Cooperation and Access to Justice for International Tourists. In particular, the definition of a tourist may have to be reconsidered in order to be more acceptable to a majority of Hague Members and a Guide could usefully complement the current text.

The suggested Hague Convention on Cooperation and Access to Justice for International Tourists would build on the HCCH's vast experience in building networks of Central Authorities in the field of international civil procedure. This report is of the opinion that the Tourism Project is compatible with the mandate of the HCCH.[…].

Overall, the Report thus expresses the view that the suggested Hague Convention on Cooperation and Access to Justice for International Tourists is both desirable and feasible, whilst being compatible with the mandate of the HCCH and work conducted in other fora."

The study analyzes (nr. 137–138) the "*Hague Convention on Cooperation and Access to Justice for International Tourists suggested by Brazil*". It builds "*on the experience of the network models it refers to and consequently offers a possible solution to the previously identified issues". It "aims to address several of the difficulties identified in Part 4339 by (notably): - imposing on contracting States the duty to provide tourists with information on their rights and legal remedies in the most appropriate venues and with special attention to the languages understood by the tourists (Article 3). - facilitating mutual understanding through the use of standard complaint forms in multiple languages (Article 4)340. - setting up an international cooperation mechanism between Central Authorities tasked with assisting tourists and coordinating actions within their State (Article 5). Assistance to tourists appears also to be a key feature of Article 6 on Competent Authorities, which must act promptly. - guaranteeing equal access to justice, in particular in respect of cautio judicatum solvi and legal aid (Articles 7 and 8)."*

And states (nr. 138): "*One of the key underlying ideas seems to be that the intervention of an Authority from the State of the trader should often be enough to convince him of the need to seriously take into account the complaint of the tourist from abroad, whilst at the same time offering him the possibility to understand this complaint in his own language. The tourist is for his part likely to know the contact details of his own relevant authority with whom he will be able to correspond in his own language and the draft Convention explicitly covers the possibility for the tourist to complain once back home (within a strict time limit). This report is of the opinion that the core cooperation mechanism set up by the suggested Hague Convention is fundamentally viable and has demonstrated its usefulness within the Mercosur and the EU (ECC-Net). The Tourism Project would build on these successes, albeit at global level. The proposed solution offers the flexibility required to meet a wide variety of difficulties encountered by tourists, whether they relate to accommodation, subsistence, transportation or else. This flexibility enables the cooperation mechanism to adapt to evolving issues, which may substantially differ over time and across countries. Nevertheless, amendments and additions could be considered in order to increase the feasibility of the Tourism Project and the practical efficiency of the Convention.*" It also suggest amendments on the definition of the tourist (without mentioning the 'nationality'), and on the reduction of the proposal to an "administrative cooperation" like the ECC-NET. At the end, it concludes (nr. 144) that it "*could be beneficial to elaborate on some of the provisions of the Brazilian proposal*", but it states that that the Brazilian draft "*constitute[s] an excellent and well-thought starting point, albeit perhaps at times lacking in details.*"

The final suggestion is to add a soft law Guide to the proposal (nr. 145): "*Some of the potentially useful details could be of a non-binding nature and in this respect a Guide complementing the current Convention could be of benefit to all involved. In particular, the relevant authorities must be properly staffed and equipped in order for the Convention to be effective. The Guide could set the minimum expectations and provide recommendations for the ideal authority. Similarly, standard operating procedures such as case handling protocols could be drafted (e.g. complaint by the tourist, preliminary examination by the receiving authority, transmission to the authority of the visited State in case of complaint back home, contact with the trader by an authority of his State, follow-up,* etc.*). Should a working group be established, one of its initial tasks could be to list the issues whose inclusion in the Convention appears opportune and whether they would be classified as essential (to be included in the Convention) or non-essential albeit important (to be included in the Guide). One should perhaps here caution against a too extensive list so as not to derail the project from the cooperation mechanism at its core. Finally, besides the Special Commission mechanism used for other Hague Conventions, consideration could perhaps be given to a more permanent liaison mechanism in order to better monitor and facilitate the implementation of the Convention."*

3 The Prospects of the so called 'Tourism Project' at the Hague Conference: new possibilities to the 'Draft of a Convention on Cooperation and Access to Justice for International Tourists'

It is clear that this new decentralized mass tourism is turning to emergent and developing countries, less prepared for the influx of visitors are driving the emergent economies to support some kind of co-operation mechanism at the Hague conference. Concerns over discrimination on the access to justice and the enforceability of judgments in tourists' redress have since occupied a center stage of the discussions at the Expert Group, but problems regarding the costs of these mechanisms and concerns whether this subject should have a priority at the Hague agenda are also present.

There are currently four models of tourist protection in Private International Law:

1. Indirect, by the establishment of substantial special uniform rules for contracts that are of interest to the sector (such as the UNIDROIT 1980 *Convention on Travel Contracts*,[44] the conventions on carriage by air of the Warsaw/Montreal system[45] or the UNWTO current *'Draft Convention on the Protection of Tourists and on the Rights and Obligations of Tourism Service Providers'*);
2. Direct, by the creation of special conflict rules to protect the consumers, also–potentially–applicable to tourists, such as the Regulation No. 593/2008 on the law applicable to contractual obligations (Rome I) of the EU[46] and the Mercosur *Agreement of Mercosur on Applicable Law to International Consumer Contracts* (MERCOSUR/CMC/DEC. 36/17).[47]

[44] See Atheniense [15].

[45] See Guimarães and Jorge [16]. And Bruno [17].

[46] Paiva [18].

[47] See Marques [19].

3. By the establishment of channels of administrative cooperation to expedite conciliation, such as the MERCOSUR Agreement on consumer visitors of 2005, or of small claims courts and administrative assistance, as established in the Regulation No. 2006/2004, revised by Regulation (EU) No. 2017/2394. The difference between the MERCOSUR system is that it focus on helping and informing the tourist at the visited country, while the EU regulation system focus on the access to justice on the country of residence of the consumers and on the co-operation between authorities to enforce the redress. This different grade of integration of authorities makesMERCOSUR system easier to enforce, because each country offers the same legal help to international tourists as to the national tourists, without discrimination.
4. By assuring a privileged access to the forum of domicile/residence of the consumer for cross-border claims and the application of consumer law as overriding mandatory rules. These cross-border claims in consumer issues, because of the small amount involved, are very costly and difficult to enforce (the judgement project at the Hague Conference would to help in this regard, but when small claims are involved, the enforcement is not foreseeable), without mentioning the existence of "*forum non conveniens*". And the foreign tourist, as a consumer, has sometimes a *forum actoris* privilege, but no special connecting factor in conflicts of law rules, except in Europe. This can be seen as an incentive to expensive and ineffective cross-border litigation in the country of origin of the tourists.

The rationale behind the existent different regimes on the international protection of tourists as consumers was the acceptance of the internationality factor of the relation, allowing the use of common connecting factors, like party autonomy or the *lex loci celebrationis*. But this rationale is not enough anymore,[48] because with the globalization of markets and the growing of mass tourism, all the distance and tourism consumptions have had incentives of the countries, so the need for a minimum level of protection and international cooperation on the subject seems to be an appropriate trend to follow. Let us see the details of the Brazilian proposal to create a global wide cooperation network to protect international tourists and the findings of the Expert Group 2018 (item A below), and the conclusions about the compatibility of the work envisaged at the Hague Conference and at the UNWTO (item B below).

3.1 The Brazilian Proposal and the Findings of the Expert Group 2018

The model chosen by the Brazilian Draft focus on the country visited. Problems in contracts and services already appear in the country of destination of tourists, but they are not addressed in such country in light of the inexistence of fast and efficient channels for these visitors to pursue. On the other hand, there is great demand for

[48] See Howells [20].

litigation in the tourists' countries of residence.[49] These are fairly inefficient and expensive cross-border litigation cases, or litigation with the trip organizers (even if, with electronic means, hiring these services directly is increasing), litigation that could be avoided with better information,[50] more administrative cooperation in the prevention and creation of conciliatory and urgent measures.

Two models have inspired the Brazilian Proposal at the Hague Conference. MERCOSUR has created two instruments (an administrative cooperation agreement in 2005, and a joint experts committee on the protection of visitors and consumers in 2012) that are now combined to allow more than 80 % of the problems to be solved with a simple intervention of the national enforcement authorities by phone, assuring information to foreign tourists and to the tourism industry regarding the rights of consumers, and also encouraging the consumer movement and the national agencies to act on behalf of foreign and national tourists.[51] The European Union has also established an EU-wide network of national consumer enforcement authorities with similar investigation and enforcement powers, under the Regulation (EC) No. 2006/2004 on Consumer Protection Cooperation now revised by Regulation (EU) No. 2017/2394 of 12 December 2017 "on cooperation between national authorities responsible for the enforcement of consumer protection laws". The European Union has created this network to protect intra-European tourists and consumers that buy on the intra-European e-commerce, the so called ECC-Net.[52] Each year this network receives around 100.000 consumer complaints from consumers residing in any of the 28 EU countries.[53] The European Union has already studied to expand this network

[49]See UFRGS research on the Brazilian case law (and information system of consumer litigation in Brazil, SINDEC, www.mj.org.br), Argentinean, Uruguayan and North American, attached to the research on the Province of Mendoza, Argentina, showing an increase of 80 % in the problems with international destinations (Brazil), D. Benitez, Informe del Derecho del turismo en Argentina, in J. Facal (Coord.), Derecho del Turismo, Montevideo, FCU (2006)232–233: "Tipo de quejas de los turistas: 1. Transporte aéreo 40 % (retraso en vuelos) 2. Alojamiento 17 % (alojamiento de alquiler) 3. Agencia de Viajes 13 % (incumplimiento de servicios) 4. Transporte automotor 11 % (demora) 5. Precios diferenciados a turistas extranjeros 8 % (hotelería y entradas en parques nacionales) 6. Alquiler de autos (calidad de los vehículos) 7. Gastronomía 2 % (sobrefacturación) 8. Otros 6 %.".

[50]See J. L. Achirica, El contrato de multipropiedad y la protección de los consumidores, CEDECS: Barcelona, 1997, p. 37 and E. I. Highton, L. A. Julia, S. Lambois, Nuevas formas de domínio-clubes de campo, cementerios, Tiempo compartido o Multipropriedad, Ad hoc, BA, 1987, p. 277.

[51]Marques [21].

[52]The ECC-Net information defines the objectives of the network: *"The European Consumer Centres Network (ECC-Net) is a network of consumer centres in the EU, Iceland and Norway. It provides information on consumer rights and assists in resolving disputes when the consumer and trader involved are based in 2 different European countries. If you live in the EU, Iceland or Norway, the European Consumer Centre in your country can- explain your rights as a consumer- help you to settle a dispute with a seller based in another EU country (or Iceland or Norway) - tell you who to contact if they can't help"*. https://ec.europa.eu/info/live-work-travel-eu/consumers/resolve-your-consumer-complaint/european-consumer-centres-network_en#find-the-consumer-centre-in-your-country.

[53]See the ECC-Net Romania, stating that in 2016, "72 % consumers travelling in the EU had problems during their travel, with 5 % less than the last year. In general, they had problems with transport delay or cancellation (mainly air transport), but also with the hotel. 29 % did not contacted

to tourists from the USA and Canada,[54] but the costs to protect consumers from Non-EU countries seem to be a barrier. The ECC-Net and its App to Inform tourists of theirs rights as consumers remains accessible only to Europeans. The study considers that the ECC-Net is not the best model for a global cooperation.

The idea is that the protection of foreign tourists–normally made *ex post* at the tourist country of the domicile, after suffering from the damage– has a chance to be more effective if made *ex ante,* and at the country visited by the tourist and with the help of the consumer protection system of such nation, preventing cross-border litigations and assuring better access to justice and legal assistance. So, the Brazilian Proposal is to create a global network of consumer agencies to help international tourists.

The Proposal of a *Convention on Cooperation and Access to Justice for International Tourists* has only 10 articles and focus on cooperation and facilitating access to justice for foreign tourists. The Preamble states that: *"international tourists should be provided with appropriate access to the courts and to alternative procedures for dispute resolution available in the State visited; with accessible information on such alternative and relevant court procedures; and with a uniform form for complaints regarding common travel and related issues as well as with an accessible channel to present such complaints so that effective action may be taken to resolve such issues in the State visited*". The aim of the proposal is stipulated in Article 1: "(a) Provide international tourists who are habitually resident in, or nationals of, any Contracting State and who are travelling to, or in, another Contracting State ("the State visited"), with access to judicial proceedings, and alternative procedures for the settlement of disputes, such as conciliation, mediation or arbitration including complaint procedures for the protection of consumers' interests available in the State visited on an equal footing with persons who are nationals of and habitually resident in that State; (b) Provide such tourists with accessible information on such procedures, and with a uniform multilingual form for complaints regarding common travel and related issues, as well as an accessible channel to present such complaints so that prompt and expeditious may be taken to resolve these issues; Establish a system of cooperation between authorities of each Contracting State."

The practical tools suggested by the Brazilian Proposal are three, as follows: information (Art. 3) and access to multilingual complaint forms (Art. 4), being received without any discrimination by national consumer agencies, and the appointment of a central authority in each country (Art. 5).[55]

---

any specialized body to help them solve their problem and 81 % think ECC Romania is a good initiative." Source: https://www.eccromania.ro/en/72-consumers-have-problems-travelling-eu/.

[54]See ECC-Net Feasibility Study Report: Assistance for Non-EU Tourists (North America), in https://www.eccireland.ie/wp-content/uploads/2015/06/Non-EU-Project-Report-2014.pdf.

[55]The text of the article 5 of the Proposal states: "(1) A Contracting State shall designate a Central Authority to discharge the duties that are imposed by the Convention on such an Authority. Federal States, States with more than one system of law or States having autonomous territorial units shall be free to appoint more than one Central Authority and shall specify the territorial or personal extent of their functions. Where a State has appointed more than one Central Authority, it shall designate the Central Authority to which any communication may be addressed for transmission to the appropriate

The First Expert Group Meeting 2018 did not focus on the Brazilian Proposal itself. The idea was to discuss the points to expand the Consultant study, and to give some examples of problems faced by the international tourists.[56] The *aide memoire* summarizes the subjects treated: Vulnerability and challenges; Definition of "tourist"; Work in other fora and compatibility; Information on the 2005 Mercosur Agreement and the ECC-Net; Relationship with the 1980 Hague Convention on Access to Justice; Expected added value of a possible new instrument; Costs and Nature of a possible future instrument. There was no conclusion regarding the cost, and on the nature of the future instrument to be elaborated (whether it would be better to have a hard or soft law instrument on the subject).

The novelty is the section on the 'expected added value of a possible new instrument'. This part states that: "*If a new instrument were to be developed, the Experts identified a number of possible expected values such instrument might add. These included that tourists might be able to obtain appropriate information, including in a language they understand, to ascertain and understand their rights, and the potentially available options to seek redress. It might also provide cooperation mechanisms among suitable bodies that can work in a concerted manner to facilitate the resolution of complaints, with a view to guaranteeing access to justice in the broadest*

Central Authority within that State. (2) Central Authorities shall–(a) Cooperate with each other and promote cooperation amongst the competent authorities in their States to achieve the purpose of the Convention; (b) Provide each other with general information on laws, including consumer protection laws, relevant to the protection of tourists' interests, and on alternative procedures for the settlement of disputes, such as conciliation, mediation or arbitration, including complaint procedures for the protection of consumers' interests, as well as relevant court procedures, such as small claims procedures, available in their State which may offer redress for issues relating to tourism service; (c) Assist international tourists who are habitually resident in or nationals of the Central Authority's State and who return from another Contracting State visited, upon their application–if a complaint procedure commenced by them according to Articles 4 and 6 in that State was not completed before their return, by contacting on their behalf the Central Authority of the State visited with a view to ensuring the follow up on such procedure, or—if no such complaint procedure was commenced by them in that State and provided they apply to the Central Authority within two weeks after their return, by providing them with information and directions enabling them to present a complaint to the competent authority in the State visited, or by forwarding a complaint on their behalf to the Central Authority of that State with a view to transmitting it to the competent authority; (d) Seek as far as possible solutions to difficulties which arise in the application of the Convention.".

[56]See conclusions on "*I. Vulnerability and challenges - 7. Experts identified that tourists in cross-border situations could experience vulnerabilities. Challenges tourists may experience include information gaps and language barriers that could lead to difficulties in accessing justice. 8. Moreover, the Experts noted that in some instances, there may be an inability to commence or continue court proceedings. Reasons include that the time spent by tourists in the location where the complaint lies is too short, or those non-resident complainants may have to provide security for costs in case of judicial proceedings. They also opined that in some instances, mediation and conciliation may require knowledge of the local language as well as the presence of the complainant in the location. 9. Some Experts suggested that small claims and online dispute resolution (ODR) mechanisms may not be suitable for the full resolution of tourism claims. 10. It was noted that agencies dealing with tourists and consumers might not be able to provide immediate help, also because there exist language barriers, as well as other issues, that prevent such help. Thus, some experts suggested that, where they do not exist, government-funded specialised agencies designed to assist tourists would be required.*"

sense, including through alternative dispute resolution, in a non- discriminatory way. The instrument might also have a preventive effect. Finally, it might create an official record of the complaint, including for subsequent use abroad."(nr. 19).

At the end of the document, the "*Experts' Group recommends to the CGAP that it mandates the Experts' Group to continue its work, with a view to assessing the need for, the nature (soft law and hard law options) and the key elements of, a possible new instrument. The composition of the Experts' Group should remain open, and, if possible, also include representatives of Stakeholders, such as the UNWTO, as well as representatives of relevant organisations and private international law experts.*" And the "*Experts' Group endorsed, and recommends that the GCAP considers, the Aide Memoire written by the Chair based on the deliberations made during the Meeting*" and "*expressed their gratitude to the Brazilian Government for their ongoing support of the Tourism Project, as well as to the Consultant for all his work, and the Permanent Bureau for the preparation of the Meeting.*"

3.2 Conclusions About the Compatibility of the Work Envisaged at the Hague Conference and at the UNWTO

One of the most important findings from the Study of the Consultant and the Expert Group is about the compatibility of the work made by the UNWTO and the future work at the Hague Conference.

The study of the Consultant focus on the compatibility of the 'Tourism Project' with the work conducted in other *fora*, in particular the UNWTO and concludes that: "*It appears that there does not seem to be a need to examine the work carried outside the UNWTO when examining the compatibility of the Tourism Project with the work conducted in other fora as a survey up to 1 December 2018 of the major global and regional organisations does not indicate any similar project to that of the Hague Conference. As for the UNWTO Framework Convention on Tourism Ethics (including its Optional Protocol) and the UNWTO current Draft Convention on the Protection of Tourists and on the Rights and Obligations of Tourism Service Providers, they do not appear to overlap or be incompatible with the Tourism Project. On the contrary, the Tourism Project seems to complement the broader agenda of the UNWTO, in particular the desire to increase the confidence of tourists as consumers in tourism service providers highlighted notably in the preamble of the UNWTO Draft Convention on the Protection of Tourists and on the Rights and Obligations of Tourism Service Providers, as well as the long-term objective of sustainable tourism. The productive working relationship established between the HCCH and the UNWTO following the contact made in early 2017 culminated in a letter of endorsement of the Tourism Project by the UNWTO in late 2017.*"

Indeed, the study of the Consultant concludes that "*none of the provisions of the draft convention under consideration overlaps or is incompatible with the Tourism Project as currently expressed in the Brazilian proposal.*" (nr. 164). And add (nr. 164

in fine): "*The work carried out by the HCCH does not seem to overlap, nor does it appear to be incompatible, with that of the UNWTO, especially the work referred to by that Member State, that is, the Draft Convention on the Protection of Tourists and on the Rights and Obligations of Tourism Service Providers. The projects are complementary. Moreover, contact had been made in early 2017 between the two institutions in order to precisely rule out any possible overlap or incompatibility. The ensuing correspondence has been very encouraging and culminated in a letter of endorsement of the Tourism Project by the UNWTO. Here is the key extract in relation to the draft Convention on the Protection of Tourists and the Rights and Obligations of Tourism Service Providers: "UNWTO´s General Assembly has requested the Secretariat to develop a Draft Convention on the Protection of Tourists and the Rights and Obligations of Tourism Service Providers (UNWTO Convention) […] Having considered the work of Hague Conference on Private International Law (HCCH) in relation to the Proposal on a Draft Convention on Cooperation and Access to Justice for International Tourists (HCCH Project), I am pleased to confirm that the HCCH Project complements work undertaken by the UNWTO in relation to […] the UNWTO Convention […]. I am also pleased to confirm that, considering their relevant scopes, there are currently no overlaps of the work undertaken by the UNWTO and the HCCH respectively*".

And it states the compatibility of the work being carried out at the Hague with other *fora* (nr. 176–177): "*The UNWTO Framework Convention on Tourism Ethics (including its Optional Protocol) and the UNWTO current Draft Convention on the Protection of Tourists and on the Rights and Obligations of Tourism Service Providers do not appear to overlap or be incompatible with the Tourism Project. On the contrary, the Tourism Project seems to complement the broader agenda of the UNWTO, in particular the desire to increase the confidence of tourists as consumers in tourism service providers highlighted notably in the preamble of the UNWTO Draft Convention on the Protection of Tourists and on the Rights and Obligations of Tourism Service Providers, as well as the long-term objective of sustainable tourism… thus lead us to the conclusion that the Tourism Project neither overlaps nor is incompatible with the UNWTO work, but rather complements it. Given the inexistence (to our knowledge) of any other global forum where similar work is being considered, we can safely conclude that the Tourism Project is compatible with the work conducted in other fora.*"

In this regard, the future work of the Hague Conference, the most important international forum for building international administrative and judicial cooperation in Private International Law issues, seems to be needed, feasible and timely.

4 Final Observations

If we want to have an overall assessment of the future of a new instrument on the protection of international tourists, it is necessary to say that the Consultant's study and the findings of the Expert Group were very positive regarding the continuation of the studies with an Expert Group at the Hague Conference. The Council on General Affairs and Policy in the 2019 Meeting has decided to have another Expert Group Meeting in the future.

The question that drives us is whether it is possible to build a network of world cooperation among all the national actors involved in the protection of consumers to protect foreign tourists.[57] The costly and inefficient international disputes, as well as the multiplication of the damage to foreign tourists, who usually are deprived of justice, could be avoided if there was a global network of tourist protection among the agents involved with consumer protection as proposed by the Brazilian government.

The proposal of the Brazilian government aims to create a network of global cooperation using the well-established bodies of consumer defense and existing national systems of consumer protection (organized by central authorities) to protect foreign tourists still in the country they visited, avoiding or at least minimizing current and future damages incurred by them.

The positive effects of such network will be very pedagogical. Through cooperation, central authorities will be able to expand national help to foreigners and identify frauds and international schemes, but also assist the individual tourist. When the international tourism is turning more and more to the less developed countries, it is only to hope that the Hague Conference prepares a new worldwide cooperation network to enhance the protection of tourists and avoid discrimination on the access of justice and alternative means of dispute resolutions. If the future legal instrument will be a hard law convention, as initially proposed by the Brazilian government, or only a soft law instrument remains open. The important action now is the subject to remain at the Hague conference agenda and to call for further Experts Groups to analyse the proposal and the complementary ways that the Consultant's study and the first Expert Group Meeting in 2018 have indicated. As the first Report of the ILA's Committee on International Protection of Consumers in 2010 states: "*Issues of consumer law are no longer national. Market globalization has changed not only the way we produce, but also the way we consume. The new 'global citizen' is also a global consumer*".[58] And more and more this 'global consumer' is an international tourist.

References

1. C. Lima Marques, Towards a global approach to protect foreign tourists, in A. Sierralta, C. Lima Marques and J. A. Moreno Rodríguez, Derecho Internacional, Mundialización y Gobernanza , CEDEP (2012) 449–455
2. C. Lima Marques; M. L. Delaloye. El rol de los principios en la proteccion internacional del consumidor: la Declaracion de Sofía de la International Law Association. In: A. Amaral Júnior; L. Klein Vieira (Org.). El derecho internacional privado y sus desafíos en la actualidad. Bogotá: Ibañez (2017) 135–154
3. J. Basedow. The Law of Open societies–Private Ordering and Public Regulation in the Conflicts of Laws, Brill/The Hague Academy of International Law (2015) 424

[57] See Marques [22].

[58] See Discussion Paper at www.ila-hq.or/en/committees/index.cfm/cid/1030.

4. C. Lima Marques. The Brazilian "Draft Convention on Co-operation in Respect of Tourists and Visitors Abroad" at the Hague Conference and the UN World Tourism Organization's Draft Convention, in j. Moreno Rodriguez; C. Lima Marques. Los servicios en el Derecho Internacional Privado–Jornadas de la ASADIP 2014
5. Marques, Claudia Lima. The Need for a Global Cooperation Network to Protect Foreign Tourists/Consumers and the comeback of Private International Law, in THE PERMANENT BUREAU OF THE HAGUE CONFERENCE ON PRIVATE INTERNATIONAL LAW, A commitement to Private International Law- Essayz in honour of Hans van Loon, Intersentia, Cambridge, 2013, p. 311ff
6. 6. Wei, Dan. A Protecção do Turista através do Direito do Consumidor. *Revista de Direito do Consumidor*, v. 83, 2012, p. 40
7. Dan, Wei. Tourist-consumer protection in Macau SAR of China as a world tourism destination, in *Revista de Direito do Consumidor*, vol. 92/2014, p. 13–24, Mar - Abr/2014, p. 14
8. Yang Yang, Consular Protection in China: Problems and Solution, International Politics Quarterly, 2013, at 17–29
9. C. Lima Marques, Towards a global approach to protect foreign tourists, in A. Sierralta, C. Lima Marques and J. A. Moreno Rodríguez, Derecho Internacional, Mundialización y Gobernanza , CEDEP (2012) 451
10. K. Tonner, Electronic Commerce and Travel Law, in T. Wilhelmsson et al. (eds.), Consumer Law in the Information Society, Kluwer, 205 (2000)
11. L. R. Atheniense. A responsabilidade jurídica das agências de viagens. Belo Horizonte: Del Rey, 2002, p. 17 e seg
12. K. Tonner, Electronic Commerce and Travel Law, in T. Wilhelmsson et al. (eds.), Consumer Law in the Information Society, Kluwer, 207 (2000)
13. R. A. Castellanos Pfeiffer. Consumer Defense in Mercosur: A Balance and Recent Challenges, in T. Bourgoignie (Ed.). L'intégration économique et la protection du consommateur, Blais (2009) 414
14. Soares, Ardyllis, A tutela internacional do consumidor turista, in *Revista de Direito do Consumidor* , vol. 82, 2012, p. 113ff
15. Atheniense, Luciana Rodrigues. *A responsabilidade jurídica das agências de viagens*. Belo Horizonte: Del Rey, 2002, p. 17ff
16. Scartezzini Guimarães, Paulo Jorge, *Dos contratos de hospedagem, de transporte de passageiros e de turismo*, Saraiva: São Paulo, 2007, p. 223ff
17. Miragem, Bruno. *Contrato de Transporte*, São Paulo: Ed. RT, 2014, p. 187ff
18. 18. R.A.M. Paiva, *Direito, Turismo e Consumo*, Renovar: Rio de Janeiro (2012), p. 236
19. Marques, Claudia Lima. Towards a global approach to protect forcign tourists: building governance through a new cooperation net in consumer and tourist issues. In: sierraltra, Anibal; Marques, Claudia Lima (orgs.). Derecho internacional, mundialización y gobernanza. Assunção: Cedep, 2012. p. 425–455
20. Howells, Geraint; Ramsay, Iain; Wilhelmsson, Thomas. Consumer law and its international dimension. In. Howells, Geraint; Ramsay, Iain; Wilhelmsson, Thomas. Handbook of Research on International Consumer Law. Elgar, 2010, p. 1
21. C. Lima Marques, Towards a global approach to protect foreign tourists. In: A. Sierralta, C. Lima Marques and J. A. Moreno Rodríguez, Derecho Internacional, Mundialización y Gobernanza , CEDEP (2012) 450.
22. Marques, Claudia Lima. Esforços atuais para incluir o tema da proteção do turista na Agenda de Trabalho da Conferência de Haia e a proposta brasileira de "Convenção de Cooperação em Matéria de Proteção dos Visitantes e Turistas Estrangeiros", in *Revista de Direito do Consumidor*, vol. 90, 2013, p. 39–64

Consumer Protection in Electronic Commerce and Online Dispute Resolution Through Mediation

Ashok R. Patil

1 Introduction

India got independence in 1947 from British crown rule and the Constitution of India came into effect on 26 January 1950. India is the seventh-largest country by area, the second-most populous country with over 1.2 billion people and the most populous democracy in the world. India is a federation with a parliamentary system governed under the Constitution of India, which serves as the country's supreme legal document. In India, the need for consumer protection is paramount in view of the ever-increasing population and the consequent need for many goods and services of which is no matching supply.

The British rule revolutionized the Indian legal system by bringing about unified nationwide modern legal system. Some of the legislations that were passed during the British regime to protect consumer interests are—the Indian Contract Act, 1872, Sale of Goods Act, 1930, Indian Penal Code, 1860, Drugs and Cosmetics Act, 1940, Agriculture Procedure (Grading and Marketing Act), 1937. Other than Constitution of India, several legislations were enacted post-independence such as Competition Act, 2002, Food Safety and Standards Act, 2006, Legal Metrology Act, 2009, the Bureau of Indian Standards, 2016, Information Technology Act, 2000 and Consumer Protection Act, 1986 to protect the consumers.

It is the State's duty to guarantee the right to live with human dignity, free from exploitation, of everyone living in it. This right to live with human dignity is enshrined in the Indian Constitution and derives its life's breath from the directive principles of state policy.[1] According to article 38 of the *Indian Constitution*, the State shall secure a social order for the promotion of the people's welfare and shall effectively

[1] The Constitution of India of 1950, article 21.

A. R. Patil (✉)
National Law School of India University, Bangalore 560072, Karnataka, India
e-mail: ashokpatil@nls.ac.in

D. Wei et al. (eds.), *Innovation and the Transformation of Consumer Law*,
https://doi.org/10.1007/978-981-15-8948-5_13

work to achieve a "social order in which justice, economic and political, shall inform all the institutions of the national life."[2] In addition, the State has a duty to raise the level of nutrition and the standard of living to improve public health, and to prohibit consumption of intoxicating drinks or drugs which are injurious to health.[3]

Due to globalisation and development of technology, Electronic Commerce (E-Commerce) has become a busting business in India today. It is the cutting edge in all areas of business today. Therefore, physical market shifting to Electronic market in India. E-Commerce has evolved and has gained importance in the present economy. E-commerce offers the consumers a wide range of products and services and also, the businesses find huge potential for consumers. Also, the number of internet users has gone up in the world including India.[4] As a result, the number of e-commerce transactions has increased multifold. A large number of new businesses and services have also evolved around the world and the concept of B2C commerce has also expanded especially inter-state and cross border transactions.[5]

E-commerce has indeed emerged as a major opportunity for India. With the phenomenal spread of mobile telephony and the advent of 4G in the country, buyers from small towns and cities are also buying online in large numbers. It is a fact that internet has dissolved the discrimination factor between the small and the big cities enabling buyers from small towns to have access to the same branded goods, and quality products which earlier was a privilege of large city buyers.

Consumer confidence primarily involves two convictions—that the consumer will get what he expects and that if things go wrong, the consumer can seek a remedy. The virtual aspect of e-commerce sale throws up newer confronts to consumer trust and confidence. The Consumer Protection law recognises several unfair trade practices such as false and misleading representation of goods and services in terms of standard, quality, grade etc., materially misleading the public as regard the price at which the goods are ordinarily sold, disparaging of goods, misrepresentations as to warranty or guarantee etc. But, what about failure on the part of the business in providing adequate disclosure of information regarding the address of the supplier, characteristics of goods and services, delivery costs, withdrawal etc. in case of such distance selling?

With the increase in e-commerce transactions, the number of disputes are bound to increase. Therefore, effective measures/mechanism for resolving these disputes is necessary and should be given importance. The e-commerce should not slow down because there is no proper dispute resolution mechanism in place. This hurts the economy of the nation considering the potential it holds in the cross border sales.

---

[2]The Constitution of India of 1950, article 38.

[3]The Constitution of India of 1950, article 47.

[4]According to a report by the Internet and Mobile Association of India and market research firm IMRB International, the number of Internet users in India is expected to reach 450–465 million by June, 2017 which is 4–8% higher than from 432 million in December 2016. It is important to note that in the report that the overall internet penetration in India is currently around 31% and in rural India 163 million internet users around 17% of total users are present.

[5]According to a report published by Forrester Research, India is the fastest growing e-commerce market in the world and could overtake USA which stands in second position after China.

An effective dispute mechanism should generally include speedy justice and convenience. Consumers including those who have small value claims should also have access to a forum. Consumers should be given an opportunity and access to assert their rights. This article analyses the present trends in consumer law in E-Commerce in India and the challenges faced in protecting the consumers in the virtual online space.

2 The Consumer Protection Act, 1986

Though there are no specific laws governing E-commerce in India, in terms of Business-to-E-consumer. The existing provisions of Consumer Protection Act,1986 is being applied to disputes in online transactions. The main object of the Consumer Protection Act, 1986 (CPA), Consumer Protection Rules, 1987, and the Consumer Protection Regulations, 2005 is the promotion of the basic rights of consumers, namely the right to safety, the right to be informed of quality, potency and purity of products, the right to have access to a variety of goods of competitive prices, the right to redress grievances and the right to consumer education. The essential feature of the Act is its provision of procedures and fora for the resolution of consumer disputes due to physical trade or online trade. The CPA has thus been amended three times in the years 1991, 1993 and 2002 to achieve this objective by plugging the gaps.

Since the CPA does not derogate from existing laws and is supplementary in nature, its provisions do not debar a consumer from going to a civil court to seek compensation for loss or damage caused to him by a defect in the goods purchased by him. Therefore, a consumer may initiate proceedings in a civil court under the law of contract, sale of goods, law of torts, or any other existing law depending on the circumstances. The CPA merely provides a separate enforcement machinery and redressal forum with the aim of giving consumers a simple and expeditious solution to consumer problems. The Act has established a hierarchy of special courts known as 'Consumer Redressal Forums' for deciding consumer disputes at three levels viz. 'District Forum' at the lower level[6] (up to 20 lakhs),[7] 'State Commission' at state level[8] (more than 20 lakhs to 1 crore)[9] and the 'National Commission' at national level[10] (more than 1 crore).[11]

Under this Act, the Consumer Dispute Redressal Agencies are given authority to provide relief to consumers who suffer losses due to defective products. The complaint can be made in relation to those goods[12] which suffer from one or more

[6]Consumer Protection Act, 1986, section 10.

[7]Consumer Protection Act, 1986, section 11(1).

[8]Consumer Protection Act, 1986, section 16.

[9]Consumer Protection Act, 1986, section 17(1)(a)(i).

[10]Consumer Protection Act, 1986, section 20.

[11]Consumer Protection Act, 1986, section 21(a)(i).

[12]Consumer Protection Act, 1986, section 2(1)(i).

defects[13]; or when goods which will be hazardous to life and safety when used are being offered for sale to the public in contravention of any standards relating to safety of such goods as required to be complied with, by or under any law for the time being in force; or if the trader could have known with due diligence that the goods so offered are unsafe to the public.[14] The CPA also prohibits "unfair trade practices".[15]

The CPA deals with the twin concepts of defect in goods and deficiency in services and provides for a comprehensive definition of consumer in section 2(1)(d) in relation to goods and services. The consumer is a person who buys any goods or hires or avails of any services for consideration. The user of such goods, with the approval of the buyer, and any beneficiary of such services with the approval of the hirer, have also been included within the ambit of the concept of consumer, enlarging its scope to a great extent. The consideration for goods or services can either be paid or promised or partly promised or covered under any system of deferred payment. However, a person who, in the case of goods, obtains the goods for resale or for any commercial purpose or who, in case of services, avails of such services, for any commercial purpose is excluded from the definition of consumer. The explanation further states that the expression 'commercial purpose' does not include use by a buyer of such goods or hirer of services, exclusively for the purpose of earning his livelihood by means of self-employment.[16]

Under section 2(1)(*f*), "defect" in goods means any fault, imperfection or shortcoming in the quality, quantity, potency, purity or standard which is required to be maintained by or under any law for the time being in force or under any contract, express or implied, or as is claimed by the trader in any manner whatsoever in relation to any goods.[17]

The expression 'service' has been defined in the Act in section 2(1)(o). 'Service' refers to any service of any description which is made available to potential users and includes, but is not limited to, the provision of facilities in connection with banking, financing, insurance, transport, processing, supply of electrical or other energy, board or lodging or both, housing construction, entertainment, amusement or purveying of news or other information, but does not include the rendering of any service free of charge or under a contract of personal service.[18] The deficiency in service is one of the grounds for filing a complaint under the Act. Presently, the majority of complaints before the adjudicatory bodies provided for in the Act relate to the deficiency in service of various service providers. The term 'deficiency' has also been defined in section 2(1)(g) of the Act. It means any fault, imperfection, shortcoming or inadequacy in the quality, nature and manner of performance which is required to be maintained by or under any law for the time being in force or has

---

[13] Consumer Protection Act, 1986, section 2(1)(c)(ii).

[14] Consumer Protection Act, 1986, section 2(1)(c)(iii).

[15] Consumer Protection Act, 1986, section 2(1)(r).

[16] Consumer Protection Act, 1986, section 2(1)(d).

[17] Consumer Protection Act, 1986, section 2(1)(f).

[18] Consumer Protection Act, 1986, section 2(1)(o).

been undertaken to be performed by a person in pursuance of a contract or otherwise in relation to any service.[19]

Some of the common issues that arise in an electronic transaction are: Is the company doing business a legitimate one and where is it located? Does the business organization/individual offering product/service provide appropriate information on terms and conditions of the purchase such as instructions for use of products, warranties, cancellation, flexibility in return/refund policies, availability of after-sale service etc.; Is the browser secure and does it encrypt personal and financial information during online transmission?; Does the browser provide comprehensive 'Privacy Policy Statement' addressing the manner in which the personal information of the customer would be used?; Is the business committed to customer satisfaction? Other issues like Fake or misleading reviews, Misleading Advertisement, Drip Pricing, Price Discrimination, Comparison portals not providing all information, Lack of quick redressal system like Online Dispute Resolution.

In the Indian context, E-commerce companies adopting inventory-based model fall within the meaning of "Intermediary" within the provision of section 2(1)(w) of Information Technology Act, 2008. Such intermediary is required to publish rules and regulations, privacy policy and user agreement for access or usage of intermediary's computer resource by any person under Information Technology (Intermediaries Guidelines) Rules, 2011.[20] On obtaining knowledge of any information being grossly harmful, harassing, defamatory, obscene or otherwise unlawful in any manner or violate any law for the time being in force, the Guidelines requires the intermediary to act within 36 h to disable such information.[21] The intermediary is also required to preserve such information and associated records for at least ninety days for investigation purposes.[22] The Rules also requires the intermediary to publish on its website the name of the Grievance Officer and his contact details by which users who suffer as a result of access to the computer resource can notify their complaints. E-commerce companies handling sensitive personal data or information of the consumer are required to comply with reasonable security practices and procedures as laid down under Information Technology (Reasonable security practices and procedures and sensitive personal data or information) Rules, 2011.

Jurisdiction of courts posed a great challenge in the early years when ecommerce cases were brought before consumer forums. Many cases were struck down due to lack of jurisdiction which the consumers had to run helter-skelter identifying the right jurisdiction, given the virtual nature of ecommerce. In a recent judgement by the National Commission in *Marwar Engineering College and Research Centre v. Hanwant Singh*,[23] the Commission has held that Consumer's place of e-commerce transaction is the jurisdiction to file a complaint.

---

[19]Consumer Protection Act, 1986, section 2(1)(g).

[20]Information Technology (Intermediary Guidelines) Rules, 2011, Rule 3(1) and 3(2).

[21]Information Technology (Intermediary Guidelines) Rules, 2011, Rule 3(4).

[22]Information Technology (Intermediary Guidelines) Rules, 2011, Rule 3(4).

[23]IV (2014) CPJ 582 (NC).

The UN Guidelines on Consumer Protection has amended in 2015 and included special emphasis on transactions taking place through ecommerce, which include fair and equitable treatment, ethical commercial behaviour, disclosure and transparency and education and awareness raising. The UN Guidelines also lays emphasis on Member States to work towards establishing consumer protection policies that encourage good business practices, ease of access to information, secure payment mechanisms, fair, affordable and speedy dispute resolution and redress, consumer privacy and data security. On the lines of these amended guidelines Government of India is coming out with new Bill called the Consumer Protection Bill, 2018.

3 The Consumer Protection Act, 2019[24]

The Consumer Protection Act, 2019 (CPA, 2019) which will come into force once it is notified by the Central Government.[25] Until that the Consumer Protection Act, 1986 is in force. Along with strengthening the existed provisions, added three new chapters on Regulatory Authority, Product Liability and Mediation.

The CPA, 2019 establishes a Consumer Protection Authority to investigate into consumer complaints, issue safety notices for goods and services, and pass orders for recall of goods and against misleading advertisements. The Regulatory Authority has a sue moto powers. Another new chapter on Product Liability added to protect the consumers in better way from injury due to defective goods and services. Consumer can file a complaint of product liability against the manufacturer. Third new chapter on Mediation aimed at simplifying the consumer dispute resolution process in the consumer forum. The National Commission or a State Commission or a District Commission, as the circumstances may be, will appoint a mediator who shall attempt to resolve the dispute between the parties by facilitating discussion between parties directly by guiding the parties in identifying issues, reducing misunderstandings, exploring different ways to compromise all in all generating options in an attempt to solve the dispute.

In its first attempt to address the concerns of consumers' right to information in ecommerce, the Consumer Protection Act, 2019 has explicitly extended the ambit to E-commerce transactions as well. Some significant provisions of the new CPA, 2019 are:

The definition of "*Consumer*' is amended to include an explanation to the expressions 'buys any goods" and "hires or avails any services" to include transactions made through any mode, offline, online through electronic means, teleshopping or direct selling or multi-level marketing. The definition '*Deficiency in service*' is amended

[24]The Gazette of India, New Delhi, 9th August 2019, Part II-section 1.

[25]Consumer Protection Act, 2019, section 1(3): It shall come into force on such date as the Central Government may, by notification, appoint and different dates may be appointed for different States and for different provisions of this Act and any reference in any such provision to the commencement of this Act shall be construed as a reference to the coming into force of that provision.

to include "*…any act of omission or commission on the part of service provider in withholding 'relevant information' which may cause damage to the consumer.*"

Failure on the part of business to allocate a 30 days cooling-off period for purchase of goods or services is also being considered to be included as 'unfair trade practice' under section 2(41)[26] of Consumer Protection Act, 2019. The same provision also attempts to provide data security on consumers' personal information disseminated on the online shopping portals.

In the context of territorial jurisdiction of consumer redressal agencies, new amendment states that a complaint may be instituted in territorial jurisdiction, where the complainant resides or personally works for gain. This is an important step towards ease of access to justice in complaints arising out of online shopping, where in most circumstances, the online store is located away from the place of consumer and provides unreasonable terms for dispute resolution. Another very important amendment is establishment of court-annexed mediation cells for the purpose of amicable redressal of consumer dispute.

4 Consumer Disputes Settlement Through ADR/ODR

The developments of the internet have provided new opportunities for business and consumers to explore new markets. Despite several changes being brought out in E-consumer protection, some challenges still pose, for instance, filing a complaint against an electronic retailer based overseas can be challenging, expensive, time consuming and it might not be clear from the website where the supplier is based. The conventional approach to jurisdiction of courts lies in territorial, pecuniary or subject-matter jurisdictions. But with the e-commerce, the question of jurisdiction gets complex.

Another challenge in cross-border consumer complaints is that the contract may be governed by the laws of the country from where the goods were supplied, rather than where it was bought. Legal action could include having to start court proceedings in the retailer's country, thus inconveniencing the consumer to a great extent. In this regard, the new UN Guidelines on Consumer Protection lays down recommendations on dispute redressal and resolution among others. The Guidelines states that the Member States should encourage development of fair, effective and transparent

---

[26]Consumer Protection Act, 2019, section 2(41), after sub-clause (*G*), the following sub-clauses are, namely:—(H) after selling such goods or rendering of such services, refuses to take back or withdraw the goods or withdraw or discontinue the service and refuses to refund the consideration thereof, if paid, within a period of thirty days after the receipt of goods or availing of services it is so requested by the consumer.

(*I*) discloses to any other person any personal information given in confidence by the consumer provided that disclosure of personal information given with express or implied consent of the consumer or under provisions of any law in force or in public interest shall not be constructed as unfair trade practice.

mechanisms to address consumer complaints, through administrative, judicial and alternative dispute resolution, including for cross-border cases.

The Supreme Court of India in *M/s Afcons Infra Ltd. v. M/s Cherian Varkey Construction Company Ltd. and Others,*[27] while enumerating matters that are suitable for Alternate Dispute Resolution (section 89 of Civil Procedure Code, 1908) held that all consumer disputes including disputes where a trader/supplier/manufacturer/service provider is keen to maintain his business/professional reputation and credibility or product popularity can be referred to ADR. In view of the above, the need for mediation in the consumer context in India has been recognised under the proposed Consumer Protection Bill, 2018. The Bill has introduced mediation in consumer cases, where disputes can be referred to mediation either at the commencement of proceeding before the Consumer Forum or at any time during the proceeding.

In *Anita Kushwaha v. Pushap Suda*[28] case Supreme Court held that 'Access to Justice' is a fundamental right and laid down four main facets of the essence of access to justice i.e., (i) The State must provide an *effective adjudicatory mechanism*; (ii) The mechanism so provided must be *reasonably accessible in terms of distance*; (iii) The process of adjudication *must be speedy*; and (iv) The litigant's access to the adjudicatory process must be *affordable*.

Mainly because of above mentioned reasons, a new way to resolve issues has evolved. Online Dispute Resolution (ODR) refers to use of ADR methods online. The use of technology to resolve disputes is the latest innovation in the field of dispute resolution. ODR is thought to supplement existing ADR methods to address disputes quickly and adequately using technology and the Internet. ODR brings considerable advantages over traditional litigation. It empowers consenting parties to create their own agreements and provides a greater degree of control over the dispute resolution process and the decision. In addition, it allows transacting parties to select neutral third parties to arbitrate, particularly professionals who are experts in the subject matter of the dispute. Compared to the constraints of procedures and precedents that judges are compelled to follow, ODR methods offer flexibility of methods and also the freedom to not be represented by a legal practitioner.

5 Online Consumer Mediation in India

Realizing enormous potential for online consumer mediation in India, the Ministry of Consumer Affairs, Government of India has sanctioned an initiative of the National Law School of India University, Bengaluru. The Online Consumer Mediation Centre (OCMC) is established at National Law School of India University, Bengaluru under the aegis of Ministry of Consumer Affairs, Government of India. The Centre aims

[27] 2010 (8) SCC 24.

[28] (2016) 8 SCC 509.

to provide for a state-of-the-art infrastructure for resolving consumer disputes both through physical as well as online mediation through its platform.

The mission of the Centre is to provide innovative technology for consumers and organisations to manage and resolve conflicts and to propel online mediation as a first choice to resolving consumer disputes. The Centre runs with a vision to provide for an innovative online mediation tool that affords consumers better access to justice through quick and easy redressal mechanism and at the same time provide opportunity for businesses to maintain good customer relations. The core Values of the Centre include Easy accessibility, Security, Confidentiality, Cost-effective, Neutrality andIntegrity.[29]

The Ministry of Consumer Affairs, Government of India has sent letters to all E-Commerce companies and Federation of Industries to make use of OCMC in settling their disputes. Also Department of Justice, Government of India has recognised OCMC and sent a letter to all States of India to make use of system.[30]

A. The process

OCMC offers two services: e-negotiation and e-mediation. To avail the services, a consumer who feels aggrieved over a sale or goods or services will have to register on the website by providing his/her Name, Age, Gender, Address, City, State, Country, Mobile No., Email, Password, Confirm Password, Identity Proof (which may be Aadhar No. or Voter ID).

After registration, the consumer will have to choose the e-commerce company against which he has grievance from the list. If the company's name doesn't appear, the Centre will add it within a day or two upon e-mail request. After selecting the company, the consumer must enter the order/bill/receipt number. Thereafter, he/she will be directed to the payment page where Rs. 100 (one hundred rupees only) has to be paid only through any of the modes prescribed.

Once the payment is made, the consumer will be taken to the e-platform where he will fill his grievance against the company and produce proofs/documents/records of grievance. The intake form requires the following details to be filled by consumer: Transaction details–Purchase date, Receipt date, value of goods/service, nature of dispute, description of issue.

Once the details are entered and documents are uploaded, the case will be put for review. OCMC will check if the case falls under scope of their rules. If yes, the case will be accepted and business will be contacted immediately. If no, then the case will be closed and there will be no refund. Consumers and businesses are required to read and understand the terms of dispute resolution through OCMC before seeking any redressal.

When the case is accepted, the parties will get chance to negotiate the dispute or escalate it to mediation. If escalated, the Centre will appoint a suitable mediator for

[29] http://onlinemediationcenter.ac.in.

[30] Apoorva Mandhani, Law Ministry Deliberates Ways to Reduce Government Litigation Accounting for 46% of Pending Cases, *available at*: http://www.livelaw.in/doj-deliberates-ways-reduce-government-litigation-accounting-46-pending-cases/.

the case. The mediator will, considering the case and circumstances, adopt various techniques to settle the case amicably.

B. **Functioning of the Centre**

The Centre offers an e-platform specially made to handle e-consumer disputes for the parties to settle amicably and out of court. The Centre performs better than the traditional courts and the consumer fora as under[31]:

I. **Scope of dispute resolution**

The Centre caters to the current need for swift remedy for e-consumers and the e-commerce companies. The Centre provides scope for resolving disputes through online negotiation and online mediation. The Centre accepts cases from those who have an agreement to resolve the dispute through mediation and also referral from regular courts and consumer fora.

II. **Regulation and applicability**

The Centre is self-regulated but follows the principles of Supreme Court Mediation Manual.[32] It has framed its own Mediation Rules and Code of Conduct for parties, mediators, the Centre and other participants. The Centre's value of transparency is visible in the effective date mentioned in the website. Most of the websites do not show the date of effectiveness of any rules, terms of use etc. The Centre also has empaneled mediators who have undergone 40-hour mediation training program as specified by the Supreme Court of India.

III. **Disclosures**

The Centre has shown great transparency in dispute resolution through publication of Mediation Rules, Code of Conduct, Terms of Use and Privacy Policy online. Also, the fee is nominal i.e. Rs. 100/- which is collected as administrative charges. Also, there is no additional and hidden charge for the dispute resolution which includes both online negotiation and online mediation.

IV. **Choice of dispute resolution**

Either party can choose for online negotiation or mediation. The parties have option to resolve it among themselves without the involvement of third party neutral. When the parties have agreed to seek help of mediator, the Centre will appoint a suitable mediator from its list of empanelled mediators published online. The parties are not given option to choose the mediator which seems to be a drawback but the fact the

---

[31]The Mediation Rules, Code of Conduct and other documents based on which the analysis is made is *available at:* website http://onlinemediationcenter.ac.in/.

[32]Mediation Training Manual of India is prepared by the Supreme Court for the purpose of training. The same is *available at*: sci.nic.in/MEDIATION%20TRAINING%20MANUAL %20OF%20INDIA.pdf.

mediators work pro bono and very minimal fee is charged shows that the parties are at a disadvantageous position.

V. **Flexibility**

a. **Flexibility in commencement**

There are no documents to be sent to the Centre. The consumer who feels aggrieved has to register himself by giving this details on the website and register the case on the e-platform after paying the fee of Rupees one hundred. All documents can be uploaded on the e-platform and during any stage of dispute resolution.

b. **Process flexibility**

The Centre provides for e-platform which can handle both synchronous and asynchronous forms of communication. The e-platform supports text based negotiation and mediation with 24X7 accessibility. This means that parties can make proposal for settlement or make any communication at any time he finds leisure and at any place. The parties at no point of time are required to come to the Centre to attend any kind of session. This kind of flexibility must be exploited by the parties. The time and energy saved is invaluable through the flexibility provided.

VI. **Power to opt out of e-platform**

The parties can opt out of the online negotiation and mediation during any stage without assigning any reasons. The role of the Centre is high here because the parties need to be educated about the benefits of online settlement including the enforcement of these settlements. It is the duty of the Centre to raise awareness of the advantages the ODR platform brings to the parties.

VII. **Timeline for dispute resolution**

The Centre as said already aims at swift resolution of disputes. The Rules strictly provide the timeframe available for parties to get the matter resolved. Settlement through negotiation must occur within 7 days and mediation within the next 23 days, if unresolved. Parties or the mediator can request for additional time in case where there is a possibility of settlement.

VIII. **Confidentiality**

The Centre offers complete confidentiality of documents and all communications including the terms of settlement agreement if agreed to between the parties. The

Centre will not disclose any communication unless mandatory under the laws of the country. The Centre's Code of Conduct prohibits taking of screenshots of the communications made and the Rules state clearly that the parties will not use this in the courts of law.

IX. **Participation**

The Centre accepts cases against all e-commerce companies. There is no limitation of number of cases that can be filed against a company. Any number of cases can be filed against any number of companies. The Centre has obtained a mandate from the Ministry of Consumer Affairs, Government of India which mandates all the e-commerce companies in India to participate in the process. Also, a letter has been obtained which states that the business organisations shall encourage the member companies to participate in the process.

X. **Other good practices**

a. **Feedback system**: The Centre has put in place a feedback form for the parties to provide their comments on the use of the e-platform. The feedback are kept confidential and will be used for improvements.
b. **Stakeholders' meetings**: There is an advisory council consisting of representatives of various stakeholders and eminent personalities. The advisory council meets periodically and reviews the working of the Centre. The suggestions of the advisory council are implemented by the Centre.
c. **Compatibility**: The e-platform is easily accessible not only on computers or laptops but mobile as well. Consumers need not worry about owning a computer to get the settlement.

The use of an e-platform such as OCMC established at OCMC holds advantage over traditional and other alternative fora. ODR will benefit the consumers in the following ways: Firstly, the consumers can file their complaints online in their home or office. Secondly, they can negotiate and try to resolve directly with the companies online. Thirdly, they get the flexibility of getting it resolved by sitting in office, home, restaurants, parks or any other place they want. Fourthly, they can give out a bid or reply to a bid at any time of the day/night they want. Fifthly, all communications are kept confidential between them. Sixthly, it is very cost and time effective. Seventhly, e-mediation process where e-mediator can be appointed online by their consent/nominated on their behalf and the whole process is also online. Eighthly, the conversation again being a record can test the impartiality of the mediator in check. Ninthly, settlement is also online which is binding and enforceable under the Arbitration and Conciliation Act, 1996[33] or as an e-contract. Lastly, e-mediation always ends in win for both parties.

C. **Limitations**

[33]Panchu [1].

There are several limitations which need to be addressed by the OCMC and the Government:

a. The Government needs to acknowledge and make resolution of disputes relating to e-commerce mandatory for all the consumers and businesses.
b. The Centre and the Government has to give awareness to the public about the advantages of resolving the disputes amicably online.
c. The Government should bring out a separate legislation for regulating mediation in the country.
d. The Centre needs to enhance the performance of the e-platform.
e. The Government should push the companies in making mediation mandatory before approaching the courts or fora.
f. The Consumer Protection Act, 2019 mandates that the Government set up mediation cells attached to district forum, state commissions and National Commission. Along with OCMC the Government can set up online mediation cells in some districts at least on a pilot basis. In order this to happen, the Government should also develop software which can be used by the consumer dispute redressal machinery.
g. Moreover, there should also be a convergence of various ministries including Ministry of Electronics and Information Technology, Ministry of Consumer Affairs, Ministry of Corporate Affairs and Ministry of Law and Justice. An inter-ministerial committee could be set up review the ODR feasibility in India.
h. The Government should also enter into agreements with the industry associations for promoting the use of online mediation centres so that there is full participation and co-operation from the businesses. Businesses also have a duty to provide the authorized officer details who will be involved in resolving the disputes and update them timely.

The above improvements can be performed if there is strong support from the Government through financial aid and assistance to the Centre. The Government should look at the role of the Centre in the long run and its relevance in the contemporary internet society. Many countries view ODR as a game changer in the dispute resolution area. India should not lag behind these developments occurring all over the world. It needs to set up a permanent online mediation centre fully supported and sponsored by the government.

6 Conclusion

The extraordinary growth of Electronic Commerce has greatly influenced the way business is being carried in the present generation. Unlike in the past, consumers have become an integral part of the growing community of global traders in the electronic market. Apart from new opportunities, it has also created numerous concerns and challenges on businesses and consumers who embark on this new course of business. E-commerce can be achieved to its fullest potential in the electronic civilization only when online consumers are afforded the same level of protection as conventional consumers.

Consumers involving in electronic commerce should be afforded adequate and transparent information about the business, products being sold and the entire transaction details. Consumer education and awareness about the use of the ecommerce platforms should be enhanced through wide media publications. Consumers will not engage in the impersonal click-and–mortar system unless they are either familiar with the business they are transacting or have the confidence that if something goes wrong they will have recourse to a quick and easy redressal of their grievance. In order to build this trust, businesses carrying out e-commerce should provide for internal mechanisms that can guarantee less expensive and effective enforcement of consumer rights.

The government must view ODR as the future. India cannot lag behind in these futuristic developments when the UNCITRAL Draft Model Rules for ODR are at developmental stage, the EU has already adopted the ODR for consumer dispute resolution. There is enormous potential for online mediation in India provided there is recognition and support from the Government. A new policy which encourages and guides the private ODR administrators is also the need of the hour.

Further the new strong comprehensive Consumer Protection Act, 2019 comes into force, then Consumer Redressal System in India will get more teeth and become strong enough to protect the E-consumers in a better way.

Reference

1. Sriram Panchu, Mediation Law and Practice, 305 (Lexis Nexis Publication, 2nd ed., 2015).

Jurisdiction and Choice of Law in Foreign-Related Tourist-Consumer Disputes in China Under the One Belt One Road Initiative—Based on Case Analysis in the Chinese Judiciary

Zhen Chen

1 Introduction

One Belt One Road Initiative, as an ambitious trade project, will inevitably promote the development of Silk Road tourism, and accordingly, an increasing amount of foreign-related tourism disputes will arise. Therefore, protecting cross-border tourist-consumer is extremely significant under the OBOR initiative. When it comes to cross-border tourist-consumer protection, multiple dispute resolution mechanisms are available for cross-border tourists, be it traditional court procedures (international litigation), or new non-court procedures (ADR or ODR). International litigation, although sophisticated, expensive and time-consuming, is still the last resort for cross-border tourists to redress their legitimate rights and interests, especially when the claim is in large amount. In this sense, international tourist-consumer protection will always remain to be 'middle class law' which focus on conflicts of laws in different jurisdictions. In order to settle foreign-related tourism disputes, jurisdiction and choice of law are two particularly important and also complicated issues in the process of foreign-related civil litigation. In particular, when Silk Road tourism in China is faced with the fast-changing technology and increasingly-popularized internet usage, E-tourism is imposing new challenges upon the traditional jurisdiction and choice of law rules.

Traditional jurisdiction and choice of law rules on foreign-related civil contract usually based on three main factors, namely, the identity of the parties, the location of the parties when they entered into a contract and the activities conducted by the parties. In terms of the identity of the parties in a tourist-consumer contract, the

Zhen Chen—LL.M (Private International Law), Wuhan University, China, 2014–2017; Ph.D. researcher (Private International Law), University of Groningen, The Netherlands, 2017-present.

Z. Chen (✉)
Groningen, The Netherlands
e-mail: zhen.chen@rug.nl

D. Wei et al. (eds.), *Innovation and the Transformation of Consumer Law*,
https://doi.org/10.1007/978-981-15-8948-5_14

tourist-consumer is always the weaker party when it comes to knowledge, information, financial status and so forth. Thus, in comparison with the other party to the travel contract, be it tour operator or travel service provider, tourist consumer is in the more disadvantaged position and has less bargaining power and experience in litigation. This is even more true when tourist consumers travel abroad and be exposed to total different culture, language, social and legal systems. Therefore, more protective rules are needed to even the imbalance power between individual tourist-consumer and travel service companies. With regard to the location of the parties, the global and dematerialization nature of the Internet and E-commerce renders this factor not as that significant as before. Moreover, the diversity of the travel forms and activities, mobility of tourist-consumers and globalization in E-tourism industry all together create more legal uncertainty and unpredictability for both tourist-consumers and tourism companies in cross-border tourist-consumer disputes. In order to provide high protection level for both international tourist and domestic tourist and make sure their access to justice is achieved best in China in this new era, it is of necessity to first examine the existing laws and current judiciary practice, identity the existing problems, and then further provide the possible solutions to improve the specific rules on jurisdiction and applicable law issues. Indeed, the clarity of jurisdiction and choice of law rules can, undoubtedly, provide legal certainty and predictability for both the tourist-consumers and the travel companies. As a result, clear and predictable rules will save time, money and energy both parties and improve the efficiency for solving relevant disputes.

Therefore, this article is centered on the question of what are the jurisdiction and applicable law rules in existing laws, how the courts apply these rules in specific cases and what are the gaps between the legislation and the judiciary in China with regard to foreign-related tourism disputes. To begin with, Part II gives a brief introduction about One Belt One Road Initiative and its stimulation effects on the development of Silk Road tourism. The following problem would be what kind of challenges that the fast-growing tourism industry, especially E-tourism, has brought in terms of tourist-consumer protection, and most importantly, what kind of rule that private international law can play in this regard. Part III comprise three separate but highly-related issues, and this section is also the most significant part of this article. Specifically speaking, it analyzes the existing problematic practices in Chinese domestic courts regarding jurisdiction, choice of law and other relevant issues. After analyzing and identifying the gap between the statutory law and the judicial practice from private international law perspective, Part IV, as a conclusion section, accordingly, generalizes the common problems and dilemmas that Chinese courts are facing with, and clarify the specific issues that have space for improvement for future legislation.

2 One Belt One Road Initiative and Cross-Border Tourist-Consumer Protection

2.1 What Is One Belt One Road Initiative?

The One Belt One Road Initiative was firstly proposed by President Xi Jinping in a speech at Kazakhstan's Nazarbayev University on September 7, 2013. This speech raised the initiative of building the Silk Road Economic Belt for the first time. Another speech made on October 3, 2013 at Indonesia's Parliament, raised the initiative of building the 21st-Century Maritime Silk Road.[1] In March 2015, the Vision and Actions on Jointly Building Silk Road Economic Belt and 21st-Century Maritime Silk Road was issued by the National Development and Reform Commission, Ministry of Foreign Affairs, and Ministry of Commerce of the People's Republic of China, with the authorization of the State Council.[2] This initiative encompasses two major parts, namely, the Silk Road Economic Belt and the 21st Century Maritime Silk Road. The Silk Road Economic Belt is a land-based network, stretching from China to Europe with a host of trade and infrastructure projects. The 21st Century Maritime Silk Road is a sea-based network throughout Asia and the Pacific with shipping lanes and port developments. The two projects, collectively, are known as "One Belt, One Road"(OBOR), "Belt and Road (B&R)", "Belt and Road Initiative (BRI)", or the "New Silk Road".

OBOR spans more than 68 countries, encompasses 4.4 billion people and accounts for 40% of the global GDP. It is a collection of interlinking trade deals and infrastructures throughout Eurasia and the Pacific.[3] High-speed and medium-speed railways were essential for the connectivity of the land-based Silk Road, therefore, infrastructure connectivity is a priority in the implementation of the OBOR initiative.[4] The initiative aims to seek common development and prosperity along the ancient Silk Road trade routes, by building a trade and infrastructure network that connects Asia with Europe and Africa.[5]

[1]The Belt and The Road, Specials, available at https://eng.yidaiyilu.gov.cn/ztindex.htm.

[2]The Plan for Building Fujian into the Core Area of the 21st-Century Maritime Silk Road, available at https://eng.yidaiyilu.gov.cn/zchj/dfgg/1465.htm.

[3]James Griffiths, Just what is this One Belt, One Road thing anyway?, available at https://edition.cnn.com/2017/05/11/asia/china-one-belt-one-road-explainer/index.html.

[4]Tseng and Lim [1].

[5]B&R Initiative to boost tourism development in all participating countries, available at https://eng.yidaiyilu.gov.cn/qwyw/rdxw/16016.htm.

2.2 OBOR Initiative and the Silk Road Tourism

At first glance, the OBOR initiative might have nothing to do with the tourist-consumer protection. Searching "tourism" in the official government website named Belt and Road Portal,[6] there are 140 related results. From the tourism-related results, it is easy to get a clear idea about what OBOR initiative has contributed to the development of Silk Road Tourism. Actually, this initiative has broadened the tourism market among OBOR countries.[7]

The OBOR countries and regions are rich in cultural and natural resources. To be more specific, in terms of the natural heritage, natural reserves and the world cultural heritage, those along the Belt and Road account for 34%, 53% and 74% respectively. The Belt and Road Initiative connects Europe, Asia and Africa not only in infrastructures, but also in resources.[8] OBOR countries account for over 70% of the global travel business. With 4.4 billion people and over 60 countries involved, the Silk Road Tourism possesses a huge market potential. OBOR countries have discussed cooperation in the fields of tourism, including transportation, facilitation, visa policy, insurance and security.[9]

While individuality and diversity is becoming a new trend of Chinese outbound travel, the tourist destinations along the Belt and Road countries can offer diverse travel services based on rich tourism resources. According to the data from the CNTA, 82.6% Chinese residents are willing to travel to these OBOR countries. Also, reservation data from travel agencies indicates that Belt and Road tourism products have become new choices of outbound travel. Visa policies also strengthen this trend.[10] In 2014, around 4 million Chinese travelers visited the EU.[11] During the 2017 "Golden Week" from October 1 to 8, almost half of the Chinese population traveled, both domestic and overseas receive a big boost. According to the data from Lvmama.com, the Belt and Road countries become popular destinations during the 7-day national holiday in 2017, such as the Czech Republic and Hungary.[12] In 2016, the Central and Eastern European (CEE) countries, such as Slovenia, Serbia, Hungary, Poland and the Czech republic, witnessed a 229 percent increase in outbound travel for Chinese tourists.[13]

[6]Belt and Road Portal, available at https://eng.yidaiyilu.gov.cn/search/newSearch.jsp?q=tourism&t_id=366&pageSize=15&qIndex=1&siteId=CMSydylyw&qIndex=1&catId=.

[7]Belt and Road creates new tourism pattern, available at https://eng.yidaiyilu.gov.cn/qwyw/rdxw/28738.htm.

[8]Belt and Road tourist city mayor's summit opens in Zhengzhou, available at https://eng.yidaiyilu.gov.cn/qwyw/hyygd/56358.htm.

[9]Lim and Tseng [2].

[10]B&R tourism promising, expert, available at https://eng.yidaiyilu.gov.cn/qwyw/rdxw/32705.htm.

[11]Belt and Road Initiative to accelerate tourism in Europe, available at https://eng.yidaiyilu.gov.cn/wtfz/mxxt/1328.htm.

[12]Facts and Figures on China's 'Golden Week' tourism boom, available at https://eng.yidaiyilu.gov.cn/qwyw/rdxw/30063.htm.

[13]CEE tourism urged to be further tapped in China, available at https://eng.yidaiyilu.gov.cn/qwyw/rdxw/19981.htm.

It is foreseeable that cross-border tourism will develop faster and occur more frequently in a much broader scope, with tourist-consumers from OBOR countries travelling for different reasons along the New Silk Road, as well as multiple tour operators and travel service companies from different countries involved. China's economic transformation has a profound impact not merely on China but on the whole world, as the U.S Department of State said long time ago.[14] The unprecedented rise of China's economic engine has made and will continue to make more countries benefit from China's economic rebirth.[15] As a result, the OBOR initiative acts as a strong stimulator and promoter to the tourism industry along the OBOR countries and regions, and attract tourists to travel abroad more frequently.

2.3 Tourist-Consumer Protection Under the Silk Road Tourism

2.3.1 Chinese Tourist-Consumers

China, as the largest population country and the second largest economy in the world, is also, unsurprisingly, the largest state of origin of international tourists.[16] According to the statistics of the China National Tourism Administration (CNTA), the number of Chinese tourists who travel abroad, also called out-bound tourists, is increasing steadily in recent years. In 2013, the number of out-bound tourist was 93.18 million, in 2014 this figure exceeded 100 million for the first time, and it reached 117 million in 2015,[17] 122 million in 2016,[18] and 130.51 million in 2017.[19] The figure for market share of inbound tourism, domestic tourism and outbound tourism of national travel agencies in 2015 was 7%, 69% and 24% respectively.[20] Also, out-bound travel have remained on an upward trend, as China's middle class continue to grow and China develops as a nation of consumers.[21] According to the prediction of World Tourism Organization, China will become the biggest tourism destination for overseas travelers and the main international tourists generating country by 2020.

[14]U.S. Department of State, *Background Note: China*, (Oct. 2007), available at http:lwww.state.govlr/pa/eilbgnl18902.htm.

[15]Evans [3].

[16]See Smed and Bislev [4].

[17]2015 China Tourism Statistics Report, available at http://zwgk.mct.gov.cn/auto255/201610/t20161018_832364.html?keywords=.

[18]2016 China Tourism Statistics Report, available at http://zwgk.mct.gov.cn/auto255/201711/t20171108_832371.html?keywords=#.

[19]2017 Data Report on Annual Tourism Market and Its Comprehensive Contribution, available at http://zwgk.mct.gov.cn/auto255/201802/t20180206_832375.html?keywords=.

[20]Report of the China National Tourism Administration on the 2015 National Travel Agency Statistics Survey, available at http://zwgk.mct.gov.cn/auto255/201609/t20160908_832363.html?keywords=.

[21]Anderson [5].

Moreover, the purchasing power of Chinese tourists is pretty high. In 2012, the purchasing power of Chinese tourists outweigh that of the USA and Germany, ranking the first in the world with an expense of 678.6 billion RMB. “Chinese tourists” is becoming a hot topic globally, while at the same time the percentage of Chinese citizens who own a passport is merely 8.7%,[22] indicating an enormous market potential. Denmark, the Netherlands, Sweden, the UK and other European countries all treat Chinese tourists as the important subjects in the future tourism activities and prepare for the visit of more Chinese tourists. However, getting China-ready is not only the strategy of European countries, but also for all the OBOR countries, especially under the construction of the Belt and Road Initiative. China is expected to send 150 million visitors to the OBOR countries in the following 5 years, and at the same time, attract 85 million visitors from the OBOR countries.[23]

2.3.2 Tourist-Consumer as the Weaker Party

Tourist-consumers are the weaker parties in comparison with tour operators or tourism service providers (airline, hotel, cruise, restaurant etc.). To be more specific, in terms of financial status, knowledge and information, tourists are generally more vulnerable, disadvantaged and less-informed. On the one hand, the bargaining power between tourists and tourism service providers is totally unequal, tourist are financially weaker and legally unexperienced. On the other hand, based on professional experiences and the dominant position, tourism service providers usually pre-drafted all the terms and provisions in a standardized travel contract, consciously avoid, reduce or transfer the potential commercial and legal risk when drafting the standardized contract without negotiating with tourists. The so-called “party autonomy” in this scenario is not a mutual and free “consumer-company autonomy”, but a unilateral and forced “company autonomy”, the “consumer autonomy” part is purposefully ignored and pitilessly devoured by the powerful company. In another word, there is no consensus foundation in the very beginning when the standardized contract is provided by the tour operators, the tourist-consumer basically can do nothing but to sign the travel contract without actually knowing what contents they have already been forced to agree. In the E-commerce context, the tourist-consumer who books flight, hotel or cruise tour online usually accept the online terms and provisions without being aware of the jurisdiction and choice of law clauses that are more favorable to the tourism service providers.

Moreover, after signing the contract, the tourists are exposed to more vulnerable circumstances, foreign country, foreign language, totally different social, cultural and legal systems and plus short-time stay. Unlike other commercial products, tourists can only check the quality of tourism service after being in the tourist destinations,

---

[22]The Number of Potential Chinese Outbound Tourists Could Double by 2020 to 240 Million, available at https://jingtravel.com/number-of-potential-chinese-outbound-tourists-double-by-2020/.

[23]New Pact to Boost Tourism under Belt and Road Initiative, available at https://eng.yidaiyilu.gov.cn/qwyw/rdxw/14473.htm.

especially under the E-tourism scenario. The electronic tourism development offers tourists more options and information, however, the information provided may be exaggerated, overwhelming or misleading. Even if cross-border tourists find something is wrong, their stay time in a foreign country is limited and there are not enough time to solve the problems. All these factors together make tourists exposed in a disadvantaged situation, even if the consumer only have to deal with domestic travel agency, the consumer may still be placed in a passive and disadvantaged position. For instance, if a Chinese tourist signs a cross-border travel contract with a domestic travel agency to enjoy a 7-day holiday in Europe, unluckily has a dispute with a foreign travel service provider and decides to initiate a lawsuit in the court where s/he is habitually resided, even if this tourist can sue in China according to Chinese Law, since China has such a wide and broad geographical area, the jurisdiction clause pre-drafted in standard travel contract may in the end prevent a Chinese tourist consumer from Hainan[24] to sue a travel agency from Heilongjiang,[25] because the distance between these two provinces is far more longer than that from Netherlands to France.[26] Therefore, cross-border tourists should be protected under more favorable rules to even the imbalance power in order to ensure tourists' access to justice being achieved best.

2.4 The Role of Private International Law Under the OBOR Initiative

Obviously, the interests of the tourists and tourism service providers are usually opposite in tourism-related disputes, which, from a legal value perspective, represent efficiency and fairness separately. How to choose between efficiency and fairness when the two values conflict with each other in the same case? Or, how to make a balance between protecting tourist-consumers and promoting the developments of tourism industry? In the field of private international law (hereinafter as PIL), the principle of weaker party protection is a basic principle,[27] the availability and application of more protective consumer rules on jurisdiction and choice of law is an intrinsic requirement and also an embodiment of this principle. When it comes to the role that PIL plays in cross-border tourist protection, it couldn't be more clear how complicated it is when consumer law, contract law, tort law, tourism law, transportation law, aviation law, maritime law all twist together in the issue of cross-border travel disputes. Moreover, the rules on conflict of laws in China are not

[24]The province located in southernmost China.

[25]The province located in northernmost China.

[26]The inconvenience and difficulty of suing a travel agency in another remote province, and the high cost of transportation and accommodation may eventually discourage tourists from seeking legal redress in the court.

[27]Bo [6].

stipulated in one single law, but are scattered in various laws, to be specific, around 420 conflict of laws rules are specified in 140 Chinese normative texts.[28]

Contrary to the booming tourism industry under OBOR initiative, the domestic legislation on tourist-consumer protection in PIL field is quite late-started and slow-developed, the awareness of protecting a tourist as a consumer still need to be promoted and enhanced. Despite the existence of current laws that aim to protect tourist consumers, it is still not enough to protect cross-border tourist consumers along the New Silk Road, especially taking into consideration of the complexity of modern travel activities and the popularity of E-commerce in tourism industry. It is more likely that in the future when Chinese tourists or foreign tourists are trying to protect themselves based on Chinese domestic laws and regulations, there are no such kind of rules to support them, or the existing rules per se are either not clear enough or not favorable to the tourist-consumers. If the more favorable protection rules for domestic tourists are still undeveloped or absent, it is hard to image that the protection rules of foreign tourists will be separately well-developed. In another word, the consumer protection rules will develop gradually as one subject in the whole legal system, if the domestic rules on tourist-consumer protection are well-developed and more advanced, both the Chinese tourists who travel abroad to a foreign country and the foreign tourist who travel to China will benefit from sound legal rules. Therefore, it is necessary to first review how and to what extent that existing Chinese PIL rules can protect tourist consumers. For instance, if a Chinese tourist booked an Italian hotel online and got injured in the hotel, which court should adjudicate this dispute? A court in China or a court in Italy? Which law should be applied to address the dispute, Chinese Law, Italian Law or the law of third country? If there are forum selection clause and choice of law agreement, the first step would be examining the validity of these clauses. Furthermore, in the absence of agreed forum and choice of law agreements, the questions would be what the legal basis for the court to exercise jurisdiction and choose the applicable law?

The questions mentioned above all fall within the scope of private international law, or conflict of laws. Private international law, although it deals with international civil and commercial issues, is still, in essence, a branch of national law within a specific jurisdiction, thus, it is of necessity to examine the legal sources of private international law in a nation. The sources of Chinese private international law include international treaties, international practices, national legislation, judicial interpretations and explanations issued by the Supreme People's Court of China, according to the General Principle of Civil Law of the People's Republic of China (GPCL).[29] First, start with the source of international treaty, under the New Silk Road Tourism, it is hard to reach an international convention that primarily focus on protecting the tourist-consumers from PIL perspective. Even if it is possible, in theory, to establish a specific and harmonized rule in an international convention among the OBOR countries and regions, in reality, this will need the efforts of many generations and take many years to reach it. Moreover, the statuary law always, unavoidably, lag behind

[28] Jin [7].

[29] Article 142 of the 1986 GPCL.

the fast development in the social society and cannot instantly reflect the social change and solve the new-emerging issues. Therefore, it is unrealistic to count on an international convention to tackle new challenges. In the absence of an international treaty, domestic private international law rules will be invoked to address foreign-related issues. For instance, in terms of choice of law rule on consumer contract, in China it is Article 42 of the Law of the People's Republic of China on Application of Laws to Foreign-related Civil Relations (hereinafter as the LALFCR).[30] The Chinese domestic courts will follow the choice of law rules like the chosen law must be substantive law,[31] the application of a foreign law should not undermine the social and public interests of China[32] and the mandatory provisions in China shall directly apply.[33]

Take a closer look at the LALFCR, instead of using the traditional wording "private international law" or "conflict of laws", this long title is kind of complicated[34] and confusing. Since PIL is related to so many fields and touches upon various issues, it is also sometimes considered not as a legal discipline at all, but as a special part of each legal branch existed in a national law.[35] As mentioned above, Chinese conflict of law rules are scattered in different legal documents. Based on the separation of civil and commercial matters in China's legislative system, the content of the LALFCR is all about civil relations (contract, tort, etc.), and commercial relations (transportation, insurance, maritime, etc.) are excluded. Clearly, Chinese 2010 Conflict Act adopted the traditional legislation system, without containing commercial relations like Maritime law, Civil Aviation Law etc., and arguably, this can be regarded as a drawback,[36] especially when cross-border tourism issues might involve the application of different laws.

3 Chinese Judicial Practice on Foreign-Related Travel Disputes

In order to answer the core questions of what is the jurisdiction rule and applicable law rule in China regarding foreign-related travel disputes, to start with, it is easier to get a clear picture about what kind of role that the existing PIL rules have already played to protect tourists in judicial practice. The cases collected and analyzed in

[30]The Law of the People's Republic of China on Application of Laws to Foreign-related Civil Relations, can also be referred as 2010 Conflicts Act, Chinese Conflict Code or Chinese Conflict Act.

[31]Article 9 of the LALFCR.

[32]Article 5 of the LALFCR.

[33]Article 4 of the LALFCR.

[34]See Nord [8].

[35]Ehrenzweig [9].

[36]See Zhongbo [10].

this article all derive from the official website, namely China Judgements Online,[37] by typing in the key words "travel contract" and "foreign-related".

These cases all have a foreign-related element, but not necessary all with a foreign plaintiff or foreign defendant, some of them involve a foreign element because the legal fact occurred abroad, even if the parties to the travel contract are all domestic ones. Pursuant to Article 2, the scope of application of the LALFCR is limited to 'foreign-related civil relations', that is, civil relations that involve one or more foreign elements. 'Foreign element' refers to (1) either or both parties are foreign citizens, foreign legal persons, foreign organizations, or stateless persons; (2) the habitual residence of either or both parties is outside the territory of China; (3) the subject matter is outside the territory of China; (4) the legal facts that establish, alter or terminate the civil relation occurred outside the territory of China, according to Article 1 of the Interpretation I of the Supreme People's Court on Certain Issues Concerning the Application of the 'Law of the People's Republic of China on Application of Law to Foreign-Related Civil Relations' (hereinafter as SPC Judicial Interpretation I of LALFCR[38]). It is noteworthy that Hong Kong, Macao and Taiwan are also treated as foreign elements in civil and commercial contracts because of their different legal system in comparison with the legal system in mainland China.[39] In accordance with Article 19 of the SPC Judicial Interpretation I of LALFCR,[40] the application of law to civil relations that involve Hong Kong and Macao also should refer to this interpretation. Therefore, Hong Kong, Marco or Taiwan-related cases are dealt with in the same rule as other foreign-related cases in Chinese courts.

Since the jurisdiction rule and the applicable law rule on foreign-related civil and commercial cases apply in a situation as long as there is a 'foreign-related element', be it an American tourist, a Hong Kong tourism service provider or the legal fact that occurred in Switzerland, the same private international law rule apply. Therefore, the reasoning of the Chinese courts in these foreign-related travel disputes can, to some extent, reflect the judicial practice in China, and thus provide foreign tourists who travel to China and Chinese tourists who travel abroad a clear picture, expectation or prediction about which court will have jurisdiction and what law will be applied to resolve their disputes when they encounter foreign-related travel disputes in the future. Additionally, through case study, it is easier to find out what is the common practice in Chinese domestic courts when dealing with foreign-related travel disputes, what are the parts that involve inconsistency and discrepancy among different domestic courts, what are the provisions that needed to be clarified to ensure legal uncertainty and what are the loopholes in legislation that needed to be plugged.

[37]http://wenshu.court.gov.cn/.

[38]The SPC Judicial Interpretation I of LALFCR was adopted by the SPC Judicial Committee at its 1563th meeting on December 10, 2012 and came into force as from January 7, 2013.

[39]Huang and Qian [11].

[40]Article 19 of the SPC Judicial Interpretation I of LALFCR.

3.1 *Jurisdiction Issue in Chinese Judicial Practice on Foreign-Related Travel Disputes*

Although this article does not touch upon the issue of recognition and enforcement of judgments. One premise of a judgment made by a country to be recognized and enforced in another foreign country is that the adjudicating court had legitimate jurisdiction. In other words, the court that exercised jurisdiction and issued the judgment is based on a ground that is acceptable according to international standards.[41] However, the practice of Chinese domestic courts is less satisfactory, and there is still a long way for Chinese courts to conduct more convincing and well-grounded jurisdiction reasoning as elaborated in the following part.

3.1.1 Missing of Jurisdiction Reasoning Part in Chinese Courts' Practice

Although the case collected all involve a foreign element, the justification of jurisdiction should be the first step before tackling the substantial dispute, sadly, not all Chinese courts justify their jurisdiction. Statistically speaking, 11 out of 21 cases had no jurisdiction reasoning part at all. It seems that some Chinese courts certainly deem that they have personal jurisdiction over Chinese parties without any doubt, there is no need to put more efforts to justify the legacy of jurisdiction, despite the fact that when it comes to the choice of law issue, many courts do elaborate and make a reasoning why Chinese law should be the governing law to address foreign-related tourism disputes.

This might mainly due to the fact that there is actually no specific provisions in Chinese law that specially deal with consumer jurisdiction rule. The absence of consumer jurisdiction rule directly leads to the missing jurisdiction reasoning part in Chinese domestic courts when foreign-related travel disputes are addressed. Although the LALFCR is regarded as Chinese PIL code, it is translated by a foreign scholar as the "Statute on the Application of Laws to Civil Relationships Involving Foreign Elements of the PRC". As can been seen from its title, the LALFCR only deals with the conflict of laws and does not touch upon conflict of jurisdictions, that is why it is also called 2010 Conflict Act/Code.[42] In this sense, the LALFCR is merely a code on the applicable law rules, not a typical PIL code that also addresses jurisdiction issues. The title of this law already indicates its limitation on the scope of application, in which three elements are emphasized, that is, foreign-related, civil relationship and application of law.

Therefore, it is not hard to image that the absence of the specific consumer jurisdiction rule will lead to the jurisdiction part being overlooked by some Chinese courts.

[41] Ten Wolde [12].

[42] See Nord [13].

In case *Foshan Guangzhilv International Travel Agency v Lin Jintian*,[43] Guangdong Foshan Intermediate People's Court identified the case as Hong Kong-related, and directly invoked Art. 551 of the Interpretation of the Supreme People's Court on the Application of the Civil Procedure Law, which stipulated that when trying civil cases involving Hong Kong, Macao and Taiwan, the People's Court may refer to special provisions applicable to foreign-related civil procedures. In other words, as mentioned above, although Hong Kong, Macao and Taiwan are not foreign countries for mainland China, their legal systems are quite different from mainland China. In this sense, laws in Hong Kong, Macao and Taiwan are different, unfamiliar and foreign to the judges in mainland courts as other foreign countries. Guangdong Foshan Intermediate People's Court merely pointed out that Hong Kong-related was also an foreign element, without specifying why the court had jurisdiction over this dispute.

Similarly, in case *Xi'an Xindaya International Travel Agency v Dr. Barsch-Supan*,[44] two American tourists want the Chinese travel agency and the deputy to pay the travel expense back after their cancellation of Tibet trip. Shaanxi High People's Court classified the case as foreign-related contract dispute, and then jumped directly to the applicable law part, without justifying why Chinese court has legitimate jurisdiction. There are also several other cases in which the courts did not mention the jurisdiction part and jumped directly to the choice of law part, such as in cases *Tong Bo v Shandong Daxinhua Yuntong Travel Agency*,[45] *Feng Yunhai v Henan Feiyang Travel Agency*,[46] *Yongan Property Insurance Company Henan Branch v Yang Junya*[47] and *Liu Peilong v Kunming Kanghui Yonghui Travel Agency*.[48]

3.1.2 Choice of Law Rule Misused on Jurisdiction Issue

Apart from courts that don't have reasoning part on jurisdiction issue, there are also some courts, 10 out of 21, that conduct legal reasoning about why Chinese courts have jurisdiction over foreign-related travel disputes. However, the existence of jurisdiction reasoning part does not mean the reasoning itself is convincing enough, in fact, conflict and inconsistency still exist in the field of judicial practice at different

[43] *Foshan Guangzhilv International Travel Agency v Lin Jintian*, Guangdong Foshan IPC, (2017) Yue 06 Min Zhong No 4445.

[44] *Xi'an Xindaya International Travel Agency v Dr. Barsch-Supan*, Shaanxi Province HPC, (2016) Shan Min Zhong No 511.

[45] *Tong Bo v Shandong Daxinhua Yuntong Travel Agency*, Shandong Province HPC, (2017) Lu Min Zhong No 1112.

[46] *Feng Yunhai v Henan Feiyang Travel Agency*, Henan Province Zhengzhou Municipality IPC, (2015) Zheng Min San Chu Zi No 307.

[47] *Yongan Property Insurance Company Henan Branch v Yang Junya*, Henan Province HPC, (2017) Yu Min Zhong No 540.

[48] *Liu Peilong v Kunming Kanghui Yonghui Travel Agency*, Kunming Railway IPC, (2017) Yun 71 Min Zhong No 11.

levels of Chinese domestic courts. As stated above, since there are no specific provisions in Chinese laws and regulations that are specially drafted to deal with consumer jurisdiction rules, consequently, there are multiple and varying legal documents that Chinese courts rely on to justify their jurisdiction. The chaos in the application of divergent legal provisions might due to the lack of relevant legislation, however, if a court resorts to the provisions of the LALFCR to justify its legitimate jurisdiction, it would make a big mistake by misunderstanding the objective and application scope of the LALFCR. As stated earlier, this 2010 Chinese Conflict Act merely focuses on choice of law rules, not jurisdiction rules. Despite this, the misuse of applicable law rule on jurisdiction issues still exists in judicial practice.

For instance, in *Henan Kanghui International Travel Agency v Thai Air Asia* case,[49] Henan Xinzheng Intermediate People's Court held that pursuant to Article 44 of the LALFCR, the place where the tort act and tort result occurred was in Xinzheng, Henan province, hereby the Xinzheng Intermediate People's Court had jurisdiction. Regardless of whether Chinese court had jurisdiction or not, the fact that the court invoked Article 44 of the LALFCR was quite wrong in the very beginning. As stated above, the LALFCR is all about Chinese conflict of law rules on different foreign-related legal relations, not touching upon jurisdiction issues at all. Article 44 of LALFCR is actually a choice of law rule on foreign-related tort liability, and thus cannot be relied on to solve jurisdiction issue. The practice of the Henan Xinzheng IPC is obviously incorrect and improper.

3.1.3 Domestic General Jurisdiction Rule Applied in Foreign-Related Dispute

In *Xue Xiujuan v Yongcheng Property Insurance Co.* case,[50] another foreign-related dispute between a tourist and an insurer operator regarding personal accident insurance of an overseas travel group, Jiangxi Nanchang Intermediate People's Court did not mention the fact that the tourist got seriously injured in a speedboat when sailing towards the Sands Island in Pattaya, Thailand, instead, the court deemed that the domicile of the defendant, Yongcheng Property Insurance Company Jiangxi Branch was located in the jurisdiction of Nanchang City, Jiangxi province, therefore, according to Article 23 of the Civil Procedure Law, the court had jurisdiction over the dispute.

Nevertheless, it is questionable to rely on Article 23 of the Civil Procedure Law to justify the jurisdiction of a foreign-related case, because Article 23 is the general jurisdiction rule that deal with domestic disputes. Article 23 is an embodiment of *actor sequitur forum rei*, which states that the plaintiff must follow the forum of the thing

[49] *Henan Kanghui International Travel Agency v Thai Air Asia*, Henan Province Xinzheng Municipality IPC, (2014) Xin Min Chu Zi No 3892.

[50] *Xue Xiujuan v Yongcheng Property Insurance Co., Ltd.* Jiangxi Branch, Jiangxi Province Nanchang Municipality IPC, (2015) Hong Min Si Chu Zi No 30.

in dispute. On the one hand, Jiangxi Nanchang Intermediate People's Court classified the dispute as foreign-related civil dispute in nature, on the other hand, the court invoked an article that addresses pure domestic jurisdiction rules to justify its jurisdiction over a foreign-related dispute. In this respect, the practice of Jiangxi Nanchang Intermediate People's Court was self-contradictory to some extent. Despite the fact that the final result of using Article 23 of the Civil Procedure Law or other provisions that deals with foreign-related jurisdiction is the same, that is, this Chinese court can exert jurisdiction. The procedural justice is still as significant as substantial justice, thus, sound and well-grounded reasoning on jurisdiction remains crucial and indispensable.

Similarly, the Guangdong Guangzhou Intermediate People's Court also invoked Article 23 of the Civil Procedure Law in Guangzhou Baiyun District Fluent Education Training Centre v Zhu Kaili,[51] an America-related and Hong Kong-related case. The court based on the factor of the defendant's domicile to exercise jurisdiction. Likewise, Shandong Rizhao Intermediate People's Court also invoked Article 23 of the Civil Procedure Law in Rizhao Oriental International Travel Agency v Chen Yan case.[52] Interestingly, what slightly different from the practice of other courts is that Shandong Rizhao Intermediate People's Court characterized the case as a travel contract dispute involving foreign element, not a foreign-related dispute, thereby in nature the case is still a pure domestic one.[53] The dispute arose when the plaintiff Chen Yan signed a 8-Western European-country travel contract with the travel agency, but got injured in Paris, France. The injured tourist argued that the travel agency failed to fulfill its obligation of guaranteeing the security of the tourist. The court reckoned that pursuant to Article 23 of the Civil Procedure Law, the domicile of the defendant was located in Rizhao, although the plaintiff was injured abroad, it didn't affect the jurisdiction of the court. Regardless of whether this case should be identified as domestic or foreign-related in nature,[54] at least the court was consistent in the practice of classification and jurisdiction. As mentioned above, Article 23 of the Civil Procedure Law is mainly about jurisdiction rule on a pure domestic issue, the court invoked this domestic rule to solve domestic jurisdiction issue, or in order to invoke domestic jurisdiction rule the court intentionally classified the case as a domestic dispute. The practice of other Chinese courts that classify a dispute as a foreign-related one on one hand, and invoke domestic jurisdiction rule provisions on the other hand, is paradoxical.

---

[51] Guangzhou Baiyun District Fluent Education Training Centre v Zhu Kaili, Guangdong Province Guangzhou Municipality IPC, (2014) Hui Zhong Fa Min Si Zhong Zi No 137.

[52] *Rizhao Oriental International Travel Agency v Chen Yan*, Shandong Province Rizhao Municipality IPC, (2016) Lu 11 Min Xia Zhong No 95.

[53] However, this classification is quite confusing and debatable, because in accordance with Article 1 of SPC Judicial Interpretation I of LALFCR, this case is clearly 'foreign-related' as the tourist got injury in Paris, France. Then the question arises as to whether it should be a domestic travel dispute with a foreign element, or a foreign-related travel dispute in nature? Putting the wording 'foreign element' and 'foreign-related' in different order, the nature of the dispute differs and accordingly the jurisdiction and applicable law rules will follow varying trajectories.

[54] The characterization of a travel dispute will be discussed later in this article.

3.1.4 Multiple but Improper Legal Documents to Justify Legitimate Jurisdiction

In case Zhu Kaili v Guangzhou Baiyun District Fluent Education Training Centre,[55] Guangdong Guangzhou Baiyu District People's Court classified it as a Hong Kong related service contract dispute. The court then conducted jurisdiction reasoning as follows, according to relevant provisions of the Answers of the SPC to Questions Concerning Economic Disputes Involving Hong Kong and Macau,[56] Article 4 of the Civil Procedure Law and Article 23 of the Civil Procedure Law, the domicile of the defendant was located in the jurisdiction of the court. Besides, the Guangzhou Baiyu District People's Court was a basic people's court approved to have jurisdiction over foreign-related commercial[57] cases.

In spite of the invoke of several provisions, the practice of this district court is still problematic. First of all, regarding the first legal document, the wording "according to relevant provisions" is quite ambiguous, the court did not specify the precise provisions. It is still unclear for the parties which particular provision was referred to justify the court's jurisdiction. In fact, "according to relevant provisions" is a commonly-used wording in Chinese courts when the court try to invoke relevant laws to justify their adjudication,[58] but still, be a little bit lazy to identify which article of that law was invoked. Likewise, in another Taiwan-related travel contract dispute heard by Fujian Zhangzhou Xiangcheng District People's Court, namely, *Zheng Yangmei v Zhangzhou Tengbang International Travel Agency,*[59] the court utilized the same wording. In this case, the tourist Huang Haizhong died in a group trip to Jinmen, Taiwan. The plaintiffs were the victim Huang Haizhong's wife, daughter, and son separately. Regarding jurisdiction within Chinese domestic court system, the district court transferred the case to Zhangzhou Intermediate People's Court in accordance with Article 18 of the Civil Procedure Law and "relevant provisions of the Minutes of the Intermediate People's Court of Zhangzhou City on the Acceptance of Foreign-related and Hong Kong-Macao-Related Cases". The court did not specify which provisions of the Minutes that it rely on by utilizing the wording of "relevant provisions".

Secondly, Article 4 of the Civil Procedure Law[60] is a worldwide-used general rule on applicable law of civil proceeding, that is, *lex fori* is the *lexi cause* of civil

---

[55]Zhu Kaili v Guangzhou Baiyun District Fluent Education Training Centre, Guangdong Province Guangzhou Municipality Baiyun DPC, (2014) Hui Yun Fa Min San Chu Zi No 15.

[56]The Answers of the SPC to Questions Concerning Economic Disputes Involving Hong Kong and Macau: the judicial proceeding of this Hong Kong related case should refer to the special provisions of the Civil Procedure Law concerning foreign-related civil proceedings.

[57]It seems that Guangdong Guangzhou Baiyu District People's Court regard this Hong Kong related service contract dispute as a foreign-related commercial dispute, not a foreign-related civil dispute.

[58]Zhen [14].

[59]*Zheng Yangmei v Zhangzhou Tengbang International Travel Agency*, Fujian Province Zhangzhou Municipality Xiangcheng DPC, (2016) Min 0602 Min Chu No 6138.

[60]Article 4 of the Civil Procedure Law stipulates that "this law must be observed when civil proceedings are conducted in the territory of PRC".

proceedings. This provision in nature is about the applicable law of the procedural issues in a domestic court, and thus cannot be relied on to decide the jurisdiction of foreign-related civil matters. Obviously, the court misused the rule of applicable law on procedural issues on the reasoning of jurisdiction part. Thirdly, as mentioned above, Article 23 of the Civil Procedure Law is mainly about jurisdiction rule on domestic issue, not dealing with jurisdiction regarding foreign-related civil issues.

At first glimpse, it seems well-grounded when the court invoked several articles from different laws to support its legitimate jurisdiction. However, the quantity of legal reference does not necessarily guarantee the quality of legal reasoning. A deeper analysis will show the weakness and insufficient ground of these legal documents, for instance, another legal document "the Answers of the SPC to Questions Concerning Economic Disputes Involving Hong Kong and Macau" has been invalid since January 18, 2013, the invoke of this provision by the court was faulty. As a matter of fact, the court seemed to endeavor to invoke as many legal documents as possible without specific in-depth analysis, as long as that legal document has a certain connection with the fact of the case in question. As a result, the cautious selection and detailed analyzation was often ignored, and the multiple legal documents invoked by a court may not even be fundamentally correct or proper.

3.1.5 Lack of Legal Document to Support Legitimate Jurisdiction

Contrary to the situation when multiple but improper legal documents are invoked, there is another situation that the court did not refer to any legal documents to justify its jurisdiction. In *Tong Bo v Shandong Daxinhua Yuntong Travel Agency*,[61] the tourist signed a travel contract with the travel agency on a 10-day 5-European Country-tour (France, Switzerland, Holland, Belgium, Germany), and got injured in a traffic accident near Mount Tilex in Switzerland on a tour bus arranged by the travel agency. Shandong Qingdao Intermediate People's Court characterized the case as a travel contract dispute, as the place of performance is overseas, the court heard the case according to the foreign-related civil and commercial proceedings. Regarding the jurisdiction issue, the court held that the domicile of the tourist and the travel agency was in Qingdao, Shandong, hence, the court had jurisdiction. However, the court did not invoke any laws or regulations to justify its jurisdiction, and this is also the case in *Lan Xinguo v Shandong Daxinhua Yuntong Travel Agency.*[62] Despite the fact that the court had legitimate jurisdiction over the dispute, as there is a foreign element in the case, the legal documents that support the legacy of jurisdiction cannot be omitted.

[61] *Tong Bo v Shandong Daxinhua Yuntong Travel Agency*, Shandong Province Qingdao Municipality IPC, (2016) Lu 02 Min Chu No 1146.

[62] *Lan Xinguo v Shandong Daxinhua Yuntong Travel Agency*, Shandong Province Qingdao Municipality IPC, (2016) Lu 02 Min Chu No 1157.

3.1.6 The Competent Court Within Chinese Domestic Courts Framework

Regarding foreign-related travel contract dispute, even though the parties agreed that Chinese court had jurisdiction, one of the disputing party may have objection to the jurisdiction level of the Chinese court, as China has four levels of jurisdiction, namely, the Basic People's Court, the Intermediate People's Court, the High People's Court and the Supreme People's Court. One of the possible disputes about the foreign-related case might be does the amount of the disputed-object determine the competent court within the framework of China's domestic courts?

In *Feng Yunhai v Shenzhen Tese International Travel agency*[63] heard by Henan High People's Court,[64] Shenzhen Tese International Travel Agency was unsatisfied with the civil ruling[65] of the Zhengzhou Intermediate People's Court and raised objections to the jurisdiction. The primary reason was based on Article 2 of the Notification of the Supreme People's Court on Adjusting the Standard of the First-Instance Civil and Commercial Cases Heard by the High People's Court and the Intermediate People's Court, which stipulates that the Zhengzhou Intermediate People's Court has jurisdiction over the first instance civil and commercial cases with a target amount of more than 3 million yuan. However, the object of this case failed to exceed the standard, hence the case should be under jurisdiction of the basic people's court. Shenzhen Tese International Travel Agency required to transfer the case to Shenzhen Luohu District People's Court, where the travel agency was located, or the courts where other defendants were located. Zhengzhou Intermediate People's Court held that the place of performance of the contract in this case was in Bali Island, Indonesia, hereby the case was foreign-related because of this foreign element. The jurisdiction of the Zhengzhou Intermediate People's Court complied with relevant provisions of the Supreme People's Court on the Centralized Jurisdiction of Foreign-related Civil and Commercial Cases. Therefore, the claim to transfer the case on the ground that the amount of the case was small cannot be supported.

When the case was appealed to its superior court, Henan High People's Court first classified the travel contract as an extra-territorial travel contract based on Article 522(4)[66] of the Interpretation of the Supreme People's Court on the Application of the Civil Procedure Law, because the traffic accident which resulted in the dispute occurred outside the territory of China. Therefore, the Provisions of the Supreme People's Court on Issues Concerning the Jurisdiction of Foreign-Related Civil and

---

[63] *Feng Yunhai v Shenzhen Tese International Travel agency*, Henan High People's Court, (2016) Yu Min Xia Zhong No 71.

[64] The judgments based on the same dispute with the same defendant but with different plaintiffs also include (2016) Yu Min Xia Zhong No 68, (2016) Yu Min Xia Zhong No 69, (2016) Yu Min Xia Zhong No 70, (2016) Yu Min Xia Zhong No 72, (2016) Yu Min Xia Zhong No 73.

[65] (2015) Zheng Min San Chu Zi No 309.

[66] It is arguable that the court did not invoke Article 1 of SPC Judicial Interpretation I of the LALFCR, which is specially drafted and issued as a guidance for Chinese domestic courts to apply the LALFCR in foreign-related civil relations.

Commercial Cases should be applied as a legal basis to exercise centralized jurisdiction. Despite the amount of the object failed to exceed 3 million, there were no people's court of the economic and technological development zone established by the state council and no basic people's courts meeting the conditions for acceptance. Thus, Zhengzhou Intermediate People's Court, as the intermediate court located in the capital of Henan province, had jurisdiction over foreign-related first-instance civil and commercial case according to Article 3 of the Provisions of the Supreme People's Court on Issues Concerning the Jurisdiction of Foreign-Related Civil and Commercial Cases.[67]

In most countries, the amount of disputed-object was the basis for dividing the range of jurisdiction within domestic framework. This is also the case in China for domestic cases, but in terms of foreign-related civil and commercial case, these rules are not strictly followed. From the reasoning parts of the courts, it is clear that the amount of disputed-object does not directly determine the competent court. The foreign-related element in a travel dispute case is an exception factor for the domestic courts not following the strict domestic jurisdiction rule. In other words, the Intermediate People's Court can exercise jurisdiction over foreign-related travel dispute even though the amount of disputed-object is far below the regulated standard.

3.1.7 The Jurisdiction Division Between the Special People's Court and the Local People's Court

The structure of Chinese court system is a two parallel system under the Supreme People's Court, one is Local People's Courts, another one is Special People's Courts. The Local People's Courts consist of High People's Court, Intermediate People's Court and Grass-roots People's Court. The Special People's Courts comprise Maritime Court, Military Court, Railway Transportation Court and Forestry Court.

In *Liu Peilong v Kunming Kanghui Yonghui Travel Agency* case,[68] Kunming Railway Intermediate People's Court classified the case as a foreign-related civil dispute, because the plaintiff was an American citizen and the accident happened in Thailand. Chinese law was applied because the parties unanimously agreed to choose Chinese law as the applicable law to settle the dispute. The applicable law is not that disputable in this case, the puzzle is about the missing jurisdiction part, why Kunming Railway Intermediate People's Court, as a special court, exercised jurisdiction, not the general Intermediate People's Court? What is the speciality of this case that distinguish it from other foreign-related civil travel dispute that caused by overseas personal injury accidents? The court per se did not give any answers or conduct any legal reasoning on its legitimacy of jurisdiction.

[67] The relevant judgements are (2016) Yu Min Xia Zhong No 68, (2016) Yu Min Xia Zhong No 69, (2016) Yu Min Xia Zhong No 70, (2016) Yu Min Xia Zhong No 71, (2016) Yu Min Xia Zhong No 72, (2016) Yu Min Xia Zhong No 73, which have almost the same reasoning and ruling with regard to the jurisdiction issue.

[68] *Liu Peilong v Kunming Kanghui Yonghui Travel Agency*, Kunming Railway IPC, (2017) Yun 71 Min Zhong No 11.

3.2 *Choice of Law Issue on Foreign-Related Travel Dispute in Chinese Judicial Practice*

3.2.1 Party Autonomy on the Application of Chinese Law in Foreign-Related Travel Dispute

In *Xi'an Xindaya International T ravel Agency v Dr. Barsch-Supan,*[69] the case was classified as foreign-related contract dispute, in which two American tourists want the travel agency and its deputy Zhang Li to pay their travel expenses back after the cancellation of Tibet trip. Escaping the jurisdiction part, the Shanxi High People's Court stated that the court respected party autonomy, and invoked Article 41 of the LALFCR to decide the applicable law. As a result, Chinese Law was applied because it was agreed by the parties. There are not much argument about the applicable law in this case, however, the identity of the two American citizens as tourists was totally ignored. The whole contract was regarded as a general contract, not a tourism contract or a consumer contract. If the two American tourists argued that American law should be applied to settle the dispute, what could be the legal basis for the court to justify that Chinese law should be the governing law?

Same as the application of party autonomy, in *Liu Peilong v Kunming Kanghui Yonghui Travel Agency* case,[70] Kunming Railway Intermediate People's Court classified the case as a foreign-related civil dispute, because the plaintiff was an American citizen and the accident happened in Thailand. Chinese law should be applied as a result of party autonomy stipulated in Art. 41 of the LALFCR, because the parties unanimously agreed to choose Chinese law as the applicable law to settle the dispute.

Likewise, in *Zhu Kaili v Guangzhou Baiyun District Fluent Education Training Centre,*[71] Guangdong Guangzhou Baiyu District People's Court classified the case as a Hong Kong-related one and invoked Article 41 of the LALFCR to apply party autonomy. Chinese law was applied because the two parties unanimously agreed to choose it. Nevertheless, the Court of Appeal, Guangdong Guangzhou Intermediate People's Court, classified the case as a foreign-related and Hong Kong-related contract dispute, not merely a Hong Kong-related service contract dispute, as Zhu Kaijia was a permanent resident of Hong Kong SAR, the subject matter of the service contract was in the USA. When it comes to the applicable law, the court also based on party autonomy, but invoked Article 3 of the LALFCR. Actually, Article 3 is a provision in the first chapter concerning the general provisions to announce that the parties have right to choose the governing law, which means it is a general principle applied to various foreign-related civil relations, not just limited in the contract field.

---

[69] *Xi'an Xindaya International Travel Agency v Dr. Barsch-Supan*, Shaanxi Province HPC, (2016) Shan Min Zhong No 511.

[70] *Liu Peilong v Kunming Kanghui Yonghui Travel Agency*, Kunming Railway IPC, (2017) Yun 71 Min Zhong No 11.

[71] *Zhu Kaili v Guangzhou Baiyun District Fluent Education Training Centre*, Guangdong Province Guangzhou Municipality Baiyun DPC, (2014) Hui Yun Fa Min San Chu Zi No 15.

The court invoked this provision to decide the applicable law, instead of Article 41, which is not quite convincing.

Apart from invoking the general provision, there is also case in which the court invoked multiple but unnecessary legal provisions to support the application of party autonomy, same as the jurisdiction part mentioned above. For instance, a Hong Kong-related contract dispute case *Weihong v Xi'an Diyawei Tourism Project Development Co.,*[72] Shanxi Xi'an Intermediate People's Court also stated that the court respected party autonomy and applied Chinese Law because the parties chose to apply the mainland law. The difference is that the court not only invoked Article 41 of the LALFCR, which is already correct and enough, but also Article 19 of the SPC Judicial Interpretation I of the LALFCR as legal basis. Indeed, Article 19 is a general provision about the reference to foreign-related civil relation when hearing the Hong Kong or Macao-related cases. It should not be invoked to justify the application of party autonomy, instead, it would be better if Article 19 was invoked after classifying the case as Hong Kong-related contract dispute, before invoking Article 41 of the party autonomy theory.

Except invoking multiple but unnecessary legal provisions, there are also cases that no legal documents were invoked to support the application of party autonomy. For example, in *Foshan Guangzhilv International Travel Agency v Lin Jintian,*[73] Guangdong Foshan Intermediate People's Court classified the case as a Hong Kong-related commercial dispute, and then decided that Chinese law should be applied because the parties had no objection to the application of Mainland law, the court hereby confirmed it without referring to any laws or regulations. In comparison with the explicit consent mentioned above, the parties in this case seemed tacitly accepted that Chinese law would be the governing law. Even though it is an implied consent, it is still the embodiment of party autonomy principle. The absence of legal documents support would inevitably derogate the public credibility of the judicial judgment.

3.2.2 The Most Significant Relationship Principle on the Application of Chinese Law in Foreign-Related Travel Dispute

In *Xue Xiujuan v Yongcheng Property Insurance Co.* case,[74] the Jiangxi Nanchang Intermediate People's Court classified the case as a foreign-related civil dispute. Since the parties didn't choose the applicable law in the travel contract, according to the most significant relationship principle stipulated in Article 41 of the LALFCR, Chinese Law should be applied. Although the court conducted legal reasoning on the applicable law, there are still two problems here. First, the court did not analyze

[72] *Weihong v Xian Diyawei Tourism Project Development Co., Ltd*, Shaanxi Province Xi'an Municipality IPC, (2017) Shan 01 Min Chu No 977.

[73] *Foshan Guangzhilv International Travel Agency v Lin Jintian*, Guangdong Foshan IPC, (2017) Yue 06 Min Zhong No 4445.

[74] Xue Xiujuan v Yongcheng Property Insurance Co., Ltd. Jiangxi Branch, Jiangxi Province Nanchang Municipality IPC, (2015) Hong Min Si Chu Zi No 30.

why Chinese Law has the closest connection with the case, it seems that the closest connection principle was mentioned first and then directly lead to the application of Chinese Law. Second, the identity of the plaintiff as a tourist or as a consumer was totally ignored, despite the fact that there is a special more protective choice of law rule on consumer contract. The same practice also show up in *Henan Zhigong International Agency v Yang Junya*[75] case heard by Henan High People's Court, the only difference is that the court classified the case as a foreign-related contract dispute, not a foreign-related civil dispute.

Similarly, in *China Dadi Property Insurance Co., Ltd. Jiangxi Branch v Xue Xiujuan* case,[76] Jiangsu High People's Court also invoked the most significant relationship principle stipulated in Article 41 of the LALFCR. However, the court also analyzed why Chinese law has the closest connection with the contract, which is more advisable. To be more specific, the court deemed that although the personal injury accident occurred in Thailand, the three parties concerned were Chinese resident, legal person and incorporated organization separately. In addition, the travel contract and the insurance contract were signed in china, thereby Chinese law should be the governing law. Clearly, the court invoked the right provision and also explained why Chinese law has the closest connection with the case. In this sense, the practice of Jiangsu High People's Court is a good example for other courts when using the closest connection principle to decide the governing law.

Nevertheless, not all courts utilized the most significant relationship principle in a professional or convincing way. Some courts relied on the closest connection principle without referring to any laws and regulations, while some did not analyze the reason of using the closest connection principle, merely listing all connecting factors without selection. To be specific, Shandong Qingdao Intermediate People's Court invoked the most significant relationship principle to apply Chinese Law in *Tong Bo v Shandong Daxinhua Yuntong Travel Agency* case, in which the tourist get injured in a traffic accident during a bus tour arranged by the travel agency in Switzerland.[77] The court, however, did not refer to any laws or analyze why Chinese law had the closest connection with the case. Luckily, when the case was appealed to Shandong High People's Court,[78] the court analyzed that based on the fact that the place of performance of the contract is overseas and the parties' domicile was in Qingdao, Shandong, in accordance with the principle of most significant relationship, Chinese Law should be applied. Actually, the fact that the place of performance of the contract is overseas should be one factor to determine the foreign-related element of the dispute, it is improper to be mentioned in parallel with the parties' domicile to justify Chinese law has the closest connection with the case. In other words, the

[75] *Yongan Property Insurance Company Henan Branch v Yang Junya*, Henan Province HPC, (2017) Yu Min Zhong No 540.

[76] *China Dadi Property Insurance Co., Ltd. Jiangxi Branch v Xue Xiujuan*, Jiangxi Province HPC, (2017) Gan Min Zhong No 248.

[77] *Tong Bo v Shandong Daxinhua Yuntong Travel Agency*, Shandong Province Qingdao Municipality IPC, (2016) Lu 02 Min Chu No 1146.

[78] *Lan Xinguo v Shandong Daxinhua Yuntong Travel Agency*, Shandong Province Qingdao Municipality IPC, (2016) Lu 02 Min Chu No 1157.

element that the place of performance of the contract is outside the territory of China, had nothing to do or had no value to prove Chinese law had closest connection with the dispute.

By contrast, concerning the same dispute occurred in the same accident but with different plaintiffs, the practice of Shandong High People's Court in *Lan Xinguo v Shandong Daxinhua Yuntong Travel Agency* case was more advisable. Instead of listing all the elements, the court picked up the factors that can prove the connection between the dispute and the Chinese law, that is, the domicile of the parties and the place where the travel contract was signed were in Qingdao, Shandong. The only imperfection is the lack of reference of Article 41 of the LALFCR.

In comparison with the absence of law reference, there is a possibility that the court invoke multiple legal documents to decide the applicable law, just as mentioned above in justification and party autonomy part. In case *Feng Yunhai v Henan Feiyang Travel Agency*,[79] the tourist got injured in a tour bus in Indonesia. Zhengzhou Intermediate People's Court invoked not only Article 41 of the LALFCR but also Article 126 of the Contract Law[80] to support the application of the closest connection principle. Specifically speaking, the domicile of the plaintiff and defendants as well as the place where the contract was signed were in China, thus the Chinese law had the closest connection with the contract. The analyzation of the connection between the case and the Chinese law has no debatable points, the disputable part is the necessity of invoking both the Contract Law and the LALFCR. In fact, the emergence of the Article 41 of the LALFCR can trace back to provisions in other laws, for instance, "General Principles of the Civil Law of the People's Republic of China" (GPCL) in 1986,[81] "Opinions of the Supreme People's Court on Several Issues concerning the Implementation of the General Principles of the Civil Law of the People's Republic of China" (for Trial Implementation) (Judicial Opinions of GPCL, 1988), Contract Law (1999),[82] "Rules of the Supreme People's Court on the Relevant Issues concerning the Application of Law in Hearing Foreign-Related Contractual Dispute Cases in Civil and Commercial Matters (2007 Rules)".[83] Therefore, it seems no need to invoke contract law, one of the legal resources of the LALFCR, to decide the governing law in this scenario.

[79] *Feng Yunhai v Henan Feiyang Travel Agency*, Henan Province Zhengzhou Municipality IPC, (2015) Zheng Min San Chu Zi No 307.

[80] Article 126 of Contract Law of the PRC.

[81] Article 145 of GPCL.

[82] Article 142 and Article 126 of Contract Law of the PRC.

[83] Article 5 of 2007 Rules.

3.2.3 The Choice of Cause of Action by the Plaintiff

There is a case heard by Fujian Quanzhou Intermediate People's Court, namely *Hong Xuanxuan v Quanzhou International Travel Agency*,[84] which was classified as a Hong Kong-related travel contract dispute. The court invoked Article 41 of the LALFCR, without explaining Chinese Law should be applied because of party autonomy, characteristic performance or most significant relationship principle. It is noteworthy that the choice of cause of action by the plaintiff also directly affect the choice of law rule. In this case, the plaintiff fell down on the wet and slippery floor in the hotel and got serious injury. Article 122 of the Contract Law provides that,

> if a party infringes upon the other party's personal and property rights and interests, due to his breach of contract, the injured party has the right to choose whether to require him to bear the liability for breach of contract or to bear the liability for tort in accordance with other laws.

In the end, the plaintiff clearly claimed that the defendant, as a tourism operator, did not fulfill the obligation of guaranteeing the tourist's security in the process of providing tourism services for the plaintiff. In another word, the tourism operator's failure to fulfill its security guarantee obligation resulted in the plaintiff's personal injury, and thus the plaintiff requested the defendant to bear the liability for breach of contract. The court, accordingly, heard the case in accordance with the legal relation chosen by the parties. However, if the plaintiff choose to sue the travel agency to bear the liability for tort, the choice of law rule would be different as a result. In this scenario, Article 44 of the LALFCR will apply, although it may turn out that Chinese law is applied in the end, the application of Chinese law is not because of party autonomy, characteristic performance or most significant relationship principle, but might because of *lex loci delicti* or common habitual residence.

3.2.4 Domestic Dispute with International Choice of Law Rule

Another interesting case is *Zhao Chengwu v Guangdong Nanhu International Travel Agency*[85] heard by Guangdong Foshan Shunde District People's Court, the plaintiff got injured in Spain due to traffic accident. Although the case is obviously foreign-related, the court did not mention the foreign-related element or classify the case as a foreign-related travel contract dispute. After classifying the case as merely a domestic travel contract dispute, in terms of the applicable law of the case, the court, however, invoked the LALFCR. The practice of the court is self-contradictory, because the classification and the choice of law rule is inconsistent in nature. This practice is the same as the jurisdiction reasoning part mentioned above, while some courts classify a case as a domestic dispute and invoke international jurisdiction rule or vice versa.

[84] *Hong Xuanxuan v Quanzhou International Travel Agency*, Fujian Province Quanzhou Municipality IPC, (2015) Quan Min Chu Zi No 968.

[85] *Zhao Chengwu v Guangdong Nanhu International Travel Agency*, Guangdong Foshan Shunde District People's Court, (2017) Yue 0606 Min Chu No 11502.

3.2.5 Co-application of Party Autonomy and the Closest Connection Principle

Even if the court classify the case as a foreign-related one, the reasoning part of the choice of law part is still paradoxical. More specifically speaking, the court invoked Article 41 of the LALFCR, which contain both party autonomy and the most significant relationship principle. First of all, the court said that the parties didn't choose the applicable law in the contract, which means party autonomy does not apply in this case. Then, the court held that both parties were domestic enterprises and individuals, and thus Chinese Law had the closest connection. The reasoning was supposed to end here and the Chinese law was applied because of the most significant relationship principle.

Nevertheless, the court added one more sentence, perhaps out of the consideration to make the application of Chinese Law more convincing, that is, both parties also believed the mainland law should be applied. This extra sentence actually leads the ground of the application of Chinese Law back to the party autonomy again, which turns out to be needless and contradictory to the court's previous reasoning. In another word, if both parties believed that Chinese mainland law should be applied, then it constituted implied consent, then party autonomy is enough to support the application of Chinese Law. If the court first mentioned the parties did not choose the applicable law, and utilized the closest connection principle to apply Chinese law, then there is no need to mention that both parties believed mainland law should be applied at the end.

3.2.6 The Missing Choice of Law Part in Chinese Judicial Practice

There are also some cases that the court classified the case as foreign-related dispute, but did not explain or prove why Chinese Law should be applied, for instance, in case *Yunnan International Travel Agency Baitalu Branch v Guan Jingjing*,[86] *Peng Shiqi v Guizhou Overseas International Travel Agency*,[87] and *Rizhao Oriental International Travel Agency v Chen Yan*.[88] It seems that the court believed that once the court had jurisdiction over a foreign-related case, the Chinese Law should be applied as a natural result, or automatically. This, however, is not always the case in private international law field. If the parties choose the forum and then the forum law must be applied, this is encouraging parties to do forum shopping. There are 4 out of 21 cases that the court did not mention why Chinese Law should be applied, but there are more cases that the court ignored the jurisdiction part, 11 out of 21. Therefore,

---

[86] *Yunnan International Travel Agency Baitalu Branch v Guan Jingjing*, Kunming Railway Transport Intermediate Court, (2017) Yun 71 Min Zhong No 20.

[87] *Peng Shiqi v Guizhou Overseas International Travel Agency*, Guiyang Municipality Yunyan District People's Court, (2017) Qian 0103 Min Chu No 5337.

[88] *Rizhao Oriental International Travel Agency v Chen Yan*, Shandong Province Rizhao Municipality IPC, (2016) Lu 11 Min Xia Zhong No 95.

jurisdiction rule should be put more emphasis than choice of law rule in the reasoning part for Chinese court.

3.2.7 The Overuse of Article 41 of the LALFCR

The choice of law rule on general foreign-related contracts, except consumer contracts, shall comply with Article 41 of the LALFCR, which is based on 'party autonomy' doctrine, 'characteristic performance' doctrine and 'most significant relationship' doctrine.[89] Actually, this choice of law rule is no difference from that of business contracts (B2B contracts). However, as we can see from above cases, Article 41 of the LALFCR is widely used by Chinese courts to determine the applicable law of foreign-related travel contract disputes.

The overuse of Article 41 of the LALFCR also indicates the underuse of Article 42 of the LALFCR.[90] However, Article 42 of the LALFCR[91] separates consumer contracts (B2C) from business contracts (B2B), which provides particular favorable choice of law rule for consumer contracts. One significant improvement in the LALFCR is to distinguish the special contracts, namely, consumer contracts and employment contracts, from the general commercial contracts, based on the inequality of bargaining power between the parties. Before this, in Chinese law, there is no distinction between consumer contract and general contract regarding choice of law issue, which may be unjust to the weaker party.[92]

Nevertheless, the existence of a protective consumer choice of law rule does not mean the rule is perfect and well-used. The biggest imperfection of this applicable law rule is about the lack of clarity on certain terminologies. Specifically, the LALFCR fails to stipulate the definition of "consumer contract", the concept of which is of extreme significance, especially under the booming Silk Road tourism activities under the OBOR initiative. Thus, the definition of "consumer" can only be deduced from domestic substantive law, namely, Law of the People's Republic of China on Protection of Consumer Rights and Interests (Consumer Protection Law).[93] Pursuant to Article 2 of the Consumer Protection Law, a consumer is a natural person who purchase or use commodities or receive services for daily use. Accordingly, a consumer contract is a contract concluded by a consumer with a trader for purchasing commodities and services for daily consumption.[94] When it comes to travel contract or tourism contract, it is still unclear whether travel contract or tourism contract is one

---

[89] Ying [15].

[90] Article 42 of the LALFCR.

[91] Article 42 of the LALFCR translated by Prof. Dr. Dan Wei goes: *The laws at the habitual residence of consumers shall apply to consumer contracts; if a consumer chooses the applicable laws at the locality of the provision of goods or services or an operator has no relevant business operations at the habitual residence of the consumer, the laws at the locality of the provision of goods or services shall apply, in* Wei [16].

[92] Zhengxin [17]; Mo [18].

[93] Article 2 of the Consumer Protection Law.

[94] Ying [19].

kind of consumer contract. It is hard to say tourism is a daily consumption service, thus, whether tourist-consumer is one kind of consumers according to the definition of Article 2 of Consumer Protection Law, and whether travel contract is one kind of consumer contracts. There are still no clear answers to these questions in Chinese relative domestic laws and regulations. As a result, the identity of a tourist as a consumer is ignored or overlooked in foreign-related travel disputes. This might also be the main reason why Article 42 of the LALFCR was not used in these disputes.

Therefore, despite the availability of special rule of applicable law for consumer contract in Chinese law, Chinese courts seem to be more favorable to invoke the rule of choice of law for general contract, that is, Article 41 of the LALFCR, instead of Article 42. While Article 42 is specially designed for consumer contract, in theory, it should be applied to provide more favorable choice of law rules for consumer protection, in practice, ironically, few courts invoke this provision to protect tourist consumers involved in foreign-related tourism disputes. Therefore, it is not hard to image in the future the existing laws is far from enough to tackle the possible disputes that generating from time-share, cruise tour, self-service tourism and E-tourism along the OBOR countries and regions.

3.3 Other Relative Issues in Chinese Judicial Practice on Foreign-Related Travel Disputes

As can been seen from the cases analyzed above, the foreign-related travel disputes vary from the cancellation of the travel contract,[95] contract fraud,[96] unsatisfactory about the contract performance,[97] nonperformance of the contract,[98] traffic accident happened in a foreign country,[99] personal damage in an Airline,[100] in a street,[101] in a Hotel Cafeteria,[102] in a speedboat,[103] tourist drowned in snorkeling activity in Thailand[104] etc. The parties involved include tourists, travel agency, travel agent and the deputy, insurance company, airline, hotel and so forth. The foreign-related element may involve an American citizen, a Thai Air Asia, a Hong Kong citizen, a Hong Kong company, a Taiwan resident, a Taiwan Travel agency, or the legal fact, for

[95](2016) Shaan Min Zhong No 511.

[96](2017) Yue 06 Min Zhong 4445.

[97](2014) Sui Yun Fa Min San Chu Zi No 15.

[98](2017) Shaan 01 Min Chu No 977.

[99](2016) Lu 11 Min Xia Zhong No 95, (2017) Yue 0606 Min Chu No 11502, (2017) Qian 0103 Min Chu No 5337, (2015) Zheng Min San Chu Zi No 307, (2017) Lu Min Zhong No 1123.

[100](2014) Xin Min Chu Zi No 3892.

[101](2016) Min 0602 Min Chu No 6138.

[102](2015) Quan Min Chu Zi No 968.

[103](2015) Hong Min Si Chu Zi No 30.

[104](2017) Yun 71 Min Zhong No 11.

instance, the travel traffic accident, occurs abroad, either in Thailand,[105] America, Switzerland,[106] Indonesia,[107] Spain,[108] or in France.[109] Or, the destination of an outbound travel contract is a foreign country, such as in Russia, Greece, Portugal, Holland, Belgium, etc.

3.3.1 The Classification of the Foreign-Related Travel Disputes Is not Accurate

It turns out the classification about the foreign-related travel disputes is not that easy in Chinese judiciary practice, in fact, different Chinese domestic courts give different answers on the similar foreign-related travel disputes. In general, there are multiple demarcations of the nature of a dispute arising from a travel contract. To be more specific, the classification of these foreign-related travel disputes by different Chinese courts varies from the foreign related travel dispute, contract dispute, travel contract dispute, commercial dispute, civil dispute, civil tort dispute, tourism dispute, to service contract dispute. The diversity of this classification lies in the vagueness of the demarcation of consumer law, travel contract and the unclear definition of tourists.

Same as traffic accident case, in *Peng Shiqi v Guizhou Overseas International Travel Agency,*[110] the plaintiff joined the defendant's tour group to Thailand, but got injured in a traffic accident while traveling in a tour coach provided by the defendant. When it comes to jurisdiction, Guiyang Yunyan District People's Court deemed that the plaintiff filed a lawsuit for breach of contract, claiming the defendant assuming the liability for breach of contract, not the liability for infringement, and also the formation of the travel contract was in Guizhou City, therefore, the case didn't apply the foreign-related jurisdiction rule. Nevertheless, in *Tong Bo v Shandong Daxinhua Yuntong Travel Agency*, the tourist got injured in a traffic accident in Switzerland, Shandong Qingdao Intermediate People's Court characterized the case as a travel contract issue, as the place of performance is overseas, the court heard the case according to the foreign-related civil and commercial proceedings. Regarding the nature of the travel contract, these two similar cases have total different classification made by two different courts. Although it seems that these two cases both involve a Chinese tourist got injured in a traffic accident that happened in a foreign country.

[105](2017) Qian 0103 Min Chu No 5337.

[106](2017) Lu Min Zhong No 1123.

[107](2015) Zheng Min San Chu Zi No 307.

[108](2017) Yue 0606 Min Chu No 11502.

[109](2016) Lu 11 Min Xia Zhong No 95.

[110]*Peng Shiqi v Guizhou Overseas International Travel Agency*, Guiyang Municipality Yunyan District People's Court, (2017) Qian 0103 Min Chu No 5337.

3.3.2 The Characterization of Travel Contract/Service Contract

In the case *Zhu Kaili v Guangzhou Baiyun District Fluent Education Training Centre,*[111] the parties had different opinions on the nature of the contract. If it is a service contract, jurisdiction and choice of law rules will follow the general rule of a general contract, but if it is a travel contract, the special rule of a consumer contract will apply, which is more favorable to the tourist-consumer. The argument about the nature of a service contract and a travel contract also inspires the further practice on classification in Chinese courts, especially under the Silk Road Tourism setting.

To be more specific, Tan Peiyi signed a registration form titled "Little Star American Starlight Journey" with the Education Training Centre. According to the content of the registration form, the Education Training Centre would organize Zhu Kaili and other performers to rehearse a program and performed at the "2014 North America Happy Spring Festival Hollywood Chinese New Year Gala". The total price was 129,200 yuan, and this price covered the accommodation, transportation, tourist destination ticket, visa, performing costume for Zhu Kaili and training fee. However, it turned out Zhu Kaili didn't perform in the Gala as promised by the training centre. Despite visiting San Francisco, San Diego, Los Angeles and other places after that, the plaintiffs sued the training centre for the reason of contract fraud.

The Guangzhou Baiyu District People's Court classified the contract as a service contract, but the Education and Training Centre claimed that the case should not be classified as a service contract dispute, there were two different types of contractual relationships between different parties in this case. First, the contract between the Education and Training Centre and Zhu Kaili was a package travel contract, which includes providing the opportunity to perform in the North American International TV Spring Festival Gala, celebrating the New Year with American children hand in hand, as well as visiting other American cities. It provides a package travel contract with a series of tours, such as transportation, accommodation and entertainment, rather than a service contract to provide only the opportunity to perform in the North American International TV Spring Festival Gala. Second, it was merely a pure travel contract between the Education and Training Centre and Tan Peiyi, Zhu Kaijia, Zhu Qingwen. These three people went to the USA only for the purpose of travelling.

On the contrary, the four plaintiffs defended that they jointly signed the contract with the Education and Training Centre as a party to the contract. The contract is mainly about the performance in the USA, despite travel services were included. The primary content of the contract was Zhu Kaili's performance on the ICN North American TV Spring Festival Gala that organized by the centre, accompanied by Zhu Kaijia, Zhu Qingwen and Tan Peiyi as family members, although they travelled around various places after the performance. In this case, is it advisable to separate the nature of the same registration form based on the different purposes of the parties? How to define the nature of a contract if it is a combination of education and travel activities? Under the New Silk Road Tourism, there are more travel projects

---

[111] *Zhu Kaili v Guangzhou Baiyun District Fluent Education Training Centre*, Guangdong Province Guangzhou Municipality Baiyun DPC, (2014) Hui Yun Fa Min San Chu Zi No 15.

that combine education activities with travel activities, what is the identity of the participant in this scenario?

3.3.3 The Characterization of Travel Contract with Dual Purposes

Another case regarding the classification of travel contract is *Gu Weilong v Xi'an Defang Investment Co., Ltd.*[112] heard by Shaanxi Xian Yanta District People's Court. The plaintiff Gu Weilong participated in a 7-day business investigation tour with a group of 20 people organized by the defendant to Japan on the theme of "pension real estate", and paid 3,2000 yuan to the defendant. The plaintiff held that there were false elements in tourist product design, route arrangement and advertising as the defendant was not a professional travel agency. Besides, the defendant had no tourism and foreign-related tourism operation qualification and entrusted the plaintiff's regiment to other companies, who organized the group in disorder and failed to provide services consistent with the travel fees, the service contract should be void and 32,000 yuan of the travel fee should be refunded.[113] However, the defendant argued that there was no contractual relationship between the two parties, thus the plaintiff was not the eligible and qualified subject to initiate the lawsuit. The payer of the contract was the Shaanxi Baile Industrial Development Co., Ltd. The contract was not a travel contract for the purpose of tourism, but a service contract.[114]

Shaanxi Xian Yanta District People's Court held that the nature of the contract was a travel contract. First, the defendant negotiated with the plaintiff by email on the ground of organizing a "survey and investigation of Japanese pension real estate activities" and arranged the plaintiff to participate in relevant activities. Although the defendant issued an invoice to the company in which the plaintiff was the legal representative, it did not affect the plaintiff's attribute as the counterpart of the contract, as the plaintiff paid the money through bank transfer.[115] Additionally, the information provided by the defendant to the plaintiff and the services specified in their agreements include arrangements for entry and exit, visas, accommodation, catering, tour buses, tour guides and scenic spots tickets. Although the defendant applied for a business visa for the plaintiff, the performance of the rights and obligations between the plaintiff and the defendant was entirely of the nature of the travel contract.[116]

In contrast, Shanxi Xian Intermediate People's Court deemed the contract was a service contract, not a travel contract, based on the object, subject and content of the contract.[117] First, the purpose of the contract was to enable the participants

[112] *Gu Weilong v Xi'an Defang Investment Co., Ltd.*, Shaanxi Province Xi'an Municipality Yanta DPC, (2015) Yan Min Chu Zi No 07364.

[113] (2015) Yan Min Chu Zi No 07364, pp. 1–2.

[114] (2015) Yan Min Chu Zi No 07364, p. 2.

[115] (2015) Yan Min Chu Zi No 07364, p. 4.

[116] (2015) Yan Min Chu Zi No 07364, p. 6.

[117] *Gu Weilong v Xi'an Defang Investment Co., Ltd.*, Shaanxi Province Xi'an Municipality IPC, (2016) Shan Min Zhong No 3012.

to understand the relevant situation of Japanese pension real estate, not to travel to Japan for sightseeing, vacation, leisure and other forms of tourism activities. Second, in terms of the content of the contract, Xi'an Defang Investment Company organized a delegation to investigate the situation of Japan's pension real estate and related pension service industry. The whole trip focused on the theme of business visit and the delegation visited many nursing homes and pension supplies exhibition halls in Japan, which is significantly different from the content of general travel contract. In this 7-day-trip to Japan, deducting the first day and the last day of the flight time, the actual inspection time is 5 days, in which two and half days were spent to organize four business inspection activities. The rest of the time was most spent on transportation, and interspersed tourist attractions visit and shopping were only for the participants to understand the local customs and economic conditions of the Japanese society. The activity cannot be identified as a tourist activity because of the mere interspersed tourist attraction visit. Third, the participants of this inspection activities in Japan were either private entrepreneurs or senior managers of the company, which was obviously different from the tourists. Fourth, GU Weilong and other members of the delegation held a short-term business visa issued by the Japanese Embassy in Beijing, not a tourist visa. Fifth, Xi'an Defang Investment Company was a legal person established by law, not a tourism operator.[118]

Despite the courts analyze the same activity, based on different perspectives, the elements were put different weights by different courts, and thus led to the discrepancy on the nature of the contract. Under OBOR initiative, the massive investment projects also attract more businessmen to go across different countries and regions along the New Silk Road, when their travel activities are mixed with business activities, or, a travel contract is concluded with dual purposes, one tricky question would be can these businessmen be regarded as tourists and thus under the protection of more protective jurisdiction and choice of law rules?

3.3.4 Mandatory Provision and Public Order Consideration About the Travel Contract

In case *Gu Weilong v Xi'an Defang Investment Co., Ltd.*, Shanxi Xi'an Yanta District People's Court also believed that the defendant had no qualification for handling outbound travel, which was a clear violation of mandatory provisions of relevant laws and administrative regulations. Pursuant to Article 52(5) of the Contract Law, contracts that violate the mandatory provisions of laws and administrative regulations are invalid, therefore, the contract in this case was invalid. Article 14 of the Interpretation of the SPC on Several Questions Concerning the Application of the Contract Law of the PRC stipulates that the "mandatory provisions" in Article 52(5) of the Contract Law refers to "mandatory provisions on effectiveness". Article 4(3) of the Measures for the Administration of Chinese Citizens' Out-bound Travel in Decree 354 of the State Council stipulates that no entity or individual shall, without

---

[118](2016) Shaan 01 Min Zhong No 3012, p. 8.

the approval of the tourism administration department of the State Council, operate the overseas tourism business without authorization or in a disguised form such as business, investigation, training etc. This provision is complementary to the licensing system for the establishment and operation of travel agencies in the Travel Agencies Regulation, which was issued by the State Council. Its legislative purpose was to strengthen the management of travel agencies, protect the legitimate rights and interests of tourists and travel agencies, maintain the order of the tourism market, and promote the healthy development of the tourism industry.[119]

The court of first instance believed that the travel contract concluded between the plaintiff and the defendant in this case was invalid, because it violated the mandatory provision on effectiveness and also and social public interests. If the travel contract of this kind was valid, the legality and validity of such travel contracts will seriously damage the interests of tourists and legally-operated travel agencies, undermine the order of China's tourism market and further damage the social public interests in China.[120] Nevertheless, the court of second instance believed that the contract was legal and valid. Specifically, the Shanxi Xi'an Intermediate People's Court deemed that the people's court can only determine the invalidity of a contract according to the laws enacted by the National People's Congress and its Standing Committee as well as the administrative regulations formulated by the State Council. Therefore, local laws and administrative regulations cannot be directly invoked as the legal basis for judging the invalidity of the contract. Mandatory provisions comprises regulatory norms and validity norms, but only by violating the mandatory provisions of laws and regulations on validity norms can the contract be considered null and void. The question based on the mandatory provision on the qualification of travel agencies might also indirectly affect the identity of an individual tourist-consumer and further influence the application of jurisdiction and choice of law rules.

3.3.5 The Challenges Caused by Self-service Tourism and E-Tourism

It can be seen that the collected cases were mainly limited to one particular travel contract, that is, a standardized package travel contract between a Chinese tourist and a Chinese international travel agency, and the dispute occurred in a foreign legal area. Relatively speaking, this kind of dispute is less complicated than a self-service cross-border tour, especially under the transformation age of tourism industry in this E-commerce era. The travel service providers and the tour operators along the OBOR countries and regions increasingly rely on internet and technology to do marketing, promoting and advertising activities. Meanwhile, the tourist-consumers are more likely to book different tourism services and products online with the popular usage of computers and smart phones. However, the availability of massive online tourism services and the convenience brought by E-tourism through online booking might

[119](2015) Yan Min Chu Zi No 07364, p. 7.

[120](2015) Yan Min Chu Zi No 07364, p. 8.

trigger complicated, expensive and time-consuming cross-border litigation for E-tourists once disputes arise. In the E-tourism scenario, parties are not confined to domestic ones,[121] the location of the parties when the travel contract is concluded is more ambiguous and less essential than that in tradition context,[122] and the activities conducted by a foreign travel companies is more hard to define.[123] For instance, if a Chinese tourist didn't sign a package travel contract with a domestic travel agency, but booked a Greek hotel through its website. Unfortunately, this Chinese tourist got injury in the hotel because of the slippery floor, when the tourist came back to China and decided to sue this Greek hotel in a Chinese domestic court that s/he was habitually resided in. Does the Chinese tourist have the right to sue a Greek hotel in a Chinese court? Does this Chinese domestic court have legitimate jurisdiction over a Greek hotel? If so, what is the legal basis? Which law should be the applicable law? If the online activities that conducted by the Greek hotel through its website can be regarded as 'engage in relevant business activities'[124] in China, then the Chinese court where the tourist-consumer has his/her habitual residence will have legitimate jurisdiction[125] and Chinese Law will be applied pursuant to Article 42 of the LALFCR.

Pursuant to Article 71 of the Tourism Law of PRC, Chinese tourists have the substantial right to file a lawsuit against either the domestic organizing travel agency or the foreign local travel agency or foreign travel service providers in a package travel contract. However, since the self-service tourist-consumer had no contract with a domestic travel agency, the tourist has to sue the foreign travel service provider directly in the court of his/her home country. As mentioned above, the special jurisdiction rule specially designed for consumer contract does not exist, Article 42 of the LALFCR, as the special protective choice of law rule for consumer contract,

---

[121] Since E-commerce enables foreign tour operators and travel service providers target Chinese tourist-consumers merely through online activities, the dispute between Chinese tourists and foreign travel companies in the cross-border context is more complicated. Even if both parties are from China, the concluded travel contract is a domestic contract, if it turns out that a Chinese travel agency act as an agent of a foreign travel operators, the dispute is still in nature foreign-related and requires the application of international jurisdiction and choice of law rules.

[122] Nowadays, with a computer and smart phone, a tourist basically can book any flight, any hotel and any travel services no matter where they are physically situated. It is difficult for an international travel company to predict where their tourist-consumers are physically located. Meanwhile, it is also difficult for the individual consumer to anticipate the location of travel service providers under the cover of the global and dematerialized Internet.

[123] The EU has 'directing test' or 'targeting test' and the USA has 'Zippo test' or 'Sliding Scale test' to examine the online activities of a business, while in China there is still no comparable or well-developed test to cope with electronic consumer disputes.

[124] As stated earlier, 'engage in relevant business activities', stipulated in Article 42 of the LALFCR, can be developed into a standard or a test to address both consumer jurisdiction issue and choice of law issue.

[125] It needs to be clarified that there is still no specific consumer jurisdiction rule in Chinese laws that the court can directly employ, the hypothesis is based on the possible further judicial interpretation from the Supreme People's Court on what constitutes the so-called 'engage in relevant business activities' stipulated in Article 42 of the LALFCR, and gradually develop a separate consumer jurisdiction rule based on this standard or test.

has its own limitation, owing to the unclear meaning of 'consumer contract' and missing standards of what constitutes 'engage in relevant business activities' for a foreign travel service providers. Therefore, a more detailed explanation of Article 42 of the LALFCR is needed in order to provide a more operational criteria for tourist-consumer protection. One possible and feasible solution is would be through further judicial interpretation issued by the Supreme People's Court. Once the criteria or test of 'engage in relevant business activities' in consumer choice of law field was established, its application can be expended to consumer jurisdiction arena. Gradually, if the established criteria or test issued by the Supreme People's Court is widely accepted and used in domestic courts, the judicial interpretation is more likely to be embodied or accepted in other relevant legislations in the future. Optimistically speaking, this might promote the reform on consumer jurisdiction legislation and fill the legislative gap in China by establishing a new and separate consumer jurisdiction rule.

4 Conclusion

Based on case analysis, this article endeavors to identify the existing problems and future challenges with regard to foreign-related travel disputes in China. It is easy to see what kind of problems and challenges are faced by Chinese courts, and also what issues need to be addressed both in the judiciary area and legislation field in order to be well-prepared for the foreseeable increasing cross-border travel disputes along the New Silk Road. To sum up, the existing problems will be concluded as follows.

4.1 The Discrepancy on Classification of the Travel Dispute

Regarding the classification about the foreign-related travel disputes, different Chinese domestic courts give different answers on the similar foreign-related travel disputes. To be more specific, the classification varies from the foreign related travel dispute, contract dispute, travel contract dispute, commercial dispute, civil dispute, civil tort dispute, tourism dispute, to service contract dispute. The further effort that can be taken by the Chinese courts is to make the classification more unified or harmonized according to relevant laws and regulations. Or, at least, with regard to the similar situation, such as traffic accident mentioned above, the practice of Chinese courts are supported to be more consistent, in order to render the judgments adjudicated by Chinese courts more convincing.

4.2 *The Definition of the Consumer Contract and Travel Contract Is Unclear*

The underuse of Article 42 of the LALFCR may first directly due to the lack of clear definition of travel contract and consumer contract in Chinese substantial law. In terms of the definition of travel contract, in comparison with other 15 kinds of named contract stipulated in the Contract Law, travel contract is merely a kind of nameless contract, while in Tourism Law, there is also no definition about the travel contract. Likewise, consumer contract is also not prescribed in Consumer Protection Law. Thus, one possible solution is to issue relevant judicial interpretation regarding the definition of travel contract and consumer contract before amending the Tourism Law, Consumer Protection Law or Contract Law, which actually takes a longer time.

4.3 *The Identity of a Tourist as a Consumer Is not Emphasized*

The identity of a tourist as a consumer is generally overlooked in Chinese judicial practice, this might also be one of the reasons that travel contract was not regarded as one kind of consumer contract, but as a general normal contract. As a result, jurisdiction rule and choice of law rule of the general contract were overused in a consumer contract,[126] and the more protective choice of law rule[127] was neglected. In addition, the definition of tourist is also unclear in Chinese domestic laws and regulations, even in the Chapter "Consumer Protection and Sharing Economy. Preliminary Ideas from the Argentine View" of the Tourism Law all the provisions are about the rights and obligations of the tourist, there is still no definition about the tourist, let alone the Contract Law or Consumer Protection Law. The absence of the definition of tourist also leads to the uncertainty of the classification of the nature of a contract when travel activities are combined with educational, recreational or business activities. Therefore, the definition of a tourist should be available in Chinese legislation, and the definition of international tourist or cross-border tourist should also be available especially under the OBOR initiative. After the availability of these definitions, the identify of a tourist as a consumer should be emphasized in order to provide more favorable protection to them.

[126] Article 23 of Civil Procedure Law and Article 41 of the LALFCR.

[127] Article 42 of the LALFCR.

4.4 *The Lack of Legislation on Consumer Jurisdiction Rule*

The absence of jurisdiction rule specially designed for consumer contract might be the main reason of many disputable practices of the Chinese courts, such as the missing reasoning jurisdiction part in foreign-related travel dispute, the lack of legal document to support jurisdiction, the multiple but unnecessary or incorrect legal documents, or, the misapplication of choice of law rule on jurisdiction issue. All these mistakes could be reduced if there is a clear and specific jurisdiction rule that specially designed to solve foreign-related consumer contract. Of course, the design of a new legislation rule on consumer contract need to coordinate and harmonize with other existing rules in relevant laws and regulations.

4.5 *The Vagueness of the Choice of Law Rule on Consumer Contract*

Article 42 of the LALFCR is the choice of law rule on consumer contract, nevertheless, as mentioned before, the biggest imperfection of this applicable law rule is about the lack of clarity on certain terminologies, such as the definition of 'consumer contract' and 'engaged in relevant business activities'. In particular, under the E-tourism situation, if the definition of 'engaged in relevant business activities' can be interpreted in a clear and specific way to the extent that a certain standard or test can be conclude and followed. This standard or test can not only be used to address choice of law issue, but also can be relied on to create a new separate consumer jurisdiction rule to tackle jurisdiction issues in the foreign-related travel disputes. Specially speaking, when a foreign tourism business operator engaged in relevant business activities according to this established standard or test in China, Chinese domestic courts can exercise jurisdiction based on their business activities conducted in China. Therefore, it is of extreme significance if the Supreme People's Court can issue a judicial interpretation to expound the meaning of the so-called 'engaged in relevant business activities' in the future.

References

1. Katherine Hui-Yi Tseng & Wen Xin Lim, *China's One Belt One Road Initiative*, Imperial College Press, July, 29, 2016, p. 12.
2. Tai-Wei Lim & Katherine Hui-Yi Tseng, *China's One Belt One Road Initiative*, Imperial College Press, July, 29, 2016, p. 5.
3. Justin W. Evans, The Magic Confluence: American Attorneys, China's Rise, and the Global Value Chain, IND. INT'L & COMP. L. REV., Vol. 18:2, at 277.
4. Karina Madsen Smed & Ane Bislev, *New Tourists at Old Destinations: Chinese Tourists in Europe*, in EMERGING POWERS, EMERGING MARKETS, EMERGING SOCIETIES, Macmillan Publishers Limited 2016, p. 235.

5. Tony Anderson, *China Practice: Advice to Wisconsin Law Firms Establishing Offices in China*, WISC. L.J., Feb. 8, 2006, at 1.
6. Qu Bo, *Issues on the Protection of Weaker Party's Interest under Private International Law*, Law Press, China, May 2009, pp. 62–63.
7. Huang Jin, *An Overview of the New Chinese Private International Law*, in International Symposium-Determination of the Law Applicable to International Contracts: A comparison between Chinese New Private International Law and EU Private International Law, Tsinghua University School of Law, March 23–29th 2011.
8. Nicolas Nord, *Comments on the Chinese New Statute on Conflict of Laws: A European Perspective*, Chinese Yearbook of Private International Law and Comparative Law, Peking University Press, 2011, Vol. 14, p. 85.
9. Albert A. Ehrenzweig, The Lex Fori-Basic Rule in the Conflict of Laws, 58 Mich.L.Rev. (Michigan Law Review) 637, Vol. 58, March 1960, p. 649.
10. Zhang Zhongbo, *Studies on the Legislation Substance and System Concerning Foreign Civil Law-Suggestions to Chinese "Application of Law Concerning Foreign Civil Law"*, Peking University Press, 2011, Vol. 14, pp. 126–127.
11. Huang J & Qian XF, *"One country, two systems", three law families, and four legal regions: the emerging inter-regional conflicts of law in China*, Duke J Comp Int'l Law (1995) 5:289–328.
12. Mathijs H.Ten Wolde, *Recognition and Enforcement of Chinese Money Judgments in Civil and Commercial Matters in the Netherlands: Law and Practice*, Chinese Yearbook of Private International Law and Comparative Law, 2017 Volume 21, Law Press. China, p. 126.
13. Nicolas Nord, *Comments on the Chinese New Statute on Conflict of Laws: A European Perspective*, Chinese Yearbook of Private International Law and Comparative Law, Peking University Press, 2011, Vol. 14, p. 72.
14. Chen Zhen, *A Brief Probe into the Existing Problems in Juridical Practice about Foreign Contracts–Based On Statistic Analysis of 109 Judgment Documents*, Jurisprudential Meditation of Luojia, Wuhan University, April, 2016, p. 60.
15. Yu Ying, *Chinese Approaches to Reform Consumer Protection law: Substantive Law and Conflict Law'*, in CONSUMER LAW AND SOCIOECONOMIC DEVELOPMENT : NATIONAL AND INTERNATIONAL DIMENSIONS, (Cláudia Lima Marques & Dan Wei, eds., 2016), pp. 81–89.
16. Dan Wei, Tourist-consumer protection in Macau SAR of China as a world tourism destination, in Revista de Direito do Consumidor, vol. 92 (2014), pp. 13–24.
17. Huo Zhengxin, 'Highlights of China's New Private International Law Act', (2011) 45 *Revue Juridique Themis* 637, 674.
18. Zhang Mo, 'Choice of Law in Contracts: A Chinese Approach' (2006) 26 *Northwestern Journal of International Law & Business* 106.
19. Yu Ying, *Chinese Approaches to Reform Consumer Protection law: Substantive Law and Conflict Law'*, in CONSUMER LAW AND SOCIOECONOMIC DEVELOPMENT : NATIONAL AND INTERNATIONAL DIMENSIONS, (Cláudia Lima Marques & Dan Wei, eds., 2016), p. 88.

Austerity and Access to Justice: Exploring the Role of Clinical Legal Education in Cambridge

Jodi Gardner and Mary Spector

> I graduated from Oxford University in 1972 frustrated by my three years study of the law. In common with many students entering university I thought that I would be embarking on a 'relevant' course of study—encountering laws, processes and personnel relating to my personal experience of the scope and impact of the legal system. In short, I thought that my studies would, to an extent, reflect my limited knowledge of life derived from the working class community in which I had lived. How wrong this proved to be.[1]

1 Introduction

Cambridge is a city of contrasts. It houses one of the oldest and most-respected universities in the world and has the highest percentage of residents with higher education qualifications in the UK,[2] however it is struggling under the weight of

[1] Lewis [32], 150.

[2] 66.8%; Centre for Cities [10], 54.

Dr. Jodi Gardner—Fellow of Law, St John's College University of Cambridge, Please contact jsg61@cam.ac.uk for any queries.

Professor Mary Spector—Associate Dean for Clinics, Professor of Law, and Director of the Civil/Consumer Clinic Southern Methodist University Dedman School of Law The authors would like to thank the Herbert Smith Freehills the University of Cambridge and St John's College for supporting the project, We also would like to thank the International Association of Consumer Law for its role in bringing the collaboration together. We benefited greatly from the helpful feedback provided by many at the IACL Conference, Indianapolis and at the IJCLE Conference Bratislava The authors were also fortunate to be assisted by Ms Ioana Crisan St John's College University of Cambridge.

J. Gardner (✉)
University of Cambridge, Cambridge, UK
e-mail: jsg61@cam.ac.uk

M. Spector
Southern Methodist University, Dallas, TX, USA
e-mail: mspector@mail.smu.edu

D. Wei et al. (eds.), *Innovation and the Transformation of Consumer Law*,
https://doi.org/10.1007/978-981-15-8948-5_15

poverty and inequality. On the basis of the Gini-Coefficient, Cambridge is the least equal city in the United Kingdom[3] (and has been for a number of years), has the third highest house prices,[4] and the third worst housing affordability ratio.[5] This poverty has significant impacts, with a life expectancy difference of 10 years between the highest ranked neighbourhood compared with the lowest.[6]

It is therefore no surprise that Cambridge has a very busy Citizens Advice Centre, which handles 36,482 advice issues in 2018 alone.[7] Anglia Ruskin University, which has its main base in Cambridge, has also recently commenced a clinical legal education program, which provides high-quality advice and assistance in family and employment law.[8] Whilst this is an important step forward in a city that had gone without a law school clinical program until 2018, many unmet legal needs still remain. The most sought after areas for Citizens Advice Cambridge were debt/money advice (27%), benefits and tax credits (23%), and housing (13%).[9] Unsurprisingly, access to assistance in these areas has been impacted drastically by recent austerity measures and government cuts. These are all areas however where legal clinics can effectively operate,[10] and correspond closely with national trends as well as with student interest.[11]

Although approximately 70% of UK law schools currently run a clinical legal education program,[12] the University of Cambridge Faculty of Law is not one of them. In this paper we begin to explore the potential for commencing a clinical program at the Cambridge Faculty of Law, and the opportunities that such a program can provide to the University, its students, and those served by such a program. We start with an examination of how the greater political and economic context in the United Kingdom has created an environment in which the need for pro bono legal assistance in vulnerable communities has arisen.

---

[3] ibid 61 (unsurprisingly followed by Oxford and London).

[4] ibid 63.

[5] ibid 66.

[6] Equality and Anti Poverty Officer Helen Crowther, Cambridge City Council [23].

[7] This is an increase of nearly 10,000 from 2017; Cambridge & District Citizens Advice Bureau [7], 3.

[8] Anglia Law Clinic [2].

[9] These both exceed the demand for employment (7%) and family (7%); Cambridge & District Citizens Advice Bueau (n 7) 3.

[10] Sylvester [44], 37.

[11] ibid 37.

[12] Kemp et al. [26], vi.

2 Developing the 'Welfare State'

Until relatively recently, the United Kingdom was widely considered a 'Welfare State'[13] that provided a decent and respectable social safety net for all citizens. The true Welfare State was developed post World War II (WWII); there were, however, significant steps taken in this direction decades earlier. Numerous government welfare schemes were enacted after World War I. These included statutory social insurance schemes for the unemployed, sick, elderly, widows and orphans. Local authorities started to run publicly funded health services, including maternal and infant welfare clinics, treatments for specific diseases (mainly venereal diseases, tuberculosis and infectious diseases), and mental health conditions. These were limited to the poor and working classes, whilst middle-class consumers were expected to cover their own medical expenses and were excluded from the social insurance schemes.[14]

This all changed after WWII, as the impact of the War led to a 'profound rethinking and reorganisation' of Britain's social services.[15] Society had become used to two novel aspects; first, a significant increase in government provision of services, and second, a higher level of taxation—to cover the costs of the War. These two issues were key to the development of a social services network in Britain.[16] The Beveridge Report (formerly known as the *Social Insurance and Allied Services Report*)[17] used the post-War experience in Britain to recommend a complete reshaping of the welfare system into a single comprehensive scheme to cover the entire population.[18]

The Beveridge Report is considered the 'founding document' of the Welfare State.[19] It provided several key policies for post-war Britain to improve welfare in the country, and was aimed to address the 'Five Giants' in the community—Want, Disease, Ignorance, Squalor and Idleness.[20] Beveridge believed that the government had three key welfare duties:

(1) the introduction of a family allowance to limit poverty in large families;
(2) the introduction of a comprehensive, nation-wide health service; and
(3) governmental responsibility for maintaining a high and stable level of employment in the country.[21]

[13]It is noted that there is considerable debate and disagreement on how 'welfare state' should be defined and whether, in fact, Britain was ever a pure welfare state: see, for example, Stewart [43], 26–31; Barry [3], 66–68; Sleeman [40], ch 1. This paper does not intend to enter this debate.

[14]Noel Whiteside, 'Private Provision and Public Welfare: Health Insurance Between the Wars' in Gladstone [22], 27. Details on the health care provided can be found at 28–32. See also Sleeman (n 13) ch 3.

[15]Sleeman (n 13) 39.

[16]For specific details of the impact of WWII on social service provision, see ibid 39–41.

[17]Sir William Beveridge, *Social Insurance and Allied Services* (HMSO London 1942).

[18]Sleeman (n 13) 41.

[19]Stewart (n 13) 17.

[20]Sleeman (n 13) 41.

[21]ibid 43.

This represented the development of a clear social safety net, a 'defining moment' in English history, and a transition to an institutional Welfare State.[22] The Report resulted in the passing of several key pieces of legislation, including the Education Act 1944, the Family Allowances Act 1945, The National Health Service Act 1946, and the National Insurance Act 1946.[23] The aim of these reforms was to expand the role of the State. The social safety net provided by the government was no longer limited to relieving the most extreme cases of poverty or inequality; it was now designed to positively promote the welfare of all citizens.[24]

In the 1970s the Welfare State in Britain was widely perceived to be in crisis, largely because the social safety net provided to citizens was considered (by some parties) to be excessively generous. This view was precipitated by a range of political and economic factors, including the election of a Conservative government, the quadrupling of oil prices creating an unprecedented level of annual inflation, the slowing down of economic growth, an actual fall in GDP, and an unprecedented increase in unemployment.[25] As a result, the 'New Right' started a campaign to roll back the Welfare State and decrease government support, particularly through the promotion of the private sector for the delivery of social services, and requiring family provision of assistance previously delivered by the State. This was continued and enhanced when Margaret Thatcher first became Prime Minister in 1979.[26] The gradual erosion of the social minimum continued for the next 15 or so years.[27] In May 1996 the Guardian published a now-infamous front-page article titled 'The End of the Welfare State'. This article discussed the ways in which both Labour and the Conservatives had chipped away at the welfare safety net created decades earlier.[28] During this process, the State began to view charity and voluntary organisations as not just complementary services, but as an alternative to government welfare provision.[29] This process has, unfortunately, yet to stop.

The UK is in the midst of crushing austerity measures which have reduced public spending across almost all government sectors.[30] When elected in 2010, the UK coalition government set about making significant changes to the welfare system, mainly in the form of large cuts to its funding.[31] This culminated in *the Spending Review 2010 Command Paper* (Spending Review 2010), which aimed to make 'net welfare savings of £7 billion a year'.[32] This was largely a response to the global

[22]David Gladstone, 'Welfare before the Welfare State' in David Gladstone (ed), *Before Beveridge: Welfare before the Welfare State* (IEA Health and Welfare Unit 1999) 3.

[23]Warwick-Booth [46], 170–171.

[24]Sleeman (n 13) 1.

[25]Lowe [34], 305.

[26]Stewart (n 13) 24.

[27]For details of this see Lowe (n 25) ch 12, particularly 305–329; Mead [36], 17–20.

[28]Stewart (n 13) 15.

[29]Lewis [31], 16.

[30]For further information on the impact of austerity, see Konzelmann [28].

[31]Lansley and Mack [29] 121–125.

[32]HM Treasury [24], 8.

financial crisis, and the savings were primarily made through a reduction of the social minimum. Many argued that this focus was quite unfair, as the poorest in society had seen very little, if any, of the benefit of the financial boom, but were the ones who suffered the most from the crash.[33] As well as reduced welfare spending, the financial crisis resulted in difficulties obtaining credit (particularly for borrowers classed as 'higher risk'), and job insecurity and instability for many people.[34] A similar program was announced in 2013, when the government proposed its 'big bang' package of benefits reforms, which aimed to further reduce spending by around £20 billion.[35]

3 Moving the Welfare State to the Community

The 'Big Society' and 'Shared Society' notions promoted by the Conservative Party further indicated an erosion of the Welfare State in favour of individual responsibility. The Conservative Government attempted to limit its responsibility for provision of the social safety net. The Beveridge Report is largely considered the 'high water mark' of the Welfare State; since the 1970s, there has been a marked decrease in the willingness of the State to address social minimum issues. It is little surprise that poverty has continued to be a significant concern, and the need for assistance clearly remains. The Government has attempted to address these issues by pushing responsibility for the social safety net from the State towards the general public. This approach can be seen in David Cameron's (failed) creation of 'A Big Society'. Cameron's 2010 speech outlined this policy, stating 'whether it is in building affordable housing, tackling youth unemployment, inviting charities to deliver public services ... the people in Britain worked out the answer to the big social problems. A big part of that answer is the Big Society'.[36] The emphasised section is highly telling, indicating a desire for the government to move away from benevolent public services, and instead putting them in the hands of charities and other community organisations.

This concept of a 'Big Society' has been highly criticised; its discourse has been dismissed by many commentators as merely a cynical attempt to allow cuts in public spending by the government.[37] The concept is highly reminiscent of Thatcher's 'responsibilisation' of society, although it also adds a further requirement that in addition to being responsible for their own individual welfare needs, people have a moral obligation to volunteer for the general betterment of their society.[38]

The problem with the Big Society concept goes deeper than government malaise—it is highly contradictory. As outlined by Kinsby,

---

[33]Warwick-Booth (n 23) 177–178.

[34]ibid 177–178.

[35]Lansley and Mack (n 31) 130.

[36]Cameron [9] (emphasis added).

[37]Kinsby [27], 485.

[38]ibid 486.

> given that the conservative critique of the state usually rests on a deeply negative and pessimistic view about human nature—with individuals viewed as selfish utility-maximisers in conflict with others, and that since they themselves know best what they want, their needs ought to be met through market rather than state mechanisms—it seems odd that Cameron is appealing to human altruism, albeit not an altruism expressed through state redistribution of resources, to prop up public services.[39]

Unsurprisingly, the Big Society concept was widely considered a disappointment that disproportionately impacted the most vulnerable.[40] An independent review completed by *The Civil Exchange* and *DHA Communications* concluded that the Big Society has 'largely failed'.[41] One of the most negative aspects of the movement was the transfer of government services to the voluntary sector, and the consequent reduction in funding. As a result, the voluntary sector lost £1.3 billion of State funding in the 2011–12 financial year alone. Whilst this had negative outcomes across the board, smaller organisations and services to disadvantaged groups were impacted to the greatest extent.[42] These drastic cuts were not replaced by an increase in contribution from voluntary or charitable organisations. Prior to the Big Society, these organisations were already frequently struggling to meet the demands of the public[43] and, post Big Society, formal volunteering and community social action actually declined.[44]

4 Access to Justice Challenges

The dismantling of the Welfare State has been particularly harmful for the legal sector and access to justice. Some of the most drastic reductions have been seen in the availability of civil legal aid as a result of the *Legal Aid, Sentencing and Publishing of Offenders Act* 2012 (UK) ('LASPO'). LASPO removed legal aid for almost all welfare benefit cases, housing matters that did not constitute 'an immediate risk to the home' and family law cases without proof of domestic violence, forced marriage or child abduction. LAPSO has been significantly criticised by a wide range of stakeholders. For example, in 2015, the House of Commons Justice Committee Report reviewed the impact of the legislation and commented that it 'harmed access

---

[39] ibid 485.

[40] Slocock et al. comment that 'the poorest in society have paid disproportionately for efforts to reduce the government deficit ... cuts in public services have hit the poorest particularly hard': [41], 57.

[41] ibid 8.

[42] ibid 32, with further discussion at 33; 'The loss of statutory income will be significantly greater each year until at least 2017–18 and there is no sign of income from other sources filling the gap. Moreover, nongovernmental funding is less likely to reach those causes which in the past have been funded by government and where needs may be greatest'.

[43] See statistics discussed in ibid 25.

[44] ibid 11. For interesting comparison, see discussion of reciprocity and undertakings in the communal domain in Chen-Wishart [13], 236–237.

to justice' whilst also failing to achieve the government's financial aims.[45] The impact of LAPSO and its financial consequences, have been vividly summarised by Prescott,

> Whatever perceived savings are attributed to these cuts are outweighed by a greater human and social cost. It has cut away at the last recourse people have against an increasingly hostile system and we all live more precarious lives because of it. The LASPO Act undermines the human right to a fair trial in the UK and entrenches the power and privilege of those who can afford the cost of legal representation.[46]

In 2018 the Bar Council of England & Wales published a report on 'Justice in the age of austerity', which looked at the impact funding cuts have had on access to justice from 2008–2018. The purpose of the paper was to 'provide an overview of the effects of austerity on the resources that government has devoted to the justice system'.[47] The Ministry of Justice experienced a reduction in funding of 27% over the decade before 2018 and this has had drastic impacts on access to justice.[48] The Legal Aid budget has been cut by 32% during this period.[49] The author comments that this 'decline in resources will be reflected in a decline in the volume and quality of the justice system and access to it'.[50] The impact of cuts in funding to legal aid has not however been equally felt across the country, with already disadvantaged regional areas being the worst hit.[51] Access to justice was further debilitated by the closure of Magistrates Courts; austerity and subsequent government cuts have meant that, in less than a decade, half of all Magistrates Courts in England and Wales have closed.[52]

The impact of funding cuts on welfare benefits cases can be likened to a one-two punch. Firstly, cuts in legal aid from LASPO, followed by the creation of the 'Universal Benefits' program. The UK Government has described this policy in the following manner:

> Universal Credit is revolutionising the welfare system by making work pay. The design and structure of Universal Credit is transformational, it focuses on replicating the world of work, encouraging claimants to take greater responsibility for their finances and incentivising them to earn more and progress in work. At the same time Universal Credit provides support for people who can't work or need help moving towards the labour market. Universal Credit

---

[45] "The Ministry of Justice has failed in three of its four objectives for LASPO: it has not discouraged unnecessary and adversarial litigation at public expense because the courts and tribunals are having to meet the costs of a significant rise in litigants in person and a corresponding fall in mediation; it has failed to target legal aid at those who need it most because it has failed to properly implement the exceptional cases funding scheme; and it has failed to prove that it has delivered better overall value for money for the taxpayer because it has no idea at all of the knock-on costs of the legal aid changes to the public purse": House of Commons Justice Committee [25], 67.

[46] Prescott [37].

[47] Chalkley [11], 4.

[48] ibid 14.

[49] ibid 14.

[50] ibid 15.

[51] Gilbert [21].

[52] Bowcott and Duncan [5].

> is already transforming lives and evidence shows people are moving into work faster and working longer with Universal Credit than under the old system.[53]

As positive as this may sound, it is widely believed that Universal Credit has been a drastic failure which has caused widespread suffering for many people. There have been significant issues with how the reforms have been carried out, which has been costly to both the government and the people reliant on the benefits for survival. The Mayor of Liverpool described the situation as 'what was once a flagship scheme to "make work pay" by rolling a range of benefits into a single payment has become a byword for institutional sclerosis and incompetence.'[54] Unfortunately the implementation of Universal Credit has occurred at the same time as the (near complete) removal of legal aid for welfare cases, meaning that vulnerable people have no ability to obtain legal assistance necessary to challenge the—often incorrect[55]—decisions being made about their eligibility for benefits.[56]

A 2017 report from Citizens Advice found that people in receipt of Universal Credit were more likely to have priority debts than those on other benefits,[57] were more likely to struggle with rent and council tax arrears,[58] and had less available income to pay creditors.[59] These problems arise from many aspects of Universal Credit, including the six week wait until their initial payment.[60] During this period, many people have no available income and therefore have to rely on credit they cannot afford, merely to cope.

The situation in the UK became so dire that, in May 2019, the Great Britain and Northern Ireland was visited by the United Nations Special Rapporteur on extreme poverty and human rights. Whilst the findings of the report are clearly the basis for concern, the mere fact that someone whose job is to investigate 'extreme poverty' felt that a visit to the UK was justified, and highlights just how dire the situation has become. The subsequent report was strongly (and unsurprisingly) critical of the austerity measures, stating that despite the UK being the world's fifth largest economy and having a 'fundamentally strong' economic, one-fifth of the population lives in poverty and approximately 5% are in extreme destitution.[61] An additional 2.5 million people are no more than 10% above the poverty line, just one financial hiccup away from falling into poverty.[62] He also criticised the 'shocking increase in the number of food banks and major increases in homelessness and rough sleeping;

---

[53] Department for Work & Pensions [17], 1.

[54] Introductory comments in Liverpool City Council [33], 3.

[55] A review of Universal Credit appeals show that more than 50% of people appealing decisions for denied benefits are successful in their case: Bulman [6].

[56] See discussion in Prescott (n 46).

[57] Drake [18], 8.

[58] ibid 10.

[59] Ibid 11.

[60] Ibid 11–14.

[61] Special Rapporteur on extreme poverty and human rights [42] 3.

[62] Ibid 6.

a growing number of homeless families',[63] and that due to austerity measures 'great misery has been inflicted unnecessarily'.[64]

A section in the Special Rapporteur's report was devoted to the 'decimation' of legal aid and the impact of LAPSO. The reduction in access to legal assistance has prevented those most vulnerable in society from claiming and enforcing their rights. This has wider ramifications, as 'lack of access to legal aid also exacerbates extreme poverty, since justiciable problems that could have been resolved with legal representation go unaddressed'.[65] The citizens of Cambridge (and the United Kingdom in general) are therefore experiencing a perfect storm of disadvantage—the impact of austerity cuts and implementation of the (flawed) Universal Credit system are occurring at a time where access to justice is being severely undermined.

5 Responding to the Challenges

One consequence of the reduction in legal aid for civil matters is an increase in demand for pro bono legal and other services from non-governmental sources. Among the primary providers of assistance to persons seeking help with legal-related problems is Citizens Advice, a national network of independent charities, staffed largely by volunteers who are not lawyers and do not provide legal advice, yet assists people matters related to debt, benefits, housing, and family relationship matters. It was originally conceived as a resource for navigating emerging social welfare schemes that arose after World War I. From the time the first 200 offices opened in September 1939, the day after the UK entered World War II, volunteers provided assistance to civilians on a range of problems that included debt resulting from lost incomes as heads of households went to war, lost ration books, locating missing loved ones, the challenges of evacuation and homelessness, as well as on questions and problems related to social welfare. By the 1970s consumer-related issues became a priority,[66] and today Citizens Advice engages in consumer education and undertakes research on consumer policy issues while also providing assistance with debt arising from utility arrears, credit cards, payday loans, overdrafts, mortgage and credit issues as well as debt collectors.[67] Indeed, in its 2017/18 annual report, Citizens Advice ranked consumer matters at the top of the list of subjects about which people sought assistance, with debt close behind at number 3.[68]

LawWorks, also known as the Solicitors' Pro Bono Group, is a charity sponsored by the Law Society that works to promote pro bono service among solicitors and at law schools. It reports that 'the reduction in the scope of legal aid has contributed to

[63] Ibid 3.

[64] Ibid 4.

[65] Ibid 10.

[66] Citizens Advice [15].

[67] Citizens Advice [14].

[68] Citizens Advice [16], 12.

an increase in the number of people going to court or tribunal without a lawyer.'[69] For example, in private family law proceedings 64% of parties were unrepresented in 2016–17, a 50% increase in five years.[70] A 2017 Ministry of Justice Report showed that those seeking help with legal problems sought assistance from 'a range of different legal and professional advisors ... with many using more than one type of provider, alongside self-help.'[71] To help meet this gap in available legal services, LawWorks has helped create and support a network of free legal advice clinics that by March 2018, numbered 229 active clinics across England and Wales. As it has done so, it has also connected 'those needing pro bono legal services with pro bono volunteers and the assistance they need, including smaller charities and not-for-profit organisations and advocates for the promotion of access to justice.[72]

Law schools have also helped to fill the justice gap, with 70% supporting pro bono law clinics staffed by students and faculty. The clinics can take many forms, but generally can be described as 'learning environment[s] where students identify, research and apply knowledge in a setting which replicates, at least in part, the world where it is practised'.[73] Although access to justice may have been one factor among many in the creation of programs at some law schools, the growth of clinical legal education in the UK initially was focused on employability and the acquisition of practical legal skills. As outlined by Drummond and McKeever, 'the conceptual basis of social justice has been superseded by a focus on educational priorities. While social justice can still be delivered, it tends to be as a consequence of a pedagogically focused initiative rather than as its mission.'[74] This is likely to be linked to the fact clinical legal education in the UK developed during a time of a functioning social safety net, one that provided legal aid for many criminal and civil matters and a strong network of free advice agencies.[75] As times have changed, however, the purpose and nature of legal clinics appears to be responding to the changes by recognising the potential to address access to justice issues. In research funded by the Legal Education Foundation, Drummond and McKeever identify both pedagogical and justice goals among the four primary objectives of UK law clinics in 2015 (1) assisting local communities, (2) developing professional capacity, (3) improving student employability and (4) meeting unmet legal need.[76]

Drummond and McKeever's research reveals a growing recognition of the 'dual purpose' associated with clinical legal education; pedagogical and justice-oriented.[77] As outlined by Drummond and McKeever, the origins of clinical education in Australia and the United States, in contrast to the UK, was 'primarily in response

[69]LawWorks [30], 8.

[70]Ibid 8.

[71]Franklyn and others [20], 192.

[72]Ibid 192.

[73]Kemp, Munk and Gower (n 12) 1 (quoting Grimes and Gibbons (1996:138).

[74]Drummond and McKeever [19], 12–13.

[75]Sylvester (n 10) 37.

[76]Drummond and McKeever (n 74) 28.

[77]For a full analysis of this, see ibid (n 74).

to a lack of accessible legal services for poor'. Indeed, as clinical education took hold in American law schools, so did the proliferation of special 'student practice rules' grounded in the dual purpose of providing access to justice while providing students with practical legal training that enable unlicensed law students to appear in courts and tribunals to argue motions and appear at trial, or take or defend depositions on behalf of consenting clients.[78] For example, Texas' student practice rules state: 'These rules are promulgated in response to the Bench and Bar of the State of Texas to the responsibility to provide competent legal services for all persons, and to establish practical training to qualified law students …'.[79] The Michigan student practice rule goes even further: 'Effective legal service for each person in Michigan, regardless of that person's ability to pay, is important to the directly affected person, to our court system, and to the whole citizenry.'[80]

Clinical legal education has the potential to respond to the challenges outlined above through the creation of law clinics designed to address some of the justice gaps experienced by local communities. As Kemp, Munk and Gower write, clinical legal education can take many forms, including, among other things, in-house advice and representation clinics, advice-only/gateway clinics, streetlaw community education projects, and specialized legal projects.[81] Whatever the form, however, clinical legal education provides 'students with an understanding of the legal environment which awaits them upon graduation and as a means to instil professional values and a sensitivity to the concept of justice'.[82] Whilst the traditional legal education provides the necessary foundation, 'there are many educational benefits that can be derived only through clinical experiences'.[83] It also provides the opportunity for students to utilise these skills to deliver critical legal services to under-served communities.

Providing students with the opportunity to engage in the 'lived reality' of the world through clinical legal education can have significant pedagogical and practical advantages. In a 2016 report, Kemp, Munk and Gower describe how, at a high level, clinical legal education can not only increase access to underserved populations, but also ensure future lawyers have the 'knowledge, skills, and values needed to help solve the world's complex problems, and a legal profession that is more skilled and committed to serving social needs'.[84] There is a plethora of evidence on the numerous benefits of clinical legal education, which does not need to be repeated at length here.[85] As outlined by Alexander and Boothby, there is 'growing pressure

[78]Rule 1 of the Texas Rules and Regulations Governing the Participation of Qualified Law Students and Qualified Unlicensed Law School Graduates in the Trial of Cases in Texas, R. 1.

[79]Ibid.

[80]Michigan Court Rule 8.120.

[81]Kemp, Munk and Gower (n 12) 2 (quoting Kerrigan & Murray (2011).

[82]Marson et al. [35], 30.

[83]Chemerinsky [12], 596.

[84]Kemp, Munk and Gower (n 12) 4 (citing Maisel (2011: 335).

[85]See, for example, Lewis (n 1); Sylvester (n 10); Marson, Wilson and Hoorebeek (n 82); Bleasdale-Hill and Wragg [4]; Drummond and McKeever (n 74); Alexander and Boothby [1]; Kemp et al. (n 12).

on Higher Education providers to produce employable graduates in a challenging graduate marketplace', and clinical legal education can assist with this challenge.[86] There are significantly more law graduates than available jobs, so anything that assists with employability will be a benefit to both students and academic institutions. For example, in 2016 over 25,000 UK students applied to study undergraduate law in England and Wales; with almost 18,000 being accepted. Even though approximately 70% of students stated that they intended to enter the legal profession, there were only 5,728 training contracts and 474 pupillages.[87] There are clearly multiple benefits to be obtained from clinical legal education, to both the community at large and to the students undertaking the work.

6 Access to Justice in Cambridge: From Pro Bono to Clinical Legal Education?

A report from the Kemp, Munk and Gower at the University of Manchester commented that Russell Group University law schools[88] are less likely to be involved in clinical legal education than some of the 'new' universities. The authors commented that this 'could be due to traditional law schools in the Russell Group being more likely to adopt the conventional doctrinal or the black-letter approach to legal scholarship'.[89] This justification is likely to apply to an even stronger degree regarding Oxbridge Law Schools, which focus on a traditional, academically-driven curriculum. Kemp, Munk and Gower further comment that the dominance of the Research Excellence Framework is also likely to have an impact on the focus areas of different universities, particularly those having a strong research-focus.[90]

Unlike most other Law Schools in the United Kingdom, the University of Cambridge is a college-based teaching institution. Whilst lectures are provided by the faculty, the majority of students' classes are taught in their individual college by their college teaching fellows. This system has a strong historical basis, but creates a number of challenges for the creation and implementation of faculty-wide programs. The resources involved in setting up and running clinical legal education is one of the biggest obstacles. Clinical legal education is relatively expensive to run, due to the small number of students who can participate in the program and the need for the students' actions to be closely supervised and monitored.[91] As outlined by Chemerinsky, 'clinical education is expensive because it requires close supervision

[86] Alexander and Boothby (n 85) 55.

[87] Ibid 59.

[88] The members of Russell Group are 24 universities (including Oxford and Cambridge) which are 'world-class' and 'maintain the very best research, an outstanding teaching and learning experience and unrivalled links with local and national business and the public sector': Russell Group [39].

[89] Kemp, Munk and Gower (n 12) 35.

[90] Ibid 35.

[91] Drummond and McKeever (n 74) 13.

of students and thus small student-faculty ratios'.[92] The recent cuts in institutional resources have resulted in challenges for the running of clinics in many law schools in the UK.[93] In addition, clinical legal education programs do not have direct links to the national Research Excellence Framework and therefore do not provide universities with the financial incentives associated with 'standard' research activities.[94] Higher education institutions are quite financially stretched, and Cambridge Faculty of Law is no exception. This is exacerbated by the intensive teaming system at the University, where students are taught in very small groups, typically only 2–3 people per class.

Despite these challenges, Cambridge Law Faculty has a strong history of being involved in pro bono activities. There are two key strands, firstly the Cambridge Pro Bono Project which was established by the Faculty to provide graduate students with the opportunity to assist preparation of legal pro bono work. There are three objectives of this project, including (1) the opportunity to engage the law in a practical way and therefore develop the skills associated with the provision of pro bono services, (2) allow the Faculty of law to 'make a meaningful and practical contribution to public interest law', and (3) facilitate the collaboration between the Faculty and the organisations undertaking pro bono work.[95] The project however focuses on policy-driven, international issues such as the legal status of transgender individuals, sexual violence offences, existing and developing human rights law, defamation and censorship, the definition of torture, and global human trafficking.[96] In addition, student participation is only for postgraduate students. Undergraduate opportunities are largely limited to the student-run Cambridge University Law Society, which comprises the second strand. It undertakes a number of locally-based volunteer projects each year, some in collaboration with law firms, others in collaboration with local charities and schools.[97] Although extremely important, neither strand claims to provide the educational benefits a well-designed program of clinical legal education can provide to students, and to the communities they serve.

Whilst there are significant benefits associated with clinical legal education, there is no utility in creating a project if the students do not want to participate. Cambridge law students are already time-poor, and have huge academic demands and pressure on them. To better understand the students' perceptions and appetite for clinical legal education, we enlisted a student to assist in developing and administering a survey of students' perceptions on clinical legal education. Of the 623 students in the Cambridge Law Faculty, 120 students—approximately 20% of the student body—completed the survey.[98] The results thus represent the opinions of 19.3% of all Law

[92] Chemerinsky (n 83) 595.

[93] For further analysis, see Bleasdale-Hill and Wragg (n 85).

[94] Drummond and McKeever (n 74) 32.

[95] The Cambridge Pro Bono Project [38].

[96] The Cambridge Pro Bono Project [45].

[97] For details see, Cambridge University Law Society [8].

[98] There are so answers which are optional, so were not completed by all students. In addition, four students did not complete some of the identifying questions (i.e. year of study).

undergraduates in the academic year 2018/19. When asked whether they would be interested in participating in clinical legal education, the response was overwhelmingly positive, with 94.2% of students wanting to be involved. Of the students who indicated that they would not be interested in participating, only one student stated that this was due to 'disinterest' in a potential program. The remaining students stated that they did not have enough time to participate in further extra-curricular activities.

When asked what areas of law they were most interested in being involved, students gave a variety of answers. The key areas were, interestingly, parts of the law that not only have already worked well in a clinical legal environment—family, debt, housing and consumer law,[99] but also correspond to the local areas of need as discussed above. When asked what motivated them to participate in clinical legal education, students were permitted to select multiple answers from a list of possible choices. Their responses reflect the 'dual purposes' of clinical legal education discussed above (namely both professional/personal benefits and giving back to the community) and were split between these two reasons, with 90% of students stating they were motivated by legal and practical experience and 82.5% being motivated by charitable purposes.

7 Conclusion

Cambridge Faculty of Law has a proud history of pro bono assistance, but pro bono only goes so far. Clinical legal education provides educational institutions with a unique opportunity to go beyond pro bono to develop programmes that embed the principles of access to justice within the curriculum. Doing so sends a message to both the students and the outside world that the institution not only recognises the ethical obligations of lawyers, but also ensures they are carried out as part of a pedagogically rigorous academic program. In this paper, we have identified some of the potential benefits of clinical legal education in a time of austerity: opportunities for students to develop key professional skills during a difficult employment market, enhancing access to justice within an under-served community and ensuring this all occurs in a strong pedagogical manner. In addition, our engagement with the students at the University of Cambridge revealed a strong interest in pro bono and clinical opportunities. Considering the specific economic and political challenges of austerity, now is the perfect time for higher education institutions, such as the University of Cambridge, to take a look at themselves and determine what role they can play in creating a fairer and more just society in their local community.

[99] Sylvester (n 10) 37.

References

1. Alexander J and Boothby C, 'Stakeholder perceptions of Clinical Legal Education within an employability context' (2018) 25 International Journal of Clinical Legal Education 53
2. Anglia Law Clinic, 'About the Clinic' Anglia Ruskin University <https://aru.ac.uk/business-and-law/economics-finance-and-law/law-clinic> accessed 16 September 2019
3. Barry N, 'Neoclassicism, the New Right and British Social Welfare' in Page RM (ed), *British Social Welfare in the Twentieth Century* (Palgrave 1999)
4. Bleasdale-Hill L and Wragg P, 'Models of Clinic and Their Value to Students, Universities and the Community in the post-2012 Fees Era' (2013) 19 International Journal of Clinical Legal Education 257
5. Bowcott O and Duncan P, 'Half of magistrates courts in England and Wales closed since 2010' The Guardian <https://www.theguardian.com/law/2019/jan/27/half-of-magistrates-courts-in-england-and-wales-closed-since-tories-elected> accessed 13 April 2019
6. Bulman M, 'Universal credit: More than half of people denied benefit have cases overturned on appeal, figures show' The Independent <https://www.independent.co.uk/news/uk/home-news/universal-credit-appeal-overturn-wrong-refused-benefit-poverty-dwp-a8649221.html> accessed 3 September 2019
7. Cambridge & District Citizens Advice Bureau, *Report of the Trustees and Financial Statements for the Year Ended 31 March 2018* (Cambridge & District Citizens Advice 2018)
8. Cambridge University Law Society, 'Pro Bono' <https://culs.org.uk/pro-bono/> accessed 16 September 2019
9. Cameron D, *Speech on the Big Society* (A Speech Delivered in Liverpool on 18 July 2010)
10. Centre for Cities, *Cities Outlook 2018* (Centre for Cities 2018)
11. Chalkley M, *Funding for Justice 2008 to 2018: Justice in the age of austerity* (Bar Council of England & Wales 2018)
12. Chemerinsky E, 'Rethinking Legal Education' (2008) 43 Harvard Civil Rights-Civil Liberties Law Review 595
13. Chen-Wishart M, 'In Defence of Consideration' (2013) 13 Oxford University Commonwealth Law Journal 209
14. Citizens Advice, 'Citizens Advice consumer work' Citizens Advice, <https://www.citizensadvice.org.uk/about-us/how-citizens-advice-works/citizens-advice-consumer-work/> accessed 13 September 2019
15. Citizens Advice, 'History of the Citizens Advice service' <https://www.citizensadvice.org.uk/about-us/how-citizens-advice-works/who-we-are-and-what-we-do/history-of-the-citizens-advice-service/> accessed 14 September 2019
16. Citizens Advice, *Annual Report: 2017/18* (August 2018)
17. Department for Work & Pensions, *Universal Credit Statistical Ad Hoc: Payment Timeliness* (Department for Work & Pensions 2017)
18. Drake C, *Universal Credit and debt* (Citizens Advice 2017)
19. Drummond O and McKeever G, *Access to Justice through University Law Clinics* (Ulster University Law School with support from The Legal Education Foundation 2015)
20. Franklyn R and others, *Findings from the Legal Problem and Resolution Survey, 2014–15* (Ministry of Justice 2017)
21. Gilbert D, 'Legal aid advice network 'decimated' by funding cuts' <https://www.bbc.co.uk/news/uk-46357169> accessed 12 December 2018
22. Gladstone D, 'Welfare before the Welfare State' in Gladstone D (ed), *Before Beveridge: Welfare before the Welfare State* (IEA Health and Welfare Unit 1999)
23. Helen Crowther EaAPO, Cambridge City Council,, 'Tackling poverty in Cambridge - The most unequal city in the UK' (*The Equality Trust*, 31 July 2017) <https://www.equalitytrust.org.uk/blog/tackling-poverty-cambridge-most-unequal-city-uk> accessed 4 September 2019
24. HM Treasury, *Spending Review 2010* (Cm Paper 7942, 2010)

25. House of Commons Justice Committee, *Impact of changes to civil legal aid under Part 1 of the Legal Aid, Sentencing and Punishment of Offenders Act 2012: Eighth Report of Session 2014–15* (House of Commons 2015)
26. Kemp V, Munk T and Gower S, *Clinical Legal Education and Experiential Learning: Looking to the Future* (University of Manchester, The School of Law 2016)
27. Kinsby B, 'The Big Society: Power to the People?' (2010) 81 The Political Quarterly 484
28. Konzelmann SJ, *The Economics of Austerity* (Edward Elgar Publishing 2019)
29. Lansley S and Mack J, *Breadline Britain: The Rise of Mass Poverty* (OneWorld Publications 2015)
30. LawWorks, *LawWorks Clinics Network Report April 2017 – March 2018* (LawWorks December 2018)
31. Lewis J, 'The Voluntary Sector in the Mixed Economy of Welfare' in Gladstone D (ed), *Before Beveridge: Welfare Before the Welfare State* (IEA Health and Welfare Unit 1999)
32. Lewis R, 'Clinical Legal Education Revisted' (2000) 13 Dokkyo International Review 149
33. Liverpool City Council, *Universal Credit: Unintended Consequences* (Liverpool City Council 2017)
34. Lowe R, *The Welfare State in Britain since 1945* (2nd edn, MacMillan Press Ltd 1999)
35. Marson J, Wilson A and Hoorebeek MV, 'The necessity of clinical legal education in university law schools: a UK Perspective' (2005) 7 International Journal of Clinical Legal Education 29
36. Mead LM, 'The Rise of Paternalism' in Mead LM (ed), *The New Paternalism: Supervisory Approaches to Poverty* (Brookings Institution Press 1997)
37. Prescott N, 'How austerity is killing legal aid and restricting access to justice' The Meteor <https://www.themeteor.org/2018/09/05/how-austerity-is-killing-legal-aid-and-access-to-justice/> accessed 5 May 2019
38. Project TCPB, 'About The Cambridge Pro Bono Project' Cambridge Faculty of Law <https://www.law.cam.ac.uk/aboutsocieties/cpp> accessed 16 September 2019
39. Russell Group, 'Our Universities' Russell Group <https://russellgroup.ac.uk/about/our-universities/> accessed 16 September 2019
40. Sleeman JF, *The Welfare State: Its Aims, Benefits and Costs* (George Allen & Unwin Ltd 1973)
41. Slocock C, Hayes R and Harker D, *Whose Society? A Final Big Society Audit* (Civil Exchange and DHA, in conjunction with Joseph Rowntree Charitable Trust and the Barrow Cadbury Trust 2015)
42. Special Rapporteur on extreme poverty and human rights, *Visit to the United Kingdom of Great Britain and Northern Ireland* (United Nations General Assembly, Human Rights Council 2019)
43. Stewart J, 'The Twentieth Century: an Overview' in Page RM and Silburn R (eds), *British Social Welfare in the Twentieth Century* (Palgrave 1999)
44. Sylvester C, 'Bridging the Gap - The Effect of Pro Bono Initiatives on Clinical Legal Education in the UK' (2003) 3 International Journal of Clinical Legal Education 29
45. The Cambridge Pro Bono Project, 'The Cambridge Pro Bono Project: Projects Completed' Cambridge Faculty of Law <https://www.law.cam.ac.uk/aboutsocieties/cpp> accessed 16 September 2019
46. Warwick-Booth L, *Social Inequality* (Sage Publishing 2013)

Role of Mandatory Arbitration in Monetary Claims Against Consumers Under Turkish Law

Orhan Emre Konuralp

1 Introduction

Consumer law is a very controversial field of contemporary world's law. The scope of consumer law enlarges day by day. As a result of this fact, law itself follows this enlargement and transforms itself. For example, in Turkish law, for non-commercial cases, attorneys are now accepted as service providers and clients of attorneys are accepted as consumers.[1] As a result of these wide definitions[2] of consumer and consumer transaction, the applicability of consumer law grows itself, thus lawmakers and lawyers face more problems to solve more than before.

In Turkey, the concept of protection of consumer became more important after the liberalization of Turkish economy in 80's. In 1995 first special act regarding consumer protection came into force and arbitral tribunals were established to settle consumer disputes.[3] However, despite the definitions in act, there was no consensus among scholars and jurisprudence neither over the jurisdiction of these arbitral tribunals nor over the definition of consumer protection.

One of these conflicted issues was the jurisdiction of consumer arbitral tribunals over the annulment of objection cases, which is very important for enforcement law. It is clear that, enforcement procedure of a dept should be important as much as court procedure itself. Annulment of objection case is one of the most crucial instruments

[1] Kurşun [1], pp. 299–301.

[2] These wide definitions about consumer law are criticized. See. Rona Serozan, *Tüketiciyi Koruma Yasasının Sözleşme Hukuku Alanındaki Düzenlemesinin Eleştirisi*, 173/4 Yasa Hukuk İçtihat ve Mevzuat Dergisi, pp. 596–597.

[3] Atalı [2], pp. 397–398.

O. E. Konuralp (✉)
Faculty of Law, Bilkent University, Ankara, Turkey
e-mail: orhankonuralp@bilkent.edu.tr

Juristische Fakultät, Univesität Regensburg, Regensburg, Germany

D. Wei et al. (eds.), *Innovation and the Transformation of Consumer Law*,
https://doi.org/10.1007/978-981-15-8948-5_16

provided to the creditor, as part of equality of arms principle. The main aim of his paper is to analyze the enforcement procedure regarding the legal character of the consumer arbitral tribunals and assess the solution of lawmakers to the problem of jurisdiction of consumer arbitral tribunals over the annulment of objection cases.

2 Legislation on Consumer Law in Turkish Law

Under Turkish law, apart from general provisions, there is a special legislation to be enforced. The main part of legislation is "Law on Consumer Protection".[4] Based on this Law, several different regulations regarding consumer protection were enacted. This law enforces not solely but in accordance with general legislation such as Civil Code, Code of Obligations and also Commercial Code. If any provision contradicts, first of all it is stated that the provision that protects consumer better will apply.[5] Additionally it could be asserted that, Law on Consumer Protection should apply, as result of principle of *lex specialis derogat legi generali*. For instance, 3rd paragraph of the 8th article of the Turkish Commercial Code states that *"provisions regarding protection of the consumers are reserved"*.[6]

Before the enactment of Law on Consumer Protection numbered 6502, former legislation, Law numbered 4077, had same name with the current one. It was enacted on 23rd February 1995 and was abrogated by the current Law. First consumer arbitral tribunals in Turkey were established by this abrogated Law, with the name "Arbitral Tribunals for Consumer Problems".[7] Despite minor differences, it could be said that former Law included almost same system for settlement of consumer disputes.

Law on Consumer Protection has very wide definitions and as a result of this fact has very wide range of scope of application. For instance, the Law on Consumer Protection defines consumer as a real person or legal entity acting for non-commercial or non-professional purposes (Art. 3-1/k). The Law defines consumer transaction as all kinds of contracts and legal procedures including the contract of work, transport, brokerage, insurance, mandate, banking and similar contracts established between consumers and real persons or legal entities, including the public legal entities, acting for commercial or professional purposes or on behalf or on account of such, in the goods and service markets (Art. 3-1/l). Additionally, the Law also defines seller, supplier and manufacturer as shown:

---

[4]Law no: 6502, Date of enactment: 7 November 2013, Promulgation Date: 28 November 2013 Official Gazette Issue: 28835. Official translation could be reached through the link: http://www.judiciaryofturkey.gov.tr/Consumer-Protection-Law-is-available-on-our-website. However, this translation is the enacted version of the Law, which was amended after the effective date. These amendments could not be found in translation, but they will be referred, as it is necessary.

[5]Kara [3], pp. 120–121.

[6]Kara [4], p. 115.

[7]Atalı [5], p. 402.

"Seller shall mean a real person or legal entities including the public legal entities offering goods or acting on behalf or on account of those offering goods to the consumer for commercial or professional purposes",

"Supplier shall mean a real person or legal entities including the public legal entities offering services or acting on behalf or on account of those offering services to the consumer for commercial or professional purposes"

"Manufacturer shall mean a real person or legal entities including public legal entities manufacturing the goods or the raw material of such goods or the intermediate goods of such, which have been presented to the consumer, and presenting themselves as the manufacturer by putting its brand, title or any other distinguishing mark on such goods."

As it could be inferred form the definitions, the scope of consumer concept in Turkish law is very wide. This wide range could be observed through the statistics. For instance, in 2017 approximately 2 million cases in private law matters were filed in Turkey.[8] 44.000 of these cases were filed in consumer courts. However, consumer courts are not the only jurisdictive authorities for consumer disputes. As it will be explained furtherly, consumer arbitral tribunals have also jurisdictive authority for certain cases. In 2017 approximately 590.000 cases were brought before the consumer arbitral tribunals.[9] Unlike courts that are organized under Ministry of Justice, consumer arbitral tribunals are organized as a part Ministry of Trade. As a result of this fact, statistics of courts and consumer arbitral tribunals are provided separately and independently. These facts illustrate that, almost ¼ of civil disputes in Turkey are consumer disputes.

3 Legal Procedure Options Under Turkish Law

Under Turkish law, applicable procedures differ, which depend on the legal character of the claim. If a claim is monetary, creditor has two options. First, creditor may file a lawsuit against the debtor and with the final decision of the court, creditor is allowed to commence an enforcement of the decision procedure. As a second option, creditor shall commence an enforcement procedure without a court decision. Main characteristic of this procedure is that, none of written proof is required. On the other hand, debtor can object this procedure without any document. However, if the objection of the debtor is set aside by the creditor, the debtor will be ordered to pay punitive damages.

However, if the claim is not monetary, such as return, repair or replace of a product, the only way provided to the creditor is filing a lawsuit. Enforcement procedure without a decision does not become effective for these kinds of claims.

---

[8]http://www.adlisicil.adalet.gov.tr/Istatistikler/1996/hukuk_pdf/hukuk-karar/2017-karar-hukuk.pdf (In Turkish).

[9]http://risk.ticaret.gov.tr/data/572b46c31a79f50cd8a22b2f/7-T%C3%BCketici%20Hakem%20Heyetlerine%20Ula%C5%9Fan%20T%C3%BCketici%20%C5%9Eikayeti%20%C4%B0statistikleri.pdf (In Turkish).

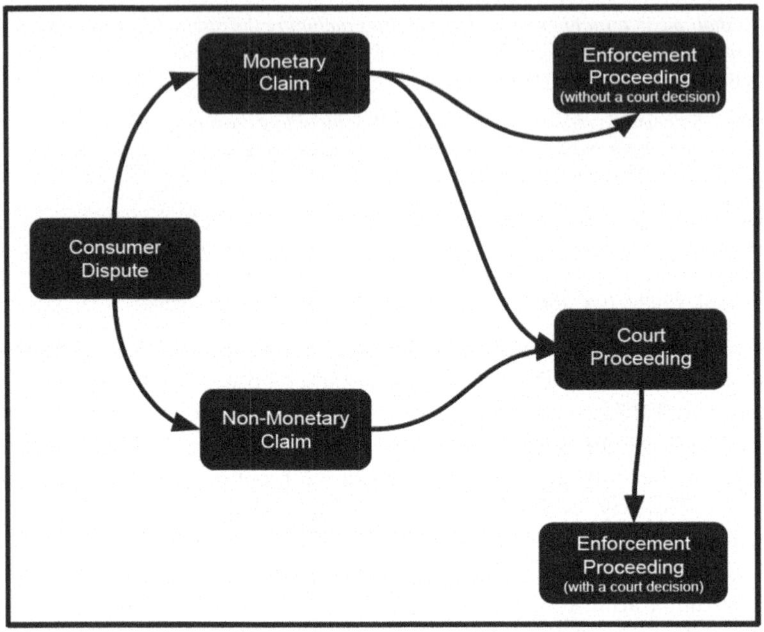

Same procedures and options apply for disputes that involve with consumer law but under Turkish law, dispute resolution system is regulated specifically. On the contrary, unlike other kind of civil disputes, Law on Consumer Protection includes special dispute resolution system for consumer disputes. Therefore, the applicability of these general enforcement procedures, which is for regular disputes, to the consumer disputes becomes controversial. The main aim of this paper to describe the legal nature of consumer disputes' settlement and to emphasize the options of creditors in consumer disputes as a follow-up question.

In order to discuss applicability of enforcement procedures, judicial system for consumer disputes should be analyzed. Turkish Law regulates consumer disputes, which exceeds 8.480 TL (which equals to 1.400 US Dollars by June 2019) differently.

4 Relationship Between the Jurisdiction of Consumer Courts and Jurisdiction of Consumer Arbitral Tribunals

Under Turkish law, if the value of a consumer dispute is above 8.480 TL, the consumer court has jurisdiction over this dispute. On the contrary, if the value of the dispute is less than 8.480 TL, the dispute can only be settled by the consumer arbitral tribunal. The decision of the consumer arbitration tribunal's is binding[10] and may be challenged to the Consumer Court.

[10] Article 70 of the Law on Consumer Protection: The decisions of the Arbitration Committees for Consumer Problems in provinces and districts shall bind the parties. See also Kara [6], pp. 653–656.

The consumer arbitration tribunal is established in every district and its members are not judges or lawyers. In other words, to settle consumer law disputes, it is not required to be a lawyer to be a member of the arbitral tribunal. For this reason the Turkish Constitutional Court does not accept the arbitral tribunal as a court. At that point, it should be added that, this decision of the Turkish Constitutional Court was given, when the former Law was enforced. Thus, there are some differences regarding the qualifications of the consumer arbitral tribunals. But these differences do not affect the importance of this decision. The Constitutional Court justified this as:

"To describe a judicial authority as a court on behalf of the Turkish the establishment of the authority, duties and powers, the functioning and trial procedures should be regulated by law. The decision-making bodies to settle the disputes to be composed of judges, by applying the techniques of judges. The appointment, retirement, rights and duties of the members shall be regulated in accordance with the principles of the independence of the courts and the guarantee of the collateral prescribed by the Constitution[11]*;*

Among the members of Arbitral Tribunal of Consumer Problems, according to Article 22 of the Law on the Protection of Consumers No. 4077, presiding member shall be the Provincial Director of the Ministry of Industry and Trade or a civil servant appointed by Director and rest of tribunal is composed of five people who shall be appointed by the chambers of artisans and consumer organizations.

Accordingly, Arbitral Tribunal of Consumer Problems do not have the qualifications of courts and court members, which is defined by the Constitution."[12]

The Constitutional Court, on the other hand, did not find dispute settlement through the consumer arbitral tribunals, instead of the court, unconstitutional. Similarly, the Constitutional Court ruled that compulsory mediation does not constitute a breach of the Constitution.[13]

Consumer arbitral tribunal members are consisted by members with different backgrounds. One of the members is appointed by the Mayor from among the expert municipal personnel in the field (Art. 66-2/a). Another member is appointed by the Bar, from among its members (Art. 66-2/b). Other member is appointed by

[11]Turkish Constitution's Article 9 (Judicial power): Judicial power shall be exercised by independent and impartial courts on behalf of the Turkish Nation.

Turkish Constitution's Article 139 (Security of tenure of judges and public prosecutors): Judges and public prosecutors shall not be dismissed, or unless they request, shall not be retired before the age prescribed by the Constitution; nor shall they be deprived of their salaries, allowances or other rights relating to their status, even as a result of the abolition of a court or a post.

Exceptions indicated in law relating to those convicted for an offence requiring dismissal from the profession, those who are definitely established as unable to perform their duties because of health, or those determined as unsuitable to remain in the profession, are reserved.

Original translation of Turkish Constitution could be reached through: https://www.anayasa.gov.tr/en/legislation/turkish-constiution/.

[12]Decision of Turkish Constitutional Court Reg. N: 2007/53 Decision N: 2007/61 Decision Date: 27 December 2007. Decision link: http://kararlaryeni.anayasa.gov.tr/Karar/Content/b3a8ce14-f034-46f0-b898-0d4429cd81f4?excludeGerekce=False&wordsOnly=False (In Turkish).

[13]Decision of Turkish Constitutional Court Reg. N: 2017/178 Decision N: 2018/82 Decision Date: 11 July 2018. Decision link: http://kararlaryeni.anayasa.gov.tr/Uploads/2018-82-ipt.docx.

the chamber of trade and industry in disputes where the seller is a merchant, or by the chamber of commerce where such are organized separately; by the union of chambers of merchants and craftsmen in provinces, and by the merchant and craftsmen chamber which has the highest number of members in districts, where the seller is a merchant and craftsmen (Art. 66-2/c). The last member is elected by the consumer organizations from among themselves. As is seen, the members of the consumer arbitration committee come from a variety of institutions and they are not guaranteed (except the member that is elected within attorneys) to have knowledge of law.

As a result of this unique character, it is not possible to classify consumer arbitral tribunals as a court. Furtherly, since the 9th article of the Constitution states that judicial power could be used solely by the courts, the duty that these tribunals fulfil, is not a part of a civil litigation system of Turkey. This dispute resolution system, thus, described as an exception for consumer disputes. Therefore, the role of consumer arbitral tribunals is described as mandatory arbitration.[14]

5 The Concept of "Denial Indemnity"

Turkish Code of Enforcement and Bankruptcy was adopted from Federal Statute on Debt Enforcement and Bankruptcy *(Bundesgesetz über Schuldbetreibung und Konkurs)* in 1934. However, it was not adopted as it is in Switzerland, instead, it has been modified. One of these differences is "denial indemnity"[15]; which is described as unique.[16]

The "denial indemnity" is an instrument of the CoEB and aims to cover the loss of creditor, which can be occurred because of the discontinuation of the enforcement procedure. On the other hand, the debtor could claim same compensation, in case of annulation of objection request of the creditor is rejected by the court. In this case, the aim of the compensation is to cover loss of debtor, who faces with an enforcement proceeding, because of a dept, that does not really exist. CoEB states that, denial compensation should be awarded to compensate the loss, which is calculated as at least 20% of the total dept that specified in enforcement procedure.[17] As a result of this legislation, either creditor or debtor do not need to prove their loss,[18] if the value of their claim for denial compensation is 20% of the debt or less. At that point, it is clear that, this is a very different concept of compensation for continental law.

---

[14] Yılmaz and Yardım [7], p. 1084; Serdar Özbek [8], p. 974; Taşpınar Ayvaz [9], pp. 291–292; Atalı [10], p. 412. Umar [11], p. 1184. In contrary see Erişir [12], pp. 51–53; Yeşilova [13], pp. 112–113. Additionally, it is also stated that, the tribunals are sui generis dispute resolution bodies. See Budak [14], pp. 79–80.

[15] See Kuru [15], p. 727; Yılmaz [16], p. 536.

[16] See Yılmaz [17], p. 683; Yeşilırmak [18], p. 220.

[17] This compensaition is not regulated by source Swiss Code. See Arslan et al. [19], p. 175.

[18] See Kuru [20], p. 263.

Because under Turkish law, which is a part of continental law, a compensation could be claimed, as long as the claimant can prove it. Moreover, Turkish Law has strict prove rules such as mandatory proving by a bill of dept.[19] Because of this difference, denial compensation is classified as a punitive damage[20] or civil penalty,[21] which is really exceptional under Turkish Law and could only be allowed specifically by the law.

This exceptional situation arises from the aim of this provision. According to several decisions of Turkish Court of Cassation *(Yargıtay)* there are two reasons behind denial indemnity. First, the legislator aims to prevent people to commence any enforcement procedure for non-existing depts, and to file an objection without any legal ground. In other words, CoEB stands creditor's and debtor's way who want to misuse this procedure. Secondly, denial indemnity has a retributive role for whom abuse the procedure.

Under the Turkish Enforcement Law, the creditor can commence an enforcement procedure without any documents or proofs in his possession, while the debtor who has no documents or proofs in his hand can file an objection to this enforcement procedure. With the objection of the debtor, the enforcement proceedings automatically stop (Art. 66 of the CoEB). The creditor who wishes to continue the enforcement proceedings has two options: Removal of the objection or annulment of the objection. If the creditor has certain documents, he can apply only to the enforcement court and request the removal of the objection. Because enforcement courts have an exclusive jurisdiction over the request of removal of objection,[22] even a valid arbitration agreement does not abolish the jurisdiction of enforcement courts.[23] The documents that creditor should submit are described by the 68th article of the CoEB as bill of dept with the signature that acknowledged by the debtor or notarized. But if the creditor does not have this kind of a document that the law seeks, the only chance of the creditor is to file a lawsuit for the annulment of the objection of the debtor. The decisions of the enforcement court do not have *res judicata* effect. In other words, the creditor may file a case in an ordinary court.

To define the jurisdictive authority for the annulment of objection, the subject of the enforcement proceedings will be taken into consideration. For example, if a case is about a commercial receivable, the commercial courts will have the jurisdiction. If this a commercial receivable is claimed through enforcement proceedings and the case for the annulment of the objection is required, the court with jurisdiction shall be the commercial courts. Similarly, if there is a consumer dispute, the court with jurisdiction will be the consumer court or the consumer arbitral tribunal according to the value of the dispute.

---

[19] 200th Article of the Turkish Code of Civil Procedure: The legal transactions made for the purpose of the birth, reduction, transfer, replacement, renewal, postponement, refusal and redemption of a right shall be proved by a bill of debt if the amount or values exceeds 2500 Turkish Lira.

[20] See Tarık Güleryüz and Zorluoğlu Yılmaz [21], pp. 347–348.

[21] Arslan et al. [19], p.175.

[22] Yilmaz [16], p. 541.

[23] 12th Chamber of the Court of Cassation, 27.02.1990, 8745/1848.

If the court decides that the claim of the claimant is lawful as a result of the annulment of objection, the objection shall be void and the enforcement proceeding shall resume. At this point, if the creditor has requested, the debtor will be sentenced to pay denial indemnity to the creditor, that is 20% of the dept. On the contrary, the court could decide that the debtor's objection is lawful. With this decision, if the debtor has requested, the court will award 20% of the dept as compensation against the creditor. To request denial indemnity, there is no need to prove the loss or to prove the damage to the requested party. In this respect, the indemnity compensation is an exceptional compensation and it is shown as an example of punitive compensation in Turkish Law.

The final decisions about the annulment of objection of the courts do have *res judicata* effect. The parties are therefore not entitled to bring same case before a court for the same dispute. This fact makes this issue more important.

If the value of the enforcement proceedings exceeds the specified limit, the jurisdictive authority for the annulment of objection will be consumer courts. Organization and procedures of the consumer courts do not differ from other courts. Therefore, there is no discussion over the case for the annulment of objection.

However, if the value of the enforcement proceedings is below the specified limit, the only jurisdictive authority, in which the annulment of objection could be filed, is the consumer arbitral tribunal. Could a delegation with no majority of lawyers be described as a court and have jurisdiction for the case of annulment of objection, which is a very technical case? In addition, should this kind of a delegation have jurisdiction over the punitive damages?

Neither the previous Law (Nr. 4077) nor the current one (Nr. 6502), until the amendment that will be mentioned, includes a direct answer for this question.[24] According to Ministry of Trade the answer to this question should be "No". As a part of a "Frequently Asked Questions" document,[25] this question is also included. At that point, this document was published, before the related amendment of the Law, in 2015, so the answer that is given should be considered for that time. The Ministry refers to the decisions of the Turkish Constitutional Court and Court of Cassation and states that, consumer arbitral tribunals have not jurisdiction over the action of annulment of objection and have not enough to grant denial indemnity.

Jurisdiction of consumer arbitral tribunals over the denial indemnity is a controversial issue. The main reason lies behind this answer is the legal nature of consumer arbitral tribunals. As it is stated above, these tribunals are not classified as a court and also consist of members with very different professional backgrounds. In case of acceptance of this approach, consumers may have not right to commence an enforcement proceeding without a court decision. Because, as a part of this proceeding, the debtor may need to file an annulment of objection lawsuit, while there is no jurisdictive authority for these cases.

---

[24] Atalı [22], p. 411.

[25] Frequently Asked Questions about Consumer Arbitral Tribunals: http://tuketici.gtb.gov.tr/data/5994288e1a79f54410c61923/SIK%C3%87A%20SORULAN%20SORULAR-%20MET%C4%B0N.pdf (In Turkish).

Some scholars state that, consumer arbitral tribunals should not have any jurisdiction over de annulment of objections cases.[26] On the other hand, some scholars asserted that, denial compensation is secondary right of the party, thus, as long as main claim arises from the consumer law, the authority with jurisdiction could grant denial compensation.[27] Furtherly, it was claimed that, the Law on Protection of Consumers should be considered as *lex posterior* and *les specialis*, therefore, jurisdictive authority for denial indemnity could not be the arbitral tribunal for consumer disputes.[28]

On the contrary, when the jurisprudence is taken into consideration, different decisions of the courts could be seen. Some decisions state that, consumer arbitral tribunals have no jurisdiction over the annulment of objection cases, therefore, for consumer dispute enforcement procedure without a court decision, is not possible. As an example, in one decision[29] of the Turkish Court of Cassation, 13th Chamber stated that, 67th article of the CoEB allows creditor to file an annulment of objection case before the "court". However, it is not possible to define consumer arbitral tribunal as a court. Consequently, if creditor does not have right to file this case, parties should not have right to apply to enforcement proceeding without a court decision. Chamber justified its decision by referring the decision of Turkish Constitutional Court's decision, that mentioned above. However, it is stated that, at the enaction date of CoEB, there was not any special dispute settlement body was established, therefore the objective of the lawmakers by saying "court" should not be interpreted as to exclude consumer arbitral tribunal from this provision.[30]

6 Applicability of Denial Indemnity in Non-Mandatory/Regular Arbitration

The unique legal character of the denial compensation and enforcement without a court decision proceeding, in general, make same issue controversial for regular arbitration. As a principle, arbitration is available for all civil matters under Turkish Law. There are some exceptions for this principle. For example, disputes about immovables or cases arising from family law are not arbitrable. This availability makes arbitration popular among people, especially for commercial disputes.

Same issue, that this article discussed, is problematic for non-mandatory arbitration too. In order to make compression between legal problems arise from similar systems, discussing these problems for non-mandatory arbitration would be beneficial.

[26] Taşpınar Ayvaz [23], pp. 302–303.

[27] See Ermenek [24], p. 610; Akif Tutumlu [25], p. 66.

[28] See Akif Tutumlu [26], p. 103.

[29] Turkish Court of Cassation 13th Chamber, http://www.resmigazete.gov.tr/eskiler/2015/06/20150605-23.pdf.

[30] Akif Tutumlu [27], p. 65.

There are two main questions to answer regarding non-mandatory arbitration. First, even if parties have an arbitration agreement, are they allowed to commence an enforcement proceeding without a court decision proceeding? Second, if parties are allowed to commence such proceeding, should arbitral tribunal have jurisdiction over the annulment of objection case? As it could be inferred, existence of the second question depends on the answer of first question. If parties are not allowed to commence an enforcement proceeding, as a legal consequence of arbitration agreement, it is not possible to discuss if the arbitral tribunal has jurisdiction over the annulment of objection case.

In Turkish doctrine, different solutions were suggested for this issue. First, it is claimed that, by being party of an arbitration agreement, parties also agreed on not to apply state judicial system, this courts and enforcement offices as well.[31] However, this approach should be regarded as a wide definition of arbitration agreement. This idea is supported with the main aim of arbitration agreement, which is to allow the tribunal to settle a dispute, but enforcement proceeding is not way to settle of dispute, instead, a way to collect through liquidation. If debtor pay in specific limited period, there would not be any dispute. On the contrary, if debtor files an objection against the enforcement proceeding, at that point, a dispute would arise. Secondly, if an arbitration agreement prevents its parties to apply enforcement proceeding, enforcement of the arbitral award becomes problematic. Since under the Turkish Law, the only way to enforce a court decision (including arbitral awards) is to commence an enforcement with a court decision proceeding,[32] unless the other party fulfills its duty intentionally.

Secondly, some scholars asserted that, arbitration agreement, itself, does not constitute a legal obstacle for application to the enforcement proceeding without a court decision.[33] On the other hand, some scholars accept that, as a result of a valid arbitration agreement, arbitral tribunal has jurisdiction over the annulment of objection cases but not over the denial indemnity compensation.[34] Finally, some scholars accept that arbitral tribunals have jurisdiction over both annulment of objection cases and denial indemnity compensation.[35] Therefore, if parties agreed to apply to the arbitration and then creditor decided to commence an enforcement proceeding, instead of bringing case before the tribunal, the debtor may object to this proceeding and creditor will have enough ground to file a annulment of objection case in an arbitral tribunal.

Unfortunately, among jurisprudence, there are different answers for this issue. In some cases, Turkish Court of Cassation ruled that, despite the arbitration agreement, parties could file an enforcement proceeding without a court decision:

---

[31] Yeşilova [28], p. 534; Dayınlarlı [29], p. 66; Deynekli and Kısa [30], p. 274; Özgür Kiraz [31], p. 307-308; Yilmaz [32], p. 541.

[32] Süral [33], pp. 1381–1382.

[33] Yavuz [34], p. 98.

[34] Pekcanıtez [35], p. 64; Pekcanıtez and Yeşilırmak [36], p. 2671; Tüysüz [37], p. 115.

[35] Yeşilırmak [38], pp. 219–220.

"Even if there is an arbitration agreement between the creditor and the debtor, the creditor may apply to enforcement without a court decision proceeding. The debtor cannot object to the proceeding as the creditor must file a case before the arbitrator."[36]

According to other decision of Court of Cassation, consumer arbitral tribunals have jurisdiction for annulment of objection cases and they have legal ground to grant denial indemnity:

"According to the established practice of the Court, the arbitrators have jurisdiction to decide on the annulment of objection proceedings and, as a result, to give a decision on the request for denial indemnity."[37]

In other decision of Court of Cassation, it is stated that, action of annulment of objection is not related with public order, thus, arbitral tribunals have jurisdiction over these cases:

"According to the article 7 of the agreement signed between the parties to the disputes arising from the contract will be settled by arbitrators. In his petition, the defendant filed an objection regarding the arbitration agreement. The annulment of the objection arising from Article 67 of the CoEB and is not related with public order. There is no legal obstacle to settle this dispute through the arbitration as it includes matters related with alienable rights of the parties."[38]

When all these decisions of the Court of Cassation are taken into consideration, it can easily be understood that, jurisprudence and scholars are not able to bring a common solution, instead, makes this issue more controversial. Additionally, these contradictions show that, lawmakers could be the only authority who would be able to provide a solution; however, any amendment has not been made on this issue, unlike the problem about the jurisdiction of the consumer arbitral tribunal.

7 Solution of the Lawmaker

The 68th article of the Law on Consumer Protection is the provision of mandatory application to consumer arbitral tribunals. Until 1st January 2018, the article was as following:

It shall be mandatory to apply to the Arbitration Committees for Consumer Problems in districts for disputes the value of which is under two thousand Turkish Liras (2.000 TL), to the Arbitration Committees for Consumer Problems in provinces for disputes the value of which is three thousand Turkish Liras (3.000 TL), and in provinces that fall under the category of metropolitan municipalities, to the provincial arbitration committees for consumer problems for disputes the value of which is between two thousand Turkish Liras (2.000 TL) and three thousand Turkish Liras (3.000 TL). Applications shall not be made to arbitration committees for consumer problems, for disputes, the value of which exceeds these.

[36] 12th Chamber of the Court of Cassation, 27.02.1990, 8745/1848.

[37] 15th Chamber of the Court of Cassation, 03.04.2008, 262/2138.

[38] 15th Chamber of the Court of Cassation, 16.05.2011, 826/2941.

However, this article was amended on 1st January 2018 by the 11th article of the Law numbered 7063[39] as following:

> ***Reserving rights of the parties that arise from Code of Enforcement and Bankruptcy****, it shall be mandatory to apply to the Arbitration Committees for Consumer Problems in districts for disputes the value of which is under* ***four thousand Turkish Liras (4.000 TL),*** *to the Arbitration Committees for Consumer Problems in provinces for disputes the value of which is* ***six thousand Turkish Liras (6.000 TL)****, and in provinces that fall under the category of metropolitan municipalities, to the provincial arbitration committees for consumer problems for disputes the value of which is between* ***four thousand Turkish Liras (4.000 TL) and six thousand Turkish Liras (6.000 TL)****. Applications shall not be made to arbitration committees for consumer problems, for disputes, the value of which exceeds these.*

As it can be seen, there are two major amendments. First, the limits that specify the jurisdiction of consumer arbitral tribunals were raised. Secondly and more importantly, from that date, the Law itself reserves the rights of the parties, that allow them to commence an enforcement proceeding without a court decision.

With this amendment, which is enforced from the beginning of 2018, the answer of this controversial issue becomes clear. From that date, it should not be any doubt on, if parties of a consumer dispute have right to commence an enforcement proceeding without a court decision. Furthermore, it becomes clear that, despite its legal character, consumer arbitral tribunal has enough ground to grant denial indemnity, in case of an annulment of objection.

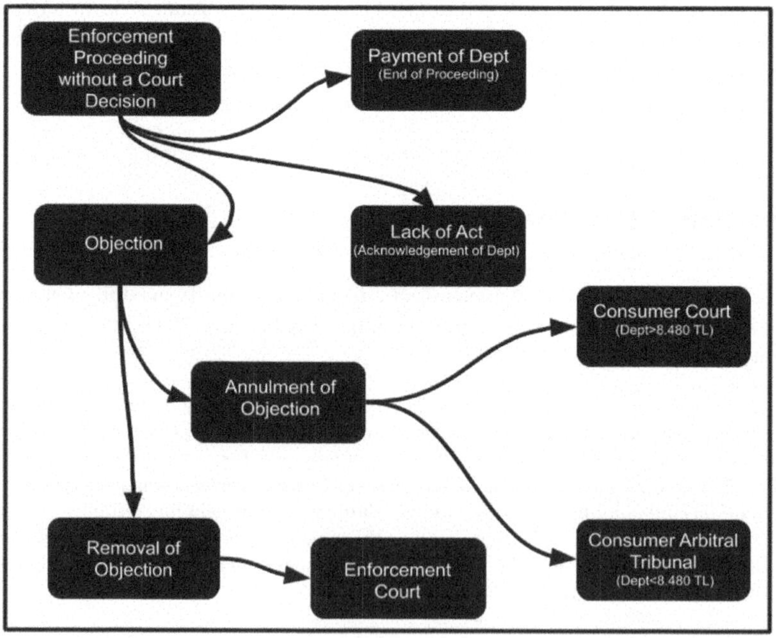

[39]http://www.resmigazete.gov.tr/eskiler/2017/12/20171220-15.htm (In Turkish).

8 Conclusion

Turkish dispute resolution system for consumer law issues is so complicated that even explaining the system is a hard job to do. This complicated system also leads very unique problems to be solved. However, as a result of the explained issued, providing a consensus usually is possible among neither scholars nor jurisprudence. This requires the transformation of legislation, to avoid any contradiction between court decisions. Since scholars has no common solution, lawmakers are forced to enforce amendments.

As it is explained, the difference between the enforcement procedures under Turkish law for monetary and non-monetary claims is one of the main reasons of lack of common approach among scholars. On the other hand, different dispute resolution bodies for same kind of disputes constitutes the other reason. It is not hard to say that, this unique structure of dispute resolution system for consumer law disputes, will lead different problems in future.

Until the enforcement of the amendment of Law on Consumer Protection, it is widely accepted that, enforcement procedure without a court decision, should not be applicable for monetary claims against consumers. It was asserted that, bringing case before the consumer arbitral tribunal should be the only way for such disputes. However, as an interesting fact, this wide acceptance did not affect lawmakers and the solution came into force as an opposite of the wide acceptance. As a quite new amendment, it is not possible the assess the approach of scholars to this amendment. However, it is possible to say that, this solution of the lawmakers may lead new problems to be solved.

References

1. Ali Suphi Kurşun, *Avukatlık Sözleşmesinin Tüketici İşlemi Bakımından Değerlendirilmesi*, 142 TBB Dergisi (2019), p. 299–301.
2. Murat Atalı, *6502 Saylı Kanun'un Tüketici Sorunları Hakem Heyetlerine İlişkin Hükümlerinin Değerlendirilmesi*, 2014 Prof. Dr. Ejder Yılmaz'a Armağan (2014), p. 397–398.
3. İlhan Kara, Tüketici Hukuku (2015), p. 120–121.
4. İlhan Kara, Tüketici Hukuku (2015), p. 115.
5. Murat Atalı, *6502 Saylı Kanun'un Tüketici Sorunları Hakem Heyetlerine İlişkin Hükümlerinin Değerlendirilmesi*, Prof. Dr. Ejder Yılmaz'a Armağan (2014), p. 402.
6. İlhan Kara, *Tüketici Hukuku* (2015), p. 653–656.
7. Ejder Yılmaz & Ertan Yardım, Milli Şerh (National Commentary) (2016), p. 1084.
8. Mustafa Serdar Özbek, Alternatif Uyuşmazlık Çözümü (2016), p. 974.
9. Sema Taşpınar Ayvaz, *Tüketici Hakem Heyetlerinin İşleyişi ve Sorunlar*, Tüketici Hukuku Konferansı Makaleler-Tebliğler (2015), p. 291–292.
10. Murat Atalı, *6502 Saylı Kanun'un Tüketici Sorunları Hakem Heyetlerine İlişkin Hükümlerinin Değerlendirilmesi*, Prof. Dr. Ejder Yılmaz'a Armağan, (2014), p. 412.
11. Bilge Umar, Hukuk Muhakemeleri Kanunu Şerhi (2014), p. 1184.
12. Evrim Erişir, *Tüketici İşlemlerinden Doğan Uyuşmazlıkların Çözümü*, Yeni Tüketici Hukuku Konferansı, (2015), p. 51–53.

13. Bilgehan Yeşilova, *6502 sayılı (yeni) Tüketicinin Korunması Hakkında Kanun'a Göre Tüketici Uyuşmazlıklarının Çözümü Usulü ve Yargılama Kuralları*, 9 Terazi Aylık Hukuk Dergisi (2014), p. 112–113.
14. Ali Cem Budak, *Tüketici Hakem Heyetleri*, 16 Special Issue Prof. Dr. Hakan PEKCANITEZ'e Armağan (2015), p. 79–80.
15. Baki Kuru, *İcra İnkâr Tazminatı*, Yargıtay Yüzüncü Yıldönümü Armağanı (1968), p. 727.
16. Ejder Yılmaz, *Tahkimde İtirazın İptali Davası ve Tahkime Elverişlilik Kuralı*, 16 Dokuz Eylül Üniversitesi Hukuk Fakültesi Dergisi (2015), p. 536.
17. Ejder Yılmaz, *İcra Tazminatı*, 2 Haluk Konuralp Anısına Armağan (2009), p. 683.
18. Ali Yeşilırmak, *Geçerli Bir Tahkim Anlaşmasının Varlığına Rağmen Genel Haciz Yoluyla Takip Yapılabilir Mi?*, 96 TBB Dergisi (2011), p. 220.
19. Ramazan Arslan & Ejder Yılmaz & Sema Taşpınar Ayvaz, İcra ve İflas Hukuku (2017), p. 175.
20. Baki Kuru, İcra ve İflas Hukuku El Kitabı (2013), p. 263.
21. M. Tarık Güleryüz & Ayça Zorluoğlu Yılmaz, *Bir Anglo – Amerikan Hukuku Müessesesi Olarak Cezalandırıcı Tazminatın [Punitive Damages] Bazı Türk Hukuku Müesseseleri ile Mukayesesi*, 141 TBB Dergisi (2019), p. 347–348.
22. Ejder Yilmaz, *Tahkimde İtirazın İptali Davası ve Tahkime Elverişlilik Kuralı*, 16 Special Issue Prof. Dr. Hakan PEKCANITEZ'e Armağan (2015), p. 541.
23. Murat Atalı, *6502 Saylı Kanun'un Tüketici Sorunları Hakem Heyetlerine İlişkin Hükümlerinin Değerlendirilmesi*, Prof. Dr. Ejder Yılmaz'a Armağan (2014), p. 411.
24. Sema Taşpınar Ayvaz, *Tüketici Hakem Heyetlerinin İşleyişi ve Sorunlar*, Tüketici Hukuku Konferansı Makaleler-Tebliğler (2015), p. 302–303.
25. İbrahim Ermenek, *Yargı Kararları Işığında Tüketici Sorunları Hakem Heyetleri ve bu Alanda Ortaya Çıkan Sorunlara İlişkin Çözüm Önerileri*, 17 Gazi Üniversitesi Hukuk Fakültesi Dergisi (2013), p. 610.
26. Mehmet Akif Tutumlu, Tüketici Hakem Heyetleri (2015), p. 66.
27. Mehmet Akif Tutumlu, 3. Tüketici Hukuku Kongresi Makale, Bildiri ve Ses Çözümleri (2014), p. 103.
28. Mehmet Akif Tutumlu, Tüketici Hakem Heyetleri (2015), p. 65.
29. Bilgehan Yeşilova, Milletlerarası Ticari Tahkimde Nihai Karardan Önce Mahkemelerin Yardımı ve Denetimi, (2008), p. 534.
30. Kemal Dayınlarlı, HUMK'da Düzenlenen İhtiyari İç Tahkim (2004), p. 66.
31. Adnan Deynekli & Sedat Kısa, İtirazın İptali Davaları (2013), p. 274.
32. Taylan Özgür Kiraz, Yargı Kararları ile Birlikte İcra Mahkemesinde İtirazın Kaldırılması (2013), p. 307–308
33. Ceyda Süral, *Hakem Kararlarının İcrası ve İptal Davası*, 16 Dokuz Eylül Üniversitesi Hukuk Fakültesi Dergisi (2015), p. 1381–1382.
34. Nihat Yavuz, İtirazın İptali ve Tahsil (Eda) Davası (2007), p. 98.
35. Hakan Pekcanıtez, *Tahkimde Açılan İtirazın İptali Davasında Hakemler İcra ve İnkâr Tazminatına Karar Verilebilir mi?*, 100 Fasikül Hukuk Dergisi (2018), p. 64.
36. Hakan Pekcanıtez & Ali Yeşilırmak, Medeni Usul Hukuku (2017), p. 2671.
37. Cemre Tüysüz, İcra ve İflâs Hukukundaki Davaların Tahkim Anlaşmasının İcrasına Etkisi (2017), p. 115.
38. Ali Yeşilırmak, *Geçerli Bir Tahkim Anlaşmasının Varlığına Rağmen Genel Haciz Yoluyla Takip Yapılabilir Mi?*, 96 TBB Dergisi (2011), p. 219–220.

Experimental Challenge for Collective Consumer Redress in Korea

Heesok Seo

1 Introduction

Consumer law in Korea only began to develop from 1980s. "Act on the Regulation of Terms and Conditions" enacted in 1986 opened the way to manage the contents of terms and conditions in a civil proceeding, and "Consumer Protection Act", which was completely revised in the same year, helped the government prepare for a system of promoting its consumer policy. This led to establishment of the mediation system for consumer dispute settlement, which is an administrative ADR system, as a means to relieve consumer damage.

Since then, as the modern consumer society characterized by mass production and mass consumption moved forward, collective consumer damage became a social issue, leading to a discussion on the system reform for consumer redress. The 2006 revision of "Consumer Protection Act" into "Framework Act on Consumers" introduced the two new systems—*Consumer Collective Mediation* and *Consumer Organization Litigation*. Established as a special system for consumer dispute settlement, the *Consumer Collective Mediation* is an ADR version of the class action that has been widely used in the United States (U.S.). The second system, *Consumer Organization Litigation*, grants consumer organizations with the right of action to prohibit the business entity's infringement of consumer rights and interests. On top of these two systems, the discussion to introduce *Consumer Class Action* has recently been on the rise with a number of legislative bills prepared and submitted to the National Assembly at the moment.

This paper aims to introduce the *Consumer Collective Mediation* system and *Consumer Organization Litigation* system from the perspective of Korean law's experimental challenge for collective consumer redress. This paper also introduces

H. Seo (✉)
School of Law at Pusan National University, Korea Consumer Law Society, Busan, South Korea
e-mail: kshskm@pusan.ac.kr

D. Wei et al. (eds.), *Innovation and the Transformation of Consumer Law*,
https://doi.org/10.1007/978-981-15-8948-5_17

the recent discussions on the introduction of class action for collective consumer redress in Korea.

2 Consumer Collective Mediation System

1. What is Consumer Collective Mediation System?

Consumer Collective Mediation is the system designed to uniformly resolve a number of consumer damages or disputes arising from factually or legally the same cause through mediation procedure by Consumer Mediation Committee (CMC), which is an administrative body for ADR. This system features the dispute settlement through collective mediation rather than class action for a uniform settlement of collective consumer disputes, considering that consumer disputes are familiar with ADR procedure. However, unlike litigation, mediation is the system for resolving a dispute through concessions and reconciliation between the parties to the dispute. Considering that the result of multiple mediations may vary even in the same case, we need to verify later whether it is effective or even possible to uniformly settle the disputes through one mediation procedure for all the consumer victims involved.

2. Cases Subject to Application

Collective mediation targets any cases which cause damage to a number of consumers in the same or similar type (Article 68, Paragraph 1[1]). More specifically, the number of consumer victims must be over 50 who suffered the same or similar damages due to the use of goods or services provided by a business entity. That is, 'collectiveness' is the first requirement. The second requirement is 'commonality'. That is, the main issue of the cases involving the same or similar damage must be legally or factually common (Enforcement Decree of the Act, Article 56). However, the collective mediation excludes from its application any cases where dispute settlement or litigation procedures under other Acts are in progress.

3. Procedure of Collective Mediation
(1) Request or Application for a Collective Mediation

Procedures for collective mediation are initiated in two ways. That is, (1) the State, a local government, the Korea Consumer Agency(KCA),[2] a consumer organization, etc. (hereinafter, "the State, etc.") may make a request to the CMC; or (2) consumers or business entities involved in a dispute may file an application to the CMC (Article

[1]Citation for the title of law—"Framework Act on Consumers"—will be omitted or just be abbreviated to "the Act" hereinafter.

[2]A specialized agency for consumer protection under the Fair Trade Commission established under the Framework Act on Consumers. It is responsible for the redress of consumer damages, consumer safety, information provision for consumers, and policy proposal etc.

68, Paragraph 1). In order for the State, etc. to be able to request collective mediation to the CMC, a consumer dispute should not be resolved through their own relief mechanisms operated by the State, etc. while the dispute meets requirements for collective mediation as discussed before. The parties involved in a consumer dispute can apply directly for collective mediation to the CMC, if the dispute meets the same requirements above.

(2) Commencement of a Procedure

In the event that there is a request or application for collective mediation, CMC must commence by its resolution a procedure for collective mediation within 60 days from the date of receipt of a request or application (Commencement of a Procedure). However, a procedure may not be commenced: ① if the dispute failed to meet the above requirements for collective mediation (collectiveness and commonality); ② if there is no reason to repeat the commencement as it is acknowledged that the dispute is subject to a preexisting settlement decision; or ③ if it is clearly acknowledged that the applicant's application details has no ground for commencement of collective mediation (Article 68, Paragraph 2). Meanwhile, the CMC may suspend by its resolution the decision to commence a procedure for dispute settlement within the period of 60 days for commencement in the events ① where testing, inspection or investigation is required to inquire into the cause of damages or ② where the representative applies to suspend the commencement of a procedure for collective mediation pursuant to Article 68-2 in order to inquire into the cause of damages ("resolution for the suspension of procedure commencement"). In this case, the suspension period cannot exceed 60 days after the given period for commencement (60 days) has elapsed (Article 68, Paragraph 3).

(3) Public Announcement of the Commencement

If the settlement committee commenced the procedure by its resolution, it must publicly announce the commencement of the procedure for at least 14 days (Article 68, Paragraph 2, and Article 58, Paragraph 1 of the Enforcement Decree of the Act). The public announcement on commencement of the procedure for collective mediation must be made in such a way as being carried in the Korea Consumer Agency's home page on the Internet and a daily newspaper with nationwide circulation (Enforcement Decree, Article 58, Paragraph 2). During this period, the CMC can receive an application from a person other than the consumer or business entity who is originally a party to be included as the party to the dispute settlement (Article 68, Paragraph 4). In this case, the CMC must notify in writing that person of the acceptance of the participation within 10 days after the end of the above announcement period (Article 68, Paragraph 2).

(4) Meetings of CMC for Mediation

If the announcement period for commencement expires and the scope of participants in the collective mediation procedure is determined, the CMC proceeds with full-scale procedures for collective dispute settlement. A case involving collective mediation is dealt with by the "Dispute Settlement Meeting" of the CMC (Article 63-2, Paragraph 1, Item 3). The dispute settlement meeting is a decision-making mechanism composed of the Chairperson, Standing Committee Members, and from 5 to 9 Committee Members designated by the Chairperson for each meeting (Article 63, Paragraph 1, Item 1).[3] A Dispute Settlement Meeting must be comprised of members who represent consumers and business entities, equally not less than one, respectively (Article 63, Paragraph 3, 2nd sentence). Before a settlement meeting is held, the Secretariat listens to the statements of the parties and conduct preliminary preparations to hold a meeting after fact-finding, testing and consultation with experts. A Dispute Settlement Meeting can pass its resolutions with the attendance of a majority of the total composition members and with the concurring vote of a majority of those present (1st sentence of the same provision).

(5) A Period for Collective Mediation

Collective mediation must be completed within 30 days from the day following the end of public announcement of procedure commencement. However, if the mediation cannot be finalized within the competent period due to any justifiable reason, the period may be extended not more than two times, by up to 30 days (within 90 days in total), respectively (Article 68, Paragraph 7).

(6) Special Conditions of the Procedure

(1) Mediation Process by the Representative Party

A. Appointment of the Representative Party

The parties who have a stake in the collective mediation may appoint 3 or less members among parties as the representative party (Article 68-2, Paragraph 1). When the parties failed to appoint the representative party, the CMC, if deemed necessary, may recommend the parties to appoint the representative party (Article 68-2, Paragraph 1).

B. Authority of the Representative Party

The parties who have appointed the representative party may perform any act only through the representative party with respect to the settlement of the relevant case (Article 68-2, Paragraph 4). The representative party may perform any act with respect to the settlement of the relevant case for parties who have appointed him/her. Yet, as for the withdrawal of settlement application, and as for the acceptance or refusal of settlement proposal, the representative party must receive a written consent from parties by whom he or she has been appointed (Article 68-2, Paragraph 3). In this way, it is for the efficiency of the procedure to allow the representative party to

[3]The CMC shall be composed of 150 or less members, including a Chairperson, of whom 5 standing members including the chairperson shall work full-time, and the other members, part-time (Article 61, Paragraph 1).

proceed with the collective mediation procedure, which referred to the U.S. Class Action or the Securities-Related Class Action Act.[4]

(2) Effect of Filing a Lawsuit during the Mediation Process

In the system of consumer mediation, mediation procedure is, in principle, suspended if the parties bring a lawsuit during the mediation procedure (Article 65, Paragraph 5). However, since application of this rule as such would cause harm to the other parties who did not bring a lawsuit, even if some of the consumers who are parties to collective mediation file a lawsuit with a court, the CMC must not discontinue its procedures but exclude such consumers from the relevant procedures (Article 68, Paragraph 6). In addition, if part of consumers who are parties to collective mediation and the business entity reach an agreement with respect to compensation of damages or if they are proceeding with dispute settlement conducted by an agency concerned under other statutes after commencement of the procedures for collective mediation, the CMC must not suspend the procedures but exclude such consumers from the relevant procedures (Enforcement Decree, Article 61).

4. Effect of Collective Mediation

(1) Notice of the Settlement Proposal and Effect of Conclusion of the Mediation

In a general consumer dispute mediation, the Chairperson of the CMC must promptly notify the parties of the contents thereof when a dispute settlement is completed—that is, when a settlement proposal is drafted (Article 67, Paragraph 1). The notified parties must notify the CMC of whether to accept the contents of the dispute settlement (settlement proposal) within 15 days from the date of receipt of the notice (Article 67, Paragraph 1, 2nd sentence). In the case of collective mediation, the acceptance or rejection of the settlement proposal is carried out by the representative party, provided, however, that such acceptance or refusal contains a written consent from the parties who appointed the representative party (Article 68-2, Paragraph 3). If there is no indication of acceptance or rejection within 15 days, it is deemed to have been accepted (Article 67, Paragraph 2, 2nd sentence). If the parties accept or are considered to have accepted the settlement proposal, the settlement proposal has the same effect as a judicial compromise/reconciliation (Article 67, Paragraph 4).

(2) Recommendation of a Compensation Plan for the Consumers Who Are Not Parties to Collective Mediation

If the business entity accepts a settlement proposal of the CMC, the CMC may recommend that a compensation plan be drawn up for consumers who are not parties

---

[4]It was enacted on January 20th, 2004 with the aim to prescribe special cases of the Civil Procedure Act with respect to "**securities-related class actions**" in order to efficiently seek a relief for collective losses arising in the course of trading securities, and ultimately to enhance the operational transparency of companies. "**Securities-related class action**" is defined as "an action for damages filed by one or more representative parties when any damage arises to many persons in the course of the trade or other transactions of securities". It was the introduction of the U.S. Class Action targeting the area of securities transactions.

to the settlement but suffered damage, and be submitted to the CMC (Article 68, Paragraph 5). The business entity who was advised to submit a compensation plan is required to inform the CMC of its acceptance of the recommendation within 15 days of receipt of the recommendation (Enforcement Decree, Article 60).

(3) Interruption of Prescription

An application or request for collective mediation pursuant to Article 68 (1) and (4) has an effect of interrupting prescription. However, if a procedure for collective mediation is terminated but a lawsuit is not instituted within 1 month from the date of termination, the application or request does not have an effect of interrupting prescription, except any of the following cases (i) where parties to a dispute accept or are deemed to accept the terms of the collective dispute settlement or (ii) where one or both parties to a dispute do not accept the terms of the collective dispute settlement (Article 68-3, Paragraph 1). In the event of interruption of prescription, the interrupted prescription runs anew when a case falls under any of the two cases above (Article 68-3, Paragraph 2).

5. Evaluation and Prospects

(1) Performance

Consumer collective mediation is intended to utilize the dispute settlement system under the administrative ADR mechanism as an alternative to the U.S. style representative-party litigation system (Class Action). Based on the results of the 12-year system operation from 2007, the average use frequency was as follows: 13 cases on average were submitted per year, of which about 8 cases were referred to the mediation procedures, and the rate of concluded mediation is 42% on average. Considering that, in the case of individual dispute settlement, about 3,000 disputes are received annually while the rate of concluded mediation is about 70%, the concluded mediation rate for collective disputes is somewhat lower than that for individual disputes.

Table: Performance of Collective Mediation

Year	Number of Requests & Applications	result			
		Acceptance	Non-Acceptance	Rate of acceptance (%)	Dismissal, Drop, etc
2007	11	5	4	55.6	2
2008	31	8	11	42.1	12
2009	34	10	11	47.6	13
2010	15	1	5	16.7	9
2011	15	4	5	44.5	6
2012	10	2	2	50.0	6
2013	10	5	–	100.0	5
2014	10	2	3	40.0	5

(continued)

(continued)

Year	Number of Requests & Applications	result			
		Acceptance	Non-Acceptance	Rate of acceptance (%)	Dismissal, Drop, etc
2015	3	–	–	–	3
2016	5	–	3	0	2
2017	5	2	1	67	2
2018	18	1	10	9	7
Total	167	40	55	42	72

(*Source* Consumer Mediation Committee)

(2) Direction of Improvement

In order to enhance effectiveness, this system needs improvements from two viewpoints. First, it is reasonable to remove the provision that allows the CMC to recommend the business entity to submit a compensation plan for consumers who are not parties to collective mediation, when the dispute was settled by the acceptance of a settlement proposal by both the parties. The provision for CMC's recommendation may protect consumers who do not join the mediation procedures and achieve the procedural goal of dispute settlement at one go. However, I think the system of recommendation is becoming a factor that weakens the effectiveness of the system by harming the business entity's trust on the system. Second, requiring all the parties of consumers to reach an agreement either by acceptance or refusal is becoming a factor that undermines by itself the merits of the mediation system, which is undesirable. Therefore, it should be desirable to improve the system by preparing a scheme that allows parties of consumers to individually accept or refuse to a settlement proposal.

3 Consumer Organization Litigation System

1. What is Consumer Organization Litigation System?

Consumer organization litigation is the system that grants a consumer organization which meets certain requirements with the right of action to prohibit or suspend the infringement of consumers' rights and interests in the event where a business entity infringes directly on the rights and interests of consumers relating to their lives, bodies, or property and such infringement continues. It was introduced in the 2006 revision of Framework Act on Consumers (Implemented on January 1st, 2008) referring to German system ('Verbandsklage'). The consumer organization litigation system features the following points: first, it grants the right of action to consumer organizations that meets certain qualification requirements; and second, it allows the claim to prohibit or suspend (omission) the business entity's infringement from continuing in the future.

Since Article 70 to Article 76 of the Framework Act on Consumers regulating the consumer organization litigation system constitute the special law of Civil Procedure Act, the Civil Procedure Act applies to matters not specified in the Framework Act on Consumers (Article 76, Paragraph 1).

2. Plaintiff

The organization that can be a plaintiff in a consumer organization litigation must fall under one of the following (1)–(3) qualifications (Article 70). (1) A consumer organization, registered with the Fair Trade Commission, that meets the following (a)–(c) requirements: (a) it aims mainly at promoting consumers' rights or interest pursuant to its articles of association; (b) the number of its regular members is at least 1,000; and (c) three years have passed since it was registered. (2) The Korea Consumer Agency. (3) The Korea Chamber of Commerce and Industry under the Chambers of Commerce and Industry Act, the federation of small and medium enterprise cooperatives under the Small and Medium Enterprise Cooperatives Act, and a nationwide economic organization prescribed by Presidential Decree. (4) A non-profit and non-governmental organization under Article 2 of the Assistance for Non-Profit, Non-Governmental Organizations Act which meets each of the following (a)-(d) requirements: (a) it is requested to institute a consumer organization litigation by at least fifty consumers who suffered legally or factually identical damages; (b) it has the actual results of activities for at least the preceding three years according to the purpose of promoting the rights and interests of consumers specified in its articles of association; (c) its number of regular members is at least 5,000; and (d) it is registered with a central administrative agency.

3. Litigation Requirements

In order for a consumer organization to file a lawsuit, the case must be where a business entity infringes directly on the rights and interests of consumers relating to their lives, bodies or property in violation of any standard under Article 20 of the Framework Act on Consumers and the infringement continues. The Article 20 of the Framework Act on Consumers provides that business entities must observe the standards of harm prevention(consumer safety), labeling, advertising, business conduct, and personal information protection determined by the State as standards for promotion of consumers' rights and interests. Thus, a consumer organization litigation can be instituted in the event of infringement and continuation of such infringement directly on the rights and interests relating to their lives, bodies, or property in violation of each standard above.

4. Application for Permission of Litigation

An organization seeking to institute a consumer organization litigation must submit to a court an application for the permission of the litigation along with a written complaint (Article 73). An application for the permission of litigation must specify parties to a dispute, plaintiff's attorney, the purport and cause of the application, the scope of the infringement of consumers' rights and interests by business entities, the date of the written request for prohibition or suspension (Article 73, Paragraph 1, Regulation on Consumer Organization Litigation by Supreme Court, Article 4). Furthermore, the application must be accompanied by the materials proving that the organization meets the qualification requirements, and a written document of the plaintiff organization requesting the business entity to prohibit or suspend the infringement of consumers' rights and interests, together with the business entity's written opinion in response to the request—however, if the business entity gives no response within a period fixed under the relevant provision, the business entity's written opinion may be omitted (Article 73, Paragraph 2).

A court must permit a consumer organization litigation, by its ruling, only in cases where all the following requirements are met (Article 74, Paragraph 1): (1) that there is any public need for permitting such litigation in the light of the protection of consumers' rights and interests and the prevention of any damage to them, because the goods or services concerned cause or might cause any danger or injury to consumers' lives, bodies or property; (2) that there is no defect in the matters entered in the application for the permission of litigation; and (3) that 14 days have passed since the organization instituting the litigation asked the business entity concerned, in writing, to prohibit and suspend the infringement of consumers' rights and interests. Parties can raise an immediate appeal against the ruling to permit or not to permit the litigation (Article 74, Paragraph 2). In the case where a ruling dismissing the litigation has become final and conclusive, it is deemed that no litigation has been filed by a consumer organization (Regulation on Consumer Organization Litigation by Supreme Court, Article 11, Paragraph 4).

5. Joinder of Pleadings and Preservative Measures

If several consumer organization litigations involving the same basis of the claims and the same defendant are pending at the same court, the court must, in principle, deliberate them in combination (Regulation on Consumer Organization Litigation by Supreme Court, Article 15). It is also possible to take preservative measures in accordance with Civil Execution Act if there is a ruling of the permission of consumer organization litigation. The preservative measure taken here will be a 'provisional disposition' to prevent the expansion or occurrence of consumer damage.

6. Effect of Final and Conclusive Judgment

When a judgment to reject a request made by a plaintiff became final and conclusive, other organizations cannot file a consumer organization litigation with regard to the same matter. However, this does not apply to cases ① when a new research result or evidence is found by an institution, which is established by the State or a local government, with respect to the rejected case after the judgment became final and conclusive; or ② when the judgment of rejection is found to have been caused by any intentional act of the plaintiff (Article 75). This is interpreted to extend the subjective extent of res judicata to other organizations in that other organizations are prohibited from filing a consumer organization litigation with regard to the same matter when a judgment of rejection became final and conclusive.

7. Evaluation and Prospects

(1) Performance of Litigation

In the early stage of the introduction of the system, a complaint was filed due to the unauthorized provision of personal information by a telecommunication company, but it was closed with withdrawal of the lawsuit as the defendant voluntarily amended the terms and conditions (*the Hanaro Telecom* case). Since December 2015, the 'Consumer Union of Korea' which is the first specialized consumer organization in Korea has filed a total of 6 lawsuits (4 cases in substance) one by one, and one of them was settled, and the remaining five cases are currently under way.

Firstly, a series of consumer organization litigations were filed in turn against three telecommunication companies (SKT, KT, LGU+) (December 17, 22, 24, 2015). The issue raised in this case was the practice of transactions and terms and conditions which restricted the customers' right of termination and did not permit the right of withdrawal in the telecommunication contract concluded by e-commerce or cold calling sales. The consumer organization lost the case in both the 1st and 2nd trials, and is currently waiting for the Supreme Court's judgment. Secondly, a complaint was filed against the Korean Smart Card Company which issues a prepaid payment means (T-money Card) used for convenient stores and transportation such as metropolitan subway, bus, taxi, etc. (December 17, 2016). In this case, there was a problem with the company's refusal to refund the charged balance in the minor's lost card, which was registered with the company's central server to take advantage of discount charge. The plaintiff lost the case in both the 1st and 2nd trials, and is currently waiting for the Supreme Court's judgment. Thirdly, a complaint was filed against KEPCO, the Korean electricity supply company, to ask for suspension of the progressive billing system, which progressively charges household electricity rates in accordance with the amount of electricity use (October 14, 2016). The plaintiff lost the case in the 1st trial, and the appeal is under way. Finally, a complaint was filed against a distributor (Hi-Mart), which restricted the right of consumers to withdraw the sales contract in e-commerce, to demand a ban on the restriction of the right to withdraw if a product package is opened (December 31, 2018)—later, the lawsuit was withdrawn with the distributor's voluntary correction (September 21, 2019).

(2) Problems and Improvement Direction

The system of consumer organization litigation has the following problems in the aspects of 'clarity of requirements' and 'effectiveness'. Together with the problems, remedies for those problems are proposed as below.

(1) Clarification of the Infringement Requirements (Article 20)

The requirement of "in violation of Article 20 (of the Framework Act on Consumers)" needs to be reviewed in terms of the clarity of a requirement. Article 20 provides compliance with the standards, which is determined by the State, of harm prevention(consumer safety), labeling, advertisement, business conduct (unfair dealing), and personal information protection. A consumer organization litigation can be instituted if business entities infringe directly on consumers' rights and interest relating to their lives, bodies, or property in violation of any of each standard above. The problem here is that it is unclear what "the standards determined by the State" means specifically. Alternatively, I think it is reasonable to specify the name of legislation (and its provisions) based on which a consumer organization litigation is to be accepted—it appears to be also appropriate to point out the types of specific infringement, but it should be more desirable to specify the legal basis (the name of legislation and specific provisions) for judgment of the illegality of the relevant act from the viewpoint of clarity.

(2) Relaxation of the Requirements for Infringement of Consumers' Rights and Interests (Directness and Continuity Requirements)

Business entities' violation of Article 20 is required to "infringe directly" on the consumers' rights and interests relating to their lives, bodies, or property and the infringement is required to continue. However, it is difficult to envisage the effectiveness of this system if the directness and continuity of infringement is required as such. In particular, if it requires infringement of the rights and interests relating to consumers' "lives or bodies", it is meaningless to demand suspension of the act of infringing their lives or bodies by litigation. It is thus recommended that this requirement be refined to such extent as "if consumers' rights and interests are infringed or likely to be infringed".

(3) Expansion of Claim Object

The object of claim in a consumer organization litigation is "prohibition or suspension of the infringement of consumers' rights and interests" (a claim for injunctive relief). However, in the case of other substantive laws that grant the right to request the prohibition or suspension of an act, all the laws grant the right to request other measures necessary to prevent the act of infringement—Civil Code, Copyright Act, Patent Act, Unfair Competition Prevention and Trade Secret Protection Act, etc.—in addition to granting the right to request prohibition (or suspension) of the infringement. No rational reason supports such restriction of the claim object to prohibition (or suspension) of an act in the system of consumer organization litigation, and it is thus necessary to expand the scope of the rights to include the right to request prevention or other necessary measures.

(4) Abolition of the Permission System for Litigation

Getting a court permission for litigation is a requirement introduced from the U.S. system of representative-party litigation (Class Action) into consumer organization litigation system in Korea. In the so-called 'opt-out' system of the U.S. class action, the system of permission to take a class action has a good reason to exist since it serves the inherent purpose of certifying a class—class certification—to proceed with a class action suit. However, there is no reason to maintain the permission system for the consumer organization litigation that allows a consumer organization to carry out proceedings and request the prohibition or suspension of business entities' infringements. It is desirable to abolish this system. Even if it is deemed by a court to be difficult to proceed with a consumer organization litigation for a procedural defect or other reasons, the court can simply dismiss the suit, and if necessary, it is possible to legislate the dismissal system.

4 Legislative Bills for Class Action

The National Assembly in Korea has recently been receiving a number of legislative bills introducing the system of class action for the redress of collective consumer damages. This is a result of the understanding that the system of collective consumer mediation cannot serve as an ultimate alternative for the redress of collective consumer damages, as Korea has experienced a number of controversial cases causing severe damages to numerous consumers—Humidifier Disinfectants Case, BMW Fire Case, VW Emission Violation Case, etc.—despite the 2006 introduction of consumer collective mediation system under the Framework Act on Consumers.

Since most of the legislative bills are based on the "Securities-Related Class Action Act", which referred to the U.S. representative-party litigation (Class Action), they are generally divided into two types: (i) one that limits the scope of application to consumer class action; and (ii) the other one, without such restriction, that targets all kinds of class. Meanwhile, there is also a legislative bill proposing the introduction of a modified class action lawsuit in which a consumer organization may institute a lawsuit seeking declaratory judgment in the 1st stage and, with a ruling in favor of the consumer organization, consumer victims may join the suit in the 2nd stage of the action. This is the legislative proposal referring to the system of class action that was recently introduced in France (2014), Japan (2016), and Germany (2018).

In the case of the legislative proposal based on the U.S. representative-party litigation, the opt-out type of class action system is advantageous to a large number of small claims for damages. However, it has been pointed out that there is a risk of depriving consumers from the right of action in that the decision will be binding on the consumers even if the representative party loses the case.

On the other hand, the consumer organization type class action system can create a synergy effect in that a consumer organization can conduct a consumer organization litigation against the same infringement, while at the same time, filing a claim for damages. It is an advantage that there is no risk of depriving consumers from the right of action in that consumers participate in the class action only in case of winning the 1st stage lawsuit by the consumer organization. But it remains a challenge how to justify granting the right of action to a consumer organization which is not a victim. In any case, if the collective mediation system and the class action system are introduced together, the number of consumers' options for the relief of collective consumer damages will increase. Much attention is to be paid towards which legislative proposal will be enacted as the legal regime for class action in the future.

5 Conclusion

As discussed above, this paper examined the two systems for the relief of collective consumer damages which were recently introduced in Korea, together with the class action system that is currently under discussion for enactment. The consumer collective mediation has its significance in the development of consumer relief system in the sense that it has aimed to facilitate the relief for collective damages by using mediation that is friendly to consumer disputes, but further efforts are needed to improve the system in that the rate of concluded mediations was not high in spite of the last 10-year operation of the system. The consumer organization litigation, the system which grants a consumer organization with the right of action to request the prohibition of business entities' infringements, is expected to have a positive effect in the aspect of strengthening the market surveillance function by private organizations. However, the requirements are too strict that the utilization rate of the system is not high, which is a problem. In the meantime, as a number of legislative proposals introducing the system of class action have been submitted to the National Assembly, the development of a new system draws attention. Introduction of the class action system should serve as a critical juncture for consumer protection in that it would offer consumers with more options for the relief of collective consumer damages. It remains to be seen how the Korean law will unfold the next chapter for collective consumer redress.

The Role of ADR in the Materialisation of Consumer Access to Justice

Jagna Mucha

1 Terminological Remarks

Reconstruction of the right of access to legal protection is difficult due to different views regarding[1] the question whether the fundamental right of access to court requires every private law dispute (including consumer disputes) to be decided by the state court of law or whether it is also possible to delegate such task to other entities,[2] such as ADR entities and thus allowing the state court to review the outcome of the dispute to the minimum extend.[3]

[1]Benöhr [1]; Tulibacka [2].

[2]European Commission, *Impact assessment accompanying the document „Proposal for a Directive of the European Parliament and of the Council on Alternative Dispute Resolution for consumer disputes (Directive on consumer ADR)" and „Proposal for a Regulation of the European Parliament and of the Council on Online Dispute Resolution for consumer disputes (Regulation on consumer ODR)"*, SEC(2011) 1408 final, p. 5; see: Gascon Inchausti [3], 31, 58.

[3]As regards the access to justice within the substantial law perspective and the role of ADR see: Sternlight [4]; Genn [5]. The author, referring to the example of mediation, indicates that its use does not facilitate access to justice from the substantial law perspective, since the parties to the mediation do not enforce their rights but aim at amicable dispute resolution. At the same time she argues that the mediator helps the parties to reach agreement and does not render judgment based on the provisions of law.

[4]Charter of Fundamental Rights of the European Union [2012] OJ C 326/391.

The following paper constitutes a part of the research conducted within the framework of the project funded by the grant no. UMO-2018/28/C/HS5/00083, 'Consumer collective redress in the group proceedings in the Polish legal system in the light of the European Union law standards-achievements and challenges', financed by the National Science Centre of Poland.

J. Mucha (✉)
Department of European Law, Institute of International Law, University of Warsaw, Warsaw, Poland
e-mail: jagna.mucha@uw.edu.pl

D. Wei et al. (eds.), *Innovation and the Transformation of Consumer Law*,
https://doi.org/10.1007/978-981-15-8948-5_18

In line with the traditional approach,[4] as described in the classical theory of the legal process, administration of justice belongs to the domain of public courts which are the best and the only competent authorities to enforce law.[5] On the other hand, in the broad sense, legal protection encompasses not only court procedures but also other out-of-court methods aiming at realisation of substantial law protection, including alternative dispute resolution methods.

In the narrow sense, the access to legal protection shall be understood as the right of access to court, constituting a vital element of the rule of law principle, upon which the European Union is based.[6] Access to legal protection means not only access to the EU courts,[7] but mainly access to the national courts and the possibility to take legal action according to the national law in order to enforce the rights granted by the EU law.[8] In the relevant literature of the subject it is stated that the right of access to court emerges from the doctrine of direct effect and primacy of the EU law.[9] Without the access to courts, being responsible for the enforcement of rights granted by legislator none of the above mentioned principles would be fulfilled. However, in light of well-developed case law of CJEU, the national law does not have to enable taking legal action at every stage of the procedure, provided that the final decision regarding EU claim can be controlled by the court of law.[10] According to the Court, "[a]ll decisions must be open to judicial scrutiny enabling their legality under EU law to be reviewed."[11]

In the subsequent part of this paper the approach of CJEU would be scrutinised, according to which the Member States may not make the right of access to courts conditional upon earlier participation in the out-of-court procedure. Leaving the discussion included therein for later, it needs to be pointed out that such statement of the Court was widely criticised in the literature of the subject concerning out-of-court consumer dispute resolution.

H. Eidenmüller and M. Engel claim that consumers who execute agreements with the ADR clause waive their right to access to justice at least for the time of lasting court procedure.[12] Quite at the same spirit, A. Nylund expresses doubts as regards the

---

[5] Council of Europe, Convention for the Protection of Human Rights and Fundamental Freedoms (European Convention on Human Rights) as amended by Protocols nos. 11 and 14, supplemented by Protocols nos. 1, 4, 6, 7, 12 and 13.

[6] See: Case C-294/83 [1986] *Les Verts* v. *European Parliament*, ECLI:EU:C:1986:166, para 23, as well as Case C-314/91 [1993] *Beate Weber* v. *European Parliament*, ECLI:EU:C:1993:109, para 8; see also: Lenaerts et al. [6].

[7] See: Biernat [7].

[8] Wróbel and Półtorak [8].

[9] Ibid., see also: Kornobis- Romanowska [9].

[10] See: Case C-69/10 *Brahim Samba Diouf v. Ministre du Travail, de l'Emploi et de l'Immigration* [2011] ECLI:EU:C:2011:524, para 56.

[11] Case C-372/09 and C-373/09 *Josep Peñarroja Fa* [2011] ECLI:EU:C:2011:156, para 63.

[12] According to those authors: "[c]onsumers also typically do not wish to waive their right of access to justice because they happened to have signed a contract purporting waiving that right. But if they later find themselves in alternative dispute resolution procedure, they are prevented from exactly such access, at least for as long as the procedure lasts or as long as they cannot terminate it."

role of ADR in facilitating access to justice. Taking as an example court mediation in the Nordic countries, the scholar states that in the case where there are no clear rules regulating the organisation of the ADR entities, their financing, training and structure of the dispute resolution system, ADR methods do not help but hinder access to justice.[13] The author claims that "[A]DR and court-connected mediation, in particular, are a black box where the mediatior is free to do many things, including pressuring the parties and being highly directive, without the parties being able to complain in an effective manner."[14]

It is worth mentioning that the narrow understanding of access to justice is anchored in the Polish Constitution also, in which such right is understood as access to courts. According to the Polish Constitution the administration of justice shall be implemented by the Supreme Court, the common courts, administrative courts and military courts and everyone shall have the right to a fair and public hearing of his case, without undue delay, before a competent, impartial and independent court.[15]

According to some Polish authors, facilitating access to ADR complies with the state obligation to materialise access to court, as set forth in the above mentioned provisions of the Polish Constitution.[16] K. Gajda-Roszczynialska and K. Weitz claim that within the framework of parties' autonomy Constitution does not exclude the possibility to resolve disputes out of the courts. They make a reservation however, claiming that "[t]he outcomes or decisions issued by ADR entities as a result of dispute resolutions cannot be classified as judicial awards issued on behalf of Republic of Poland, and the legality of such outcomes or decisions rendered in the civil disputes shall be controlled by state judicial power."[17] Therefore, in spite of the limited scope of the formal objections which may be raised in such a case at the state court, this is the state court and not the ADR entity who facilitate access to justice. Nothing prevents however the ADR system to complement judicial system of justice. Following this line of reasoning A. Bieliński states that "[t]he right of access to court, identified with dispute resolution by the state courts may be and shall be complemented by out-of-court mechanisms (...) It's seems that only if the system of legal protection is constructed in such [twofold] way, it reaches the expectation of the modern society, functioning in the environment which is subject to many dynamic changes of different character and in conditions fostering creation of conflicts."[18]

Noteworthy, majority of the constitutions of the Member States, including Poland, do not mention explicitly the term "access to justice", which would cover the use of

---

Horst Eidenmüller, Martin Engel, 'Against false settlement: designing efficient consumer rights enforcement system in Europe', [2014] 29 Ohio St. Journal on Dispute Resolution 261.

[13]Nylund [10].

[14]Ibid. 334.

[15]Constitution of the Republic of Poland as of 2 April 1997, (Journal of Laws as of 1997, no. 78 position. 483, as amended), Article 175 in connection with Article 45.

[16]Weitz and Gajda-Roszczynialska [11].

[17]Ibid., [self- made translation].

[18]Bieliński [12], [self- made translation].

out-of-court dispute resolution methods.[19] In spite of this, in some Member States, including i.a. Lithuania, the possibility to use out-of-court dispute mechanisms is derived from the provisions regarding consumer protection which impose the promotion of the use of mediation as a means of dispute resolution. Quite opposite, in the constitutions of Hungary and Portugal, there are explicit references to ADR, which emerges directly from the access to justice notion.[20]

In view of the above mentioned considerations there are no doubts that access to state courts is not sufficient to ensure efficient consumer protection in the EU. Therefore, E. Łętowska indicates that under the EU law there is a need to create a different, broader approach, according to which access to justice shall be understood as all-kind means, undertakings and procedures aiming at realization of substantial-law norms, including not only access to state courts but also any methods alternative to the court procedures.[21] Quite in the same spirit K. Gajda claims that traditional, narrow understanding of legal protection remains contrary to the EU law. The author observes that the issue of ensuring efficient consumer protection shall be considered broadly since it relates not only to the efficiency of justice system and court procedures enabling consumer redress but also to the alternative, out-of-court consumer dispute resolution methods.[22]

2 Access to Justice in the EU Law

Under the EU law access to justice it is enshrined in Article 47 of CFR, granting individuals right to the effective legal protection against infringements of their substantive rights. In line with this provision the right to the effective access to justice shall encompass: (i) the right to effective remedy before a tribunal, (ii) the right to fair and public hearing within the reasonable time by an independent and impartial tribunal previously established by the law, (iii) the right to be advised, defended and represented, as well as right to legal aid.

In the legal system of the Council of Europe, the right to access to justice is guaranteed by Article 6 ECHR which provides the right to fair trial and Article 13 of the ECHR which grants the right to an effective remedy.

The comparison of the provisions of Article 47 of the CFR with the provisions of Article 6 in connection with Article 13 of the ECHR shows that the wording of Article 47 para 1 of the CFR corresponds with Article 6 para 1 of the ECHR[23] and the

---

[19] On the access to justice in the constitutions of particular Member States see: Storskrubb and Ziller [13].

[20] Weitz and Gajda-Roszczynialska, Ibid. (18), 29.

[21] Ewa Łętowska, *Europejskie prawo umów konsumenckich* (CH Beck 2004) 376.

[22] Gajda [14].

[23] See: Case C-619/10 *Trade Agency Ltd v. Seramico Investments Ltd* [2012] ECLI:EU:C:2012:531, para 52; Case C-199/11, *Europese Gemeenschap v. Otis NV and others* [2012] ECLI:EU:C:2012:684, para 47.

wording of Article 47 para1 of the CFR corresponds with Article 13 of the ECHR. In spite of this convergence it needs to be pointed out that the scope of the protection provided by CFR and ECHR is different.[24] Article 6 of ECHR is applicable only in the determination of civil rights and obligations provided by the national law or in the criminal cases regarding charges raised against the individual. On the other hand, Article 47 of CFR, in spite of referring to all rights and freedoms recognised by the EU law, including any economic, social and cultural rights, does not ensure such complex system of protection.[25] CFR is applicable to the individuals only when the Member States are implementing the EU law.[26] In other words, an individual may recall the rights mentioned in Article 47 of CFR before the state court only when the case has the EU character, that is when its subject matter is encompassed by the scope of application of the EU law or when this subject matter remains in relation to the EU law.[27] If the case has a purely domestic character, the national court is not obliged to verify the compliance of the case with the EU standards of fundamental rights, including access to justice right. Additionally, Article 13 of ECHR determines the right to effective remedy before a national authority (not only before the court) in case of violation of rights and freedoms, as set forth in ECHR. On the other hand, under Article 47 of CFR, the right to effective remedy and fair trial before a tribunal shall be applicable to all the rights and freedoms granted under the EU law and it is not limited to the scope of CFR.

In spite of the fact that both systems differ as for the scope of their application, principles and conditions determined by CJEU and ECHR respectively, in both regimes the right to effective legal remedy is enforced mainly at the national level. It follows from the well-developed case law of CJEU that the efficient judicial protection of fundamental rights, enshrined in Article 47 CFR was derived from the constitutional tradition common to the Member States as well as from interpretation of Article 6 in connection with Article 13 of ECHR. It implies that the case law of ECHR remains essential for the interpretation of fundamental rights codified in CFR as long as these rights correspond to the rights guaranteed by ECHR. The above mentioned relation is confirmed explicitly by Article 52 para 3 of CFR (Table 1).

2.1 The Principle of Effective Judicial Protection

The development of the concept of the right to effective legal remedy and the right to court in the EU system was originated in the Luxembourg case law. As a result, in the EU law the principle of effective judicial protection of fundamental rights was created, which was acknowledged as a general principle of law.

---

[24] See: Bisztyga [15].

[25] European Union Agency for Fundamental Rights (FRA), *Handbook on European law relating to access to justice* [2016] 23.

[26] It follows from Article 51 of the CFR; in the literature of the subject see: Kowalik-Bańczyk [16].

[27] Grzeszczak and Szmigielski [17].

Table 1 Compartive sheme the scope of Article 6 of ECHR, Article 13 of ECHR and Article 47 of CFR

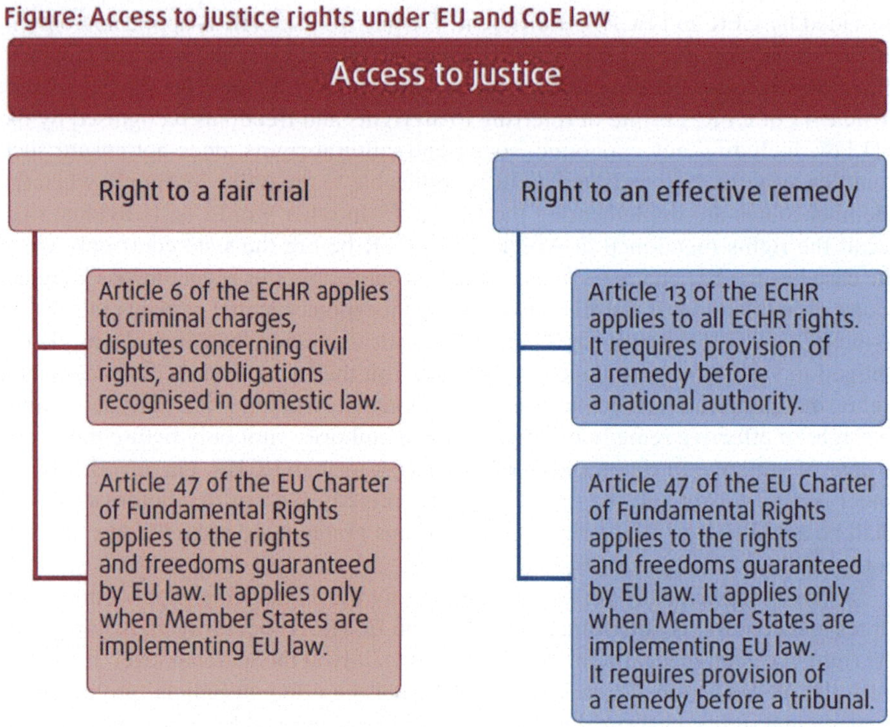

Source European Union Agency for Fundamental Rights (FRA), *Handbook on European law relating to access to justice,* Luxemburg 2016, p. 21

For the first time CJEU referred to this principle in the historical case C-14/83 *von Colson*, answering in the preliminary ruling the question of the German court regarding, i. a. effects of the sanctions for the breach of the prohibition of the discrimination by the employers.[28] In this case the Court stated that the Member States have an obligation to guarantee "real and effective judicial protection" (germ. *tatsächlichen und wirksamen Rechtschutz*).[29] The Court considered these obligations as undefined demand, derived from the general rule of efficiency, saying that the national provisions cannot make it practically impossible or excessively difficult to enforce the rights granted under the EU law.[30]

[28]Council Directive 76/207/EEC on the implementation of the principle of equal treatment for men and women as regards access to employment, vocational training, and promotion and working conditions [1976] OJ L 39/40.

[29]Case C-14/83 *Sabine von Colson and Elisabeth Kamann v. Land Nordrhein-Westfalen* [1984] ECLI:EU:C:1984:153, para 23.

[30]See: Wróbel [18]; Zawidzka- Łojek [19].

In the subsequent case law CJEU recalled explicitly the issue of effective judicial protection, i. a. in the landmark decision in the case *C-222/84 Johnston.*[31] CJEU stated there that the Member States are obliged "[t]o introduce into their legal systems such measures as needed to enable all people (…) to pursue their claims by judicial process."[32]At the same time the Court claimed that the requirement of judicial control reflects a general principle of law which underlines the constitutional tradition common to the Member States.[33] Therefore, the principle of effective judicial protection gained an importance of primary law. The Court recalled that the sources of this principle are laid down in Articles 6 and 13 of ECHR, constituting the right to fair trial and the right to the effective legal remedy. Such approach was clearly influenced by former case law of ECHR which interpreted the above mentioned provision of ECHR. The position of CJEU, as regards this principle was maintained and developed in the subsequent case law.[34]

Since the Treaty from Lisbon came into force, CJEU in the case law does not recall Article 6 and Article 13 of ECHR, using a formula according to which the principle of efficient judicial protection, being a general rule of the EU law is enshrined in Article 47 of CFR.[35] In the literature of the subject it is emphasised that such wording is intentional as it aims at stressing the origin of this principle, which constitutes one of the fundamental rights guaranteed in Article 47 of CFR.[36]

2.2 *Access to Court Right and Obligatory Participation in the ADR Proceedings*

In the relevant literature of the subject it is pointed out that the right of access to court enshrined in Article 47 para 2 of CFR entails the necessity to ensure the judicial protection of the claims derived from the EU law. It involves the right to bring an action to court and to commence legal proceeding, which fulfills the criteria of efficiency and equivalence.[37] It is worth noting at this point that according to the well-developed case law of CJEU, the national law does not have to provide the access to court at every stage of proceedings, since the absence of a remedy at

[31]Case C-222/84, *Marguerite Johnston v. Chief Constable of the Royal Ulster Constabulary* [1986] ECLI:EU:C:1986:206.

[32]Ibid., para 17.

[33]Ibid., para 18.

[34]Case C-432/05 *Unibet (London) Ltd i Unibet (International) Ltd* v. *Justitiekanslern* [2007] ECLI:EU:C:2007:163, para 37; Case C-402/05 P and C-415/05 P *Yasin Abdullah Kadi* and *Al Barakaat International Foundation v. Council of European Union* [2008] ECLI:EU:C:2008:461, para 335; Case C-12/08 *Mano Car Styling SA* v. *Dervis Odemis* [2009] ECLI:EU:C:2009:466.

[35]Case C-279/09 *DEB Deutsche Energiehandels- und Baratungsgesellschaft mbH* v. *Bundesrepublik Deutschland* [2010] ECLI:EU:C:2010:811, para 31; Case C-457/09 *Claude Chartry* v. *Belgium* [2011] ECLI:EU:C:2011:101, para 25.

[36]Wróbel and Półtorak, Ibid. (10), 1169.

[37]Ibid.

every stage of the procedure does not constitute an infringement of the right to an effective remedy. However, undoubtedly the legality of the final decision, adopted in relation to the claims granted by the EU law must be subject to thorough review by the national court.[38]

It needs to be mentioned also that the right to submit to court the claims safeguarding rights which individuals derive from the direct effect of the EU law may become dependent on exhausting other available measures (for example participation in ADR or administrative proceedings). Such condition does not infringe on the requirement of efficient judicial protection provided that it is introduced without prejudice to the principle of equivalence, according to which the out-of-court procedure must not be less favourable than the procedure governing similar domestic actions and cannot not make it impossible or excessively difficult in practice to exercise the rights conferred by the EU law.[39]

In some circumstances the requirement to participate in other than court proceedings in order to commence these proceedings may infringe the principle of efficiency. For purpose of the discussion conducted here there are two judgments of CJEU which are particularly significant: case C-410/01 *Fritsch, Chiari & Partner* and C-320/02 *Grossmann Air Service.*[40] The Court stated there that making access to the judicial review procedures set forth in the EU law conditional on prior application to a conciliation commission is contrary to the EU law's objective of speed and effectiveness. According to the Court, "[p]rior application of conciliation commission inevitably has the effect of delaying the introduction of the judicial review procedures which the EU law requires Member States to establish." Additionally, the Court stated that the conciliation commission does not have the powers which the EU law requires to be granted by the Member States to the bodies responsible for carrying out the judicial review procedures, so that referrance to it does not ensure the effective application of the relevant EU law. In line with the above mentioned case the law national law cannot deprive entities of the right to take an action to court in case when out-of-court procedure was not commenced.

The above mentioned approach of CJEU changed in the case law passed later. In the landmark decision in case C-317/08 *Alassini*[41] the Court verified the compliance of the national law imposing obligation of the prior out-of-court settlement procedure with the principle of effective judicial protection.[42] The Court stated there that following factors show that a mandatory settlement procedure does not make it impossible or excessively difficult in practice to exercise the rights which individuals

---

[38]Case C-69/10 *Brahim Samba Diouf,* Ibid. (11), para 56; Case C-372/09 and C-373/09 *Josep Peñarroja Fa,* Ibid. (13), para 63.

[39]Case C-228/98 *Charalampos Dounias* v. *Ypourgio Oikonomikon* [2000] ECLI:EU:C:2000:65, paras 64–67.

[40]Case C-410/01 *Fritsch, Chiari & Partner, Ziviltechniker GmbH and Others* v. *Autobahnen- und Schnellstraßen-Finanzierungs-AG (Asfinag)* [2003] ECLI:EU:C:2003:362, paras 31–35; Case C-320/02 *Grossmann Air Service, Bedarfsluftfahrtunternehmen GmbH & Co. KG* v. *Republik Österreich* [2004] ECLI:EU:C:2004:93, paras 41–43.

[41]Case C-317/08- 320/08 *Alassini and others.* v. *Telecom Italia SpA* [2010] ECLI:EU:C:2010:146.

[42]See: Prince [20].

derive from the EU law: (i) the outcome of the settlement procedure is not binding for the parties concerned and thus it does not prejudice their right to initiate legal procedure, (ii) the settlement procedure does not result in a substantial delay for purposes of bringing legal proceedings, (iii) for the duration of the settlement procedure the period for the time-barring of claims is suspended, (iv) there are no fees for the settlement procedures before an ADR body.[43] Taking the above mentioned into consideration, the Court stated that the national legislation which imposes prior implementation of an out-of-court settlement procedure does not violate the principles of equivalence, effectiveness and the principle of effective judicial protection. However, the Court determined the obligatory settlement procedure of a dispute– which admittedly serves the purpose of public interest and is proportionate measure—is a hindrance in access to court.

Another interesting problem raised by CJEU in this case regarded the electronic means of the mediation proceeding. The Court indicated that if the settlement procedure could be accessed only by electronic means, the exercise of the rights conferred in the EU law "[m]ight be rendered in practice impossible or excessively difficult for certain individuals—in particular, those without access to the Internet."[44] In such scenario the obligatory settlement procedure would constitute the clear breach of the right of access to court.

CJEU adjudicated also on the question of the compliance of the ADR proceedings which result in the decision binding to the parties with the principle of effective judicial protection.[45] In the case C-168/05 *Mostaza Claro,*[46] the Court confirmed the arbitrability of consumer disputes provided that the conditions set forth in the directive 93/11/EWG are satisfied. In this case the company initiated arbitration proceeding against the consumer who did not refuse to bring legal proceedings. Within the arbitration proceedings Mostaza Claro presented arguments on the merits of the dispute, but she did not repudiate the arbitration proceedings or claim that the arbitration agreement was null and void. The arbitration proceedings subsequently took place and the arbitrator found against her. As a result the consumer contested the arbitration decision before the state court, who requested the preliminary ruling from CJEU. The Court stated that even if the consumer has not pleaded invalidity of the arbitration agreement in the course of the arbitration proceedings, limiting it to the action for annulment before the national court, the national court is obliged to determine, whether the arbitration agreement is void and annul that award, where that agreement contains an unfair term.[47]

---

[43]Case C-317/08- 320/08 *Alassini and others,* Ibid. (43) paras 54-57.

[44]Ibid, para 58.

[45]See: Mucha [21]; Norbert Reich, 'Party autonomy and consumer arbitration in conflict: A „Trojan horse" in the access to justice in the E.U. ADR-Directive 2013/11?', [2015] 4 Penn. St. J.L. & Int'l Aff. 306.

[46]Case C–168/05 *Mostaza Claro* p. *Centro Móvil Milenium SL* [2006] ECLI: EU:C:2006:675.

[47]Ibid., para 39.

The reasoning of the Court as regards the validity of the arbitration clause in consumer contracts was further developed in the case C-40/08 *Asturcom.*[48] In this case the arbitration proceeding was initiated by the trader who demanded from the consumer the payment of the overdue invoices for the telecommunication services. As a result of arbitration proceeding, which took place without the participation of the consumer, the arbitral tribunal rendered award in which the consumer was ordered to pay due amounts. Since the consumer did not initiate the proceedings for annulment of the arbitration award, it became final and the trader brought an action before the national court for the enforcement of arbitration award. However, the national court indicated that the arbitration clause in the contract was unfair, since: (i) the costs incurred by the consumer in travelling to the seat of the arbitration tribunal were greater than the amount at issue in the dispute in the main proceedings, (ii) the seat is located at a considerable distance from the consumer's place of residence and its location is not indicated in the contract and (iii) the arbitral tribunal itself draws up the contracts which are subsequently used by telecommunications undertakings. Since the consumer did not raise any objections to the arbitral award, the national court was not sure whether it should verify the validity of the arbitration clause *ex officio.* However, CJEU had not doubts that in such case "[t]he national court or tribunal hearing an action for enforcement of an arbitration award which has become final and was made in the absence of the consumer is required, where it has available to it the legal and factual elements necessary for that task, to assess of its own motion whether an arbitration clause in a contract concluded between a seller or supplier and a consumer is unfair. (…). If that is the case, it is for that court or tribunal to establish all the consequences thereby arising under national law, in order to ensure that the consumer is not bound by that clause".[49]

The interdependence of the participation in the arbitration proceeding and materialisation of access to court right was also verified by the Court in the case C-342/13 *Sebestyén.*[50] The national court was provided the guidance on how to verify, whether the arbitration clause included in the consumer contract shall be regarded as unfair term within the meaning of directive 93/13/EWG. The Court found there that it is the responsibility of the national court (i) to assess, whether the arbitration clause has the object or effect of excluding or hindering the consumer's right to take legal action or exercise any other legal remedy and (ii) to take account of the fact that the communication to the consumer, before the conclusion of the contract at issue, of general information on the differences between the arbitration procedure and ordinary legal proceedings, cannot alone make it possible to rule out the unfairness of that clause.[51]

---

[48]Case C-40/08 *Asturcom Telecomunicaciones SL p. Cristina Rodriguez Nogueira* [2009] ECLI:EU:C:2009:615.

[49]Ibid., para 59.

[50]Case C-342/13 *Katalin Sebestyén* p. *Zsolt Csaba Kővári, OTP Bank, OTP Faktoring Követeléskezelő Zrt, Raiffeisen Bank Zrt* [2014] ECLI: EU:C:2014:1857.

[51]Ibid., para 36.

In light of the discussion conducted herein it is also worth mentioning one of ECHR judgment in which the Court stated that failure of the authorities to enforce the final arbitral award may constitute a breach of Article 6 para 1 of the ECHR.[52] In spite of the fact that the *Regent Company* case referred to herein did not involve consumer being a party of the dispute, the case is worth scrutinising due to the meaning of the final arbitral award rendered to the benefit of the trader. The ECHR stated there that non-enforcement of the final arbitral award cannot be justified by the insolvency of the state-owned company which was ordered to pay the due amounts to the trader. It is noteworthy that according to the ECHR the continued non-enforcement of the final arbitral award violates the right of the trader to access to justice.[53]

3 Conclusions

From the above discussion on the consumer access to justice one may draw the following conclusions. Firstly, it emerges from the analysis of the legislation that under the EU law the access to justice is understood as the right to an effective judicial remedy and the right of access to court. Alternative dispute resolution methods are clearly not involved in the above mentioned categories of rights. Therefore, one cannot claim that the participation of consumers in the ADR procedure materialises their right of access to justice.

However, it follows from the analysis of the case law of CJEU that the access to justice right can be restricted by imposing an obligation of the prior out-of-court settlement procedure. The above mentioned restriction will not breach the right to effective judicial protection provided that: (i) the outcome of the procedure will not be binding to the parties, (ii) the procedure does not result in a substantial delay for the purposes of bringing legal proceedings, (iii) for the duration of the settlement procedure the period for the time-barring of claims is suspended, (iv) there are no fees for the settlement procedures before the ADR body. Additionally, the binding character of the decision rendered within the out-of-court procedure does not breach itself the right to an effective judicial protection. CJEU confirmed the arbitrability of the consumer disputes unequivocally, indicating –however—that it is the obligation of the national courts to verify the potential unlawfulness of the arbitration clause. The above mentioned obligation is imposed on the state courts either within the setting aside or enforcement procedure initiated by a party. The right to the effective legal protection is materialised by the state courts, reviewing the decisions rendered by the ADR entities.

Admittedly, it seems to be undisputed that the judicial system of legal protection shall be complemented by the out-of court methods which will allow to decrease the workload of courts on the one hand and simultaneously increase the number of

---

[52] *Regent Company v. Ukraine* App no. 773/03 (ECHR, 3 April 2008), para 60.

[53] Ibid.

consumer seeking redress on the other. In this sense, ADR methods will facilitate the consumer access to justice.

References

1. Iris Benöhr, 'Consumers' access to justice and procedural rights' in Iris Benöhr (ed.), *EU consumer law and human rights* (Oxford Scholarship Online, Oxford, 2013) 175.
2. Magdalena Tulibacka, 'Europeanization of civil procedures: in search of a coherent approach' [2009] CMLR 1527, 1565.
3. Fernando Gascon Inchausti, 'Specific problems of cross-border consumer ADR: what solutions?' in Michael Stürner, Fernando Gascon Inchausti, Remo Caponi (eds.), *The role of consumer ADR in the administration of justice* (Sellier European Law Publisher, Münich, 2015), 31, 58.
4. Jean R. Sternlight, 'Creeping mandatory arbitration: is it just?' [2005] SLR 1631, 1675.
5. Hazel Genn, 'What is civil justice for? Reform, ADR and access to justice', [2012] 24 YJLH 397, 417.
6. Koen Lenaerts, Ignance Maselis, Kathleen Gutman, *EU procedural law* (Oxford EU Law Library, Oxford University Press, 2014) 2.
7. Stanisław Biernat, 'Dostęp osób prywatnych do sądów unijnych po traktacie z Lizbony (w świetle pierwszych orzeczeń)' [2014] EPS 12, 19.
8. Andrzej Wróbel, Nina Półtorak, 'Komentarz do artykułu 47 Karty Praw Podstawowych', in Andrzej Wróbel (ed.), *Karta Praw Podstawowych Unii Europejskiej, Komentarz* (C.H. Beck, Warszawa 2012) 1169.
9. Dagmara Kornobis- Romanowska, 'Zasada pierwszeństwa prawa wspólnotowego w praktyce ETS i sądów krajowych' [2004] PPE, 35.
10. Anna Nylund, 'Access to justice: Is ADR a help or hindrance?' in Laura Ervo, Anna Nylund (eds.), *The future of civil litigation- access to courts and court-annexed mediation in the Nordic countries* (Springer 2014) 325, 344.
11. Karol Weitz, Katarzyna Gajda-Roszczynialska, 'Alternatywne metody rozwiązywania sporów ze szczególnym uwzględnieniem mediacji' in Andrzej Torbus (ed.), *Mediacja w sprawach gospodarczych. Praktyka – teoria – perspektywy* (Ministerstwo Gospodarki 2015) 31.
12. Andrzej Bieliński, 'Prawo do sądu a alternatywne metody rozwiązywania sporów ze szczególnym uwzględnieniem mediacji' in Łukasz Błaszczak (ed.), *Konstytucjonalizacja postępowania cywilnego* (Presscom 2015), 406, 407.
13. Eva Storskrubb, Jacque Ziller, 'Access to justice in European comparative law' in Francesco Francioni (ed.), *Access to justice as a human right* (Oxford University Press 2007), 177, 203.
14. Katarzyna Gajda, 'Dochodzenie roszczeń konsumenckich' in E. Nowińska, P. Cybula (eds.), *Europejskie prawo konsumenckie a prawo polskie* (Zakamycze 2005) 544, 545.
15. Andrzej Bisztyga, 'Europejska Konwencja Praw Człowieka a Karta Praw Podstawowych Unii Europejskiej- stan kompatybilności czy konkurencyjności?' [2011] PPK 179, 188.
16. Krystyna Kowalik-Bańczyk, 'Bezpośrednie stosowanie Karty Praw Podstawowych w krajowym postępowaniu sądowym gwarancją skuteczności prawa UE', [2011] EPS 40, 46.
17. Robert Grzeszczak, Artur Szmigielski, 'Sądowe stosowanie Karty Praw Podstawowych UE w odniesieniu do państw członkowskich– refleksje na podstawie orzecznictwa Trybunału Sprawiedliwości i praktyki sądów krajowych', [2015] EPS 11, 18.
18. Andrzej Wróbel, 'Autonomia proceduralna państw członkowskich. Zasada efektywności i zasada efektywnej ochrony sądowej w prawie Unii Europejskiej' [2005] Ruch Prawniczy, Ekonomiczny i Socjologiczny, 45, 47.
19. Anna Zawidzka- Łojek, 'Prawo Unii Europejskiej a prawo państw członkowskich' in Anna Zawidzka- Łojek, Robert Grzeszczak, Adam Łazowski (eds), *Prawo Unii Europejskiej, Vademecum* (EuroPrawo 2015) 234.

20. Sue Prince, 'Access to court? 'Encouraging' consumers to use court-connected mediation in small claims and other cases' in Pablo Cortés, *The new regulatory framework for consumer dispute resolution* (Oxford University Press 2016) 83.
21. Jagna Mucha, 'Arbitration of consumer disputes in the relevant case law of the European Court of Justice' in Anita Garnuszek, Laura Mazur, Aleksandra Orzeł (eds.), *Quo vadis arbitrażu? Quo vadis arbitration?* (Warszawa 2013) 350, 368.

The National Consumer Defense System and the Consumidor.gov.br Platform: From Conflict to Consensus

Leonardo Bessa and Ana Tarter

1 Introduction

The protection of the consumer has normative prominence in Brazil. The text of the Federal Constitution indicates the relevance of the theme in more than one device.[1] At the same time, there is a structure composed of several public agencies and private entities that, directly or indirectly, have the attribution of implementing and

[1] The Federal Constitution of Brazil provides for the protection of consumers in three main articles: art. 5, XXXII, which considers consumer protection as a fundamental right; the art. 170, V, which lists consumer protection as a principle of the Economic and Financial Order; and, finally, art. 48 of the ADCT, which determined that the elaboration of the Consumer Defense Code by the National Congress should be carried out within 120 days of the promulgation of the Constitution.

Leonardo Bessa—Justice attorney of MPDFT—Ministério Público do Distrito Federal, Phd in Civil Law from the University of the State of Rio de Janeiro-UERJ; Master of Law from the University of Brasilia-Unb; Law professor at UniCeub—Centro Universitário de Brasília-DF.

Ana Tarter—PhD student in Law from the University of Brasilia-Unb; Master of Law from the IDP Instituto Brasiliense de Direito Público.; Assistant Director of Brasilcon—Instituto Brasileiro de Política e Direito do Consumidor.

L. Bessa (✉)
Ministério Público do Distrito Federal, Brasília, Brazil
e-mail: leoroscoe@globo.com

University of the State of Rio de Janeiro-UERJ, Rio de Janeiro, Brazil

L. Bessa · A. Tarter (✉)
University of Brasilia-Unb, Brasília, Brazil
e-mail: luisatarter@gmail.com

A. Tarter
UniCeub—Centro Universitário de Brasília-DF, Brasília, Brazil

IDP Instituto Brasiliense de Direito Público, Brasília, Brazil

Brasilcon—Instituto Brasileiro de Política e Direito do Consumidor, Brasília, Brazil

D. Wei et al. (eds.), *Innovation and the Transformation of Consumer Law*,
https://doi.org/10.1007/978-981-15-8948-5_19

defending consumer rights. In addition to this situation, the debate on the out-of-court settlement of disputes has expanded since the enactment of Law 13.105/15, the new Code of Civil Procedure, encourages the negotiation and extra-judicial settlement of conflicts.

This paper, taking into account the purposes of the 17th Conference of the International Association of Consumer Law and its objective of sharing international models and experiences, presents a panorama of Brazil's National Consumer Defense System (SNDC). To do so, it indicates the structure and main attributions of public agencies and civil entities that, directly or indirectly, promote consumer protection in Brazil. It is demonstrated that, despite a praiseworthy normative delineation, the numbers and analysis of indicators show a high index of lawsuits, which provokes critical reflections on the functioning and effectiveness of the SNDC.

In this presentation, in addition to exposing indicators that points out to constant disregard for consumer rights, a relatively new tool is presented by the National Consumer Secretariat, which has been very useful in reducing consumer disputes. We present indicators that points to a constant disregard for consumer rights and it is featured the relatively new tool of the National Consumer Secretariat that has been very useful in reducing consumer disputes: the consumidor.gov.br platform.

Legal actions concerning consumer law have a great influence on the high volume of lawsuits in the Judiciary of Brazil. It is the third most demanded theme of all courts.[2] Thus, understanding the volume and profile of processes involving consumer law is a necessary condition not only to ensure the effectiveness of the fundamental right to consumer protection, listed in art. 5 of the Federal Constitution, but also to enable a sound administration of justice.

In spite of all normative protection—constitutional and infraconstitutional –, in addition to the entire structure of the National System of Consumer Protection—SNDC, the number of lawsuits filed indicate a weak effectiveness of consumer law.

Taking into account that each judicial proceeding in Brazil has an average cost of R $ 2,000.00 per year for public coffers and an average processing time of 5 years for (according to CNJ data), Brazil faces a clear procedural effectiveness problem which leads to the negative consequence of encouraging the general violation of the law.

In this scenario, there is a growing need to make use of alternative conflict solutions to deal with the current stock of processes and to avoid new ones. In the midst of the Digital Era, nothing more natural than using digital platforms for negotiation, mediation and arbitration, such as the platform consumer.gov.br.

In the practical world, it is a common practice to create profiles and register consumers (which led to the need to create a legal framework to deal with

[2]It should be noted that 80 million cases were processed in the Brazilian Judiciary in 2017. These results can be verified in a study prepared by the National Justice Council (CNJ). The complete material is available in http://www.cnj.jus.br/files/conteudo/arquivo/2018/04/28383cca082cb68ac79144e7b40f5568.pdf. Acesso em: 14/03/2019.

consumer databases in Brazil).[3] The platform consumer.gov.br evaluates and exposes companies by the same (or similar) mechanisms used to evaluate consumers.

2 National System of Consumer Protection—SNDC

The Law nº 8.078/1990 (Code of Consumer Protection- CDC), the main federal norm that governs consumer relations, was not content to just stipulate rights in favor of the consumer. It went beyond and established a National System of Consumer Protection (SNDC), with the objective of enabling the articulation of public and private entities that have the attribution and duty to protect the consumer, aiming at the desired social effectiveness of the law.[4]

The configuration of the National System of Consumer Protection and its proposal of articulation between the entities and bodies that compose it are justified by the great size of the Country (Brazil has 8.516,000 Km^2 area).

The SNDC is an instrument to enable the National Consumer Relations Policy to "meet the needs of consumers, respect for their dignity, health and safety, protection of their economic interests, improvement of their quality of life, as well as transparency and harmony of the relations of consumption "(article 4, caput, of the CDC).

In this sense, art. 105 of Law 8.078/1990 establishes that the National System of Consumer Defense—SNDC is composed of federal, state, and municipal agencies and private consumer protection entities. The National Consumer Secretariat—Senacon, a federal body that is part of the structure of the Ministry of Justice, is responsible for coordinating the System (article 106 c/c and Decree 2.181/1997, with the new text conferred by Decree 7.738/2012).

In order to understand the public bodies and entities that are part of or collaborate with the National Consumer Defense System—SNDC, it is not enough to analyze Title IV of the CDC (composed of articles 105 and 106): the articles that establish the attributions of these entities are distributed by the entire Consumer Protection Code (Articles 4, 5, 6, 44, 55-60, 82, 97, 102, 107), as well as other legal acts.

The following items will be used to indicate and explain the main bodies and entities that implement the consumer's right, their respective functions and mode of operation.

---

[3] To better understand the legislation on registration and databases of consumers in Brazil, see for everyone BESSA, Leonardo Roscoe. *Cadastro Positivo*: comentários à Lei 12.414, de 09 de junho de 2011. São Paulo: Revista dos Tribunais. 2011.

[4] In this respect, Marcelo Sodré teaches that the National System "traz a ideia de uma extensão geográfica e cultural. A junção dos conceitos *sistema* e *nacional* leva à conclusão de que todas as instituições políticas ou sociais que exercem algum papel para a consecução dos fins almejados (sejam eles quais forem), dentro de um campo pré-fixado (um país), devem compor um todo organizado. A ideia central é de que um Sistema Nacional deve abarcar todas as entidades que atuam em um determinado tema, sejam públicas ou privadas, em todas as esferas da federação do Estado Nacional. (...) Pode-se afirmar, então, que o conjunto de entidades do Sistema Nacional de Defesa do Consumidor é composto pelas entidades, públicas ou privadas, que atuam em torno deste tema". *Formação do Sistema Nacional de Defesa do Consumidor*, p. 155.

2.1 *PROCON*

Procon is the simplified designation of state and municipal consumer protection agencies. Its main attribution is to apply, directly, administrative sanctions to suppliers that violate consumer protection rules, all in accordance with the provisions of arts. 55 to 60 of Law 8.078/1990 and Decree 2.181/1997.

In Brazil, any offense to the consumer protection rule may lead to the application of the administrative sanctions indicated in art. 56.[5] It should be emphasized that it is not only the violation of consumer law established by Law 8.078/1990 that imposes administrative penalties, in fact, any offense against any rule that seeks to protect the material and moral interests of the consumer may lead to administrative penalty. The caput of art. 56 is clear in the sense that sanctions are applied in the face of infringements of consumer protection rules, not infringements of the Consumer Protection Code.

According to art. 56 of the CDC, the following administrative sanctions may be applied to suppliers who violate consumer protection standards: fine, seizure of the product, destruction of the product, revocation of the registration of the product with the competent body, prohibition of manufacture of the product, suspension of the supply of products or services, temporary suspension of activity, withdrawal of license of the establishment or activity, prohibition, total or partial, establishment, work or activity, imposition of counterpropaganda.

It should be noted that Procon, in the analysis of possible infringement of consumer law, should, of course, interpret the legal rule and define, in the specific case and for the purposes of applying the administrative sanction, if there was an offense against the consumer's right. In this work, in the context of the contractual protection of the consumer and to define abusiveness of a particular clause, it is also legitimate to interpret the contractual provision.[6]

---

[5]The application of sanctions stems from Procon's police power. It has punitive and pedagogical character. A single consumer offense is sufficient to allow for the incidence of penalties under the CDC. "The understanding in the Superior Court of Justice that the administrative sanction provided for in article 57 of the Consumer Protection Code is based on the Police Power that Procon holds to apply fines related to the violation of the provisions of Law no. 8,078/1990, regardless of whether the claim is made by a single consumer, by ten, one hundred or thousands of consumers. "(AgInt in REsp 1,594,667/MG, Rel. Min. Regina Helena Costa, J. 04.08.2016, DJe 17.08.2016).

[6]In this regard, the Superior Court of Justice (STJ) stated: "Procon, although it does not have jurisdiction, may interpret contractual clauses, since the Public Administration, by means of organs of administrative judgment, exercises control of legality, which does not is confused with the jurisdictional function proper, even though "the law will not exclude from the appreciation of the Judiciary an injury or threat to law" (article 5, XXXV, CF/1988). The succinct motivation that allows the exact understanding of the decision is not confused with non-existent motivation. The administrative sanction imposed by Procon is legitimated by virtue of its police power (administrative administrative activity) to commence fines related to the transgression of Law 8.078/1990, upsetting the review of the proportionality of the penalty fixed in the statement of Precedence 7/STJ. (REsp 1,279,622/MG, 06.08.2015, Rel. Min. Humberto Martins, DJe 17.08.2015). In a ruling handed down in 2017, the Court points out that "the Superior Court of Justice has consolidated the understanding that it is Procon's responsibility to analyze contracts and impose fines and other penalties, pursuant to arts.

Procon, in addition to the application of administrative sanctions, also carries out important work to inform consumers' rights and to promote conciliation between the parties. Usually, there is a telephone number to answer questions and provide information to interested parties. In addition, booklets are published on various topics of consumer interest, all with the aim of attending to the duty to educate and inform the consumer (articles 4, IV and 6, II, CDC).

The injured consumer, before filing an action, has the alternative of going to Procon and making a complaint to the agency for breach of the consumer protection standard. In practice, once the consumer situation is resolved and the agreement is signed, the body invariably closes the procedure.[7]

In addition to serving as an attenuating circumstance in the imposition of the administrative penalty, Procon has another relevant practical repercussion. Some Procons disclose, annually, based on art. 44 of the CDC, a list of establishments that do not respect consumers' rights. This relationship is known as a bad suppliers registry and should indicate the existence of substantiated complaints, as well as "whether or not the complaint was answered by the supplier".[8]

Finally, it should be noted that, although it is not common, Procon or any other organ of the public administration, direct or indirect, although without legal personality, is, by virtue of the provisions in art. 82, III, of the CDC, authorized to file a

---

56 and 57 of the CDC and 18 and 22 of Decree 2.181/97. "(REsp 1,652,614/ GO, Rel. Min. Herman Benjamin, J. 06.04.2017, DJe 27.04.2017).

[7]Strictly speaking, the situation should not have that outcome. Compliance with consumer pretension should serve as a maximum mitigating factor, never as a basis for closing. It is the duty of the administrative authority to apply the sanctions indicated in art. 56 whenever there is an offense, even if later corrected or mitigated, to the consumer's right. The purpose of the application of sanctions is preventive and repressive. It does not seek the indemnification of the consumer, but rather that the distressed supplier does not return to do the same kind of injury. In this line of reasoning, art. 25, III, of Decree 2.181/1997 establishes that it is only an attenuating circumstance "to have the violator adopted the pertinent measures to minimize or immediately repair the effects of the injurious act". In this direction, that is, that the purpose of the administrative action is not to obtain the compensation of the damage of the consumer, it is possible to apply a sanction on account of injury news to the right of the consumer that has already been repaid by virtue of individual action filing. Therefore, even the consumer with a favorable decision in the Court can make a representation with Procon, for application of administrative penalty - the filing of action does not prevent or prejudice that the same matter be referred to Procon. The incidence of civil sanction does not exclude the administrative or penal sanction, as foreseen in the caput of art. 56 of the CDC. In addition, the Judiciary may, even after the judgment, submit to Procon for breach of the consumer protection standard for the application of an administrative sanction, for pedagogical purposes, that is to say, that the supplier does not retake the same offense. On the subject, there are judgments of the STJ: RMS 22.241-RN, j. 07.11.2006, rel. Min. Eliana Calmon, DJ 20.11.2006); REsp 1,164,146, rel. Min. Luiz Fux; RMS 21,520-RN, rel. Min. Teori Albino Zavascki, 1st T., j. 08.08.2006, DJ 17.08.2006).

[8]The establishment of a Procon in the municipality, as well as the modernization of the organ, depend basically on the political will of the mayor and the city council. In addition to 27 state Procons, the number of municipalities with Procons does not reach 900, many with absolutely precarious functioning, without a job plan and salaries. It may occur, therefore, that in some State or Municipality there is, for example, Procon or the Consumer Police, or that the structure of a certain body, due to lack of human and material resources, is so deficient that it is impossible effectively carry out its functions.

collective action to protect the diffuse, collective and individual homogeneous rights of the consumer.

2.2 *Office of the Public Interest Attorney (Public Consumer Defense Office)*

The Office of the Public Interest Attorney (Prosecution Service or Public Prosecutor's Office) is an institution to which prosecutors and prosecutors belong. The functions of the organ are numerous and varied. A few years ago, the prosecutor was invariably associated with that of the criminal prosecutor, especially as an accuser at the jury court. The scenario is different nowadays.

In the last three decades, several laws have expanded the prosecution's chances, with emphasis on the 1988 Constitution. The institution is now recognized as an important body for the defense of collective rights related to the environment, urban planning, public patrimony, people with disabilities, consumers, children and adolescents.[9]

Since the Public Prosecutor's Office has absolute financial, administrative and functional autonomy (Article 127 of the Federal Constitution), it is understood that the institution or even the consumer defense attorneys do not formally form part of the National System of Consumer Protection. The discussion is not very useful. The fact is that the Public Prosecutor, as a relevant actor in the area of consumer protection, integrating or not the System, should seek to act in an articulated manner with other Public Prosecutors, Public Defenders, Procons, civil entities, regulatory agencies, with all which, directly or indirectly, promote the protection of consumer interests.

The Code of Consumer Protection (Law 8.078/90), when referring to the implementation of the National Consumer Relations Policy, provides, in art. 5, that the Public Authority will have, among other instruments, the "Institution of Public Prosecutor's Offices for Consumer Protection, within the scope of the Public Prosecutor's Office".

The effective creation of a Consumer Protection Office in a particular Public Prosecutor's Office depends on the institution's internal organization. As a rule, in the state capitals there is one or more promoters with exclusive attribution of protection of consumer rights (Consumer Protection Office). In smaller cities it is different: the same promoter who acts in other areas, such as family and criminal, also has the function of protecting the collective rights of consumers.

---

[9]On the subject, the Federal Constitution states: "The Prosecution Service is a permanent institution, essential to the jurisdictional function of the State, which is responsible for defending the legal system, the democratic regime and the unavailable social and individual interests" (article 127). and that it is the institutional function of the body to promote civil inquiry and public civil action "for the protection of public and social heritage, the environment and other diffuse and collective interests" (article 129, III).

The Office of the Attorney General for Consumer Protection is part of the Public Prosecution Service and basically acts to protect consumers' interests and collective rights. The law, when referring to such interests, refers to diffuse, collective and individual homogeneous rights (articles 81 and 82 of the CDC).[10]

2.3 *Public Defender's Office*

The Federal Constitution establishes the obligation of the State to offer legal assistance to the poor. Among the fundamental rights listed in art. 5 of the Basic Law, item LXXIV states that "the State shall provide full and free legal assistance to those who prove insufficient resources".

According to art. 134 of the Federal Constitution, the Public Defender's Office, is an essential institution for the jurisdictional function of the State, being responsible for legal guidance and defense, to all degrees, of the needy, that is, people who do not have the resources to hire private attorney.

In a country of poor and needy population, the importance of the role played by public defenders in the most varied social relations is quite obvious. This relevance contains differentiated nuance in the conflicts arising from consumer relations. While the middle-class consumer can absorb small injuries practiced by the market (for example, charging an undue tariff by the bank in the amount of R $ 27.00), with no greater impact on the family budget, the same does not occur with the one who, receiving a salary minimum per month, should support the whole family. The "small injuries" practiced by the suppliers can represent 20, 30, up to 50% of their monthly gain, to the detriment of amounts destined for food and other basic necessities.

The Office of the Public Defender serves the injured consumers, who do not have enough resources to hire private attorney, and is responsible for filing actions to defend their individual interests.

In recent years, in addition to the work to safeguard individual interests, the Public Defender of several states has stood out in the collective defense of consumers, bringing actions against public civil actions to solve in a single process injuries to consumers that repeat and multiply.

Before the new writing of art. Law No. 7,347/1985, the resistance of some courts to accept the legitimacy of the Public Defender's Office was unreasonable, since art.

[10]The CDC conceptualizes the species of collective rights in its art. 81 and, in art. 82, which establishes that, among other entities, the Public Prosecutor's Office is entitled to promote the defense of consumers' interests and rights: "Art. 81. The defense of the interests and rights of consumers and victims may be exercised individually or jointly. Single paragraph. The collective defense shall be exercised in the case of: I - diffuse interests or rights, understood as such, for the purposes of this code, indivisible transindividuals held by persons undetermined and bound by actual circumstances; II - collective interests or rights, so understood, for the purposes of this Code, transindividuals, of an indivisible nature held by a group, category or class of persons linked to one another or to the other party by a legal relationship; III - homogeneous individual interests or rights, thus understood as arising from common origin. Art. 82. For the purposes of art. 81, sole paragraph, are concurrently legitimized: I - the Public Prosecutor, [...]".

82, III of the CDC is quite clear in giving legitimacy to "entities and organs of the Public Administration, direct or indirect, even without legal personality, specifically intended to defend the interests and rights protected by this Code."[11]

The Public Defender's Office, in short, is an institution that, independently of formally integrating the National System of Consumer Protection, directly exercises consumer protection, both individually and collectively.

2.4 Consumer Police Department

The Consumer Police Office is a civil police body whose primary responsibility is to investigate criminal offenses against consumer relations through a police investigation or a detailed statement.

The CDC contains a mechanism designed to encourage Brazilian states to establish "police stations specialized in serving consumers who are victims of criminal offenses" (article 5, III). In practice, however, very few cities have a specific police station to investigate criminal offenses the victims of which are consumers.

Due to the principle of legal reserve, which establishes that "there is no crime without prior law that defines it, nor punishment without prior legal notice" (Article 5, XXXIX), it should be noted that only the conduct that, in theory, constitute infraction (crime or criminal contravention) must be brought to the attention of the police station. Most of the civil and administrative illicit acts carried out by suppliers are, for lack of a specific criminal classification, absolutely indifferent to criminal law. In the face of news of a crime against consumer relations, the Consumer Police Office has the duty to investigate the fact, by means of a police inquiry (articles 4 to 23 of the Code of Criminal Procedure) or a detailed term (article 69 of Law 9,099/1995), all its circumstances and authorship. Once the investigations have been completed, the police investigation or termination will be sent to the prosecutor with a criminal assignment, who will decide whether to file a criminal suit against the alleged perpetrators or to close the procedure.[12]

---

[11]Until January 15, 2007, when Law 11.448 was issued, there was unjustified resistance regarding the legitimacy of the Public Defender's Office for the filing of collective actions. The aforementioned law ended the controversy, because, when conferring new wording on art. 5 of Law No. 7.347/1985, expressly establishes that the Public Defender's Office has "the legitimacy to propose the principal action and the injunction".

[12]The criminal functions of the Public Prosecution Service may or may not belong to the Consumer Protection Justice Promoter, depending exclusively on the internal organization of the institution. In any case, the prosecutor who has criminal powers, in addition to offering a complaint, as the holder of the criminal action, must follow the investigations carried out in the police proceedings, and may, if appropriate, determine the execution of several investigative proceedings, such as testimony witness or expertise.

2.5 Civilian Consumer Protection Entities

Alongside state consumer protection bodies are civilian or non-governmental consumer protection organizations. These are private, non-profit associations established on the initiative of a group of individuals for the individual or collective defense of the rights and interests of the consumer, for the purpose of educating the consumer, carrying out diffusion activities and scientific research of this branch of law,, to promote, directly or indirectly, the greater effectiveness of consumer law in the Country.[13]

On two occasions, the CDC expressly indicates the duty of public authorities to encourage the creation and development of associations representing consumer interests (Articles 4, II and 5). It is the objective of the National Consumer Relations Policy to "encourage the creation and development of representative associations" of consumer interests.

Associations linked to consumer law constitute a means of organizing civil society to defend their interests. Although there has been a growing awareness of the Brazilian citizen about the importance of organizing in order to demand respect for their rights, there are still few consumer protection associations, in contrast, for example, with the countries of Europe.[14]

Consumer protection associations, in general, carry out rights awareness work, through campaigns, booklets, magazines, etc. They are also legally authorized, after one year of incorporation, to file collective actions that may benefit both associates and other consumers who find themselves in a similar situation (article 82, IV, of the CDC).

---

[13]"O direito do consumidor, ao lado de outros dos denominados novos direitos típicos da pós-modernidade, como o direito ambiental, guarda uma característica extremamente louvável e que, em boa medida, é uma das razões de sua crescente efetividade, tanto entre nós, quanto na experiência do direito europeu, de influência marcante no Brasil. Trata-se do papel ativo que reserva às diversas organizações da sociedade civil, a qual é expressamente estimulada pelo Código. Este estímulo à auto-organização dos consumidores é perceptível na legitimação das associações para interposição da ação coletiva, assim como na sua participação no SNDC, o que lhe determina a atuação coordenada na formulação de políticas públicas, mobilização da sociedade, educação para o consumo e colaboração com os órgãos públicos na repressão às infrações aos direitos dos consumidores" (Bruno Miragem, *Comentários*, p. 1161).

[14]The first civil associations for consumer protection were formed in the mid-1970 s, therefore, before the edition of Law 8.078/1990 (Code of Consumer Protection). By the way, reference is made to Marcelo Sodré who states that In the mid-1970 s, the first consumer protection entities began to appear. In the scope of civil society, ADOC - Consumer Protection and Defense Association of Curitiba (26.10.1976) and APC - Consumer Protection Association of Porto Alegre (19.05.1976). It should be noted, however, that these entities and others that have emerged have always had extreme difficulty in acting, either because of the novelty of the theme, or because of the lack of organization of civil society (we still lived an authoritarian government) or even by the absolute lack of support by the federal government. (*Formation of the National System of Consumer Protection*, page 131).

2.6 Other Entities that Defend Consumer's Rights

In addition to public and private entities that have the specific function of defending consumer rights, there are several others that, indirectly, also play this role.

They are state bodies created to monitor certain economic activities that, of course, affect the interests of consumers, such as Anatel—National Telecommunications Agency, which operates in the area of fixed and mobile telephony. Aneel—National Electric Energy Agency, ANP—National Petroleum Agency, ANS—National Supplementary Health Agency, Embratur—Brazilian Institute of Tourism, Inmetro—National Institute of Metrology, Standardization and Industrial Quality, Anac—National Civil Aviation Agency, Central Bank of Brazil, CVM—Securities Commission and Susep—Superintendency of Private Insurance.

At the state level, reference should be made to Health Surveillance, which, among other functions, receives complaints from consumers regarding public health issues, such as the hygiene of establishments and the marketing of deteriorated and unfit foods.[15]

2.7 National Consumer Secretariat

The art. 105 of the CDC establishes that the National System of Consumer Defense—SNDC is integrated by federal, state, Federal District and municipal agencies and private consumer protection entities. As demonstrated, there are a number of public and private entities that promote consumer advocacy or, more broadly, consumer law enforcement. In this myriad of entities, the National Consumer Secretariat—Senacon, which is part of the Ministry of Justice, has the attribution of promoting integration and harmony between these various bodies.[16]

---

[15]It is argued in doctrine whether or not such bodies are part of the National System of Consumer Protection. The same arguments presented in relation to the Public Prosecutor's Office and the Public Defender's Office are valid here. The discussion has no major practical repercussions, since, integrating or not the System, all have the duty to act in an articulated and harmonious way with the public agencies that have the main function of consumer protection, thus fulfilling the constitutional guideline of consumer protection by the State (article 5, XXXII, of the CF) and the principle of efficiency of public administration (article 37, caput, of the CF). Regarding the subject, Bruno Miragem observes that it seems to us beyond doubt that all the organs that are directly or indirectly linked to consumer protection are naturally members of the SNDC. This action, in the case of public bodies linked to the Administration, is usually manifested in the attributions of the body, which may be both the formulation of public policies for consumer protection and the regulation and supervision of the consumer market and the economic sectors that the make up. Thus, along with the public bodies directly involved in consumer protection, which at the state and municipal level are generally identified by the acronym Procon, SNDC also includes all the bodies that carry out their own consumer defense activities, including in this way the Public Prosecutor's Offices the Public Defenders, the regulatory agencies of public services, among others (Bruno Miragem, *Comments*, pp. 1143–1144).

[16]By 2012, Senacon's duties were with the Department of Consumer Protection and Defense. Decree 7,738/ 2012 changed the structure of the body. The DPDC, in accordance with Decree 7.738, now

The attributions of Senacon are listed in art. 106 of the CDC, and also in art. 3 of Decree 2.181/1997. It is important to highlight the attribution of "planning, elaborating, proposing, coordinating and executing the national consumer protection policy"; "Provide consumers with ongoing guidance on their rights and guarantees"; "To encourage, including financial resources and other special programs, the formation of consumer protection entities by the population and by state and municipal public agencies" and "to develop other activities compatible with their purposes."

There is no subordination, as already mentioned, between the National Consumer Secretariat and the civil entities and entities that make up SNDC. In practice, however, there is an effort and movement of the SNDC actors to act in an integrated and articulated way.

The legislation allows Senacon to apply the administrative sanctions envisaged to face offense to the consumer protection standard (article 56 of the CDC). It is fundamental, however, to rationalize its activities and avoid parallel oversight of the same fact, that the work is integrated with the Procons and other federal agencies to exercise the indirect guardianship of the consumer to avoid conflicting positions and discussion regarding the bis in idem.

It is remarkable the increase of the activities developed by the National Consumer Secretariat. Among several actions, this article highlights the implementation, in June 2014, of the platform consumer.gov.br, which will be dealt with in the following item.

3 The Consumer.gov.br Platform

The platform consumer.gov.br, conceived based on principles of transparency and social control, is a public service focused on solving consumption conflicts over the Internet. In summary, a free and public service that enables the resolution of consumer conflicts in a fast and unbureaucratized way, through direct communication between consumers and suppliers.[17]

The main novelty of Consumidor.gov.br is to enable direct contact between consumers and companies, in a public and transparent environment, without the intervention of the Public Authority in the individual treatment. In addition, the platform provides essential information to the design and execution of public consumer protection policies, as well as encourages market competitiveness by improving the quality of products, services and customer service.

This tool is not an administrative procedure and is not a traditional service provided by the consumer protection agencies that make up the SNDC. In this sense, the use

---

has the function of "supporting the National Consumer Secretariat in the fulfillment of the powers established in Law 8.078/ 1990". The art. 2 of Decree 2.181/ 1997, with the new wording conferred by Decree 7.738/ 2012, states: "The National Consumer Registry of the Ministry of Justice and the other Federal, State, Federal District, Municipal and the civil defense consumer organizations".

[17] According to explanations offered in the Senacon's own virtual page, it is "a new public service for alternative solution of consumption conflicts through the internet, which allows direct interaction between consumers and companies".

of this service does not exclude the possibility of State assistance provided by the State and Municipal Procons, Public Defenders, Public Ministry and Special Civil Courts.

As it is a service provided and maintained by the State, the participation of companies will only be allowed to those who formally join the service, by signing a term in which they undertake to invest all efforts to solve the problems presented by consumers. The consumer, in turn, must properly identify himself and undertake to present all the data and information related to the reported complaint.

The data recorded in the complaints feed into a public database with information on the suppliers that obtained the best resolution and satisfaction rates in the handling of complaints. The performance of the participating companies can be monitored from the "Indicators" functionality, which provides indexes on the number of completed complaints per company, percentage of solution, consumer satisfaction with service, average response time and response percentage.

With the purpose of expanding access to the platform, Senacon has been seeking the formalization of partnerships with other public entities, notably Procons, Public Defenders, Judiciary and Public Prosecutor. Specifically within the scope of the Judiciary, the platform Consumidor.gov.br has been used in strategic actions aimed at the incentive and perfecting of extra-judicial methods for settling consumer conflicts with a focus on the reduction and prevention of litigation.

Projects such as the one implemented in the Court of Justice of Rio Grande do Sul in partnership with SENACON—called "Solução Direta-Consumidor" (Direct-Consumer Solution)—increase the visibility of the platform for the alternative solution of consumer conflicts, in order to avoid the filing of a judicial process. In this case, the history of the attempt to solve the problem by the consumer on the platform can be extremely useful in the case of filing a lawsuit, as indicative of demonstrating the resistance by the supplier to redress the violated interests of the consumer.[18]

3.1 *Indicators of Platform*

From June 2014 (launch of the platform consumer.gov.br) to December 2017, more than 980 thousand complaints were registered on the platform, more than 780 thousand users registered on the site and more than 400 companies already serve their consumers through this channel.

In order to use the service, the consumer must first check if the company on which he/she wants to file a complaint is included in the list of companies that are members of the platform (companies voluntarily join the service by signing a term in which

[18]The "Direct-Consumer Solution" Project, the pioneering agreement between the Court of Justice and the National Consumer Secretariat, allows a platform to be disclosed directly on the court website and also offered in the balance sheets of the special statements, as an alternative to the judicialization. demand. Public officials were advised to pass on to citizens as instructions for the use of the registrar as requested claims. See more in https://www.tjrs.jus.br/site/processos/conciliacao/consumidor.html Access in 27/03/2019.

they undertake to know, analyze and invest all available efforts to solve the problems presented).

After the consumer register on the site and filed the complaint, the time period of 10 (ten) days for the company's manifestation begins. During this time, the company has the opportunity to interact with the consumer before posting their final response. The consumer then has up to 20 (twenty) days to comment on the response received and to classify the demand as Resolved or Unresolved and also indicate the degree of satisfaction with the service rendered by the company.

The idea is to establish that only if the problem is not solved in the platform that it will be necessary to resort to a Procon or, eventually, to Justice. The more problems that are solved at the pre-administrative level, the less conflict will overwhelm the Procons, and the fewer they will reach the Judiciary.

The average solution index of the companies in Consumidor.gov.br in 2017 was 80.6% and the average response time was 6.3 days. It stands out, in the index of solution, the Telecommunications segment that had the highest index within the platform, 88.6%.[19]

The differential of this new channel of communication in relation to those offered by the suppliers themselves is that the companies registered in the platform must demonstrate a differentiated disposition to listen and serve the consumer, since their position will be under the watchful eye of the consumer protection agencies and other consumers of civil society. In other words, accredited companies are exposed and, frankly and openly, participating in healthy competition: the one that most respects the interests and rights of the consumer wins. The virtual platform, with the dissemination of quality of service and number of resolution of demands, allows the consumer to make a comparison between suppliers and, consequently, to make better choices.

In addition to being an interesting alternative for dispute resolution between suppliers and consumers, the platform provides the State with essential information for the elaboration and implementation of public consumer protection policies and encourages competitiveness in the market by improving quality and customer service. The way the companies will operate will be closely monitored by SENACON—National Consumer Bureau, Procons and by civil society as a whole.

The platform is a relevant tool for providing data and indicators to suggest, in a collective perspective, public policies of consumer protection, in compliance with the constitutional mandate that establishes that it is the duty of the State to carry out the protection of consumer interests, the vulnerable part in consumer relations (article 5, XXXII of CF/1988).

It should always be remembered that, in terms of conflict resolution, society should not expect or depend only on judicial protection, especially in the context of the Brazilian socio-political-economic reality and the increasing number of conflicts submitted to the Judiciary. In this context, by enabling the quick consensual solution

[19]This information can be verified in the Open Data available on the platform consumer.gov.br.

of consumer disputes, the platform addresses the idea of access to the just legal order, as developed by Kazuo Watanabe.[20]

4 Conclusions

The platforms aimed at reducing judicial involvement in matters of consumer disputes promote the rescue of the idea that a judicial proceeding is justified only if a previous attempt at a resolution is not successful. The public platform for alternative solutions to consumer conflicts, consumer.gov.br, serves well for this purpose by allowing direct interaction between consumers and participating companies, which undertake to analyze and respond to the demands of their consumers in up to ten days—much shorter than what usually takes the course of a judicial process.

Conceived on the basis of the principle of transparency and social control, the tool enables the resolution of consumer conflicts in a fast and unbureaucratic way, as it brings consumers and suppliers together to present a consensual solution without the direct intervention of the Public Authority. In this scenario, it is the responsibility of the managing bodies of the platform, namely SENACON, Procons, Public Defenders, Public Prosecutors, among others, to monitor and approve compliance with the Website Terms of Use, which rules are enforceable both for companies and for consumers.

With the expansion of the SENACON partnership agreements with the Courts of Justice, consensual solutions to consumer disputes will play an even more important role in the analysis of cases by the Judiciary. This scenario, therefore, gives consumers the quicker search for the solution of their consumer issues while challenging companies to present, when appropriate, quick and effective solutions to the problems that may be questioned.

This still challenging scenario proposes to change the culture of litigation that permeates consumer relations in Brazil, which concerns not only the consumer, but also organizations and companies. Thus, combining this proposal with a coordinated action of the SNDC, as well as the regulatory models of the regulatory agencies, it is possible that, in the near future, consumer protection will abandon its characterization as the third most demanded issue of the Brazilian courts.

Reference

1. Watanabe, Kazuo. *Acesso à Justiça e sociedade Moderna. Participação e processo.* São Paulo: Revista dos Tribunais, 1988, p. 129.

[20]In the actor's conception, the problem of access to justice can not be studied in the narrow limits of the existing judicial organs. It is not only a matter of making access to justice as a state institution possible, but also facilitating access to a just legal order. Watanabe [1], p. 129.

European Air Passengers' Rights: *The Concept Of' Extraordinary Circumstances' and the Enforcement of the Right to Compensation*

Marianne Hundahl Frandsen

The European Regulation (EC) No 261/2004 establishes rights for air passengers. The passengers have the right to compensation in case of delay or cancellation unless it *"is caused by extraordinary circumstances which could not have been avoided even if all reasonable measures had been taken"*.[1] The compensation is a fixed amount of money depending on time of delay and route length.[2]

The purpose of the concept of 'extraordinary circumstances' is to limit the liability for airlines in the case of specified situations. The Regulations' preamble 14 lists examples of those situations and preamble 15 provides detailed explanation of the concept. Case law show that it is difficult to apply the concept in practice. Since 2005, the CJEU has ruled on nine cases about 'extraordinary circumstance', which has giving a decisive and clearer interpretation of the concept.[3] Denmark has 6 cases from supreme and high court and more than 15.000 cases from the Danish transport authority.

An overview of the content can be illustrated by the following:

[1] Article 5,3.

[2] Article 7 and case C-402/07 (…) paragraph 61.

[3] From 2008 – December 2018: C-294/10, C-195/07 (…), C-12/11, C-315/15, C-394/14, C-402/07 (…), C-257/14, C-549/07, C-501/17. Other cases are delete from the register with no access now; see for example C-396/06.

The research presented in this abstract is a part of my PhD thesis, which is still in progress: "The Danish passengers' legal position".

M. H. Frandsen (✉)
Aalborg University, Aalborg, Denmark
e-mail: hundahl@law.aau.dk

D. Wei et al. (eds.), *Innovation and the Transformation of Consumer Law*,
https://doi.org/10.1007/978-981-15-8948-5_20

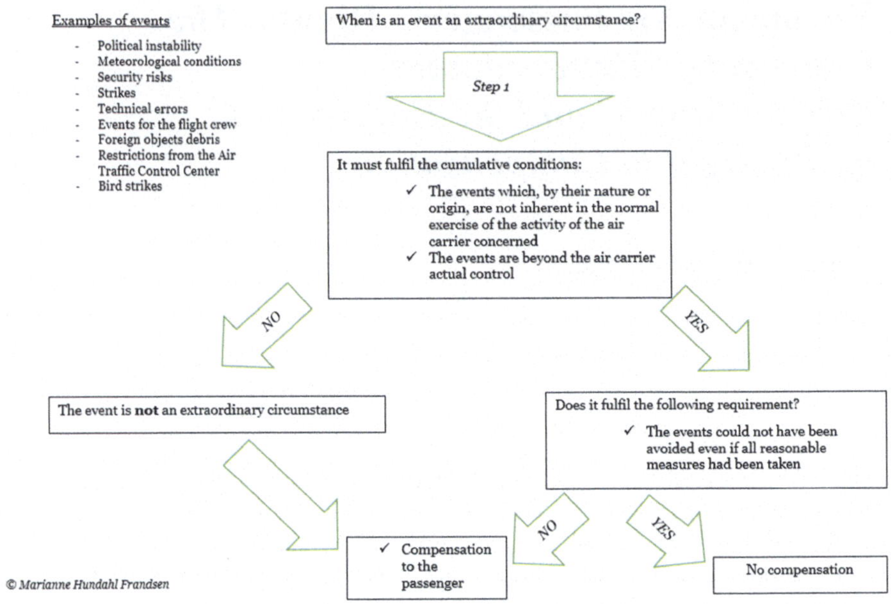

1 The Procedure of Enforcement

The passenger must apply for compensation through the airline company. The airline can deny compensation, if it can prove that the delay or cancellation is caused by an 'extraordinary circumstance'. If the passenger is not satisfied with the airline's respond or if it has not responded within 6 weeks, the passenger can complain to the Danish transport authority. The transport authority has 5 months to decide the case. If it decides in favour of the passenger and the airline does not respect their ruling, the passenger can go to court. The passenger can for free get help and advice from the European Consumer Centre Denmark after the first contact with the airline.

As an alternative to the formal procedure, the passenger can choose to send the claim to a private company, who will claim the compensation on behalf of the passenger. Denmark has four private companies that offer to take legal action against the airline in return for receiving a percentage of the passengers' compensation.[4] The companies charge between 19.8 and 25.0%, if they win and nothing if they lose ('no cure no pay'). One company claims to win 98% of their cases.[5] Another company claims to have helped more than 290.200 passengers.[6] With these numbers, it seems

[4] www.Flypenge.dk, www.flyfhjaelp.dk (www.refundmore.com), www.flyforsinkelse.dk and www.airhelp.com.

[5] https://flyhjaelp.dk/?gclid=EAIaIQobChMIoJD6j7Pc3gIVVeh3Ch2MQQRFEAAYASAAEgKb3fD_BwE.

[6] https://flyforsinkelse.dk/om-os.

to be a need for those companies. The private companies have resulted in fewer cases at the transport authority, while city courts have gotten even more.[7]

In a consumer protection perspective, there are pros and cons of the use of private companies: For example, the passenger is dependent on the company to take the case. However, the passenger safe a lot time in return of some 'compensation-money' and sometimes the amount of money is more than what the flight tickets have cost. The development of private companies was not the intention by the EU, and the concept of 'extraordinary circumstances' remains difficult and unclear.

[7]There are about 1.500 cases pending alone in the court of Copenhagen.

Specialized Courts and Consumer's Defense: The Overindebtedness Case

Patrícia Antunes Laydner and Káren R. Danilevicz Bertoncello

Due to the significant increase in the number of judicial cases and the crisis faced by justice in Brazil, there is a tendency to specialize the judicial activity by adopting specific mechanisms aiming to concentrate cases of a particular nature—such as collective rights, health, the environment and, more recently, cases involving business issues—in the hand of a small number of judges.

However, such specialization on specific cases can also have harmful effects, especially with regard to the increase of role conflicts that end delaying the resolution of claims. The delimitation of roles becomes a complicated task especially in cases of transversal rights and factual situations concerning different branches of law, contributing to the increase of conflicts and making it more difficult to understand the judiciary. One could also question whether specialization would influence the impartiality of the judge or not. It is necessary to pay special attention to possible side effects resulting from the limitation of roles once structural issues and budgetary problems could harm certain forms of specializations in the judiciary.

The present hypothesis aims to illustrate the risks of specialization and role distribution from the empirical study undertaken with consumers' over-indebtedness, devoid of legal protection in Brazil, which can be solved through personal insolvency proceedings or contract revision requests. In this context, some magistrates from the State of Rio de Janeiro started to adopt certain roles for business Courts in order to process and to judge contractual relations where they could identify the insolvency of the debtor, then it was possible to limit the percentage of payment to creditors as a way to preserve and guarantee an existential minimum, the right to basic conditions of life, for debtors.

P. Antunes Laydner (✉)
Université de Paris Sud, Paris, France
e-mail: palaydner@tjrs.jus.br

K. R. Danilevicz Bertoncello (✉)
Universidade Federal Do Rio Grande Do Sul, Porto Alegre, Brazil
e-mail: Krdb@tjrs.jus.br

D. Wei et al. (eds.), *Innovation and the Transformation of Consumer Law*,
https://doi.org/10.1007/978-981-15-8948-5_21

Therefore, in order to understand the specialization of judges in the concrete case and from the adopted parameters, some reflections were raised prospecting consequences in social relations, such as: to what extent is the fundamental right provided for in Article 5, XXXII, of the Brazilian Federal Constitution ("The State shall promote the defense of consumers") being preserved? Could the overindebted consumer be equated with the insolvent businessperson? Would this comparison allow judicial integration when restructuring liabilities, despite the absence of legal provisions? If admitted, would the court be responsible for determining the criteria of creditors case by case when restructuring liabilities? Lastly, would the judge specialized in business issues provide consumers with the fundamental right provided for in Article 5, XXXII, of the Brazilian Federal Constitution considering that the same judge is customarily used to interpret the Law from a corporate point of view as to protect and satisfy creditors?

Therefore, a general analysis of the context of specialized Courts in the Brazilian System (A) should be done before addressing the issue of role adequacy for dealing with overindebted consumers by the specialized protection of business Courts.

A. The context of Court Specialization in Brazil

As mentioned in the introduction, there is currently a tendency in Brazil to create specialized Courts for different subjects. Whether this trend is due to several factors justifying the adoption of concentrated models of role limitation (1) or not, it is also necessary to take into account possible drawbacks of specialization (2).

1. The specialization of court jurisdiction as a trend

Within each legal system, several factors lead to the definition of the people responsible for having decision-making power. In general, the complexity of the facts, the importance of the legal interests protected and the desire to unburden jurisdictional authorities are the grounds for measures to justice reorganization. Therefore, it is affirmed that "the complexity and the increasing number of legal rules may lead to the specialization of courts, while the increase in the number of cases leads to multiple jurisdictions or to separate them into different forms of judgement",[1] and that the judicial crisis leads to new forms of judicial organization.[2]

For those who defend court specialization, this mechanism would speed up the processes to get final judgements, making them more effective and contributing to the standardization of decisions (an essential aspect in Brazil, where the system of precedents is not adopted). In this sense, a study carried out by the University of Denver[3] states that among what justifies the specialization in the specific case of

[1] F. Kernaleguen, Institutions judiciaires, Paris, LexisNexis, 2013, 5e édition, p. 75.

[2] L. Cadiet, J. Normand, S. A. Mekki, Théorie générale du procès, Paris, Puf, 2013, 2e éd., p. 425.

[3] G. Pring et C. Pring, « Specialized Environmental Courts and Tribunals at the Confluence of Human Rights and the Environment », Oregon Review of International Law, n 2, 2009, available in http://www.eufje.org/images/DocDivers/Rapport%20Pring.pdf (consulté le 01.10.15).

environmental law is: (a) the reduction of time required for judgement of cases, (b) the reduction of delays, (c) the improvement in the quality of decisions and uniformity of interpretation and application of law. Indeed, because it involves an internal reorganization that allows for new divisions of the workload and the unburdening of certain courts, it is possible to find in court specialization one of the possible answers to the problem of efficiency of justice.

One of the elements that lead to specialization is precisely the complexity of the Law, which is not a recent phenomenon and was very clearly described by Jean CARBONNIER at the end of the fifties: "from east to west one may notice that legal civilizations which are believed to be so distinct suffer from the same evils: bureaucracy, technocracy, managerialism. Urbanization, industrialization, wars, economic crises, as well as the proliferation of diplomas of Law (…) were decisive for the development of an enormous, artificial and complex Law designed and applied by law firms, yet felt by the people, like a foreign body."[4]

Indeed, from the advance of the postmodern society, Law is marked by globalization, fast communication and development of new technologies, which leads to a critical degree of complexity.

The difficulties inherent to the so-called complexity are many: perplexity, legal insecurity, instability of norms. Citizens have difficulties understanding and accessing the Law, and they also feel lost against the constant flow of extraordinarily complex rules and regulations. The legislator, who is a victim but also a perpetrator of complexity, is engaged in a fight between external pressure and the problematic maintenance of system coherence. Public agents, economic agents, they all find themselves immersed in a system whose complexity (see synonym) makes it almost inaccessible. As explained by Mireille DELMAS-MARTY, the complexity of the law is an inevitable phenomenon, which represents a new realism "adapted to the complexity of the real world",[5] leaving no alternative for its solution than that of "turning disorder into another kind of order", by the use of adapted mechanisms.[6]

Besides the complexity, it is a fact that the Brazilian judicial system has been facing a crisis, illustrated by the difficulties found regarding the excessive volume of cases, budgetary restrictions and difficulties to reduce the number of old processes. The Brazilian judicial system, often criticized by the media and citizens, is object of constant studies and reforms. Problems that are commonly associated with public discontent are the slowness of the judiciary, high operational costs and difficulties in accessing justice.[7]

---

[4]J. Carbonnier, Observations sur le colloque réalisé à Varsovie, du 10 au 16 septembre 1958, portant sur « Le concept de la légalité dans les pays socialistes », *in* Écrits, Textes rassemblés par R. Verdier, Paris, PUF, 2008, p. 1166.

[5]M. Delmas--Marty, «Préface» *in* M. Doat, J. Le Goff et P. Pé´drot, dir., Droit et complexité, pour une *nouvelle intelligence du droit vivant (actes du colloque de Brest de 2006, 2007), Rennes, PUF, 2007, p. 7.*

[6]*Ibid.*, p. 12.

[7]Therefore, check E. Capellari, "A crise do Poder Judiciário no contexto da modernidade: a necessidade de uma definição conceitual", Revista de Informação Legislativa, a. 38, n. 152, out/dez. 2010, p. 137. E. Von Mülhen et G. Masina point to certain possible causes

In order to try to solve the increasing number of cases, the Brazilian system has been adopting methods of judicial organization influenced by private management models. Due to this phenomenon, which is not exclusive to the Brazilian system, the discussions about the administration of Justice started to change its course and are not only restricted to law professionals anymore. Under the control of the Brazilian National Council of Justice,[8] mechanisms of strategic management are increasingly adopted by the courts, and specialization is part of this framework. The use of private models, however, also brings some drawbacks. For Paul MARTENS, management irruption in public administration represents a new kind of standardization of the work of judges. For him, behind these seemingly harmless "magicians", the statisticians and the accountants, hide "gurus of neoliberal revolution" that tend to progressively replace reflection by performance, strengthening productivity, competition and a type of quality which can be understood as singularly quantitative.[9]

The spirit of a constant pursuit of productivity is also reflected in the adoption of specialization systems, usually geared to the dynamization of jurisdictional provision, which does not necessarily complement the active defense of rights, especially if we take into account the difficulties arising from specialization.

2. Challenges faced by specialization

Jurisdictions are considered by the Brazilian Federal Constitution as unique expressions of the same power[10] and follow different classifications depending on how the power is shared within the judicial structure. The rules about the judicial organization are not resulting from chance and do not concern the interests of the judicial power and the desires of productivity exclusively. On the contrary, as it is a public service intended to meet the interests of the community, justice must be organized in order to administrate the number of cases demanded but also guarantee access to justice and equal treatment to all citizens, as well as the effectiveness of judgements. The judicial organization is, therefore, both a "starting point" and a "turning point",

for this crisis: a precarious and disproportionate structure to the volume of cases demanded, excessive growth in cases, the large number of lawyers entering the market each year, the complexity and instability of the legislative system. "O princípio da razoável duração do processo", *in* F.C. Machado, R.B. Machado, dir., A reforma do Poder Judiciário, São Paulo, Quartier Latin, 2006, p. 145.

[8]According to G. Mendes, former president of the Supreme Court and Brazilian National Council of Justice, improving the provision of the justice as a public service implies the untiring pursuit of an evolution in administrative management, to reduce costs and to maximize the effectiveness of resources. *In* A Reforma do Sistema Judiciário no Brasil: elemento fundamental para garantir segurança jurídica *ao investimento estrangeiro no País* (speech given at the l'OCDE in May/2009) http://www.stf.jus.br/repositorio/cms/portalStfInternacional/portalStfAgenda_pt_br/anexo/discParisport1.pdf (consultado em 19.02.14).

[9]P. Martens, «Préface» in B. Frydman, E. Jeuland, dir., Le nouveau management de la justice et l'indépendance des juges, Paris, Dalloz, 2011, p. 2.

[10]According to Article 92 of the Federal Constitution, the Judiciary Power is one in Brazil, but divided into several bodies, such as the Federal and State Courts, Labor Court, Military Court, Electoral Justice and Superior Courts.

once the resolution of a conflict depends to a large extent on the court to which it is assigned.[11]

Competence and Jurisdiction are first and foremost a manifestation of power,[12] which is understood as the "extension of the power to judge belonging to a jurisdiction".[13] Thus, specialization necessarily involves a limitation of the power of the judge. This limitation affects the specialized judge, whose jurisdiction is generally framed by regulations limiting his area, but it also reduces the power of other judges who, due to a new delimitation of competence and jurisdiction, will be deprived of contact with the respective matter. It is not uncommon, therefore, that certain specialization initiatives run into internal resistance.[14]

The resistance can be even higher when one thinks of the influence that specialization can exert on the impartiality of the judge and the principle of natural justice. This principle, taken initially from Italian doctrine, relies on an idea of equality between the parties. It is widely adopted in Brazil and aims to guarantee that the parties are judged by a judge previously defined by law, it also implies the generality and predictability of the system of competence and jurisdiction division, prohibiting the existence of exemption courts. Although specialization courts and exemption courts do not communicate, there is resistance to specialization justified by this principle[15] and the impartiality of the specialized judge is questioned.

As Ricardo LORENZETTI points out, there is always the risk that the highly specialized judge will give greater importance to issues of his knowledge, to what he is familiar with, as if it were a unique subject, which can also lead to judicial activism and the imbalance of the system.[16] If it seems challenging to oppose to specialization using the particular argument of impartiality, one must not forget that the specialized judge tends to adopt a more direct approach to the issues he is concerned with. If this does not prevent the adoption of more effective systems of allocation of competences and jurisdiction, it must at least be taken into account when setting such roles.

Moreover, one must not forget that the more specialized jurisdictions are, the higher is the probability of arising problems regarding the choice of what court can decide on each matter. The boundaries between different competences are never

[11] E. Jeuland, Droit processuel général, Paris, Montchrestien, 2012, 2ème édition, p. 119.

[12] Within the Judiciary of each nation, the various bodies that constitute the jurisdictions are organized in such a way as to allow the work of the judicial power within the limits of competence and jurisdiction of each body, and according to the amount of jurisdiction assigned to each body. A. G. Carneiro, Jurisdição e competência, São Paulo, Saraiva, 2013, p. 73.

[13] E. Jeuland, *op. cit.*, p. 349.

[14] V. P. De Freitas e A. M. Agostini discuss an internal resistance of the judiciary to accept the fragmentation of the jurisdiction, *in* "A especialização da jurisdição ambiental como garantia de efetividade do direito fundamental ao meio ambiente ecologicamente equilibrado", Revista da AJURIS, v. 39, n. 128, dezembro 2012, http://livepublish.iob.com.br/ntzajuris/lpext.dll/Infobase/2b0a/2b91/351d?fn=documentframe.htm&f=templates&2.0 (consulté le 27.06.14).

[15] In a criminal claim for money laundering, for example, the offense against the principle of natural judge has been alleged because the judgement was awarded by a specialized federal Court, the allegation was eventually dismissed by the Supreme Court of Justice. (RHC no 59420/SP, relator Min. Ericson Maranho, 15.12.15.).

[16] R. Lorenzetti, Teoria da decisão judicial, São Paulo, Revista dos Tribunais, 2009, p. 57.

definite and the possibilities of increasing conflicts—which can end up delaying the judgement[17]—cannot be disregarded.

This risk is mainly present regarding cross-border rights or involving multidisciplinary matters. Some issues can be analyzed, at least in theory, from the point of view of different branches of law. This is the case in situations of over-indebtedness, which, as well shall see, require the protection of the system of consumer defense code but also run the risk of being considered as a situation of insolvency.

B. The over-indebted consumer in Brazilian Law

The Consumer Defense Code, Law n. 8.078/90, provides for in its Article 4, I, as an integral principle of the National Consumer Relations Policy as follows: "acknowledgement of consumer vulnerability on the consumer market". Therefore, the law recognizes this principle as an absolute presumption with regard to the individual consumer and has focused attention on the different types of vulnerabilities identified in consumer relations as a way to protect consumer fragility.[18]

The subject is also pointed out in international studies, given the apparent imbalance. It seems intuitive to verify the need for different levels of protection with regard to the over-indebted consumer. Such interpretation does not act contrary to the constitutional provision that determines the protection of the consumer. In this sense, "consumer vulnerability can take many different forms and affect consumers differently depending on where their vulnerability lies at. For example, economic vulnerability impacts many consumers negatively when participating in the market. Research suggests that consumers tend to be overly optimistic about their future income and do not take into account the probability of illness, divorce, accident, loss of a job that results in financial difficulty".[19]

After defining the premise of consumer vulnerability, we must note the inexistence of legal precept aiming at the treatment of the situations of over-indebtedness in Brazil. Currently, Bill n. 3515 which provides for the prevention and treatment of over-indebtedness in Brazil, was approved by the Federal Senate, but it is subject to discussion in the Chamber of Deputies. This bill was inspired in the voluntary work

---

[17]The judge may deny his competence and jurisdiction for a specific case in Brazil, but if the judge addressed does not comply with it, a conflict may arise. This shall then be analyzed by the higher court if the judges are members of the same court. As longs as the conflict is not solved, the case shall be suspended. The lack of competence and jurisdiction may also be required by the parties involved and the respective decisions challenge appeal, which can also delay the trial. In case of conflict of competence and jurisdiction between members of different courts, the Superior Court of Justice shall decide upon this fact, this court is also overburdened and responsible for the appeals concerning federal laws. In this context, it is common to see issues of competence and jurisdiction being raised by the parties as a defense strategy aimed precisely at delaying the analysis of the case.

[18]According to MARQUES, Cláudia Lima; MIRAGEM, Bruno. *O novo direito privado e a proteção dos vulneráveis*. São Paulo: Revista dos Tribunais, 2014.

[19]Tekman, Nezihe. Vulnerable consumer: a new yardstick for the European consumer law? *In Consumer Protection: current challenges and perspectives*. Porto Alegre: Orquestra, 2017, p. 40.

of the Brazilian Judiciary as a result of joint action with the academy (UFRGS, Prof. Cláudia Lima Marques).[20]

This pioneering project aims to insert back in the social scenario the consumer under over-indebtedness situation. This goal is obtained throughout conciliation hearings—within or outside of the course of legal action. These hearings serve to renegotiate with all the creditors at once. A judge coordinates the work during the hearing proposing the renegotiation with each debtor according to the financial possibilities of the person afflicted with the over-indebtedness making sure it will be set aside a minimum amount as a living stipend.

In this context, it is up to the consumer to choose the voluntary procedure, adopted as a self-assessment available by the Judiciary Power, as an alternative dispute resolution method.[21] The disadvantages could be the absence of compulsory attendance of creditors to conciliation hearings or the filling of lawsuits to review clauses. Actions claiming for review are commonly filled in Brazil as a way to question abusive clauses and charges that contribute to the excess of debts, although initially, the credit concession itself did not consider the consumer's repayment capacity.[22]

Regarding the discussion of legal claims for reviewing contractual clauses, the filling is directed to civil courts, aiming at limiting the percentage of discounts in the consumer's salary for payment of the loan. However, some judges decided to interpret the consumer's declaration of over-indebtedness and the respective questioning of abusive clauses in loan agreements as a self-declaration of civil insolvency, which is the reason why such cases were referred to business Courts such as Judicial Recovery.

The Rio de Janeiro Court of Justice[23] understood that the consumer's request did not authorize the interpretation of its declaration as self-insolvency, and determined that it should be decided in the civil courts. Then, the judicial decision recognized the possibility of a new payment plan without the agreement of creditors, a condition that is required in the system of civil insolvency, as provided for in article 783 of the Brazilian Code of Civil Procedure. Furthermore, the order to grant credit started to be considered as a way to provide responsible credit, as the chronological order is part of the decision regarding whom the consumer would pay first.[24]

---

[20]Bertoncello, Káren Rick Danilevicz; LIMA, Clarissa Costa de. ADHESION TO THE PROJECT 'IT IS NICE TO CONCILIATE'—THE NATIONAL COUNCIL OF JUSTICE/ CNJ PIONEER PROJECT: "THE TREATMENT OF THE SITUATION OF THE CONSUMER OVERINDEBTEDNESS". *Revista de Direito do Consumidor,* São Paulo, n. 63, pp.173–201, jul./set.2007.

[21]Ramos, Fabiana D'Andrea; Ferreira, Vitor Hugo do Amaral. Consumer protection and ADR: comments about vulnerability. *In Consumer Protection: current challenges and perspectives.* Porto Alegre: Orquestra, 2017, pp. 185–197.

[22]About this, LIMA, Clarissa Costa de. LIMA, Clarissa Costa de; Bertoncello, Káren Rick Danilevicz. *Superendividamento aplicado:aspectos doutrinários e experiência no Poder Judiciário.* Rio de Janeiro: GZ, 2009.

[23]Porto, Antônio José Maristello; Sampaio, Patrícia Regina Pinheiro. Superendividamento e insolvência civil no Rio de Janeiro: um estudo empírico. *Revista de Direito Empresarial*, Fórum, Rio de Janeiro, set.-dez/2014, pp. 51–70.

[24]Nesse sentido, situam-se as decisões proferidas nos julgados: Agravo de Instrumento n.0034238-26.2012.8.19.0000, Apelação n.0369073-03.2008.8.19.0001, Apelação n.379317-49.2012.8.19.001.

It is important to highlight that the procedure provided for in the Brazilian Code of Civil Procedure for cases of civil insolvency remains under the provision of the Code of Civil Procedure from 1973, pursuant to Article 1052 of the Code of Civil Procedure from 2015. Therefore, the creditor has in the Brazilian juridical scenario the provision of the Code of Civil Procedure on articles 748 and 786 to the hypothesis of civil insolvency of the debtor (person and not a company) when the debts exceed the amount of all the debtor's assets. However, this is not a system to treat the over-indebtedness because it configures a modality of 'enforcement for a certain amount against the debtor' suing the debtor for a specific amount. The insolvency declaration can be by the initiative of the creditor or even of the debtor and has as an effect the anticipation on the payments deadline, the gathering of all his/her patrimony susceptible of pledge (the actual and those acquired during the course of the lawsuit) and the 'enforcement by bankruptcy law of its creditors/all the creditors can sue the debtor having some of them preference on the amount of the credits obtained. In this type of action called 'enforcement', the causes that generate the over-indebtedness are not investigated, its goal is to define the state or patrimony of the debtor and to declare who are the creditors that are going to be taken part in this collective action of 'enforcement'. In other words, there is no similarity between the relief systems found in Comparative Law,[25] and they do not aim to prevent social problems related to the over-indebtedness.[26]

Therefore, the analysis of the judicial decisions in question is in full harmony with the doctrine investigating the extension of the interpretation of Article 480 of the Civil Code[27] and Article 4, III, of the Consumer Defense Code, which provides for the incidence of good-faith in consumer relations. According to Cláudia Lima Marques, the recognition of the "general duty of renegotiation in long-term contracts" is based on the duties of cooperation, good-faith and the alteration of circumstances in terms of equity (*exceção de ruína,* a term coming from German Law).[28] One of the aims of good-faith, according to the German doctrine, is the correction and adaptation in case of changing circumstances,[29] and so serving as the basis of the duty of renegotiation in case of a breach.

The application of the principle of good-faith as a way to analyze the conditions under which credit is granted and the identification of over-indebtedness have also been outlined by decisions taken by the 23rd Civil Chamber of the Court of Justice of

[25]See also: Kilborn, Jason J. Comportamentos econômicos, superendividamento; estudo comparativo da insolvência do consumidor: buscando as causas e avaliando soluções. *Direitos do consumidor endividado.* São Paulo: Revista dos Tribunais, 2006.

[26]Bertoncello, Káren R. Danilevicz; LIMA, Clarissa Costa de. ADHESION TO THE PROJECT ' IT IS NICE TO CONCILIATE'—THE NATIONAL COUNCIL OF JUSTICE/ CNJ PIONEER PROJECT: "THE TREATMENT OF THE SITUATION OF THE CONSUMER OVERINDEBTEDNESS". *Revista de Direito do Consumidor,* São Paulo, n. 63, pp. 173–201, jul./set.2007.

[27]Article 480 do CC: "Se no contrato as obrigações couberem a apenas uma das partes, poderá ela pleitear que a sua obrigação seja reduzida, ou alterado o modo de executa-la, a fim de evitar a onerosidade excessiva.".

[28]Marques, *Contratos...,* p. 245.

[29]Marques, *Contratos...,* p. 186.

Rio Grande do Sul.[30,31] The judgement initially declared competence and jurisdiction for judging a case in which the conditions for granting a credit card were questioned, and then to define the abusive appropriation of the entire income of the consumer to pay the debt with the respective identification of the over-indebted situation of the consumer.[32]

1 Initial Conclusions

The decisions undertaken by the two Higher Courts regarding the identification of situations of over-indebtedness of consumer indicate the need to approve the Bill n. 3515, in particular, because the regulation of such issue both from a material and a procedural point of view must be based on the global view of the social phenomenon. After all, if the aim of the law of judicial reorganization (Law. 11.101/2005) is to preserve the social character of companies acting towards wealth and also worker

[30] JUÍZO DE RETRATAÇÃO. APELAÇÃO CÍVEL. CONTRATO DE CRÉDITO PESSOAL. SUPERENDIVIDAMENTO DE DIREITO E DE FATO. BOA-FÉ OBJETIVA NUMA VERSÃO DE EQUIDADE E ABUSO DE DIREITO. PECULIARIDADE DO CASO CONCRETO EM QUE SE FIXA A TAXA DOS JUROS REMUNERATÓRIOS EM 12% AO ANO. MANTIVERAM O DESPROVIMENTO DO APELO DO RÉU E PROVIMENTO DO APELO DO AUTOR, EM JUÍZO DE RETRATAÇÃO. UNÂNIME. (Apelação Cível Nº 70071338305, Vigésima Terceira Câmara Cível, Tribunal de Justiça do RS, Relator: Clademir José Ceolin Missaggia, Julgado em 25/09/2018).

[31] APELAÇÃO CÍVEL. AÇÃO REVISIONAL. CONTRATO DE CARTÃO DE CRÉDITO. SUPERENDIVIDAMENTO DE DIREITO E DE FATO. BOA-FÉ OBJETIVA NUMA VERSÃO DE EQUIDADE E ABUSO DE DIREITO. PECULIARIDADES DO CASO CONCRETO EM QUE SE FIXA A TAXA DOS JUROS REMUNERATÓRIOS LIMITADA EM 12% AO ANO. CASO EM QUE O LIMITE DE CRÉDITO CONCEDIDO É INCOMPATÍVEL COM A CAPACIDADE ECONÔMICA DO CONSUMIDOR. 1. Juros Remuneratórios. Do caderno processual, extrai-se que o autor é aposentado e beneficiário da Assistência Judiciária Gratuita. Na fatura com vencimento em agosto de 2010, verifica-se que o limite total de crédito que lhe foi conferido era de R$ 6.320,00 e o total da fatura era de R$ 8.841,00 e a do mês anterior era de 7.197,89 sendo que as despesas lançadas são mínimas e a dívida aumentou de forma progressiva e exacerbada, chegando a R$ 11.453,10 em 20 de dezembro do mesmo ano. 2. Capitalização. Ausente previsão contratual de forma expressa, deve ser afastada em qualquer periodicidade. 3. Comissão de permanência. Inexiste interesse processual se não há previsão contratual tampouco cobrança na fatura acostada aos autos. Pedido de afastamento não conhecido. 4. Juros moratórios. Os juros moratórios decorrem de previsão legal e são limitados em 1% ao mês. Inteligência da Súmula nº. 379 do Superior Tribunal de Justiça. Mantida a cobrança. POR MAIORIA, DERAM PARCIAL PROVIMENTO AO APELO DO AUTOR, VENCIDO O DESEMBARGADOR CLADEMIR JOSÉ CEOLIN MISSAGGIA QUE DAVA PARCIAL PROVIMENTO EM MAIOR EXTENSÃO. (Apelação Cível Nº 70068400480, Vigésima Terceira Câmara Cível, Tribunal de Justiça do RS, Relator: Clademir José Ceolin Missaggia, Julgado em 27/03/2018).

[32] Agravo de instrumento n.70068130376: CONTRATO DE CARTÃO DE CRÉDITO. COMPETÊNCIA EXCLUSIVA DAS VIGÉSIMA TERCEIRA E VIGÉSIMA QUARTA CÂMARAS CÍVEIS. COMPETÊNCIA DECLINADA. (Agravo de Instrumento Nº 70068130376, Décima Sexta Câmara Cível, Tribunal de Justiça do RS, Relator: Paulo Sérgio Scarparo, Julgado em 29/01/2016) e AGRAVO DE INSTRUMENTO. CONTRATOS DE CARTÃO DE CRÉDITO. AÇÃO REVISIONAL. RETENÇÃO DE PROVENTOS DE APOSENTADORIA CREDITADO

protection, it seems urgent to recognize the importance of the legal protection of the over-indebted consumer, as a natural person who is a member of a family.

The initial thoughts indicated by the global analysis of over-indebtedness and the preservation of the principle of the dignity of human being, as constitutionally guaranteed by Article 1, III, show that: "The problem of debtor and creditor perspectives in bankruptcy is also one of rival-form ambiguity. If one sees the perspective of only the debtor or the creditor, one is observing less than the full picture. If one is unaware that another image exists, the image one sees appears complete. But more than the image exists. Development of a complete bankruptcy system requires that we consider the perspective of both debtors and creditors."[33]

Considering the social repercussion of the phenomenon, the effects go beyond family consequences to achieve collective well-being: "In the bankruptcy context, dual perspectives are insufficient. There is yet another perspective to consider: the interest of the community."[34]

EM CONTA-CORRENTE. SALDO DEVEDOR DE CHEQUE ESPECIAL. SUPERENDIVIDAMENTO. 1. DA UTILIZAÇÃO DO PROVENTOS DO AUTOR PARA COBRIR SALDO DEVEDOR—As instituições financeiras não podem se valer da integralidade do pensionamento do correntista que lhe é confiado em depósito para abater saldo devedor da conta-corrente.—De acordo com o disposto no art. 7º, X, da CF, o salário do trabalhador tem caráter alimentar e inviolável, pois se destina ao seu sustento e ao de sua família. 2. SUPERENDIVIDAMENTO—Na espécie, caracterizado o superendividamento, tendo em vista o débito contraído pelo autor com a instituição financeira ré, de forma a minar seus vencimentos ao ponto de não conseguir mais manter o necessário para a mantença do seu mínimo existencial. 3. TUTELA ANTECIPADA—Demonstrada prova inequívoca do alegado e a verossimilhança da alegação associadas a uma das hipóteses previstas nos incisos I e II do art. 273 do CPC, vai deferida a liminar no sentido de proibir a utilização dos proventos de aposentadoria do autor, para cobrir saldo devedor junto à instituição bancária. - No que tange ao pedido de estorno das verbas salariais já utilizadas, deve-se aguardar ou a angularização ou o final da instrução processual, quando novos elementos deverão aportar ao feito, permitindo, melhor exame. AGRAVO DE INSTRUMENTO PARCIALMENTE PROVIDO. (Agravo de Instrumento Nº 70068130376, Vigésima Terceira Câmara Cível, Tribunal de Justiça do RS, Relator: Ana Paula Dalbosco, Julgado em 18/02/2016).

[33]Gross, Karen. *Failure and forgiveness: rebalancing the bankruptcy system.* New Haven: Yale University Press, 1999, p.18.

[34]*Idem, ibidem*, p. 19.

Toward Regulatory Mass Redress Schemes—Mass Redress in Financial Mis-selling Scandals in the U.S., the U.K. and South Korea

Youkyung Huh

1 Introduction

Collective actions such as class litigation, once hailed as the conventional go-to remedy for mass harm, have proved to be expensive, inefficient, and ineffective.[1] Alternative dispute resolution systems (ADR), online dispute resolution (ODR) systems, and collective forms of ADR/ODR[2] are increasingly gaining attention as possible solutions.[3] In some nations, the role of the consumer ombudsman has come to the fore. *Regulatory redress schemes*, often used in tandem with consumer ombudsmen systems, are the newest redress "technology,"[4] and they are the focus of this paper. The term "regulatory redress" refers broadly to a situation where the "intervention of a public authority" ensures recompense for injured consumers.[5] This regulatory power can include both "soft" influence (where a public authority might be able to persuade, conciliate, or mediate redress) and "hard" enforcement (where a public authority requires a redress scheme).

This paper analyzes case studies from three nations that have recently used regulatory redress schemes to address widespread financial mis-selling scandals. In response to the inappropriate sales of credit card add-on products in the United

[1] *See generally* CHRISTOPHER HODGES & STEFAAN VOET, DELIVERING COLLECTIVE REDRESS: NEW TECHNOLOGIES (Hart Publishing, 2018).

[2] Some ADR bodies have the capacity to aggregate individual claims and decide them collectively, while others do not. *Id*. at 2.

[3] *See* [1].

[4] HODGES & VOET (2018), *supra* note 1, at 7.

[5] *Id.* at 153.

Y. Huh (✉)
Busan, Korea
e-mail: kantorka60@gmail.com

D. Wei et al. (eds.), *Innovation and the Transformation of Consumer Law*,
https://doi.org/10.1007/978-981-15-8948-5_22

States, the Consumer Financial Protection Bureau (CFPB) ordered financial companies to repay consumers whom these deceptive practices harmed.[6] In the United Kingdom, the Financial Conduct Authority (FCA) and the Financial Ombudsman Service (FOS) ordered and managed consumer redress schemes that reimbursed millions of consumers who were mis-sold payment protection insurance (PPI) policies.[7] In South Korea, the Financial Supervisory Service (FSS) advised financial companies to repay consumers for mis-sold credit card add-on products.

It is not a coincidence that the regulatory case studies that I have chosen all involve harm to consumers caused by financial products. Regulatory mass redress works exceptionally well in the financial services sector because, unlike any other industry, it is a heavily regulated industry that offers regulators unique opportunities to access information and intervene at an early stage. The wide variety of enforcement mechanisms available to financial regulators creates incentives for the regulated entities to offer redress voluntarily and promptly. Further, as the consumer harm that financial products cause can easily be widespread, inconspicuous, and of low-value in individual cases, it is likely that policymakers have come to consider regulatory mass redress as an attractive alternative to traditional class action litigation.

Regulatory redress schemes operate in the broader milieu of each nation's unique civil justice system and financial regulatory architecture. In the U.S. and the U.K., financial authorities promulgate, impose, and operate explicit legal mandates, guidelines, and procedures regarding consumer restitution or redress schemes. In contrast, the South Korean case lacks a legal basis for its consumer redress scheme and is much more informal.

What these regula tory redress schemes have in common is that they can be very accessible, effective, and efficient, particularly in low-value but widespread financial mis-selling cases. However, regulatory redress schemes are not without drawbacks. Critics argue that consent replaces the rule of law, and administrative actions replace due process.[8] They also raise the concern that the new processes emphasize efficiency over the right to a fair trial by an independent judiciary that will consider the evidence and apply the law.[9] Thus, designing an optimal regulatory redress scheme becomes a balancing act between efficiency gains and due process. This paper reflects on the implications of these three case studies and proposes various factors that legislators should consider when designing regulatory redress schemes.

---

[6]See *Factsheet* CONSUMER FINANCIAL PROTECTION BUREAU: ENFORCING FEDERAL CONSUMER PROTECTION LAWS (Jul. 2017), https://www.consumerfinance.gov/documents/5074/201707_cfpb_factsheet_enforcing-federal-consumer-protection-laws.pdf [https://perma.cc/P5LK-52UN]; CONSUMER FINANCIAL PROTECTION BUREAU, CFPB Orders Bank of America to Pay $727 Million in Consumer Relief for Illegal Credit Card Practices (Apr. 9, 2014), https://www.consumerfinance.gov/about-us/newsroom/cfpb-orders-bank-of-america-to-pay-727-million-in-consumer-relief-for-illegal-credit-card-practices/ [https://perma.cc/KCX7-XJ8E].

[7]*See generally,* [2].

[8]Legg [3].

[9]*Id.*

2 Delivering Consumer Redress

2.1 Pathways to Delivery

Modern consumer protection policy appropriately places consumers' rights to redress at its center.[10] There are several pathways to delivering redress for consumer harm, although some are more effective and efficient than others. Here, I briefly survey the options available to consumers around the world and examine recent global trends and discussions.

Access to judicial redress is the most common form of recompense available to harmed consumers in most nations.[11] Legislators modify traditional civil procedures, however, when they seek to redress the imbalance between the consumers and the industry that stem from information and bargaining power asymmetry.[12] Further, in the consumer and competition area, many cases involve mass injuries, where harm is widespread but individual claims are small. In this situation, it is rational for individual consumers to choose *not* to litigate because their expected benefits from a court claim do not justify the related costs.[13]

Collective redress has successfully extended the protection of the law to consumers for whom individual civil actions have proven unviable. Collective redress in the form of *judicial class litigation* is the most well known scheme.[14] In a class action suit, a group of individuals who have suffered the same or similar loss or harm can resolve their claims (with the same or similar legal or factual issues) against a defendant in a single litigation. Class action mechanisms allow a day in court for low-value individual cases arising from a broad-based consumer harm, which would otherwise not be possible.

Many variations of class action mechanisms exist. The U.S.-style of these is the most well known and the most widely used.[15] Recently, however, jurisdictions that are in the process of adopting a class action system, or of reforming their existing system, have consciously rejected the litigation-friendly culture of the U.S., and are instead devising mechanisms that suit their own jurisdictions.[16] For example, when considering the collective redress system for the EU, the EU Commission's 2018 proposal on collective redress sets higher barriers to litigation that typically apply to

---

[10]*See* [4].

[11]*Id.* at 6 ("available to all UNCTAD member states" which consists of 195 nations across the world). *See* UNCTAD, Membership of UNCTAD and of the Trade and Development Board, https://unctad.org/en/Pages/About%20UNCTAD/UNCTADs-Membership.aspx [https://perma.cc/U2N8-JXC3].

[12]UNCTAD (2018), *supra* note 10, at 6.

[13]*See* [5].

[14]*See* Hodges, *supra* note 13; UNCTAD (2018), *supra* note 10, at 6.

[15]*See* Hodges, *supra* note 13, at 11.

[16]*See,* e.g., Japan, Korea, and the EU.

the U.S.[17] South Korea, which is currently contemplating class action reform, also tends to opt for a more limited, EU-style collective redress.

Regardless of the specific form (U.S.-style or EU-recommended style), court-led consumer redress has proven to be expensive, inefficient, and ineffective as a remedy for mass harm.[18] Court proceedings (whether collective or not), present challenges for consumers, including the lengthy duration of the procedures, the associated high costs (especially if the action fails), and the complexity of laws and procedures.[19] Some commentators even argue that litigation-based actions are "old technologies" compared to some of the newer options that this paper discusses below.[20]

Policymakers have developed alternative dispute resolution (ADR) methods as alternatives to costly litigation. ADR is a way of settling a complaint out of court with the assistance of impartial dispute resolution bodies such as conciliators, mediators, arbitrators, ombudsmen, and complaint boards. ADR is an attractive option for consumer disputes because it is easier, faster, and less expensive than going to court. This option first appeared in the U.S., then spread to other countries, including Canada, Australia, South Korea, and several in Europe. The EU directive on consumer ADR sets forth the quality criteria that it requires ADR bodies to meet to ensure that they resolve disputes in an effective, fair, independent, and transparent manner.[21]

Another new form of redress is online dispute resolution (ODR). The digital dimension of the market has grown in importance as consumers purchase and transact more online. ODR consists of mechanisms for resolving disputes by using electronic communication.[22] It can offer simple, efficient, fast, and low-cost out-of-court solutions.[23] Major online platforms like eBay and Paypal were the first to develop ODR.[24] ODR platforms can manage significantly more complaints than can any court system.[25] Emulating these private ODR systems, more countries are adopting

---

[17]EU, The New Deal. The EU style collective redress is opt-in style, whereas US style is opt out, loser pay model, generally lower amounts of compensation and allowing for representative action.

[18]*See* Hodges (2012), *supra* note 13, at 18; *See generally,* HODGES & VOET (2018), *supra* note 1.

[19]UNCTAD (2018), *supra* note 10, at 6. Alexander Biard, *Collective Redress in the EU: A Rainbow Behind the Clouds?*, 18 ERA FORUM 189, 195 (2018), https://doi.org/10.1007/s12027-018-0509-4 [https://perma.cc/3DX2-6JEJ] (citing an evaluation report of the EU, "in practice affected persons do not use them due to the rigid conditions sent out in national legislation, the lengthy nature of procedures or perceived excessive costs in relation to the expected benefits of the actions.").

[20]*See generally* [6].

[21]European Parliament, Directive 2013/11/EU of the European Parliament and of the Council of 21 May 2013 on Alternative Dispute Resolution for Consumer Disputes and Amending Regulation (EC) No. 2006/2004 and Directive 2009/22/EC (June 18, 2013), https://eur-lex.europa.eu/legal-content/EN/TXT/?uri=celex%3A32013L0011 [https://perma.cc/L9SC-VB2W].

[22]PABLO CORTÉS, ONLINE DISPUTE RESOLUTION FOR CONSUMERS IN THE EUROPEAN UNION 85 (Routledge, 2011) (Note. 1 states, "ODR is understood as any method used to settle disputes that are conducted mainly through the use of ICT (i.e., automated negotiation, assisted negotiation, online mediation, online arbitration, cybercourts, etc.).

[23]European Parliament, *supra* note 21.

[24]UNCTAD (2018), *supra* note 10, at 9.

[25]*Id.*

ODR, or at least some of its elements, as part of their public redress mechanisms.[26] For example, in accordance with the 2018 EU directive, the European Commission operates an online dispute resolution site through which any consumer who bought goods or services online from an EU trader can file a complaint.[27]

One final option for consumer redress is the ombudsman. Operating in a number of nations, consumer ombudsman schemes offer a type of specialized ADR system that provides some form of redress; can systematically assess individual issues to analyze complaint patterns; and draw broader implications on a specific product or industry.[28]

Consumer ombudsman work in cooperation with regulators. They can formulate recommendations in light of their systemic analysis, inform legislation or rule changes, and give feedback to traders.[29] While some consumer ombudsmen provide general services for overall consumer complaints, such schemes generally work best in specialized areas, such as the financial services, communications, or energy sectors.[30] The most significant benefit of ombudsmen is their ability to provide collective redress. Although both ADR and ODR have their advantages, they are limited as mechanisms for *collective* consumer redress because traditionally, they provide only *individual* redress for consumers,[31] and individual redress is still an inefficient way to resolve mass harm. Consumer ombudsman schemes that work in tandem with regulatory authorities and allow regulatory mass redress, thus, offer a promising solution for mass consumer harm.

2.2 Regulatory Mass Redress

This paper uses the term "regulatory redress" to refer broadly to a generic term of the redress made that consumers receive through the "intervention of an administrative authority."[32] As noted in the previous sections, courts are not the only institutions in which consumers rely on redress. ADR, ODR, and ombudsman schemes provide alternatives to court remedies. As the following case studies will show, more examples

[26] Some ODR practices have elements of the dispute resolution carried out offline (e.g., in South Korea) an ODR scheme managed by the Korean IT Industry Promotion Agency incorporates offline (e.g., face-to-face method). See Okkyeong Bang, Current Practices of ODR in Korea (Sept. 21, 2012), http://uncitralrcap.org/wp-content/uploads/2015/11/Day2_Panel1_2_Okkyeong-Bang_Current-Practices-of-ODR-in-KOREA.pdf [https://perma.cc/8JYC-EV5X].

[27] European Parliament, *supra* note 21.

[28] *See* HODGES & VOET, *supra* note 1 at 212; *see* Waye & Morabito, *supra* note 3.

[29] *See* HODGES & VOET, *supra* note 1.

[30] *Id.*

[31] Collective Redress, *supra* note 20, at 67.

[32] HODGES & VOET, *supra* note 1, at 153 uses the phrase "intervention of a *public* authority" in defining regulatory redress (emphasis added). To differentiate from courts, I intentionally use the term "administrative authority" as a way to clarify that I am excluding in-court remedies from the term of "mass regulatory redress."

are emerging in which the public authorities that enforce consumer protection laws are shifting their attention to restitution for wronged consumers rather than just focusing on the deterrence of wrongdoing.[33] In addition, the UN Guidelines on Consumer Protection also offer administrative options for consumer redress.[34]

Administrative authorities with investigative, regulatory, supervisory, or enforcement powers regarding consumer laws or specific industries can intervene to require traders to recompense harmed consumers.[35] One example of such an administrative authority is the public official responsible for consumer law enforcement, such as the Consumer Ombudsman in Nordic countries: Denmark, Finland, Norway, and Sweden.[36] In these nations, the administrative authority can bring a case to the court to seek collective redress.[37] Other nations have sector-based administrative authorities that can intervene to seek consumer redress. The financial regulators who hold this role appear in this paper's case studies.

I deliberately use "intervention" in its broadest sense to encompass the variety of redress schemes that exist globally. Borrowing from the typology of Hodges and Voet (2018), regulatory power includes "soft" influence—approval—and "hard" influence—coercion.[38] Soft influence exists where a public authority might be able to persuade, conciliate, or mediate redress. This public authority might have formal enforcement powers that indirectly influence the payer to rectify the harm that it has caused.[39] Making voluntary redress could potentially reduce the likelihood and magnitude of a formal enforcement action or criminal penalty against the perpetrator.[40]

The second type of regulatory intervention can come in the form of the approval of a public authority or the court. The UK Financial Conduct Authority's approval for a redress scheme is an example of this kind of intervention.[41] A public authority-approved scheme has the particular advantage of ensuring autonomy, flexibility, and speed, while also scrutinizing the fairness of the redress terms.[42] We can also understand the term "approval" as covering a settlement or an agreement between the regulated entity and the public authority.

Finally, there is "hard" enforcement, where a public authority requires a redress scheme. An obvious case would be where the authority orders a person or a company

[33]The case studies on the US, the UK, and South Korea set forth in this paper exemplifies this phenomenon. *See also* HODGES & VOET, *supra* note 1, at 153–210.

[34]As per the United Nations Guidelines for Consumer Protection, which provide: Governments should establish or maintain legal and/or administrative measures to enable consumers or, as appropriate, relevant organizations to obtain redress through formal or informal procedures that are expeditious, fair, inexpensive, and accessible.

[35]HODGES & VOET, *supra* note 1, at 153.

[36]*Id.* at 160.

[37]*Id.* at 153.

[38]*Id.* at 154. (As seen below, this would be the case for most financial authorities).

[39]*Id.*

[40]*Id.*

[41]*Id.* at 156.

[42]*Id.* at 156.

to compensate the injured party.[43] One example of this is the FCA's power to compel firms to initiate and administer mandatory consumer redress schemes under s404 of the Financial Services and Market Act (FSMA). Another example is the Consumer Ombudsman of Denmark's ability to initiate a class action on behalf of consumers.[44]

As the case studies below will demonstrate, in real world cases the typology is not always clear; sometimes regulators employ several mechanisms at the same time. Nonetheless, it is useful to distinguish the range of options available to the relevant authorities.

3 Case Studies: Recent Regulatory Mass Redress Schemes

3.1 The United Kingdom

The U.K. has seen an increasing preference for alternative means of collective redress instead of litigation. The country has instituted a robust regulatory redress scheme, which proved its worth in the case of mis-sold PPI insurance. This scandal was the largest in the nation's history. Since 2011, people who complained about mis-sold PPIs have received about £34 billion in recompense.[45] The PPI consumer redress case is still ongoing, as the FCA set August 19, 2019, as the deadline for complaints. The FCA has yet to publish the final report that will provide a definitive review of the overall impact of FCA's measures and draw the PPI issue to a close.[46]

(1) **Mis-selling of Payment Protection Insurance (PPI)**

As far back as the 1970s, but mostly between 1990 and 2010, banks, lenders, and various providers sold as many as 64 million payment protection insurance (PPI) policies to British consumers.[47] The sellers bundled PPI with credit products such as loans (personal loans, business loans, and student loans), credit cards, store cards, catalogue credit, overdrafts and mortgages, loan secured on homes in addition to the mortgage, home improvement loans (such as for remodeling, furniture, car financing or something bought on credit, such as a sof a—this may have been called a "finance

---

[43] *Id.* at 157.

[44] *Id.*

[45] *Monthly PPI refunds and compensation,* FINANCIAL CONDUCT AUTHORITY, *available at* https://www.fca.org.uk/data/monthly-ppi-refunds-and-compensation [https://perma.cc/F5HT-XLTM].

[46] *Monthly PPI Refunds and Compensation,* FINANCIAL CONDUCT AUTHORITY (Dec. 7, 2019), https://www.fca.org.uk/data/monthly-ppi-refunds-and-compensation [https://perma.cc/965X-ZKUJ].

[47] *Payment Protection Insurance Complaints Deadline Progress Report,* Financial Conduct Authority (Dec. 24, 2018), https://www.fca.org.uk/ppi-complaints-deadline-progress-report [https://perma.cc/26BT-N7ZQ]; *See also* NATIONAL AUDIT OFFICE, *Financial Services Mis-selling: Regulation and Redress,* HC Paper No. 851 (2016).

agreement" or "hire purchase.").[48] Sometimes a PPI came as a standalone product, unrelated to a specific type of credit.[49] The sellers marketed PPI under different names, such as "accident, sickness and unemployment (ASU) insurance," "account cover," "credit insurance," "credit protection," "loan care," "loan insurance," "loan protection," "loan repayment insurance," "mortgage payment protection insurance (MPPI)," "payment cover," and "protection plan."[50]

PPI was mis-sold in the following ways. Sometimes the seller did not make it clear that the customer was purchasing PPI; some told customers that they could not get credit unless they purchased PPI with their loans; in some cases, the sellers did not properly explain the terms and conditions of PPI; the commission associated with the PPI and included in its cost was unfair.[51] Sometimes PPI policies were unnecessary or unsuitable for the consumer because the consumer was ineligible to claim the benefits payable under the policy or was unlikely to need the protection.[52]

The combined effect of the long duration of the PPI sales period, the length of time since the products were sold (i.e., decades in some cases), the variety of PPI-related products and sales channels, the variations of how PPI was branded (named), and the unclear, even abusive nature of many of PPI sales was detrimental to the purchasers. Consumers were often unaware of their coverage or unsure whether they had PPI, and lacked the relevant paperwork or statements to check on their status.[53] This created a significant obstacle for mass consumer redress, eventually forcing the FCA to lead a proactive large-scale communications campaign that involved advertising, PR, social media, and partners.[54]

(2) **Regulator's Response and Consumer Redress**

The magnitude and duration of PPI mis-selling was substantial. The UK financial authorities' efforts to manage the intervention, which spans over two decades, continue to evolve. Overall, the now-defunct Financial Services Authority ("FSA")

---

[48] *Payment Protection Insurance Explained*, FINANCIAL CONDUCT AUTHORITY (Apr. 29, 2019), https://www.fca.org.uk/ppi/ppi-explained [https://perma.cc/7EPR-CNPQ].

[49] *What is PPI and Did I Have it?*, FINANCIAL OMBUDSMAN SERVICE, https://www.financial-ombudsman.org.uk/ppi/what-is-ppi.html [https://perma.cc/SX29-95SZ].

[50] *How to Check if You Had PPI*, FINANCIAL CONDUCT AUTHORITY (Aug. 7, 2019), https://www.fca.org.uk/ppi/how-to-check [https://perma.cc/W662-F5HX].

[51] *What is PPI and Did I Have it?*, FINANCIAL OMBUDSMAN SERVICE https://www.financial-ombudsman.org.uk/ppi/what-is-ppi.html [https://perma.cc/7D7K-H7MV].

[52] *PPI: Complaints We Deal With,* FINANCIAL OMBUDSMAN SERVICE (June 7, 2019), https://www.financial-ombudsman.org.uk/ppi/how-does-the-ombudsman-resolve-ppi-complaints.html. [https://perma.cc/VS39-4MTQ].

[53] Financial Conduct Authority, *Policy Statement PS 17/3: Payment Protection Insurance Complaints: Feedback on CP16/20 and Final Rules and Guidance* 23 (2017), https://www.fca.org.uk/publication/policy/ps17-03.pdf. [https://perma.cc/R5ZQ-CZCU].

[54] *See* Financial Conduct Authority, *Payment Protection Insurance Complaints Deadline Progress Report* (2018), https://www.fca.org.uk/publication/corporate/ppi-complaints-deadline-progress-report.pdf. [https://perma.cc/L3YH-V355].

and its successor, the FCA, have combined supervisory and regulatory tools[55] and formal enforcement actions (i.e., fines), with a system of regulatory redress for consumers.

The FSA, which regulated financial services until April 2013, took up the mis-selling of PPI as soon as it assumed oversight of the insurance business in 2005. In that first year, the FSA immediately conducted a thematic review of PPI sales practices,[56] and in 2009 it banned firms from selling single premium PPIs.[57] From 2006 to 2010 the FSA imposed 24 enforcement actions against the mis-selling of PPI, with fines totaling £12.6 million.[58]

Working in cooperation with the FSA/FCA, the Financial Ombudsman Service ("FOS") sought to resolve individual complaints between consumers and businesses. In principle, consumers first had to complain to the financial services firms. Those dissatisfied with the response could then bring the case to the FOS. The number of complaints concerning payment protection insurance that consumers filed with the "FOS jumped from 1,315 in 2006 to 104,597" in 2011,[59] and continued to increase massively after that, with 400,000 new PPI claims filed in both 2012–13 and 2013–14.[60] This upsurge in complaints presented a major challenge to the FOS and significantly strained its resources, as it found it necessary almost to triple in size as it took on new case handlers and adjudicators.[61]

The number of PPI complaints piling up at the FOS and the FOS's referral to the FSA to investigate the wider implications of the complaints compelled the FSA to take a systemic approach to the problem. Accordingly, the FSA created increasingly specific regulations and adopted a focused supervisory regime to handle the complaints.[62] In 2010, this resulted in "Policy Statement 10/12"—the FSA's announcement of the structure by which it would handle PPI complaints more fairly and consistently, and reduce the FOS's heavy caseload.[63] Among other things, Policy Statement 10/12 amends the Complaints Sourcebook ("DISP"), the FSA's earlier

---

[55] *See* Ferran, *supra* note 7, at 256.

[56] *Id.* at 255 (citing FSA, The Sale of Payment Protection Insurance: Results of Thematic Work (November 2005); FSA, The Sale of Payment Protection Insurance: Mystery Shopping Results (November 2005)).

[57] *Id.* at 254 (citing FSA, *Update on FSA Work on the Sale of PPI*, (FSA/PN/012/2009, 20 January 2009); FSA, *FSA Wants All firms to Stop Selling Single Premium PPI* (FSA/PN/031/2009, 24 February 2009)).

[58] *Id.* at 260 (citing FSA, The Assessment and Redress of Payment Protection Insurance Complaints (PS10/12), at p. 4)); *See also Clydesdale Bank F ined £20,678,300 for Serious Failings in PPI Complaint Handling*, Financial Conduct Authority (Apr. 14, 2015) https://www.fca.org.uk/news/press-releases/clydesdale-bank-fined-%C2%A320678300-serious-failings-ppi-complaint-handling [https://perma.cc/F33R-D27R].

[59] *Id.* at 255 (citing Financial Ombudsman Service, Annual Review 2010/11, at 41).

[60] National Audit Office, *Financial Conduct Authority and Financial Ombudsman Service, Financial Services Mis-selling: Regulation and Redress* 10 (2016).

[61] *See id.*

[62] *See* Ferran, *supra* note 7, at 263.

[63] Financial Services Authority, *Policy Statement 10/12: The Assessment and Redress of Payment Protection Insurance Complaints* (2010) [hereinafter Policy Statement 10/12].

set of relevant rules. The revised sections include explanations of how firms should handle and assess PPI complaints and how they should deal with evidence and redress regarding these sales.[64] Policy Statement 10/12 also presented the way in which the FSA planned to monitor firms' behavior regarding PPI complaints, requiring the firms to provide it with sample files of PPI complaints, governance structures, internal procedures, papers, and minutes of senior management meetings about PPI.[65]

Encouraging consumers to file PPI claims was an important aspect of the FSA/FCA's approach to the PPI scandal. In 2012, the FSA issued guidance on how companies should contact consumers so as to facilitate PPI claims.[66] In 2013, the FCA, published empirical field research about ways to encourage consumers to seek redress.[67] That paper recommended small changes like adding a message to 'act quickly' to a plain envelope, using an FSA logo in the letterhead; using salient bullets; simplifying the body of the letter; and including in the text an explanation that the claims process would only take five minutes. These served to increase the consumer response rate.[68]

To ensure robust and consistent consumer redress, the FSA/FCA's supervisory work also included a program of oversight and review of the progress of consumer redress. The authorities kept track of the monthly and annual number of complaints to firms, the complaint uphold rates, and the amount of PPI redress paid by month and years.[69] It asked firms to conduct self-assessments, to review complaint handling failures, and to provide the resulting information to the authorities. It also required them to hold regular meetings with the FCA.[70]

In 2017, the FCA issued "Policy Statement 17/3," which, among other matters, set August 29, 2019 as the deadline by which consumers must file their PPI complaints or lose their rights to have them assessed; presented its communications campaign to inform the consumers of this deadline; and imposed the requirement that the financial industry fund the consumer communications campaign.[71] In accordance

---

[64] National Audit Office, *supra* note 60, at Appendix 1 Final Handbook text.

[65] National Audit Office, *supra* note 60, at 58.

[66] Financial Services Authority, *Finalized Guidance, Payment Protection Insurance Customer Contact Letters (PPI CCLs)—Fairness, Clarity and Potential Consequences* (2012).

[67] Adams and Hunt [7].

[68] *Id.* (*See also* Becky Rowe, Jenny Holland, & Ruby Wootton, Financial Conduct Authority: Understanding PPI Redress from a Consumer Perspective, FINANCIAL CONDUCT AUTHORITY (Nov. 2015) https://www.fca.org.uk/publication/consultation/understanding-ppi-redress-consumer-perspective.pdf. [https://perma.cc/8V4E-9ERH]).The FCA also commissioned behavioral research to understand the mindsets of complaining and non-complaining consumers, and ways to encourage people to complain).

[69] Financial Conduct Authority, Thematic Review, Redress for Payment Protection Insurance (PPI) Mis-sales Update on Progress and Looking Ahead, TR 14/14 (2014).

[70] *Id.* at 15–17.

[71] Financial Conduct Authority, *Policy Statement PS17/3 Payment Protection Insurance Complaints: Feedback on CP 16/20 and Final Rules and Guidance* (2017) (hereinafter "Policy Statement 17/3").

with Policy Statement 17/3, the FCA launched a media campaign that has led millions of additional consumers to seek redress.[72]

(3) **Implications**

Commentators have hailed the UK financial sector's regulatory redress scheme as a very successful system, especially compared to court-led civil justice systems.[73] They describe the exercise as an "integrated voluntary, regulatory, and Ombudsman redress," and notes that "various techniques can be integrated into a holistic practical approach."[74] The system makes both voluntary redress and regulatory redress available to consumers. The redress could be considered "voluntary" in a sense that it first asked consumers to file a complaint with the firms (rather than the FOS). Also, in an early stage of the PPI scandal, the firms "voluntarily" repaid the consumers, even before the FSA set guidelines and rules. We can consider the plan a "regulatory" redress because in both 2010 and 2017 the FSA/FCA amended its Handbook (by way of Policy Statements 10/12 and 17/3) and set rules and guidelines for firms to follow. Along with this, the FOS, addressed individual claims and set the redress standard for them.[75]

It is worth noting that a collective action litigation might have been unfeasible or very ineffective and costly in this situation, because authorities would have had to review each "mis-selling" case individually in light of its specific circumstances; for example, some consumers were more informed than others, and some actually needed the PPI while others did not.[76] It would have been difficult to put the vast variety of products and sales channels involved into one "class." As such, I have not found evidence of any attempt to establish a consumer class (aggregated) litigation, nor of

---

[72]Financial Conduct Authority, *Payment Protection Insurance Complaints Deadline Progress Report* 6 (2018), https://www.fca.org.uk/publication/corporate/ppi-complaints-deadline-progress-report.pdf. [https://perma.cc/CZD5-EL22]. (according to the FCA, during the first ten months of its campaign, it received 8.4 million inquiries, an increase of 40% monthly compared their immediate pre-campaign level, while consumers made 3.7 million complaints, 63% more than in the 10 months before the campaign) (One can view an example of a media campaign, featuring a robotic head of Arnold Schwarzenegger, on Youtube at https://www.youtube.com/watch?v=zS9wMHXZ4Ts [https://perma.cc/ULB8-CG2A], or https://www.youtube.com/watch?v=cfwk0bAAfPk [https://perma.cc/959Q-V6CQ]).

[73]Hodges & Voet, *supra* note 1, at 248; Rebecca Money-Kyrle, *Collective Enforcement of Consumer Rights in the United Kingdom* (March 01, 2015) (referencing 'Im Namen des Verbrauchers? Kollective Rechtsdurchsetzung in Europa/In the Name of Consumers? Collective Rights Enforcement in Europe', Schmidt- Kessel M, Strünck C and Kramme M (eds), JVW Publishing (2015), available at SSRN: https://ssrn.com/abstract=2661980 (commenting, "[w]hilst general criminal and civil justice mechanisms currently in force have failed to deliver, there are other administrative and regulatory routes that provide avenues to collective enforcement of consumer rights in the UK)).

[74]Hodges & Voet, *supra* note 1, at 252.

[75].

[76]Emma Ann Hughes, *FCA Hits Back at Claims it Overwhelmed FOS*, FY Advisor (Sept. 18, 2018), https://www.ftadviser.com/regulation/2018/09/11/fca-hits-back-at-claims-it-overwhelmed-fos/ [https://perma.cc/84LU-T5X7] (the FCA stated that, "In many instances the nature of the (PPI) complaint is quite specific to the individual.").

Parliamentary, consumer, or other policy calls to propose such class action-related solution.[77]

3.2 The United States

In the United States, the Consumer Financial Protection Bureau ("CFPB") charged several banks with "deceptive acts or practices" in connection with their marketing of credit card add-on products. The CFPB, which Congress created as a response to the Global Financial Crisis of 2008, issued several enforcement actions ordering consumer redress for such deceptive selling. Since the very beginning of the CFPB's operations, it has embraced its role as a financial cop, even describing itself as a "cop on the beat."[78] As such, consumer redress (i.e., restitution or consumer refund) has been an important component of the CFPB's enforcement actions, as it required the banks in question to refund billions of customers' money.[79]

(1) **Misconduct Related to Credit Card Add-on Product Sales**

Credit card add-on products are additional, optional services that credit card companies provide.[80] Both banks and bank-authorized third-party vendors sold "credit protection" or "identity monitoring" as additions to a customer's account. There was a wide variety of these products, with a diverse scope and design. Just to give one example, between 2010 and 2012, Bank of America marketed credit card payment protection products that allowed customers to request that the bank cancel some amount of credit card debt in the event of certain hardships, like involuntary unemployment or disability, and certain life events, such as entering college or retirement.[81] This optional coverage required a monthly or annual membership fee but the bank did not always present this clearly to its customers, and engaged in deceptive practices that I describe below in detail.[82]

CFPB's supervisory oversight discovered that some banks were engaging in high-pressure, confusing, and deceptive promotional practices when marketing the products, including the inadequate disclosure of important terms and conditions. Some of them enrolled consumers in programs, and even billed them, without the customers'

---

[77] HODGES & VOET, *supra* note 1, at 257.

[78] McDonald [8].

[79] *See* Peterson [9].

[80] *See What are Credit Card "Add-On" Products?* CONSUMER FINANCIAL PROTECTION BUREAU (Aug. 8, 2016), https://www.consumerfinance.gov/ask-cfpb/what-are-credit-card-add-on-products-en-1541/ [https://perma.cc/L58D-S2E9].

[81] *See* CFPB Orders Bank of America to Pay $727 Million in Consumer Relief for Illegal Credit Card Practices, CONSUMER FINANCIAL PROTECTION BUREAU (Apr. 9, 2014), https://www.consumerfinance.gov/about-us/newsroom/cfpb-orders-bank-of-america-to-pay-727-million-in-consumer-relief-for-illegal-credit-card-practices/ [https://perma.cc/83PV-9SUN].

[82] CONSUMER FINANCIAL PROTECTION BUREAU, *supra* note 80.

affirmative knowledge or consent. In some cases, a bank would bill consumers for services that it had not performed or activated. CFPB's consumer complaint database associated these deceptive marketing and sales practices with credit card add-on products.[83]

Some of the sales methods involved soliciting via telemarketing. For example, in the Bank of America case, the bank's Call Center Representatives ("CSRs") solicited the cardholders who called the bank to activate their cards, encouraging them to enroll in the add-on products.[84] Bank of America misled some consumers about the enrollment process for these products, telling them that there were additional steps necessary in order to enroll, while in reality, it was registering these consumers in the add-on products during these calls, and charging the unsuspecting customers for them.[85]

(2) **Regulator's Response and Consumer Redress**

One of the CFPB's first enforcement actions, in 2012, was against the deceptive selling of credit card add-on products.[86] The action stemmed from an examination that identified the deceptive marketing tactics of Capital One Bank (U.S.A.), N.A.'s vendors, who pressured or mislead consumers into paying for "add-on products" such as payment protection and credit monitoring when they activated their credit cards.[87] In this action, the CFPB ordered Capital One to refund approximately $140 million to two million customers and to pay an additional $25 million penalty. The CFPB grounded its enforcement actions on sections 1053 and 1055 of the Consumer Financial Protection Act of 2010 (CFPA).[88]

Together with this first enforcement action, the CFPB also exercised its supervisory powers by issuing CFPB Bulletin 2012-16, "Marketing of Credit Card Add-on Products."[89] The Bulletin, outlines the CFPB's expectations for institutions under its supervision and their service providers to offer credit card add-on products in compliance with Federal consumer financial law.[90] The CFPB presents guidelines regarding marketing materials, employee incentive or compensation programs, and

---

[83] Consumer Financial Protection Bureau, *supra* note 80. https://www.consumerfinance.gov/policy-compliance/guidance/supervisory-guidance/bulletin-marketing-credit-card-add-on-products/.

[84] Consent Order at 7, *In re* Bank of America, (No. 2014-CFPB-0004) https://files.consumerfinance.gov/f/201404_cfpb_bankofamerica_consent-order.pdf [https://perma.cc/5XDN-7HQM].

[85] Consumer Financial Protection Bureau, *supra* note 81.

[86] *See* CFPB Probe into Capital One Credit Card Marketing Results in $140 Million Consumer Refund, Consumer Financial Protection Bureau (July 18, 2012), https://www.consumerfinance.gov/about-us/newsroom/cfpb-capital-one-probe/ [https://perma.cc/VRZ2-QQSP].

[87] Consumer Financial Protection Bureau, *supra* note 86.

[88] 12 U.S.C. Sections 5563 and 5565.

[89] *Bulletin Re: Marketing of Credit Card Add-On Products*, Consumer Financial Protection Bureau (July 18, 2012) https://www.consumerfinance.gov/policy-compliance/guidance/supervisory-guidance/bulletin-marketing-credit-card-add-on-products/.

[90] *See id.*

scripts and manuals related to credit card add-on products.[91] In addition, the Bulletin stipulates that "institutions that offer credit card add-on products should employ compliance management programs"[92] that include certain items that are intended to provide guidance for financial companies to follow.[93]

After the initial enforcement action against Capital One Bank, the CFPB issued a series of subsequent actions ordering financial companies to repay consumers for deceptive marketing.[94] In 2013, it required American Express to refund an estimated $59.5 million to more than 335,000 consumers because of deceptive marketing concerning credit card add-on products.[95] In 2015, Citibank paid $700 million to about seven million consumers in relief for illegal credit card practices related to credit card add-on products and services.[96] In 2016, Bank of America had to provide $727 million consumers with refunds for deceptive marketing related to credit card add-on products.[97]

What is important about this series of consumer redress actions is the CFPB's dedication to making it easy for consumers to receive relief. Its consent orders usually included very detailed terms about how the consumers should receive redress. The orders laid out the terms of a "Redress Plan"[98] or "Remediation Plan."[99] It required the redress plan to include the following: (1) Convenient repayments to consumers—if the consumers were still customers of the relevant bank, they would receive a credit to their accounts, and if they were no longer bank credit card holders, they would receive a check in the mail.[100] The CFPB did not require consumers to take any action

---

[91] *See id.*

[92] *Id.* at 5.

[93] McDonald, *supra* note 78, at 243 (Some commentators have criticized the CPFB's use of bulletins, stating: "The practice of publishing bulletins that officially do not have the effect of law, but nonetheless are otherwise relied upon in enforcement proceedings, contributes to a perception that agencies intentionally bypass the notice-and-comment requirements required for rulemaking through backdoor measures, that is, by issuing guidance documents.").

[94] *Consumer Financial Protection Bureau: Enforcing Federal Consumer Protection Laws (2016)*, Consumer Financial Protection Bureau, https://files.consumerfinance.gov/f/documents/07132016_cfpb_SEFL_anniversary_factsheet.pdf [https://perma.cc/BG3A-XYLU].

[95] *See CFPB Orders American Express to Pay $59.5 Million for Illegal Credit Card Practices*, Consumer Financial Protection Bureau (Dec. 23, 2016), https://www.consumerfinance.gov/about-us/newsroom/cfpb-orders-american-express-to-pay-59-5-million-for-illegal-credit-card-practices/ [https://perma.cc/T45U-NRW4].

[96] *See CFPB Orders Citibank to Pay $700 Million in Consumer Relief for Illegal Credit Card Practices*, Consumer Financial Protection Bureau, (July 21, 2018) https://www.consumerfinance.gov/about-us/newsroom/cfpb-orders-citibank-to-pay-700-million-in-consumer-relief-for-illegal-credit-card-practices/[https://perma.cc/ZNA2-336C].

[97] Consumer Financial Protection Bureau, *supra* note 81.

[98] Consumer Financial Protection Bureau, *supra* note 81.

[99] Capital One Bank, (USA), No. 2012-CFPB-0001 (2012), *available at* https://files.consumerfinance.gov/f/201207_cfpb_consent_order_0001.pdf [https://perma.cc/5F5M-V6XK].

[100] In re Bank of America, *supra* note 96; Consumer Financial Protection Bureau, *supra* note 86.

to receive their repayment.[101] (2) Calculation methods for restitution or monetary relief.[102] (3) Requirements on a written letter to consumers from the bank, notifying them of the redress including the relevant requirements on the envelope containing the letter.[103]

To help inform consumers, the CFPB also published a blog post for Capital One customers explaining the announcement and the refund process. The statement on CFPB's blog emphasized the convenient repayment process:[104]

> Convenient repayment for consumers: If the consumers are still Capital One customers, they will receive a credit to their accounts. If they are no longer a Capital One credit card holder, they will receive a check in the mail. Consumers are not required to take any action to receive their credit or check.

The CFPB also posted a general blog post to all consumers informing them how to "Stop Mystery Credit Card Fees" from their card issuers.[105]

(3) **Implications**

The CFPB consent order-type of consumer redress scheme is unique in that it does not require consumers to file a complaint or take any action, but instead "automatically" repays them with credit or a check. The CFPB consistently uses this method of redress in all of its consent orders related to credit card add-on products. Although this automatic repayment method is immensely convenient and favorable to the consumer, it does raise the concern that the CFPB might be inappropriately imposing a blanket restitution plan for instances of deception or mis-selling that usually require individual review to determine the extent of the bank's culpability toward each customer. One possible reason why such a broad-based plan makes sense is that consent orders, which are a type of settlement between a private party and an administrative agency,[106] were the legal instrument that the CFPB employed, and there is a degree of flexibility allowed for this.[107] Another possibility is that in many cases, the sales representatives used a common sales script, which created a pattern of behavior that the CFPB could apply to a range of cases. In those instances, the CFPB and the regulated entities could issue a blanket, automatic refund to eligible customers. Finally, it is also possible that the redress amounts for these types of credit card add-on products were typically low, while individual screenings of each deception or mis-selling would be more costly than a blanket refund to all consumers in a particular sale.

Once a firm has entered into a consent order with the CFPB, it must abide by the terms of the Bureau's order and is subject to the Bureau's oversight regarding

---

[101] *Id.*

[102] In re Capital One Bank *supra* note 96 at 15–17.

[103] *Id.* at 17.

[104] Markus [10].

[105] Hillebrand [11].

[106] Jackman and Delnero [12].

[107] *See* [13] (similarly, courts have afforded the FTC a wide discretion for cease and desist orders in enforcing deceptive and unfair practices).

implementation of the order. As such, we can characterize the CFPB consent order as a "hard" enforcement, where a public authority mandates a consumer redress scheme.[108]

3.3 South Korea

In South Korea there was a widespread mis-selling scandal in which credit card companies mis-sold Debt Cancellation and Debt Suspension (DCDS) products to millions of consumers.[109] The Financial Services Service (FSS), Korea's primary financial regulatory agency, stepped in and compelled the relevant financial companies to provide redress to the defrauded consumers.

(1) Misconduct Related to DCDS Products Sale

DCDS products, which Samsung Card first introduced in 2005, are a type of insurance service that credit card companies offer customers. The products come with fees that the companies add to the monthly bills. The fees vary depending on the total monthly card usage and the rates fixed by card companies. The service allows customers to cancel or suspend payments in the event of death or illness.

As of the end of 2016, 2.7 million customers had signed up for this product. The related average monthly charge was about 6 USD (6574 KRW). Between 2012 and 2016 the product created a total revenue of more than 10 billion USD (1.18 trillion KRW).

DCDS products were usually mis-sold sold by way of various aggressive telemarketing techniques. For example, company representatives often failed to get the consumer's explicit consent; sometimes they did not mention that products came with a fee for the service (i.e., they promoted the product as a VIP customer service, confusing consumers into thinking that the products were free, when in fact fees were charged). Sometimes the telemarketer spoke so quickly that it was impossible for the consumer to comprehend the complicated terms.

The most common type of consumer misunderstanding was about the way that the company assessed the fees for DCDS. It did so with the formula of multiplying a multiplier (i.e., 0.5%) to the "remaining credit card balance at the end of the month." Often, the product marketing promised that "the fee would usually be less than a dollar or less than ten dollars." Some consumers misunderstood that the fee would be a flat fee, when in fact it fluctuated commensurate to the amount of the month-end

---

[108]In theory, since the financial companies can voluntarily choose to (or decline to) enter a consent order, the CFPB's consent order-type of regulatory redress can also be understood as a voluntary regulatory redress.

[109]This section was largely adapted from an article that the author wrote in Korean. Youkyung Huh, *Consumer Friendly Consumer Redress—A Comparative Case Study on Consumer Redress in Large Scale Mis-selling Scandals-*, [소비자친화적인 금융소비자 피해구제 대규모 불완전판매에 대한 소비자 피해구제 사례 연구를 중심으로] S. Kor. Bus. L. Assoc., 32 Bus. L. Rev. 317 (2018).

balance. At times, the scope and meaning of "balance" was unclear to the consumer. In most cases this term included not only credit card balances but also the sum of other credit services that the credit card company offered (i.e., short-term loans, installment loans and revolving credit) which typically came to much more than just the monthly credit card bill. In other words, depending on the type of contract, the company often carried over the total amount of the installment or the revolving amount from the previous month, including it in the next month's "balance" for the purpose of calculating DCDS fees. If a customer had a significant balance, than the fees could run up to tens or hundreds of dollars, considerably more than the amount that telemarketers had promoted.

As a result of this kind of fraudulent sale, DCDS-related complaints filed with the Korea Consumers Agency (KCA) and the FSS increased significantly after 2010. In 2015–2016, DCDS-related complaints ranked at the top of all credit card-related complaints, and mis-selling was the most common factor (78.6%) of all such DCDS-related complaints.

(2) **Regulator's Response and Consumer Redress**

The increase of DCDS consumer complaints after 2010 triggered the FSS to issue a series of regulatory actions relating to DCDS products. In 2013, the FSS required the credit card companies to lower DCDS fees.[110] In 2015, the FSS prepared a comprehensive review of the business conduct of all credit card companies. In May 2016, the FSS entered into a Memorandum of Understanding (MOU) with the credit card companies seeking to improve business conduct. From November to December 2016, the FSS reviewed the credit card companies' performance of the MOUs. In this process the FSS found the credit card companies had mis-sold the DCDS and advised the companies to repay the mis-sold funds to the consumers. The FSS determined that 650 thousand customers were eligible for reimbursements amounts of 23 million USD (KRW 26.1 trillion). As the problem persisted, in 2016 the authorities banned new sales of DCDS products altogether (although customers who already bought DCDS products remained subscribed unless they cancelled their subscriptions).[111]

The credit card companies' consumer redress procedures were not uniform. In some cases, the companies automatically repaid amounts even though the consumers had not filed a complaint. The companies themselves identified and reached out to this group of customers in order to make restitution. But in other instances, the companies made redress payments only if the consumers individually filed complaints with them. When consumers did this, the credit card company would listen to the recording of the sale, and if it deemed it a mis-selling, then the consumers were eligible for a repayment.

Many consumers were not aware of widespread mis-selling and of their eligibility to redress; in fact, many did not even realize that they had subscribed to DCDS services. As such, the FSS required the credit card companies to notify DCDS customers in writing, at least once a year, (i) of the fact that the customer

[110]Lee [14].

[111]Lee [15].

had enrolled in DCDS services, (ii) of the monthly fees for the product, (iii) of the scope of the services, and (iv) of the fact that consumers were eligible to cancel the services if they deemed them unnecessary. The companies also had to notify DCDS consumers of the past three months' worth of fees for the product through text messages. The FSS required the credit card companies to operate call centers with numbers dedicated for DCDS products so that consumers could confirm their DCDS subscription status and cancel the service if they so chose. The local media and social network services (internet portals, etc.) also published information about the DCDS mis-selling scandal. This helped many consumers become aware of the product, allowing them to file complaints with their credit card companies.

In September 2017, however, the Board of Audit and Inspection (BAI) of Korea,[112] a national audit agency, published a report that found the FSS' handling of the DCDS mis-selling scandal deficient. According to the report, the scope of DCDS subscribers who were eligible for redress was much broader than that which the FSS had initially identified. The BAI found that the FSS had wrongly excluded more than 2.2 million consumers from its initial consumer redress scheme. The BAI noted the likelihood that these consumers were not aware of mis-selling and that the FSS had been wrong in not devising a way to protect them as well.

As of this date, there is no evidence that the FSS has publicly orchestrated another, broader mis-selling consumer redress scheme for the DCDS products. The Korea Consumer Agency's consumer call centers continued to receive complaints about DCDS mis-selling as late as 2018, so it appears that there is still a large number of consumers who might be eligible for redress. As of 2018 March, 2.1 million customers still received DCDS services.

The BAI audit results and the existence of consumer complaints as late as 2018 show the importance of properly informing eligible consumers in a consumer redress scheme. We have seen above that the FSS publicized its redress scheme through media exposure, occasional discussions in SNS posts, and direct notification from the credit card companies. Nevertheless, these attempts were not sufficient to reach all (potentially) mis-sold consumers and to encourage them to seek redress.

(3) **Implications**

The FSS intervened in problematic sector at an early stage by using both its formal and its informal supervisory powers. It is important to note that the FSS "advised" the credit card companies to offer redress, but could not *legally* "require" them to do so. Korean legal academics categorize these types of "advisories" as a type of "administrative guidance (*Haengjungjido*),"[113] which has no binding legal effects on the parties that receive them. These so-called advisories, however, have a de

[112]The Korean constitution created the BAI as a public agency with the primary function of the auditing and inspecting the accounts and the work of government agencies. Responsibilities & Functions, Board of Audit and Inspection, (http://english.bai.go.kr/bai_eng/html/about/responsibilities.do?mdex=bai_eng8) [https://perma.cc/DWH5-8YJ5] (last visited Aug. 5, 2019).

[113]Article 2 (3) of the Korean Administrative Procedure Act stipulates that "The term "administrative guidance" [(*Haengjungjido*),] "means an administrative action, such as guidance, recommendation,

facto power which can compel financial companies to abide by them.[114] Because administrative guidance is not legally binding, the agency needs no specific legal ground to issue one and can use them informally and flexibly in a wide variety of situations.

Indeed, there is no legal ground for consumer redress under Korean law. The FSS can only "advise," or recommend, redress through informal administrative advisories and agreements (taking the form of MOUs) between the regulator and the financial companies.

The informal 'advisory' method has both advantages and disadvantages. On the one hand, the regulators can be flexible in designing redress schemes that are not available in the letter of the law. On the other hand, precisely because there are no clear legal guidelines regarding consumer redress, it is up to the good will of the financial companies to design and manage a robust restitution scheme. The DCDS redress scheme above showcases both—the FSS could flexibly intervene at a relatively early stage and "advise" the credit card companies to offer redress, but as the BAI chided, the FSS was also hesitant in using its informal powers and so did not intervene as forcefully as it might have, had it the formal authority to do so. When the credit card companies chose not to operate a robust redress arrangement, the FSS did not have the power to follow up on the advisory by, say, imposing administrative fines, sanctions, or penalties. This leaves consumers who are not aware of their rights in an undesirable limbo status.

4 Why Regulatory Mass Redress Works Well For The Financial Sector

The case studies above all present the mis-selling of similar financial products. Although the three relevant nations operated redress schemes against the framework of very different legal and cultural backgrounds, the results of delivering mass redress to millions of low-value claims were identical.[115]

Why is the financial sector an area to which regulatory redress schemes are so appropriate? Would it be preferable for this area to develop mass regulatory schemes? In short, would it be more effective for countries to adopt a formal regulatory redress

advice by an administrative agency to encourage or discourage a particular person regarding performance of certain acts, within the scope of duties or affairs under its jurisdiction in order to realize specific administrative aims…" Korean Administrative Procedure Act, Act No. 12347, Jan. 28, 2014, art. 2(3) (S. Kor.).

[114]In part, this is because financial authorities have a wide variety of enforcement tools that can be implemented to encourage a voluntary redress scheme (*See infra* section IV). Another reason can be attributed to the Korean of tradition of a strong state led economy where authorities have a strong influence over the industry beyond the black letter of the law.

[115]*See supra* Section II. B. Waye & Morabito *supra* note 3. Other nations, like Italy and Australia, have also instituted formal mass regulatory redress schemes.

scheme or for them to activate informal redress schemes, especially in the financial sector? This section will examine these questions.

First, more than most other industries, the financial services sector is heavily regulated. This creates unique opportunities for regulators to access information and intervene at an early stage. Financial companies are under constant on-site and off-site supervision through bank examinations and various reporting and approval requirements. In their supervisory role, financial regulators can also have informal interactions (such as meetings, calls, and emails) with regulated entities. The benefit of the constant supervisory function of a financial regulator is that it can detect problems and intervene at an early stage. Access to a wealth of information through the supervisory function also remedies the difficulties in gathering information that are often present in an in-court consumer redress case. The discovery procedure in certain jurisdictions (i.e., the US) alleviates this problem, but in some nations (i.e., South Korea), practitioners find it hard to come up with evidence in instances of financial harm. Regulatory redress, instigated or ordered by a financial regulator, answers this problem.

Second, financial regulators are armed with a variety of enforcement tools to invoke or supplement consumer redress, and these enhance the effectiveness of a redress scheme. In addition to the supervisory process, regulators have their own investigatory powers to help them reach an enforcement decision. Regulators have an array of tools for enforcing laws, including criminal and administrative penalties, and powers such as cease and desist orders and injunctions against infringement. These actions alone might have deterrence effects, but they cannot redress consumer harm, and so are not helpful to defrauded customers. The value of this array of enforcement tools lies in the fact that they can induce or influence a regulated entity to implement a swifter and more robust redress plan.[116] In nations where authorities do not have mandatory redress powers, regulators can derive a de facto power to encourage a voluntary redress from de jure enforcement powers. In other words, regulatory redress is effective because it can be used in tandem with other enforcement tools.[117]

Third, the consumer harm that financial products cause can easily be widespread, inconspicuous, and of little value on an individual level. The case studies on mis-sold PPI and credit card add-on products illustrate this point. Unlike defective manufactured goods, the consumer harm that financial services contracts generate can go unnoticed for months or even years. In the UK, PPI consumers were unaware of the scandal for decades. Consumers easily overlooked financial charges on their monthly bills (especially in low amounts), even when companies added them illegally. Other examples of low-value but widespread harm in the financial sector abound. For example, in Ireland, about 160,000 people were eligible to claim between €100 and €200 each for having been mis-sold a credit card protection policy.[118] In Latvia, it

---

[116] HODGES & VOET, *supra* note 1, at 154.

[117] Hodges *supra* note 13, at 19, 20.

[118] *Collective Redress for All Europeans*, BEUC: THE EUROPEAN CONSUMER ORGANISATION, https://www.beuc.eu/collective-redress-all-eu-consumers#examples [https://perma.cc/A8ZS-SQQE] (last visited Aug. 6, 2019). However, Ireland does not have a collective redress system to facilitate this restitution.

took more than two years for anyone to notice that a large consumer credit company was misleading consumers with respect to interest rates on credit cards.[119] Regulatory consumer redress, especially "automatic" redress schemes where financial companies pay refunds even to consumers who have not filed a consumer complaint is particularly useful for these types of small amount cases.[120]

Finally, it is foreseeable that digitalization in the financial sector will create more possibilities for inconspicuous, widespread harm. The rapid evolution of technology in the financial area has fundamentally changed the way that companies sell these services, while diminishing consumers' ability to understand the financial transactions. This increased consumer vulnerability will inevitably lead to an increase in unfair and deceptive trade practices, including fraud and mis-selling, as well as account hacking and data theft.[121]

5 Designing an Optimal Regulatory Redress Scheme

5.1 Balancing Benchmarks

The three case studies show that regulatory redress schemes operate in the broader milleu of each nation's unique civil justice system and financial regulatory architecture. The customs and traditions, the cultural factors, and the nature of existing relationships between authorities and regulated entities also contribute to the various approaches. Despite these differences, however, we can derive common benchmarks that legislators should consider when designing an effective regulatory redress scheme.

First, a regulatory reparations scheme that is set against judicial redress can be efficient, even though it raises concerns about the right to fair trial and due process. Judicial redress is tedious and resource-intensive but it demonstrates the most reverence to the rule of law. The right to a fair trial, with an independent judiciary that considers the evidence and applies the law, gives way in a regulatory redress scheme to efficiency and expediency. Some types of regulatory redress schemes replace due process with the voluntary consent of the regulated.[122] For example, the use of consent orders in the US CFPB case study bypasses any procedural requirements for adjudication and allows the administrative agency and the parties involved to

---

[119] *Id.*

[120] The case study on the CFPB refunding consumers is a good example of this.

[121] *G20/OECD Policy Guidance: Financial Consumer Protection Approaches in the Digital Age*, OECD 13, 14 (2018), http://www.oecd.org/g20/G20-OECD-Policy-Guidance-Financial-Consumer-Protection-Approaches-digital-age.pdf [https://perma.cc/XNL6-YZHS].

[122] Micheal Legg, *Many wrongs can make a right: how mass redress schemes can replace court action*, THE CONVERSATION (Nov. 24, 2015), http://theconversation.com/many-wrongs-can-make-a-right-how-mass-redress-schemes-can-replace-court-action-51118) [https://perma.cc/9RCL-4E8J].

resolve an agency-initiated proceeding without the time and expense of a formal administrative hearing.[123] In the Korean FSS case study, we saw that there was no legal framework for imposing the redress scheme; there, the authorities' informal advice and recommendation replaced the rule of law. However, in this situation, where regulatory redress procedures lack the minimum procedural guarantees of a court-led redress or a formal enforcement action, such a scheme might infringe on the consumer's right to a fair trial or to due process for the participating parties.[124]

Second, procedural rules for court-led remedies usually have safeguards to ensure openness and transparency, characteristics that some regulatory redress schemes lack. The schemes can set aside hearings, the publication of the content and documents of files, transcripts of statements, and rules on ex parte communication. More "formal" regulatory redress schemes can have more procedural mechanisms to enhance transparency. For example, the FSA/FCA formalized the UK PPI redress scheme through Policy Statements, revisions of relevant sections of the Handbook, and written guidance. That the UK financial regulators published consultation papers seeking feedback from the industry, consumers, and other stakeholders before they set forth new rules shows a high degree of transparency and openness regarding the rules and procedures that they applied to the PPI redress scheme. Critics of the CFPB's frequent use of consent orders argue that it used these orders as a way to evade formal rulemaking, something that the CFPA allowed it to do.[125] In this way, however, the critics argue, the CFPB deprived companies of fair notice of prohibited conduct[126] This claim brings to the fore the necessity that procedures for regulatory redress schemes be transparent, so that participating parties and interested stakeholders can assess the fairness of the redress.

5.2 Design Factors

With the basic benchmarks of efficiency, fairness, due process, transparency, and openness in mind, we now turn to the policy decisions involved in designing a specific regulatory redress scheme.

---

[123] 12 C.F.R. section 1081.120 (c) (3) (v) (2012). By submitting an offer of settlement, the person making the offer waives, subject to acceptance of the offer, judicial review by any court.

[124] For example, Article 6 of the European Convention on Human Rights notes the following: "In the determination of his civil rights and obligations or of any criminal charge against him, everyone is entitled to a fair and public hearing within a reasonable time by an independent and impartial tribunal established by law." Y.B. Eur. Conv. on H.R.

[125] *See* 12 U.S.C. section 5531(b) (2010). McDonald (2018), *supra* note 78.

[126] Jackman & Delnero, *supra* note 106.

a. *Ceiling Amount or Threshold Issues*

First, we need to identify the extent of the need for mass redress and whether there should be a ceiling amount of compensation that can be awarded via regulatory redress schemes. Regulatory mass redress schemes are most effective for low-value claims because consumers are less likely to seek redress for them in court (while there is an increased chance that they will do so for high-value claims). The higher the stakes in individual cases, the greater the necessity for a fair trial, judicial consideration of the evidence, and the application and interpretation of the law. Voluntary redress or "soft" regulatory redress (such as administrative advice or inducement) becomes less likely in high-value cases where regulated entities are unlikely to settle.[127]

b. *The Right to Appeal and Court Participation*

Another policy option is to determine the degree to which the regulated entity should be allowed to appeal or whether a court action is required to complete the redress. By definition, in a voluntary redress scheme (i.e., a consent order) the regulated entity agrees to forgo judicial review. However, a mandatory framework, where a public authority can coerce a redress scheme, raises constitutional issues of the right to appeal and the right to be heard.[128] A middle ground arrangement could be a model where administrative authorities can bring a case to court to seek collective redress (here it is the regulators who initiate the regulatory actions for redress), but where the court ultimately determines the extent or format of any redress.[129]

c. *How to Reach Out to Consumers*

A recurring theme in collective action is to how to determine the class; that is, should it be an opt-in, where a class member needs to take affirmative action to be included in the group, or an opt-out, where a customer need do nothing at all in order to part of the final outcome. A similar policy choice in regulatory redress schemes is to determine whether consumers must file a complaint or take action to receive restitution (as in the UK PPI redress case) or whether the redress is "automatic," so that consumers automatically receive payments through their bank accounts or mailed checks (as in the US CFPB consent order). If the scheme requires consumers to take action in order to receive refunds, authorities must implement sufficient measures to ensure that the members of the relevant "class" are aware of the possibility of harm.[130]

---

[127]*See* [16]. In this case the FSS attempted to impose a voluntary redress scheme, but the redress amount per consumer that it determined was ten times more than the amount that regulated entity believed appropriate. The large amount at stake and the differences in legal interpretation of the terms and conditions of the insurance contract contributed to the lawsuit.

[128]*See* Hodges, *supra* note 13, at 18.

[129]*See supra* Section II. B.

[130]The UK's PPI case shows that the FCA took great care to publicize the PPI's mass harm. The Korean DCDS case demonstrates the pitfalls of regulatory redress when members of a potential "class" are not properly notified. The US CFPB case shows how simple an automatic redress can be from the consumer's perspective.

Thus, there is a necessary policy choice between the "automatic" payment method (consumers need not take action for redress) and the "opt-in" payment method (in which consumers must file a complaint with the firm or relevant authorities in order to receive payment).

d. *The Degree of Autonomy or Self-regulation of the Regulated Entity*

A final policy decision concerns the degree of the financial companies' discretion in administering regulatory redress schemes. Even when authorities order mandatory repayment, they might still be flexible in the way that the firm manages the redress scheme and handles individual claims. In other cases, the authorities themselves might determine the specific formula that calculates the repayment amounts. Generally speaking, more regulation (less discretion) creates a fairer and more level field among consumers and firms, while allowing self-regulation and a higher degree of autonomy can enhance market efficiency, as firms can find a specific solution that best fits their case.[131]

6 Conclusion

Several countries have successfully deployed regulatory mass redress schemes, proving that these can be potent alternatives to slow and inefficient court-led collective actions. For mass harm, regulatory mass redress is a great improvement over the conventional individual form of ADR or ODR. Thus, regulatory redress schemes, often used in tandem with consumer ombudsmen systems, are rightfully called the newest redress "technology"[132] and deserve more attention from policymakers and academia.

The case studies show wide variations among the regulatory redress schemes that different nations use, which has made it difficult for policymakers to identify this technique as a distinct solution for mass harm. The discrepancies have also made it difficult for them to pinpoint commonalities among the plans and categorize the necessary policy decisions. This article clarifies the issue by presenting some of the relevant considerations—the efficiency gains, the right to a fair trial, due process concerns, and the degree of openness and transparency. Based on these points, policymakers must make specific design choices such as determining a threshold necessary to activate a redress scheme, or the prescribed maximum amount of repayment that a regulatory redress scheme will offer. Determining the extent of the court's contribution, including a party's right to appeal a regulatory redress order, is also an important policy choice. As a more practical matter, figuring out how to reach harmed consumers and repay them is yet another direction in which nations have greatly diverged. Finally, legislators must establish the degree of autonomy that they will allow the firms in managing their redress schemes.

---

[131] *See* [17].

[132] *See generally* HODGES & VOET, *supra* note 1.

There are no correct answers to any of the policy choices. Among other factors, the extent of the harm and the expected amount of redress for a typical case are relevant and will vary from case to case. In addition, a nation's tendency to allow industries to self-regulate or its deference to regulatory authority are also important considerations when determining the rigidity of a regulatory redress scheme.

What is clear is that *regulatory mass* redress—not court litigation and not redress of individual cases—is the most efficient way to deal with certain types of mass harm that occur frequently in certain industries. The case studies in this paper illustrate that the financial sector is an area in which mass harm occurs commonly and that regulatory mass redress has been an effective way to tackle it.

Given that the concept of regulatory mass redress is a relatively novel way to compensate harmed consumers, I hope that this paper will stimulate research on the regulatory mass redress cases of other nations and lead to additional discussion about the policy choices involved in designing optimal redress schemes, as well as to the further development of new techniques for consumer redress.

References

1. Vicki Waye & Vince Morabito, *Collective Forms of Consumer Redress: Financial Ombudsman Service Case Study*, 12 J. CORP. L. STUDIES 1, 1 (2012).
2. Eilis Ferran, *Regulatory Lessons from the Payment Protection Insurance Mis-selling Scandal in the U.K.*, 13 EUR. BUS. ORG. L. REV. 247 (2012).
3. Micheal Legg, Many Wrongs Can Make a Right: How Mass Redress Schemes Can Replace Court Action (Nov. 23, 2015), http://theconversation.com/many-wrongs-can-make-a-right-how-mass-redress-schemes-can-replace-court-action-51118 [https://perma.cc/9MTZ-C964].
4. United Nations Conference on Trade and Development, Dispute Resolution and Redress at 1 (Jul. 9–10, 2018), https://unctad.org/meetings/en/SessionalDocuments/cicplpd11_en.pdf) [https://perma.cc/Y66Q-MLJM] [hereinafter UNCTAD (2018)].
5. Christopher Hodges, *Current Discussions on Consumer Redress: Collective Redress and ADR*, 13 ERA Forum 11, 16 (2012).; UNCTAD (2018), *supra* note 10, at 6.
6. Christopher Hodges, *Collective Redress: The Need for New Technologies,* 42 J. CONSUMER POL'Y REV. 59 (2018) [hereinafter Collective Redress].
7. Paul Adams & Stefan Hunt, *Encouraging Consumers to Claim Redress: Evidence from a Field Trial*, FCA OCCASIONAL PAPERS, Apr. 2013.
8. Kevin M. McDonald, *Who's Policing The Financial Cop on The Beat—A Call for Judicial Review of The Consumer Financial Protection Bureau's Non-Legislative Rules*, 35 REV. BANKING & FIN. L. 225, 227 (2015).
9. Christopher L. Peterson, *Consumer Financial Protection Bureau Law Enforcement: An Empirical Review,* 90 TUL. L. REV. 1057 (2016).
10. Kent Markus, *How will the Capital One order handle refunds?* Consumer Financial Protection BUREAU (July 18, 2012), https://www.consumerfinance.gov/about-us/blog/capital-one-order-refunds/ [https://perma.cc/CSK2-6RFD].
11. Gail Hillebrand, *How to stop mystery credit card fees,* CONSUMER FINANCIAL PROTECTION BUREAU, (July 18, 2012), https://www.consumerfinance.gov/about-us/blog/stop-mystery-credit-card-fees/ [https://perma.cc/8DY8-X99J].
12. Stefanie H. Jackman & Daniel L. Delnero, *CFPB's Systemic Regulation of Four Industries: Enforcing Broader Changes* Via *Consent Order,* 31 LEGAL BACKGROUNDER 16, 1 (2016).

13. August Horvath, John Villafranco, & Stephen Calkins, ABA SECTION OF ANTITRUST LAW CONSUMER PROTECTION LAW DEVELOPMENTS 259 (2009).
14. Eun-Joo Lee, *Card companies cut DCDS charges*, KOREA JOONGANG DAILY (Apr. 18, 2013), http://koreajoongangdaily.joins.com/news/article/article.aspx?aid=2970323 [https://perma.cc/2RV9-AT4X].
15. Kyung-min Lee, *Regulator inspects card firms ahead of fee reduction*, THE KOREA TIMES (Aug. 7, 2019), http://m.koreatimes.co.kr/pages/article.asp?newsIdx=258702 [https://perma.cc/6EAU-GBJT].
16. Park-Eun Jee, *Samsung Life defies FSS, sues policyholder*, KOREA JOONGANG DAILY (Aug. 14, 2018), http://koreajoongangdaily.joins.com/news/article/article.aspx?aid=3051875 [https://perma.cc/V3JR-RXKT].
17. Pablo Cortes, *Accredited online dispute resolution services: creating European legal standards for ensuring fair and effective processes,* 17 INFO. & COMM. TECH. L. 221, 223-24 (2008).

Macao's Experience in Building Cross-Border Tourists Consumers Dispute-Solving System

Dan Wei and Gloria Ka In Pun

1 World's Tourism Development and Its Significance

In pace with the global economic growth, effects of globalization and coordination regarding tourism policies among countries, tourism has become a worldwide rapid-growing economic sector and has been experiencing a continuous growth in recent decades. In 2018, travel and tourism sector contributed $8.8 trillion and created 319 million jobs to the global economy, occupying 10.4% of the global gross domestic product (GDP),[1] while international tourist arrivals reached up to 1.4 billion,[2] experiencing eight consecutive year of sustained growth.[3] Tourism is undoubtedly an important industry to boost the development of global economy, yet it is also a pillar to many countries' economy and culture integration as it stimulates consumption, creates job opportunities and fosters culture exchange, thus to help countries elevate their recognition in international society. To ensure a sustainable development of tourism industry, consumer protection is a paramount task. Tourism industry generates abundant positive effects to a country, when the most obvious effect lies on the great increase of economic activities, consumers then become the actual contributors behind. Therefore, it is necessary to set up a complete help-seeking mechanism to

[1]"Travel & Tourism continues strong growth above global GDP." World Travel & Tourism Council, February 2019, https://www.wttc.org/about/media-centre/press-releases/press-releases/2019/travel-tourism-continues-strong-growth-above-global-gdp/.

[2]"International Tourist Arrivals Reach 1.4 billion Two Years Ahead of Forecasts." World Tourism Organization, January 2019, https://www2.unwto.org/press-release/2019-01-21/international-tourist-arrivals-reach-14-billion-two-years-ahead-forecasts.

[3]"Travel & Tourism continues strong growth above global GDP." World Travel & Tourism Council, February 2019, https://www.wttc.org/about/media-centre/press-releases/press-releases/2019/travel-tourism-continues-strong-growth-above-global-gdp/.

D. Wei (✉) · G. Ka In Pun
University of Macau, Macao, China
e-mail: danwei@um.edu.mo

D. Wei et al. (eds.), *Innovation and the Transformation of Consumer Law*,
https://doi.org/10.1007/978-981-15-8948-5_23

reinforce consumer confidence as they are always at the weak and vulnerable position when dealing especially with cross-border consumer dispute. Only when consumers are appropriately protected and they feel confident at involving in economic activities, all the other strategies concerning with sustainable development of tourism industry can be carried on.

2 Macao's Tourism Development Under Its Multiple Roles

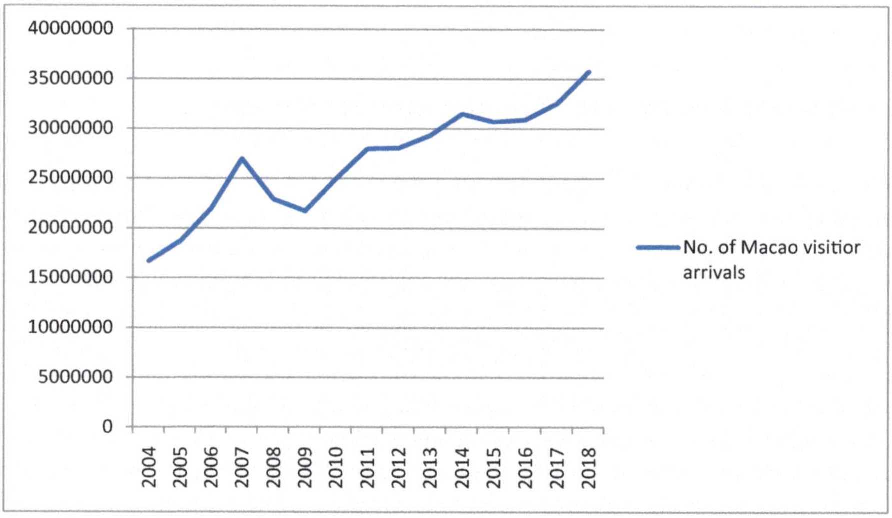

The number of Macao visitor arrivals since 2014

As a special administrative region of China, Macao has transformed from a small fishing village into an international city whose GDP per capita gained the first place among all the Asian cities in 2018.[4] In the past decade, Macao experienced a drastic increase in tourists, reaching 35,803,663 visitors in 2018, half more than in 2008, in which the largest proportion of tourists is from Mainland China.[5] According to the World Travel and Tourism Council, in 2017, Macao's reliance on international tourism spend was the greatest among the world, occupying 97.3% of the total

[4]"List of Asian countries by GDP per capita." Statistics Times, March 2019, http://statisticstimes.com/economy/asian-countries-by-gdp-per-capita.php, source from: International Monetary Fund World Economic Outlook (October-2018).

[5]Tourist arrivals, Macao SAR Statistics and Census Service Bureau, 2018, https://www.dsec.gov.mo/Statistic.aspx?NodeGuid=251baebb-6e5b-4452-8ad1-7768eafc99ed.

gross domestic product.[6] On 18 February 2019, the outline development plan for the Guangdong-Hong Kong-Macao Greater Bay Area was officially launched. It further clarified and emphasized on Macao's three important roles in its development orientation, they are 'one centre, one platform, one base', which implies to build Macao into a world centre for tourism and leisure, a service platform for economic and trade cooperation between China and Portuguese-speaking countries, and a cooperation and exchange base which promotes the coexistence of diversified cultures under the mainstream of Chinese culture.[7] Along with the above roles, the importance of tourism to Macao's economy and the aim of sustainable development of economy, tourist consumers' protection is an indispensable job. It is essential for Macao to establish dispute-solving system to fully protect consumers from any loss resulting from lack of resolution mechanism, so as to maintain Macao's international image.

3 Tourist Consumer Protection Mechanism in Macao and Its Innovation

During travel, physical safety is one of the most concerning questions. For this reason, Macao SAR has set up the Tourism Crisis Management Office (GGCT), a strategic coordination committee whose mission is to guarantee immediate and effective operational measures to be taken and provide assistance when Macao SAR residents encounter emergent situations resulted from serious accidents, catastrophes or calamities abroad, as well as tourists who are involved in similar situations when travelling in Macao SAR.[8] In addition, Tourism Crisis Management Office has established a 24 h hotline for tourists and residents to seek help under urgent circumstances and is responsible to manage Macao SAR's travel alert system. Macao SAR's travel alert system covers 77 countries or tourist destination and is categorized into three levels, each level represents different degree of threat. It aims to raise tourists' and residents' awareness, and to facilitate their decision through an easy and timely dissemination of information about crisis situations, emergencies or catastrophes affecting different parts of the world.[9]

In spite of physical safety, the most frequent problem encountered by tourists is consumer disputes. In 1988, Macao government launched its first consumer protection law. It gave definition to the word 'consumer', listed out consumers' rights and indicated the prohibition of harmful activities to consumers. Nevertheless, as

[6]FIGURE 12: RELIANCE ON INTERNATIONAL TOURISM SPEND, 2017, from City Travel & Tourism Impact 2018, World Travel and Tourism Council, https://www.wttc.org/-/media/files/reports/economic-impact-research/cities-2018/city-travel--tourism-impact-2018final.pdf.

[7]"澳门各界:《粤港澳大湾区发展规划纲要》带来新机遇", Liaison Office Of The Central People's Government In The Macao S.A.R., February 2019, http://www.zlb.gov.cn/2019-02/20/c_1210063766.htm, source from: 中新社.

[8]Mission of Macao SAR Tourism Crisis Management Office, https://www.ggct.gov.mo/en/mission.

[9]"Macao SAR Government Implements Travel Alert System", http://mtt.macaotourism.gov.mo/201703/en/contents/1/620.html?1488349519.

years passed, Macao has entered into a new and economically fast-growing era where economic structure changed and tourism has become the most important industry in Macao. As a result, consumer protection law should be correspondingly adjusted according to the current situation. In 2019, Macao SAR Executive Council finished discussing the draft bill of the New Consumer Protection Law. The draft bill took the experience and legal system of the nearby countries and places for reference, its content mainly focuses on a more thorough clarification on consumer rights, establishment of different mechanisms to monitor traders' behavior and safeguard consumers' interest, as well as setting up a cooling-off period for consumers and endowing Macao SAR Government Consumer Council authority to punish and monitor.[10]

3.1 Macao SAR Government Consumer Council

To put consumer rights protection into implementation, Macao SAR Government Consumer Council was set up in 1988 on the basis of Consumer Protection Law. Its objective is to express its opinion regarding policies defined by the Macao SAR Government's Administration in respect of consumer rights protection and promotion on essential measures for protecting those rights[11] whereas its other major responsibilities are to promote actively consumer rights protection,[12] to study and transfer consumers' objection and complaints to the responsible department and to provide resolution mechanism such as mediation, arbitration to cases involving small consumer disputes. In order to better foster consumer rights protection task, Macao SAR Government Consumer Council established a number of innovative mechanisms, they are consumer arbitration centre and certified shop.

3.2 Macao SAR Consumer Arbitration Centre

Established in 1998, Macao SAR Consumer Arbitration Centre is the first arbitration center in Asia-Pacific region which specializes in handling consumer disputes and provides a free, fair, efficient and effective dispute-solving method other than judicial litigation to both consumers and traders, reducing their economic and time cost when encountering disputes. It aims to settle small consumer disputes occurred in Macao SAR, with the amount of 100,000 Macao Patacas or less, as well as to provide

[10] 行政會完成討論 «消費者權益保護法» 法律草案,Macao SAR Government Portal, March 2019, https://www.gov.mo/zh-hant/news/274088/, source from: Macao SAR Executive Council.

[11] Introduction of Macao SAR Government Consumer Council, https://www.consumer.gov.mo/AboutUS/Intro.aspx?lang=en.

[12] Performance pledge of Macao SAR Government Consumer Council, https://www.consumer.gov.mo/AboutUS/commitment.aspx?lang=en.

information, mediation and arbitration services. If a consumer thinks he has suffered a loss due to the purchase of defective products, unsatisfactory service, or being forced to purchase goods or services at an unreasonable price, consumer may bring relevant documents to the Consumer Arbitration Centre for help. If trader cherishes his business' goodwill and wishes to settle dispute with consumers, he may also approach the Consumer Arbitration Centre for information and assistance.[13] Once a trader joins the Consumer Arbitration Centre, trader must accept the settling of disputes by Consumer Arbitration Centre when the relevant dispute is occurred in Macao, its amount is of 100,000 Macao Patacas or less, and the settlement is agreed or requested by the consumer. In addition, Macao SAR Government Consumer Council promised in its performance pledge that cases concerning with consumer arbitration service will be followed up within 12 days after the acceptance of application for arbitration.[14] It takes normally an average of one to two months to solve a case through mediation and arbitration, some of the cases can even be concluded within one month.[15]

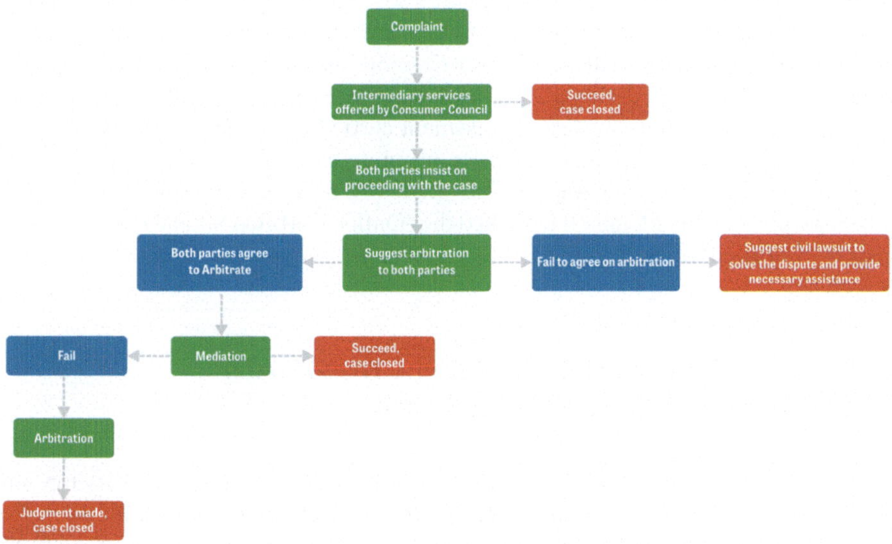

Macao SAR consumer arbitration flow chart. Arbitration flow chart of Macao SAR Consumer Arbitration Centre, https://www.consumer.gov.mo/CAC/Intro.aspx?lang=en

[13]Introduction of Macao SAR Consumer Arbitration Centre, https://www.consumer.gov.mo/CAC/Intro.aspx?lang=en.

[14]Performance pledge of Macao SAR Government Consumer Council, https://www.consumer.gov.mo/AboutUS/commitment.aspx?lang=en.

[15]"消費爭議仲裁中心 處理600個案70%和解", BASTILLE POST, June 2017 https://www.bastillepost.com/macau/article/674601-%E6%B6%88%E8%B2%BB%E7%88%AD%E8%AD%B0%E4%BB%B2%E8%A3%81%E4%B8%AD%E5%BF%83-%E8%99%95%E7%90%86600%E5%80%8B%E6%A1%8870%E5%92%8C%E8%A7%A3.

3.3 *Certified Shop*

For the purpose of elevating consumer confidence in Macao traders, Macao SAR Consumer Arbitration Centre set up an 'Adherent' Scheme. By joining the 'Adherent' Scheme, traders make a promise to consumers as they become obliged to resolve every consumer dispute, thus to increase the efficiency and effectiveness of resolving disputes between both parties, to better protect consumers' rights and to enhance the traders' reputation. In order to become an 'Adherent', traders must promise to agree to submit and resolve consumer disputes in the Consumer Arbitration Centre if disputes cannot be settled through negotiation. This agreement represents that if the dispute between consumer and 'Adherent' cannot be settled under Macao SAR Government Consumer Council's coordination, traders must attain resolution through making use of the efficient, fair and free services provided by Macao SAR Consumer Arbitration Centre after satisfying relevant conditions. With the objective to demonstrate the principle of 'honesty and trustworthiness', Macao SAR Government Consumer Council established the 'Certified Shop' system in 2001. If shops have joined as 'Adherents' for over a year, abide by the Regulations and Undertakings of Certified Shops and pass the assessment of the Consumer Council, the 'Adherents' will be awarded the emblem of 'Certified shops'.[16] This system does not only enforce consumer rights protection through the strict assessment carried out by Macao SAR Government, it indeed also encourages traders to promote business in an honest behavior. Furthermore, as online consumption has gradually become common, Macao SAR Government Consumer Council launched the 'Online Certified Shops' system on the basis of 'Certified Shop'.[17]

4 Macao's Experience in Building Cross-Border Consumers Dispute-Solving System

Analyzing from the rapid development of Macao tourism industry and its top ten tourist-source markets in the past decade, Macao hosts tourists from all over the world each year. Among all the tourist-source markets, the number of tourists from Mainland China, Hong Kong SAR and Taiwan has increased significantly, occupying the top three positions over the past ten years.[18] Due to Macao's diversified tourist-source markets and its major economic reliance on tourists from Mainland China and Hong Kong SAR, plus the close cooperation and joint development of the Guangdong-Hong Kong-Macao Greater Bay Area, Macao SAR noticed the needs

[16]Regulations and undertakings of Macao SAR Certified Shops, https://www.consumer.gov.mo/Shop/promise.aspx?lang=en.

[17]Introduction of Macao SAR Certified Shops, https://www.consumer.gov.mo/Shop/Intro.aspx?lang=en.

[18]Top ten visitor source markets, Macao Tourism Data Plus, 2008-2018, https://dataplus.macaotourism.gov.mo/Publication/Report?lang=E.

and urgency of setting up both interregional and international consumer disputes-solving mechanism. Until now, it has built alliance with a total number of 40 regional and international members.[19]

4.1 *International Consumers' Dispute-Solving Mechanism of Macao*

In respect of the international consumer dispute, Macao SAR Government Consumer Council has initiated cooperation with the Consumer Association of Singapore, Directorate-General for Consumer Affairs of Portugal, International Consumer Organization for Portuguese-speaking Countries, CONSUMARE, Portuguese Economic and Food Safety Authority and the Portuguese Association for Consumer Protection so far. When tourists or Macao SAR residents encounter consumer disputes during their travel to Macao or Singapore, they can seek help from the respective local consumer association after returning to their place of residence. The consumer dispute will then be settled through case transfer and information exchange. On the other hand, taking advantage of Macao SAR as a service platform between China and Portuguese-speaking countries, the Cooperation Agreement for dealing with consumer complaints in the Greater Bay Area has designated Macao SAR Government Consumer Council to be the consumer complaints' transferring platform between cities in Greater Bay area and Portuguese consumer organizations. In 2018, Macao SAR Government Consumer Council established partnership with the Portuguese Association for Consumer Protection by signing collaboration agreement. Macao SAR Government Consumer Council then officially becomes a transferring platform between consumer organizations in Mainland China and in Portugal, and the related cases will be transferred to the respective consumer organization within 15 days.[20] For the moment, statistic regarding to Macao's international cases referral is not available.

4.2 *Macao's Interregional Consumer Disputes Resolution Scheme*

According to 'One country, two systems', a constitutional principle of the People's Republic of China, Macao SAR's and Hong Kong SAR's capitalist system remain

---

[19] Alliance of Macao SAR Government Consumer Council, https://www.consumer.gov.mo/AboutUS/allide.aspx?lang=en.

[20] "澳消委會為大灣區與葡消保組織搭建合作平台　簽署備忘錄建立轉介消費個案機制及處理原則", Macao SAR Government Information Bureau, April 2018, https://www.gcs.gov.mo/showNews.php?DataUcn=123749&PageLang=C, source from: Macao SAR Government Consumer Council.

unchanged while Mainland China adopts socialism as its economic and social system. Despite the principle 'One country, two systems', China's current situation is of 'one country, two systems, three legal systems and four jurisdictions'. Due to the history background, the legal systems of Macao SAR, Hong Kong SAR and Mainland China are different. Macao SAR belongs to civil law family; Hong Kong SAR follows common law tradition while the legal system of Mainland China is the socialist system of laws with Chinese characteristics[21] which is largely influenced by civil law tradition. Therefore, the consumer disputes resolution schemes established on the basis of respective consumer law between Macao SAR, Hong Kong SAR and Mainland China are not unified. Nevertheless, along with the fast-growing development of tourism industry and the close cooperation between cities in Guangdong-Hong Kong-Macao Greater Bay Area, cross-border economic activities between Mainland China and Macao are increasing drastically, thus bringing more consumer disputes correspondingly. For this reason, it is necessary and urgent to set up an interregional consumer dispute-solving system on the basis of collaboration agreement.

4.2.1 Interregional Consumers' Dispute-Solving Collaboration Agreement

Over years, Macao SAR Government Consumer Council has been working hard on promoting consumer rights protection through cross-border dispute-solving scheme. After considering the tremendous quantity of tourists from Mainland China, Macao SAR Government Consumer Council has signed collaboration agreements on consumer rights protection with several cities in Mainland China, including Beijing, Tianjin and Liaoning etc. When consumers from Macao or related cities encounter consumer dispute during cross-border consumption, they can seek help from or make complaints towards any consumer association of the involved parties. Information regarding the complaint cases will be sent to the tourists' visited region where disputes are occurred for resolution. Lastly, result will be sent back to the consumer association where complaints are accepted. The above complaint transferring system successfully provides efficient and effective services to consumers.

4.2.2 Cooperation Between Macao and Other Cities in Greater Bay Area on Consumer Disputes Resolution

The mutual cooperation between Guangdong-Hong Kong-Macao Greater Bay Area and the sustainable development of Macao tourism industry foster cross-border consuming activities. In order to enforce and safeguard consumers' confidence, Macao SAR Government Consumer Council has been concentrating on improving

[21] "The Socialist System of Laws with Chinese Characteristics," The State Council Information Office of the People's Republic of China, October 2011, http://www.scio.gov.cn/zfbps/ndhf/2011/Document/1036756/1036756.htm.

consumer rights protection services and increasing the flexibility of dispute resolution. With this aim, the Secretary for Economy and Finance of Macao SAR revised the Regulations of Consumer Arbitration Centre, allowing Macao SAR Consumer Arbitration Centre to conduct cross-border mediation and hearing through long-distance information transmission, such as web video conference.[22] That is to say, after returning to place of habitual residence, tourist consumers can still receive a fair and reasonable judgement from Macao SAR Consumer Arbitration Centre. The revision elevates Macao SAR Consumer Arbitration Centre's utilization rate and contributes to Macao's future development in the area of cross-border consumer dispute resolution.

On 15 March 2018, in accordance with the collaboration agreement on protection of consumer rights, Macao SAR Government Consumer Council and Zhuhai Association for Consumers' Rights and Interest Protection initiated Macao-Zhuhai the cross-border arbitration service.[23] If Zhuhai's residents encounter consumer disputes in Macao and request Macao SAR Consumer Arbitration Centre for settling, even though consumers have already retuned to Zhuhai, they can still participate in arbitration's process under the coordination of Zhuhai Association for Consumers' Rights and Interest Protection.

On 10 April 2018, Macao SAR Government Consumer Council, together with the consumer associations of Hong Kong SAR and the 9 municipalities in Guangdong–Hong Kong-Macao Greater Bay Area, signed a memorandum of cooperation regarding consumer protect in Greater Bay Area.[24] It enforces the sharing of information and regional interaction among consumer associations of the 11 cities in Greater Bay Area, as well as established a cooperation mechanism for transferring complaint cases.

On 31 May 2019, Guangdong Province Consumer Council signed the Guangdong-Hong Kong Collaboration Agreement on Consumers' Rights Protection and Guangdong-Macao Collaboration Agreement on Consumers' Rights with Hong Kong SAR Consumer Council and Macao SAR Government Consumer Council respectively. In addition, the Consumers Complaints Transferring Platform in Guangdong-Hong Kong-Macao Greater Bay Area was officially launched. From then on, consumers from Guangdong Province, Macao SAR and Hong Kong SAR can make complaints through logging into the platform website, putting 'one net transfer' into practice. Subsequently, the platform will transfer the related cross-border consumer dispute to the competent consumer associations for resolution.

22"修改澳門消費爭議仲裁中心規章 跨域調解及審判增旅客消費消心", Macao SAR Government Portal, January 2018, https://www.gov.mo/zh-hant/news/229623/, source from: Macao SAR Government Consumer Council.

23"消費爭議仲裁中心成立20年出版特刊 提升服務本月中實行澳珠跨域仲裁服務", Macao SAR Government Portal, March 2018, https://www.gcs.gov.mo/showNews.php?PageLang=C&DataUcn=122899, source from: Macao SAR Government Consumer Council.

24"澳消委會為大灣區與葡消保組織搭建合作平台 簽署備忘錄建立轉介消費個案機制及處理原則", Macao SAR Government Information Bureau, April 2018, https://www.gcs.gov.mo/showNews.php?DataUcn=123749&PageLang=C, source from: Macao SAR Government Consumer Council.

The Consumers Complaints Transfer Platform in Guangdong-Hong Kong-Macao Greater Bay Area provides one-stop service and reduces the time needed for transferring documents. On the other hand, as the platform is of bidirectional operation, consumers can acknowledge the case's most updated situation while traders can also check on the case's information and consumers' opinions etc.[25]

The innovative 'one net transfer' system was launched under the initiative of Guangdong-Hong Kong-Macao Greater Bay Area. The Greater Bay Area comprises the two Special Administrative Regions of Hong Kong and Macao, and the nine municipalities in Guangdong Province. As the fourth largest bay area in the world, the greater bay area had a combined population of around 70 million in 2017[26] and contributed $16,419.7 billion of GDP in 2018.[27] Its main objectives include facilitating in-depth integration within the region, promoting coordinated regional economic development and developing an international first-class bay area ideal for living, working and travelling.[28] The 'one net transfer' system brings giant convenience and assistance to Greater Bay Area's development as it connects the 11 cities and acts as a form of enforcement to safeguard consumers' rights during cross-borders consumption through accelerating dispute resolution's efficiency, reducing dispute-settling time and encouraging both consumers and traders to promote economic activities. A complete platform for dealing with consumer dispute is unquestionably beneficial to the development of such an economically fast-growing bay area.

4.2.3 Zhuhai Hengqin New Area's Utilization of Macao SAR's Consumer Dispute-Solving Mechanism and Its Own Innovative System

Hengqin is a coastal island tucked into the southern corner of Zhuhai city in Guangdong province. As Hengqin is closely adjacent to Macao, in pace with the completion of Hong Kong-Zhuhai-Macao Bridge, it became the only continental region that connects Macao and Hong Kong. Hence, Hengqin has been selected as a New Area in order to enhance economic ties with Hong Kong and Macao with the objectives to cultivate an international, legalized and market-oriented business environment[29] and

[25]"大灣區快線: 灣區消費投訴 一網跨境轉辦", 文匯報, June 2019, http://paper.wenweipo.com/2019/06/01/CN1906010010.htm.

[26]Overview of Guangdong-Hong Kong-Macao Greater Bay Area, https://www.bayarea.gov.hk/en/about/overview.html.

[27]"Statistics of the Guangdong-Hong Kong-Macao Greater Bay Area." HKTDC Research-Hong Kong Economy, June 2019, http://hong-kong-economy-research.hktdc.com/business-news/article/Guangdong-Hong-Kong-Macau-Bay-Area/Statistics-of-the-Guangdong-Hong-Kong-Macao-Greater-Bay-Area/bayarea/en/1/1X000000/1X0AE3Q1.htm.

[28]Overview of Guangdong-Hong Kong-Macao Greater Bay Area, https://www.bayarea.gov.hk/en/about/overview.html.

[29]Introduction of Hengqin New Area of Zhuhai, China (Guangdong) Pilot Free Trade Zone, http://en.hengqin.gov.cn/ftze/About/201503/3993a81884be4a9b98cf98a8a6e6b722.shtml.

to foster the sustainable development of Macao's economy. Base on the above objectives, Hengqin becomes the first city in Mainland China which utilized Macao SAR's 'Certified Shop' scheme and set up 'Hengqin Certified Shop' model.[30] By hanging the 'Henqin Certified Shop' plaque in business premises, it can elevate consumers' confidence and accelerate consumption rate. Besides, the abundant benefits of joining 'Hengqin Certified Shop' brings an effect that traders are more likely to regulate their trading behavior by complying with the evaluation regulation of 'Hengqin Certified Shop', thus to cultivate a safe environment for consumption. In addition, Hengqin also reached a great success on innovating consumer rights protection mechanism. For instance, in 2016, Hengin initiated the 'Pre-claim' system and the small consumer dispute arbitration.[31] Regarding the 'Pre-claim' system, its functional operation is as follow. When the consumer disputes occurred between consumers and traders cannot be resolved after Zhuhai Hengqin New Area Consumer Association's coordination, consumers can then request to utilize the 'Pre-claim' system after satisfying certain conditions. Subsequently, Zhuhai Hengqin New Area Consumer Association will transfer the case to Zhuhai Arbitration Commission for resolution. If Zhuhai Arbitration Commission's ruling identified trader's responsibility on compensation, Zhuhai Hengqin New Area Consumer Association will transfer the amount of compensation from the special fund account to the consumer within a specified time while trader needs to deposit the compensation amount back into the account. If trader did not put back the pre-claimed amount within the designated time, Zhuhai Hengqin New Area Consumer Association will pursue the compensation through legal process.[32] The 'Pre-claim' system uses a large degree of enforcement to protect consumers' interests as it ensures the ruling's fulfillment and strongly increase the utilization of arbitration services.

4.3 A Closer Look on the Effectiveness of Interregional Enforcement Cooperation

The cooperation between consumer councils across the Guangdong-Hong Kong-Macao Greater Bay Area has attained a great success in recent years. In the past three years, consumer councils across Guangdong Province have settled more than 1500 cross-border consumer dispute cases and retrieved losses valued at $2.07 million.[33] The big achievement on interregional consumer rights protection should be credited

[30]"横琴新区:创新型消费维权体系", 人民网, July 2016, http://expo.people.com.cn/n1/2016/0708/c403808-28537702.html.

[31]"横琴新区:创新型消费维权体系", 人民网, July 2016, http://expo.people.com.cn/n1/2016/0708/c403808-28537702.html.

[32]"横琴创新型消费维权体系 探索先行赔付制度", December, 2018 http://news.zh51home.com/artical/150325.html, source from: 南方网.

[33]"New website helps Greater Bay Area consumers report complaints." CHINA DAILY.COM.CN, June 2019, http://www.chinadaily.com.cn/a/201906/02/WS5cf39c49a3104842260bf0ce.html.

to the joints efforts made by the consumer councils from different cities. To continue the success and to further enlarge consumer rights protection work, the harmonization of consumer law is the core task. As mentioned in the above paragraphs that China' current situation is of 'one country, two systems, three legal systems and four jurisdictions', the difference in legislation and law enforcement is the major obstacle in establishing a complete and unified consumer rights protection mechanism. Henceforth, it is necessary to ensure the unification in the area of legislation and law enforcement as this can motivate cross-border consumption and contribute in cultivating a safe and friendly business environment.

5 A Comparative Study with the Cross-Border Dispute Resolution Network in European Union

The European Union is a unique economic and political union between 28 EU countries.[34] As cross-border consumption has become a very common global economic activity, the European Union has been devoting itself to work on consumer protection. To help consumers solve consumer disputes, the European Commission provides several dispute resolution tools and established the European Consumer Centres Network (ECC-Net). ECC-Net comprises 30 centres covering the EU, Iceland and Norway with the aim to provide consumers with information on their rights related to their cross-border purchases of goods and services, to advise them in case of problems and to assist them with complaint handling so that they can take full advantage of the internal market.[35] In addition, the ECC-Net also contributes to further enhance consumer confidence across the European Union. ECC-Net achieved great success on its objectives. In 2018, ECC-Net provided direct assistance to over 118,000 consumers and serve as contact points for Online Dispute Resolution platform designed to help EU consumers solve online shopping problems.[36]

Similar to the European Union, the Guangdong-Hong Kong-Macao Greater Bay Area adopts a consolidated single market and has a combined economy under the initiative of economic integration. For this reason, the success of both European Union's and Greater Bay Area's efforts on protecting consumer's rights through building cross-border dispute-solving mechanisms have proven the needs of a global and continuous consumer rights protection work.

---

[34] "The EU in brief" on European Union's official website, https://europa.eu/european-union/about-eu/eu-in-brief_en.

[35] European Consumer Centres Network (ECC-Net) on European Commission's official website, https://ec.europa.eu/internal_market/scoreboard/performance_by_governance_tool/european_consumer_centre_network/index_en.htm.

[36] European Consumer Centres Network (ECC-Net) on European Commission's official website, https://ec.europa.eu/internal_market/scoreboard/performance_by_governance_tool/european_consumer_centre_network/index_en.htm.

6 Demonstration on Macao's Success in Consumer Rights Protection Through Interregional and International Cooperation Among Administrative Authorities

The goal of perfecting tourist consumer rights protection cannot be achieved by relying only on one single region's or country's efforts. Indeed, it depends on interregional and international cooperation between institutions. The success of cross-border collaboration on protecting consumer rights between Macao SAR and other cities is an evident example. On 9 to 10 July 2019, the United Nations Conference on Trade and Development (UNCTAD) held the third session of Intergovernmental Group of Experts on Consumer Protection Law and Policy in which representatives from over 100 countries, consumer organizations and law experts from all over the world participated, including Macao SAR Consumer Council. The meeting mainly focused on discussion relating to worldwide consumer protection problems and all participants have made a consensus that revision of consumer protection laws or proposal of new laws is an essential tool to overcome challenges encountered when putting consumer protection work into practice.[37] The consensus is identical to Macao SAR's aim on its consumer law revision and is in line with the spirit of United Nations Guidelines for Consumer Protection.

The United Nations Conference on Trade and Development (UNCTAD) stated in paragraph no. 36 of the United Nations Guidelines for Consumer Protection, revised in 2015, that Member States should encourage the development of fair, effective, transparent and impartial mechanisms to address consumer complaints through administrative, judicial and alternative dispute resolution, including for cross-border cases, as well as in paragraph no. 78 that Member States should, in particular, address the cross-border challenges raised by such activity, including enforcement cooperation and information-sharing with other Member States, and should also cooperate with the relevant stakeholders in the tourism-travel sector.[38] As shown in the United Nations Guidelines for Consumer Protection, UNCTAD is strongly supporting the settlement of cross-border disputes through cross-border cooperation. On the other hand, the UNCTAD also indicated in its Manual on Consumer Protection that the current route to international consumer protection for individuals passes by way of institutional, rather than judicial solutions due to the intrinsic difficulty of filing judicial cases across borders, the lack of definite inter-agency cooperation agreements of a judicial nature and the little guarantee of success in long distance litigation.[39] That is to say, nowadays, the resolution of international consumer disputes through non-judicial procedures has become a common route and is highly preferred by tourist

---

[37]"Macao Consumer Council attended UNCTAD meeting as Chinese delegates with State Administration for Market Regulation representative." Macao SAR Government Portal, July 2018, https://news.gov.mo/detail/en/N18GRxt2f7?0, source from: Macao SAR Government Consumer Council.

[38]United Nations Guidelines for Consumer Protection, United Nations Conference on Trade and Development, 2016, https://unctad.org/en/PublicationsLibrary/ditccplpmisc2016d1_en.pdf.

[39]"Manual on Consumer Protection", United Nations Conference on Trade and Development, July 2018, p. 58, https://unctad.org/en/PublicationsLibrary/ditccplp2017d1_en.pdf.

consumers. This emphasizes once again the needs of cross-border cooperation among administrative authorities. With regards to the United Nations Conference on Trade and Development's promotion on cross-border dispute-solving cooperation, Macao has indeed achieved successfully this vision through implementing consumer law on interregional and international consumer dispute-solving collaboration and carried out UNCTAD's promotion in recent decade.

Besides, the Hague Conference on Private International Law has been working on the 'tourism project' from a hard law perspective, with the theme presented by Brazil: the protection of international tourists as consumers. The Government of Brazil has formulated several documents on this subject, such as the proposal on draft conventions on cooperation and access to justice for international tourists, on cooperation in respect of the protection of tourists and visitors abroad, accompanied by a justification and a multilingual complaint form and on cooperation in respect of the protection of tourists and visitors abroad and Explanatory Memorandum on the topic of tourist protection.[40] The above proposal aims to count on the Hague Conference prepare a new worldwide network of global cooperation to enhance international tourist protection and to avoid discrimination on the access of justice through a multilateral convention among countries and the establishment of complaint platform. In fact, as we can see, Macao SAR has already put the vision of Hague Conference's 'tourism project' into practice for years. Though Macao's experience at consumer dispute resolution through multilateral agreements and cooperation is not much, its success in settling cross-border consumer disputes through bilateral collaboration has proven that the 'tourism project' of Hague Conference with the objective to protect tourist consumers through conventions is both desirable and feasible.

To create a safe global business environment under tourism's rapid development, cross-border cooperation is an indispensable mean. As Macao is an international city with multiple roles, tourism industry's great contribution to Macao's economy is unquestionable. Therefore, in order to correspond to Macao's roles of being a world centre for tourism and leisure and the service platform between China and Portuguese-speaking countries, Macao SAR Government has been exerting itself in improving consumer's weak position when resolving consumer disputes through revising consumer law, establishing better mechanisms on consumer rights protection and setting up cross-border collaboration schemes. Even though there is still a long path to perfect consumer rights protection, this meaningful task can definitely be achieved with the global joint efforts on cross-border consumer rights protection cooperation.

[40]Protection of tourists, Hague Conference on Private International Law, https://www.hcch.net/en/projects/legislative-projects/protection-of-tourists.

Part III
The Transformation of Consumer Laws

The Need for a Transnational Coordination Mechanism for Complaints of International Tourists

Dan Wei and Hongling Ning

1 Introduction

Fueled by global economic upswing, increased air capacity and visa facilitation, international tourism has experienced steady and strong growth worldwide for many years since 1990. From 2011 to 2018, tourism exports had grown even faster than merchandise exports (+3%) for seven consecutive years. Revenues from international tourism reached a total USD 1.7 trillion in 2018, accounting for 29% of global service exports and 7% of overall exports of goods and services.[1] Worldwide international tourist arrivals increased to 1.4 billion in 2018.[2] Meanwhile, it is estimated that international tourism numbers and confidence are still on the rise.

However, it is submitted that, with the increase of international tourists, dissatisfied tourists will almost inevitably also increase. With the recognition of the weakness and vulnerability of tourists in cross-border situations, there is an increasing need to protect the interests of international tourists among shareholders of the tourism.

It is noteworthy that China remains the world's largest source country for outbound tourism in terms of expenditure. Chinses tourists travelling aboard totally spent 257.7 billion US dollars in 2017.[3] The number of outbound Chinese tourist amounted to 149. 72 million in 2018.[4] On average, each Chinese tourist spent about US $800 per oversea travel in 2018.[5] But for some destinations, the average expenditure was even

[1] UNWTO [15].
[2] UNWTO [16].
[3] UNWTO [14].
[4] MCT [8].
[5] MCT [9].

D. Wei (✉) · H. Ning
Faculty of Law of the University of Macau, Taipa, Macau
e-mail: danwei@um.edu.mo

D. Wei et al. (eds.), *Innovation and the Transformation of Consumer Law*,
https://doi.org/10.1007/978-981-15-8948-5_24

higher, for instance, the average expenditure of each Chinese tourist in Finland was €1262, far exceeding tourist from other countries.[6]

But every coin has two sides. In recent years, deliberate fraud, attack, stolen or robbery against Chinese tourists happened in some travel destinations such as Columbia, Brazil, France and so on. In addition, accidents including traffic accident, drowning death happened from time to time. The accident happened near coast of the island of Phuket in Thailand in 2018 is a fatal lesson for Chinese tourists. Obviously, China has a stronger interest than others in the protection of their nationals abroad.

This article tries to explore, in the context of the world trend providing protection of international tourists as consumers, how would China contribute to the effort of advancing protection of international tourists, so as to benefit both Chinese outbound tourists and others as well. It first explores the identity of tourists as consumers within the framework of domestic law and judicial practice of China; then it elaborates that international tourists including Chinese tourists are in a weaker position and even vulnerable. On basis of that, it asserts that a transnational coordination mechanism for complaints of international tourists is in need.

2 Tourists as Consumers

2.1 Tourists as Consumers in Laws and Regulations

In Chinese Law, though not specifically mentioned, tourists are as one kind of consumers could be easily and clearly presumed from provisions in Tourism Law of the People's Republic of China[7] and Law of the People's Republic of China on the Protection of Consumer Rights and Interests.[8] Article 92 of Tourism Law is about dispute settlement mechanism between a tourist and a tourism operator, it reads as follows:

In the case of any dispute between a tourist and a tourism operator, the dispute may be settled through any of the following means:

(1) *negotiation between two parties*;
(2) *application to the consumer association, tourism complaint acceptance institution or relevant mediation organization for mediation*;
(3) *application to the arbitration institution for arbitration in accordance with the arbitration agreement reached between the tourist and the tourism operator*;
(4) *lawsuit brought to the people's court.*

[6]MCT [7].

[7]Tourism Law of the People's Republic of China was adopted in 2013, and was amended twice in 2016 and 2018 respectively.

[8]Law of the People's Republic of China on the Protection of Consumer Rights and Interests was adopted in 1993, and was amended twice in 2009 and 2013 respectively.

According to Article 36 of Law on the Protection of Consumer Rights and Interests, *CHINA CONSUMERS' ASSOCIATION is* an organization with the aim of protecting legitimate rights and interests of consumers. One of its functions is to deal with complaints from consumers and conduct investigations and mediations regarding the complaint issues.

As a tourist could plea for the help of *CHINA CONSUMERS' ASSOCIATION* whose objective is to protect consumers, it is no doubt that tourists are as one kind of consumers and accordingly they could invoke Law on the Protection of Consumer Rights and Interests.

Moreover, in a judicial interpretation document, Provisions of the Supreme People's Court on Several Issues Concerning the Application of Law in the Trial of Cases about Tour Disputes,[9] Article 6 stipulates:

Where, in a standard contract, notice, statement, bulletin, etc., *a tour operator makes any unfair or unreasonable provisions on tourists, or reduces its liability or exempts itself from liability for any damage to the legitimate rights and interests of tourists, and a tourist claims that such provisions are void according to Article 24 of the Law on Protection of Consumer Rights and Interests, the people's court shall support such a claim.*

Therefore, it is no doubt that a tourist is a kind of consumer in Chinese law.

In fact, not only China, but also the world generally treats tourists as consumers. In the United Nations Guidelines for Consumer Protection adopted by the 70th United Nations General Assembly on 22 December 2015,[10]measures on tourism are included at paragraph 78 under section K "Measures relating to specific areas":

Member States should ensure that their consumer protection policies are adequate to address the marketing and provision of goods and services related to tourism, including, but not limited to, travel, traveler accommodation and timeshares. Member States should, in particular, address the cross-border challenges raised by such activity, including enforcement cooperation and information-sharing with other Member States, and should also cooperate with the relevant stakeholders in the tourism-travel sector.

Likewise, in the Report of the Secretary-General to the General Assembly of World Tourism Organization(UNWTO) on 20 July 2017, it mentions that the primary objective of the draft UNWTO Convention on the Protection of Tourists and on the Rights and Obligations of Tourism Service Providers is "to establish uniform rules to ensure and promote an appropriate degree of protection of tourists, in order to protect tourists as consumers".[11] Therefore, it could be seen that generally tourists are viewed as a special kind of consumers in the world.

[9]Provisions of the Supreme People's Court on Several Issues Concerning the Application of Law in the Trial of Cases about Tour Disputes, Interpretation of Law [2010] No. 13, 26 October 2016.

[10]Resolution adopted by the General Assembly [12].

[11]Report of the Secretary-General [11].

2.2 Tourists as Consumers in Judgments

In judicial practice, tourists are also treated as consumers. For instance, in a case "Gao Kunhua v. YUHENG Jewelry Shop" published by Yunnan High Court, a tourist named Gao Kunhua was cheated by YUHENG Jewelry Shop and bought counterfeit products, the court concluded that YUHENG Jewelry Shop committed civil fraud, thus applied Article 55 of Law on the Protection of Consumer Rights and Interests and exerted punitive damages to the YUHENG Jewelry Shop.[12]

Some commentator argued that the identity of a tourist, including a tourist traveling aboard, as one kind of consumer is generally absent and unclear in both Chinese domestic laws and judgements concerning travel-contract disputes involving foreign element; Consequently, when it comes to the choice of law, the People's Courts usually apply Article 41 of the Law of Application of Law for Foreign-related Civil Relations of People's Republic of China (LALFCR)[13] which is for a general contract, instead of Article 42 of the LALFCR that provide more favorable choice of law rule for a consumer.[14] In our view, this is really a misunderstanding.

In the case China Dadi Property Insurance Co., Ltd. Jiangxi Branch v. Xue Xiujuan,[15] examined by the commentator Zhen Chen, the tourist Xue Xiujuan concluded a travel contract with Jiangxi Ganzhong International Travel Agent, because of adverse weather she got injured in Thailand. When came back she sued the travel agent and the insurance company for compensations. Both the first instance court and the appeal court explicitly invoked Law of the People's Republic of China on the Protection of Consumer Rights and Interests. The appeal court Jiangxi High People's Court mentioned that according to Article 18 of Law of the People's Republic of China on the Protection of Consumer Rights and Interests and Article 7 and 8 of Provisions of the Supreme People's Court on Several Issues Concerning the Application of Law in the Trial of Cases about Tour Disputes, the travel agent as an operator of tourism services has the obligation to guarantee the personal and property safety of the tourists. It could be seen clearly that in judges' view, a tourist is as one kind of consumer who is under the protection of Law of the People's Republic of China on the Protection of Consumer Rights and Interests.

However, as Xue Xiujuan chose the cause of action as contract breach instead of tort, Jiangxi High People's Court applied Article 41 rather than Article 43 to determine the governing law. It is noteworthy that non-application of Article 42 of LALFCR doesn't necessarily indicate denying the status of a tourist as a consumer. Article 42 is as follows:

The laws at the habitual residence of consumers shall apply to consumer contracts; If a consumer chooses the applicable laws at the locality of the provision of goods or

---

[12]YNFY [18].

[13]Law of Application of Law for Foreign-related Civil Relations of People's Republic of China was adopted on 28 October 2010.

[14]Zhen Chen [19].

[15]China Dadi Property Insurance Co., Ltd. Jiangxi Branch v. Xue Xiujuan, Jiangxi Province HPC, (2017) Gan Min Zhong No. 248.

services or an operator has no relevant business operations at the habitual residence of the consumer, the laws at the locality of the provision of goods or services shall apply.

It is hard to say Article 42 is more favorable to a consumer indeed. The first sentence of Article 42 may be deemed a *prima facie* evidence of advantage to a consumer because it provides that the law of the country of the consumer's habitual residence will be applied in the circumstance of a consumer-contract dispute. However, as service providers are usually located in foreign countries when a consumer travels aboard, the law of the country where the commodities and services be supplied by the supplier should be applied according to the second sentence. This means non-application of the first sentence is the normal result. But it doesn't mean the level of protection at the travel destination is lower or higher than China, instead, the level of protection depends on substantive provisions of different travel destinations. So, Article 42 is critiqued by many scholars. For example, Yuying asserted that although the objective of limiting party autonomy was to protect the weak consumer, such objective may not be realized, because Article 42 ignored the substantive standard provided by local law.[16]

In the authors' view, what really matters is the application of Article 42 will normally lead to application of foreign law since service providers are usually outside China, which is certainly inconvenient as the People's Courts are unfamiliar with foreign law. By contrast, Article 41 respects party autonomy and in case of no party agreement the People's Court could determine the applicable law according to doctrine of the most significant relationship. This means application of Article 41 would easily lead to application of Chinese law. Maybe this is the primary reason why People's Courts are reluctant to apply Article 42 of the LALFCR. As could be seen from cases cited by the Zhen Chen, in almost all of the judgements, Chinese law is the applicable law. Besides, in this case, since all the three parties are Chinese(enterprises), it is unreasonable to apply foreign law to settle the travel-contract dispute performed in a foreign country.

Therefore, in view of the clear words in Tourism Law, Law on the Protection of Consumer Rights and Interests and the judicial interpretation issued by SPC mentioned above, it is incorrect to presume the non-identity of a tourist as a consumer just from the non-application of Article 42 of the LALFCR. Indeed, the research method itself is somewhat problematic. The empirical research is on the basis of selecting cases by key words "travel contract" and "foreign-related", which means relevant judgements are already classified as "travel contract" involving foreign element, rather than "consumer protection" by the cause of action. Moreover, all, or nearly all of these cases concern a travel contract dispute between a Chinese tourist and a Chinese international travel agent, so application of Chinese law is a reasonable result. Thus, it is no surprise that in these cases Article 42 of LALFCR is ignored.

---

[16] Yu Ying [17].

3 International Tourists as Weaker Consumers

3.1 International Tourists

Is a tourist a consumer just like a regular consumer that consume goods and services, or does his/her consumption activities distinguishable from ordinary consumers that demand special attention? It is argued that if a consumer is the weaker party to a contract with a local trader, the tourist in cross-border situations may be deemed the weakest party.[17] A few factors contribute to the weaker consumer status of an international tourist, such as linguistic obstacle, diverse cultures and short-time stay.

When try to seek judicial redress, an international tourist would face more cross-border obstacles. The first challenge is information gaps. The tourists may not know his/her rights under the law of the visited country, whether and to what extent their damage would be compensated, where to get legal assistance and how to access justice. The inability to communicate with the local language may even increase such difficulties. The second challenge would be the short-term stay. It is more likely that the tourist could not commence or continue the court proceeding within limited visa period. The situation would be even worse if case delay can be used strategically. Third, even if physical presence at the court is not necessary and the representation of a party by a lawyer is permitted, the cost of judicial proceeding and the lawyer fee may exceed the damages, let alone the possibility of failure.

In sum, diversified rules on consumer protection in different countries, the lack of effective redress channels in international tourism, no compensation for redress effort may let a tourist give up resolving disputes with tourism service/goods providers. And this in turn make tourists the prime targets of fraud. In this vain, some commentator asserted that "the traveler is prompted into a more fragile condition than the regular consumer when buying goods and services because he/she is out of his domicile or jurisdiction, usually for a medium or short period of time."[18] Besides, an international tourist is easily to be the victim of racism, xenophobia or other bias. In such circumstances, a tourist is a vulnerable person.[19]

3.2 Chinese Outbound Tourists

When compared with other international tourists, Chinese tourists may face more difficulties. A Chinese tourist is usually perceived as wealthy carrying luxury goods or a lot of cash but unable to protect himself/herself properly, so attack against

---

[17] HCCH [4].

[18] Maria Goretti Sanches Lima [5], p. 4.

[19] Maria Goretti Sanches Lima [5], p. 1.

Chinese tourists happened from time to time.[20] In fact, not all Chinese tourists are pretty wealthy, but most of them are extremely weak when facing robbery, mugging or any other attack. Besides violence, Chinese tourists are generally not good at, sometimes unwilling or unable to, insist on their rights when tourism service/goods providers commit contract breaches or tort. One reason may be the language barriers. It is still difficult for many Chinese tourists to communicate smoothly in English. And this shortcoming would decrease their confidence in rights protection. Another reason may be the traditional culture of weary litigations,[21] which can be made use of by some service/goods providers.

Very few Chinese tourists would opt for seeking redress in the tourism destination. By contrast, foreign tourists such as Americans are more prone to initiate a lawsuit to get their loss back. For example, the case Xi'an Xindaya International Travel Agency v. Dr. Barsch-Supan[22] was initially initiated by two Americans against a Chinese and a Chinese travel agent for returning back travel fees.

Even when Chinese tourists come back, they seldom sue foreign service/goods providers. When searching judgements dealing with foreign-related travel-contract disputes on the website of China Judgments Online, one could easily find that Chinese tourists usually choose to sue the Chinese travel agent with whom he/she had ever concluded a travel contract. Besides the travel agent, in some cases a Chinese insurance company affording insurance liability either for the travel agent or for the tourist was also added as a defendant, just as the case China Dadi Property Insurance Co., Ltd. Jiangxi Branch v. Xue Xiujuan mentioned above. However, the travel agent's liability is limited to give reasonable notice and reminding. This means if a tourist got injured during the travel, he/she may not get full compensation for the fees and costs incurred. For example, in the abovementioned case China Dadi Property Insurance Co., Ltd. Jiangxi Branch v. Xue Xiujuan, Jiangxi High People's Court held that the tourist herself should bear 20% of the damages.

Nonetheless, by using the package travel, tourists could sometimes benefit from the associated safety net. By concluding a travel contract, the travel agent or tour operator has a general obligation to ensure the safety and rights of tourists. In case of disputes regarding their experiences abroad, tourists could make complaints against the Chinese travel agent or tour operator in China or access domestic dispute resolution mechanism. Moreover, by joining group tour, individuals could enjoy the convenience and protection of Approved Destination Status (ADS) agreements. Since 1995, China has concluded ADS agreements with 130 countries.[23] Travel agents in mainland China can only sell package tours to countries granted ADS by China. Chinese tourists going through designated travel agents will benefit from simplified

[20]See SPM (2017) Chinese tourists robbed in Paris hotel car park by four attackers armed with tear gas. https://www.scmp.com/news/china/society/article/2118471/chinese-tourists-robbed-paris-hotel-car-park-four-attackers-armed. Accessed 7 August 2019.

[21]See He Qinhua [3].

[22]Xi'an Xindaya International Travel Agency v. Dr. Barsch-Supan, Shaanxi Province HPC, (2016) Shan Min Zhong No. 511.

[23]MCT [6].

and facilitated procedures for tourism visa, as well as basic consular protection from the approved destinations.

In recent years, thanks to the fast development of digital economics, there is a rapid boom in low cost travel among new generation without using all-inclusive package travel. They arrange travel routes themselves, order airlines, book hotels and other services through online platforms. In other words, they explicitly or implicitly establish goods or service contract directly with foreign tourism service providers, or even assume all the risk themselves in some circumstances such as self-driving. This style of tourism put them in an added vulnerability.

On 5 July 2018, a tour boat capsized off the coast of the island of Phuket after a storm, with dozens of Chinese passengers being dead or missing. Though Thailand's Ministry of Tourism and Sports committed to give compensation to families of the victims and the inured, the amount of compensation for each was far from enough. Most of these Chinese outbound tourists traveled by themselves, they ordered the boat service from online travel platforms such as Xiecheng, Feizhu, Mafengwo and so on. When negotiations failed, some families had ever initiated judicial proceedings in China with the help of lawyers against the relative Chinese online platforms and some travel agent. However, since the third-party platform is not the ultimate service supplier, families and the injured could hardly ask the platform to afford too many liabilities. Taking into consideration of the legislative gap, some had given up. While it is without any doubt that the Thailand boat company should be liable to all loss, no one tried to sue it in Thailand.

Therefore, it could be seen that Chinese tourists and their families are in general too weak to protect their rights. If without intervention and positive compensation by Thailand government, their condition could even be worse. With the booming of individual international tourists, there is an increasing need of setting up a transnational mechanism to protect Chinese outbound tourists who are unable or unwilling to initiate a lawsuit.

4 The Need for Establishing a Transnational Coordination Mechanism for Complaints

4.1 Current International Approach for Tourist Protection

According to UNWTO, "tourist" means a person taking a trip which includes an overnight stay to a main destination outside his/her usual environment, for less than a year, for any main purpose (business, leisure or other personal purpose) other than to be employed by a resident entity in the country or place visited. On basis of this definition, international law specifically addressing tourist protection is quite limited.

In 1970s, International Convention on Travel Contracts (CCV) was concluded under the auspices of the International Institute for the Unification of Private Law (UNIDROIT). It is about the content of a travel contract, i.e., it establishes uniform rights, obligations and liabilities between a traveler and a travel organizer or intermediary. This convention was signed in 1970, and came into force in 1976. However, up to now, only six countries, namely Argentina, Benin, Cameroon, Italy, San Marino, Togo, have signed and ratified CVV.[24] Though CCV is still open for accession, its influence seems quite limited. The main reason may be that the travel contract is usually concluded between a traveler and a domestic travel agent, which is in fact a domestic contract. Disputes regarding travel contracts could be resolved within the same jurisdiction. This means international law is almost irrelevant in this respect.

Nowadays, due to the increasing world trend of mass travel without using the service of a travel agent or tour operator, many cross-border tourists don't benefit from associated protection any more, hence, the requests for effective international agreements governing tourist-consumers and tourism service providers loom up.

In response, UNWTO created a working group in 2011 to elaborate an international convention for the protection of tourists as consumers to improve tourist confidence in the tourism sector. In 2017, a draft UNWTO Convention on the Protection of Tourists and on the Rights and Obligations of Tourism Service Providers was put out as a report, though the draft convention had not been fully finalized yet. It is composed of a general part and three independent annexes, i.e., assistance in emergency situations, package travel and accommodation. The main purpose of the draft convention is to establish uniform standards and recommended practices for state parties to ensure an appropriate degree of protection for tourist-consumers and to clarify rights and obligations of tourism service providers. Nonetheless, the level and scope of protection for tourist-consumers in the draft convention are to some extent limited.

Another effort to advance the protection of international tourists is made by Hague Conference on Private International Law (HCCH). Distinct from UNWTO focusing on substantive rules, HCCH addresses the issue of access to justice for international tourists. Due to a proposal made by Brazil in respect of a possible future Convention on Co-operation and Access to Justice for International Tourists (Tourism Project) in 2013,[25] HCCH began to consider the Tourism Project. In February 2018, the Permanent Bureau of HCCH submitted a final report named Study on the desirability and feasibility of further work on the Proposal on a Draft Convention on Co-operation and Access to Justice for International Tourists to the Council on General Affairs and Policy of the Conference.[26] Currently, HCCH is still proceeding with the Tourism Project.

While the work of UNWTO on uniform substantive rules and the effort of HCCH on access to justice are both highly appreciated, there is still a long way to go. Some commentator asserted that cooperation among states on the access to judicial procedures for an international tourist would entitle the tourist to a legal personality and capacity of a special consumer worldwide, but in practice, this is not necessarily

---

[24]UNIDROIT [13].

[25]Brazil [1].

[26]HCCH [4].

effective and not fully automatic yet.[27] From the viewpoint of a tourist, even if there were proper legal provisions guaranteeing his/her rights and the access to justice in the visited country, it still seems unfeasible due to short-length stay and various obstacles, especially for small claims.

4.2 The Need for a Transnational Coordination Mechanism for Complaints

The concept of access to justice could also be understood in the broadest sense, including efficient and effective complaint channels and alternative dispute resolution mechanisms for cross-border tourists. Considering the weaker position and the vulnerability of tourists traveling aboard, assistance to tourists should be a key feature in the effort of providing protection for international tourists. In this respect, a transnational coordination mechanism dealing with complaints from tourists seems more effective.

The intervention of an authority from the destination state should in general be enough to convince service/goods provider of the necessity to seriously take into consideration of the complaint by the foreign tourist, while at the same time help the service/goods provider understand the complaint in his/her own language. The tourist is more willing to contact the authority of his/her own country either before or after come back. Thus, cooperation and coordination between authorities of the two countries would offer the international tourist practical convenience and help.

In fact, the models proposed by Brazil include setting up an international cooperation mechanism between competent authorities tasked with assisting tourists and coordinating actions within their states, and such a cooperation mechanism is deemed fundamentally viable by HCCH.[28] Article 5 of the proposal provides:

(1) *a contracting state shall designate the competent authority or authorities responsible to act on a complaint presented in accordance with Article 4. If more than one competent authority is designated, one of these authorities shall be designated as the competent authority to which complaints under this Convention may be addressed.*
(2) *The competent authority should maintain a public website on which the complaint form, in all the languages referred to in Article 4, shall be published.*
(3) *Competent authorities should take directly or through public authorities or other bodies having responsibilities for, or a legitimate interest in, the cessation or prohibition of infringements of the laws (including consumer protection laws)that protect the tourist's interest, all appropriate steps, including by providing information, practical assistance, and refer to the appropriate institutions in charge of providing legal advice or of alternative procedures, or to*

[27] Maria Goretti Sanches Lima [5].
[28] HCCH [4].

the relevant court, to try and resolve the issue relating to tourism service that is the object of the complaint.

(4) *They shall act promptly and expeditiously, taking into the account of the usual short period during which tourist stay in their State and in the place visited, and paying due regard to special needs of persons of disabilities.*

(5) *They shall keep a register of complaints and of the action taken upon those complaints in accordance with the laws of their State.*[29]

Chinese tourists in general prefer seeking administrative relief. According to government statistics, in 2018 the number of complaints made by tourists through the National Complaint Platform 12301 amounted to 1447,[30] far exceeding the number of lawsuit cases. So Chinese tourists would benefit from such a transnational coordination mechanism for complaints. That is to say, the establishment of a dedicated transnational tourist complaint body/mechanism is in line with the interests of China.

Of course, provisions on the function of such a transnational coordination mechanism for complaints could be clearer. For example, how do it protect tourists' interests? Does it offer mediation or compensation for tourists? Or the competent authority just conduct investigation and impose sanctions on service/goods providers. Obviously, the former is more favorable and useful for tourists. Hence, an all-around function of such a mechanism should be in principle emphasized.

5 Conclusion

Over past several decades, international tourism has become one of the most important industries in the world. All world regions enjoyed robust growth in recent years. It is predicted that international arrivals will continue to grow, while at the same time, almost inevitably, dissatisfied tourists will also increase. China is a key player in international tourism in terms of departures/expenditures. The boom of outbound tourists also reinforces the pressure on states, particularly China, to guarantee effective protection for their nationals abroad.

Within the domestic law framework of China, a tourist is deemed as a kind of consumer. If a dispute with a tourism operator arises, the tourist may make an application for mediation to CHINA CONSUMERS' ASSOCIATION. The tourist can also invoke provisions of Law on the Protection of Consumer Rights and Interests to protect his/her rights and interests. The practice of identifying a tourist as a kind of consumer is in line with the world trend of protecting tourists as consumers.

Furthermore, an international tourist is a weaker consumer that call for more attention. A tourist coming from abroad may experience challenges such as language barriers, culture obstacles, information gaps and so on. Moreover, the short-length stay would often constitute a bar to access to justice. Due to the Chinese culture of

---

[29] Brazil [2].

[30] Renmin [10].

preferring conciliation over litigation and the position of China as a top one spending country, Chinese outbound tourists may face more challenges or even risks.

Therefore, despite the appreciated effort of UNWTO and HCCH, a transnational coordination mechanism dealing with complaints from tourists is in line with the interests of China. It would be more attractive and appealing to Chinese outbound tourists, and other tourists as well. The responsibility of such a mechanism should be providing comprehensive assistance to international tourists as far as possible.

References

1. Brazil (2013) Proposal by the Government of Brazil: Draft Convention on co-operation in respect of the protection of tourists and visitors abroad and Explanatory Memorandum on the topic of tourist protection. Available at: https://assets.hcch.net/docs/1565f420-ac8f-4c13-9d71-3839fff28e58.pdf. Accessed 7 August 2019.
2. Brazil (2015) Proposal by the Government of Brazil on a draft convention on co-operation and access to justice for international tourists. Available at: https://assets.hcch.net/docs/74b12153-45a4-45fa-a86e-814fa5bf9d2a.pdf. Accessed 7 August 2019.
3. He Qinhua (1993) The Historic Observation of Extensive and Weary Litigations: A Few Thoughts About Chinese and Western Legal Traditions. Legal Science 3: 10–15.
4. HCCH (2018) Final report concerning a possible future Convention on Co-operation and Access to Justice for International Tourists. Available at: https://assets.hcch.net/docs/18e70dec-83ae-4a15-ac6f-309440cf74bc.pdf. Accessed 7 August 2019.
5. Maria Goretti Sanches Lima (2018) Traveller Vulnerability in the Context of Travel and Tourism Contracts: A Comparison of Brazilian and EU Law. Springe, Berlin.
6. MCT (2018a) Outbound travel destination country where area business has been officially launched. Available at: http://zt.mct.gov.cn/cjyzl/gltl/201507/U020180724606008331724.jpg. Accessed 7 August 2019.
7. MCT (2018b) The total expenditure of Chinese tourists in Finland far exceed other tourists. http://zt.mct.gov.cn/cjyzl/dtxw/201803/t20180320_860909.shtml. Accessed 7 August 2019.
8. MCT (2019a) Tourism Market in 2018. http://zwgk.mct.gov.cn/auto255/201902/t20190212_837271.html?keywords=. Accessed 7 August 2019.
9. MCT (2019b) The Report of outbound Chinese tourism in 2018: The Average Expenditure of Each Chinese is about US $ 800. http://whs.mof.gov.cn/pdlb/mtxx/201903/t20190328_3207566.html. Accessed 7 August 2019.
10. Renmin (2019) Tourism Complaint Ranking List in 2018. http://travel.people.com.cn/n1/2019/0222/c41570-30897023.html. Accessed 7 August 2019.
11. Report of the Secretary-General of UNWTO, A/22/10(I)(c), Madrid, 20 July 2017. Available at: http://cf.cdn.unwto.org/sites/all/files/pdf/a22_10_i_c_unwto_convention_on_the_protection_of_tourists_en_0.pdf. Accessed 7 August 2019.
12. Resolution adopted by the General Assembly on 22 December 2015, A/RES/70/186. Available at: https://undocs.org/A/RES/70/186. Accessed 7 August 2019.
13. UNIDROIT (1970) International Convention on Travel Contracts. Available at: https://legacarta.intracen.org/instrument/053627-international-convention-travel-contracts/. Accessed 7 August 2019.
14. UNWTO (2018) UNWTO Tourism Highlights (2018 Edition). Available at: https://www.e-unwto.org/doi/pdf/. https://doi.org/10.18111/9789284419876. Accessed 7 August 2019.
15. UNWTO (2019a) Exports From International Tourism Hit USD 1.7 Trillion. http://www2.unwto.org/press-release/2019-06-06/exports-international-tourism-hit-usd-17-trillion. Accessed 7 August 2019.

16. UNWTO (2019b) International Tourist Arrivals Reach 1.4 billion Two Years Ahead of Forecasts. http://www2.unwto.org/press-release/2019-01-21/international-tourist-arrivals-reach-14-billion-two-years-ahead-forecasts. Accessed 7 August 2019.
17. Yu Ying (2011) Comments on Article of 42 of LALFCR. Law Review2: 65–70.
18. YNFY (2017) Ten Typical Tourism Cases in Yunnan Province published by Yunnan High Court. http://ynfy.chinacourt.gov.cn/article/detail/2017/09/id/3337716.shtml. Accessed 7 August 2019.
19. Zhen Chen (2019) Jurisdiction and Choice of Law in Foreign-Related Tourist-Consumer Disputes in China under the One Belt One Road Initiative—Based on Case Analysis in the Chinese Judiciary. Paper presented at the 17th conference of the International Association of Consumer Law, Indiana University, Indianapolis, 13–15 June 2019.

The Supply of Products and Services to LGBTI Consumers Under the Social Function of the Contract

Laércio da Silva

1 Introduction

The purpose of this paper is to study the social function of the contract in the context of the provision of products and services to LGBTI consumers. The hypothetical-deductive, hermeneutic, dialect and argumentative methods will be used. As for theoretical framework, it's taken the book "Social Function of the Contract: an essay about your meanings and usages", from Luís Gustavo Haddad, and the Michel Foucault's books about the history of sexuality. Initially, a briefing about the LGBTI community is taken. Then, a dialectical and hermeneutical analysis between the principles of the social function of the contract versus the freedom to contract is taken, presenting, in the following step, the conclusions.

In the consumer market, globally, the dissemination of many products and services has been done by exploring the universe of the LGBTI community. Gays, lesbians, bisexuals, transgenders, among other members of the mentioned social community, have been exposed[1] in the advertising booths that offer products and services of several strong brands[2] in the market, such as Coke, C&A, among others. LGBTI voices and speeches are exposed, the social exclusion which they were victims is heard, phrases with great impact are presented and acclaimed, all this embedded in the product or service in divulgation.

The phenomenon above is a clear example of the massive contracting of products and services coupled with a delicate aspect of society, with collective connotations,

[1] Available on: https://www.youtube.com/watch?v=wxEwmSyxAEw.

[2] Available on: https://www.youtube.com/watch?v=i_OACwYHyMw.

Laércio da Silva, Bachelor of Law and Mastering Student at The Center of European and German Studies. Ex-President of the Association of Consumer Law in the State of Bahia, Brazil. Lawyer.

L. da Silva (✉)
Universidade Federal de Viçosa, Viçosa, Brazil
e-mail: laercio.neto@gmail.com

D. Wei et al. (eds.), *Innovation and the Transformation of Consumer Law*,
https://doi.org/10.1007/978-981-15-8948-5_25

which is, the systemic violence and social exclusion of the LGBTI community, which apparently reverts to inclusion, respect and tolerance in advertising of the products and services offered. It is exalted exactly the point which is persecuted, despised and, really often, detached from society: the LGBTI human being, in all its extension in being. This type of allusion to the LGBTI community by the private market reverberates, contractually, what is known as the social function of the contract.

In addition to the effects between the parties of the contract, which means the satisfaction of the opposing interests between the contractual parties, any contract concluded must obey, respect, the social function. In general terms, the social function fulfills the contract when it is attentive to its social environment, connecting itself to the social reality that presents around its context of celebration, instead to remain inert, in total estrangement from the society that surrounds it. Furthermore, a contract that has exclusively economics connotations, which aims the circulation of goods and services, even if it harm important social, historical or cultural heritage or, for example, reinforce stigmas and processes of social exclusion, that profile of contract works against the social function that all contract is required to have.

In the same social space destined to the contracting of goods and services, in which the divulgation of diverse products and services exploring the universe of the LGBTI community is announced, so as to enhance it and to include it, it's also heard about the fence of the supply of products and services to consumers, because they are LGBTI, such as the marriage cake that was denied to a homoaffective couple in the United States of America, supported by a decision of the Supreme Court[3] of that country, as well as having the supply of services to modify the sexual orientation and gender identity in countries such as the United States of America, Ecuador and Peru.

The paper, indeed, proposes a dialectical and hermeneutic study about the social function versus the freedom to contract in the supply of products and services to LGBTI consumers. It's a general objective to study the incidence of the social function of the contract in the relations of consumption occurred in the bulge or involving the social community in focus, and as for a specific objective it's taken a brief foreshortening about the LGBTI community, presenting, then, the conclusions.

2 Brief Understandig of LGBTI Community

Some sectors of society need special attention, which is dispensed to others that little or no discrimination, stigmatization suffer. Law, as a social science, focused on the laws that exist and are applied for the correct functioning of society, must, more than any other, sensitize social segments that remain outside the margin, to the current legal order, which means, they do not have the same rights as other people because of some dullness, some restriction, exclusion, non-legitimate discrimination.

[3]Read more on: https://www.acidigital.com/noticias/confeiteiro-e-novamente-processado-por-se-negar-a-fazer-bolo-com-conteudo-gay-25473.

In our society, where pre-established models of behavior, of affective relationships and family formation are noted, the issues surrounding the LGBTI theme, as well as their human rights, are obviously problematic, diminished, and difficult. Michel Foucault, discussing the history of sexuality in the 4 volumes of the book, brings relevant reflections[4] on the subject. It is from this contextualization that the LGBTI matters are born and takes place.

Thus, what it's still understood in the field of sexuality is evidently attached to the function of procreation and for the constitution of family-within the idea of a heterosexual family. All those who differ from this orientation find obstacles[5] depending on the family context, place or country where they live around the planet, among other variants. It is a retreaded human aspect, excluded in fact, seriously confined to the more gray and violent meanders of the society.[6]

It means that LGBTI people are expected not to talk about, to interdict, to not exist and to render mute the LGBTI matters: this is how the LGBTI's body, sexuality and modus vivendi around the world are treated, in fact with eradicating treatments and intentions.[7]

It's kown that power is all around society and influences people and institutions.[8] Power is a part of society. It is from this structuring of power and discourse of the society, now in focus, that the disruption, subjugation and silencing of LGBTI are installed and maintained.[9] Regarding the outline of this scenario that it's possible to understand the systemic violence against LGBTI being.

In the instances of discursive production, it is seen that repression of the community and LGBTI being clearly occurs.[10] Only what is in accordance with the dominant

---

[4]Sexuality is kept inside home. The conjugal family confiscates it. And it absorbs it entirely in the serious function of reproducing. Around the sex, shut up. The couple, legitimate and procreative, dictates the law. Foucault [1], p. 8.

[5]If it is necessary to give a way to illegitimate sexualities, which will bother elsewhere: that they disturb where they can be reinscribed, if not in the circuits of production, at least profit. Foucault [1], p. 9.

[6]The rendezvous and the house of health will be such places of tolerance: the prostitute, the client, the ruffian, the psychiatrist and his hysteric ... (...) Outside these places, modern Puritanism would have imposed its threefold decree of interdiction, non-existence and mutism. Foucault [1], p. 8.

[7]The repression is deeply established, has solid roots and reasons, weighs on sex in such a rigorous way that a single denunciation would not be able to free us; work can only be long. Thus, it is to be expected, therefore, that the effects of liberation in regard to this repressive power will be delayed. Foucault [1], pp. 16–17.

[8]The important point will be to know in what forms, through which channels, flowing through which discourses, power manages to reach the most tenuous and most individual of conducts, which paths allow it to reach the rare or almost imperceptible forms of desire, in what way power penetrates and controls daily pleasure—all with effects that may be of refusal, blockade, disqualification, but also incitement. Foucault [1], p. 17.

[9]It is necessary to search for the instances of discursive production (which, of course, also organize silences), power production (which sometimes have the function of interdicting), the production of knowledge (which errors). Foucault [1], p. 18.

[10]The interdiction of certain words, the decency of expressions, all censures of the vocabulary could well be only secondary devices with respect to this great subjection. They are ways to make it morally acceptable and technically useful. Foucault [1], p. 34.

morality and, still, useful in the technical understanding of the word, useful for something technical, justify the existence of LGBTI in society. Sexuality, indeed, is an aspect of the human being that attracts great vigil, control, and is object of intense debate.[11] Surrounded by all sides, the minimal expression of sexuality was simply forbidden. It was believed that it's better to control it or it could not exist in a normal and fluid way.

In several contexts and places around the world, one or all of these elements act, partially or jointly, to eradicate or suppress LGBTI from the social fabric, in clear manifestation of a systemic violence against this minority group.[12] Note that in a chapter not very old in history, it is reported, for example, that by 1969 homosexual acts were considered illegal in the United States, as in much of the world.[13] These data indicate the low level of awareness of society on the subject and the evident dehumanization of the LGBTI community, consequently.

According to the report of the Inter-American Commission on Human Rights, organized by the Organization of American States (OAS) in 2015, it is noticed that, even today, more than 45 years ago, there are high levels of violence against LGBTI people.[14] Thus, the very nature of LGBTI, expressed in its naturalness of being who it really is, in addition also the affectivity between the mentioned members, are persecuted, violated, strongly attacked.[15]

The mentioned report of the Inter-American Commission on Human Rights brings important critics and information.[16] The imposition of sexual orientation as heterosexual, the obligatory division between male and female gender, believing in the hierarchy of the masculine over the feminine, it's in the bosom of contemporary society.[17]

[11] An agricultural worker from the village of Lapcourt, with a rather simple spirit, employed seasonally from one corner to another, fed here and there by a little charity and by the worst of the works, living in farms or stables, is denounced. (…) In the ferns of a patch, he had obtained some caresses from a girl, as he had already done, as he had seen do, as they did around him (…) The small country pleasures could have become, from a certain moment, the object not only of a collective intolerance, but of a judicial action, of a medical intervention. Foucault [1], p. 35.

[12] Medical examination, psychiatric investigation, pedagogical report, and family controls may well have as their overall and apparent goal to say no to all errant or unproductive sexualities. Focault [1], p. 50.

[13] At the time, several treatment clinics for homosexuals were in full operation, where shocks, sterilization, castration and even lobotomy were applied. Gorisch [2].

[14] Many manifestations of such violence are based on the aggressor's desire to" punish" those identities, expressions, behaviors or bodies that differ from traditional norms and gender roles "or" to the male/female binary system. Available on: http://www.oas.org/pt/cidh/docs/pdf/ViolenciaPessoasLGBTI.pdf.

[15] This violence is directed, among others, to public demonstrations of affection between persons of the same sex, and the expressions of " femininity" perceived in men or "masculinity" in women. Available on: http://www.oas.org/pt/cidh/docs/pdf/ViolenciaPessoasLGBTI.pdf.

[16] Societies in the Americas are dominated by rooted principles of heteronormativity, cisnormativity, sexual hierarchy, sex and gender binaries, and misogyny. Available on: http://www.oas.org/pt/cidh/docs/pdf/ViolenciaPessoasLGBTI.pdf.

[17] These principles, combined with generalized intolerance against people with sexual orientations, identities and expressions of gender and diverse bodies; legitimize violence and discrimination against LGBTI people. Violence against LGBTI people exists as a consequence of social contexts,

Thus, the commission recommends that the Inter-American Commission on Human Rights—IACHR, the OAS Member States adopt comprehensive measures to combat discrimination, social and cultural prejudices and stereotypes against LGBTI people.

The consultation on the IACHR report also points out the existence of the provision of therapeutic services to change the natural expression of gender identity and sexuality of members of the LGBTI community.[18] Submission to therapeutic treatments, hospitalization in clinics and rapes, in addition to other inhuman treatments reported, make up the daily life of some LGBTI in the Americas and worldwide.

The Human Rights Commission has also received information about the existence of centers for the "treatment" for LGBT people in Ecuador, Peru, the Dominican Republic and the United States, "noting that" the person under "treatment" is enclosed in a center, interned in a "clinic", and most of the time against their own will or through false pretenses and submitted to very rigid regimes. It should be noted that, in accordance with that report, therapeutic cures "include inhuman or degrading treatment, including acts of sexual violence, as part of the"[19] procedure to modify their sexual orientation or gender identity. These data indicate, one hand, serious and clear violations of human rights and, on the other hand, disobedience to the world's health councils and bodies, which do not allow or recommend this type of treatment in medical clinics regarding gender identities or sexual orientation.

The community in question, therefore, is a social segment that has lived, for centuries and more centuries, in the margins of the juridical order, and still lives without many of its basic and fundamental rights, such as the simple right to a dignified life and personal liberty, for example, properly ensured. Only in 2011, through Resolution of the Human Rights Council, the United Nations (UN), in a General Assembly, declared that LGBTI rights are human rights - General Assembly Resolution L9, which stipulates that all the peoples of the UN must fight against prejudice and modify their discriminatory legislation, recognizing the LGBTI as a human being.

When it comes to law and the protection of the target community, over the last ten years more than 40 countries around the world have come to conceive the homosexual relationship as a family entity, equating it in rights and duties with the already established relationship heterosexual. By consulting the UN interactive map[20] of countries that have legalized same-sex marriage, it is noted that the above-cited number of 40 countries have recognized the legality of same-sex marriage, sometimes by court order, sometimes by legislative amendment. Although not included in the UN list,

---

societies and states that do not accept, and that actually punish sexualities, identities and bodies that do not fit the social patterns of corporality. Available on: http://www.oas.org/pt/cidh/docs/pdf/ViolenciaPessoasLGBTI.pdf.

[18]The information received refers to cases in which LGBT people or those perceived as such are subjected to supposed therapeutic treatments, hospitalized in clinics or camps, and victims of physical abuse. Women are also subject to rape and other acts of sexual violence as a form of punishment for their sexual orientation and gender identity, real or perceived. Available on: http://www.oas.org/pt/cidh/docs/pdf/ViolenciaPessoasLGBTI.pdf.

[19]Available on: http://www.oas.org/pt/cidh/docs/pdf/ViolenciaPessoasLGBTI.pdf.

[20]Available on: http://internap.hrw.org/features/features/marriage_equality/.

India was, more recently, the country that changed its old understanding and began to protect as legal the affective relationship, after a major decision from the Supreme Court.

In Brazil, the first change occurred in 2011, after the Federal Supreme Court (STF) understand the constitutionality of the union between people of the same sex in he judgment of the Action called "Non-compliance with Basic Precept" (ADPF). Several other rights, such as the marriage itself, registered in the civil registries, as well as the adoption of children, inclusion as beneficiary of health insurance, were discussed and granted after the trial of this process. The latest change in the news concerns the change in the civil registry of the names of transsexuals to their social name in the register, which is, the one that is socially endowed, judged favorably by the Supreme Court in the Action ADI 4.275.

Although the scenario appears to be advancing towards the achievement of basic rights in the LGBTI community, the legislation of 73 countries around the world establish homosexuality is a prohibited conduct and constitutes a crime. From 73 countries, 13 of them attribute the death penalty to homosexual conduct, according to the map drawn up by the International Association of Lesbian, Gay, Bisexual, Transgender and Intersex (ILGA).[21] This type of legislation obstructs the establishment of the most basic human rights in the social grouping in focus, contributing, around the world and especially in the countries where they have cogent force, to the maintenance of homophobia and violence against the LGBTI community.

Insisting on the theme of homophobia, there was an immense controversy about the advertising referring to the Valentine's day of the Brazilian perfumery brand "O Boticário". In the Valentine's day advertisement, there were exposed several couples exchanging gifts, among them were homosexual couples composed by both men and two women. By consulting the YouTube platform,[22] where the publicity was reproduced, it was possible to verify a series of offensive attacks, some phrases like "death to the gays". The controversy was so intense that ended up with a Representation in the National Council for Self-Regulatory Publicity (CONAR), No. 088/15, refuted and filed unanimously by said council. It is reported that more than a thousand of emails were sent to CONAR with a request for cassation of the advertising in focus.

Therefore, taking into consideration all the explanation made in the paragraphs above, the juridical and social relevance of the theme is evident. The LGBTI Community is faced with a stigmatized social segment, excluded, sometimes even persecuted by some more aggressive sectors of the society, which violates the Brazilian constitutional principles of human dignity, equality and social solidarity. Thus, the social function of the contract in the supply of products and services to LGBTI consumers, notably in order to understand the relevance of the effects of a contract not only between the parties, but from the impact they can have on society, is clearly relevant when it comes to the target community.

---

[21] Available on: https://ilga.org/downloads/2017/ILGA_WorldMap_ENGLISH_Overview_2017.pdf.

[22] Available on: https://www.youtube.com/watch?v=p4b8BMnolDI.

3 The Social Function of the Contract *Versus* the Freedom to Contract

The idea of the social function of the contract arises more exactly in Brazilian law after the promulgation of the Brazilian Civil Code in 2002, inserted in the civil legislation through the article 421 and 2.035.[23] The aim of the social function is to bring social connotations to the private\economic relations between the parties, the idea of an effective social function and not merely symbolic, which affects and regulates hiring between private individuals.[24]

With the advancement of technology, the approach of different cultures and countries, the massive contracting of products and services is a common place, with a daily existence and importance. Civil legislation needs to be in pace with the updating of society, and this is often possible by handling the general clauses available.[25] In other words, this means constructive dialogue with society, application of the law in line with social matters instead of denying it.[26]

General clauses are very common in law worldwide and it's a sophisticated legal technique, aiming at the best and improved application of the law. Many troubles in life of society don't find a solution in the law and needs the usage of general clauses to overcome that debility. Moving forward in the theoretical framework of this paper, it is necessary to clarify that the social function is very important because it express social needs in the private law.[27] Thus, it's not possible to understand companies without collective interference in society, which leads to a second consequence, the

[23] According to the only literal sense of these provisions, the social function of the contract is: (i) basis for the exercise of contractual freedom; (ii) limit for the exercise of this freedom; (iii) guaranteed by certain precepts of public order. HADDAD, Luís Gustavo. Social function of contract: an essay on its uses and meanings. 1 ed. Publishing company Saraiva: São Paulo, 2013. Kindle arquive, position 174.

[24] The code still gave high importance to the protection of the social function of the contract, since it qualified as cogent the rule contained therein. HADDAD, Luís Gustavo. Social function of contract: an essay on its uses and meanings. 1 ed. Publishing company Saraiva: São Paulo, 2013. Kindle arquive, position 174.

[25] A non-totalitarian code has windows open for the mobility of life, bridges that link it to other normative bodies—even the extra-legal ones—and avenues, well-trodden, that link it, dialectically. Martins [3], p. 131.

[26] General clauses constitute a legislative technique characteristic of the second half of the century, which arose as a response to specific and certain problems of daily life, seeking desirable results for the common good and social utility. General clauses have intentionally vague and open meanings, being marked the advantage of mobility, in addition to acting technically as metanorms. MARTINS COSTA, Judith. Reflections on the principle of the social function of contracts. FGV Journal of Law, v. 1, n. 1. São Paulo: 2005, p. 41.

[27] In general terms, is the expression of sociality in Private Law, projecting in its normative corporations and in the different legal disciplines the constitutional guideline of social solidarity (Federal Constitution of Brazil, article 3, III; "by combining the factors of production (labor, capital and human resources) and the agents of the economic process (consumer, worker and entrepreneur), companies undoubtedly have a trans-individual or community dimension.. HADDAD, Luís Gustavo. Social function of contract: an essay on its uses and meanings. 1 ed. Publishing company Saraiva: São Paulo, 2013. Kindle arquive, position 259.

observance of these same companies with principles, social, macro, trans individual commandments. Therefore, contracts can not harm the collectivity or determined people.

The current super connected planetary context, with mass offerings of products and services to nations and partners worldwide, gives the great business an unquestionable power over society. This planetary influence must be accompanied, inspected, and preferably channeled to the realization of the higher purposes present in the Constitution of the Federative Republic of Brazil.[28] In other words, the freedom to contract now has to be linked to healthy, dignified, and above all inclusive, solidarity and egalitarian social parameters.

Relevant questioning arises, then, from this point on in this brief essay. In a concrete case, how is it possible to identify a violation to the social function of the contract? On the basis of which grounds can be identified a violation of the social function required by law.[29] Thus, it is important to point out the criteria for analyzing the social function of the contract, since its incidence between private individuals and their reflections on the society is notorious.

The jurists defends that, regarding the application of the social function of the contract, it's necessary to follow the juridical reasoning based on consequences.[30] The central ideia is that "the new paradigm seeks a forward-looking and regulatory view that seeks to identify the individual and collective costs, gains and incentives that will be generated by two or more competing decisions in a given case."[31] Thus, by weighing factors such as costs, gains and individual and collective incentives, as pointed out in the above quotation, an adequate result will be achieved in the sense of a contract observing its social function or not.[32]

In this sense, under the aegis of the social function of the contract, a contract that reinforces situations of social vulnerability, that refuses to provide services to

[28]The jurists studying the Brazilian Civil Code indicate that hence the immediate reference, soon after the freedom to contract, to the social function of the contract; hence the reason why freedom and social function are interwoven, generating a new idea, that of (private) solidarity. HADDAD, Luís Gustavo. Social function of contract: an essay on its uses and meanings. 1 ed. Publishing company Saraiva: São Paulo, 2013. p. 43.

[29]Both parties, as well as third parties and society in general, are real or potential beneficiaries of the profits generated by the contract, whether it is seen as an institution or as a general type. The contract acquires new roles and to a certain extent substitutes for the law in the organization of social life. HADDAD, Luís Gustavo. Social function of contract: an essay on its uses and meanings. 1 ed. Publishing company Saraiva: São Paulo, 2013. Kindle arquive, position 482.

[30]HADDAD, Luís Gustavo. Social function of contract: an essay on its uses and meanings. 1 ed. Publishing company Saraiva: São Paulo, 2013. Kindle arquive, position 1704.

[31]HADDAD, Luís Gustavo. Social function of contract: an essay on its uses and meanings. 1 ed. Publishing company Saraiva: São Paulo, 2013. Kindle arquive, position 1701.

[32]By assessing the consequences, it will be possible to find out if the solution or decision in question is universalizable and can be applied to all the identical or equivalent cases without causing unsustainable situations. HADDAD, Luís Gustavo. Social function of contract: an essay on its uses and meanings. 1 ed. Publishing company Saraiva: São Paulo, 2013. Kindle arquive, position 1712.

consumers, even if it is stocked, or that treats people unequally, which is based on unlawful discrimination, is not according to the social function of the contract.[33]

The juristic explicitly states that the freedom to contract is a "situated freedom, it is necessary to seek to situate it, ascertaining its surroundings, the environment in which it moves and develops, and the meanings that the expression connotes"[34]. It is inside this and to this environment that private autonomy contracts, and it is therefore unreasonable to conceive of a contract being celebrated in total isolation from the social environment that surrounds it.[35]

The phenomenon of contractual trans individuality is already present. It means that "contracts are, above all, social facts. In varying degrees and measures can affect—and positively affect—who did not take part of them."[36] It is, in a nutshell, the approach and study of the contract, in addition to its effects between parties, it is necessary to examine external effects to them, collective effects, for example, if they accentuate or attenuate factors of social vulnerability\ exclusion.[37]

The legal jurists teach that "the aim of the true social function of the contract involves the presence of diffuse interests, coupled with the individual interests of the parties.".[38] With massive contracts and globalization, it's difficult to imagine the contracts worldwide without your power and influence in society and, obviously, your collective impact. To consume is a human necessity and those who owner the big market owns our necessities—and naturally have power above us all.

The freedom to contract, therefore, is exercised within society itself, and often pervades and regulates life between individuals in a more intense and daily way than the Law itself that emanates from the State. If the contract is made and is daily present in the community, in the society, it is important that we do it in accordance with the principle of social function so that situations of vulnerability and social exclusion are not reinforced or expanded. It is appropriate to exercise the freedom to contract

---

[33]The monitoring of the fulfillment of the social function of the contracts turns to the analysis of the overall effects of contracts and contractual arrangements for the organization of the economy and society. HADDAD, Luís Gustavo. Social function of contract: an essay on its uses and meanings. 1 ed. Publishing company Saraiva: São Paulo, 2013. Kindle arquive, position 1726.

[34]MARTINS COSTA, Judith. Reflections on the principle of the social function of contracts. FGV Journal of Law, v.1, n.1. São Paulo: 2005, p. 45.

[35]The environment of the freedom to contract is the community. Every community is a permanently instituted and permanently creative historical-social dimension of meanings. MARTINS COSTA, Judith. Reflections on the principle of the social function of contracts. FGV Journal of Law, v.1, n.1. São Paulo: 2005, p. 45.

[36]MARTINS COSTA, Judith. Reflections on the principle of the social function of contracts. FGV Journal of Law, v.1, n.1. São Paulo: 2005, p. 54. .

[37]A much broader phenomenon—the phenomenon of trans individuality—that, in contemporary procedural law, has expression in the instruments that protect diffuse and collective interests. Based on this finding lies the perception of trans individual efficacies deriving from the principle of social function. MARTINS COSTA, Judith. Reflections on the principle of the social function of contracts. FGV Journal of Law, v.1, n.1. São Paulo: 2005, p. 54.

[38]THEODORO JÚNIOR, Humberto. The contract and its social function. 4ed. Forense Publisher: São Paulo, 2014. p. 57.

with a very careful management, always considering, the social function that any contract is required to have.

4 Conclusion

It's important to note that the dissemination of several products and services, exploring the universe of the LGBTI community, which includes gays, lesbians, bisexuals, transgenders, among other members of the social minority in focus, reinforces contract management in the sense of its social function, applying an important clause present in law, the social function of the contract.

The usage of advertising for the mass hiring of products, when it explores a delicate aspect of society, with collective amplitude, such as homophobia, it helps to face systemic violence against the LGBTI community, for example, and apparently reverberates positive effects towards the cure of social exclusion. It accomplishes the social function of the contract to include in mass advertisings a person which is persecuted, despised and, more often, detached from society: the LGBTI human being, in all its extension in being. The allusion to the LGBTI community by the private market reverberates, contractually, what is understood as the social function of the contract. Explore and try to overcome social pains and problems, pointing out better outings to the world – here is a suitable understanding of the social function of the contract.

The social function is really fulfilled when the contract is attentive to its social environment, connecting itself to the social reality of its context of celebration, instead of being indifferent to the society that surrounds it, neutral to the problems of the community. A purely economic contract, which deals with the movement of goods and services, damaging relevant social, historical or cultural heritage, or which, for example, reinforcing stigmas and processes of social exclusion, undermines the social function that any contract is required to have.

In the same social space destined to the contracting of goods and services, in which the dissemination of various products and services exploring the universe of the LGBTI community is announced, so as to enhance it and include it, it is also known the refusal to provide products and services to consumers, because they are LGBTI, such as the marriage cake that was denied to a homoaffective couple in the United States of America, supported by a decision of the Supreme Court of that country, as well as having equal alteration of sexual orientation and gender identity in countries such as the United States of America, Ecuador and Peru, according to information gathered by the Inter-American Commission on Human Rights in a report explored during the lines of this paper.

It's important to conclude that, positively and negatively, the contracting of goods and services and publicity can reverberate, in the society, aspects of inclusion or social exclusion, contributing to reduce or worsen systemic violence against people and communities, such as in the case of LGBTI. To permit, therefore, the conclusion of contracts for goods and services to disregard the social function of the contract is clearly against the Brazilian legal system. These types of contracting should be inhibited or prohibited because they contribute to discriminatory processes, so that they should be changed in order to observe the social reality, basically the environment around.

References

1. Focault, Michel. *History of sexuality: the will to know.* 4 ed. Publishing company: Paz & Terra: São Paulo, 2017.
2. Gorisch, Patrícia. *The Recognition of LGBT Human Rights: From Stonewall to the UN*. 4 ed. Publishing company Appris: Curitiba, 2014.
3. Martins Costa, Judith. *Private Law as a "system under construction"—the general clauses in the Brazilian Civil Code Project. Journal of the Courts*, n. 753. São Paulo: RT, 1998.
4. Focault, Michel. *History of sexuality: use of pleasures*. 1 ed. Publishing company: Paz & Terra: São Paulo, 2017.
5. Focault, Michel. *History of sexuality: the care of self*. 1 ed. Publishing company: Paz & Terra: São Paulo, 2017.
6. Borillo, Daniel. *Homophobia: history and criticism of a prejudice.* Publishing company: Autentica, Belo Horizonte, 2010.
7. Ambrose, Tom. *Heroes and exiles: gay icons through the ages*. Publishing company: Autentica, Belo Horizonte, 2010.
8. Dias, Maria Berenice. *Homoaffection and LGBTI rights*. 6 ed. Publishing company Revista dos Tribunais: São Paulo, 2014.
9. Marques, Cláudia Lima; Benjamin, Antônio Herman V; Miragem, Bruno. *Consumer Law Legal Doctrine*. 4. ed. ampl. rev. São Paulo: Publishing company Revista dos Tribunais, 2012.
10. Miragem, Bruno. *Consumer rights course*. 5 ed. ampl. rev. São Paulo: Publishing company Revista dos Tribunais, 2014. p. 122.
11. De Godoy, Claudio Luiz Bueno. *Social function of the contract*. Publishing company Saraiva: São Paulo, 2007.
12. Fachin, Luiz Edson. *Critique of legal legalism and positivist historicism: an essay for an exercise in dialogue between history and law, in the perspective of contemporary* Civil Law. Dialogues on Civil Law. Rio de Janeiro: Publishing company Renovar, 2002.
13. Facchini Neto, Eugênio. *The social function of private law*. Revista da AJURIS—Association of Judges of Rio Grande do Sul, v. 43, n. 105, year XXXIV. Porto Alegre: Publishing company AJURIS, March 2007.
14. Foucault, Michel. *In defense of society. Course at the Collège de France* (1975–1976). Translated by Maria Ermentina Galvão. São Paulo: Publishing company Martins Fontes, 1999.
15. Godoy, Cláudio Luiz Bueno. *Social function of the contract*. São Paulo: Saraiva, 2004 GOMES, Rogério Zuel. Teoria contratual contemporânea. Rio de Janeiro: Publishing company Forense, 2004.
16. Grau, Eros Roberto. *Contractual management*. In France, Limongi (organizer). Encyclopedia Saraiva de Direito, v. 32. São Paulo: Publishing company Saraiva, 1977.
17. Lôbo, Paulo Luiz Neto. *Contract and social change*. Forense Magazine n. 722, Rio de Janeiro: Publishing company Forensic.
18. Mancebo, Rafael Chagas. *The social function of the contract*. São Paulo: Publishing company Quartier Latin, 2006.
19. Martins Costa, Judith. *The general clauses as factors of mobility of the legal system. In Journal of Legislative Information*. Brasília: Sub-secretary of Technical Issues of the Federal Senate, 1991.

20. Meirelles, Jussara. *The being and the have in the Brazilian codification*. In Fachi, Luiz Edson (coordinator). Rethinking the fundamentals of contemporary Brazilian civil law. Rio de Janeiro: Publishing company Renovar, 1998.
21. Poulantzas, Nicos. *The State, the Power, the Socialism*. São Paulo: Publishing company Graal (Peace and Earth), 2000.
22. Rousseau, Jean-Jacques. *The social contract. The great philosophers of law*. São Paulo: Publishing company Martins Fontes, 2002.
23. Silva, Luis Renato Ferreira da. *The social function of the contract in the new Civil Code and its connection with social solidarity*. In SARLET, Ingo (organizer). The new Civil Code and the Constitution. Porto Alegre, Publishing company Livraria do Advogado, 2003.
24. Negreiros, Teresa. *Contract Theory: new paradigms*. 2 ed. Rio de Janeiro: Publishing company Renovar, 2006.

Consumer Protection in the Case of Public Service Provision: Innovations in Brazil

Carlos Eduardo Dieder Reverbel

1 Introduction

The present article intends to open the discussion brought by Law 13.460/17 that was regulated only 30 years after the Constitution of the Federative Republic of 1988 and 20 years after and Constitutional Amendment n° 19/98. Fortunately the Public Power has supplied the legislative gap promised by the non-self-executing norms of the Constitution.

In this article, we will analyze Law 13.470/17. In addition to the introduction and conclusion, the article is divided into three parts: the first deals with non-self-enforcing standards that depend on complementation; the second deals with public services and consumer protection. Finally, we deal with the regulation of the protection of the public service user, dividing the matter into four topics: user and consumer; user and public service; police power and public service; duties and rights of users of public services. As the subject is brand new, we do not have specific doctrine dealing with it. We explored the subject not yet written by administrative and consumerist doctrine.

Carlos Eduardo Dieder Reverbel is professor of Constitutional Law in undergraduate and graduate Law School of the Federal University of Rio Grande do Sul (UFRGS). Master and Doctor of Constitutional Law by UFRGS. Doctor of State Law by USP (São Paulo University). Coordinator of UFRGS's Specialization Program in State Law. Member of BRASILCON.

C. E. D. Reverbel (✉)
Federal University of Rio Grande do Sul (UFRGS), Porto Alegre, Brazil
e-mail: reverbel@rmad.com.br

D. Wei et al. (eds.), *Innovation and the Transformation of Consumer Law*,
https://doi.org/10.1007/978-981-15-8948-5_26

1.1 *Non-self-executing Norms Within the Brazilian Constitution*

The 1988 Brazilian Constitution was so benevolent with its promises for the future. It created, shall we say, a great expectation within our society with regards to a number of forthcoming promises. The classical doctrine of American Constitutional Law—Cooley,[1] Story—deals with material such as *non-self-executing norms*. It was Rui Barbosa[2] who inaugurated the subject in Brazil.[3] In this way, within our Constitution there is an extensive list of material that depends on regulation and needs to be complemented.[4] On this list we have the participation of the public service users in the direct and indirect administration of those services. Article 37, § 3, of the Brazilian Constitution regulated this subject. Now, public service consumers have the proper means to revendicate the correct application of the law.

Among these rules, it appears precisely the Article **37, §3**, changed by the constitutional amendment 19/98, which refers to the Ordinary Legislator the regulation of the form of participation of users in direct and indirect administration, mainly with regard to dissatisfaction with the services provided by the public power, specifically regulating items I, II and III of article 37, paragraph 3 of the 1988 Brazilian Constitution.[5]

The 13.460/17 law regulated the article 175, items II and IV, of 1988 Brazilian Constitution, since such provision mentions that it is incumbent upon the public authority to provide public services, determining that the regulatory act shall decide on the rights of users and the obligation to maintain adequate services. Moreover, for the public services provided through instruments of delegation, the article 1, § 3, of law 13.460/17 deals with this, in a way that such Legal Diploma applies "subsidiarily to the provisions of this Law to public services provided by private individuals".

On the other hand, it should be mentioned that Constitutional Amendment N° 19/98 established a period of **120 days** for the National Congress to regulate the provisions of Paragraph 3, items I, II and III of Article 37 of the Constitution.[6]

[1]Cooley [3], p. 101.

[2]Barbosa [1], p. 488.

[3]Ferreira filho [6], p. 41. Silva [12], p. 88.

[4]The very Brazilian Consumer Code is a good example. Suffices to see the text from Article 48 of the Provisional Dispositions of the 1988 Brazilian Constitution: "O Congresso Nacional, dentro de cento e vinte dias da promulgação da Constituição, elaborará código de defesa do consumidor" (The House of Representatives, in one hundred and twenty days from the enactment of this Constitution, will make a Consumer Protection Code).

[5]See: Rezende De Oliveira [11].

[6]We transcribe here the text from the Article 37, § 3°, I, II e III of the Brazilian Constitution, with the wording determined by the Constitutional Amendment n° 19/1998 *in verbis:* Paragraph 3. The law shall regulate the forms of participation of users in governmental entities and in entities owned by the Government, especially as regards: I—claims relating to the rendering of public services in general, the provision of user services being ensured, as well as periodical assessment, both external and internal, of the quality of services; II—the access of users to administrative records and to information about Government initiatives, with due regard for article 5, items X and XXXIII;

This omission has been extended over time. We experienced a delay of almost **30 years**, if we count from the 1988 Constitution; **20 years** of delay, if we count from the Constitutional Amendment n° 19/98. This demonstrates, to a certain extent, a leniency of the public power itself, of the Congressmen, towards the consumers who are the beneficiaries of these public services. It is curious to note that it was the National Congress (Article 27 of Constitutional Amendment N° 19) that delimited the 120-day deadline for the regulation of the matter, having neglected it for nearly 20 years. This is the central problem of non-self-enforcing norms: they depend on the political will of the Legislators.

The pressure for regulation should come from society, from consumers, from recipients of public services.[7] Nowadays, the pressure has come from the Judiciary, or rather from the Lawyers. In 2013, the Federal Council of the Brazilian Bar Association (article 103, VII, of the 1988 Brazilian Constitution) filed a Direct Action of Unconstitutionality (DAU) by Default with the purpose of publishing the promised law. The DAU request intended that the Code of Consumer Protection be applied subsidiarily until the law was published. Without success in this *desideratum*, the Judge-Rapporteur determined that Congress should comply with the judicial determination in 120 days. As the powers are independent, although harmonic with one another (article 2 of Brazilian Constitution) and the separation of powers cannot be abolished (article 60, §4, item III of Brazilian Constitution), the judicial decision was not honored by the parliamentarians. Only in 2015 the House of Representatives took the initiative and approved global substitute amendment, resending the Bill to the Federal Senate, which finally approved the substitute with minor amendments, on 06.06.2017. It was only on June 26, 2017 that the matter was finally regulated, sanctioned and published in the Official Gazette, with the edition of Law 13.460/2017,[8] which we will analyze in more detail.[9]

III—the rules of a complaint against negligence or abuse in the exercise of an office, position or function in government services. (Brazil. Constitution of the Federal Republic of Brazil [2].

[7]The Brazilian Federal Senate presented the Bill no. 439/1999, that has the goal to regulate the subject matter. After three years the bill has been sent to House of Representatives, where it took the identification of Bill no. 6.953/2002. Due to the slowness of the Legislative Branch, the Brazilian Bar Association (OAB) proposed a Direct Action of Unconstitutionality (DAU) by Default no. 24. In this action was requested the application of the Bill before its final approvation, all in accordance with the cases judged for by the Brazilian Superior Justice Court (STJ). REsp 1.659.509/SE. Second Panel. Judge-Rapporteur. Min. Herman Benjamin. j. 02/05/2017. DJe 12/05/2017; BRAZILIAN SUPERIOR COURT OF JUSTICE (STJ). AgInt no REsp 1.569.566/MT. Second Panel. Judge-Rapporteur. Min. Herman Benjamin. J. 07/03/2017. DJe 27/04/2017; BRAZILIAN SUPERIOR COURT OF JUSTICE (STJ). AgRg no AREsp 239.416/RJ. First Panel. Judge-Rapporteur. Min. Napoleão Nunes Maia Filho. j. 26/02/2013. DJe 06/03/2013; BRAZILIAN SUPERIOR COURT OF JUSTICE (STJ). AgRg no AREsp 183.812/SP. Second Panel. Rel. Min. Mauro Campbell Marques. j. 06/11/2012. DJe 12/11/2012. Justice Dias Toffoli granted the provisional injuction, but decided to not apply the Consumer Bill subsidiarily and provisionaly. See: Souza Dos Santos [13].

[8]Souza Dos Santos [13].

[9]It's interesting to mention that, in the Brazilian State of São Paulo, since 1999, the matter is regulated by the State Act no. 10.294, that regulates the protection and the defense of the user of the public services in the State of São Paulo.

1.2 Public Services and Consumer Protection

The Public Service, by its nature and purpose, must be provided—in the form of the law, directly or through concession or permission—by the Public Power, for the benefit of the administered and the community. Supported by legality and the **Supremacy of Public Interest** over the Interest of the Particular. The common good comes before and goes beyond private interest. It is anterior and posterior. Thus, in Brazilian Public Law, the principle of supremacy of the public interest prevails.

The Public Service provided by the State must, on the other hand, meet the expectations and the wishes of the citizen. Law N°. 8.987 of February 13, 1995, when dealing with the provision of public services by way of concession or permission, defines, in Article 6, paragraph 1, which means to be the full and adequate attendance of users in the provision of these services, *in verbis*: *Adequate service is that which satisfies the conditions of regularity, continuity, celerity, efficiency, safety, up-to-date, generality, courtesy in its provision and modicity of tariffs.*

That is, the administration wants to see its fundamental right to provide the public service effectively, with **continuity** (permanent public service, uninterrupted); **celerity** (the common good has priority and needs to be met within a reasonable time), **efficiency** (the objective must be well achieved, prohibiting, if necessary, the right to strike), **economicity** (not always the lowest price, but fair price); **safety** (protection against danger and losses, with reliability and continuity); destined to the generality of the administered, service provided with **courtesy, education, fairness** of tariffs—fair price.

The citizen feels, *cœteris paribus*, a consumer of these services. The public service user wants to see the performance of this service as if it were provided by the private sector, in any relationship of consumption. Law 13.460/2017, unlike the Concessions Law, sets out in article 4, the principles that the Public Service must follow, namely: *regularity, continuity, effectiveness, security, up-to-date, generality, transparency and courtesy*. The Concessions Law 8.957/95 mentions that the public service must **meet certain conditions**. The current law 13.460/17 indicates that the public service must **observe the principles**.

Article 2 of Law 13.460/17 considers as public service all administrative activity of direct or indirect provision of goods or services to the population, **exercised** by a body or entity of the public administration. The term used is improper. The service is **owned** by the Administration, but may be **exercised** or **provided** by different persons (provided by third parties) to the person who holds the title.[10] Therefore, the Law affects every public service that is provided by the private sector as occurs, for example, with notaries and registrars.[11]

Law 13.460 of June 26 2017 (composed of 07 chapters, 25 articles and 2421 words) is a landmark in Brazilian Administrative Law. Effectively, from it, a Code of Consumer Protection for the Public Service User is designed for the near future. This law has the originality of proposing the theme, raising the question, directing

---

[10] See Eidelwein [5], paper presented to the final graduation in Law.

[11] Ramon Alvares [10].

the course of future debates. The issue is set and has its own rules. Its developments will depend on time, case law and its own acceptance by public entities linked to compliance with it. Let us see what, in fact, it regulates.

1.3 The Regulation of Public Service User Protection by Law 13.460/17

(A) **User and Consumer**

Law 13.460/17 compatibilizes the concepts of "user" and "consumer". These concepts, not always correctly collated, are linked with public services directly offered by the public administration to users.[12] In this aspect, the provison of article 1, § 2, of law 13.460/17 deserves to be highlighted. This article determines that the application of this law does not move away from the necessity to enforce the specific regulatory norms, or move away from the necessity to enforce Law 8.078/90, when characterized as consumer relation.

In public services provided directly by the Public Administration and those provided in the modality of concession and permission the Code of Consumer Defense is applied. The combined Reading of article 7, of Law 8.987/95; of article 22, of Law 8.078/90 and article 1, § 2, II, of Law 13.460/17 show the ample protection of consumers by the legislators. The normative texts mentioned reinforce the thesis of an increase in consumer protection when directly related to public services. The subject lacked regulation, but a few sparsely distributed legislations did not lose the opportunity to highlight the importance of these fundamental rights.

(B) **User and Public Service**

Law 13.460/17 defined what it is to be a public service user, and, with a certain originality, conceptualized that the Brazilian Constitution didn't define, the concept of public service and the user appearing in article 2, subsection I and II. User, therefore, is a private individual or company that benefits from or uses, effectively or potentially, public services.

Public Service,[13] as defined in the new statute, is the administrative activity or the direct or indirect supply of goods and services to the people, exercised by the public

[12] On the subject matter, see Maffini et al. [8], pp. 409–420.

[13] In what concerns the concept of public service: "(…) even having made such a delimitation, there is, nevertheless, controversy over the definition of public service, especially by the absence of a legal definition. Anyway, it is possible to found, in the several conceptual formulas elaborated by the scholars, a set of elements used to define public services, in a strict sense. In first place, we have a "**MATERIAL ELEMENT**" that limits the notion of public services to the activities executed for the benefit of the community, considered as a unity (even if the service's fruition could be individualized) or to the State itself, for the indirect use for the community. There is no need that the service be provided in favor of all the members of the society. Likewise, the public service will not be mischaracterized, in itself, by the fact that only a minority of the society could enjoy the service.

administration. The legal text, in spite of the absence of an express disposition, is seen as encompassing the fulfilment of public service by an individual, provided that it is authorized by the public administration.

The Article 4°, Law 13.460/17 stablishes the parameters to the **concept of adequate public service**. In general terms, such parameters do not differ from those of Article 6°, § 1°, Law 8.987/95 that regulated **public services** provided by concession or permission. Comparing both statutes above mentioned, we see that in the text of Law 13.460/17 there is no reference to the **price adequacy**, that is a clear requirement in Law 8.987/95, because the public services provided directly by the State—object of Article 37, § 3° from the Brazilian Constitution—generally do not demand payment. Therefore, both the Scholars and the case law must deal with the question of the public services provided by the public administration by delegation—by concession or permission.

The Brazilian Constitution attributes to the Federal Government the exploitation, directly or by authorization, concession or permission the services and installations of electric energy (art, 21, XII, "b"). In the hypothesis of delegation of the service to a state company from a member state—in spite of Article 1° from Law 13.460/17 refers public services made directly or indirectly by the public administration, the statute regulating the issue must be the 8.987/95, because of the adequacy of the rules about concessions and permissions. The specialty of the subject matter determines the application of the rules concerning concessions and permission of public service that demands, also, **price adequacy**.

As told above, we have to see the collectivity as a whole, indivisible and, if we conclude that the service contemplates the collectivity, direct or indirectly, the material element is fulfilled. Besides that, there is the "**SUBJECTIVE OR ORGANIC ELEMENT**", established in Article 175 of the Brazilian Constitution, in view of which only the service provided by the State could be considered public service. This element requires state control over the public service, either executing it by its inner organs, or by individuals, and in this case will be essential its legitimation by regular means, such as delegation, concession of public service, permission etc. Lastly it is necessary a "**FORMAL ELEMENT**", that refers to the need of a legal qualification, in statutory law, of the activity as a public service, as well as its submission to rules of public law which derogate from private law. This last element or criteria of definition of public service brings with it, also, one of the main consequences of its definition, that is, the effect of a peculiar legal regime that, as we shall see, will cause significant state regulation. Therefore, in a formal meaning, an activity could be considered a public service only if thus qualified by the Constitution or, in some special cases, by the statutes. A service does not become a public service, therefore, only by the desire of its author, but by the qualification from the law. On the other hand, still on the formal notion of public service, we have an activity that is heavily regulated by the State and that, by this very reason, cannot be framed in the notion of free Initiative that is adequate to other species of economic activity. Unifying these elements of definition, as well as some moderations required by the modern notion of public services, Paulo Modesto (Reforma do Estado, formas de prestação de serviços ao público e parcerias público-privadas: demarcando as fronteiras dos conceitos de serviços público, serviços de relevância pública e serviços de exploração econômica para as parcerias público-privadas, p. 25) defines it as the "activity of administrative action, concrete, under the direct and immediate execution by the State and its delegates, made available directly to determined or indetermined users, under the Public Law regime, compulsory, egalitarian and continuous, seeking to satisfy collective needs, controlled by the Government" (Maffini [7], pp. 221–222, our translation). See also, Couto E Silva [4], pp. 45–74.

(C) Police Power and Public Service

It is uncontroversial—since Law 13.460/17—the application of the Consumer Code in the provision of public services by the public Administration. On the other hand, we cannot apply neither Law 13.460/17 nor Law 8.078/90 (the Brazilian Consumer Code) in cases in which the public administration is **not** providing public services and when, even in the context of public services, there is **no consumer relation**. In other words, the public organs that do not provide public services are freed from those regulations when they exercise **police power**, as seen in the regulatory agencies.

On the other hand, we could consider the application of Law 13.460/17 in the hypothesis in which theses agencies offer a public service to the citizen, because these agencies exercise its **police power** over **economic activities** to guarantee **user's rights**, the user is a true consumer of the services regulated. Therefore, the relation between the **individual** and the **supervisory organ** can be configured as a provision of public service, as the supervisory organ seeks to answer the user's reclamations. Law 13.460/17 do not deal with the **police power** exercised by a **Regulatory Agency**. On the other hand, Law 13.460/17 is applicable in the hypothesis of a consumer claiming to the Regulatory Agency that has been abuse of power from the organ responsible by the execution of the public service.[14]

(D) Rights and Duties of the Users of the Public Services

In addition to the rights expressly stated in the consumer Code, the users have a list of **subjective rights** pertinent to the adequate execution of public services (arts. 5° and 6°, Law 13.460/17), these rights are accompanied by its corresponding **duties,** addressed to the users (Article 8°). In this respect, we must also highlight Article 7°, Law 13.460/17,[15] that deals with the **User's Service Letter**, instrument of user information "about the services provided by the organ or entity, the access forms to these services and its commitments and quality standards to the public attendance". In the Brazilian Federal Government, the Ad-Law in this subject matter is the Presidential

[14]Maffini et al. [8], p. 410.

[15]"Article 7° The organs and entities here regulated must publish a User's Service Letter. § 1° The User's Service Letter must inform the user about the services provided by the organ or entity, the access forms to these services and its commitments and quality standards to the public attendance. § 2° The User's Service Letter must provide clear and precise information about each of the services provided, presenting, as a minimum, information about: I—the services provided; II—requisites, documents, ways and information necessary to access the service; III—main steps to the service process; IV—Deadline to the public service; V—way in which the service will be executed and VI—places and ways for the user to manifest on the service execution. § 3° Besides the information described in § 2°, the User's Service Letter must detail the commitments and quality standard about, as a minimum, the following aspects: I—service priorities; II—wait time forecast; III—communication mechanism with the users; IV—procedures to receive and answer users manifestations and V—mechanism of consult, by the users, about the progress of the service requested and eventual manifestations. § 4° The User's Service Letter will be periodically updated and will be permanently published in the electronic site of the organ of entity in the internet.

§ 5° Specific Decree, approved by each branch and federative level, will dispose about the operationalization of the User's Service Letter.

Decree 9.094, from July 17, 2017, that also seek to simplify the service provided to the users of public services, as well as ratify the dispensation of signature recognition and document authentication in documents produced in the country.

Law 13.460/17 regulated the **user's power to manifest** (Article 2°, V). This rule defines **manifestations** as follows: "reclamations, denunciations, suggestions, praises and other pronunciations from users about public services and the behavior of public agentes in providing and supervising such services". It is interesting to see that the statute used the word "**manifestation**" and not "**claim**", unlike Article 37, § 3°, from the Brazilian Constitution, both in its original wording as in the current writing, combined with § 3°, I, from Article 37 of the Brazilian Constitution. Anyway, the institute of manifestation (or claim), regulated in arts. 9° to 12, Law 13.460/17, is an important instrument of social control offered to the collectivity, to the enhancement of the public services provided by the public administration.[16]

Still deserves attention, in what concerns to the protection of the users of public services, arts. 18 to 22[17] Law n° 13.460/17, that regulates the Users Councils (advisory bodies), that seeks to monitor and evaluate the adequacy of the services provided by the public administration. Besides, it is also possible to impose instruments of continuous evaluation of these public services, as stated in arts. 23 and 24[18] Law n° 13.460/17.

Lastly, we must underline that Article 25, Law Lei 13.460/17, stablished a *vacatio legis* different to each of the federal entities, taking the number of inhabitants as the criteria. Therefore, the Law will come into force in the deadline of: **I—three hundred and sixty days** for the Union, the member states, the Federal District and the cities

[16]In what relates to the social control provided by the manifestation (or claim) see Pereira [9].

[17]"Article 18. Besides other ways provided by the statutes, the participation of the users in monitor and evaluation of public services will be made by user's councils. Single Paragraph. The user's councils are advisory bodies with the following attributions: I—monitor the service provision; II—participate in the service evaluation; III—propose enhancements in the service provision; IV—contribute to define directives to the adequate user attendance and V—monitor and evaluate the ombudsman activity. Article 19. The Council's composition must observe criteria of representativeness and plurality of the interested parts, seeking equilibrium in the representation. Single Paragraph. The representatives will be chosen in a process open to the public and different for each kind or user to be represented. Article 20. The user's council could be consulted for the indication of the ombudsman. Article 21. The participation of the user in the council will be considered relevant public service without remuneration. Article 22. Specific Decree from each Branch and federal level will regulate the operation of the user's councils.

[18]Article 23. The organs and public entities ruled in this statute must evaluate the services provided, in the following aspect: I—user satisfaction with the service provided; II—quality of user attendance; III—fulfilment of commitments and deadlines defined to the provision of the services; IV—Amount of manifestations from the users and V—measures adopted by the public administration to the enhancement of the provision of the services. § 1° The evaluation will be performed by satisfaction poll that will be done annually, or by any other way that guarantees statistical significance to the results. § 2° The result from the evaluation must be published in the organ's or entity's site, including the ranking of the entities with bigger occurrence of claims from the users in the period of the evaluation mentioned in § 1° and will serve as aid to reorient and adjust the services provided, in special with regard to the fulfilment of the commitments and quality standards published in the User's Service Letter. Article 24. Specific Decree from each Branch and federative level will regulate the evaluation of the effectivity and the satisfaction levels from the users.

with over five hundred Thousand inhabitants; **II—of five hundred and forty days** to the cities with between on hundred Thousand and five hundred Thousand inhabitants; and of **III—seven hundred and twenty days** to the towns with less than one hundred thousand inhabitants. The deadline seems to be sufficient to the implementation of the legal regime instituted by Law 13.460/17, especially if we consider the long delay in the subject matter regulation.

2 Conclusion

This essay sought to present the legal regime instituted by Law 13.460/17, for the defense of users of public services provided by the Public Administration. Although the exact understanding of the institutes provided by Law 13.460/17 can only occur from the doctrinal and jurisprudential maturation of the legal diploma, it is undeniable that, together with Law 8.987/95 and the Consumer Protection Code, it will serve as an important instrument to protect users of public services. None of this will occur without the Government's willingness to improve the quality of its services, which encompasses another matter, such as a reform of the administration as a whole, seeking greater efficiency in the management of public affairs, so that consumers of this service feel fully integrated into the Social and Democratic State of Law.

References

1. Barbosa, Ruy. Comentários á Constituição Federal Brasileira (coligidos e ordenados por Homero Pires). Vol. II. São Paulo: Saraiva& Cia., 1933.
2. Brazil. Constitution of the Federal Republic of Brazil: Constitutional text of October 5, 1988, with the alterations introduced by Constitutional Amendments no. 1/92 through 72/2013 and by Revision Constitutional Amendments no. 1/94 through 6/94. Translated and revised by Istvan Vajda, Patrícia de Queiroz Carvalho Zimbres and Zanira Tavares de Souza. 6th ed. Brasília: The Federal Senate, Undersecretariat of Technical Publication, 2013. Available in http://www.stf.jus.br/repositorio/cms/portalStfInternacional/portalStfSobreCorte_en_us/anexo/Constitution_2013.pdf. Access in Apr 20, 2019.
3. Cooley, Thomas M. A treatise on the constitutional limitations which rest upon the legislative power of the states of the American union. 4ª ed. Boston: Little, Brown, and Company, 1878.
4. Couto E Silva, Almiro do. Privatização no Brasil e o Novo Exercício de Funções Públicas por Particulares. Serviço Público "Á Brasileira"?, In: *Revista de Direito Administrativo*, n° 230, outubro/dezembro, Rio de Janeiro: Renovar, 2002, pp. 45–74.
5. Eidelwein, Arthur. *Lei 13.460 a sua aplicação subsidiária caso o serviço seja prestado por particular.* Porto Alegre. 2018. UFRGS, monografia apresentada.
6. Ferreira Filho, Manoel Gonçalves. *Curso de Direito Constitucional.* 40ª ed. São Paulo: Saraiva. 2015.
7. Maffini, Rafael. *Elementos de Direito Administrativo*, Porto Alegre: Livraria do Advogado. 2016.
8. Maffini, Rafael.; Pedrollo, Gustavo Fontana; Ramos, Letícia Ayres; Oliveira, Rodrigo Führ de; Heinen, Juliano. Serviço público e as noções jurídicas de "usuário" e de "consumidor": em torno do estatuto dos usuários de serviços públicos (lei 13.460/17). In: JAEGER JUNIOR,

Augusto; REVERBEL, Carlos Eduardo Dieder; MARTINI, Sandra Regina. *O movimento do saber*: uma homenagem para Claudia Lima Marques. Porto Alegre: RJR. 2017. pp. 409–420.
9. Pereira, Paulo Ricardo Maroso. *Direito de reclamação do usuário de serviço público*: um instrumento de controle social no atual modelo de administração pública brasileira. (Masters Dissertation) – Law Postgraduate Program, Federal University of Rio Grande do Sul. Porto Alegre, p. 219, 2017. Available in http://hdl.handle.net/10183/169479. Access in Apr. 03, 2019.
10. Ramon Alvares, Luís. *Breves Apontamentos sobre a aplicação da Lei 13.460/2017 no Direito Registral Imobiliário*. Published at October, 03, 2017utubro de 2017,. Available in: http://iregistradores.org.br/breves-apontamentos-sobre-a-aplicacao-da-lei-13-4602017-no-direito-registral-imobiliario/. Access in: Apr. 03, 2019.
11. Rezende De Oliveira, Rafael Carvalho. *Lei de Defesa do Usuário do Serviço Público avança na proteção dos direitos básicos*. Revista Consultor Jurídico, Jun., 10, 2018. Available in: https://www.conjur.com.br/2018-jul-10/rafael-oliveira-lei-defesa-usuario-avanca-pro tecao-direitos Access in: 03.25.2019.
12. Silva, José Afonso da. *Aplicabilidade das normas constitucionais*. São Paulo: Malheiros, 2008.
13. Souza Dos Santos, Júlio César. *A tutela dos direitos dos usuários dos serviços públicos: breves apontamentos sobre a Lei n° 13.460/17*. Revista FIDES: v. 8 n. 2 (2017): 16ed., p. 233. Available in http://www.revistafides.ufrn.br/index.php/br/article/view/329. Access in: 03.26.2019.

Developing Micro, Small and Medium Enterprises in Nigeria Through Standardisation

Felicia N. Monye and Phebean O. S. Arumemi

1 Introduction

In Nigeria, standardisation has been part of the system since the enactment of the Standards Organisation of Nigeria Act 1971 (48 years ago) which was repealed and replaced by the Standards Organisation of Nigeria Act 2015.

Over the years, the Standards Organisation of Nigeria (SON), the standards-making body for Nigeria has developed numerous standards covering different product fields. Strengthened by the expanded functions and powers conferred by the 2015 Act, the Organisation has intensified its standardisation activities to cover new areas of national interest. Currently, standards developed or adopted by SON cover the following sectors: civil/building, chemical technology, electrical-electronics, food-codex, mechanical, textile-leather and services.

Currently, a major area of focus is development of standards for products mostly produced by Micro, Small and Medium Enterprises (MSMEs) with the aim of empowering the operators to key into the Federal Government's Economic Recovery and Growth Plan (ERGP), a plan aimed at diversifying the economy of the country. To empower MSMEs to produce products that are competitive at local and international markets, SON has adopted various measures including development of MSMEs-related standards; procurement of testing facilities that can be utilised by all producers including MSMEs; sale of standards to MSMEs at subsidised rates; education of MSMEs on application of standards; participation of MSMEs in the

F. N. Monye (✉)
Faculty of Law, University of Nigeria, Enugu Campus, Standards Organisation of Nigeria (SON), Nsukka, Nigeria
e-mail: felicia.monye@unn.edu.ng

P. O. S. Arumemi
Standards Organisation of Nigeria (SON), Lekki Lagos, Nigeria
e-mail: phebean.arumemi@son.gov.ng

D. Wei et al. (eds.), *Innovation and the Transformation of Consumer Law*,
https://doi.org/10.1007/978-981-15-8948-5_27

standards-making process; and product certification through the Mandatory Conformity Assessment Programme (MANCAP) and the Standards Organisation of Nigeria Conformity Assessment Programme (SONCAP) both applicable to all manufacturers irrespective of size. In addition, Nigeria being a member of the African Organisation for Standardisation (ARSO) and International Organisation for Standardisation (ISO) has participated and adopted some international standards thereby achieving uniformity and facilitating access to foreign markets.

Application of standards in small businesses is being promoted as a veritable tool for addressing issues relating to quality, consumer confidence, competition, optimal deployment of resources, reduction in waste and maximisation of profit for economic development.

This paper examines some MSMEs-related standards developed by SON and other measures put in place by the Organisation to build the capacities of MSMEs to achieve improved quality and safety of products and services offered to consumers by this sector.

2 Functions of SON

Section 5 enumerates the functions of the Standards Organisation of Nigeria. Among others, the functions include measures to ensure compliance with the standards designated and approved by the Council; investigations as necessary into the quality of facilities, materials and products whether imported or manufactured in Nigeria; evaluation of quality assurance activities, including certification of systems, products and laboratories throughout Nigeria. Other functions include compilation of inventory of products requiring standardisation; establishment of mandatory conformity assessment programme for locally manufactured products; registration of all manufactured products distributed, marketed and consumed throughout Nigeria; import and export product surveillance, certification and conformity assessment; training and accreditation of training institutions and organisations for purposes of international standards; investigations into production premises and raw materials; establishment of relevant quality assurance systems including certification of production sites for regulated products; and any other activity likely to assist in the performance of the functions conferred on the Organisation under the Act.

The above functions are applicable to all manufacturers in Nigeria including MSMEs. But in relation to the latter, the Organisation has mapped out some strategies aimed at strengthening the capacities of operators in this sector to produce safe and good quality products. Some of the measures are discussed in subsequent paragraphs.

Table 1 Classifications adopted by National Policy on MSMEs

S/N	Size category	Employment	Assets (naira, million) (excluding land and buildings)
1	Micro enterprises	Less than 10	Less than 10
2	Small enterprises	10–49	10 - less than 100
3	Medium enterprises	50–199	100 - less than 1,000

3 Meaning of MSMEs and SMEs

It is deemed necessary to define the acronyms 'MSMEs' and 'SMEs' as they are often used interchangeably without giving a thought to the distinct features of each. For the purpose of this paper, the definition contained in the National Policy on MSMEs[1] is adopted. This uses a classification based on dual criteria: employment and assets (excluding land and buildings), as follows: (Table 1)

From the foregoing definitions, it can be argued that some enterprises which are referred to in informal circles as SMEs are indeed micro enterprises as the capital base of most of such businesses is less than the sum stipulated for SMEs. To qualify as a small enterprise, the enterprise must employ 10–49 persons and have a capital base of 10 to less than 100 million naira. The corresponding figures for medium enterprises are as shown in the last row of the table. For the purpose of this paper, the encompassing term "Micro, Small and Medium Enterprises (MSMEs)" is used to cover all enterprises that come within any of the above definitions.

4 Importance of MSMEs to the Nigerian Economy

It is widely acknowledged that MSMEs make significant contributions to the Gross Domestic Product of Nigeria. Writing with particular reference to SMEs, Oyelaran-Oyeyinka notes that in light of recent events in the Nigerian macroeconomic environment, SMEs have compelling growth potential and like other emerging economies are likely to constitute a significant portion of GDP in the near future.[2] The author notes that in terms of opportunities, SMEs have significant untapped growth potential, strong export and employment potentials but face huge gaps in infrastructure, poor financial support and credit environment and high levels of unskilled workforce.[3] He notes that the vital role of Government in providing an enabling environment for SMEs cannot be overemphasised.[4]

[1]The National Policy on MSMEs, Federal Republic of Nigeria, 2015.

[2]https://www.cbn.gov.ng/fss/wed/SME_Issues,%20Challenges%20and%20Prospects_Oyeyinka%20Banji.pdf accessed 19 March 2019.

[3]Ibid 6.

[4]Ibid 11.

The Federal Government of Nigeria has demonstrated commitment to MSMEs development through the establishment of an Agency, the Small and Medium Enterprises Development Agency of Nigeria (SMEDAN) and a Council, the National Council on Micro, Small and Medium Enterprises to promote MSMEs development. Similarly, programmes such as the Economic Recovery and Growth Plan (ERGP),[5] and the Nationwide MSMEs Clinics being organised by the Office of the Vice President of the Federal Republic of Nigeria in various states of the Federation to facilitate MSMEs development have been supportive. The aim of the MSMES Clinic is to create platforms (clinics) where key trade and industry-related Federal Government agencies and MSMEs interact in business forums. The programme serves as a one-stop-shop for diagnosing and proffering solutions to challenges faced by the entrepreneurs. Each Forum holds for two days with a day of the event devoted to interactions with the Vice President. The clinics have been held in different cities across the country as part of the strategies for making it easier for MSMEs to do business in Nigeria.[6]

In May 2018, the Director-General of the Small and Medium Enterprises Development Agency of Nigeria (SMEDAN), disclosed that there were about 37.1 million Micro, Small and Medium Enterprises (MSMEs) operating in the country; contributing 48.7% to the Gross Domestic Product (GDP) and 7.2% to export.[7]

This level of contribution to GDP is indeed, significant; but the percentage contribution to export is worrisome. To reverse this trend, SON has taken up the task of developing MSMEs through standardisation and quality assurance to achieve global competiveness. This has resulted in an impressive number of standards for products that are popular with the MSMEs.

5 Major Challenges Faced by MSMEs in Nigeria and Ameliorating Measures by Some Agencies

MSMEs in Nigeria face some teething challenges which inhibit growth and maximisation of potentials. These include finance, multiple taxes, high cost of infrastructure, fierce competition from similar imported products and acute power shortage. The last item has necessitated the use of power generating sets by operators at exorbitant costs thereby increasing the cost of production and prices of products and services. Some measures taken by relevant agencies to ameliorate these challenges are considered below.

[5] The Nigeria Economic Recovery and Growth Plan, 2017–2020.

[6] http://nmsmeawards.com.ng/about-msme-clinic/ accessed 01 April 2019.

[7] https://www.businesspost.ng/2018/05/20/37m-msmes-contribute-47-8-to-nigerias-gdp-smedan/, accessed 19 March 2019.

6 CBN Measures

Finance appears to pose the greatest problem as many MSMEs find it difficult to access bank loans at affordable rates. To ameliorate this problem, the Central Bank of Nigeria (CBN) has, over the years, introduced some financial measures to assist MSMEs to access funds from designated financial institutions. A major step in this regard was the launch by CBN of the MSME Development Fund on 15 August 2013 with a share capital of N220 billion. The main objective of the Fund is to provide low interest funds to the MSME sub-sector of the Nigerian economy through the Participating Finance Institutions (PFIs). The specific objectives are to enhance access by MSMEs to financial services; increase productivity and output of microenterprises; increase employment and create wealth; and engender inclusive growth.[8]

Eligible activities that are financed under the Fund include agricultural value chain, services, cottage industries, artisans, trade and commerce and any income generating business as may be prescribed by the CBN from time to time. Eligible MSMEs are able to obtain a long term single digit loans. This reduces the cost of borrowing and enhances the earning capacity of operators in addition to job creation for the teeming unemployed population.

In addition, CBN has issued successive guidelines to regulate the system[9] and other financial measures to enhance the participation of MSMEs in the economic development of the country.[10]

7 SMEDAN Measures

The Small and Medium Enterprises Development Agency of Nigeria (SMEDAN) is charged with the responsibility of promoting small scale enterprises in Nigeria. As contained in Sect. 8 of the Small and Medium Scale Enterprises Development Agency Act, 2003 (as amended), the responsibilities of the Agency include stimulating, monitoring and coordinating the development of the MSMEs sub-sector; initiating and articulating policy ideas for small and medium enterprises growth and development; promoting and facilitating development programmes, instruments and support services to accelerate the development and modernisation of MSME operations; serving as vanguard for rural industrialisation, poverty reduction, job creation and enhanced livelihoods; linking MSMEs to internal and external sources of finance, technology, technical skill development and management; intermediating between MSMEs and Government; and collaborating with other institutions in both public

---

[8] Ibid.

[9] https://www.cbn.gov.ng/devfin/smefinance.asp accessed 20 March 2019; see also CBN website for other measures operated to enhance the contribution of MSMEs to the national economy.

[10] https://www.cbn.gov.ng/devfin/smefinance.asp accessed 20 March 2019 –https://www.cbn.gov.ng/search/runsearch.asp?q=MSME accessed 30 March 2019.

and private sectors to create a good enabling environment for businesses in general and MSMEs in particular.[11]

Measures put in place by SMEDAN to enhance the efforts of MSMEs include creation of Business Support Centres in different parts of Nigeria;[12] information on various loan facilities;[13] Conditional Grant Scheme (CGS) for Micro Enterprises in Nigeria;[14] and Entrepreneurship Development Programmes for MSMEs.[15]

8 SON Measures

Irrespective of measures put in place by the Government and regulatory agencies to encourage the growth of MSMEs, the most crucial factor is the outcome of the measures as reflected in the level of acceptability of the products produced by the operators. An essential factor that influences the acceptability of a product is quality. This in turn is influenced by application of the relevant standard in the production of the product. This is where the crucial role of the Standards Organisation of Nigeria comes into play. By responding to market needs and developing well-articulated standards for the MSMEs sector, the Organisation supports the operators' efforts to produce quality and safe products that can compete favourably in local and foreign markets. SON has demonstrated remarkable strength in this regard through measures and standards that are MSMEs-oriented, some of which are discussed below.

8.1 Training on Application of Standards

Mindful of the centrality of standards to quality of products and services, the Organisation has packaged some programmes aimed at enhancing the capacity of MSMEs to apply product standards. Such programmes include mentorship during factory inspections; sector-based stakeholders workshops; and an ACP-TBT sponsored train-the-trainer programme held in 2015.

---

[11] See also, https://smedan.gov.ng/index.php/who-we-are/smedan-mandate.html accessed 04 April 2019.

[12] https://smedan.gov.ng/index.php/zonal-office/business-support-centers.html accessed 05 April 2019.

[13] http://smedan.gov.ng/cip/ accessed 05 April 2019.

[14] https://smedan.gov.ng/index.php/dg-s-office/news/203-smedan-unveils-conditional-grant-scheme-cgs-for-micro-enterprises-in-lagos.html accessed 05 April 2019.

[15] https://smedan.gov.ng/index.php/15-departments/enterprise-development-and-promotion/edp-programmes/41-entrepreneurship-training-programme-edp.html accessed 05 April 2019.

8.2 *Participation in the Standards Development Process*

SON operates the policy of the International Organisation for Standardisation (ISO) and African Organisation for Standardisation (ARSO) on stakeholder engagement. In line with this policy, the Organisation involves key stakeholders in the standardisation process. In particular, operators of MSMEs are included in all Technical Committees on Standards Elaboration. The aim is to give the operators the opportunity to make input and gain from the expertise of other stakeholders participating in the process. This, apart from empowering the participants with the knowledge to apply the standards when approved, positions them to serve as change agents among other operators of MSMEs.

8.3 *Sale of Standards to MSMEs at Subsidised Rates*

In order to assist MSMEs to apply standards and thereby produce products that are acceptable in local and international markets, SON offers product standards to the operators at subsidised rates. This is meant to encourage more operators to embrace the application of standards with a view to achieving product quality and safety.

8.4 *Product Certification*

Product certification is one of the tools employed by SON to ensure compliance with prescribed standards. Certification activities of SON dates back to 1976 when two products manufactured by Lever Brothers Nigeria Limited (now, Unilever Nigeria Plc) were certified. This Scheme has continued and has been embraced by more manufacturers over the years. A certification scheme which all manufacturers are required to subscribe to is the Mandatory Conformity Assessment Programme (MANCAP) introduced in 2006 with the objective of assessing locally manufactured products in Nigeria to ensure conformity with minimum requirements of the Nigerian Industrial Standards (NIS). This programme is aimed at safeguarding the safety and health of consumers of made-in-Nigeria products. A further aim is to promote fair competition at both domestic and international markets in the overall interest of economic and industrial development of Nigeria.[16]

Since inception, an increasing number of companies have been subscribing to the MANCAP Certification Scheme. As regards the MSMEs, SON offers subsidised certification charges with the aim of encouraging the operators to subscribe to the Scheme. A streamlined duration of 60 days for certification to the MANCAP certification has been impactful. The following table shows the statistics of MSME products that have been certified in the last four years (Table 2).

[16]For more information on this programme, see http://son.gov.ng/mancap/ accessed 19 March 2019.

Table 2 MSMEs with certified products

Year	No. of MSMEs with certified products	No. of certified products
2016	485	933
2017	767	1,186
2018	632	1,151
Jan–March 2019	69	127
Total 2016–March 2019	1,953	3,398

The above statistics demonstrate the interest of MSMEs to authenticate the quality and safety of products produced by them through certification. This, in a way, mirrors the attitude of consumers towards products that bear certification marks. This is not to say that Nigeria has achieved her potential in this sector given the number of MSMEs operating in the country which stood at 37.1 million according to the statistics released by the Small and Medium Enterprises Development Agency of Nigeria (SMEDAN) in 2013.[17] There is, therefore, a compelling need to implement rigorously the various measures mapped out by SON to develop the skills of MSMEs in application of standards and participation in the certification Scheme.

Baring statistical data, one can say with reasonable certainty that many cottage industries and micro enterprises operating in the rural areas for local markets are not aware of product standards relating to products being produced by them.

It is pertinent to note that producers of products meant for export readily seek certification because the relevant authorities including SON will not endorse a product that is not certified. In fact, once a product is certified, it becomes export ready. This means that certification for the local market qualifies a product for the international market. The only exception is where specific parameters beyond the scope of the relevant Nigerian Industrial Standard (NIS) are set by the importing country. In this case, the Product Type Certification will apply. This involves issuance of certificates of conformance to applicable standards or contractual documents for products to facilitate export trade. The process applies to specific consignments meant for export by the applicant. The objective is to ensure that locally manufactured products meant for export conform to relevant Nigerian industrial standards as well as the quality requirements of the importing country including packaging. This is done on an individual basis following a formal application to SON by the company concerned. The applicant is required to provide all necessary details of the product, processes, packaging and intending country for the export. After inspection of the production processes, the consignment and samples of the product, a Certificate of Conformance will be issued for the particular consignment upon approval.[18] The MSMEs are being encouraged to take advantage of the Product Type Certification to meet the needs of their clients.

[17] SMEDAN and National Bureau of Statistics Collaborative Survey: Selected Findings, 2013.

[18] Source: http://son.gov.ng/product-certification/, accessed 21 March 2019.

It follows that in the case of products meant for export, the producer has no hiding place. It is hoped that with time, all manufacturers in Nigeria will see the need to voluntarily key into the certification scheme as a matter of good business practice and thus reduce the coercive efforts of SON to bring about compliance.

8.5 Awareness Creation and Education of MSMEs on Application of Standards

SON uses different platforms including awareness workshops to promote the application of standards and the role of the Organisation as a business facilitator rather than as a regulator of mandatory application of standards. This position aligns with the Federal Government's programme on ease of doing business issued through an Executive Order 001 of 18 May 2017. The aim is to demystify the perceived role of the Organisation as elitist and fit for only large companies. SON makes efforts to take the message of standards to the grassroots to empower local producers to meet the expectations of consumers. Among other things, the awareness exercise includes information on social and economic benefits of standards to users. Increased awareness is expected to produce some multiplier effects such as increased voluntary application by operators, improved quality of products and services and improved patronage of made-in-Nigeria products—outcomes which support the goal of diversification being pursued by the Federal Government.

The awareness programmes provide interactive platforms for proffering solutions to challenges relating to standards and certifications. Additionally, the programmes provide opportunities for collating data on products requiring standards development. Awareness programmes for MSMEs form part of the annual work plan of SON thus buttressing the premium placed on this sector. In fact, not less than two hundred (200) awareness creation programmes are held annually at a monthly average of sixteen (16) programmes across the thirty-six (36) states and the Federal Capital Territory. Some examples are:

a. Flag off of subsidy in the sale of standards- Nasarawa, Benue, Anambra, Katsina (2016);
b. Zero rejects of agricultural exports- Kano, Benue, Enugu, Lagos, Port Harcourt and Maiduguri (2017);
c. Nationwide training workshops on zero tolerance for substandard products- (2017/2018);
d. Participation in the National MSMEs Clinics for engagement on application of standards in 21 states (2017/2018);
e. Participation in various annual and sectorial conferences organised by Business Membership Organisations across the country provide opportunities for speaking on application of standards;
f. Training of Sorghum Farmers and Processors on Application of Standards, Kano- 2018;

g. Training on Metrology Calibration Services, Bauchi (2019);
h. Annual engagement of National Youth Service Corp Members undergoing skills acquisition and enterprise development;
i. Mentorship programmes on application of standards integrated into factory inspections.

The Organisation's presence in One-Stop-Shop Investment Centres for MSMEs, an offshoot of the Nationwide MSMEs Clinics also creates valuable platforms for engaging with the MSMEs on standardisation. These centres currently exist in the Federal Capital Territory (FCT), Abia, Kwara, Cross Rivers, Osun, Oyo, Osun and Plateau states.

8.6 Communication Strategies

Apart from dedicated MSMEs awareness creation programmes, SON features public enlightenment programmes on radio, television and social media. 'Standard and You' runs on National Television Authority and Channels TV on a weekly basis. In addition, a live *pidgin* English radio programme—"*Laughter on the Loose*", runs on WAZOBIA FM 99.5 on Tuesdays in Abuja and Thursdays in Lagos. The programme engages MSMEs through live discussions and phone-in on issues relating to standards and certification. It further promotes awareness on consumer rights and benefits of patronising certified local products. SON also interacts with stakeholders on social media (Twitter—@SONNigeria; facebook—facebook@sonnisnigeria as well as through toll free lines on 07056990099 and 08002255766).

8.7 Provision of Testing Facilities

SON has acquired impressive number of facilities for testing various made-in-Nigeria products. This saves manufacturers including the MSMEs the burden of having to acquire personal testing facilities at exorbitant prices. Operators are free to take samples of products and materials to SON facilities for conformity assessment. Subsidised testing charges are offered to MSMEs by SON.

8.8 Other Measures

SON operates other measures which serve as incentives for MSMEs to adopt the application of standards. One of such measures is a dedicated MSMEs Desk to assist MSMEs with necessary information to enhance compliance to standards and conformity assessment.

In the area of import, SON grants the SONCAP import permit to MSMEs at subsidised service charges for importation of raw materials and equipment. SONCAP is defined by SON as a pre-shipment verification of conformity to standards. The process is used to verify that products to be imported into Nigeria are in conformity with the applicable NIS or approved equivalents and technical regulations before shipment.[19]

A further incentive is the recommendation of MSMEs with certified products for financing. This is a powerful tool as it sends a positive signal to the prospective lender that the products offered by the concerned MSME are to be trusted. This window is also aimed to encourage voluntary patronage of standards and certification by MSMEs.

9 Standardisation Activities of SON

Standards developed or adopted by SON cover seven broad fields, namely, Civil-Building, Chemical Technology, Electrical-Electronics, Food-Codex, Mechanical, Textile-Leather and Service Standards. As at 31 March 2019, the Organisation had a total of 1,184 national and 1,425 adopted standards, known as the Nigerian Industrial Standards (NIS), with access to thousands of international standards from: International Organisation for Standardisation (ISO), International Electrotechnical Commission (IEC), ASTM International (formally American Society for Testing and Materials), Codex Alimentarius, African Organisation for Standardisation (ARSO), Economic Community of West African States (ECOWAS) and International Telecommunication Union (ITU). Apart from protecting the health and satisfying the needs of consumers, product and service standards assist operators to save costs, reduce waste and produce products that compete favourably in local and foreign markets. The standards development process prioritises stakeholders' involvement and engagement using the guiding principles for global best practice in standards development. Every stage of the standard development process is communicated through media notification for involvement.

Although the same standards are applicable to all manufacturers in a given line of product or service, by a deliberate policy to empower MSMEs to improve on the quality and safety of products offered to consumers, SON has taken a step further to undertake the development of new standards for indigenous products and services that are popular among MSMEs. The aims are to ensure safety of products and services and achieve sustainability of businesses through increased patronage and profits. For instance, service standards to provide operational guidance for skilled workers are being elaborated to enhance and continuously improve on the quality of services that have been embraced by many MSMEs. The list includes Standards for Fashion Designing and Tailoring, Car Washing, Auto Mechanical Works, Electrical Wiring, Carpentry, Hair dressing, Cobbling, Plumbing and Masonry. In the product

[19]Source: http://son.gov.ng/soncap/ accessed 22 March 2019.

field, SON has also elaborated an impressive number of new standards that can easily be applied by MSMEs. Examples are Standard for Clean Cook Stove—Biomass Type (NIS 1000: 2018), Standard for Paste Ink (NIS 1033: 2018), Specifications for Plaster of Paris (P.O.P) Emulsion and Screed Emulsion Paints (NIS 1034: 2018) Standard for Sport Mat Part 1—Landing Mat for Pole Vault and High Jump (NIS 908-1: 2018), Standard for Duvet (NIS 1040: 2018) Standard for Multipurpose Sofa Bed (NIS 830: 2018) Standard for Couch Mattress (NIS 1042: 2018) Standard for Solid Foam Chair and Seat Support (NIS 1043: 2018), Standard for Reflective Safety Garment (NIS 071: 2018) Standard for Elasticated Disposable Baby Diaper (NIS 880: 2018) and Safety and Performance Requirements for Motorcycle Assembly (NIS 889: 2018).

In the Food and Codex sector are the following new standards: Standard for Dried and Smoked Fish (NIS 982: 2018), Standard for Ready to Cook Quick Frozen Plantain Chip (NIS 1045:2018), Standard for Rice Flour (NIS 810: 2018), Standard for Icing Sugar (NIS 732: 2018), Standard for Fura (NIS 735: 2018), Standard for Ready-to-Cook Quick Frozen Yam Chips (NIS 1048: 2018), Standard for Mango Juice (NIS 1019: 2018), Standard for Aloe Vera Drinks (NIS1006: 2018), Standard for Guava Juice (NIS 1018: 2018), and Standard for Coconut and Pineapple Juice (NIS 1002: 2018). For ease of reference, some of these standards are shown in the Table 3.

As noted above, in addition to national standards, SON also adopts international standards relevant to the needs of Nigeria. The objective is to achieve uniformity and facilitate access to foreign markets. Some newly adopted standards which can be said to have particular bearing on MSMEs are listed in the Table 4.

Standards presented in the above tables (Tables 3 and 4) were selected by purposeful sampling method based on the authors' perception of products and services that are particularly suitable for MSME operation. At the risk of repetition, it must be emphasised that every manufacturer, big or small, with the requisite expertise is free to engage in any field of activity and must comply with the relevant standards applicable to that field. Thus, nothing prevents a large enterprise from engaging in any of the products listed in the above tables.

10 Examination of Selected Standards Relevant to MSMEs

It is mandatory for all manufacturers operating in Nigeria to comply with minimum standards relating to products manufactured by them. This means that no standards are reserved for any particular group of manufacturers based on size. However, the current drive of Nigeria to diversify the economy has created the need to empower MSMEs to contribute more significantly especially in areas that are suited for small scale operations. This has created the need to develop new standards for products that can easily be handled by MSMEs.

It must be emphasised that the fact that a particular standard is targeted on MSMEs does not mean that other manufacturers cannot apply such standards. As stated above, standards developed by SON are applicable to all manufacturers in the product field

Table 3 List of standards that support MSMEs

S/N	Title of standard	Reference code
1	Standard for Clean Cook Stove—Biomass Type	NIS 1000: 2018
2	Standard for Paste Ink	NIS 1033: 2018
3	Specifications for Plaster of Paris (P.O.P) Emulsion and Screed Emulsion Paints	NIS 1034: 2018
4	Standard for Sport Mat Part 1—Landing Mat for Pole Vault and High Jump	NIS 908-1: 2018
5	Standard for Duvet	NIS 1040: 2018
6	Standard for Multipurpose Sofa Bed	NIS 830: 2018
7	Standard for Solid Foam Chair and Seat Support	NIS 1043: 2018
8	Standard for Reflective Safety Garment	NIS 071: 2018
9	Standard for Elasticated Disposable Baby Diaper Safety	NIS 880: 2018
10	Performance Requirements for Motorcycle Assembly	NIS 889: 2018
11	Standard for Dried and Smoked Fish	NIS 982: 2018
12	Standard for Ready to Cook Quick Frozen Plantain Chips	NIS 1045:2018
13	Standard for Rice Flour	NIS 810: 2018
14	Standard for Icing Sugar	NIS 732: 2018
15	Standard for Fura	NIS 735: 2018
16	Standard for Ready-to-Cook Quick Frozen Yam Chips	NIS 1048: 2018
17	Standard for Mango Juice,	NIS 1019: 2018
18	Standard for Aloe Vera Drink	NIS1006: 2018
19	Standard for Guava Juice	NIS 1018: 2018
20	Standard for Coconut and Pineapple Juice	NIS 1002: 2018

covered by the standard. As a matter of obligation, all manufacturers, large, medium or small involved in the production of the product concerned are required to comply with the minimum or maximum specification bench marks for a particular product.

For purposes of illustration, three newly elaborated MSMEs-oriented standards selected from the Food-Codex are examined here. The choice of this sector is informed by the fact that most of the products covered by this sector are very popular with consumers.

11 Standard for Dry Beans—NIS 1030: 2018

'Beans' is a very popular food item in Nigeria. In fact it can be regarded as one of the staple foods in Nigeria. Apart from serving as a popular food item on its own, a lot of other food products are derived from it such as bean cake and bean pudding popularly called *moi moi* in many communities. It is also served with rice as a popular

Table 4 Selected adopted MSMEs-related standards

S/N	Title of standard	Reference code
1	Cycles Safety Requirements for Bicycles for Young Children	NIS ISO 8098: (2014) 2018
2	Bicycle Tyres and Rims- Part 2: Rims	NIS ISO 5775: (2015) 2018
3	Standard for Quick Frozen Fish Fillets	NIS CAC 90:(2016) 2018
4	Standard for Quick Frozen Shrimps and Prawns	NIS CAC 92: (2017) 2018
5	Standard for Canned Crab Meat	NIS CAC 90: (2016) 2018
6	Standard for Canned Fin Fish	NIS CAC 119: (2016) 2018
7	Standard for Burnt Clay Bricks—Specifications	NIS ARS 1302: (2016) 2018
8	African Traditional Medicine- Minimum Requirements for Registration of Plant Based Traditional medicines.	NIS ARS 954: (2016) 2018
9	Guidelines for use on various types of cement	NIS ARS 1304: (2016) 2018
10	Toilet Soap—Specifications	NIS ARS 489: 2019
11	Laundry Soap—Specifications	NIS ARS 490: 2019
12	White Sugars—Specifications	NIS ARS 58: 2019
13	Code of Practice for Packaging and Transport of Fresh Fruit and Vegetables	NIS CAC/CRP 44: 2019
14	Raw Cane Sugar Specifications	NIS ARS 875: 2019
15	Standard for Quick Frozen Vegetables	NIS CODEXSTAN 320: 2019
16	Standard for Guavas	NISCODEXSTAN 215: 2019
17	Standard for Lime	NIS CODEXSTAN 213: 2019
18	Standard for Canned Sweet Corn	NISCAC 18: 2019
19	African Traditional Medicine—Aloe Vera	NIS ARS 956-1:2019
20	Tourism—Sustainability and Eco-Labelling Requirements	NIS ARS/AES 04: 2019

delicacy. Another interesting thing about this product is that it is grown by numerous farmers, big and small scattered all over the country but with a huge concentration in the northern parts of Nigeria. Before the development of the standard under consideration, the issues of quality and safety were determined by the knowledge and skills of the farmers gathered from mentorship or piecemeal trainings where available. It is, therefore, not surprising that the Standards Organisation of Nigeria should take interest in developing a standard for this product to ensure that consumers derive the needed satisfaction from this popular food item.

11.1 Scope and Definition

This standard is a modified adoption of African Standard ARS 864:2013: Dry Beans—Specification. The new standard specifies requirements and methods of sampling and test for dry beans intended for human consumption. It requires farmers and handlers to ensure availability of quality and safe dry beans throughout the year—(clause 1). The standard defines dry beans as thresh field and garden beans, whole, broken, and split commonly used for human consumption—(3.1).

11.2 Quality Requirements

Clause 4.1.1 stipulates the minimum requirements for dry beans. By this clause, dry beans shall be:

a. the dried mature grains of *Phaseolus vulgaris* Linn;
b. well-filled, clean, wholesome, uniform in size and shape;
c. free from substances which render them unfit for human consumption or processing into or utilisation thereof as food;
d. free from abnormal flavours, musty, sour or other undesirable odour, obnoxious smell and discoloration; and
e. free from micro-organisms and substances originating from micro-organisms, fungi or other poisonous or deleterious substances in amounts that may constitute a hazard to human health.

The above requirements can be said to be self-explanatory. The overall effect of the requirements is that dry beans should be wholesome and fit for human consumption. Other requirements specified are grading, characteristics and test methods. A table is used to denote the specific requirements.

11.3 Contaminants

Clause 5 specifies the maximum limits of contaminants to which dry beans must comply with. Included in this clause are metal contaminants and pesticide residues. The clause states the parameter limits for testing compliance with the specified maximum levels of contaminants and residues as specified in the standard.

11.4 Hygiene

Clause 6 enjoins producers to prepare and handle dry beans in accordance with appropriate provisions of ARS 53. It is provided that when tested with the specified method, dry beans shall not contain any substance originating from microorganisms in amounts which may represent a hazard to health. The microbiological limits and micro-organism limits test methods are stated in the clause.

11.5 Packaging

Clause 7 contains the packaging requirements. It provides that dry beans shall be packed in suitable packages which shall be clean, sound, free from insect, fungal infestation and the packing material shall be of food grade quality and shall be securely closed and sealed. Beans should be packaged in containers which should safeguard the hygienic, nutritional, technological and organoleptic qualities of the product. Furthermore, each package shall contain dry beans of the same type and the same grade designation. In the case of beans presented in bags, the bags shall also be free of pests and contaminants.

11.6 Labelling and Sampling

Clause 8 states that each package of dry beans shall be legibly and indelibly marked with the following: product name as—Dry Beans; variety; grade; name, address and physical location of the producer/packer/importer; lot/batch/code number; net weight in kg; the declaration—'Food for Human Consumption"; and storage instruction as—"Store in a cool dry place away from any contaminants". Other labelling requirements are crop year; packing date; best before date; instructions on disposal of used package; country of origin; and a declaration as to whether or not the dry beans were genetically modified. To ensure that the batch has complied with the prescribed standard, it is required that each pack shall be marked with the MANCAP logo and the corresponding number.

Clause 8.2 states the labelling requirements for non-retail containers. Cause 9 adopts the sampling method contained in ISO 13690.

12 Standard for Ground Rice—NIS 810:2018

Rice, the product from which rice flour is produced is also one of the staple foods in Nigeria. Probably due to changing tastes of consumers or the need for variety, rice flour has assumed a considerable level of popularity in Nigeria. A reason which may be adduced for this is the fact that Nigerians are known for consuming solid foods of which pounded yam was the most popular. With time, other cereals began to be processed into flour and fast began to be accepted as viable substitutes for pounded yam. These cereal products are easy to prepare into solid foods thus satisfying the needs of consumers that are addicted to such foods. Rice flour is a popular example of such cereal-based food items in Nigeria.

This changing demand has in turn resulted in the influx of producers into rice flour business. This has thus necessitated the development of this standard. As stated in the Foreword to the standard, processing, trade and consumption of rice flour in

Nigeria have witnessed a steady increase making the elaboration of this standard imperative to ensure safety, quality and fair trade practices.

12.1 Scope and Definitions

This standard specifies the essential quality requirements, safety, packaging, labeling, reference test methods and sampling for rice flour from milled rice—clause 2. Clause 3 defines different varieties of rice including de-husked rice, milled rice, paddy rice and parboiled rice. Rice flour is defined as flour milled from white or parboiled rice.

Clause 4 prescribes the essential and optional ingredients. The essential ingredient is white rice that meets the requirements of NIS 338: 1997. A table is used to specify the permissible levels of optional ingredients.

12.2 Quality Requirements

General and specific requirements are provided for in clause 5. The general requirements are that rice flour shall be free from rancidity, objectionable odour, insects, rodent hair and other extraneous materials. Table 2 contains the specific requirements. In addition, it is stipulated that rice flour shall not contain microorganisms in such a level as shall constitute any danger to health of the consumer. The permissible limits of microbial contaminants, mycotoxins and metallic contaminants are specified in Tables 3, 5 and 6 respectively.

12.3 Hygiene

Clause 6 requires that rice flour shall be produced under Good Manufacturing Practice (GMP) and handled in accordance with relevant sections of the recommended International Code of Practice—General Principles of Food hygiene (CAC/RCP1–1969—REVA 4-2003) as amended and National Agency for Food and Drug Administration and Control (NAFDAC) Guidelines for Food Hygiene Practice, 2004.

12.4 Packaging, Labelling and Storage

Clause 7 specifies the requirements for packaging, labelling and storage of rice flour. As part of the packaging requirements, rice flour shall be packed, transported and stored in containers which preserve the hygiene and organoleptic qualities of the product. Further, the packaging materials shall be such as to protect the product against bacteria and other contaminants; it shall protect the product as far as possible against any infiltration of moisture, insect infestations and leakage. The packaging material shall not impact any odour, taste and any other extraneous property to the product and shall not result in contamination of the product with the substance of which the packaging material is made.

Clause 7.2 adopts the provision of Codex Alimentarius Commission for Food Labelling (4th Edition, 2005), the NAFDAC Regulations (2005) on the Labelling of Pre-Packaged Food and in addition, specifies the following:

a. Name of the product presented on the principally displayed panel of the label and not obstructed by printed or graphics in bold capital letters of the same color size;
b. Name and location address of the manufacturer or importer;
c. Batch number or code number;
d. Date of production and best before date;
e. Country of origin;
f. NAFDAC Registration number; and
g. MANCAP NIS logo and certificate number

12.5 Sampling and Analysis

Clauses 8 and 9 specify criteria for sampling and analysis. Among other requirements, the product shall be sampled and analysed using the international reference methods stated in the clause.

13 Standard for Fura—NIS 735:2018

Fura is a local food popular in the northern parts but now generally consumed in different parts of Nigeria. As noted in the Foreword to the standard, Fura is an indigenous food product made mainly from millet grain. The product can be obtained from other grains and is consumed in different forms in most parts of the country. It is further noted that in recent times, the product is fast becoming a popular beverage known by various names in different parts of the continent. This popularity informed the development of this standard to guide the production and quality of the product for safety and fair-trade practices.

13.1 Scope and Definitions

This standard specifies the quality and safety requirements, labelling, storage, packaging, sampling and test method for Fura—(clause 1). The term 'Fura' is defined by clause 3 as a pregelatinized millet-based product usually mixed with water and/or spices and presented in solid form as dough ball or in powdered form or granules. Millet which is the main ingredient for Fura is defined as the threshed grain of the species defined in the scope of Nigerian Industrial Standard (NIS 467:2003).

13.2 Presentation

Clause 4 provides that Fura shall be presented in solid form as dry, clean and in various shapes as dough ball or in granules or powder form.

13.3 Ingredients

Clause 5 specifies the essential and optional ingredients for Fura. The essential ingredients are millet grains and water. It is required that the millet grains used in the preparation of Fura shall meet the requirements of NIS 467:2003. The water used shall also comply with the Nigerian Industrial Standards listed in this clause.

Clause 5.2 specifies the optional ingredients which include spices (any of the following individually or in combination—ginger, red pepper, clove, mint, kimba known as Negro Pepper, chili powder and black pepper) and sweeteners such as white refined sugar, brown refined sugar, white plantain sugar, glucose, dextrose, sucrose, fructose, maltose and galactose. The standard prohibits the use of artificial and non-nutritive sweeteners for the production of Fura.

The standard allows the use of some fortificants and anti-oxidants listed in Clauses 5.2.3 and 5.2.4 to enhance the nutritional value of Fura.

13.4 Quality Requirements

Clause 6 lays down the general and specific requirements. It is required that the colour, odour, taste and texture of Fura shall be characteristic of the product. It prohibits the presence of foreign matter (hair strands, sand, or insects and insect parts). Tables are used to specify the specific requirements; microorganism and mycotoxin tolerance limits. It is provided that Fura shall comply with the pesticide residue limits established by Codex Alimentarius Commission for Pesticide Residue in Food (CAC Vol. 2B—2000). Limits of metallic contaminants and toxins established by Codex Alimentarius Commission for Contaminants and Toxins in Food and Feed.

(Codex Stan 193—1995 (Amendment 2010) are adopted.

13.5 Hygiene

Clause 7 provides that Fura shall be produced under Good Manufacturing Practice (GMP) and handled in accordance with the relevant section of the Recommended International Code of Practice-General Principles of Food Hygiene (CAC/RCP 1-1969-Rev 4- 2003) and the National Agency for Food and Drug Administration and Control (NAFDAC) Guidelines for Food Hygienic Practices, 2004.

13.6 Packaging, Transport, Labelling and Storage

Clause 8 provides that Fura shall be packed, transported and stored in suitable, clean, sound, strong, airtight food grade containers such that the containers should safeguard the hygienic and organoleptic properties of the product. In addition, the packaging material shall protect the product against leakages, seepages, moisture, insects, microbial and other contaminations. Other packaging requirements include weights of packages and storage conditions.

Clause 8.5 adopts the provisions of Codex Alimentarius Commission on labelling of pre-packaged foods (Codex Stan 1-1985, Rev. 6-2008). It is further required that the name of the product shall be Fura and shall be clearly and indelibly written on the package. The form of presentation of the product such as instant powdered Fura or pulverized should also be stated. A complete list of ingredients used shall be declared on the label in descending order of proportion. Other requirements which must be declared include net weight in the metric system of measurement, name and full location address of the manufacture/packer and/or distributor of the product; manufacture date, best before or expiry date; information for storage, handling, preparation and disposal of packaging materials; MANCAP NIS logo and NAFDAC Registration Number.

13.7 Sampling

Clause 9 states the general sampling requirements, criteria for conformity and test methods. Tables are used to specify the specific requirements.

14 Observations

The above selected standards demonstrate the concerted efforts of SON to develop standards for products that are popular among the MSMEs. The standards also demonstrate the responsiveness of the Organisation to the changing demands of consumers. Just like other innovative measures introduced by SON in recent years, it is too early to assess the practical impact of these standards. Most of the producers are located in different parts of the country with some operating as one-man businesses. SON needs to intensify outreach programmes to ensure that these standards are embraced by the target operators.

15 Impact of SON Measures on the Acceptability of MSME Products by Consumers Within and Outside Nigeria

The positive impact of SON's measures on the acceptability of MSMEs products by consumers within and outside Nigeria is evident from the 2016 Report of MSME Stakeholders Perception Survey conducted for the Standards Organisation of Nigeria (SON) by NOI Polls supported by the UKAID-ENABLE II Project.[20] 94% of respondents acknowledged that SON's activities provided market advantages over the uncertified products of competitors. This result no doubt implies consumer acceptability of certified products. Also, a Federal Government's initiative promoting the patronage of locally made products in Government procurements through an Executive Order 003[21] is expected to drive up production. Standards and certification services are available to support the implementation of the Order as a means of enhancing the acceptability of locally made products and services.

16 Other Measures that Should Be Considered by SON to Encourage MSMEs to Apply Standards

16.1 Deployment of Technology

Despite the remarkable efforts of SON at reaching all MSMEs in Nigeria through the State Offices, a lot of grounds still need to be covered in view of the large size of the country. Technology is therefore anticipated to hold the solution. The Federal Government through the Federal Ministry of Industry, Trade and Investment (FMITI), is set to launch the SMEs online portal which is expected to serve as a one-stop-shop solution to MSMEs access to respective ministries, departments and agencies. In addition, SON could introduce an APP in the form of hand-held devices that facilitate access to information and participation in standards development and

[20]Source: The MSME Stakeholders Perception Survey Report for the Standards Organisation of Nigeria (2016) p 30.

[21]Executive Order 003- On support for local contents in public procurement by the Federal Government, 2017.

implementation processes from the comfort of the user's home or office. This will enhance access and application of standards.

16.2 Communication Materials in Local Languages

As part of the measures to encourage small scale producers scattered all over the country particularly in the rural areas to apply product standards, SON should deploy communication materials and standards in local languages of host communities to create better understanding of standards. Although finances and sustainability of implementation may constitute key impediments of these initiatives, in the long run, remarkable benefits will accrue to both producers and consumers.

17 Conclusion

This paper discloses that the current innovative approaches of SON have impacted positively on quality of products manufactured by MSMEs. This is reflected in the increased number of MSMEs products that have received the certification of the Organisation. On the flip side is the finding that many MSMEs face considerable challenges which must be addressed in order to achieve the desired goals. In addition, the paper discloses that many MSMEs are yet to embrace the standardisation and certification schemes as demonstrated by the disparity between the number of MSMEs in Nigeria and the number of products in the sector that have been certified.

It is too early to assess the full impact of the measures being implemented by SON to encourage the application of standards and improve the quality and safety of products made by MSMEs. As seen from the selected standards discussed above, most of the MSMEs-related standards are relatively new just like the various measures being implemented by SON. As shown in earlier sections, the number of MSMEs applying for MANCAP certification is on the increase. A few of the operators have been able to obtain certification for export. These developments are very interesting leading to the conclusion that the goal of improving the quality of products and services offered by this sector will be achieved.

The Role of International Consumer Policy in Fostering Innovation and Empowering Consumers to Make Informed Choices

Kara D. Nottingham and Izabel Cardozo

1 Introduction

This study addresses the topic of consumer policy from an international law perspective, exploring the content and evolving meaning of the right to information in the age of fast-paced scientific and technological advancement, according to the United Nations Guidelines for Consumer Protection ("the Guidelines"), which were adopted in 1985 and last revised in 2015.[1]

The revision of the Guidelines in 2015, and its new text, have attributed enhanced responsibility for businesses and governments in building consumer knowledge and education, so that consumers are equipped to make informed choices. The "Principles for Good Business Practices", now embedded in the Guidelines, highlight the responsibility of businesses to provide truthful, relevant, and non- misleading information concerning their products and services, while also avoiding deceptive or abusive practices. Since its latest revision, the Guidelines have established a role for businesses to upskill consumers' awareness and knowledge of risks, through consumer education initiatives.

[1] See United Nations Guidelines on Consumer Protection ("the Guidelines"), available online at https://unctad.org/en/PublicationsLibrary/ditccplpmisc2016d1_en.pdf (last accessed on 12 March 2019).

Kara D. Nottingham and Izabel Cardozo are Counsel and Assistant General Counsel, respectively, at Philip Morris International in Lausanne, Switzerland. Kara holds a JD from William & Mary School of Law in Williamsburg, Virginia (USA), and LLM in International Dispute Settlement from the Graduate Institute—University of Geneva (Switzerland). Izabel holds a law degree from the University of the State of Rio de JaneirovUERJ and a LLM in Constitutional Law from The Catholic University of Rio de Janeiro—PUC/RJ (Brazil). This paper represents the views of the authors and not necessarily the organization where they work.

K. D. Nottingham (✉) · I. Cardozo
Philip Morris International, Lausanne, Switzerland
e-mail: kara.nottingham@pmi.com

D. Wei et al. (eds.), *Innovation and the Transformation of Consumer Law*,
https://doi.org/10.1007/978-981-15-8948-5_28

As regulation often lags behind the speed of product development, the Guidelines encourage businesses to educate consumers on product innovation and new technologies. Where regulatory gaps exist, businesses should be able to disseminate accurate and truthful information to avoid the risk of consumers being left in the dark, unable to make an informed decision on whether or not to consume a new product. The free flow of information, including relevant scientific information provided from producers to consumers, contributes to more innovation, enabling better and informed consumer choices.

This study is divided into three parts. Part (I) will address the meaning of the consumer right to information in the age of innovation, using the Guidelines as a framework. Part (II) will discuss how courts in different jurisdictions have addressed the issue of the provision of information to consumers, based on consumer rights and/or commercial speech theories. Part (III) will look at how the provision of scientific information to consumers can propel innovation and behavior change.

2 The Meaning of the Consumer Right to Information in the Age of Innovation

2.1 The Foundations of the Right to Information

At its core, the right to information is a corollary of freedom of expression, which is embedded in the international human rights framework.[2] The Universal Declaration of Human Rights (UDHR), in its Article 19, and the International Covenant on Civil and Political Rights (ICCPR), in its Article 19(2), state that individuals have a right to freedom of expression, which includes the right to receive information. This principle has also been incorporated into regional human rights frameworks and enforced by regional human rights judicial mechanisms, including the European Court of Human Rights (ECtHR), the African Court of People and Human Rights, and the Inter-American Court of Human Rights.[3]

In this connection, Article 10 of the European Convention on Human Rights (ECHR) reiterates that the right to freedom of expression includes the right to receive

[2]The international human rights framework is composed of the Universal Declaration of Human Rights (hereinafter UDHR), adopted by the United Nations General Assembly (hereinafter the UNGA) on 10 December 1948, the International Covenant on Civil and Political Rights (hereinafter the ICCPR), adopted by the UNGA on 16 December 1966, and the International Covenant on Economic, Social and Cultural Rights (hereinafter ICESCR), adopted by the UNGA on 16 December 1966, which together form the "International Bill of Human Rights"; See also, Office of the High Commissioner for Human Rights [1].

[3]The European Convention on Human Rights (hereinafter the ECHR) was opened for signature on 4 November 1950 and came into force on 3 September 1953. The African Charter of Human and People's Rights was adopted on 27 June 1981 and entered into force on 21 October 1986. The American Convention on Human Rights was signed on 22 November 1969 and entered into force on 18 July 18 1978.

and impart information and ideas. This concept is similarly expressed in Article 9 of the African Charter of Human and People's Rights, and Article 13 of the American Convention on Human Rights. Jurisprudence from the European Court of Human Rights supports this proposition, in applying the principle that Article 10 guarantees not only the freedom of the press to inform the public, but also the right of the public to be properly informed.[4] Information that is of the public interest should be disclosed, to allow individuals to participate in public governance and debates of legitimate public concern.[5]

The African Commission on Human and People's Rights has declared that the right of the public to receive information is a core tenet of a democratic society,[6] providing regional reinforcement for similar statements made by United Nations Human Rights Council and the General Assembly.[7] The African Court of Human Rights has determined that the right to freedom of expression, including the right to receive information, can only be infringed if the restrictions put in place are proportionate and for a legitimate public concern.[8] The Inter-American Court of Human Rights has reiterated this concept.[9]

The international human rights framework is clear in delineating the right of individuals to receive accurate information to allow them to make informed decisions and to participate in public governance. Information accessibility also entails the right to seek, receive, and impart information and ideas concerning products. While within the human rights context, the scope of discussion typically relates to political speech—commercial speech is another form of communication which also receives varying levels of protection in various jurisdictions. While each jurisdiction has a different approach, this paper posits that consumers should be provided more, rather than less information, and businesses should be able to engage in truthful non-misleading communications as a means of informing the public. The more information the public receives, the better equipped they are to make informed decisions.

Information accessibility, and the ability to communicate to consumers, are key in the context of rapid technological innovation and advancement which facilitates the

---

[4]European Court of Human Rights, The Sunday Times v. The United Kingdom, Case No. 6538/74, 26 April 1979, at para. 66.

[5]European Court of Human Rights, Magyr Helsinki Bizottsag v. Hungary, Case No. 18030/11, 8 November 2016, at para. 161.

[6]See African Commission on Human and People's Rights, Article 19 v. Eritrea, Comm. No. 257/03, 30 May 2007.

[7]See Report of the Special Rapporteur on the Promotion and Protection of Freedom of Expression, A/71/373, 6 September 2016, http://www.un.org/ga/search/view_doc.asp?symbol=A/71/373 (last accessed on 12 April 2019). The Human Rights Council and the General Assembly have referred to freedom of expression as one of the essential foundations of a democratic society and one of the basic conditions for its progress and development.

[8]The African Court of Human and People's Rights, Lohé Issa Konaté v. The Republic of Burkina Faso, App. No. 004/2013, 5 December 2014, at para. 133. The case is in the context of criminalization for defamation.

[9]Inter-American Court of Human Rights, Gomes Lund et al. ("Guerrilha do Araguaia") v. Brazil, App. No. 004/2013, 24 November 2010, at paras. 197–202.

creation of new products. The right to receive, seek, and impart information takes on various dimensions, and understanding the foundational basis for these principles is key to coming up with effective consumer policies. The right to information also has roots in the principle of autonomy, which will be explored in further detail below.

2.2 *Respect for Autonomy*

As an ethical principle, autonomy provides recognition for the fact that individuals, i.e. consumers, should have the ability to freely express their will and their choices. The term autonomy comes from the Greek phrase autos which means self, in combination with the word nomos which means rule, governance or law.[10] In ethics and political philosophy, autonomy is the state or condition of self-governance, or leading one's life according to reasons, values, or desires that are authentically one's own.[11]

Autonomy, or personal autonomy, is one of the ethical foundations to many moral and political rights and freedoms. Personal autonomy can be defined as the ability to conduct life in a manner of one's own choosing. Within the sphere of human rights, the concept of personal autonomy is closely linked to the right to privacy[12] and the freedom to make choices. This term relates to:

> (…) a person's ability to make his or her own rules in life and to make decisions independently. The idea that people must be free to shape their own lives is central to most accounts of autonomy. In general, autonomy means that a subject is the best expert on his/her interests. It is the reason why this subject should be able to make his/her own laws, particular rules of conduct or follow the values that are acceptable to him/her in practice. In general, any action or act can be described as autonomous only if the agent gives preference to this action, and this decision is independent and corresponds with his/her plan of action. In other words, we can talk about autonomy only when the freedom to choose and to make ethical decisions is guaranteed.[13]

In the field of bioethics, to respect an autonomous agent is to acknowledge that person's right to hold views, to make choices and to take actions based on personal values and beliefs.[14] This principle is the basis for the practice of "informed consent" in the physician/patient relationship regarding health care. Before any treatment can be given to a patient or procedure performed, patients must give informed consent. The process of informed consent is an opportunity for a doctor to provide information to their patients about the risks, benefits, and alternatives of a certain procedure, so

[10]Sakellari [2].

[11]Taylor et al. [3].

[12]The International Covenant on Civil and Political Rights, Article 17: ("1. No one shall be subjected to arbitrary or unlawful interference with his privacy, family, home or correspondence, nor to unlawful attacks on his honour and reputation. 2. Everyone has the right to the protection of the law against such interference or attacks.").

[13]Gumbis et al. [4].

[14]Beauchamp and Childress [5].

that they can take an informed decision about the medical treatment they wish to follow.[15]

Respect for autonomy is also engrained in consumer laws and relates to the right of consumers to make informed choices according to their own needs and preferences. To ensure respect for consumers' autonomy, governments should provide a framework under which consumers can receive reliable, accurate and non-misleading information about the choices of products that are available to them. This is particularly true when products can have an impact on the health of consumers. This information is usually supplied and provided by businesses, in the form of commercial speech. The overlay between the principle of autonomy, the right to information, and commercial speech, is even more relevant in the context of new innovative or technological products on the market, which consumers may be unfamiliar with and need information concerning the form of usage, benefits and potential risks.

These two fundamental principles, the right to information and the concept of autonomy (or the right to make informed choices), are embedded in the modern notions of consumer rights and consumer protection. The next section will explore the political origins of consumer policy, and the right to be informed in relation to products, goods, and services.

2.3 The Political Origins of Consumer Rights

Many scholars believe that the modern concept of consumer protection first appeared in a political declaration made by President Kennedy to the United States Congress in 1962, entitled the Special Message to the Congress on Protecting the Consumer Interest. In this speech, President Kennedy recognized the importance of consumers as a political and economic group, and called upon Congress to take actions to protect their interests. The historic speech recognized that technological progress posed both opportunities and difficulties for consumers. Consumers benefited from a much wider variety of consumer goods, but were rarely provided with the information they needed to make informed choices. The following sections of the speech illustrate this point:

> [t]he march of technology – affecting, for example, the foods we eat, the medicines we take, and the many appliances we use in our homes – has increased the difficulties of the consumer along with his opportunities; and it has outmoded many of the old laws and regulations and made new legislation necessary. The typical supermarket before World War II stocked about 1,500 separate food items – an impressive figure by any standard.
>
> But today it carries over 6,000. Ninety percent of the prescriptions written today are for drugs that were unknown 20 years ago. Many of the new products used every day in the home are highly complex. The housewife [or house husband] is called upon to be an amateur electrician, mechanism, chemist, toxicologist, dietitian, and mathematician – but she [or he] is rarely furnished the information she [or he] needs to perform these tasks proficiently.
>
> Nearly all of the programs offered by this Administration – e.g., the expansion of world trade, the improvement of medical care, the reduction of passenger taxes, the strengthening of mass

[15] Coggon and Miola [6].

> transit, the development of conservation and recreation areas and low-cost power – are of direct or inherent importance to consumers. Additional legislative and administrative action is required, however, if the federal Government is to meet its responsibility to consumers in the exercise of their rights (Emphasis added).[16]

Stemming from this declaration, four policy areas have been identified, which shaped the basic rights of consumers: (i) the right to safety; (ii) the right to be informed; (iii) the right to choose; and (iv) the right to be heard. The right to be informed entails the right of consumers to be provided all the facts they need to make informed choices, as well as the right to be protected against fraudulent, deceitful, or misleading information, advertising, labeling, or other practices.

The right to information is essential to empowering consumer choice. A delicate balance must exist between the rights of consumers, and the shared responsibility of governments and businesses, to provide consumers with truthful information on products and services.

Over the years, political support has grown globally for enhancing the rights of consumers. The "right to be informed" has been tangibly furthered through the implementation of national laws and development of court jurisprudence which protect this right. The United Nations, through its Guidelines, established a global framework and strong political will to encourage the adoption of laws around the world which further the rights of consumers. These Guidelines, and relevant revisions which have taken place over the years to reflect the reality of the evolving rights of consumers due to technological innovation and advancement, will be explored in detail below.

2.4 United Nations Guidelines for Consumer Protection

2.4.1 Background

Prior to the issuance of the Guidelines in 1985, member states already started to assess responsibilities for businesses in the context of consumer goods, through issuing the United Nations Set of Principles and Rules on Competition, also known as The Set of Multilaterally Agreed Equitable Principles and Rules for the Control of Restrictive Business Practices (the "Set Principles").[17] The Set Principles reflect a multilateral agreement on competition policy.[18]

---

[16]Kennedy [7].

[17]See The Set of Multilaterally Agreed Equitable Principles and Rules for the Control of Restrictive Business Practices (hereinafter the Set Principles), https://unctad.org/en/docs/tdrbpconf10r2.en.pdf (last accessed on 8 April 2019). Resolution 35/63 was adopted by the United Nations General Assembly at its thirty-fifth session on 5 December 1980, whereby the Set principles were pronounced. One of the stated objectives of the Set Principles is "to attain greater efficiency in international trade and development, (...), such as through: (...) (c) encouragement of innovation.".

[18]See United Nations Conference on Trade and Development explanation of the Set Principles, https://unctad.org/en/Pages/DITC/CompetitionLaw/The-United-Nations-Set-of-Principles-on-Competition.aspx (last accessed on 8 April 2019). The Set Principles (i) provide a set of equitable rules for the control of anti-competitive practices; (ii) recognize the development dimension

On 9 April 1985 the General Assembly of the United Nations unanimously adopted the Guidelines, which were then again revised in 1999 and 2015.[19] The Guidelines are an internationally recognized set of minimum objectives for consumer protection. They are a form of policy advice for member states, with flexibility to be imposed into national laws in a manner which respects local circumstances and tradition.[20]

Given the international unanimous consensus with which the Guidelines were adopted, some scholars believe "they have a chance of developing into customary law and becoming binding laws in the future."[21] The Guidelines were one of the first international documents explicitly recognizing the right of consumers to make informed decisions in accordance with their individual wishes and needs—placing a responsibility on member states to ensure these protections are engrained in their local laws.

The adoption of the Guidelines has reinforced the increasing recognition in recent years that consumer policy can no longer be seen as being of purely local concern and must be seen in an international context.[22] In addition, given that there is recognition that "consumer rights are sufficiently important and have been unanimously accepted by UN member states as basic principles (…)," there is a presumed universal need to ensure a stable and high level of protection.[23]

The Guidelines are said to have shaped consumer laws in over 100 countries, and thus can potentially be viewed as embodying universally recognized standards for consumer-related legislation.[24] This demonstrates direct acceptance of consumer rights at an international level, and sets a framework to encourage governments to promote consumer protection in the areas of consumer information, choice, and education.[25]

Over time, the Guidelines have been adapted to take into consideration innovations and advancements, like the internet and e-commence, and were revised in 1999 and 2015. Product innovation creates a new set of dynamics and responsibilities for businesses and governments. An analysis of the revisions to the Guidelines shows that businesses now have more of a role to play in upskilling the awareness of consumers through communication initiatives. The evolution of the Guidelines to highlight the increased onus placed on businesses, and the delicate balance that must be achieved between business and governments, will be assessed below.

---

of competition law and policy; and (iii) provide a framework for international cooperation and exchange of best practices.

[19] As a general rule, guidelines and declarations issued by international organizations assist countries in implementing their national laws. These soft law documents do not trigger binding obligations on member states. Nevertheless, guidelines provide useful information and guidance for member states to interpret and implement laws in their national jurisdictions.

[20] Wei [8].

[21] Benöhr and Micklitz [9].

[22] Harland [10].

[23] Benöhr, supra note 21 at p. 25.

[24] Wei, supra note 20.

[25] Id.

2.4.2 Revision of the Guidelines

The Guidelines were last revised in 2015 to reinforce one of the underlying objectives of providing consumers with relevant information on products and services, so they can make better and more informed choices.[26] Over time, a textual review and analysis of the Guidelines from 1985, to 1999, and then 2015, shows that: (i) there is an emphasis on the empowerment of consumers to make decisions for themselves, echoing the principle of autonomy; (ii) businesses have an enhanced responsibility to educate consumers, and to provide truthful, relevant, non-misleading information concerning their products, which should in turn be allowed to reach consumers and be subject to government scrutiny and enforcement; and (iii) effective policies require a delicate balance between the roles of governments, businesses, and consumers themselves.

One of the most important changes made in the 2015 revision of the Guidelines is to section III(5)(e). Instead of access "of" consumers to adequate information, the Guidelines were changed to read access "by" consumers to adequate information enabling informed choices according to their individual wishes and needs.[27] These changes were interpreted as follows:

> What is the underlying philosophy of the Guidelines? They promote a 'choice' model of consumer protection tempered by information and education, along with certain protection. A key aspect of this Revision is the emphasis on knowledge. Information and knowledge complement a choice model, for without information and the ability to use that information there can be no informed choice, optimum or otherwise. In addition to promoting global flows of knowledge, there is an interesting change to the preposition in the General Principles concerning adequate information for informed choices. Instead of access 'of' consumers, this now reads access 'by' consumers. 'By' connotes a more positive involvement of consumers with information (Emphasis added).[28]

Notably, the 2015 revision of the Guidelines also places enhanced emphasis on the duty of businesses, through addition of the new "Principles for Good Business Practices" section. Older versions of the Guidelines had fewer references to direct business responsibilities. The previous versions primarily addressed governments, to ensure that member states put the proper frameworks in place to regulate the activities of businesses.

---

[26]The Handbook, supra note 21. Gael Pearson, The UNGCP Guidelines: Some Comments, at pp. 40–41.

[27]The Guidelines, supra note 1, at §III(5)(e). ("4. Member States should develop, strengthen or maintain a strong consumer protection policy, taking into account the guidelines set out below and relevant international agreements. In so doing, each Member State must set its own priorities for the protection of consumers in accordance with the economic, social and environmental circumstances of the country and the needs of its population, and bearing in mind the costs and benefits of proposed measures. 5. The legitimate needs which the guidelines are intended to meet are the following: [...] (e) Access by consumers to adequate information to enable them to make informed choices according to their individual wishes and needs.").

[28]Supra, note 26.

In the beginning, the 1985 version of the Guidelines included limited references to responsibilities for businesses.[29] The United Nations Economic and Social Council adopted revisions to the Guidelines in 1999, with the primary purpose of adding provisions on sustainable consumption. The 1999 revisions slightly enhanced the reference to responsibilities on businesses, introducing a new section II(7).[30]

Fast forwarding to the digital era of technological advancement and the internet, the newly revised 2015 version of the Guidelines incorporate a whole section entitled "Principles for Good Business Practices." This section, in its entirety, provides as follows:

> (11) The principles that establish benchmarks for good business practices for conducting online and offline commercial activities with consumers are as follows:
>
> (a) Fair and equitable treatment. Businesses should deal fairly and honestly with consumers at all stages of their relationship, so that it is an integral part of the business culture. Businesses should avoid practices that harm consumers, particularly with respect to vulnerable and disadvantaged consumers:
>
> (b) Commercial behaviour. Businesses should not subject consumers to illegal, unethical, discriminatory or deceptive practices, such as abusive marketing tactics, abusive debt collection or other improper behaviour that may pose unnecessary risks or harm consumers. Businesses and their authorized agents should have due regard for the interests of consumers and responsibility for upholding consumer protection as an objective.
>
> (c) Disclosure and transparency. Businesses should provide complete, accurate and not misleading information regarding the goods and services, terms, conditions, applicable

29United Nations General Assembly Resolution on Consumer Protection, A/RES/39/248, 16 April 1985, https://www.un.org/documents/ga/res/39/a39r248.htm (last accessed on 8 April 2019). ("Section IIIA(10): Appropriate policies should ensure that goods produced by manufacturers are safe for either intended or normally foreseeable use. Those responsible for bringing goods to the market, in particular suppliers, exporters, importers, retailers and the linked (hereinafter referred to as 'distributors') should ensure that while in their care these goods are not rendered unsafe through improper handling or storage that while in their care they do not become hazardous through improper handling or storage. Consumers should be instructed in the proper use of goods and should be informed of the risks involved in intended or normally foreseeable use. Vital safety information should be conveyed to consumers by internationally understandable principles wherever possible. Section IIIB(20): Promotional marketing and sales practices should be guided by the principle of fair treatment of consumers and should meet legal requirements. This requires the provision of the information necessary to enable consumers to take informed and independent decisions, as well as measures to ensure that the information provided is accurate. Section IIIB(22): Governments should, within their own national context, encourage the formulation and implementation by business, in co-operation with consumer organizations, of codes of marketing and other business practices to ensure adequate consumer protection. Voluntary agreements may also be established jointly by business, consumer organizations and other interested parties. These codes should receive adequate publicity. Section IIIF(35): Business should, where appropriate, undertake or participate in factual and relevant consumer education and information programmes.").

30Department of Economic and Social Affairs [11]. ("Section II(7) All enterprises should obey the relevant laws and regulations of the countries in which they do business. They should also conform to the appropriate provisions of international standards for consumer protection to which the competent authorities of the country in question have agreed (Hereinafter references to international standards in the guidelines should be viewed in the context of this paragraph.)").

fees and final costs to enable consumers to take informed decisions. Businesses should ensure easy access to this information, especially to the key terms and conditions, regardless of the means of technology used.

(d) Education and awareness-raising. Businesses should, as appropriate, develop programmes and mechanisms to assist consumers to develop the knowledge and skills necessary to understand risks, including financial risks, to take informed decisions and to access competent and professional advice and assistance, preferably from an independent third party.

(e) Protection of privacy. Businesses should protect consumers' privacy through a combination of appropriate control, security, transparency and consent mechanisms relating to the collection and use of their personal data.

(f) Consumer complaints and disputes. Businesses should make available complaints-handling mechanisms that provide consumers with expeditious, fair, transparent, inexpensive, accessible, speedy and effective dispute resolution without unnecessary cost or burden. Businesses should consider subscribing to domestic and international standards pertaining to internal complaints handling, alternative dispute resolution services and customer satisfaction codes (Emphasis added).[31]

The shared responsibility between business and governments in relation to the dissemination of information and education programs is highlighted in the following sections:

42. Member States should develop or encourage the development of general consumer education and information programmes, including information on the environmental impacts of consumer choices and behaviour and the possible implications, including benefits and costs, of changes in consumption, bearing in mind the cultural traditions of the people concerned. The aim of such programmes should be to enable people to act as discriminating consumers, capable of making an informed choice of goods and services, and conscious of their rights and responsibilities. In developing such programmes, special attention should be given to the needs of vulnerable and disadvantaged consumers, in both rural and urban areas, including low- income consumers and those with low or non-existent literacy levels. Consumer groups, business and other relevant organizations of civil society should be involved in these educational efforts.

46. Businesses should, where appropriate, undertake or participate in factual and relevant consumer education and information programmes.[32]

These additions put an enhanced responsibility on businesses to have a proactive role in providing consumers with information to guide their decisions. The new critical provisions, Section 11(c), Section 11(d), and Section 42, show that the responsibility for education and awareness-raising is split between both government and businesses—representing a paradigm shift in the role of businesses to upscale the knowledge of consumers. Section 11(d) now encourages businesses to develop the knowledge and skills necessary for consumers to understand risks associated with products.

The provisions outline a balance among the roles of all parties involved in consumer policy. On the government side, frameworks should enable consumers

[31] The Guidelines, supra note 1, at §IV.

[32] Id. at §§42 and 46.

Fig. 1 Information and the roles of governments, businesses and consumers

to access information which is provided in relation to the full range of products and services available for consumption. Governments are also expected to provide consumer education and adequate law enforcement to curb the potential for any abusive practices. Businesses, in turn, have a responsibility to communicate truthfully and accurately to ensure that they do not mislead consumers. Consumers should then exercise their rights autonomously, making informed decisions. This delicate balance among the different roles is illustrated in the visual representation (Fig. 1).

Under the current text of the Guidelines, approaches to consumer policy that allow providing more (not less) information to consumers, should be encouraged. Further support for this approach is found in Section 5 (k), which states that "the global free flow of information" is one of the guiding principles and objectives of the Guidelines. Section 28 also calls on Member States to "encourage all concerned to participate in the free flow of accurate information on all aspects of consumer products."

This balanced policy approach proves to be more relevant in the case of newly emerging technologies and product innovations, which may not be explicitly covered by existing regulations. Ideally, regulation should indicate to manufacturers which information standard they must comply with.

However, as regulation is always a few steps behind innovation, there is a legitimate case for manufactures to provide such information despite regulatory gaps.

3 Different Policy Approaches to the Provision of Information to Consumers

3.1 Comparative Law Review

In some jurisdictions, businesses have a fair amount of discretion in providing consumers with product related information. In the United States, for instance, the Supreme Court has granted constitutional protection to "commercial speech", i.e. speech which communicates an economic interest and provides information to consumers.[33] Commercial speech protections can help facilitate the dialogue between businesses and consumers, and allow for the free flow of information to guide decision-making.

In the United States commercial speech is a relevant tool available for businesses to keep consumers abreast of new products and services. As an example, a 2012 decision by the Second Circuit Court of Appeals recognized as commercial speech that merit protection the provision of truthful and non- misleading information about unapproved off-label use of prescription drugs.[34]

Although commercial speech can be considered a constitutional feature particular to the United States, other jurisdictions also protect commercial speech, or have framed the concept in different ways—in some instances as a right or freedom and in others as an obligation or duty—providing a certain degree of protection to the information.

The next section will analyze how courts have approached the provision of information to consumers by examining selected jurisprudence in the United States, Canada, Germany, the European Union, and Brazil. As stated above, the United States provides stronger safeguards for commercial speech.

Canadian protections for commercial speech mirror the American approach, but can be more restrictive. In Germany, the Constitutional Court grants protection to commercial speech and will not allow blanket bans on advertising or commercial information, especially if it involves truthful and non-misleading content. In Europe, the Court of Justice of the European Union (CJEU) recognizes a certain degree of protection for commercial speech, but in concrete cases this protection does not always fully materialize.[35] The CJEU is willing to accept restrictions on commercial speech justified on the basis of health, or other relevant public interests. While Brazilian Courts have not developed their own "commercial speech"

---

[33]Oxana Gassy-Wright (Under the Direction of Peter J. Spiro), Commercial Speech in the United States and Europe, University of Georgia School of Law LLM Theses and Essays, at p. 15, https://digitalcommons.law.uga.edu/cgi/viewcontent.cgi?referer=https://www.google.com/&httpsredir=1&article=1016&context=stu_llm (last accessed on 12 April 2019); See also Securities and Exchange Commission v. Wall Street Publishing Institute Inc. dba Stock Market Magazine, 851 F.2d 365 (U.S.C.A. DC Cir. 1988); See also Central Hudson Gas & Electric Corp. v. Public Service Commission (hereinafter Central Hudson), 447 U.S. 557 (1980).

[34]See US v. Caronia, 703 F.3d 149, 163, 168–169 (2d Cir. 2012).

[35]Gassy-Wright, supra note 33, at p. 5.

doctrine, they have recognized a consumer right to receive adequate information, which is considered an autonomous right that needs to be fulfilled by businesses.

Of course, varied political, legal, and cultural traditions lead to varying degrees of protection for information provided by businesses. With all due respect for varied approaches, this paper contends that in order for businesses to fulfill the "Principles for Good Business Practices" and inherent responsibilities delineated in the newly revised Guidelines, the act of providing truthful non- misleading information to consumers in relation to new and innovative products should receive some level of protection, in order to spur product innovation and equip consumers with the requisite knowledge to guide their decisions.

3.1.1 Commercial Speech in the United States

Free speech is viewed as one of the foundational tenets of a democratic society, and can be used as an instrument for the achievement of truth through knowledge.[36] Commercial speech can be defined as speech that is "concededly an advertisement and refers to a specific product and is motivated by commercial interest," or speech that is used for advertising or profit.[37] The justifications for protecting commercial speech include that commercial speech helps to influence the free market economy, and the free market allows for the free flow of information and free choice (autonomy).

Until the mid-1970s, however, the Supreme Court did not consider that commercial speech was protected by the First Amendment. In a series of cases culminating in Virginia State Board of Pharmacy

v. Virginia Citizens Consumer Council Inc (1976), the Supreme Court changed course and decided that the First Amendment's protections extended to purely commercial speech. In Virginia Pharmacy, the Court struck down a Virginia regulation that prohibited pharmacists from advertising the price of prescription drugs.

In that case, the rationale for First Amendment protection of commercial speech was the interest both of the individual consumer and society generally in the free flow of commercial information, which was viewed as indispensable to informed economic choice.[38] Justice Blackmun, writing for the Court, argued that there was a listener's right to receive advertising and also considered that an alternative approach

---

[36] Id., at p. 1.

[37] Id., at p. 15.

[38] See Virginia State Board of Pharmacy v. Virginia Citizens Consumer Council Inc., 425 U.S. 748 (1976); See also ERIC BARENDT, FREEDOM OF SPEECH, Oxford University Press, (2d. ed. 2005), at pp. 400–401. In the course of the decision the Court provided three reasons why commercial speech should be entitled to First amendment protections. ("The first focused on the interests of consumers in the free flow of commercial information: '[T]hat interest may be as keen, if not keener by far, than his interest in the day's most urgent political debate.' Secondly, society has a strong interest in the unimpeded flow of commercial information, partly because that information may have a public interest component, but more generally because the flow is important in enabling

could be to assume that the information is not in itself harmful—and that people will act in their own best interest if they are well informed. Justice Blackmun suggested that the best approach is open the channels of communication rather than to close them.

While commercial speech receives constitutional protection in the United States, review and survey of jurisprudence from the Supreme Court shows that there is an intermediate level of protection for the dissemination of truthful and non-misleading information about products and services.[39] The Central Hudson case laid out a four part test to determine whether or not commercial speech should be protected.[40] This test, articulated below, has been used consistently to determine whether or not commercial speech will receive protection from the Court:

> For commercial speech to come within that provision, it at least must concern lawful activity and not be misleading. Next, we ask whether the asserted governmental interest is substantial. If both inquiries yield positive answers, we must determine whether the regulation directly advances the governmental interest asserted, and whether it is not more extensive than is necessary to serve that interest.[41]

The test lies first in determining whether or not the communication could be misleading. A check will also be done to ascertain if the government interest in controlling or limiting the commercial speech is substantial and if the regulation directly advances such interest. Finally, the Court will review whether the restriction imposed extends further than necessary. This approach provides more leeway to businesses to communicate. At the same time it ensures that misleading statements do not receive protection under the First Amendment.

The 44 Liquormart (1999) case was critical in highlighting the rationale of the Court in providing protections for commercial speech.[42] In this case, liquor retailers challenged Rhode Island statutes prohibiting advertisement of liquor prices. The Supreme Court held that a complete ban on such advertisements violated the First Amendment. The Supreme Court gave deference to the ability of businesses to provide truthful non-misleading information to the public.

The language of the Supreme Court in the 44 Liquormart case again reiterates that there must be a delicate balance between businesses, governments, and individuals, in shaping effective policies. This balance, along with an emphasis on the principles of autonomy and the free flow of information, was expressed in the following passage:

> Precisely because bans against truthful, nonmisleading commercial speech rarely seek to protect consumers from either deception or overreaching, they usually rest solely on the offensive assumption that the public will respond 'irrationally' to the truth. Linmark, 431

---

consumers to make informed choices, which cumulatively are essential to the working of a free-enterprise economy. Thirdly, for the state to justify its ban on the publication of drug prices with the argument that otherwise consumers would be attracted to go to low-cost, low-quality pharmacist is unacceptable paternalism.").

[39]Gassy-Wright, supra, note 33, at p. 5.

[40]Central Hudson, supra note 33.

[41]Id., at 566.

[42]44 Liquormart, Inc. v. Rhode Island, 517 U.S. 484 (1996).

> U.S., at 96, 97 S.Ct., at 1620. The First Amendment directs us to be especially skeptical of regulations that seek to keep people in the dark for what the government perceives to be their own good. That teaching applies equally to state attempts to deprive consumers of accurate information about their chosen products (…).[43]

Also crucial is the impact commercial speech may have on broader societal changes. In Bigelow v. Virginia, the Supreme Court is said to have recognized, for the first time, the correlation between commercial speech and social development, in upholding the ability to make available to the public abortion services and daily rates.[44]

An interesting evolution of the commercial speech doctrine can also be evidenced in a 2012 decision by the Second Circuit Court of Appeals in Caronia v. United States. In this case the Court extended the First Amendment protection to the diffusion of truthful and non-misleading information on unapproved off-label use of prescription drugs. The court held that a salesperson who promoted unapproved off-label—yet scientifically justified—uses of a drug (in this case, the anti-narcolepsy drug Xyrem®) could not be held liable for violating the Food, Drug, and Cosmetics Act (FDCA).

According to the Second Circuit Court of Appeals ruling, the particular FDCA restrictions imposed on such speech violated the First Amendment.[45] In this ruling the Court noted that prohibiting the promotion of off label drug use, while simultaneously allowing off-label drug use, would interfere with the ability of patients to receive relevant information. The Court reasoned that "such barriers to information about off-label use could inhibit, to the public's detriment, informed and intelligent treatment decisions."[46] The Court gave deference to the free flow of information and revealed a policy approach which gave heightened protection to the value of truthful and non-misleading communication.

3.1.2 Commercial Speech in Canada

The Canadian Charter of Rights and Freedoms (the Charter) is the supreme law of Canada and the main source of constitutionally guaranteed rights and freedoms.[47] In

---

[43] Id., at 503.

[44] See Bigelow v. Virginia, 421 US 809 (1975); See also Batra [12].

[45] Caronia, supra note 34. ("[O]ff-label drug usage is not unlawful, and the FDA's drug approval process generally contemplates that approved drugs will be used in off-label ways. In effect, even if pharmaceutical manufacturers are barred from off-label promotion, physicians can prescribe, and patients can use, drugs for off-label purposes. As off-label drug use itself is not prohibited, it does not follow that prohibiting the truthful promotion of off-label drug usage by a particular class of speakers would directly further the government's goals of preserving the efficacy and integrity of the FDA's drug approval process and reducing patient exposure to unsafe and ineffective drugs.").

[46] Id.

[47] The Canadian Charter of Rights and Freedoms §2(b). ("Everyone has the following fundamental freedoms: (…) (b) freedom of thought, belief, opinion and expression, including freedom of the press and other media of communication.").

Ford v. Quebec (A.G.) (1988), the Supreme Court of Canada stated that the freedoms guaranteed in the Charter "should be given a large and liberal interpretation" and that there is "no sound basis on which commercial expression can be excluded from the protection of s. 2(b) of the Charter."[48] The Supreme Court based its opinion on the welfare enhancing argument that individuals were able to make improved economic choices, as well as the proposition that the making of market choices was "an important aspect of individual

self-fulfillment and personal autonomy":

> Over and above its intrinsic value as expression, commercial expression, which, as has been pointed out, protects listeners as well as speakers plays a significant role in enabling individuals to make informed economic choices, an important aspect of individual self-fulfilment and personal autonomy. The Court accordingly rejects the view that commercial expression serves no individual or societal value in a free and democratic society and for this reason is undeserving of any constitutional protection. (Emphasis added).[49]

In Irwin Toy Ltd. v. Quebec (A. G) (1989), the majority decision begins with an analysis of what constitutes "expression" under Section 2(b) of the Charter. In this case the Supreme Court gave "expression" a very broad scope and decided that "if the activity conveys or attempts to convey meaning, it has expressive content and prima facie falls within the scope of the guarantee."[50] After deciding that expression is to be defined broadly, the majority restated and summarized the reasons for protecting freedom of expression as set out in Ford v. Quebec.[51]

These cases show that the Supreme Court of Canada proclaimed recognition for commercial speech protections, recognizing benefits to both speakers and listeners.[52] The Canadian approach, however, is different from the doctrine in the United States, as the Supreme Court of Canada usually assesses the value of the expression at issue, as part of the justification process under the Charter. Based on this assessment, restrictions on commercial speech, due to their content, are more easily justified.[53]

---

[48] Supreme Court of Canada, The Attorney General of Quebec v. La Chaussure Brown's Inc., Valerie Ford, McKenna Inc., Nettoyeur et Tailleur Masson Inc. and La Compagnie de Fromage Nationale Ltée A.G. (hereinafter Ford v. Quebec), Docket No. 20307, 2 SCR 712 (1988).

[49] Id., at para. 59.

[50] Supreme Court of Canada, The Attorney General of Quebec v. Irwin Toy Limited, Docket No. 20074, 1 S.C.R. 927 (1989).

[51] Id. ("We have already discussed the nature of the principles and values underlying the vigilant protection of free expression in a society such as ours. They were also discussed by the Court in Ford (at pp. 765–67), and can be summarized as follows: (1) seeking and attaining the truth is an inherently good activity; (2) participation in social and political decision making is to be fostered and encouraged; and (3) the diversity in forms of individual self-fulfilment and human flourishing ought to be cultivated in an essentially tolerant, indeed welcoming, environment not only for the sake of those who convey a meaning, but also for the sake of those to whom it is conveyed.").

[52] Roach and Schneiderman [13], Cullen and Tso [14].

[53] Id.

3.1.3 Freedom of Speech in Germany

Germany is one jurisdiction within the European Union that also provides for strong protections for freedom of speech, including commercial statements, typically upholding the right of businesses to provide essential, non-misleading information to consumers.

For example, in the case Nuklearmedizin im Briefkopf, the German Constitutional Court recognized the interest of third parties in receiving truthful and non-misleading information as a factor to be considered in the balancing test required by constitutional law. This case involved advertising signs placed by a doctor. The German Constitutional Court annulled restrictions on the ability of a radiologist to make certain statements in his letterhead. In making its decision, the German Constitutional Court held that:

> The legally protected interest [Rechtsgut] of public health and the resulting advertising ban to avoid the commercialization of the profession of doctors, which is undesirable from the point of view of health policy, do not justify the general prohibition of information on the specifics of the exercise of the profession, irrespective of its intent and purpose or its informative value for third parties (…) Insofar as the references are fact-based and non- misleading, they are permitted (…) This follows from Art. 12(1)GG (Emphasis added).[54]

In another case, the German Constitutional Court (BVerfG) overruled the civil court decision prohibiting the dissemination of three publications by a physician who sold vitamin supplements. The complainant published books and brochures and engaged in a public debate with the pharmaceutical industry stating that many diseases are caused by a lack of vitamins, which could easily be avoided through consumption of vitamin supplements. In issuing its judgment and allowing the dissemination of the information, the Constitutional Court recognized the general importance of the consumers' interest in receiving information about publicly discussed health issues.[55]

In general, business communications will receive protection in Germany if they aim to contribute to a debate of public interest (like health).[56] The German Federal Court for private and criminal law ("Bundesgerichtshof") has also recognized the interests of the majority of consumers in the dissemination of truthful information, in showing that objectively correct information is worthy of a higher level of protection.[57]

In the medical context, recognition has been given for the ability of a charitable foundation whose purpose is to provide consumer information and advice on health issues, to provide information on doctors in its patient information services,

---

[54] BverfG, 1 BvR 166/89 (1993)—Nuklearmedizin im Briefkopt, and subsequently BVerfG, 1 BvR 1147/01 (2002)—Bezeichnung von Klinik-Arzten als Spezialisten in Faltblatt.

[55] BVerfG, 1 BvR 2041/02 (2007), Pharmakartell.

[56] BVerfG, 2 BvR 1915/91(1997)—Warnungen auf Tabakerzeugnissen, at para. 46.

[57] BGH, judgment of 15 February 1996—I ZR 9/94 (juris)—Der meistverkaufte Europas, para. 28 = GRUR 1996, 910.

specifying special treatment options, therapy facilities, and the specialist title.[58] In upholding its justifications, the Court noted that it is in the essential interest of patients to be informed about special treatment methods, and also that the "guiding model of the autonomous citizen and patient, would be also undermined by a corresponding ban on information (…)."[59]

3.1.4 Commercial Speech in the European Union

Jurisprudence at the level of the European Union shows recognition of some degree of protection to "commercial speech", although both the ECtHR and CJEU give deference to member states in determining the restrictions deemed necessary to protect other relevant values, like public safety, health or security, which may conflict with commercial speech.[60]

For state interference with commercial speech to be considered legitimate by the ECtHR, it has to: (i) be prescribed by law; (ii) pursue one or more of the legitimate aims set out in Article 10, paragraph 2, ECHR; and (iii) be necessary in a democratic society to achieve such aims.

A review of jurisprudence of the ECtHR shows that the necessity test is less strict with regard to commercial statements than in the case of political speech. This means that member states enjoy a wider "margin of appreciation" to regulate commercial matters, which implies that they may interfere with commercial speech to a greater extent than would be allowed with regard to other kinds of expression. In other words, the ECtHR is usually more willing to accept the regulation of advertising than it is to accept the regulation of noncommercial speech.[61]

In Casado Coca versus Spain, the ECtHR examined whether the Barcelona Bar Association violated Article 10 of the ECHR in sanctioning a lawyer for advertising his practice in the local newspapers, which was considered in breach of an advertising

---

[58] District Court Kiel, judgment of 10 November 1998- 16 O 19/98- Patienteninformationsdienst.

[59] Id. at para. 39.

[60] The Convention, supra, note 2 at 10§2. ("The exercise of these freedoms [freedom to hold opinions and to receive and impart information and ideas], since it carries with it duties and responsibilities, may be subject to such formalities, conditions, restrictions or penalties as are prescribed by law and are necessary in a democratic society, in the interests of national security, territorial integrity or public safety, for the prevention of disorder or crime, for the protection of health or morals, for the protection of the reputation or rights of others, for preventing the disclosure of information received in confidence, or for maintaining the authority and impartiality of the judiciary.").

[61] The doctrine of "margin of appreciation" allows the governments of the Party States some discretion, subject to the European Court of Human Rights supervision, in balancing freedom of speech with conflicting interests such as reputation, privacy, and the right to a fair trial. See, e.g., European Court of Human Rights, Church of Scientology v. Sweden, Case No. 7805/77, 5 May 1979. ("The level of protection must be less than that accorded to the expression of 'political' ideas, in the broadest sense, with which the values underpinning the concept of freedom of expression in the Convention are chiefly concerned.").

ban imposed by the Bar regulation.[62] The Court provided in depth reasoning for how Article 10 guarantees freedom of expression, and also covers some forms of communications in a business context.[63]

The dicta in the Casado Coca v. Spain case implied recognition that restrictions on the provision of truthful information to consumers will be subject to close scrutiny by the ECtHR. According to the reasoning of the Court, attempts to ban or restrict purely factual business communications may be challenged, based on a potential violation to Article 10, as it impinges on freedom of expression and the free flow of information. However, at the end the ECtHR found that a violation of Article 10 had not occurred and that local authorities were better placed to regulate the advertising of legal services.

The ECtHR allows for a broader "margin of appreciation" or discretion when reviewing national policies that restrict commercial advertising.[64] In practice, this leads to an overall weaker level of protection of commercial speech. This weaker scope of protection implies that the ability of businesses to communicate with consumers in the European Union can be more easily restricted.

Alongside the ECtHR, the CJEU also has a significant body of jurisprudence addressing issues related to commercial speech. This study focuses on selected cases where consumer protection was included in the rationale of the decisions.

In GB-INNO-BM v. Confederation du Commerce Luxembourgeois, the CJEU addressed a question of commercial advertising and the free movement of goods.[65] The case involved the advertising of sales offers with a price reduction through leaflets, informing the duration of the offer and the prices previously charged, which was prohibited by the Luxembourg legislation but permitted by the regulations in force in Belgium. The CJEU decided that the restrictions imposed by the Luxembourg legislation were unjustified and did not protect consumer interests.

---

[62]European Court of Human Rights, Casado Coca v. Spain, Case No. 15450/89, 24 February 1994, at paras. 35–51.

[63]Id. at paras. 35, 49, and 51. ("For the citizen, advertising is a means of discovering the characteristics of services and goods offered to him. Nevertheless, it may sometimes be restricted, especially to prevent unfair competition and untruthful or misleading advertising. In some contexts, the publication of even objective, truthful advertisements might be restricted in order to ensure respect for the rights of others or owing to the special circumstances of particular business activities and professions. Any such restrictions must, however, be closely scrutinized by the Court, which must weigh the requirements of those particular features against the advertising in question; to this end, the Court must look at the impugned penalty in the light of the case as a whole." […]"The Court would first point out that Article 10 guarantees freedom of expression to 'everyone'. No distinction is made in it according to whether the type of aim pursued is profit-making or not. […]"In the Commission's view, banning practically all advertising by members of the Bar appeared to be excessive and scarcely compatible with the right to freedom of expression, which includes the freedom to impart information and its corollary, the right to receive it. The applicant's notice set out particulars that were wholly neutral (his name, occupation and business address and telephone number) and did not contain information that was untrue or offensive to fellow members of the Bar. He was therefore entitled to impart that information, just as his potential clients were entitled to receive it.").

[64]Johnson and Ho Youm [15].

[65]See Court of Justice of the European Union, GB-INNO-BM v. Confederation du Commerce Luxembourgeois, Case No. 362/88, E.C.R.I-667, (1990).

The Court stated that community law establishes a link between consumer protection and providing information to consumers, which implies providing more, rather than less, information. The Court stated that by providing information, the consumer is given a voice in decisions which involve him (or her).[66]

In Neptune Distribution Snc v. Ministre de l'Economie et des Finances (France) a request was made for a preliminary ruling concerning the prohibition to label and advertise natural mineral waters, suggesting characteristics which the water did not possess.[67] In this case, the CJEU reaffirmed the need to provide accurate and transparent product information to consumers, which would be "closely related" to the protection of human health. Through using this reasoning, the Court found that the message at issue could mislead consumers, so the Court accepted the restrictions on speech that had been imposed by the French government.[68]

In another case, involving the alleged advertisement of prescription drugs, the CJEU made a clear distinction between "information" content versus "advertising" content of commercial communications, stating that "material which is purely informative, without promotional intent, is not covered by the provisions of [the] directive relating to advertising of medicinal products."[69] The Court found that in order for

---

[66]Id., at paras. 14, 15, and 18. ("The question thus arises whether national legislation which prevents the consumer from having access to certain information may be justified in the interest of consumer protection. It should be observed first of all that Community policy on the subject establishes a close link between protecting the consumer and providing the consumer with information. [...] The existence of a link between protection and information for consumers is explained in the introduction to the second programme [of the European Economic Community for a consumer protection and information policy]. There it is stressed that measures taken or scheduled in accordance with the preliminary programme contribute towards improving the consumer's situation by protecting his health, his safety and his economic interest, by providing him with appropriate information and education, and by giving him a voice in decisions which involve him. [...] It follows from the foregoing that under Community law concerning consumer protection the provision of information to the consumer is considered one of the principal requirements. Thus Article 30 cannot be interpreted as meaning that national legislation which denies the consumer access to certain kinds of information may be justified by mandatory requirements concerning consumer protection.).

[67]Court of Justice of the European Union, Neptune Distribution SNC v. Ministre de l'Économie et des Finances (Minister for Economic Affairs and Finance), Case No. 157/14, 17 December 2015.

[68]Id at paras. 65 and 74. ("The need to ensure that the consumer has the most accurate and transparent information possible concerning the characteristics of goods is closely related to the protection of human health and is a question of general interest [...] which may justify limitations on the freedom of expression and information of a person carrying on a business or his freedom to conduct a business.)." ("Since the freedom of expression and information laid down in Article 11 of the Charter has, as is clear from Article 52(3) thereof and the Explanations Relating to the Charter as regards Article 11, the same meaning and scope as the freedom guaranteed by the ECHR, it must be held that that freedom covers the use by a business, on packaging, labels and in advertising for natural mineral waters, of claims and indications referring to the sodium or salt content of such waters.").

[69]Court of Justice of the European Union, MSD Sharp & Dohme GmbH, Case No. 316/09, 5 May 2011, at para. 32.

a communication to be qualified as an advertisement, it must bear a promotional purpose. Information which is purely informative does not amount to advertising.[70]

In the food context, the CJEU has considered disproportionate and unjustified in light of consumer protection arguments, a general prohibition of health claims, combined with a prior authorization system for the labelling and presentation of foodstuffs, imposed by food regulations in Austria. Such a requirement resulted in a failure to fulfill obligations on the approximation of the laws of member states relating to the labeling, presentation and advertising of foodstuffs.[71]

In that case, the CJEU also observed that the Austrian government had not produced any evidence that a system of ex post control of foodstuffs would be ineffective. The Court also clarified that, in case of doubt as to whether the message can mislead consumers or not, the national authorities should take "into account the presumed expectations of an average consumer who is reasonably well informed and reasonably observant and circumspect."[72]

3.1.5 Protection of Consumer Information in Brazil

Brazil is another jurisdiction which favors the free flow of information enabling individuals to make better consumer choices. While not through the use of the doctrine of "commercial speech," consumer information receives a high level of

[70] Id., at para. 48. ("Having regard to all of the foregoing, the answer to the question referred is that Article 88(1)(a) of Directive 2001/83 must be interpreted as meaning that it does not prohibit the dissemination on a website, by a pharmaceutical undertaking, of information relating to medicinal products available only on medical prescription, where that information is accessible on the website only to someone who seeks to obtain it and that dissemination consists solely in the faithful reproduction of the packaging of the medicinal product, in accordance with Article 62 of that directive, and in the literal and complete reproduction of the package leaflet or the summary of the product's characteristics, which have been approved by the authorities with competence in relation to medicinal products. On the other hand, the dissemination, on such a website, of information relating to a medicinal product which has been selected or rewritten by the manufacturer, which can be explained only by an advertising purpose, is prohibited. It is for the referring court to determine whether and to what extent the activities at issue in the main proceedings constitute advertising within the meaning of that directive.").

[71] See Court of Justice of the European Union, Republic of Austria v. Commission, in joined Case Nos. C-421/00, C-426/00 and C-16/01, 23 January 2003. ("37. While Article 2(1) of Directive 79/112 prohibits, first, all statements relating to the preventing, treating and curing of a human disease, even if they are not liable to mislead the purchaser, and, second, misleading statements relating to health, it is clear that the protection of public health, assuming that risks relating thereto are nevertheless conceivable in a particular situation, cannot justify a system as restrictive of the free movement of goods as that which results from a procedure of prior authorisation for all health-related information on the labelling of foodstuffs, including those which are manufactured lawfully in other Member States and are in free circulation. 38. Less restrictive measures exist for the prevention of such residual risks to health, such as, for example, an obligation on the manufacturer or distributor of the product in question, in the event of any uncertainty, to furnish evidence of the accuracy of the facts mentioned on the labelling (see, to that effect, Commission v. Austria, paragraph 49").).

[72] Id.

protection in Brazil.[73] The Courts clearly place an obligation on businesses to give more, rather than less information to consumers—to guide their decisions. Similar to other freedom of expression provisions around the world, Article 5 of the Brazilian Constitution provides as follows:

> The expression of thought is free, except for anonymity.[74]
>
> The expression of intellectual, artistic, scientific and communication activities will be free and independent of censure.[75]
>
> Access to information is ensured to everyone and the confidentiality of the source shall be safeguarded, whenever necessary to the professional activity.[76]

In 2007 the Superior Court of Justice handed down an important ruling determining the level of information that a business should provide to consumers in order to fulfill its obligation under the Consumer Protection Code. The case involved the labeling of a food product that contained gluten. Brazilian food regulations required standard labeling for products containing gluten ("this product contains gluten"). Although the producer had complied with the labeling requirements set by the food regulation, in a legal action filed by the Federal Public Prosecutor's Office, the Superior Court of Justice understood that such requirements were insufficient to provide the consumer with the level of information they needed to protect their health, placing a higher burden on businesses.

The Superior Court of Justice ruled that manufacturers should always strive to go beyond labeling requirements established under food law (special law) if this proves to be necessary to meet their general duty to inform under the Consumer Protection Code (consumer law). The Superior Court of Justice highlighted that, under the consumer protection law, the right to information was an autonomous right that posed an autonomous obligation on businesses. The decision went further stating that labeling requirements provided under food regulation set minimum standards, which did not replace the general information obligations set forth by the consumer protection law.[77]

---

[73] With respect to the consumer right to information, see Article 6, items II and III, of the Brazilian Consumer Protection Code: "The following are basic consumer rights: [...] II - education and information about the adequate level of consumption for products and services, ensuring freedom of choice and equality in hiring processes; III - adequate and clear information about different products and services, with correct specification of quantity, characteristics, composition, quality, price and taxes, as well as the risks presented.".

[74] Article 5(iv) of the Brazilian Constitution (Freedom of Thought).

[75] Article 5(ix) of the Brazilian Constitution (Freedom of Expression).

[76] Article 5(xiv) of the Brazilian Constitution (Access to Information).

[77] See Superior Court of Justice of Brazil, Special Appeal No. 586316-MG, 17 April 2007. ("The duty of information requires a positive and active behavior, (…) Positive and active behavior means that the consumer protection microsystem is not compatible with half-information, semi-information, proto-information or partial information, regardless of the term being chosen. Information is either given in full, or is not information in the legal (and practical) sense attributed to it by the CDC. (…) If the requirements of the special legislation that governs a specific product or service are not sufficient to properly inform the consumer, it is up to the manufacturer—the most knowledgeable

Stating that the product "contains gluten", as required by the existing food regulation, was not enough to keep consumers well informed. Businesses were required to add an additional message that "gluten is harmful for people with celiac disease", even though this message was not prescribed by the existing food regulation. The Court acknowledged that "if the requirements of the special legislation that governs a specific product or service are not sufficient to properly inform the consumer, it is up to the manufacturer—the most knowledgeable about the products and services on sale—to offer complementary information."[78] This ruling demonstrates that businesses are encouraged to complement labeling information prescribed by special regulations, if necessary to fulfill the consumer right to information.

4 Propelling Innovation Through Information

4.1 Providing Scientific Information to Consumers

Communication of scientific information presents unique opportunities in the context of consumer policy. One of the first studies analyzing the effects of disseminating scientific information to consumers in relation to consumer behavior and product development/innovation was produced in 1990.[79] The objective of the study was to assess advantages and risks of allowing producers to provide consumers with scientific information that could help them make better dietary choices, as well as the effects this policy approach could have in terms of fostering product innovation. The study also identified policy approaches that could help deter consumer deception, while not inhibiting the dissemination of truthful science-based claims. It provided a number of examples where this approach proved to be advantageous for consumers, highlighting that "[t]he gain to consumers from incorporating evolving scientific discoveries into basic decisions about food and product choices can be enormous."[80]

One case study confirming the proposition that providing scientific information to consumers could have a positive impact on consumption behavior and product development, involved the ready-to-eat cereal market in the United States. Prior to 1984, health claims were not allowed on the labeling of food in the United States. However, upon a change in the food legislation, the Kellogg Company started to claim that All Bran cereal was high in fiber and that diets high in fiber could benefit

about the products and services on sale—to offer complementary information.(...) Only the well informed consumer may in fact fully enjoy the economic benefits of the product or service it has been provided, as well as to adequately protect itself from risks arising thereof. (...) Strictly speaking, the obligation to inform, nowadays has a true autonomous nature (...) (unofficial translation))," https://stj.jusbrasil.com.br/jurisprudencia/4092403/recurso-especial-resp-586316 (last accessed on 15 April 2019).

[78] Id.

[79] Ippolito [16].

[80] Id.

consumers by reducing health risks. Other cereal companies then responded with similar claims for their own high fiber cereals, while producers not using high fiber cereals in their portfolio were nudged to reformulate their products to match consumer expectation and competitors' offers.[81]

By the year 1987 consumers substantially increased their consumption of high-fiber cereals, with the greatest increase occurring in the groups that previously consumed the least amount of fiber cereal. The profile of the cereal market then correspondingly changed. Market shares for high fiber cereals increased and more cereals with high fiber content were circulating on the market and being purchased.[82]

This study also noted that when information is provided by producers, it can be more effective and far-reaching than non-producer information disseminated by state educational campaigns, which may typically benefit segments of society with higher education. Another finding was that producers have higher incentives to innovate and introduce better products to the market if they can highlight certain aspects of their products, while consumers can use the information provided to make better choices.

Another case study showing that the provision of scientific information to the consumer through food labeling can positively impact product development and innovation is related to industry "trans fatty acid" (TFA). Consumption of TFA increases the risk of coronary heart disease, and possibly also the risk of sudden cardiac death and diabetes according to public health studies. In 2002, Canada passed regulations requiring mandatory TFA food labeling, which came into force on most packaged foods by 2005. A study published by the European Journal of Clinical Nutrition assessed both grocery and restaurant foods likely to contain TFA in Canada in 2005–2007, the period following mandatory labeling of TFA content.[83] The conclusions were that food manufacturers and restaurants took the opportunity to reformulate their products, to reduce TFA content, increasing content of unsaturated fats, which could provide health benefits to consumers.[84]

---

[81] See Publication Before the Department of Health and Human Services Food and Drug Administration, in the Matter of Request for Comments on First Amendment Issues, Docket No. 02 N-0209, Comments of the Staff of the Bureau of Economics, the Bureau of Consumer Protection, and the Office of Policy Planning of the Federal Trade Commission, 13 September 2002, https://www.ftc.gov/sites/default/files/documents/advocacy_documents/ftc-staff-comment-food-and-drug-administration-concerning-first-amendment-issues/fdatextversion.pdf (last accessed on 12 April 2019).

[82] Ippolito, supra note 79.

[83] Ratnayake et al. [17].

[84] Id. ("Among the major grocery and restaurant food products in Canada that might contain TFA in 2005–2007, nearly half

(42%) contained X5% TFA on initial assessment. Many were subsequently discontinued or reformulated to reduce TFA; in those assessed more than once, nearly three-quarters had undergone reformulation, with average reduction to p2% TFA. Following reformulation, only one product had unchanged content of cis unsaturated fats; all others had increased cis unsaturated fats, most with absolute increase X10% of fatty acids and half with absolute increase X20%. The total fat content was generally unchanged.(...)[T]his first large-scale contemporary assessment of TFA contents and reformulations suggests that, at least in industrialized nations with food labeling, rather than replacing TFA with SFA or increasing total fat content, food manufacturers/restaurants are generally taking advantage of costs and efforts of reformulation as an opportunity to not only reduce TFA but

As evidenced by the cereal and TFA case studies, improvements to health can be achieved through the introduction of new and innovative consumer goods on the market, or by reformulation of existing products. In both cases a change in the regulatory frameworks, which allowed consumers to receive more information about products, also encouraged producers to improve their respective product offerings. In the cereal case, researchers were also able to detect a change in consumption patterns related to high fiber cereals.

For those behavior and market changes to happen, it was key that consumers received the essential information they needed on new products, via labeling, education campaigns, or other means. In these cases, regulatory policies which encourage the provision of information, can have the effect of "[t]apping into the resources of the private sector to promote products based on scientific relationships."[85] This type of fact-based dissemination of information can inform decision-making and product innovation in parallel.

Scientific innovation may create what can be categorized as "imperfect information".[86] Unlike the case of asymmetric information, where producers know relevant information about the product that consumers do not, in cases of imperfect or missing information, relevant product information does not exist or is contradictory. This situation could arise when the long term health effects of a product are unknown, or when scientific opinions differ about the health consequences of consumption. Even in those cases, the government can take a policy stance to provide consumers with the fullest information possible. This situation was described in more detail by the United States Department of Agriculture as follows:

> Another type of information problem that may occur in food markets is that of imperfect information. Unlike the case of asymmetric information, where producers know relevant information about the product that consumers do not, in cases of imperfect or missing information, relevant market information does not exist or is contradictory. This situation could arise when the longterm health effects of a food or food attributes are unknown, or when scientific opinions differ about the health consequences of consumption. In these cases, the government might require full disclosure of even preliminary or contradictory information to provide consumers with the fullest information possible. Hadden (1986, p. 263) argues 'It is a perversion of the intent of information provision to wait until full knowledge is available before labeling products.' Indeed, if such information is valuable to consumers, it could improve market efficiency as in the case of asymmetric information.[87]

If a policy standard is adopted which requires absolute certainty before any claims or communications on products are allowed, consumers will lose the potential benefits of receiving the information earlier.[88] Keeping consumers in the dark about

---

also increase the content of cis unsaturated fats. Such reformulation may provide additional health benefits beyond those due to lower TFA content. Most of the assessed food manufacturers and restaurants have global reach, and these findings should encourage food and restaurant industries in other regions that it is possible to reformulate foods to both eliminate industrial TFA and improve overall fatty acid composition.").

[85]Supra, note 79, at p. 440.

[86]United States Department of Agriculture [18].

[87]Id.

[88]Ippolito, supra note 79, at p. 433.

scientific developments will lead consumers to use outdated information on which to base their decisions.[89]

In the context of tobacco, this raises questions about what level of information should be provided to consumers on innovative and emerging nicotine containing products, such as e-cigarettes and heated tobacco, which may potentially be less harmful alternatives to conventional cigarettes. Recognizing that alternative nicotine containing products may have the potential to reduce public health harms associated with smoking, some governments have adopted regulatory frameworks that allows information to be provided to adult legal aged smokers about those alternatives.[90] The fact that these products are subject to stringent regulations, including mandatory disclosure regimes, should not keep adult legal aged consumers from being properly informed and updated on scientific advancement and innovation that concerns new products.

4.2 Education Campaigns: A New Way of Communicating with Consumers

Making consumers aware of the latest scientific evidence will help inform their decisions. To ensure that the information on new and innovative products gets to consumers, governments and businesses should use appropriate means of communication, including education campaigns.

Section 11(c), Section 11(d), and Section 42 of the Guidelines indicate that the responsibility for consumer education and awareness-raising is split between both government and businesses. Section 11(d) now calls on businesses to develop the knowledge and skills necessary for consumers to understand risks associated with products. Interestingly, businesses are now engaging in more education campaigns with consumers, especially for new technological products that consumers may not be familiar with.

In this connection, revisions to the Vienna Convention on Road Traffic have paved the way for automated vehicles.[91] In 2017 Waymo (formerly part of Google) was the first company to create "the world's first public education campaign for self-driving cars," which sought to increase knowledge regarding self-driving technology.[92] The campaign partnered with "Mothers Against Drunk Driving," attempting to raise awareness on the possibilities to reduce drunk driving crashes through the use of autonomous vehicles. The campaign entitled "Let's Talk Self-Driving" was geared towards educating the public about this new technology.

Other companies such as Intel and Uber were also slated to release statements and advertisements concerning the new technology. Driverless cars have the ability to

---

[89] Id., at pp. 438–439.

[90] See, e.g., U.K. Department of Health [19]; See also New Zealand Ministry of Health [20].

[91] See United Nations Economic Commission for Europe (UNECE) Press Release [21].

[92] See Engadget [22].

reduce accidents significantly. When commercialized, consumers need to be aware of the potential risks and benefits, and also how to use them. A parallel can be drawn to recent education campaigns which are informing consumers about better options than smoking, such as quitting or switching to less harmful alternatives.[93] Communication efforts and education campaigns discussing new technologies are aligned with the spirit and letter of the Guidelines.

4.3 Conclusion

The theoretical foundations for freedom of expression, respect for autonomy and consumer protection support the notion that individuals should be provided with truthful non-misleading information, in order to guide their autonomous decisions. The newly revised version of the Guidelines places an enhanced responsibility on businesses to provide information to consumers.

Reviewing the jurisprudence pertaining to commercial speech and consumer protection in selected jurisdictions around the world shows that, while approaches are different and there is a spectrum of communication restrictions and freedoms, overall there is recognition of the benefit of providing essential information to consumers. This benefit must be considered and weighed against potential risks underlying the product and broader public concerns. The delicate balance between businesses and governments, envisioned in the Guidelines, can be achieved through allowing communication and simultaneously encouraging substantiation of claims and effective enforcement measures to quell deceptive practice.

In order to fulfill responsibilities under the "Principles for Good Business Practices" section of the Guidelines, while in parallel propel product innovation forward, businesses should be able to communicate science-based information to consumers. As science and technology continues to evolve, approaches which open the gateways of communication to consumers will encourage product innovation, development, and advancements, which may ultimately have a positive impact on society.

References

1. Office of the High Commissioner for Human Rights, Human Rights Framework, https://www.ohchr.org/EN/Issues/Migration/Pages/HumanRightsFramework.aspx (last accessed on 15 April 2019).
2. E. Sakellari, (2003), Patient's autonomy and informed consent, Cus Nurs Web J, Issue 13, (2003), http://www.researchgate.net/publication/241752332. (last accessed on 10 April 2019).
3. James Taylor, Autonomy, Ethics and Political Philosophy, Encyclopedia Britannica, https://www.britannica.com/topic/autonomy (last accessed on 15 April 2019).

[93] https://www.pmi.com/unsmoke.

4. Jaunius Gumbis, et. al., Do Human Rights Guarantee Autonomy?, Cuadernos Constitucionales de la Cátedra Fadrique Furió Ceriol no. 62/63, (2011), at pp. 77–93, http://www.corteidh.or.cr/tablas/r26750.pdf (last accessed on 10 April 2019).
5. Tom L. Beauchamp & James F. Childress, Principles of Biomedical Ethics, (Oxford University Press, 5th edn. 2001), at p. 63.
6. John Coggon and José Miola, Autonomy, Liberty, and Medical Decision-Making, The Cambridge Law Journal (2011), at pp. 523–547.
7. John F. Kennedy, Special Message to the United States Congress on Protecting Consumer Interest, 15 March 1962, https://www.jfklibrary.org/asset-viewer/archives/JFKPOF/037/JFKPOF-037-028 (last accessed on 8 April 2019).
8. Dan Wei, Consumer Protection in the Global Context: The Present Status and Some New Trends, Consumer Law and Socioeconomic Development National and International Dimensions, (1st ed. 2017)(Claudia Lima Marques and Dan Wei eds.), at p. 10.
9. Iris Benöhr and Hans W. Micklitz, Consumer Protection and Human Rights, Handbook of Research on International Consumer Law (hereinafter the Handbook), (1st ed. 2011), (Geraint G. Howells, I. Ramsay, Thomas Wilhelmsson eds.), at pp. 23–26.
10. David Harland, The United Nations Guidelines for Consumer Protection, Journal of Consumer Policy (1987), Vol. 10, Issue 3, https://doi.org/10.1007/BF00411533 (last accessed on 8 April 2019).
11. Department of Economic and Social Affairs, United Nations Guidelines for Consumer Protection (as expanded in 1999), New York 2003, https://unctad.org/en/PublicationsLibrary/UN-DESA_GCP1999_en.pdf (last accessed on 8 April 2019).
12. Narain Batra, The First Freedoms and America's Culture of Innovation, the Constitutional Foundations of The Aspirational Society, (2013), at pp. 116–117
13. Kent Roach and David Schneiderman, Freedom of Expression in Canada, Supreme Court Law Review (2013), 61 S.C.L.R. (2d), p. 2., https://www.law.utoronto.ca/utfl_file/count/documents/Schneiderman/Chapter%2010%20Roach%20Schneiderman.pdf (last accessed on 15 April 2019).
14. Richard Cullen and Kevin Tso, Commercial Free Speech – A Critical Reconsideration, Australian Journal of Asian Law, Vol. 17 No. 2 (2016), Article 2, at p. 7.
15. Bruce E.H. Johnson, Kyu Ho Youm, Commercial Speech And Free Expression: The United States And Europe Compared, Journal of International Media & Entertainment Law, 2009, at pp. 159– 197, https://www.dwt.com/files/Publication/22af8b44-1950-4390-b6dd-27a527358802/Presentation/PublicationAttachment/a9a37bde-c417-4191-9916-2b564bfc36e7/pubs_Johnson_CommercialSpeech.pdf. (last accessed on 12 April 2019).
16. Pauline M. Ippolito, The Regulation of Science-Based Claims in Advertising, Journal of Consumer Policy, 13(4):413–445, Kluwer Academic Publishers (1990), https://www.researchgate.net/publication/251270405_The_Regulation_of_Science-Based_Claims_in_Advertising (last accessed on 13 April 2019).
17. Ratnayake, et. al., Nationwide product reformulations to reduce trans fatty acids in Canada: when trans fat goes out, what goes in?, European Journal of Clinical Nutrition, https://www.nature.com/articles/ejcn200839.pdf (last accessed on 13 April 2019).
18. United States Department of Agriculture, Economic Research Service, Mandatory Labeling, Economics and Food Labeling, https://www.ers.usda.gov/webdocs/publications/41203/18890_aer793d.pdf?v=0 (last accessed on 14 April 2019).
19. U.K. Department of Health, Towards a smoke-free generation: a tobacco control plan for England, July 2017, available online at: https://assets.publishing.service.gov.uk/government/uploads/system/uploads/attachment_data/file/630217/Towards_a_Smoke_free_Generation_-_A_Tobacco_Control_Plan_for_England_2017-20222_pdf (last accessed on 14 April 2019).
20. New Zealand Ministry of Health, Ministry of Health position statement – Vaping products, October 2017, available online at https://www.health.govt.nz/our-work/preventative-health-wellness/tobacco-control/vaping-smokeless-including-heated-tobacco (last accessed on 14 April 2019).

21. United Nations Economic Commission for Europe (UNECE) Press Release, UNECE Paves the Way for Automated Driving by Updating UN International Convention, 23 March 2016, https://www.unece.org/info/media/presscurrent-press-h/transport/2016/unece-paves-the-way-for-automated-driving-by-updating-un-international-convention/doc.html (last accessed on 14 April).
22. Engadget, "Waymo Ad Campaign Get Public Behind Self-Driving Cars," https://www.engadget.com/2017/10/09/waymo-ad-campaign-get-public-behind-self-driving-cars/ (last accessed on 14 April 2019).

Consumer Law in Senegal and What Potential Threats to the Welfare of Consumers in the Ecowas Region

Jean Karim Coly and Luis Alexandre Winter Carta

1 Introduction

Digital technology is an important leverage to change the living conditions of the population, particularly disadvantaged, and provides opportunities for modernization and promotion of socio-economic sectors with high growth potential, through the techniques and production technologies but also trade in goods and services.

Based on the digital sector performance, Senegal wishes to accelerate the main growth drivers for the improvement of production capacity and innovation in growth sectors.

The option chosen is to accelerate the spread of digital technology in the priority sectors identified in the Senegal Emergent Plan (PSE in French), on the one hand, promote access to basic social services (health, education, financial services), and also significantly increase productivity by focusing on the increased use of digital technology in the fields of agriculture, livestock, fisheries and trade.

Senegal Emergent Plan (PES in French) aims to transform Senegal into an emerging country in 2035, "with a socially responsible society and the rule of law." It is in this context that identified a number of areas including development, essential to achieving this goal, including that of the digital economy.

Indeed, the digital economy is a cross-cutting area which includes all production, distribution and consumption of goods and services related to telecommunications and information technology and communication, their uses as heart or medium in industrial processes, economic and societal.

So, with all this evolution of information technology and communication in Senegal, no how not to care with the safety of Senegalese consumers. For this,

J. K. Coly (✉) · L. A. W. Carta
Pontifical Catholic University of Paraná, Curitiba, Brazil
e-mail: jeankarino@gmail.com

L. A. W. Carta
e-mail: lacwad@gmail.com

D. Wei et al. (eds.), *Innovation and the Transformation of Consumer Law*,
https://doi.org/10.1007/978-981-15-8948-5_29

the study of our first chapter, we will systematically analyze the vulnerability of the Senegalese consumer, but also to see the devices that Senegal has put in place to protect consumers against the risks of globalization has increased the Production of goods and services. This brings us to a so-called consumer society.

In the second chapter, we will study the risks Consumer situation in relation to community integration and globalization. Today, regional integration shows that Senegal is part of community organizations at the sub regional and regional or continental (WAEMU, ECOWAS, OHADA African Union), therefore potential threats to the well-being of the consumer ECOWAS member countries is not negligible. Like any community space, free movement of goods and services is generally lavished. This means that the Senegalese consumer will be in direct contact with products from another country of the space where may be the observation of product security rules do not meet the same standards as in Senegal.

2 Consumer Law in Senegal

The consumer law is born from the desire to provide the consumer facing professional protection that the law of contracts did not seem sure enough her.[1]

Thus, "the use of modern technology in today's societies, development and technical and scientific progress in human life, and also the need of human society in their use, have led to increased level production of goods and services. This remarkable evolution of human society will eventually set up a so-called consumer society. "[2]

Thus Thomas Diatta, points out that in this consumer society, there is a category of people called professionals who produce goods and services they offer to another segment of the population called consumers. In the relationship between consumer and professional, he has always been and always raises the question of safety first. According to the author, this question of consumer safety is acute throughout the world, particularly in Africa and Senegal.[3]

Thus, Professor Jean-Pascal Chazal, supports the idea to affirm the need to protect the consumer, he calls vulnerable to the professional person.

According to Chazal, by definition of the word vulnerable means the person or thing that may be injured. In a first direction, the injury (vulnus) is a synonym of wound, bodily injury. But quickly, even in classical Latin, "vulnerare" takes a figurative sense. It is used, for example, the damage to public order. Therefore, the vulnerable is one that can be injured in a physical sense but also in the sense imaged, one that is likely to be the victim of an infringement of its heritage, its property, its interests. The consumer seems to be vulnerable under these two senses.[4]

[1]Rzepecki [8].

[2]http://sendroit.over-blog.com/article-la-securite-du-consommateur-senegalais-90993080.html.

[3]Id.

[4]Chazal [1], pp. 00–00.

The CHAZAL professor, says that the vulnerable person in its consumer business, may suffer bodily injury in connection with the use of defective goods. It may also suffer pecuniary injury, which is the most common case in practice.[5] So according to Chazal, the idea of potential injury should be preferred here. For if the consumer has to be protected by the law, it is not because he is always injured, but because it is likely to be for the simple reason that defends evil, he is not well equipped to deal with his partner-opponent what the professional.[6]

The concept of "consumer safety", or more precisely the consumer's physical security poses enormous problems in his apprehension. Certainly, the words that made up the isolation are not elusive but mostly the term taken as a whole that is difficult to define. For example, to define the concept of consumer, it is important to distinguished it from related concepts such as the user, the user and the client. The user is a person who uses a public service, as opposed to the customer who is the one who uses the services of a private company.[7]

In terms of the consumer's definition may be debatable, but when it comes to consumer safety, it is quite clear that the consumer, as protected by consumer law, is the person who is offered or accept a contract offer for a good or service for non-business purposes. All individuals are therefore consumers at a time of day. At night when the baker buys flour to make bread for her children, it becomes consumer. By cons, in the day when he contracts for the purpose of his work, he acts as a professional.[8]

So to return to the notion of security, it can be difficult to define, but it must be understood as the state of mind of a person who feels calm and confident. It is feeling well or ill founded, to be free from danger and risk. But here the security word refers to the idea of protection against risks that can threaten the physical integrity of the person.[9]

This for when we talk about consumer safety, the aim, not rules that would protect specifically and only the consumer, but the rules concerning the safety of that on which door customer activity.[10] Henceforth we will talk protection that is so in fact the safety of these goods and services that the consumer is likely to get.

To return to the purpose of this, that is what interests us here is the protection of the Senegalese consumer.

So let us first interested in the geographical position of the Senegalese consumer. As we can see Senegal is a country crossroads (air, sea, road and rail). As such, it constitutes the stop and the bridge transit of most products within the African economic market in general and particularly in the West African economic market.

---

[5]id.

[6]id.

[7]Security of Senegalese consumer. Available on: http://sendroit.over-blog.com/article-la-securite-du-consommateur-senegalais-90993080.html. Published on December 2, 2011. Accessed 03.21.2019.

[8]Id.

[9]id.

[10]id.

Thus, in this country are meeting a variety of products manufactured locally or imported that are offered to Senegal consumer. And this diversity of products offered to the Senegalese consumer may subject to various risks related to the consumption.

But be reminded that there is another problem that causes Senegalese consumers to these products at risk. Most Senegalese consumers are not rich. So with the poverty that plagues the Senegalese population, not to mention the economic crisis, are pushing these consumers to lower products cost without worrying about his safety and health. In addition to his carelessness, the Senegalese consumer faces an economy which is heavily dominated by the informal sector. This segment manufactures and distributes products to consumers sometimes in complete disregard of the rules of hygiene and health and safety products.

Indeed, since independence until today, Senegal in its logic of protection of natural interests of the consumer has taken a series of laws and regulations to protect the health of people in general and especially the consumer. But one can also add health regulations on hygiene and specific texts for certain commodities, reinforce this legal arsenal of control for food safety.[11]

So include some examples in texts on:

- The health safety control of foodstuffs is governed in Senegal by a basic law: the 66-48 law of 27 May 1966.
- The Basic Law is supplemented by two decrees of general application, the 68-507 and 68-508 laws of 7 May 1968.

The first specifies the import control conditions and measures of practical operating food.

The second decree treats control procedures, sampling, data entry and analysis in law enforcement fraud.

For drugs and other pharmaceutical products, there are also texts at this level. Only non-food consumer products and risk products (GMOs) that are yet on the market are not subject to regulation. Parliament seems to have focused on food, drug and pharmaceutical protection at the expense of other products that may also pose risks to the safety and health of the consumer. Next to this legislation, Senegal has set up official services control products.

In this regard we have:

- The Directorate of Plant Protection Phytosanitary Control by Legislation Division and Quality.
- The Directorate of Oceanography and Fisheries by the (Office of Control of fisheries products and regional fishery services).

The National Service of Health in connection with the Ministry of Commerce (Division of Consumer Affairs and Quality).

Thus, with such a device we realize that the security of Senegalese consumer is not fully guaranteed. So, to protect consumer safety, Senegal has put in place mechanisms for prevention and management of risks related to consumption. This means that

[11]id.

safety must be considered in all its entirety. Senegalese Consumers should also be framed in their contracts with professional requiring security there.[12] Although the basic law, decrees and provisions on pharmaceutical drugs and specialties, there is some prevention and risk management with the control enactment and criminal or administrative sanctions as mentioned above, but it should recognize that this device is still insufficient. For, it may be noted that the major problem of Senegal today is the enactment of the Consumer Code or a law on general product safety is lacking.

The organization of the United Nations esteem in the guidelines "that governments should develop or maintain a strong consumer protection policy of drawing guidelines that aim to meet the legitimate needs below:

> Protection of consumers against risks to theirhealth and safety; Promotion and protection of economic interests of consumers; Consumer access to the information needed to make an informed choice 'according to their wishes and needs; Consumer education 'notably concerning the socio-economic impact and environmental choices they make; Possibility for consumers to obtain effective redress; The right to form groups and consumer organizations and other relevant groups and possibility 'for these organizations' to assert their views in decisions affecting them; Promotion of sustainable consumption patterns.[13]

For the United Nations Organization "Governments should provide or maintain adequate infrastructure to develop and implement consumer protection policy and monitor its implementation. It is important to ensure particularly that the consumer protection measures are implemented to the benefit of all sectors of the population including the rural population and the poor."[14]

So consumer protection must remain a key concern for regulators.

In fact, the regulated operators are required to observe a strong work ethic and oriented towards satisfying the needs of consumers.

However, despite this gloomy diagnosis of the current state of Senegalese legislation, necessary to remember that the Senegalese consumer is not totally defenseless against risks that products may present for the 2002-23 was law in Article 5 has the same regulatory body is responsible for handling disputes between consumers and traders and that it must: "(…) act either as a peacemaker is to decide disputes between the licensing authority and dealers between companies in regulated sectors and between those airlines and consumers"[15]

Note also, in case of realization of risks and damages are suffered by a consumer, "one can assume that it can engage the responsibility of the manufacturer or distributor on the basis of common law and even to some extent that of the state. Civil law, criminal law, administrative law and EU law would be a great contribution to the

---

[12]Id.

[13]United Nations Conference on Trade and Development 'Principles United Nations Guidelines for Consumer Protection (as expanded in 1999)' New York and Geneva '2001 UNCTAD/DITC/CLP/Misc.21' p. 3.

[14]id.

[15]Statement of reasons law No. 2002-23 of 4 September 2002 'with regulatory framework for dealers to utility companies. Available at: https://www.ofnac.sn/resources/pdf/Lois/loi%20n%202002-23%20du%204%20septembre%202002%20portant%20cadre%20de%20regulation%20ARTP.pdf. Accessed 07.03.2019.

protection of consumer safety. This protection goes far beyond the scope of consumer law."[16]

"In view of the provisions of Law 2002-23, we have in Senegal essentially ten bodies that have a comparable mission to a mission control whether horizontal or sectoral, and in various fields such as: telecommunications and mail, electricity, water, consumer markets, broadcasting, public procurement, transport, oil and gas, and infrastructure.[17]"

Thus, between theory and practice, the gap is still deep and all organs do not play efficiently their role of protecting the interests of Senegalese consumers.

3 What Potential Threats to the Welfare of Consumers in the ECOWAS Region

Indeed, the situation of consumers with respect to community integration and globalization that knows the world in recent years is really worrying in regard to potential threats to the welfare of consumers in ECOWAS member countries. Thus, in the case of Senegal, is a country fully integrated into the market economy. Today, regional integration shows that Senegal is part of community organizations at the sub regional and regional or continental level (WAEMU, ECOWAS, OHADA African Union). But let us interested especially on the two community areas namely UEMOA and ECOWAS, including Senegal made figure of economic power. Then, as in most community spaces, the free movement of goods and services is generally lavished. So, this is what will make the Senegalese consumer to be in direct contact with products from another country of the space where may be the observation of product security rules do not meet the standards. Like so said Thomas Diatta, in these two areas, there are not to our knowledge a policy to protect the safety of consumers as is the case in the European Community area.[18] But recently in November 2018, the workshop, which opened in Ouagadougou, had as main objective the strengthening of consumer protection mechanism in Africa in general, and within the Community in particular. To do this, during the work, the participants from the ECOWAS member countries have approved the Community regulatory framework for consumer protection and the mechanism for consumer representation in the institution's quality infrastructure bodies.[19]

---

[16]Security of Senegalese consumer. Available on: http://sendroit.over-blog.com/article-la-securite-du-consommateur-senegalais-90993080.html. Published on December 2, 2011. Accessed 03.21.2019.l.

[17]Limitations of consumer protection by the regulatory authorities by Momar Ndao [5].

[18]Security of Senegalese consumer. Available on: http://sendroit.over-blog.com/article-la-securite-du-consommateur-senegalais-90993080.html. Published on December 2, 2011. Accessed 03.21.2019.

[19]Consumer protection [7].

In most of the cases, the requirement of consumer safety is seen as a ratification the fundamental rights of consumers in the safety and health. But it should be noted that there's few studies that examine the issue of consumer safety in the least developed countries (LDCs), particularly those who specialize in this area in the countries of Africa if was to make the comparison in particular with studies that focus primarily on the West.

This for the Organization for the Harmonization of Business Law in Africa (OHADA) has as main objective to allow some clarity, modernity and transparency in relation to the understanding, practice and the judicial application of the law business.

In the words of Thomas Diatta, which claims that:

> Through the uniform acts of OHADA heard intervene in commercial law, corporate law, collective procedures, the sales law, transportation law, labor law, accounting law and enforcement procedures. This is fundamentally a right of African economic affairs. Thus one may wonder if there is a consumer protector and especially one that would protect their safety in this fundamentally economic law. Business law is closely linked to that of consumption, is consumer protection in the field of sovereignty of member states or OHODA? If it is the responsibility of OHADA, what is done to ensure consumer protection, since there is little or almost no legal framework at Member State level? These observations are also valid for the UEMOA and ECOWAS.[20]

Indeed, Thomas Diatta, shows his concern by questioning the very existence of a law that would protect consumer safety, especially the Senegalese consumer at the OHODA but also valid for UEMOA and ECOWAS. Since their main objectives is the development of trade in the sub-region and intends trade, we necessarily expect to see the important role that consumers play so it is crucial that these community organizations can reflect on protection devices their consumers and especially one that would protect their security in a legal framework in the Member States.

Because according to Ngom, "the common competition policy in the space of ECOWAS must contribute directly to the welfare of consumers, because people promoting providing them with a plurality of similar products, competitive or substitutable. It should also benefit companies that will grow their customer base and innovate, thereby increasing their competitiveness."[21]

It is in this context that this last workshop of ECOWAS held in Ouagadougou has been highly anticipated for the validation of the Community regulatory framework

---

[20]Security Senegalese consumer. Availableon: http://sendroit.over-blog.com/article-la-securite-du-consommateur-senegalais-90993080.html. Published on December 2, 2011. Accessed 21/03/2019.

Original text:"A travers des actes uniformes l'OHADA a entendu intervenir dans le droit commercial, le droit des sociétés, les procédures collectives, le droit de la vente, le droit du transport, le droit du travail, le droit comptable et les voies d'exécution. Il s'agit d'un droit des affaires africain fondamentalement économique. C'est ainsi que l'on peut se demander s'il existe un dispositif protecteur des consommateurs et surtout un qui protégerait leur sécurité dans ce droit foncièrement économique. Le droit des affaires étant intimement lié à celui de la consommation, la protection du consommateur est-elle du domaine de la souveraineté des Etats membres ou de l'OHODA? Si elle est de la compétence de l'OHADA, qu'est-ce qui est fait pour assurer la protection du consommateur, étant donné qu'il existe peu ou presque pas d'encadrement juridique au niveau des Etats membres? Ces observations sont également valables pour l'UEMOA et la CEDEAO".

[21]Ngom [6].

project developed according to the UN guide to consumer protection and the representatives of the designation mechanism consumer associations and sensitizing them to the platform and be able to use it.

So this is to suggest, firstly, a more suitable environment for activities of independent organizations working for the protection of consumer rights and are regularly the cause of actions to inform and protect consumers we are and, secondly, a mechanism for consumer associations in the region to be represented in the organs of the regional quality infrastructure. According to him, the development of this framework comes into line with the quality policy of ECOWAS (Ecoqual) adopted in 2013 by the Heads of State and Government. Also, it aims to ensure the economic competitiveness of the region through the provision of quality goods and services and world-class, and the appropriate consumer protection and environmental conservation.[22]

4 Final Considerations

Even though Senegal has established an outstanding device for the protection of consumers, we realize that the security of the Senegalese consumer is not fully guaranteed.

However, faced with the increasing vulnerability of consumers from advanced technology and business skills, information and consumer protection should be strengthened more than ever.

It is also necessary to have information comparable, reliable and easy to use (especially in cross), to collect reliable data on how the market serves the interests of consumers, empowering advocacy organizations consumers, particularly in some member countries, and to improve information and educational tools used. He also recalled the need to strengthen the rights of consumers, particularly in a cross border context.

References

1. Chazal, Jean Pascal. **Vulnérabilité et droit de la consommation**. Cohet-Cordey, Frédérique. Colloque sur la vulnérabilité et le droit, Mar 2000, Université P. Mendès-France, Grenoble II, France. Presses Universitaires de Grenoble, pp. 00–00, 2000.
2. Conference Des Nations Unies Sur Le Commerce Et Le Developpement. **Principes directeurs des nations unies pour la protection du consommateur** (tel qu'étendus en 1999)' New York et Genève' 2001 UNCTAD/DITC/CLP/Misc.21' p. 3Id.
3. Diatta, Thomas. **La Sécurité du consommateur sénégalais**. Disponible sur: http://sendroit.over-blog.com/article-la-securite-du-consommateur-senegalais-90993080.html. Publié le 2 décembre 2011. Consulté le 21/03/2019.

[22]Security of Senegalese consumer. Available on: http://sendroit.over-blog.com/article-la-securite-du-consommateur-senegalais-90993080.html. Published on December 2, 2011. Accessed 03.21.2019.

4. Expose Des Motifs **loi n° 2002-23 du 4 septembre 2002 portant cadre de regulation pour les entreprises concessionnaires de services publics**. Disponible sur: https://www.ofnac.sn/resources/pdf/Lois/loi%20n%20200223%20du%204%20septembre%202002%20portant%20cadre%20de%20regulation%20ARTP.pdf. Consulté le 07/03/2019.
5. Ndao, Momar, Limites de la protection des consommateurs par les autorités de régulation, 2008. Disponible sur: https://www.memoireonline.com/11/09/2890/m_Limites-de-la-protection-des-consommateurs-par-les-autorites-de-regulation3.html#toc7. Consulté le 07/03/2019.
6. Ngom Mbissane, «**Intégration régionale et politique de la concurrence dans l'espace CEDEAO** » , Revue internationale de droit économique, 2011/3 (t.XXV), pp. 333–349. DOI: https://doi.org/10.3917/ride.253.0333. URL: https://www.cairn.info/revue-internationale-de-droit-economique-2011-3-page-333.htm.
7. Protection du consommateur: **La CEDEAO renforce le mécanisme**. Disponible sur: https://www.leconomistedufaso.bf/2018/12/03/protection-du-consommateur-la-cedeao-renforce-le-mecanisme/. Consulté le 25/03/2019.
8. Rzepecki, Nathalie. **Droit de la consommation et théorie générale du contrat**.Nouvelle édition [en ligne]. Aix-en-Provence: Presses universitaires d'Aix-Marseille, 2002 (généré le 27 février 2019). Disponible sur Internet: http://books.openedition.org/puam/479. ISBN: 9782821853379. DOI: https://doi.org/10.4000/books.puam.479.

Jean KarimColy PhD student in Economic Law at the Pontifícia Universidade Católica of Paraná (PUCPR)/Brazil. Master in Economic Law at the Pontifícia Universidade Católica of Paraná (PUCPR)/Brazil. Bachelor degree in International Relations IMAN/Dakar. Researcher in the UNINTER scientific initiation program in the Contemporary Theory of Jurisdiction and Public Law, with the tripartite project of the Authority and the New World Order - Courts, Administration and International Parliaments.

Luis Alexandre Winter Carta He holds a Bachelor's degree in law from the Federal University of Paraná (1984), specializing in philosophy of education, Pontifical Catholic University of Paraná (1988), master's degree in Latin American integration from the Universidade Federal de Santa Maria (2001) and PhD in integration of Latin America by the USP/PROLAM (2008). He is currently professor at the Pontifical Catholic University of Paraná on graduation (where he was coordinator between 1987 to 1989), in post lato sensu where coordinates the specialization in law, logistics and international business, and the doctoral sensu, in master's and doctoral degrees. Former professor and former " (2005–2010) of law school international school Curitiba, professor of the Centro Universitário Curitiba and FAMEC. This 1984 Attorney-at-law and legal consultant, working mainly on the following themes and areas: contracts, regional integration, MERCOSUR, international relations, maritime law, customs law, international economic law and international law. Coordinator of the NEADI (www.neadi.com.br). Member of Centre of Arts of Paraná and the Institute of Lawyers of Paraná.

A Behavioral Economic Analysis of Consumer Withdrawal Rights in the USA, EU, and Japan

Koju Hirose

1 Introduction

Withdrawal rights for consumer transactions in the USA and the EU have been analyzed and compared in both the USA and the EU. This study aims to introduce, analyze, and compare two studies in the USA[1] and the EU,[2] which discussed withdrawal rights for consumer transactions utilizing economic theories. The Consumer Rights Directive[3] was adopted on October 25, 2011, after the Proposal for a Directive of the European Parliament and of the Council on Consumer Rights.[4] Since the consumer's withdrawal right in distance selling contracts has been proposed in this Proposal for a Directive of the European Parliament and of the Council on Consumer Rights, these two studies discussed the justification of withdrawal rights for consumer transactions. Promises must be kept (*pacta sunt servanda*). However, the consumer's right to withdraw from a contract is allowed on conditions favorable to consumers. There is therefore a need to define and clarify the basis for justification for it. This study attempts to organize and review the points of arguments by comparing the consumer's withdrawal rights in the USA, the EU, and Japan, as well as discussing the benefits of the behavioral economic analysis of these rights.

---

[1]Ben-Shahar and Posner [1].

[2]Eidenmüller [2].

[3]Directive 2011/83/EU of the European Parliament and of the Council of 25 October 2011 on consumer rights, amending Council Directive 93/13/EEC and Directive 1999/44/EC of the European Parliament and of the Council and repealing Council Directive 85/577/EEC and Directive 97/7/EC of the European Parliament and of the Council [2011] L304/64.

[4]COM (2008) 614 final.

K. Hirose (✉)
National Institute of Technology, Kitakyushu College, Fukuoka, Japan
e-mail: hirose@kct.ac.jp

D. Wei et al. (eds.), *Innovation and the Transformation of Consumer Law*,
https://doi.org/10.1007/978-981-15-8948-5_30

2 Consumer Withdrawal Rights in the Distance Selling Contract and the Door-to-Door Sales Contract

This chapter will give a simple introduction of the characteristics and the period of consumer withdrawal rights in the distance selling contract and the door-to-door sales contract.

A. USA

In the USA, consumers have the withdrawal right in the door-to-door sales, although the laws regulating door-to-door sales differ for each state. The cooling-off period under the federal rule (16 C.F.R. §429) gives the consumer the right to cancel any sale resulting from a door-to-door transaction, without any penalty or obligation, for three business days from the date on which the contract was signed.

On the other hand, the federal rule does not give the consumer the withdrawal right in the distance selling contract.

16 C.F.R. §429.1 is as follows:

§429.1 The Rule.

In connection with any door-to-door sale, it constitutes an unfair and deceptive act or practice for any seller to:

(a) Fail to furnish the buyer with a fully completed receipt or copy of any contract pertaining to such sale at the time of its execution, which is in the same language, e.g., Spanish, as that principally used in the oral sales presentation and which shows the date of the transaction and contains the name and address of the seller, and in immediate proximity to the space reserved in the contract for the signature of the buyer or on the front page of the receipt if a contract is not used and in bold face type of a minimum size of 10 points, a statement in substantially the following form:

> You, the buyer, may cancel this transaction at any time prior to midnight of the third business day after the date of this transaction. See the attached notice of cancellation form for an explanation of this right.

The seller may select the method of providing the buyer with the duplicate notice of cancellation form set forth in paragraph (b) of this section, provided however, that in the event of cancellation the buyer must be able to retain a complete copy of the contract or receipt. Furthermore, if both forms are not attached to the contract or receipt, the seller is required to alter the last sentence in the statement above to conform to the actual location of the forms.

(b) Fail to furnish each buyer, at the time the buyer signs the door-to-door sales contract or otherwise agrees to buy consumer goods or services from the seller, a completed form in duplicate, captioned either "NOTICE OF RIGHT TO CANCEL" or "NOTICE OF CANCELLATION," which shall (where applicable) contain in ten point bold face type the following information and statements in the same language, e.g., Spanish, as that used in the contract.

NOTICE OF CANCELLATION
[enter date of transaction]
(Date)
You may CANCEL this transaction, without any Penalty or Obligation, within THREE BUSINESS DAYS from the above date.
If you cancel, any property traded in, any payments made by you under the contract or sale, and any negotiable instrument executed by you will be returned within TEN BUSINESS DAYS following receipt by the seller of your cancellation notice, and any security interest arising out of the transaction will be cancelled.
If you cancel, you must make available to the seller at your residence, in substantially as good condition as when received, any goods delivered to you under this contract or sale, or you may, if you wish, comply with the instructions of the seller regarding the return shipment of the goods at the seller's expense and risk.
If you do make the goods available to the seller and the seller does not pick them up within 20 days of the date of your Notice of Cancellation, you may retain or dispose of the goods without any further obligation. If you fail to make the goods available to the seller, or if you agree to return the goods to the seller and fail to do so, then you remain liable for performance of all obligations under the contract.
To cancel this transaction, mail or deliver a signed and dated copy of this Cancellation Notice or any other written notice, or send a telegram, to [Name of seller], at [address of seller's place of business] NOT LATER THAN MIDNIGHT OF [date].
I HEREBY CANCEL THIS TRANSACTION.
(Date)
(Buyer's signature)

(c) Fail, before furnishing copies of the "Notice of Cancellation" to the buyer, to complete both copies by entering the name of the seller, the address of the seller's place of business, the date of the transaction, and the date, not earlier than the third business day following the date of the transaction, by which the buyer may give notice of cancellation.
(d) Include in any door-to-door contract or receipt any confession of judgment or any waiver of any of the rights to which the buyer is entitled under this section including specifically the buyer's right to cancel the sale in accordance with the provisions of this section.
(e) Fail to inform each buyer orally, at the time the buyer signs the contract or purchases the goods or services, of the buyer's right to cancel.
(f) Misrepresent in any manner the buyer's right to cancel.
(g) Fail or refuse to honor any valid notice of cancellation by a buyer and within 10 business days after the receipt of such notice, to: (i) Refund all payments made under the contract or sale; (ii) return any goods or property traded in, in substantially as good condition as when received by the seller; (iii) cancel and return any negotiable instrument executed by the buyer in connection with

the contract or sale and take any action necessary or appropriate to terminate promptly any security interest created in the transaction.

(h) Negotiate, transfer, sell, or assign any note or other evidence of indebtedness to a finance company or other third party prior to midnight of the fifth business day following the day the contract was signed or the goods or services were purchased.

(i) Fail, within 10 business days of receipt of the buyer's notice of cancellation, to notify the buyer whether the seller intends to repossess or to abandon any shipped or delivered goods.

[37 FR 22934, Oct. 26, 1972, as amended at 38 FR 30105, Nov. 1, 1973; 38 FR 31828, Nov. 19, 1973; 53 FR 45459, Nov. 10, 1988; 60 FR 54186, Oct. 20, 1995]

B. EU

In the EU, consumers have the withdrawal rights in the distance selling contract and the off-premises contract. The consumer shall have a period of 14 days to withdraw from a distance selling or off-premises contract, without giving any reason, and without incurring any costs.

Unlike in the USA, consumers in the EU have a period of 14 days to withdraw from a distance selling contract. In the USA, the federal rule does not give the consumer the withdrawal right in the distance selling contract.

Article 9 of the Consumer Rights Directive is as follows:

Article 9

Right of withdrawal

1. Save where the exceptions provided for in Article 16 apply, the consumer shall have a period of 14 days to withdraw from a distance or off-premises contract, without giving any reason, and without incurring any costs other than those provided for in Article 13(2) and Article 14.
2. Without prejudice to Article 10, the withdrawal period referred to in paragraph 1 of this Article shall expire after 14 days from:

   (a) in the case of service contracts, the day of the conclusion of the contract;
   (b) in the case of sales contracts, the day on which the consumer or a third party other than the carrier and indicated by the consumer acquires physical possession of the goods or:
      (i) in the case of multiple goods ordered by the consumer in one order and delivered separately, the day on which the consumer or a third party other than the carrier and indicated by the consumer acquires physical possession of the last good;
      (ii) in the case of delivery of a good consisting of multiple lots or pieces, the day on which the consumer or a third party other than the carrier and indicated by the consumer acquires physical possession of the last lot or piece;

(iii) in the case of contracts for regular delivery of goods during defined period of time, the day on which the consumer or a third party other than the carrier and indicated by the consumer acquires physical possession of the first good;

(c) in the case of contracts for the supply of water, gas or electricity, where they are not put up for sale in a limited volume or set quantity, of district heating or of digital content which is not supplied on a tangible medium, the day of the conclusion of the contract.

3. The Member States shall not prohibit the contracting parties from performing their contractual obligations during the withdrawal period. Nevertheless, in the case of off- premises contracts, Member States may maintain existing national legislation prohibiting the trader from collecting the payment from the consumer during the given period after the conclusion of the contract.

C. Japan

In Japan, consumers have the withdrawal rights in the door-to-door sales.

Unlike in the USA and the EU, consumers in Japan have a period of 8 days to withdraw from the door-to-door sales contract. In contrast, consumers in the USA and the EU have a period of 3 business days and 14 days respectively to withdraw from the door-to-door sales contract.

On the other hand, consumers in Japan do not have the withdrawal rights in the distance selling contract. However, consumers have limited rights to withdraw from the distance selling contract, which consumers cannot have if the seller had indicated special provisions on withdrawal of an offer or cancellation of a contract in its advertisement. This system is called the return system in Japan. In the return system, the seller has an option to give consumers withdrawal rights, but consumers do not have the option to waive or to ask for it.

Article 9(1) and 15-3(1) of the Act on Specified Commercial Transactions[5] are as follows:

(Withdrawal of an Offer or Cancellation of a Door-to-Door Sales Contract)
Article 9(1)
If a seller or a service provider has received an offer for a sales contract for goods or specified rights or an offer for a service contract for services at a place other than an office or other such location; if a seller or a service provider has received an offer for a sales contract for goods or specified rights or an offer for a service contract for services at an office or other such location from a specified customer; if a seller or a service provider has entered into a sales contract for goods or specified rights or a service contract for services at a place other than an office or other such location (excluding if the seller or the service provider received the offer at an office or other such location and entered into the sales contract or the service contract at a place other than an office or other such location); or if a seller

[5]See http://www.japaneselawtranslation.go.jp/law/detail/?ft=1&re=01&dn=1&x=67&y=10&co=01&ia=03&ky=特定商取引&page=6.

or a service provider has entered into a sales contract for goods or specified rights or a service contract for services at an office or other such location with a specified customer, the person who made the offer or the purchaser or the service recipient (hereinafter referred to as the "offeror or counterparty" in this Article to Article 9-3) may withdraw the offer for a sales contract or a service contract or cancel the sales contract or the service contract (hereinafter referred to as the "withdrawal of an offer or cancellation" of a contract in this Article) in writing; provided, however, that this does not apply once eight days have passed after the date on which the offeror or counterparty received the document referred to in Article 5 (or after the date on which the offeror or counterparty received the document referred to in Article 4, if the offeror or counterparty received the document under Article 4 at an earlier date than that on which the offeror or counterparty received the document referred to in Article 5) (if the offeror or counterparty did not withdraw the offer or cancel the contract before the end of that period because of having been under the misapprehension that information about the withdrawal of an offer or cancellation of the contract that the seller or the service provider had misrepresented to the offeror or counterparty, in violation of the provisions of Article 6, paragraph (1), was true, or because the offeror or counterparty was overwhelmed due to the seller's or the service provider's use of intimidation, in violation of the provisions of paragraph (3) of that Article, the first part of this paragraph does not apply once eight days have passed after the date on which the offeror or counterparty received a document delivered thereto by the seller or the service provider pursuant to the provisions of order of the competent ministry that contains a notice to the effect that the offeror or counterparty may withdraw the offer or cancel the sales contract or service contract).

(Cancellation of a Contract in Mail Order Sales)

Article 15-3(1)

When a seller that has advertised terms and conditions for selling goods or specified rights through mail order sales has received an offer for a sales contract for those goods or specified rights or entered into a sales contract for those goods or specified rights, the person making the offer or the purchaser (simply referred to as the "purchaser" in the following paragraph) may withdraw the offer for the sales contract or cancel the sales contract (hereinafter referred to as a "withdrawal of an offer or cancellation" of a contract in this Article) during the period up until eight days have passed since the date on which the purchaser is delivered the goods or is transferred the specified rights; provided, however, that this does not apply if the seller had indicated special provisions on withdrawal of an offer or cancellation of a contract in its advertisement (if the sales contract is an electronic consumer contract prescribed in Article 2, paragraph (1) of the Act on Special Provisions to the Civil Code Concerning Electronic Consumer Contracts and Electronic Acceptance Notice (Act No. 95 of 2001) or in any other cases specified by order of the competent ministry, this means if the seller had indicated special provisions in its advertisement and had also indicated those special provisions by a method other than an advertisement that is specified by order of the competent ministry).

3 Economic Analysis

Ben-Shahar and Posner analyzed the relationship between depreciation costs and information benefits. Ben-Shahar and Posner discussed that "(the right to withdraw) allows buyers to learn about goods and services that they purchase and to reject them if they value these goods and services less than they thought; and if sellers are protected from depreciation losses, the doctrine should work a Pareto improvement."[6] Moreover, Ben-Shahar and Posner advocated the effectiveness of a default rule for consumer withdrawal rights and discussed that "the optimal contract containing a right to withdraw need not be mandatory."[7]

Eidenmüller advocated that withdrawal rights are necessary for experience goods and supported it with an example of purchasing clothes through distance selling (i.e., mail order), where the consumer has to purchase the good before knowing whether it is comfortable or not.[8] On the other hand, withdrawal period is unnecessary for search goods (such as unpacked fruits as the quality can be immediately ascertained) and credence goods (such as medical services since the non-professional consumer will find it difficult to ascertain the quality at any rate).[9] However, in the case of experience goods, 'information asymmetries' (an economics term describing insufficient product information) between the seller and the buyer lead to market failure due to 'adverse selection' (i.e., consumer selects a low-quality good due to information asymmetries instead of selecting a high-quality good in a functioning market).[10] In such a situation, consumers only pay low prices for experience goods of which they cannot ascertain its quality, and high-quality goods remain unsold, thereby leading to a market collapse.[11] An effective solution for this situation is 'signaling' (i.e., indicator providing information indirectly). For example, if the buyer is unable to obtain accurate information about the good directly, he/she will expect the 'signal' (information conveyed by the seller about the good's supposed high quality) to be accurate. Withdrawal rights thus function as 'signals' in such situations since the consumer can withdraw from the contract after making the purchase even without product information.[12] This way, sellers are able to sell goods without much product information by sending signals, consumers will not withdraw from the contract as long as they are not unpleased, and high-quality goods sellers will not have to contend with high withdrawal rates or the associated expenses.[13] Eidenmüller also explained why mandatory law is inappropriate for withdrawal rights in the distance selling

[6]Ben-Shahar and Posner, supra note 1, at 20.

[7]Id.

[8]Eidenmüller, supra note 2, at 8.

[9]Id., at 7–8.

[10]Id., at 8.

[11]Id., at 8–9.

[12]Id., at 9.

[13]Id.

context since consumers want the good's price to be lowered if they are not entitled to withdrawal rights.[14] Eidenmüller advocated that "(in the distance selling context,) vendors should be obliged to provide consumers an option to contract with a withdrawal right".[15]

Eidenmüller discussed three different rationales, information asymmetries, exogenously distorted preferences of the consumer, and endogenously distorted preferences, which may justify granting withdrawal rights in particular case settings. Eidenmüller also advocated that "exogenously distorted preferences justify providing a mandatory withdrawal right in the doorstep selling context – but not for all contracts concluded off-premises"[16] and "endogenously distorted preferences justify providing a mandatory withdrawal right with respect to timesharing agreements, credit contracts, and life insurance contracts".[17]

4 Behavioral Economic Analysis

A comparison of the legal provisions in the USA, the EU, and Japan has revealed that consumers do not have the option to waive or to ask for withdrawal rights in the distance selling contract. Eidenmüller advocated that "(in the distance selling context,) vendors should be obliged to provide consumers an option to contract with a withdrawal right".[18] On the other hand, human beings often maintain the status quo. Even if consumers have consumer withdrawal rights, consumers might not exercise their rights because of status quo bias. Behavioral economic analysis will be important for withdrawal rights in the distance selling contract, because 'status quo bias' for the possibility of consumers to exercise their rights should be considered. Further research would be required for this aspect. The length of the period is another contentious issue because there are various elements for consideration, for example, the consumer might be busy during the period. It might be useful to conduct behavioral economic analysis using accurate statistical data to anticipate consumer behavior in the withdrawal period.

Consumers are human beings and therefore might be able to be irrational and diverse. Eidenmüller indicated that "many systematic deviations from the assumption of fully rational behavior have been discovered by cognitive psychologists" and applied behavioral economic analysis (incorporating availability bias, status quo bias for instance) to justify consumer withdrawal rights.[19] Behavioral economic analysis might be useful to explain endogenously distorted preferences.

---

[14] Id.

[15] Id., at 23.

[16] Id., at 23–24.

[17] Id., at 24.

[18] Id., at 23.

[19] Id., at 16–18.

Eidenmüller distinguished contracts by utilizing economic theories.[20] A distinction between search goods, experience goods, and credence goods is useful to justify consumer withdrawal rights. However, we should also be cognizant that withdrawal rights alone are insufficient to protect consumers for search goods and credence goods. It is difficult to say that withdrawal rights are not needed for search goods and credence goods because consumers might be able to exercise the withdrawal right. We should research consumer behavior and vendor behavior in withdrawal period by utilizing behavioral economic analysis.

Behavioral economic analysis might be helpful to anticipate consumer behavior and to draft efficient consumer protection laws, where accurate statistical data will be required. For future studies, I'd like to conduct research using accurate statistical data to anticipate consumer behavior.

5 Conclusion

Since the legal provisions for withdrawal rights in distance selling are very different between the USA and the EU, research in this area has led to further studies on the distinction of contracts as well as advancing research on consumer behavior in each type of contract. It is of noteworthy mention that behavioral economics has been applied fruitfully in the comparison and analyses of the consumer's withdrawal rights. If we are able to come up with proposals to better the society as a whole by analyzing allocation of resources not only for consumers but for honest and dishonest companies as well, it might be beneficial to apply these economic theories to clarify and define the judgment criteria for justice and fairness. On the other hand, there is a need to define the nature of each contract to prove the rationale for justifying the consumer's right to withdraw from it, and the application of economic theories is expected to clarify the nature of each contract. Studies conducted in the USA and the EU on the consumer's withdrawal rights by applying economic theories have centered around the analyses of justification basis of these rights for each type of contract via an economical distinction of these contracts. For instance, the contracts drafted nowadays are complicated and diversified, such as online sales contract and door-to-door sales contract. In fact, the laws of the USA, the EU, and Japan present different stipulations concerning the consumer's withdrawal rights for each type of contract. Therefore, the individual provisions, such as provisions for the withdrawal period and legal consequences, differ between contracts. In particular, the scope and application of the mandatory rule and the default rule are different in the USA, the EU, and Japan, and have been the topic of many discussions and disputes. Advances in science and technology have transformed the structure of the market, such as recycling, digital contents, the Internet, and corporate mergers, resulting in further complication and diversification of the contents of contracts. We can therefore expect to create a new classification of contracts by applying economic theories to

[20] Id., at 7–24.

it. Moreover, these studies have attempted to perform a psychological analysis of the relationship between law and consumer behavior based on behavioral economics to propose legal provisions to build a better society. Behavioral economic analysis is expected to be able to anticipate consumer behavior and to draft efficient consumer protection laws. For future studies, I'd like to conduct research on accurate statistical data to anticipate consumer behavior.

References

1. Omri Ben-Shahar and Eric A. Posner, *The Right to Withdraw in Contract Law*, John M. Olin Program in Law and Economics Working Paper No. 514, pp. 1–23 (2010) [https://chicagounbound.uchicago.edu/cgi/viewcontent.cgi?article=1566&context=law_and_economics].
2. Horst Eidenmüller, *Why Withdrawal Rights?*, European Review of Contract Law, 7(1), pp. 1–24 (2011).

The Spectacle of Life in Assisted Human Reproduction: A Short Essay

Marcos Catalan and Carla Froener

Human reproduction is a succession of events generally beginning, at least for now, with the union of male and female germ cells and ending with the successful birth of another live human being. This process went through an apotheosis of change in July of 1978, when the world first heard of Louise Joy Brown—the world's first test-tube baby—and since then it has provoked many smiles of joy, but it has also become an enormous marketing opportunity.

In the next few pages we will quickly explore the challenges of human reproduction and the questions arising from the intersection of (a) the changes of configuration of Brazilian families (b) the rising demand for assisted reproduction (c) the market expansion and the legal limits it almost crosses and (d) the non-disclosure of common risks involved in the medical procedures.

The plan described presupposes that there is no doubt that the architecture of contemporary families has been heavily influenced by a important part of "promethean" technical advances in genetics, biotechnology, robotics and trans-humanism ad, at the same time, that important mutations ascended from the fractures opened by the friction between Law and Society in the fields that were earlier sowed by the Pandectists with the seeds of conceptual purism.

One of these important mutations is the eudemonist family.

This paper was produced during the project *Consumer protection adrift*: an attempt to measure the state of the art, in the jusconsumerist protection, in the Brazilian Superior Court of Justice [407142/2018-5] financed with resources of the National Council for Scientific and Technological Development—CNPq.

M. Catalan (✉)
Faculdade de Direito do Largo de São Francisco, Universidade de São Paulo, São Paulo, Brasil
e-mail: marcoscatalan@uol.com.br

M. Catalan · C. Froener
Universidade LaSalle, Canoas, Brasil

D. Wei et al. (eds.), *Innovation and the Transformation of Consumer Law*,
https://doi.org/10.1007/978-981-15-8948-5_31

For them, the most important thing is the way in which they exercise their freedom, with or without legal permission, in multiple spaces of coexistence, tenderness and affection spread through the phenomenological dimension.

Eudemonism and technology.

Since 1988, in Brazil, a family does not presume marriage anymore, as previously determined by our laws. The formation of a family does not presuppose sexual relations, or even people of different genders. The fact is that, nowadays, normally diarchic factors seem to have influenced the fall of the model of family that submitted wife and children to the head of the family—the man—who held the power of ownership over his family. In the current Brazilian legal structure of family, children are not even necessary. Double income, no kids: one in five couples, in Brazil, has no children and feel no obligation to have them.

Children, today, are almost always—specially among the most cultured strata of society, we conjecture—derived from projects of life conceived through the whims of Libera. In case children are dreamt of, desired, or chosen, the recent technological advances allow for the overcoming of biological limitations that were, up until recently, insurmountable.

Actually, we all know that the technical advances have changed the natural presupposed causal relation in the field of reproduction, allowing, for instance, procreation with no sexual contact, the dissociation between genetic ascendance, motherhood and gestation, and also, egg fusion.

Along with it, women's emancipation has also influenced human reproduction. Pregnancy keeps being delayed and thus made more difficult. Data from Brazil's Health Ministry show that the percentage of mothers at the age of 30 or more has risen from 22.5% in the beginning of the century to over 30% in 2012.

Well.

It is evident that assisted human reproduction may make viable the exercise of parenthood in this and in other innumerous contexts, prescinding even the use of gametes or another person's uterus for the experimentation in independent productions or in co-parenting, even though these phenomena have been receiving legal support influenced by ideological, religious, geographic and political points of view. We also cannot ignore inherent risks associated with birth power, especially those related to the questionable availability of Family status.

But we don't want to get into that subject now.

Let us go back to human reproduction and the practices emerging from the field of genetic selection, in situations in which there are very thin lines dividing the expectations of parent candidates and their projects from practices that are dangerously close to those of eugenics. And when this does not happen, the mapping of genetic profiles from donors and providers of gametes emerges as another troublesome question in Brazil: people have had their physical, intellectual and genetic characteristics listed in catalogs that up until recently listed phone numbers and addresses.

Humans have turned into merchandise.

Life has been offered and sold in websites and billboards, enabling the experience of the genetic fetish of filiation, especially when we have in mind the selected group that can afford these experiences.

In Debord's *La société du spectacle*, human beings are spectators who experience with each choice they make situations oscillating between contemplative states and some low level of interaction, with choices that are not always their own selections, among them, obviously, parenthood.

In Brazil, long before assisted human reproduction started being available to the general public, television exploited the idea, as of the image was a curious precursor of reality.

In 1990 the *novela* "*Barriga de Aluguel*" premiered. In vitro fertilization and surrogacy permeated the plot in which the biological mother of the child, and author of the parenting project, fought for custody with the surrogate mother, who became a step mother of the baby. In 2012, the *novela* "*Fina Estampa*" told the story of a woman whose eggs were manipulated, without her consent, and implanted in another woman's womb, who desired a child and wanted to have one naturally, in spite of her diagnosed infertility.

It is curious to note how both stories ended in dramatic legal battles that questioned who were the real parents of the children, even though themes such as the ethical and legal limits of assisted human reproduction or the complexity of experimental parenthood projects were never discussed.

From fiction to daily life, it is important to note that television tends to describe the technology involved in human reproduction as extremely simple, accessible and harmless—using images of smiling women and children—with no reference whatsoever as to the extremely low rates of success and the high financial cost commonly associated with the procedures.

This is an extremely relevant matter.

A lot of dramatization and almost no information.

Even though in Brazil there are recognized principles of (a) consumers rights (b) the myriad of rules listed in consumers legislation with the mandate to warn, communicate, explain, guide and give notice, and (c) the normative power of the principle of the child's best interest. And we are not even talking about the preoccupation with human dignity when we notice that lives were turned into consumer goods.

With permission from Law, or at its margin, almost always walking a thin line or taking cover in uncertainty zones, the Market has expanded and colonized human reproduction with its practices and discourses.

It is hard not to notice how economic rationale has infiltrated the practice of medicine in this field also. Diagnosis and therapies, pharmaceutical drugs and prosthetics, equipment and children are sometimes talked about as if they were clothes, shoes, cell phones or television sets.

Infertility, from the 1960's and into the 1980's, was thought of as a pathology to be solved through adoption, but later became known as a personal problem for which there are obviously solutions that can be bought or financed.

In support of this fact, we have that in Brazil, in 2015 alone, 141 human reproduction clinics have implanted 73,472 embryos. However, we do not know how many babies were born.

Human reproduction became a product to be consumed.

Colonized by the market, and less and less spontaneous. Specialists commonly are suggested by Gynecologists in the private sector. People submit themselves to very costly procedures and high probability of being unsuccessful. Also, we must not forget how common are the diagnoses of "infertility with no apparent cause".

At the same time, it is possible to identify reports showing that medical research about the causes of infertility or low fecundity rates are not encouraged enough: it seems that it is much more lucrative to invest in sophisticated techniques of reproduction, mostly because, apparently, the cure for infertility is a one-time sale, and assisted reproduction is a service that can be bought many times over, even in the successful cases, because there is always the possibility of a new child.

There are many other ethical issues masked by the spectacle of assisted human reproduction. The harvesting of eggs is preceded by hormonal treatments with many risks, including, in the most extreme cases, the death of the donor. Gamete donation might be followed by infections. Monitoring of embryonic implants require invasive exams. The rates of failure, ectopic pregnancy and miscarriages are high. Multiple gestations and premature babies are also very common scenarios. And the issue of the destination of left-over embryos is rarely discussed.

And what about the physical and mental health of people searching assisted reproduction, men and women who have only experienced anxiety and frustration through their innumerous attempts of fertilization? What about people who have a hard time owning their life stories and cannot tell if the emptiness they feel is because of the absence of children or the illusion of rebuilding a marriage corroded by time?

Perceptibly, from our point of view, a lot of what happens in Brazil does not consider some very important issues of the Law: information, prevention and precaution.

The manufacturer's authorised representative in the EU is Springer Nature Customer Service Centre GmbH, Europaplatz 3, 69115 Heidelberg, Germany. If you have any concerns regarding our products, please contact ProductSafety@springernature.com

Printed and bound by CPI Group (UK) Ltd, Croydon, CR0 4YY
23/09/2026
02221532-0011